AF905588

Arbitration and Human Rights

Toms Krūmiņš

Arbitration and Human Rights

Approaches to Excluding the Annulment of Arbitral Awards and Their Compatibility with the ECHR

Springer

Toms Krūmiņš
COBALT
Rīga, Latvia

ISBN 978-3-030-54236-8 ISBN 978-3-030-54237-5 (eBook)
https://doi.org/10.1007/978-3-030-54237-5

© The Editor(s) (if applicable) and The Author(s), under exclusive license to Springer Nature Switzerland AG 2020
This work is subject to copyright. All rights are solely and exclusively licensed by the Publisher, whether the whole or part of the material is concerned, specifically the rights of translation, reprinting, reuse of illustrations, recitation, broadcasting, reproduction on microfilms or in any other physical way, and transmission or information storage and retrieval, electronic adaptation, computer software, or by similar or dissimilar methodology now known or hereafter developed.
The use of general descriptive names, registered names, trademarks, service marks, etc. in this publication does not imply, even in the absence of a specific statement, that such names are exempt from the relevant protective laws and regulations and therefore free for general use.
The publisher, the authors and the editors are safe to assume that the advice and information in this book are believed to be true and accurate at the date of publication. Neither the publisher nor the authors or the editors give a warranty, expressed or implied, with respect to the material contained herein or for any errors or omissions that may have been made. The publisher remains neutral with regard to jurisdictional claims in published maps and institutional affiliations.

This Springer imprint is published by the registered company Springer Nature Switzerland AG
The registered company address is: Gewerbestrasse 11, 6330 Cham, Switzerland

For my son Jēkabs

Foreword

This monograph by Toms Krūmiņš is based on his thesis, successfully defended at the University of Copenhagen in May 2019. The topic of *Arbitration and Human Rights* is significant and controversial both from a practical and a theoretical point of view. It is also susceptible to many different approaches and limitations. Hence, the subtitle—*Approaches to Excluding the Annulment of Arbitral Awards and their Compatibility with the ECHR*. The monograph is an expanded and updated version of the thesis with also significant reorganization of the text so that it is accessible to both academics and practitioners.

During the second half of the twentieth century (international), arbitration has been gaining unprecedented acceptance by disputing parties and national legislators alike and has established itself as the prime dispute resolution method for commercial disputes. At the same time, the arbitral subject matter has significantly increased to also cover issues that may partly pertain to "public interest". Arbitral awards also appeared to be "invincible". There have been proposals for arbitral awards to be made immune from any challenge at the courts of the place where they were made, and the 1958 New York Convention of the Recognition and Enforcement of Foreign Arbitral Awards (NYC) significantly limited the grounds on which an award may be resisted recognition and enforcement. Given the importance of arbitration, however, public attention and interest have also increased.

Against such a background, the main issue the book addresses is whether it would be necessary to continue to use setting aside proceedings of arbitral awards made in the context of international commercial arbitration. The topic is approached from the standpoint of disputing parties and their procedural human rights as well as public international law obligations states assume under the European Convention of Human Rights (ECHR). Would it then be acceptable to limit further or even exclude judicial scrutiny of arbitral awards either by mutual consent of disputing parties or a statutory exclusion at the seat of arbitration? Would such exclusion enhance the efficiency of international arbitration without any significant compromise or sacrifice of due process? Would the exclusion of setting aside proceedings under national arbitration laws be compatible with the rule of law and due process?

I have written on other occasions that the NYC provides appropriate checks and balances for international arbitration and in the (quite typical) event of an arbitration taking place in a neutral place, not connected to the disputing parties or the subject matter of the arbitration, setting aside procedures would be both inconvenient and unnecessary.[1]

In this critical thematic junction, Toms Krūmiņš covers a series of well-defined research questions and his analyses are carried out with great care and precision. The outcome is an innovative monograph that substantially and persuasively debates the interaction of (procedural) human rights and arbitration.

Chapter 1 sets outs the scene and provides the reader with a roadmap of how the research and the arguments unfold.

Chapter 2 provides a useful and targeted overview of the ECHR (particularly useful for arbitration academics and practitioners with limited knowledge of European Human Rights).

Chapter 3 discusses comprehensively the interaction of arbitration and the ECHR, and it introduces the main scope of the monograph, covering both issues of application of the ECHR to arbitration, waiver of such application, Article 6 ECHR (right to fair trial) and its relevance and potential application to arbitration. In this respect, this chapter already discusses the issue of setting aside proceedings and the lack of such proceedings in national arbitration laws and any potential human rights implications.

Chapter 4 discusses approaches to the setting aside of awards and related issues, such as jurisdiction for such proceedings, time limits and justification and grounds for the application of setting aside of awards.

Chapter 5 explores exclusion agreements, i.e. various approaches that national legislators have adopted to allow for the possibility of limiting and even excluding setting aside proceedings for arbitrations within their jurisdiction. The chapter also discusses whether such limitation and exclusion are provided for in the context of delocalization of arbitration or on different bases.

Chapter 6 explores specific national law approaches towards exclusion of setting aside proceedings with particular focus on Latvia, and other jurisdictions which abandoned with exclusion (e.g. Belgium and Malaysia) and some which still have an exclusion (e.g. Kyrgyzstan). The focus on Latvia is well justified not only

[1]Loukas Mistelis, "Delocalization and its Relevance in Post-Award Review", in Fabien Gelinas and Frederic Bachand (eds.), *25 Years of the UNCITRAL Model Law*, Juris 2013, pages 165–179; Loukas Mistelis, "Setting Aside of Arbitral Awards and Forum Shopping in International Arbitration: Delocalization, Party Autonomy and National Courts in Post-Award Review", in Franco Ferrari (ed), *Forum Shopping in the International Commercial Arbitration Context*, Sellier 2013, pages 277–296; also "Nulidad de laudos arbitrales y forum shopping en arbitraje internacional: delocalizacion, autonomia de las partes y cortes nationales en las revisions post-laudo", in Hector Flores Senties (ed), *Retos Contemporaneos del arbitraje internacional*, Tirant lo Blanche 2018, pp 263–284 [chapter in book], ISBN978-84-9190-3456-8 (in Spanish; and "Anulação de sentença arbitral e forum shopping em arbitragem internacional: Delocalização, autonomia des partes e cortes locais na fase de controle pose-sentença arbitral", *Revista de Arbitragem e Mediação*, vol. 60/2019, p. 259–281, Jan–Mar 2019, DTR\2019\24187 (in Portuguese).

because it is the author's home jurisdiction but also because it appears to be one of the few jurisdictions in the world which has decided not to statutorily provide a setting aside of arbitral awards made within the jurisdiction.

Chapter 7 provides a synthesis and a critical reflection of the interaction of setting aside proceedings and the ECHR and in particular Article 6. In addition, it makes recommendations for setting aside proceedings which would be compatible with the ECHR.

Chapter 8 offers a summary of findings and conclusions both in respect of voluntary exclusion of setting aside proceedings but also in respect of statutory exclusions.

I commend the author for successfully taking on the task of exploring such a complex and novel topic, for conducting significant research and for making such a difficult topic accessible to both practitioners and academics. The published outcome is a significant contribution to arbitration scholarship and provides intriguing insights and food for thought. Congratulations are warranted and well deserved.

London
July 2020

Prof. Loukas Mistelis

Preface

This book marks the end of a years-long journey—a journey that began quite some time ago and has now materialized in this monograph. Looking back at it, I understand that this book and the PhD thesis, defended at the University of Copenhagen in May 2019 that this book in a slightly amended and modified manner largely reflects, is only a *finale* to that journey.

I have been fortunate enough to have been blessed by the presence of many different key people throughout this journey. In hindsight, each of them has played a pivotal role in the development of my personal and professional life, and either directly or indirectly provided also his or her own unique input in the making of this book.

Above all, I am immeasurably grateful to my mother who has always supported me no matter how difficult the circumstances at times were. Without your right decisions at the very early stages of my life and continuous support later on, I would certainly not be where I am today.

I also wish to express my deepest gratitude to all those whose support and encouragement have in one way or another contributed greatly to this still unimaginable end result.

First and foremost, it is my beloved fiancée Linda after 4 years of law studies in the Netherlands and initial hesitation to take this step, it was you who eventually persuaded me to come back home to Latvia in 2014. It is here where the journey to this book truly began. I am very thankful for your everlasting support and sacrifice.

I also wish to thank my dear friend Aleksandrs Ļeščinskis who encouraged me to apply for the vacant PhD position and Dace Silava-Tomsone for equally encouraging me to certainly make use of this opportunity. Without your encouragement, I would never have done it. I equally wish to thank Professor Frank Diedrich for clearing my initial doubts, Professor George Ulrich and Dr. Mārtiņš Mits for believing in me at the very beginning of my PhD studies, my supervisors—Professor Clement Salung Petersen and Dr. Gaļina Žukova for your continued and invaluable mentorship and guidance, Professor Giuditta Cordero-Moss for your helpful suggestions, the staff at the Riga Graduate School of Law (in particular Ligita Gjortlere) and the PhD School, Faculty of Law, University of Copenhagen for your continued practical support, the members of my PhD defence committee—Associate Professors Sylvie Cécile Cavaleri of the University of Copenhagen, Inga Kačevska of the University of Latvia, and Professor Loukas Mistelis of the Queen Mary University of London. I express particular appreciation to Professor Mistelis for kindly agreeing to provide his thoughts on the subject matter of this book in the form of a foreword. Last but not least, I wish to thank the editorial team of Springer, in particular Anke Seyfried, Boopalan Renu and Monica Janet Michael for your continued assistance in making this happen.

This journey has officially come to an end.

With a hope for a more balanced and effective framework of international arbitration oriented towards the protection of arbitrating parties' human rights—

Rīga
July 2020

Toms Krūmiņš

Contents

Abbreviations

AALCO	Asian-African Legal Consultative Organization
ACHPR	African Charter on Human and Peoples' Rights
ACHR	American Convention on Human Rights
AIAC	Asian International Arbitration Centre
BCCP	Belgian Code of Civil Procedure
BIT	A bilateral investment treaty
CAS	Court of Arbitration for Sport
CEPANI	The Belgian Centre for Arbitration and Mediation
CIETAC	China International Economic and Trade Arbitration Commission
CJEU	Court of Justice of the European Union
DIS	The German Arbitration Institute
ECCI	Estonian Chamber of Commerce and Industry
ECHR	European Convention for the Protection of Human Rights and Fundamental Freedoms
ECmHR	European Commission of Human Rights
ECtHR	European Court of Human Rights
EU	European Union
FCCP	French Code of Civil Procedure
HKIAC	Hong Kong International Arbitration Centre
IBA	International Bar Association
ICC	International Chamber of Commerce
ICCPR	International Covenant on Civil and Political Rights
ICSID	International Centre for Settlement of Investment Disputes
ISDS	Investor-State Dispute Settlement
LCCI	Latvian Chamber of Commerce and Industry
LCCP	Latvian Code of Civil Procedure
LCIA	London Court of International Arbitration
LSSR	Latvian Soviet Socialist Republic
LSSR PCC	Latvian Soviet Socialist Republic People's Council of Commissioners (*Tautas Komisāru Padome*)

PILA	Swiss Private International Law Act
Pre-war CPL	Russian Civil Procedure Law of 1864
RCAKL	Regional Centre for Arbitration, Kuala Lumpur
SAA	Swedish Arbitration Act
SAIC	Singapore International Arbitration Centre
SCC	The Arbitration Institute of the Stockholm Chamber of Commerce
SIAC	Singapore International Arbitration Centre
TFEU	Treaty on the Functioning of the European Union
UDHR	United Nations Universal Declaration of Human Rights
UNCITRAL	United Nations Commission on International Trade Law
USSR	Union of Soviet Socialist Republics
ZPO	German Code of Civil Procedure (*Zivilprozessordnung*)

Chapter 1
Introduction

1.1 Setting the Scene

The necessity of court involvement in arbitration proceedings is axiomatic. Even though arbitration, as a private dispute settlement mechanism, in its nature endeavours to free itself from the constraints of public authorities, the *great paradox of arbitration*, as Jan Paulsson has put it,[1] is in the fact that it also seeks the cooperation of the very same public authorities.

The success and effectiveness of arbitration proceedings is therefore inconceivable without the support of, and also control by national courts. Arbitration does not exist in a legal vacuum—it is not only regulated by the laws of the seat of arbitration and the rules of procedure chosen by the parties, but its success also heavily depends on court involvement throughout the life-cycle of arbitration.

The rationale behind court involvement in arbitration proceedings is two-fold, i.e. to assist and to control. On the one hand, national courts assist parties and arbitral tribunals with various procedural tasks, such as the appointment and challenging of arbitrators, summoning and hearing of witnesses, taking of evidence, issuing of interim measures and other procedural orders.[2] On the other hand, courts also exercise a supervisory function and act as guardians for the protection of party expectations

[1] Paulsson (2013), p. 30.

[2] In institutional arbitration, whereby arbitration proceedings are administered by a party-chosen arbitral institution, some of the listed tasks are entrusted to and carried out primarily by the chosen arbitral institution pursuant to its procedural rules. Nevertheless, even in such cases national courts remain important players and are the only ones 'possessing coercive powers which could rescue the arbitration if it is in danger of foundering'. See Lord Mustill in *Copee Levalin NV v Ken-Ren Fertilisers and Chemicals* [1994] 2 Lloyd's Rep. 109 at 116, HL acknowledging that: '[t]here is plainly a tension here. On the one hand the concept of arbitration as a consensual process reinforced by the ideas of transnationalism leans against the involvement of the mechanisms of state through the medium of a municipal court. On the other side there is the plain fact, palatable or not, that it is only a Court possessing coercive powers which could rescue the arbitration if it is in danger of foundering'.

© The Editor(s) (if applicable) and The Author(s), under exclusive license to Springer Nature Switzerland AG 2020

T. Krūmiņš, *Arbitration and Human Rights*,
https://doi.org/10.1007/978-3-030-54237-5_1

and fundamental rights, as well as the legitimacy of arbitration proceedings per se.[3] Although both aspects of court involvement in arbitration proceedings raise thought-provoking questions when put in perspective of the main theme of this book, i.e. arbitration and human rights, the essence of the present contribution limits itself to perhaps the most widely discussed issue of court control over arbitration—the so-called setting-aside proceedings.

As long as arbitration has existed, arbitration proceedings and the ensuing arbitral awards have been subject to some form of judicial control. Already in Roman law arbitration *ex compromisso* depended on a close supervision by the praetor.[4] Similar control mechanisms, both in more stringent or lenient forms, have survived the centuries and remain vital also in contemporary relationship between arbitration and the State.

Traditionally, judicial control over arbitration was exercised mostly at the enforcement stage.[5] A court, presented with a request to recognize and enforce an arbitral award, would formally review that arbitral award's compliance with certain fundamental procedural principles and parties' rights and either grant or deny its enforcement against the award debtor in that particular State. Generally, this is true also in contemporary arbitration where court control plays important role especially at the recognition and enforcement stage. However, enforcement proceedings are solely concerned with the actual enforcement of an arbitral award, and not with questions pertaining to its validity. If a defective arbitral award violating one of the parties' procedural rights for some reason is nevertheless recognized and enforced by national courts, the aggrieved party, apart from opposing the recognition and enforcement of the defective arbitral award, had no opportunity to contest the validity of such an arbitral award. In order to remedy this procedural injustice, a separate action, i.e. an action for the setting aside of an arbitral award at the seat of arbitration, was developed.[6]

The setting-aside, annulment or challenge of an arbitral award[7] implies a decision of a court at the seat of arbitration to the effect that the arbitral award has no legal force. It is a review by a State court at the seat of arbitration of an arbitral award in order to confirm that the arbitral award (and the underlying arbitration process) complies with, on the one hand, certain fundamental procedural principles and rules and, on the other hand, that State's overriding mandatory provisions and public policy. The setting aside of an arbitral award is considered as the mirror for the action of recognition and enforcement. It is possible only on very limited grounds generally

[3] For a general overview of the different roles that national courts may play during the life-cycle of arbitration proceedings see, e.g. Kerr (1985), p. 34.

[4] See, e.g. Roebuck and De Loynes de Fumichon (2004), p. 96.

[5] Van den Berg (2014), p. 3.

[6] Ibid., pp. 3–4.

[7] When referring to the action of setting-aside these terms are used interchangeably. For examples of the different expressions used in national arbitration legislations see, e.g. Poudret and Besson (2006), p. 703. Hereinafter in this book judicial review of an arbitral award by means of setting aside proceedings will be interchangeably referred to as the 'setting aside', 'challenge' or 'annulment' of an arbitral award.

resembling the same grounds as for the refusal of recognition and enforcement of an arbitral award. As aptly put by Prof. Park, the setting aside of an arbitral award is seen as a form of risk management whereby courts remedy violations of fundamental procedural rights during arbitration proceedings.[8]

Judicial control of arbitration proceedings and the eventual arbitral award by means of setting-aside proceedings has been perhaps the most widely debated aspect of court involvement in arbitration proceedings. Judicial control and the necessity of court involvement for the smooth and efficient functioning of arbitration per se is an accepted fact and not a matter of intellectual controversy.[9] What is, however, a matter of intellectual controversy and at the heart of this book and the discussion regarding judicial controls over arbitration in general, is a question of the exact depth and extent of such control. Considering that States are generally free to 'apply whatever measures of judicial control'[10] of arbitration they deem necessary, various approaches and attitudes towards regulating arbitration have emerged.

Generally, on the one hand, there are the so-called *minimalists*, favouring *low-intensity* court control[11] and *delocalized* arbitration, arguing that an international arbitral award is 'not anchored in any national legal order [but] is a decision of international justice, whose validity must be ascertained with regard to the rules applicable in the country where its recognition and enforcement are sought.'[12] On the other hand, there are the *maximalists*, i.e. States where arbitration as an alternative dispute settlement mechanism is subjected to a more careful judicial scrutiny. And then there are the majority that are trying to find a healthy balance between arbitral autonomy and judicial scrutiny.

As a result, inter alia, of the differing approaches vis-à-vis judicial controls over arbitration, a relatively recent legal phenomenon has emerged—many States have modified their arbitration laws with a view to seemingly enhance the efficiency of arbitration process and allow parties, under certain conditions, to exclude the application of setting-aside proceedings through the conclusion of the so-called *exclusion agreements*—agreements permitting contractual exclusion of the right to challenge an arbitral award before courts at the seat of arbitration. The Swiss Private International Law Act ('PILA') and its Article 192(1) in this regard can be considered as the pioneer[13] an example later followed by many other hubs of international arbitration, such as France, Sweden, Belgium and others.

---

[8] Park (2001), p. 595 et seq.

[9] Sattar (2010), p. 73.

[10] Craig (1988), p. 174.

[11] Paulsson (2013), p. 144.

[12] This view is taken from the famous case *Société PT Putrabali Adyamulia v Société Rena Holding et Société Moguntia Est Epices*, Cour de Cassation, 29 June 2007, 05-18.053 and represents the French school of thought.

[13] Art. 192(1) of the PILA provides: '[w]here none of the parties has its domicile, its habitual residence, or a place of business in Switzerland, they may, by an express statement in the arbitration agreement or in a subsequent agreement in writing, exclude all setting aside proceedings, or they may limit such proceedings to one or several of the grounds listed in Article 190, paragraph 2.'.

It is true that by loosening the *lex arbitri* and minimizing judicial scrutiny over arbitration proceedings, on the one hand, and giving more procedural autonomy to arbitrating parties, on the other hand, many States strive for more attractiveness when it comes to choosing a venue and the *lex arbitri* applicable to arbitration proceedings. An arbitration-friendly legal environment is one of the most important prerequisites that parties consider when choosing an arbitral seat.[14] Since international arbitration proceedings are capable of raising significant amount of revenue, States tend to experiment with their *lex arbitri* with a view to attract more international arbitrations.[15]

Relatively recently, one of such *legislative experiments*, namely Article 192(1) of the PILA, was challenged before the European Court of Human Rights ('ECtHR' or the 'Court'). On 1 March 2016, the ECtHR delivered a judgment in the case of *Tabbane v. Switzerland* in which the Court examined the compatibility of Article 192(1) of the PILA with Article 6(1) of the European Convention for the Protection of Human Rights and Fundamental Freedoms ('ECHR' or the 'Convention') which, inter alia, guarantees everyone the right of access to a court.[16] By applying certain well-established legal principles pertaining to the relationship between arbitration and human rights, in particular under the ECHR, the Court concluded that parties, provided certain pre-conditions are fulfilled, have full autonomy to renounce in advance the application of setting-aside proceedings, and that Article 192(1) of the PILA does not violate Article 6(1) of the ECHR and the right of access to a court.[17]

The Court's decision in the *Tabbane v. Switzerland* case raises a question whether arbitrating parties indeed have an absolute autonomy to exclude in advance the application of setting-aside proceedings—a mechanism that verifies, inter alia, whether an arbitral award complies with such seemingly *non-waivable* rights as the right to a fair hearing and the right to an independent and impartial tribunal. This is especially true when an arbitral tribunal has issued a declaratory award or an award dismissing all or some of the claims. Such an arbitral award would not require any further enforcement, and thus also a control by State courts in the recognition and enforcement proceedings.

Moreover, somewhat further developing the issue of compatibility of exclusion agreements with the ECHR and trying to similarly ascertain the limits of ECHR Member States' discretion vis-à-vis regulation of setting-aside proceedings in their national arbitration law, another thought-provoking phenomenon relates to a situation where the setting-aside mechanism is simply non-existent in the applicable *lex arbitri*. This is the case in Latvia—the author's home country—which is the only Member State of the Council of Europe that does not provide in its national law a mechanism

---

[14] See, e.g. Queen Mary University of London, White & Case (2018) 2018 International Arbitration Survey: The Evolution of International Arbitration, p. 9. http://www.arbitration.qmul.ac.uk/research/2018/. Accessed 21 May 2020.

[15] Berger (1993), pp. 1–6. See also Illmer (2011), p. 646 citing a study that estimated 'the total value of the fees generated by the main European arbitration centres not including ad hoc arbitration at around EUR 4 billion per year'.

[16] *Tabbane v. Switzerland*, App. No. 41069/12, ECtHR, 1 March 2016.

[17] Ibid., para. 36.

for challenging arbitral awards. To some extent the current Latvian approach echoes the *innovative* (albeit severely criticized and later also abandoned Article 1717(4) of the Belgian Code of Civil Procedure ('BCCP') (as amended on 27 March 1985) that abolished setting-aside proceedings for arbitral awards issued in Belgium unless one of the parties to arbitration proceedings was Belgian. Apart from Latvia (and formerly to some degree also Belgium), complete statutory unavailability of setting-aside proceedings is characteristic also to few other States, e.g. formerly Malaysia and currently Kyrgyzstan.

Although in recent years there have been vivid academic discussions about the necessity of setting-aside proceedings,[18] apart from the unsuccessful, and later also abandoned, Belgium's attempt to eliminate setting-aside proceedings, only a handful of States have endeavored to do away with setting-aside proceedings altogether. The mechanism for challenging arbitral awards is still a prevalent method of judicial control over arbitration proceedings that States are generally reluctant to give up. Moreover, even though some States provide for a statutory possibility to exclude the application of setting-aside proceedings, due to the severe consequences that such an exclusion entails, arbitrating parties are generally cautious and hesitant to exclude their right to challenge arbitral awards.[19]

In the wake of the *Tabbane v. Switzerland* case, many questions arise in this regard pertaining not only to the exact extent of party autonomy to exclude the application of setting-aside proceedings, but also to the extent to which States are free to regulate setting-aside proceedings in their national arbitration law and still be considered as complying with their obligations under the ECHR. Despite the Court's conclusions in the *Tabbane v. Switzerland* case, one must ask—is party autonomy in this regard truly unlimited? Is it permissible to exclude in advance also such seemingly non-waivable rights as the right to a fair hearing and the right to an independent and impartial tribunal, both embodied in Article 6(1) of the ECHR? Would an exclusion agreement in different circumstances nevertheless lead to its incompatibility with the Convention? Similarly, do ECHR Member States have an absolute obligation to put in place an effective mechanism providing for the setting aside of a possibly defective arbitral award or is total non-availability of setting-aside proceedings compliant with the ECHR?

Answers to these questions have been seemingly left open after the Court's *Tabbane v. Switzerland* ruling and the present book will address them. Despite certain principles and guidelines that the ECtHR has established over the years in various arbitration-related cases brought before it, the exact extent of the relationship between arbitration and human rights, especially certain procedural human rights, such as the right to a fair trial enshrined in Article 6(1) of the ECHR, is still somewhat obscure. At least to the extent to provide concrete answers to the above questions.

The ECtHR's ruling in the *Tabbane v. Switzerland* case suggests that arbitrating parties have full autonomy to exclude their right to challenge an arbitral award before

---

[18] See, among other sources, Van den Berg (2014).

[19] For Switzerland, see Van den Berg (2014), p. 15 Dasser (2007), p. 471. For Sweden, see, e.g., Heuman and Jarvin (2006), p. 536. Generally, see Chap. 5.

State courts. This conclusion entails the balancing of two competing interests—judicial control and the legitimacy of arbitral awards, on the one hand, and party autonomy and willingness for an increased finality, on the other hand. Provided that the exclusion is voluntary and attended by certain minimum safeguards commensurate to its importance, the latter, as interpreted by the ECtHR, seemingly prevails over the former.

However, it is questionable whether full exclusion of setting-aside proceedings is *permissible* in all circumstances. Since the very first ruling on the interplay between arbitration and the ECHR[20] the general interpretation of applicability of ECHR norms to arbitration proceedings has been governed by the so-called *waiver theory* which entails that parties, by concluding an arbitration agreement, waive certain rights guaranteed by Article 6(1) of the ECHR.[21] Nevertheless, the ECtHR has also held that a '[w]aiver may be permissible with regard to certain rights but not with regard to certain others [and that a] distinction may have to be made even between different rights guaranteed by Article 6'.[22]

Until now the ECtHR has not clearly established which rights are *waivable* and which, on the other hand, are so fundamentally important in a democratic society that the signing of an arbitration agreement does not impair their applicability to arbitration proceedings and the resulting arbitral award. It is argued that the category of *non-waivable* rights include, inter alia, the right to a fair hearing and the right to an independent and impartial tribunal, both of which have been considered to be part of broader procedural public policy.[23]

Generally, grounds for setting aside an arbitral award include, inter alia, also grounds that pertain to violations of what have been characterized as *non-waivable* rights within the meaning of Article 6(1) of the ECHR.[24] An arbitral award may be set aside by courts at the seat of arbitration both for violations of due process and an improper constitution of an arbitral tribunal. If the right to challenge an arbitral award is either voluntarily excluded in advance or simply does not exist in the applicable national arbitration law in the first place, there is no opportunity for parties to object against potential violations of their *non-waivable* rights.

The indefinite relationship between arbitration and the ECHR, especially the somewhat obscure distinction between *waivable* and *non-waivable* rights of Article 6(1) of the ECHR, provides ample room for a normative discussion and analysis on the most appropriate regulatory approach to exclude setting-aside proceedings in national arbitration law—an approach that would most correspond with the Court's own established principles pertaining to the dichotomy between arbitration and the ECHR, in particular the right to a fair trial under Article 6(1) of the ECHR.

The ECtHR's ruling in the *Tabbane v. Switzerland* case seemingly provides an answer to the question on compatibility of exclusion agreements with the ECHR,

---

[20] *X. v. the Federal Republic of Germany*, App. No. 1197/61, ECmHR, 5 March 1962.

[21] See Sect. 3.4.

[22] *Suovaniemi and others v. Finland*, App. No. 31737/96, ECtHR, 23 February 1999.

[23] See Sects. 3.4.3.3, 7.2.2.1 and 7.2.2.3.

[24] See Sect. 4.4.1.

in particular, the right to a fair trial under Article 6(1) of the ECHR. However, on a closer look, it raises more questions than it provides answers, both as to the accuracy and comprehensiveness of the Court's conclusions, as well as the role of the indefinite distinction between *waivable* and *non-waivable* rights of Article 6(1) of the ECHR and its impact on the validity of exclusion agreements under the ECHR. Equally, although the former approach in Belgium in statutorily excluding the application of setting-aside proceedings altogether was severely criticized by many,[25] it witnessed little attention from the perspective of its compatibility with the ECHR.[26] To this date there has been little scholarly contribution analyzing the interplay between the availability of setting-aside proceedings under national arbitration law, on the one hand, and certain procedural human rights as provided for in the ECHR, in particular the right to a fair trial under Article 6(1) of the ECHR, on the other hand.

The overall aim of this book is three-fold. First, it provides comprehensive and critical analysis of the dichotomy between arbitration and the ECHR, in particular the right to a fair trial under Article 6(1) of the ECHR. As said, despite certain established principles, the exact extent of the relationship between arbitration and the ECHR, in particular the right to a fair trial under Article 6(1) of the ECHR, is still somewhat obscure. Second, by first briefly introducing the challenge mechanism per se, this book then more in detail explores the various different legislative ways how States have approached statutory exclusion of setting-aside proceedings. It not only analyzes different States' (e.g. Switzerland, France, Belgium, Sweden and others) national laws that provide arbitrating parties with the possibility to voluntarily exclude setting-aside proceedings, but also introduces the reader to more *exotic* examples of national laws that exclude setting-aside proceedings altogether (e.g. formerly Belgium and Malaysia, currently—Kyrgyzstan and Latvia). Lastly, by examining the various different legislative approaches to excluding the application of setting-aside proceedings from the viewpoint of their compatibility with the ECHR, in particular the right to a fair trial under Article 6(1) of the ECHR, this book puts forward certain *de lege ferenda* recommendations as to the most appropriate, ECHR-compatible approach to regulating setting-aside proceedings in national arbitration law.

1.2 Organization of the Book

Chapter 2 provides a succinct overview of the ECHR, its enforcement machinery, general rules of applicability and its underlying principles of interpretation—all geared towards better understanding the relationship between arbitration and the ECHR.

Chapter 3 introduces the main theme of the present book—arbitration and the ECHR. It provides comprehensive and up-to-date analysis of the interplay between arbitration and the ECHR, in particular by introducing the different approaches of

[25] See Sect. 6.2.

[26] See, in particular, Jaksic (2002), pp. 285–318.

applicability of the ECHR to arbitration and examining the existing ECtHR case law regarding the relationship between arbitration and human rights norms enshrined in the ECHR, in particular the right to a fair trial under Article 6(1) of the ECHR. This chapter is intended as an all-encompassing examination of the ECtHR's practice and attitude towards arbitration, geared towards the more specific subject focus of this book, namely setting-aside proceedings, in particular, exclusion agreements and the phenomenon of total lack of setting-aside proceedings in national arbitration law.

Chapter 4 introduces the main more specific subject focus of this book, i.e. the annulment mechanism—its genesis, theoretical underpinnings and various procedural issues, such as jurisdiction, time-limits etc. More emphasis, however, will be put on the actual grounds on which an arbitral award may be annulled. This will be done by succinctly looking at each annulment ground provided in the 1985 United Nations Commission on International Trade Law ('UNCITRAL') Model Law on International Commercial Arbitration ('UNCITRAL Model Law'), i.e. an instrument that has been said to depict a general consensus in this regard.[27]

Chapter 5 is dedicated to the issue of exclusion agreements. It looks at various approaches that States have adopted when introducing a possibility to exclude the application of setting-aside proceedings in their national arbitration laws. For this purpose, a comparative analysis will be carried out of the most common ECHR Member States' legislative approaches and provisions permitting voluntary exclusion of setting-aside proceedings. These States include Switzerland, France, Sweden and Belgium. Chapter 5 also includes a brief overview of other States' approaches to regulating the exclusion of setting-aside proceedings, both those States that adopt a more liberal approach, as well as those that look at the exclusion of setting-aside proceedings more restrictively or take an intermediate approach in that regard.

Chapter 6 looks at the phenomenon of total lack of setting-aside proceedings in national arbitration law. This is not only the case of Latvia—the author's home country, but also other States—both formerly (e.g. Belgium, Malaysia) and presently (e.g. Kyrgyzstan). The focus, however, will be on the case of Latvia, by providing a brief historical overview of the legislative development of arbitration in Latvia in general, and a more *in concreto* look at the issue of setting-aside proceedings in Latvian arbitration law, both from a historical and a contemporary perspective, with a view to understand the underlying reasons why the Latvian legislature has decided not to statutorily regulate the mechanism for challenging arbitral awards.

Chapter 7 critically reflects on the contemporary relationship between arbitration, in particular setting-aside proceedings, and the ECHR and aims to determine the extent to which States are free to regulate setting-aside proceedings in their national arbitration law and still be considered as complying with their obligations under the ECHR, in particular the right to a fair trial under Article 6(1) of the ECHR. It moreover provides certain *de lege ferenda* recommendations as to the most appropriate, ECHR-compatible approach to regulating setting-aside proceedings in national arbitration law.

---

[27] Born (2014), p. 3187.

Chapter 8 provides a concise conclusion, summarizing the main findings of this book.

References

Berger KP (1993) International economic arbitration. Kluwer Law and Taxation Publishers, Deventer, Boston

Born G (2014) International commercial arbitration, 2nd edn. Kluwer Law International

Craig WL (1988) Uses and abuses of appeal from awards. Arbitr Int 174–227. https://doi.org/10.1093/arbitration/4.3.174

Dasser F (2007) International arbitration and setting aside proceedings in Switzerland: a statistical analysis. ASA Bull 25:444–472

Heuman L, Jarvin S (eds) (2006) The Swedish Arbitration Act of 1999 five years on: a critical review of strengths and weaknesses. Juris Publishing

Illmer M (2011) Brussels I and arbitration revisited. Rabel J Comparative Int Private Law 75(3):645–670

Jaksic A (2002) Arbitration and human rights. Peter Lang, Frankfurt am Main

Kerr M (1985) Arbitration and the courts: The UNCITRAL model law. ICLQ 34(1):1–24

Park WW (2001) Why Courts review arbitral awards. In: Briner R et al (eds) Law of international business and dispute settlement in the 21st century, Liber Amicorum Karl-Heinz Bockstiegel. Carl Heymanns Verlag KG, Köln/Berlin/Bonn/München, pp 595–606

Paulsson J (2013) The idea of arbitration. Oxford University Press

Poudret JF, Besson S (2006) Comparative law of international arbitration. Sweet & Maxwell, United Kingdom

Roebuck D, Loynes De, de Fumichon B (2004) Roman arbitration. Holo books. The Arbitration Press, Oxford

Sattar S (2010) National Courts and international arbitration: a double-edged sword? J Int Arbitr 27(1):51–73

Van den Berg AJ (2014) Should the setting aside of the arbitral award be abolished? ICSID Rev 1–26. https://doi.org/10.1093/icsidreview/sit053

Chapter 2
The ECHR: In Brief Perspective

2.1 A General Overview

It was not until after the Second World War that specific catalogues of human rights and freedoms emerged in the international arena. As a response to the horrific violations of human rights during the Second World War, international community was determined to seize the moment and draft international human rights instruments that would serve as means to avoid such violations in future.[1] The very first instrument of such a kind was the United Nations Universal Declaration of Human Rights (Universal Declaration) adopted by the United Nations General Assembly in 1948 that for the first time recognized and set out universally protected 'inalienable rights of all members of the human family'.[2]

The Member States of the recently established Council of Europe drew inspiration from the Universal Declaration and in 1950 signed regionally applicable human rights instrument that would serve similar ends—the ECHR. It entered into force three years later and since then has provided a coherent system for the protection of the most fundamental human rights and freedoms in Europe.

The rights and freedoms set out in the ECHR were derived from the Universal Declaration and essentially can be categorized into two generations. The first and most predominant generation of *civil and political* rights protects the enjoyment of the most basic human rights, including, among others, the right to life, freedom of speech, freedom of religion and also the right to fair trial. The second-generation rights, labelled as *economic, social and cultural* rights, developed especially after the Second World War and include, inter alia, the right to education, social rights, and freedom of association and other rights.[3]

---

[1] Rainey B et al. (2014), p. 3.

[2] Preamble of the United Nations Universal Declaration of Human Rights.

[3] In recent years, separate categories of third and fourth generation human rights have also been developed. More on the evolution of human rights, please see, e.g., Pocar (2015) and Macklem (2015).

© The Editor(s) (if applicable) and The Author(s), under exclusive license to Springer Nature Switzerland AG 2020

T. Krūmiņš, *Arbitration and Human Rights*,
https://doi.org/10.1007/978-3-030-54237-5_2

The ECHR primarily addresses civil and political rights, and also with regard to the applicability of the ECHR to arbitration, the first-generation rights, especially the right to a fair trial enshrined in Article 6(1) of the ECHR, have had the greatest impact. Certain first and second-generation rights and freedoms are additionally provided in the Protocols to the ECHR that, on a voluntary basis, have been signed by many Member States of the ECHR. For the purposes of applicability of the ECHR to arbitration, the most important right not directly stipulated in the text of the ECHR itself is the right to protection of property enshrined in Article 1 of Protocol 1 to the ECHR. The ECtHR has repeatedly recognized that an arbitral award can constitute a 'possession' within the meaning of Article 1 of Protocol 1 to the ECHR.[4]

International law, including international human rights law, creates obligations for its subjects. As regards the traditional subjects of international law, i.e. States, the ECHR in this respect is straightforward. Article 1 of the ECHR requires its Member States to secure to everyone within their jurisdiction the rights and freedoms guaranteed in the ECHR and its Protocols, provided that the respective Protocol has been signed and ratified.[5] Human rights are not created by States—they 'derive from the inherent dignity of the human person'[6] and pertain to an individual solely because of his or her qualities as a human being. By signing and adhering to the ECHR, Member States thus have an obligation to recognize, respect and protect such rights.[7]

In order to ensure the abovementioned engagements undertaken by the Member States[8] the ECHR also established an enforcement mechanism that, although witnessed a major reform in 1998, has effectively carried out its main task, i.e. to provide a platform for Member States, persons, non-governmental organization and groups of people to bring applications concerning alleged violations of their Convention rights and freedoms, and also to ensure that Member States comply with their respective obligations under the Convention.

2.2 The ECHR's Enforcement Mechanism

Without an effective mechanism for ensuring the protection of the rights and freedoms enshrined in the Convention, the purpose and practical relevance of the Convention would be endangered. Therefore, with the entry into force of the ECHR two separate organs were created to ensure that ECHR Member States comply with their respective

[4]See, e.g. *Stran Greek Refineries and Stratis Andreadis v. Greece*, App. No. 13427/87, ECtHR, 9 December 1994, para. 62; *Regent Company v. Ukraine*, App. No. 773/03, ECtHR, 3 April 2008, para. 61; *Kin-Stib and Majkić v. Serbia*, App. No. 12312/05, ECtHR, 20 April 2010, paras. 83–85.

[5]Protocols to the ECHR. http://www.coe.int/en/web/conventions/search-on-treaties/-/conventions/treaty/results/subject/3. Accessed 21 May 2020.

[6]Preamble of the ICCPR.

[7]See Sect. 2.5.

[8]Art. 19 of the ECHR.

obligations thereunder. Following a major institutional reform in 1998, currently the task of overseeing the compliance with the Convention is vested in one single institution, namely the ECtHR. However, a great number of arbitration-related cases were decided prior the 1998-reform under the 'old regime'.

Initially, the Convention established two organs—the European Commission of Human Rights ('ECmHR' or the 'Commission') and the Court.[9] The vast majority of arbitration-related cases were decided by the former Commission that under the 'old regime' was entitled to hear applications and decide on their admissibility or inadmissibility. If an application was declared inadmissible (which was mostly the case with arbitration-related applications), the case was closed. If, however, the Commission declared an application admissible, it continued with considering the merits of the case and prepared a report as to whether there had been a violation of the ECHR or not.[10] Only after an application survived the 'admissibility stage' before the Commission it would be further referred to the Cabinet of Ministers or the Court for final examination.[11]

Although, as mentioned, the majority of arbitration-related applications did not get pass the 'admissibility stage', the Commission's admissibility decisions continue to have an effect as important sources for the interpretation and application of the Convention.[12] This is especially true for arbitration-related cases decided by the ECtHR in which the Court greatly relies on principles and rules established by the former Commission in its admissibility decisions.

Due to the significant increase of applications and also the rapidly increasing number of Member States of the Council of Europe in the beginning of 1990s, there was a pressing need to restructure the Convention's enforcement mechanism in order to make it more efficient. A solution was found by signing of Protocol 11 that amended the Convention and as of 1 November 1998 replaced the former Commission and the Court with a new permanent Court that since then oversees both—admissibility and merits stages of application.[13]

The Convention distinguishes between two types of applications that can be brought before the ECtHR—inter-state applications filed by one State against another and individual applications filed by 'any person, non-governmental organization or group of individuals claiming to be the victim of a violation [...] of the rights set [out in the Convention]'.[14] The overwhelming majority of applications are brought by individuals. Notably, all arbitration-related applications decided by the ECtHR (or

[9] Former Art. 19 of the ECHR.

[10] Former Art. 30 of the ECHR. For more detail see Rainey et al. (2014), p. 8, Mikaelsen (1980), pp. 15–17; Zwart (1994), pp. 26–27.

[11] Rainey et al. (2014), p. 8.

[12] Ibid., p. 20.

[13] Protocol 11 to the Convention for the Protection of Human Rights and Fundamental Freedoms, restructuring the control machinery established thereby. https://www.coe.int/en/web/conventions/full-list/-/conventions/rms/090000168007cda9. Accessed 21 May 2020.

[14] Art. 34 of the ECHR.

the former Commission) have been brought by individuals, therefore further short overview of admissibility requirements will concern individual applications only.

2.3 Admissibility of Individual Applications

Article 34 of the ECHR provides that:

> The Court may receive applications from any person, nongovernmental organization or group of individuals claiming to be the victim of a violation by one of the High Contracting Parties of the rights set forth in the Convention or the Protocols thereto. The High Contracting Parties undertake not to hinder in any way the effective exercise of this right.

The right to file an individual application has been described as 'a key component of the machinery for protecting the rights and freedoms set forth in the Convention'.[15] Indeed, it gives any individual the right to address the Court with applications of alleged violations of the rights and freedoms provided in the Convention. However, what exactly falls into the category of 'any person, nongovernmental organization or group of individuals'? Although parties to commercial arbitration may include private individuals and public entities, international commercial arbitration disputes are primarily disputes between two or more corporate entities. Therefore, a question arises to what extent a corporate body is protected under the ECHR and is entitled to lodge an application.

It is said that the Convention's founding fathers never thought of excluding corporate bodies from the protective regime of the ECHR.[16] Corporate bodies and their right to file applications before the ECtHR are included within the scope of the term 'nongovernmental organizations'. Although the first versions of the Convention's text also referred to 'corporate persons' and 'corporate bodies' under Article 35 of the ECHR, the final version settled for the benefit of the broader term of 'nongovernmental organizations'.[17] This, however, does not mean that by broadening the scope of application it was intended to exclude corporate bodies.[18]

The fact that the Convention also applies to corporate entities (as far as the right to file an individual application is concerned) has been long affirmed also by the Court. Since its first judgment concerning an individual application by a corporate claimant in 1979,[19] the Court has repeatedly affirmed that corporate bodies have rights to file applications regarding alleged violations of the Convention's rights and freedoms.[20]

---

[15] *Mamatkulov and Askarov v. Turkey*, Apps. No. 46827/99, 46951/99, ECtHR, 4 February 2005, at 122.

[16] Emberland (2006), pp. 3–4.

[17] Van den Muijsenbergh and Rezai (2012), p. 48.

[18] Emberland (2006), p. 35.

[19] *The Sunday Times v. United Kingdom*, App. No. 6538/74, ECtHR, 26 April 1979.

[20] See, e.g., cases reported in European Court of Human Rights, Factsheet—Companies: victims or culprits, July 2013. http://www.echr.coe.int/Documents/FS_Companies_ENG.pdf. Accessed 21 May 2020.

A separate question is the extent to which legal entities are protected under the ECHR and, in particular, the specific rights and guarantees enshrined in the ECHR that also apply to companies. The most obvious right whose violation can be invoked also by corporate bodies is the right to fair trial under Article 6(1) of the ECHR, however, other rights, e.g. the right to property, may be equally important.[21]

As mentioned, for one reason or another, a great deal of arbitration-related applications before the ECtHR (or previously the Commission) have not survived the admissibility stage and advanced to the analysis of the case on merits. This is due to the Convention establishing several grounds of inadmissibility that are briefly summarized below.

2.3.1 Procedural Grounds of Inadmissibility

Article 35 of the ECHR provides for certain admissibility criteria that must be complied with in order for an application to be considered before the ECtHR.

First, prior to filing an application with the Court it is necessary to exhaust all domestic remedies.[22] This requirement is based on the principle of subsidiarity and the assumption that national authorities should first have an opportunity to remedy alleged violations of the ECHR. The non-exhaustion of national legal remedies has also been a ground for inadmissibility for certain arbitration-related applications, in particular also with regard to setting-aside proceedings.[23]

Secondly, Article 35(1) of the ECHR stipulates that an application shall be filed 'within a period of six months from the date on which the final decision was taken'. If an application is brought after the said period of time, the Court has the right to declare it inadmissible.[24]

Article 35 of the ECHR also lists several other procedural grounds of inadmissibility pursuant to which an application will not be dealt with by the Court. These

---

[21] See Sect. 3.3.2.

[22] Generally on the exhaustion of domestic legal remedies see, e.g. Rainey et al. (2014), pp. 34–36; Harris et al. (2014), pp. 47–61. European Court on Human Rights: Practical Guide on Admissibility Criteria. http://www.echr.coe.int/Documents/Admissibility_guide_ENG.pdf. Accessed 21 May 2020.

[23] The ECHR has in numerous cases refused to hear arbitration-related applications arguing that by failing to apply for the setting aside of an arbitral award the applicant has failed to exhaust all domestic legal remedies. See, e.g. *R. v. Switzerland*, App. No. 10881/84, ECmHR, 4 March 1987; *Hedland v. Sweden*, App. No. 24118/94, ECmHR, 9 April 1997. In case the applicable national arbitration law does not even provide for a possibility of setting aside an arbitral award (e.g. the case of Latvia), such an argumentation would not be applicable.

[24] Art. 35(2)(a) of the ECHR. For more information see, e.g., European Court on Human Rights: Practical Guide on Admissibility Criteria, pp. 34–35. http://www.echr.coe.int/Documents/Admissibility_guide_ENG.pdf. Accessed 21 May 2020. See also Harris et al. (2014), p. 73.

include cases where applications are anonymous,[25] the matter at hand is substantially the same as a matter already examined by the Court, or cases where the Court considers that there has been an abuse of the right of individual application.[26]

2.3.2 *Grounds of Inadmissibility Relating to the Court's Jurisdiction*

In addition to procedural grounds of inapplicability, an application may also be dismissed if it falls outside the scope of the Court's jurisdiction. The following grounds of inadmissibility must be examined by the Court *ex officio* and they concern (i) questions of who can file an application against whom (*ratione personae*); (ii) the subject matter of an application (*ratione materiae*); (iii) the application of the Convention in time (*ratione temporis*) and (iv) in place (*ratione loci*).

Ratione personae The Court's competence *ratione personae* has two components. The question of who can bring an application before the ECtHR was already answered—the Convention provides for two types of applications, namely inter-state (Article 33 of the ECHR) and individual applications (Article 34 of the ECHR), provided persons have been 'victims of a violation by one of the Member States of the rights set forth in the Convention or the Protocols thereto.'[27]

The second component of the Court's jurisdiction *ratione personae* relates precisely to the above quoted passage of Article 34 of the ECHR, namely that an application can only be brought for violations committed by a Member State of the ECHR. It is not possible for an individual to bring an application regarding an alleged violation of the Convention by another individual.[28] Generally, the *ratione personae* criteria requires that the alleged violation of the Convention's right or freedom has been committed by a Member State or its authorities, such as courts, police forces etc.[29] It is the ECHR Member States that are bound by the Convention and are required to secure to everyone the rights and freedoms guaranteed therein. If put in the perspective of arbitration-related cases, the requirement that an alleged violation has been committed by a Member State, or at least can be imputable to it, becomes particularly significant.

Arbitration proceedings do not proceed in a legal vacuum. National courts are often required to assist arbitral tribunals or parties to the arbitration proceedings

---

[25] Art. 35(2)(b) of the ECHR. For more information see, e.g., Rainey et al. (2014), pp. 39–40. See also European Court on Human Rights: Practical Guide on Admissibility Criteria, pp. 35–37. http://www.echr.coe.int/Documents/Admissibility_guide_ENG.pdf. Accessed 21 May 2020.

[26] Art. 35(3)(a) of the ECHR. For more information see, e.g., Harris et al. (2014), pp. 79–81. See also European Court on Human Rights: Practical Guide on Admissibility Criteria, pp. 37–40. http://www.echr.coe.int/Documents/Admissibility_guide_ENG.pdf. Accessed 21 May 2020.

[27] Art. 34 of the ECHR. More on the 'victim' requirement see, e.g., Zwart (1994), pp. 50–71.

[28] *X v. United Kingdom*, App. No. 6956/75, ECmHR, 10 December 1976; *Durini v. Italy*, App. No. 19217/91, ECmHR, 12 January 1994.

[29] Harris et al. (2014), p. 81.

with various procedural matters. Although it is evident that the Convention does not produce direct horizontal effect, i.e. it cannot be directly invoked by one individual against another, it does not mean that the Convention produces no horizontal effect at all.[30]

Article 1 of the ECHR requires Member States to 'secure to everyone within their jurisdiction the rights and freedoms defined in [the Convention]'. This requires not only to abstain from interferences with the enjoyment of such rights and freedoms, i.e. a negative obligation, but also requires Member States to put in place effective safeguards against possible violations of particular rights by private individuals, i.e. a positive obligation.[31] The latter in essence produces an indirect horizontal effect, meaning that States may be held responsible for failure to provide sanctions for violations of human rights committed by private individuals within their jurisdiction.[32]

For example, in one landmark arbitration-related case, i.e. *Jakob Boss Söhn KG v. the Federal Republic of Germany*,[33] the former Commission, while recognizing that by concluding an arbitration agreement arbitrating parties renounce the right to have their case determined in court proceedings for the conduct of which a Member State is responsible under the Convention, explicitly stated that:

> This does not mean, however, that the respondent State's responsibility is completely excluded [...] as the arbitration award had to be recognised by [...] courts and be given executory effect by them. The courts thereby exercised a certain control and guarantee as to the fairness and correctness of the arbitration proceedings which they considered to have been carried out in conformity with fundamental rights and in particular with the right of the applicant company to be heard.[34]

Consequently, it is not disputed that ECHR Member States have a positive obligation to ensure that arbitration proceedings within their jurisdiction comply with certain fundamental *fair trial* standards. The question, however, is to what extent Member States have such an obligation? Until now, neither the former Commission nor the Court has provided a clear-cut answer to this question.

Ratione materiae The Court's jurisdiction *ratione materiae* relates to the substantive subject matter of an application and, at least with regard to the applicability of the Convention to arbitration proceedings, can be seen as the most important threshold before a case can be heard by the Court. For a successful application there has to be a violation of one or more of the rights expressly or impliedly guaranteed and protected by the Convention's or its Protocols' provisions. The very first discussions relating to the applicability of the Convention to arbitration centered around the notion of their inapplicability *ratione materiae*.[35] It was argued, for example, that neither the

---

[30] Jaksic (2007), p. 162.

[31] See Sect. 2.5.

[32] Harris et al. (2014), p. 82, Jaksic (2007), Samuel (2004), p. 426, Petrochilos (2004), p. 112.

[33] *Jakob Boss Söhn KG v. the Federal Republic of Germany*, App. No. 18479/91, ECmHR, 2 December 1991.

[34] Ibid.

[35] See in more detail Sect. 3.2.

letter nor the spirit of the Convention suggests that it should apply to arbitration[36] and that an arbitral tribunal cannot be considered as a 'tribunal established by law' within the meaning of Article 6(1) of the ECHR.[37] However, as will be explained,[38] the abovementioned arguments and other objections against the applicability of the Convention to arbitration proceedings have been rebutted both by scholars and, most importantly, also the Court itself.

Ratione temporis The Convention does not produce retroactive effect. An application will not satisfy the requirement *ratione temporis* if it relates to events taking place before the Convention or its Protocols thereto entered into force in the respective Member State.[39] As regards arbitration proceedings, this would require that the alleged violation occurred after the Convention entered into force in the State of the seat of arbitration (or the State of recognition and enforcement if the alleged violation occurs there).

Ratione loci Compatibility with the Convention *ratione loci* requires that alleged violations of the Convention's rights and freedoms occur within the jurisdiction of a Member State of the ECHR.[40] This requirement derives from Article 1 of the ECHR and with regard to arbitration proceedings is not seen as troublesome. Whenever the seat of arbitration (or the State of recognition and enforcement if the alleged violation occurs there) is within one of the ECHR Member States, the requirement *ratione loci* will be satisfied.

2.3.3 Grounds of Inadmissibility Relating to Merits

Although the abovementioned formal requirements may be satisfied, an application may still be rejected on grounds of merits.

Firstly, Article 35(3)(a) of the ECHR provides that the Court will reject an application as inadmissible if it is 'manifestly ill-founded'. This criterion requires the Court to make a preliminary analysis of the substance of an application and is seen as the most common ground for declaring an application inadmissible.[41] This is true also for arbitration-related cases that have mostly been declared 'manifestly ill-founded'

[36] See, e.g., Jarrosson (1989), p. 574, Krings and Matray (1982), p. 256, Giunio (2000), p. 39. Generally, see Sect. 3.2.

[37] Jarrosson (1989), p. 592, Benedettelli (2015), p. 633.

[38] See Sect. 3.2.

[39] Rainey et al. (2014), pp. 87–89. See also European Court on Human Rights: Practical Guide on Admissibility Criteria, pp. 46–52. http://www.echr.coe.int/Documents/Admissibility_guide_ENG.pdf. Accessed 21 May 2020.

[40] More in detail on *ratione loci* see, e.g., Rainey et al. (2014), pp. 89–102. See also European Court on Human Rights: Practical Guide on Admissibility Criteria, pp. 45–46. http://www.echr.coe.int/Documents/Admissibility_guide_ENG.pdf. Accessed 21 May 2020.

[41] Harris et al. (2014), p. 78.

by the former Commission or the Court.[42] Only a handful of arbitration-related cases have resulted in a judgment establishing a violation of the Convention or its Protocols thereto.

In essence, declaration of an application 'manifestly ill-founded' requires a *prima facie* examination of the merits of an application and conclusion by the Court that the submitted allegations are unsubstantiated or that there is no violation of the rights and freedoms provided in the Convention or its Protocols.[43] In such a way, an application is declared inadmissible already at the very beginning without the need to proceed with its examination on merits that would result in a judgment.[44]

The second ground of inadmissibility relating to the merits of an application is a relatively new ground introduced by Protocol 14 in 2010 and is currently enshrined in Article 35(3)(b) of the ECHR. An application may be rejected by the Court if the applicant has not suffered a significant disadvantage. Under this criterion, the Court will examine whether (i) the applicant suffered a significant disadvantage; (ii) whether respect for human rights would in any event require an examination of the case; and (iii) whether the case was duly considered by a domestic tribunal.[45] While there is no hierarchy among the criteria, the Court has noted that the first aspect is at the core of this admissibility criterion.[46]

2.4 Interpretation of the ECHR

In order to better understand the dichotomy between arbitration and the ECHR per se and, in particular, to search for the most appropriate, ECHR-compatible approach to regulating setting-aside proceedings in national arbitration law, it is necessary to

---

[42] See, e.g., *Firma Heinz Schiebler KG v. the Federal Republic of Germany*, App. No. 18805/91, ECmHR, 2 December 1991; *Jakob Boss Söhn KG v. the Federal Republic of Germany*, App. No. 18479/91, ECmHR, 2 December 1991; *Nordström-Janzon and Nordström-Lehtinen v. the Netherlands*, App. No. 28101/95, ECmHR, 27 November 1996; *Pastore v. Italy*, App. No. 46483/99, ECtHR, 25 May 1999; *Suovaniemi and others v. Finland*, App. No. 31737/96, ECtHR., 23 February 1999; *R v. Switzerland*, App. No. 10881/84, ECmHR, 4 March 1987; *Tabbane v. Switzerland*, App. No. 41069/12, ECtHR, 1 March 2016 and others.

[43] Harris et al. (2014), p. 78, Rainey et al. (2014), p. 40.

[44] European Court on Human Rights: Practical Guide on Admissibility Criteria, p. 82. http://www.echr.coe.int/Documents/Admissibility_guide_ENG.pdf. Accessed 21 May 2020.

[45] See, e.g., *Korolev v. Russia*, App. No. 25551/05, ECtHR, 1 July 2010; *Savu v. Romania*, App. No. 29218/05, ECtHR, 11 October 2011; *Kiousi v. Greece*, App. No. 52036/09, ECtHR, 20 September 2011; *Rinck v. France*, App. No. 18774/09, ECtHR, 19 October 2010.

[46] *Shefer v. Russia*, App. No. 45175/04, ECtHR, 13 March 2012, paras. 17–18 where the Court acknowledged that 'the question of whether the applicant has suffered a 'significant disadvantage' is at the core of this admissibility criterion [...] The general principle *de minimis non curat praetor* underlies the logic of Article 35 § 3 (b), which strives to warrant consideration by an international court of only those cases where violation of a right has reached a minimum level of severity. Violations which are purely technical and insignificant outside a formalistic framework do not merit European supervision [...] The assessment of this minimum level is, in the nature of things, relative and depends on all the circumstances of the case'.

concisely reflect also on the principles and notions that the Court takes into account when interpreting the Convention and deciding a particular case.

2.4.1 General Rules of Interpretation

First and foremost, due to the particular character of the ECHR as an international treaty, it has to be interpreted according to the international law rules on the interpretation of treaties that can be found in the 1969 Vienna Convention on the Law of Treaties ('Vienna Convention').[47] Article 31 of the Vienna Convention provides that 'a treaty shall be interpreted in good faith in accordance with the ordinary meaning to be given to the terms of the treaty in their context and in the light of its object and purpose.' Having considered it as a reflection of customary international law, the Court had recognized and taken into account the above stated general principle of interpretation even before the Vienna Convention entered into force.[48] In later judgments the Court has confirmed the importance of the Vienna Convention in interpreting the Convention and deriving other interpretation techniques thereof that will be considered in brief below.[49]

2.4.2 The Object and Purpose of the Convention

In interpreting the Convention, the Court puts great emphasis on its object and purpose—an interpretive method laid down by the Vienna Convention and further elaborated by the Court in numerous cases. The object and purpose of the Convention stems, inter alia, from its Preamble and has been generally identified as 'the

---

[47] 1969 Vienna Convention on the Law of Treaties. https://treaties.un.org/doc/publication/unts/volume%201155/volume-1155-i-18232-english.pdf. Accessed 21 May 2020.

[48] Harris et al. (2014), p. 65. The Vienna Convention entered into force on 27 January 1980, however, the Court had referred to the general principles of interpretation enshrined in the Vienna Convention already earlier in, e.g. *Golder v. United Kingdom*, App. No. 4451/70, ECtHR, 21 February 1975, paras. 29–30.

[49] See, in particular, *Saadi v. United Kingdom*, App. No. 13229/03, ECtHR [GC], 29 January 2008, para. 62 where the Court summarized its approach regarding interpretation of the ECHR in the following way: '[u]nder the Vienna Convention on the Law of Treaties, the Court is required to ascertain the ordinary meaning to be given to the words in their context and in the light of the object and purpose of the provision from which they are drawn [...] The Court must have regard to the fact that the context of the provision is a treaty for the effective protection of individual human rights and that the Convention must be read as a whole, and interpreted in such a way as to promote internal consistency and harmony between its various provisions [...] The Court must also take into account any relevant rules and principles of international law applicable in relations between the Contracting Parties [...] Recourse may also be had to supplementary means of interpretation, including the preparatory works to the Convention, either to confirm a meaning determined in accordance with the above steps, or to establish the meaning where it would otherwise be ambiguous, obscure or manifestly absurd or unreasonable [...]'.

protection of individual human rights'[50] and the maintenance and promotion of 'the ideals and values of a democratic society'.[51]

An example of the Court recognizing and applying the doctrine of the 'object and purpose' of the Convention is the well-known *Golder v. United Kingdom* case, where despite the absence of a clear wording in Article 6(1) of the ECHR the Court recognized and read the right of access to a court into the broader right to fair trial provided in Article 6(1) of the ECHR.[52] Since then, the implied right of access to a court has been recognized in numerous cases.[53] The right of access to a court is also one of the most frequently invoked rights in arbitration-related cases before the ECtHR. Also with regard to the availability of setting-aside proceedings in national arbitration law, the right of access to a court plays an important role. Even more so, in absence of a right of access to a court by means of setting-aside proceedings, parties would not be able to enjoy other rights of Article 6(1) of the ECHR, especially the so-called *non-waivable* rights, such as the right to a fair hearing and the right to an independent and impartial tribunal.

2.4.3 Evolutive Interpretation

The content of the Convention's rights and freedoms is not static and has changed over times. The Convention does not contain an exhaustive list of detailed principles that would cover every aspect of our fundamental rights and freedoms.[54] It is rather seen as a 'bill of rights' providing only general principles, subject to further interpretation

---

[50] *Soering v. United Kingdom*, App. No. 15038/88, ECtHR, 7 July 1989, para. 87.

[51] Rainey et al. (2014), p. 7.

[52] *Golder v. United Kingdom*, App. No. 4451/70, ECtHR, 21 February 1975, at 36 where the Court considered that 'the right of access [to a court] constitutes an element which is inherent in the right stated by [Article 6(1)]. This is not an extensive interpretation forcing new obligations on the Contracting States: it is based on the very terms of the first sentence of [Article 6(1)] read in its context and having regard to the object and purpose of the Convention, a lawmaking treaty [...] and to general principles of law.'.

[53] See, e.g., *Kuzmenko v. Ukraine*, App. No. 49526/07, ECtHR, 9 March 2017, para. 25; *Baka v. Hungary*, App. No. 20261/12, ECtHR [GC], 23 June 2016, para. 120; *Cudak v. Lithuania*, App. No. 15869/02, ECtHR [GC], 23 March 2010, para. 54; *Markovic and others v. Italy*, App. No. 1398/03, ECtHR [GC], 14 December 2006, para. 92.

[54] For example, when the Convention was signed in 1950 it was hard to envisage that overseeing the protection and enjoyment of human rights on the Internet, would become the every-day life of the Convention's controlling mechanisms. See, e.g., the extensive report on internet cases prepared by the Research Division of the ECHR. European Court of Human Rights, Research Division, Internet: Case-Law of the European Court of Human Rights (June 2015). http://www.echr.coe.int/Documents/Research_report_internet_ENG.pdf. Accessed 21 May 2020.

by the Court.[55] Therefore, in order to successfully deal and respond to the ever-changing present day conditions, the Court already in 1978 developed the so-called evolutive or dynamic interpretation of the Convention.[56]

It was first adopted by the Court in the famous *Tyrer v. United Kingdom* case where the Court stated that 'the Convention is a living instrument which [...] must be interpreted in the light of present-day conditions.'[57] Since then, it has been widely recognized in other cases[58] and, as will be seen, bears importance also with regard to the Convention's application to arbitration.

2.4.4 Common Standards

In interpreting the Convention, the Court will also give due consideration to the fact that there exists a consensus among many Member States as regards a certain matter. The Court has relied on comparative surveys of the laws of the Member States in cases relating to, for example, the right to respect for private and family life of same-sex couples,[59] the retention of DNA samples,[60] recognition of the gender identity of transsexuals[61] and others. It has been argued that the justification for relying on national law standards when interpreting an international treaty is the fact that the Convention itself has been inspired by European 'common law' and that a deviation from generally accepted practices among the Member States would undermine the trust in the Convention.[62]

---

[55] Benedettelli (2015), p. 641.

[56] Generally on the principle of evolutive interpretation see, e.g., Rainey et al. (2014), pp. 73–78.

[57] *Tyrer v. United Kingdom*, App. No. 5856/72, ECtHR, 25 April 1978, para. 31.

[58] See, e.g., *Mitzinger v. Germany*, App. No. 29762/10, ECtHR, 9 February 2017, para. 41; *Austin and Others v. the United Kingdom*, Apps. No. 39692/09, 40713/09 and 41008/09, ECtHR [GC], 15 March 2012, para. 53; *Bayatyan v. Armenia*, App. No. 23459/03, ECtHR [GC], 7 July 2011, para. 102; *Christine Goodwin v. the United Kingdom* App. No.28957/95, ECtHR [GC], 11 July 2002, para. 75; *Kress v. France*, App. No. 39594/98, ECtHR [GC], 7 June 2001, para. 70.

[59] *Schalk and Kopf v. Austria*, App. No. 30141/04, ECtHR, 24 June 2006, at 93 stating that 'a rapid evolution of social attitudes towards same-sex couples has taken place in many member States [and] a considerable number of member States have afforded legal recognition to same-sex couples'.

[60] *S. and Marper v. United Kingdom*, Apps. No. 30562/04 and 30566/04, ECtHR [GC], 4 December 2008 where the Court referred to the consensus in the great majority of the Member States: 'the strong consensus existing among the Contracting States in this respect is of considerable importance and narrows the margin of appreciation left to the respondent State in the assessment of the permissible limits of the interference with private life in this sphere. The Court considers that any State claiming a pioneer role in the development of new technologies bears special responsibility for striking the right balance in this regard.'.

[61] *Christine Goodwin v. United Kingdom*, App. No. 28957/95, ECtHR [GC], 11 July 2002, paras. 84–85.

[62] Harris et al. (2014), p. 11.

The common standards doctrine may also help in the search for the most ECHR-compatible approach to excluding setting-aside proceedings under national arbitration law. Since there are already a handful of States permitting voluntary exclusion of setting-aside proceedings, the common standards interpretive method, especially after the ECtHR's decision in the *Tabbane v. Switzerland* case, carries slightly less weight for arguing that such exclusion agreements in their entirety are contrary to the ECHR. This, however, does not mean that there is no room for arguing that such agreements, by excluding also the grounds of challenge of an arbitral award that pertain to the *non-waivable* rights, may lead to a violation of the ECHR. The same holds true for a legislative approach that excludes the availability of setting-aside proceedings altogether. Currently, Latvia is the only ECHR Member State that does not statutorily regulate setting-aside proceedings. Other ECHR Member States, despite some of them expressly providing for an opportunity to exclude such a right, nevertheless statutorily regulate and provide arbitrating parties with a possibility to challenge arbitral awards before their courts.

2.4.5 *Margin of Appreciation*

The doctrine of margin of appreciation is at the heart of the Convention's system, its interpretation and the relationship between the Convention's controlling bodies, on the one hand, and ECHR Member States, on the other hand. Being perhaps one of the most extensively commented principles of interpretation of the ECHR,[63] the principle of margin of appreciation gives the ECHR Member States a certain discretion in fulfilling their obligations under the ECHR.

The margin of appreciation reflects the subsidiary relationship between the Convention's controlling organs and the ECHR Member States. It is said that the latter is initially and primarily responsible for ensuring that the rights and freedoms provided in the ECHR are observed within their territory.[64] The Convention's controlling organs, especially the ECtHR, are there only to supervise the actions or omissions of the Member States whenever a Convention's right or freedom is at stake. The said doctrine was first elaborated in the *Handyside* case in 1976:

> State authorities are in principle in a better position than the international judge to give an opinion on [...]'necessity' of a 'restriction' or 'penalty' [...] [I]t is for the national authorities to make the initial assessment [...]
>
> Consequently, [Article 10(2)] leaves to the Contracting States a margin of appreciation. This margin is given both to the domestic legislator ('prescribed by law') and to the bodies, judicial amongst others, that are called upon to interpret and apply the laws in force [...]
>
> Nevertheless, [Article 10(2)] does not give the Contracting States an unlimited power of appreciation. The Court, which, with the Commission, is responsible for ensuring the observance of those States' engagements [...] is empowered to give the final ruling on whether a

[63] See, among others, Yourow (1996), Arai-Takahashi (2001), Legg (2012).

[64] Harris et al. (2014), p. 17.

> 'restriction' or 'penalty' is reconcilable with freedom of expression as protected by [Article 10]. The domestic margin of appreciation thus goes hand in hand with a European supervision. Such supervision concerns both the aim of the measure challenged and its 'necessity'; it covers not only the basic legislation but also the decision applying it, even one given by an independent court.[65]

Since then, the margin of appreciation doctrine has been applied in numerous cases,[66] especially relating to the Convention's rights and freedoms that are not absolute and may be subject to restrictions imposed by the Member States. Article 6(1) of the ECHR and the right of access to a court is one of such provisions.

It is well-known that the right of access to a court is not absolute and restrictions or waivers may be permissible in certain circumstances.[67] Similarly to other procedural human rights, also the right of access to a court 'by its very nature calls for regulation by the state, regulation which may vary in time and place according to the needs and resources of the community and of individuals'.[68] Thus, State parties are given a certain margin of appreciation in establishing limitations to the right of access to a court. Nevertheless, such limitations must not 'restrict or reduce the access left to the individual in such a way or to such an extent that the very essence of the right is impaired'.[69] In addition, every limitation to a right of access to a court must have a legitimate aim and there has to be a reasonable degree of proportionality 'between the means employed and the aim sought to be achieved'.[70]

The degree or scope of the margin of appreciation varies according to circumstances, the subject matter, context and background of the case.[71] For example, Member States enjoy a narrow margin of appreciation when 'a particularly important

[65] *Handyside v. United Kingdom*, App. No. 5493/72, ECtHR, 7 December 1976, paras. 48–49.

[66] See, e.g., *Evans v. United Kingdom*, App. No. 6339/05, ECtHR [GC], 10 April 2007; *Hämäläinen v. Finland*, App. No. 37359/09, ECtHR [GC], 16 July 2014; *Dickson v. United Kingdom*, App. No. 44362/04, ECtHR [GC], 4 December 2007; *Kart v. Turkey*, App. No. 8917/05, ECtHR [GC], 3 December 2009; *Sahin v. Germany*, App. No. 30943/96, ECtHR [GC], 8 July 2003; *Abdulaziz, Cabales and Balkandali v. United Kingdom*, App. Nos. 9214/80; 9473/81; 9474/81, ECtHR, 28 May 1985; *Mathieu-Mohin and Clerfayt v. Belgium*, App. No. 9267/81, ECtHR, 2 March 1987.

[67] See, e.g., *Golder v. the United Kingdom*, para. 38; *Philis v. Greece*, Apps. No. *12750/87; 13780/88; 14003/*88, ECtHR, 27 August 1991, para. 59; *De Geouffre de la Pradelle v. France*, App. No. 12964/87, ECtHR, 16 December 1992, para. 28; *Stanev v. Bulgaria*, App. No. 36760/06, ECtHR [GC], 17 January 2012, para. 241.

[68] *Golder v. United Kingdom*, App. No. 4451/70, ECtHR, 21 February 1975, para. 38 quoting the so-called Belgian linguistics case, Apps. No. 1474/62; 1677/62; 1691/62; 1769/63; 1994/63; 2126/64, ECtHR, 23 July 1968, para. 5.

[69] *Ashingdane v. the United Kingdom*, App. No. 8225/78, ECtHR, 28 May 1985, para. 57.

[70] See, e.g., *Fayed v. the United Kingdom*, App. No. 17101/90, ECtHR, 21 September 1994, para. 65; *Markovic and Others v. Italy*, App. No. 1398/03, ECtHR, 14 December 2006, para. 99; *Ashingdane v. the United Kingdom*, para. 57.

[71] *Hämäläinen v. Finland*, App. No. 37359/09, ECtHR [GC], 16 July 2014, para. 109.

facet of an individual's existence or identity is at stake'[72]; ethnic or racial discrimination is involved[73]; or when a case concerns an 'intimate aspect of private life'.[74] On the other hand, Member States will have a wider discretion in cases concerning public emergency,[75] national security[76] or protection of morals.[77]

In addition, Member States will have a wide margin of appreciation when 'there is no consensus within the Member States of the Council of Europe, either as to the relative importance of the interest at stake or as to the best means of protecting it [...]'[78] The margin of appreciation doctrine has been also applied in a handful of arbitration-related cases.[79] The search for the most ECHR-compatible approach to excluding setting-aside proceedings under national arbitration law inevitably also implies consideration of ECHR Member States' margin of appreciation to regulate such proceedings in their national law. Despite continuous doubts as to the necessity of setting-aside proceedings in contemporary framework of international commercial arbitration, there remains a common consensus (a *common standard*) among States on the importance of setting-aside proceedings for the protection of both such States' own interests, as well as the interests of arbitrating parties.

2.4.6 *Proportionality and Fair Balance*

Equally important is the principle of proportionality and the notion of fair balance developed by the ECtHR, in particular with regard to the rights and freedoms that are subject to restrictions, such as the right of access to a court.

Whenever ECHR Member States limit or restrict a Convention right or freedom, such a limitation must have a legitimate aim and there has to be a reasonable degree of proportionality 'between the means employed and the aim sought to be achieved'.[80]

---

[72] *Evans v. United Kingdom*, App. No. 6339/05, ECtHR [GC], 10 April 2007, para. 77.

[73] *D.H. and others v. Czech Republic*, App. No. 57325/00, ECtHR, 13 November 2007.

[74] *Dudgeon v. United Kingdom*, App. No. 7525/76, ECtHR, 22 October 1981, para. 52.

[75] *Brannigan and McBride v. United Kingdom*, Apps. No. 14553/89, 14554/89, ECtHR, 26 May 1993.

[76] *Klass and others v. Germany*, App. No. 5029/71, ECtHR, 6 September 1978; *Leander v. Sweden*, App. No. 9248/81, ECtHR, 26 March 1987.

[77] *Handyside v. United Kingdom*, App. No. 5493/72, ECtHR, 7 December 1976.

[78] *Evans v. United Kingdom*, App. No. 6339/05, ECtHR [GC], 10 April 2007, para. 77. In *Petrovic v. Austria*, App. No. 20458/92, ECtHR, 27 March 1998, the Court considered that '[t]he scope of the margin of appreciation will vary according to the circumstances, the subject matter and its background; in this respect, one of the relevant factors may be the existence or non-existence of common ground between the laws of the Contracting States'.

[79] See, e.g., *Transado-Transportes Fluviais Do Sado, S.A. v. Portugal*, App. No. 35943/02, ECtHR, 16 December 2003; *Tabbane v. Switzerland*, App. No. 41069/12, ECtHR, 1 March 2016.

[80] See, e.g., *Fayed v. the United Kingdom*, App. No. 17101/90, ECtHR, 21 September 1990, para. 65; *Markovic and Others v. Italy*, App. No. 1398/03, ECtHR, 14 December 2006, para. 99; *Ashingdane v. the United Kingdom*, para. 57.

The test of proportionality is invoked not only with regard to the rights and freedoms expressly stipulated in the Convention, but also with regard to impliedly guaranteed rights, such as the right of access to a court, and also in determining whether a positive obligation has been satisfied.[81]

The principle of proportionality has been of significance also in arbitration-related cases, e.g. the *Tabbane v. Switzerland* case where the proportionality between the Swiss legislator's aims and the means employed to achieve such aims, inter alia, convinced the ECtHR in finally determining that Article 192(1) of the PILA and parties' voluntary exclusion of a right to challenge an arbitral award is compatible with Article 6(1) of the ECHR and the right of access to a court.[82]

Additionally, the principle of proportionality is somewhat supplemented by the Court's developed notion of fair balance 'between the demands of general interest of the community and the requirements of the protection of the individual's human rights'.[83] Although not expressly indicated, the Court relied on the notion of fair balance also in the *Tabbane v. Switzerland* case where, in the Court's view, a fair balance was appropriately struck between the general interests of the Swiss legislature to provide for a possibility to exclude the annulment action and the principle of party autonomy.[84]

2.4.7 Other Principles of Interpretation

Over the years, the ECtHR has developed and relied on other equally important principles that have proved to be significant when interpreting the Convention and the rights and freedoms stipulated therein.

For example, in interpreting the Convention the Court also considers the Convention's *travaux préparatoires*, or preparatory works, in order to confirm a particular assumption.[85] Similarly, the ECtHR aims to interpret the Convention consistently as a whole in order to achieve internal harmony between its provisions.[86] Moreover,

---

[81] Harris et al. (2014), p. 13 citing *Mathieu-Mohin and Clerfayt v. Belgium*, App. No. 9267/81, ECtHR, 2 March 1987; *Fayed v. the United Kingdom*, App. No. 17101/90, ECtHR, 21 September 1994; *Rees v. United Kingdom*, App. No. 9432/81, ECtHR, 17 October 1986 and *Gaskin v. United Kingdom*, App. No. 10454/83, ECtHR, 7 July 1989.

[82] *Tabbane v. Switzerland*, App. No. 41069/12, ECtHR, 1 March 2016, para. 34.

[83] *Soering v. United Kingdom*, App. No. 15038/88, ECtHR, 7 July 1989, para 89.

[84] *Tabbane v. Switzerland*, App. No. 41069/12, ECtHR, 1 March 2016, para. 34.

[85] See, e.g. *Lithgow and others v. United Kingdom*, Apps. No. 9006/80; 9262/81; 9263/81; 9265/81; 9266/81; 9313/81; 9405/81, ECtHR, 8 July 1986, para. 117; *James and others v. United Kingdom*, App. No. 8793/79, ECtHR, 21 February 1986, para 64 where 'confronted with a text whose interpretation has given rise to such disagreement, the Court considers it proper to have recourse to the *travaux préparatoires* as a supplementary means of interpretation (see Article 32 of the Vienna Convention on the Law of Treaties).' See also *Nolan and K. v. Russia*, App. No. 2512/04, ECtHR, 12 February 2012.

[86] *Stec and others v. United Kingdom*, Apps. No. 65731/01 and 65900/01, ECtHR [GC], 12 April 2006; *Saadi v. United Kingdom*, App. No. 13229/03, ECtHR [GC], 29 January 2008, para. 62;

although the Court has sometimes relied on the 'common law' of the Member States, the Convention's terms will generally be interpreted autonomously, i.e. without reference to how a particular term is understood in the laws of Member States.[87] Additionally, the Court has repeatedly held that the Convention is designed to 'guarantee not rights that are theoretical or illusory but rights that are practical and effective'.[88] The principle of effectiveness is therefore an important element in interpreting Member States' positive obligations.

As will become evident, these and other of the above-mentioned principles of interpretation of the ECHR have been significant also in shaping the understanding of and determining the scope of application of the ECHR to arbitration. The case of *Tabbane v. Switzerland*, as a pivotal example contributing to the understanding of the relationship between the ECHR and setting-aside proceedings in particular, confirms the importance of the said principles. Equally, such principles can be used in examining the limits and comprehensiveness of the *Tabbane v. Switzerland* ruling and, more specifically, in search for the most appropriate ECHR-compatible legislative approach to excluding the application of setting aside proceedings in national arbitration law.

2.5 Member States' Obligations Under the ECHR

The Convention does not only set forth rights and freedoms that every individual shall enjoy solely because of his or her qualities as a human being living in a democratic society. The protection of such rights and freedoms rests not only in the supervisory function of the Convention's controlling organs, but, according to the principle of subsidiarity and the doctrine of margin of appreciation, primarily in the obligations assumed by Member States when signing and ratifying the Convention.

The primary point of departure for deriving Member States' obligations under the ECHR is Article 1 of the ECHR, providing that '[t]he High Contracting Parties shall secure to everyone within their jurisdiction the rights and freedoms defined in Section I of this Convention'.

Generally, international human rights law categorizes States' obligations in three categories: (i) to respect; (ii) to protect; and (iii) to fulfil/secure human rights and

Austin and Others v. the United Kingdom, Apps. No. 39692/09, 40713/09 and 41008/09, ECtHR [GC], 15 March 2012, para. 54 where the Court held that 'the Convention must be read as a whole, and interpreted in such a way as to promote internal consistency and harmony between its various provisions'.

[87] See, e.g., *Allen v. United Kingdom*, App. No. 25424/09, ECtHR [GC], 12 July 2013, para. 95; *König v. Germany*, App. No. 6232/73, ECtHR, 28 June 1978, para 88.

[88] See, e.g. *Salduz v. Turkey*, App. No. 36391/02, ECtHR [GC], 27 November 2008, para. 51; *Imbrioscia v. Switzerland*, App. No. 13972/88, ECtHR, 24 November 1993, para. 38.

freedoms.[89] The obligation to *respect* entails the respect of human rights and freedoms by abstaining from unwarranted interference thereof. The obligation to *protect* requires States to protect individuals from interference with such rights by third parties. Lastly, the obligation to *fulfil* or *secure* requires States to adopt specific legislative measures for the full realization of such rights and freedoms.

The terminology used by the ECtHR in this regard is somewhat different since the Court refers to a dichotomy of States' obligations under the Convention, i.e. *negative* and *positive* obligations. Nevertheless, it has also been recognized that, despite the different wording and approach in categorizing States' obligations, the substance remains intact—obligations to *respect* are negative obligations, however, obligations to *protect* and *fulfil* are positive obligations.[90] Irrespective of the method of categorization, failure to comply with such obligations will give rise to a responsibility of a Member State for the breach of its obligations under the ECHR.

Although Article 1 of the ECHR speaks only of *securing* such rights and freedoms, by now it has been generally established that the *securing* of the Convention's rights and freedoms is much broader, at least with regard to the required obligations on part of ECHR Member States.[91] It entails both the fulfillment of negative obligations and also positive obligations. As seen, negative obligations require Member States to refrain from interference with the enjoyment of the Convention's rights and freedoms, however, positive obligations require Member States to take actual positive steps, i.e. 'to do something',[92] by adopting measures for safeguarding a Convention right or freedom. The Court has confirmed the dichotomy of negative and positive obligations on many occasions.[93]

As will explained, Article 6(1) of the ECHR and the right of access to a court 'by its very nature calls for regulation by the State',[94] thus requiring a positive action on behalf of a State, i.e. to legislate. Regulation of setting-aside proceedings under national arbitration law similarly requires a positive action on behalf of a State. Therefore, further brief focus will lie on positive obligations under the ECHR only.

---

[89] Generally on the tripartite obligations of States see, e.g., Shue (1996), Harris et al. (2014), p. 22, Koch (2009), pp. 14–21.

[90] Harris et al. (2014), p. 22.

[91] Ibid., p. 21.

[92] As argued by the applicants in the so-called *Belgian linguistics* case, Apps. No. 1474/62; 1677/62; 1691/62; 1769/63; 1994/63; 2126/64, ECtHR, 23 July 1968. Later the ECtHR has more precisely defined positive obligations as 'a positive duty on the State to take reasonable and appropriate measures to secure the applicants' rights'. See *Powell and Rayner v. United Kingdom*, App. No. 9310/81, ECtHR, 21 February 1990, para. 41.

[93] See, among others, *Marckx v. Belgium*, App. No. 6833/74, ECtHR, 13 June 1979, para. 31; *Abdulaziz, Cabales and Balkandali v. United Kingdom*, Apps. No. 9214/80; 9473/81; 9474/81, ECtHR, 28 May 1985, para. 67; *Airey v. Ireland*, App. No. 6289/73, ECtHR, 9 October 1979, para. 32. More recently see, e.g., *Söderman v. Sweden*, App. No. 5786/08, ECtHR [GC], 12 November 2013, para. 78; *A.-M.V. v. Finland*, App. No. 53251/13, ECtHR, 23 March 2017, para. 71.

[94] See, e.g. *Kart v. Turkey*, App. No. 8917/05, ECtHR [GC], 3 December 2009, para. 79. Generally, see Sect. 3.3.1.1.

2.5.1 *Positive Obligations*

The Convention was signed with the aim to avoid the horrific violations of fundamental human rights during the Second World War—an aim that essentially required States to observe mainly negative obligations, i.e. not to interfere with the enjoyment of fundamental human rights by individuals within their jurisdiction. Although some positive obligations are explicitly present in the Convention's text or follow therefrom,[95] their recognition and development on a broader scale did not happen until late 1960s and the Court's judgment in the *Belgian linguistics* case.[96] Since then, the Court has developed the concept of positive obligations to the extent that now almost every right and freedom guaranteed in the Convention entails both a negative and also a positive obligation on behalf of the Member States.[97]

A positive obligation can be defined as 'a positive duty on the State to take reasonable and appropriate measures to secure the [...] rights [guaranteed in the Convention]'.[98] Being an expression of two of the abovementioned tripartite obligations, namely obligations to 'protect' and 'fulfil', positive obligations require Member States to carry out certain measures in order to comply with their commitments under Article 1 of the ECHR. Taken in conjunction with the rights and freedoms guaranteed in Section I of the ECHR, Article 1 of the ECHR is seen as the legal basis for Member States' positive obligations vis-à-vis individuals within their jurisdiction.[99]

The purpose of positive obligations is to guarantee an effective enjoyment of the rights and freedoms provided by the Convention. Article 1 of the ECHR requires that Member States *secure* such rights and freedoms, and *securing* may also entail the taking of necessary legislative or other means in order to achieve that aim. The guarantee of effectiveness of the Convention's rights and freedoms is seen as an inherent element in the rights and freedoms that the Convention provides.[100] This,

---

[95] See, e.g., art. 13 of the ECHR and the right to an effective remedy.

[96] *Belgian linguistics* case, Apps. No. 1474/62; 1677/62; 1691/62; 1769/63; 1994/63; 2126/64, ECtHR, 23 July 1968, para. 3 where the Court held that '[t]he negative formulation ['no person shall be denied the right to education'] indicate [...] that the Contracting Parties do not recognise such a right to education as would require them to establish at their own expense, or to subsidise, education of any particular type or at any particular level. However, it cannot be concluded from this that the State has no positive obligation to ensure respect for such a right as is protected by Article 2 of the Protocol (P1-2). As a 'right' does exist, it is secured, by virtue of Article 1 (art. 1) of the Convention, to everyone within the jurisdiction of a Contracting State'.

[97] Akandji-Kombe J (2007) *Positive obligations under the European Convention on Human Rights: A guide to the implementation of the European Convention on Human Rights*, Human rights handbooks, No. 7, p. 6. Council of Europe, Directorate General of Human Rights.

[98] See, e.g. *Powell and Rayner v. United Kingdom*, App. No. 9310/81, ECtHR, 21 February 1990, para. 41.

[99] Akandji-Kombe J (2007) *Positive obligations under the European Convention on Human Rights: A guide to the implementation of the European Convention on Human Rights*, Human rights handbooks, No. 7, pp. 6–7. Council of Europe, Directorate General of Human Rights.

[100] For example, in *Airey v. Ireland*, App. No. 6289/73, ECtHR, 9 October 1979, para. 32 the Court stressed that 'in addition to this primarily negative undertaking, there may be positive obligations inherent in an effective respect for private or family life'. Similar conclusions have been drawn also

in turn, is linked with the afore mentioned principle of effectiveness that entails that the Convention shall 'guarantee not rights that are theoretical or illusory but rights that are practical and effective'.[101]

Generally, the domain of positive obligations is predominately occupied with the Convention's procedural safeguards, such as the right to fair trial under Article 6(1) of the ECHR and the right to an effective remedy provided in Article 13 of the ECHR that mainly require Member States to take positive steps, i.e. to legislate. ECHR Member States are therefore under an obligation to provide an effective legislative framework that gives due effect to their obligations under the Convention. The Court has repeatedly held that failure to do so will engage Member States' responsibility for breach of their commitments under the ECHR.[102]

Considering that the main focus in this book lies on the guarantees of Article 6(1) of the ECHR, including the right of access to a court, it must be mentioned that also with regard to the right of access to a court the ECtHR has ruled that it not only requires Member States to abstain from interfering with such a right of access, but it also requires Member States to effectively legislate in order to guarantee individuals within their jurisdiction the respective right of access to a court.[103] Even though, as will be explained in more detail below,[104] the right of access to a court and the respective obligation of Member States to legislate is not absolute, the obligation per se exists. The possibility to limit the right of access to a court is seen as an exception, rather than the main rule requiring that 'all litigants should have an effective judicial remedy enabling them to assert their civil rights'.[105]

Positive obligations are closely linked with the question of horizontal applicability of the Convention. In fact, it is said that 'the establishment and development of the horizontal effect of the Convention by the European Court is, in its entirety, a consequence of the theory of positive obligations.'[106] This book focuses solely on the evident indirect applicability of the Convention's rights and freedoms among individuals, i.e. an indirect horizontal effect. Although some scholars have suggested that

in more recent cases. See, e.g. *Malec v. Poland*, App. No. 28623/12, ECtHR, 28 June 2016, para. 66; *A.-M.V. v. Finland*, App. No. 53251/13, ECtHR, 23 March 2017, para. 71.

[101] *Salduz v. Turkey*, App. No. 36391/02, ECtHR [GC], 27 November 2008, para. 51. More recently see, e.g. *Cudak v. Lithuania*, App. No. 15869/02, ECtHR [GC], 23 March 2010, para. 65; *Carmel Saliba v. Malta*, App. No. 24221/13, ECtHR, 29 November 2016, para. 65.

[102] See, e.g. *C.N. and V. v. France*, App. No. 67724/09, ECtHR, 11 October 2012, para. 108; *Rantsev v. Cyprus and Russia*, App. No. 23965/04, ECtHR, 7 January 2010, para. 285; *Young, James and Webster v. United Kingdom*, Apps. No. 7601/76, 7806/77, ECtHR, 13 August 1981, para. 49.

[103] See, e.g. *Golder v. United Kingdom*, App. No. 4451/70, ECtHR, 21 February 1975, para. 38; *Waite and Kennedy v. Germany*, 26083/94, ECtHR [GC], 18 February 1999, para. 59; *Sabeh El Leil v. France*, App. No. 34869/05, ECtHR [GC], 29 June 2011, para. 47.

[104] See Sect. 3.3.1.1.

[105] See, e.g. *Sabeh El Leil v. France*, App. No. 34869/05, ECtHR [GC], 29 June 2011, para. 46.

[106] Akandji-Kombe J (2007) *Positive obligations under the European Convention on Human Rights: A guide to the implementation of the European Convention on Human Rights*, Human rights handbooks, No. 7, p. 15. Council of Europe, Directorate General of Human Rights.

the Convention also establishes direct effect vis-à-vis individuals,[107] the consensus is that the ECHR does not produce such effects.[108] Article 1 of the ECHR only addresses Member States of the ECHR and individual applications may be submitted to the Court, provided that an individual claims 'to be the victim of a violation by one of the High Contracting Parties'.[109] This is confirmed by the lack of ECtHR judgments on the direct horizontal applicability of the Convention.[110]

Indirect horizontal effect of the Convention, on the other hand, has by now been generally established both by the ECtHR case-law and doctrine. This means that Member States can be held responsible for violations committed by individuals against other individuals within their jurisdiction. The ECtHR has repeatedly established that Member States' positive obligations 'may involve the adoption of measures designed to secure respect for [the Convention's rights] even in the sphere of the relations of individuals between themselves'.[111] Shortcomings in national legislation and the lack of such measures as are necessary in order to guarantee the Convention's rights and freedoms will therefore engage the responsibility of the defaulting Member State.

Of course, the mere fact that an individual has breached another's rights and freedoms under the Convention cannot lead to a finding against a Member State within whose jurisdiction the violation has occurred.[112] The respective violation must be somehow imputable to the Member State either due to some sort of failure in the legal order to remedy such violations or an otherwise inadequate legal intervention. Moreover, the Court has held that similarly to negative obligations, also with regard to positive obligations a 'regard must be had to the fair balance that has to be struck between the competing interests of the individual and of the community as a whole'.[113] A similar weighing of interests is carried out when analyzing the whether or not restriction of a particular right guaranteed by the ECHR has been reasonably proportionate.

---

[107] See, e.g. Clapham (2006).

[108] See, e.g. Harris et al. (2014), p. 23.

[109] Article 34 of the ECHR. See also, among others, *Durini v. Italy*, App. No. 19217/91, ECmHR, 12 January 1994.

[110] Ziemele I (2009) Human Rights Violation by Private Persons and Entities: The Case-Law of International Human Rights Courts and Monitoring Bodies, p. 12. EUI Working Papers, Academy of European Law.

[111] See, e.g. *Söderman v. Sweden*, App. No. 5786/08, ECtHR [GC], 12 November 2013, para. 78; *Mikulić v. Croatia*, App. No. 53176/99, ECtHR, 7 February 2002, para. 57; *Phinikaridou v. Cyprus*, App. No. 2389/02, ECtHR, 20 December 2007, para. 47; *Putistin v. Ukraine*, App. No. 16882/03, ECtHR, 21 November 2013, para. 34.

[112] Akandji-Kombe J (2007) *Positive obligations under the European Convention on Human Rights: A guide to the implementation of the European Convention on Human Rights*, Human rights handbooks, No. 7, p. 14. Council of Europe, Directorate General of Human Rights.

[113] See, e.g. *Phinikaridou v. Cyprus*, App. No. 2389/02, ECtHR, 20 December 2007, para. 47. See also *Putistin v. Ukraine*, App. No. 16882/03, ECtHR, 21 November 2013, para. 34; *Van Kuck v. Germany*, App. No. 35968/97, ECtHR, 12 June 2003, para. 70.

2.6 Summary

The above short chapter has briefly introduced the Convention, its enforcement mechanism and the various methods of interpreting the ECHR, often trying to connect the said issues with the more specific point of focus of this book, i.e. setting-aside proceedings and, in particular, exclusion of setting-aside proceedings by means of both the so-called exclusion agreements and legislative vacuum in this regard. This book's specific focus lies not only on the setting-aside mechanism, but also on the ECHR, and the dichotomy between the two. Therefore, understanding of the basics of the ECHR, albeit on a very superficial basis, is indispensable for further delving into the matter.

References

Arai-Takahashi Y (2001) The margin of appreciation Doctrine and the principle of proportionality in the jurisprudence of the ECHR. Intersentia

Benedettelli MV (2015) Human rights as a litigation tool in international arbitration: reflecting on the ECHR experience. Arbitr Int 31(4):631–659

Clapham A (2006) Human rights obligations of non-state actors. Oxford University Press, United Kingdom

Emberland M (2006) The human rights of companies: exploring the structure of ECHR protection. Oxford University Press, United Kingdom

Giunio M (2000) Right to a fair trial and efficiency of arbitral proceedings. Croat Arbitr Yearb 7:31

Harris D et al (2014) Harris, O'Boyle & Warbrick: law of the European Convention on Human Rights, 3rd edn. Oxford University Press, United Kingdom

Jaksic A (2007) Procedural guarantees of human rights in arbitration proceedings: a still unsettled problem? J. Int. Arb. 24(2):159

Jarrosson C (1989) L'arbitrage et la Convention européenne des droits de l'homme. Rev Arbitr 4:573–607

Koch IE (2009) Human rights as indivisible rights: the protection of socio-economic demands under the European Convention on Human Rights. Martinus Nijhoff

Krings E, Matray L (1982) Le juge et l'arbitre. Rev. dr. int. et dr. comp. 227

Legg A (2012) The margin of appreciation in international human rights law: deference and proportionality. Oxford University Press, United Kingdom

Macklem P (2015) Human rights in international law: three generations or one? Lond Rev Int Law 3(1):61–92

Mikaelsen L (1980) European Protection of Human Rights: the practice and procedure of the European Commission of Human Rights on the admissibility of applications from individuals and states. Stijthoff & Noordhoff

Petrochilos G (2004) Procedural law in international arbitration. Oxford University Press, United Kingdom

Pocar F (2015) Some thoughts on the universal declaration of human rights and the generations of human rights. Intercultural Hum Rights L Rev 10:45

Rainey B et al (2014) Jacobs, White, and Ovey: The European Convention on Human Rights, 6th edn. Oxford University Press, United Kingdom

Samuel A (2004) Arbitration, alternative dispute resolution generally and the European Convention on Human Rights: an Anglo-Centric view. J Int Arbitr 21(5):413, 426

Shue H (1996) Basic rights: subsistence, affluence, and U.S. Foreign Policy, 2nd edn. Princeton University Press

Van den Muijsenbergh W, Rezai S (2012) Corporations and the European Convention on Human Rights. Pacific McGeorge Glob Bus Dev Law J 25(1):43

Yourow HC (1996) The margin of appreciation Doctrine in the dynamics of European Human Rights Jurisprudence. Martinus Nijhoff

Zwart T (1994) The admissibility of human rights petitions: the case law of the European Commission of Human Rights and the Human Rights Committee. Martinus Nijhoff, Dordrecht/Boston/London

Chapter 3
Arbitration and the ECHR

3.1 Introduction

Traditionally, arbitration and human rights have been viewed as two distinct, unrelated and independent areas that have little or no bearing on each other. Indeed, at first sight it may be hard to see what both disciplines have in common. Arbitration, on the one hand, is a private dispute settlement mechanism by means of which parties aim to avoid the jurisdiction of ordinary courts for various practical, economic or political reasons. The notion of human rights, on the other hand, in its essence stems from natural law and generally refers to the 'freedoms, immunities, and benefits that [...] all human beings should be able to claim as a matter of right in the society in which they live'.[1] Recently, however, it has become evident that human rights do have implications on arbitration proceedings and vice versa. This is not only true as regards investment arbitration—a matter that will not be further explored in this book[2]—but also as regards commercial arbitration. The Court's ample case law regarding the dichotomy between arbitration and the ECHR is an undeniable confirmation of this.

As has become evident, the ECHR is primarily addressed to its Member States that are under an obligation to secure to everyone within their jurisdiction the Convention's rights and freedoms. Arbitration, on the other hand, is a private dispute settlement mechanism by means of which arbitrating parties aim precisely at avoiding the involvement of State machinery at the seat of arbitration proceedings. Or do they?

Indeed, in the best-case scenario, arbitration proceedings commence, take place and are terminated without the need for involvement of national courts at the seat of arbitration. Arbitrating parties honour their own agreement to settle any disputes or controversies by means of arbitration and consequently also voluntarily carry out the final arbitral award. However, when the commencement of arbitration, its actual proceedings or the compliance of the final award encounters difficulties, only State

[1] Garner (2014), p. 858.

[2] Generally on human rights in investment arbitration, please see, e.g., Dupuy et al. (2009), Mouyal (2016).

© The Editor(s) (if applicable) and The Author(s), under exclusive license to Springer Nature Switzerland AG 2020

T. Krūmiņš, *Arbitration and Human Rights*,
https://doi.org/10.1007/978-3-030-54237-5_3

courts are the ones 'possessing coercive powers which could rescue the arbitration if it is in danger of foundering'.[3]

Even more so, when signing an arbitration agreement, parties believe that a sufficient and reasonable degree of procedural fairness will be present throughout arbitration proceedings, guaranteeing both parties an equal opportunity to be heard and making sure that the final arbitral award will be a product of fair proceedings decided by impartial, objective and independent arbitrators.[4] However, what if one of the parties was not provided with equal treatment during arbitration proceedings and certain fundamental procedural rights were therefore violated? What if the arbitral tribunal rejected parties' submitted evidence without a sufficient reason or the arbitral tribunal was simply bias in deciding the whole case? Arbitration proceedings, like any other mechanism for settling disputes, involves competing interests, different views and certainly opposing beliefs of which one of the involved parties ought to be responsible. Therefore, tactical techniques and making use of all the available procedural tools for reversing an unfavorable outcome of a case is inevitable and certainly will take place prior, during and after the arbitration proceedings.

A problem, however, arises when the aggrieved party is precluded from seeking court assistance that would remedy procedural inconsistencies resulting from unfair arbitration proceedings. What if the applicable *lex arbitri* did not provide for an opportunity to challenge incorrectly assumed arbitral jurisdiction? Or there was no possibility to challenge the impartiality and independence of arbitrators before State courts? Or the national arbitration law did not provide a mechanism for challenging and setting aside arbitral awards on the basis of violations of fundamental procedural human rights? When agreeing to arbitrate and *escape* the jurisdiction of State courts, arbitrating parties certainly do not envisage that in case of fundamental procedural violations there would be no possibility to remedy such violations before State courts.

This is well illustrated, inter alia, also by the generally seldom and reluctant use of the so-called exclusion agreements. It is said that setting-aside proceedings function as a form of risk management whereby courts remedy violations of fundamental procedural rights during arbitration proceedings.[5] Therefore, even though arbitrating parties agree to subject themselves to arbitration instead of State courts, they generally want to retain the right to address State courts with applications of alleged violations of their rights of due process during arbitration proceedings. At least with regard to the rare use of exclusion agreements this is explained due to 'the prudence of the parties, who are more concerned about certainty than about rapidity and economy, at least when significant interests are at stake'.[6]

---

[3]Lord Mustill in *Copee Levalin NV v Ken-Ren Fertilisers and Chemicals* [1994] 2 Lloyd's Rep. 109 at 116, HL acknowledging that: '[t]here is plainly a tension here. On the one hand the concept of arbitration as a consensual process reinforced by the ideas of transnationalism leans against the involvement of the mechanisms of state through the medium of a municipal court. On the other side there is the plain fact, palatable or not, that it is only a Court possessing coercive powers which could rescue the arbitration if it is in danger of foundering'.

[4]Born (2009), p. 1001.

[5]Park (2001), p. 595.

[6]Van den Berg (1992), p. 273.

Generally, various international instruments relating to international arbitration,[7] national arbitration laws,[8] and institutional arbitration rules,[9] require that arbitration proceedings are carried out according to certain well-established fundamental principles aimed at protecting parties' fundamental procedural rights during arbitration proceedings. A separate discussion that will not be addressed in detail in this book relates to a question of whether arbitral institutions and arbitral tribunals are directly bound by the provisions of ECHR that similarly require to observe certain procedural human rights.[10] This is the case as regards compulsory or statutory arbitration,[11] however, if parties have voluntarily agreed to submit their dispute to arbitration, the role of the Convention is not as straightforward.

Human rights arguments as a basis for arguing that the outcome of arbitration proceedings had been unjust and violated fundamental procedural safeguards are seemingly used as *ultima ratio* argumentation, i.e. when all other attempts to remedy the alleged injustice have been exhausted and proved to be non-satisfactory.[12] It is evident that the ECHR does not produce direct horizontal effect and addresses only its Member States that may be held responsible for violations of the Convention's rights and freedoms. However, this does not mean that Member States' responsibility for violations of individual's rights and freedoms by other individuals is entirely excluded. ECHR Member States have a positive obligation to guarantee that violations of the Convention's rights and freedoms are sufficiently remedied within their jurisdiction. This, in turn, gives legitimate basis for arguing that such a remedial positive obligation also covers violations of fundamental human rights during arbitration proceedings.

---

[7] For example, art. 18 of the UNCITRAL Model Law requires that 'the parties shall be treated with equality and each party shall be given a full opportunity of presenting his case.' Similarly, the fulfilment of parties' due process rights is implied in art. V of the New York Convention that provides that a foreign arbitral award may be refused recognition and enforcement if, inter alia, '[t]he party against whom the award is invoked was not given proper notice of the appointment of the arbitrator or of the arbitration proceedings or was otherwise unable to present his case' or '[t]he composition of the arbitral authority or the arbitral procedure was not in accordance with the agreement of the parties, or, failing such agreement, was not in accordance with the law of the country where the arbitration took place'.

[8] National arbitration laws similarly require that parties' due process rights shall be respected during arbitration proceedings. See, e.g. art. 1699 of the BCCP, sec. 18 of the Danish Arbitration Act, art. 1036(2) of the Dutch Code of Civil Procedure, sec. 732 of the Estonian Code of Civil Procedure, sec. 22 of the Finish Arbitration Act, sec. 1042(1) of the ZPO, art. 28(1) of the Lithuanian Law on Commercial Arbitration, arts. 19–23 of the Latvian 2015 Arbitration Law.

[9] See, e.g. art. 14(4) of the LCIA Arbitration Rules (2014); arts. 23(2) and 40 of the SCC Arbitration Rules (2017); art. 22(4) of the ICC Arbitration Rules (2017).

[10] See briefly Sect. 3.4.1. See also, e.g., Petrochilos (2004), pp. 151–158.

[11] *Bramelid and Malmström v. Sweden*, Apps. No. 8588/79 and 8589/79, ECmHR, 12 October 1982; *Hedland v. Sweden*, App. No. 24118/94, ECmHR, 9 April 1997; *Cantafio v. Italy*, App. No. 14667/89, ECtHR, 12 December 1992.

[12] See, e.g. discussion on the *Tabbane v. Switzerland* case in Sect. 5.2.4.

Before looking at certain ECHR provisions that may impact arbitration proceedings and subsequent ECHR Member States' obligation to ensure that such proceedings are in compliance with the Convention's rights and freedoms, several approaches of application of the ECHR to arbitration will be introduced. Such approaches are the result of different schools of thought on theory of arbitration and dividing opinions whether or not the Convention shall be applied to arbitration or not.

3.2 Arbitration and the ECHR: Approaches of Application

Since the very beginning of the discussion on the interplay between arbitration and the ECHR, the question of the applicability of ECHR to arbitration has divided legal scholars. Some have argued that the Convention is completely inapplicable to arbitration proceedings, others, on the other hand, that the Convention's rights and freedoms shall be directly applicable to arbitration proceedings. While the former Commission and the ECtHR have confirmed an intermediary position, i.e. that the Convention's rights and freedoms are indirectly applicable to arbitration proceedings, it is still relevant to look at the arguments for and against a complete non-applicability or applicability of the ECHR to arbitration.

3.2.1 Absolute Non-applicability

Although the signing of the ECHR in 1950 coincided with the period when arbitration started to regain its popularity as a method for solving international and also national commercial disputes,[13] the founding fathers of the ECHR did not foresee that human rights guarantees as established in the ECHR could have implications on arbitration proceedings and vice versa. Neither the *travaux préparatoires*, nor the text of the ECHR itself contains an express reference to arbitration.[14] The lack of reference to arbitration in the ECHR is also advanced as an argument by the opponents to the applicability of human rights norms to arbitration.[15]

Notwithstanding that the former Commission and the ECtHR had already somewhat addressed the question of applicability of the ECHR to both compulsory and voluntary arbitration,[16] generally the first scholarly debates concerning the said issue

---

[13] For more detailed information on the increasing use and development of international commercial arbitration since the second half the twentieth century see, e.g., Born (2014), pp. 93–97.

[14] Lew et al. (2003), p. 91, Landrove (2006), p. 74, Benedettelli (2015), pp. 640–641.

[15] See, e.g., Jarrosson (1989), p. 574, Krings and Matray (1982), p. 256, Giunio (2000), p. 39.

[16] See, e.g. *X. v. the Federal Republic of Germany*, App. No. 1197/61, ECmHR, 5 March 1962; *Bramelid and Malmström v. Sweden*, Apps. No. 8588/79 and 8589/79, ECmHR, 12 October 1982.

appear only in the 1980s.[17] Many scholars denied direct applicability of the Convention's human rights provisions to arbitration proceedings. Among others, French jurist Jarrosson in his seminal article *L'arbitrage et la Convention européenne des droits de l'homme* advanced several arguments against the applicability of the ECHR to arbitration proceedings.[18]

Jarrosson referred to the Convention's letter and spirit according to which the applicability of the ECHR to arbitration should be undesirable and unnecessary. He asserted that there is no reference to arbitration or arbitrator in the Convention or its *travaux préparatoires.*[19] Apart from the civil limb of Article 6 of the ECHR, he saw no other provision in the Convention that could have bearing on arbitration.[20] Moreover, Jarrosson argued that the Convention's spirit implies that only its Member States should be responsible for violations of the Convention's rights and freedoms.[21] Arbitral tribunals are private bodies that cannot be considered as State organs and therefore cannot trigger liability under the Convention.[22] In addition, he asserted that an arbitral tribunal cannot be considered as a 'tribunal established by law' within the meaning of Article 6(1) of the ECHR.[23]

Later, other scholars, such as Jaksic and Benedettelli, have elaborately rebutted these arguments of non-applicability.[24] According to them, the lack of reference of arbitration in the ECHR does not per se mean that the Convention is not applicable to arbitration.[25] Similarly, over the years it has become evident that there are also other Convention's provisions—apart from Article 6(1) of the ECHR—that may have bearing on arbitration, such as Article 1 of the Protocol 1 to the ECHR.[26] Also, the ECtHR itself has stipulated that 'a tribunal established by law' within the meaning of Article 6(1) of the ECHR 'is not necessarily to be understood as signifying a court of law of the classic kind, integrated within the standard judicial

---

[17] See, among others, Flauss (1986), Jacot-Guillarmod (1990), pp. 281–295, Matscher (1987), p. 226, Moitry (1989), Jarrosson (1989), p. 574.

[18] Jarrosson (1989).

[19] Ibid., p. 576. Similar observations have been made by other scholars. See, e.g. Krings and Matray (1982), p. 256, Giunio (2000), p. 39.

[20] Jarrosson (1989), pp. 576–577.

[21] Ibid., pp. 578–579.

[22] See, e.g. Besson (2006), p. 401.

[23] Jarrosson (1989), p. 592.

[24] Jaksic (2002), pp. 183–187, Benedettelli (2015), pp. 640–642.

[25] Benedettelli argues that the ECtHR 'considers the Convention as 'a living instrument' which must be interpreted 'in the light of present day conditions' and not solely in accordance with the intentions of its drafters'. See Benedettelli (2015), p. 641. Jaksic (2002), p. 184.

[26] Ibid. See also *Stran Greek Refineries and Stratis Andreadis v. Greece*, App. No. 13427/87, ECtHR, 9 December 1994, para. 62; *Regent Company v. Ukraine*, App. No. 773/03, ECtHR, 3 April 2008, para. 61; *Kin-Stib and Majkić v. Serbia*, App. No. 12312/05, ECtHR, 20 April 2010, para. 83–85.

machinery'.[27] Consequently, it is said that arbitral tribunals are also considered as 'tribunals established by law' within the meaning of Article 6(1) of the ECHR.[28]

Additionally, Jarrosson argued that the application of the ECHR to arbitration is simply useless due to the Convention's rights and guarantees of due process already being guaranteed by different international conventions and various national arbitration laws. Therefore, in Jarrosson's opinion, the fact that arbitration is outside the scope of the ECHR does not mean that arbitration proceedings are subject to violations of fundamental procedural human rights: such rights are ensured by international conventions, i.e. the New York Convention, and national arbitration laws.[29]

However, the Convention's guarantees, such as the right of access to a court, become vitally significant, in particular, when no similar rights and freedoms exist in the applicable national regulatory framework.[30] For example, the Convention's safeguards will play significant role in a case when the applicable *lex arbitri* does not provide for a right to contest the jurisdiction of an arbitral tribunal before the State courts or in a case where parties are statutorily precluded from challenging an arbitral award and address before State courts possible violations of due process during the arbitration proceedings.

Many subsequent scholars adding to the debate on the applicability of the ECHR to arbitration refer to Jarrosson as a scholar arguing solely in favour of a complete non-applicability of the ECHR to arbitration.[31] This, however, is not entirely true since Jarrosson, albeit impliedly, also recognized the indirect horizontal effect and the fact that Member States may still be held liable for violations of the ECHR whenever they are involved in arbitration proceedings, either by assisting in issuing interim measures or during the setting-aside proceedings.[32]

Various national judicial bodies have also argued for direct inapplicability of the ECHR to arbitration. For example, in the 1980s the Swiss Federal Tribunal held that the ECHR does not apply to arbitration proceedings.[33] Later, however, it changed its

[27] *Lithgow and Others v. the United Kingdom*, Apps. No. 9006/80; 9262/81; 9263/81; 9265/81; 9266/81; 9313/81; 9405/81, ECtHR, 8 July 1986, para. 201.

[28] Besson (2006), p. 397, Landrove (2006), pp. 79–82, Benedettelli (2015), p. 642, Jaksic (2002), p. 186, Petrochilos (2004), p. 153.

[29] Jarrosson (1989), p. 594 where the author asserts [in original in French] '[O]n s'aperçoit que les arbitres qui violeraient le principe d'égalité des parties, verraient leur sentence annulée. Tel serait le cas si le tribunal arbitral avait péché par manque d'indépendance, ou s'il n'avait pas respecté le principe du contradictoire, ou encore s'il avait porté atteinte aux droits de la défense dans une mesure suffisante pour que l'on puisse dire qu'il n'y a pas eu en l'espèce de «cause entendue équitablement» [...] Même en faisant abstraction des conventions internationales, l'étude comparative des différents droits nationaux révèle une grande similitude dans les droits procéduraux garantis, et l'on ne voit pas quel principe serait protégé par la Convention européenne des droits de l'Homme et oublié par les autres conventions ou lois nationales sur l'arbitrage.'

[30] See *mutatis mutandis* discussion on the Latvian Constitutional Court's *Hiponia* case in Sect. 6.5.1.4.

[31] See, e.g. Jaksic (2007).

[32] Jarrosson (1989), pp. 586–587.

[33] Landrove (2006), p. 96.

approach and held that the ECHR, in particular, Article 6(1) of the ECHR, applies also to arbitration proceedings.[34] Similarly, with regard to a complaint that arbitral proceedings administered by the ICC International Court of Arbitration violated Article 6(1) of the ECHR, the French *Cour de Cassation* held in the *Cubic Defence* case that the ECHR only concerns its Member States and their jurisdiction, and not a non-profit organization that is not a judicial body.[35]

The fact that the ECHR does not directly apply to voluntary arbitration can be also read into the Convention's controlling bodies' rulings.[36] At the same time, and more importantly, the former Commission has also clearly stressed that the ECHR is nevertheless indirectly applicable to arbitration and Member States are responsible for guaranteeing the fairness and correctness of arbitration proceedings.[37]

Generally, it is no longer disputed that the ECHR is applicable to arbitration. The question, however, is whether such applicability is direct or indirect. The majority of scholars believe that the ECHR is not directly applicable to arbitration and before arbitral tribunals, albeit at the same time they recognize its indirect applicability and resulting obligations on behalf of ECHR Member States for violations of the Convention's rights and freedoms during arbitration proceedings.[38] Considering that the former Commission and also the ECtHR have both recognized the indirect effect of the Convention's provisions to arbitration, debates on the complete inapplicability of the ECHR to arbitration have seemingly only theoretical, rather than practical value.

---

[34] Ibid. [in referring to *X. v. Y.* 30 April 1991, ATF 117 Ia 166 (1991) and the unreported *Hitachi v. SMS* 30 June 1994, ATF, 15 Bull. ASA 99 (1997) and *Egemetal v. Fuchs*, 28 April 2000, ATF 126 III 249 (2000)].

[35] *Sociéte Cubic Defense Systems Inc. v. Chambre de Commerce Internationale*, Cour de Cassation (1 Ch. civile), 20 February 2001, Rev. Arb. 511 (2011). See also *Sociéte Cubic Defense Systems Inc. v. Chambre de Commerce Internationale*, Cour d'Appel de Paris (1 Ch. A), 15 September 1998, Rev. Arb. 103 (1999).

[36] See, e.g. *Nordström-Janzon and Nordström-Lehtinen v. the Netherlands*, App. No. 28101/95, ECmHR, 27 November 1996 where the Court stated that '[i]n some respects—in particular as regards publicity—it is clear that arbitral proceedings are often not even intended to be in conformity with Article 6 (Art. 6), and the arbitration agreement entails a renunciation of the full application of that Article.' As will be seen later, this and, in particular, other arguments by the former Commission in this case have been severely criticized and later also overruled by the ECtHR.

[37] *Jakob Boss Söhn KG v. the Federal Republic of Germany*, App. No. 18479/91, ECmHR, 2 December 1991 where the Commission observed that the 'applicant company had voluntarily entered into an arbitration agreement and thereby renounced its right to have its civil rights determined in court proceedings for the conduct of which the State is responsible under the Convention [...] This does not mean, however, that the respondent State's responsibility is completely excluded [...] as the arbitration award had to be recognised by [...] courts and be given executory effect by them. The courts thereby exercised a certain control and guarantee as to the fairness and correctness of the arbitration proceedings which they considered to have been carried out in conformity with fundamental rights and in particular with the right of the applicant company to be heard'.

[38] See, e.g. Kaufmann-Kohler and Schultz (2004), p. 198, Kurkela and Turunen (2010), p. 2, Benedek et al. (2007), pp. 275–276, Landrove (2006) pp. 90–93, Poudret and Besson (2006), pp. 65–66, Petrochilos (2004), pp. 112–13 and 163–165.

3.2.2 Direct Applicability

Another approach to the applicability of the ECHR to arbitration that finds support merely in the theoretical works of some scholars and will be looked at only briefly relates to the direct applicability of human rights norms in arbitration proceedings and before arbitral tribunals. Scholars that argue for the direct applicability of the ECHR in arbitration proceedings, such as Jaksic and, contrary to his previous views,[39] also Besson, point to the quasi-judicial function of arbitral tribunals and view arbitral tribunals as part of the State machinery.[40]

In fact, the underlying line of reasoning for directly applying the ECHR to arbitration and before arbitral tribunals can be seen as impliedly based on the very theoretical postulates of arbitration in general. What is the source of power vested in arbitral tribunals? Is it the State at the seat of arbitration that delegates certain *judicial* functions to arbitral tribunals and in essence *permits* arbitration within its jurisdiction?[41] Or is it arbitrating parties without whose agreement to arbitrate an arbitral tribunal would have no legal basis and jurisdiction?[42] If one supports the former, i.e. the so-called jurisdictional theory of arbitration, it is no surprise that arbitral tribunals are put on par with the State's judicial organs and thus are required to directly observe the Convention's human rights guarantees.

For example, Besson, after stipulating that in his opinion '[a]rbitrators are substitutes for judges and they exercise a jurisdictional mission even if their intervention is conditional upon an agreement between parties'[43] continued with a reference to a somewhat paradoxical situation:

> [I]f the courts of the contracting States shall apply and ensure respect for the Convention rights when they review an arbitral award, it is not satisfactory to deny the corresponding duty of the arbitrators to also respect the same provisions, especially because they have a duty to make sure that their award will not be set aside by the courts of the seat of arbitration.[44]

---

[39] Poudret and Besson (2006), p. 67.

[40] Jaksic (2002), pp. 203–204, Besson (2006), p. 402, Moitry (1989), p. 115 where the author is of the opinion that the standards of impartiality and independence should be also directly guaranteed in arbitration proceedings where the arbitrators are chosen by the parties.

[41] Among others favouring the so-called jurisdictional theory of arbitration, see the seminal work of Mann (1967) where the author argues that '[t]here is a pronounced similarity between the national judge and the arbitrator in that both of them are subject to the local sovereign. If, in contrast to the national judge, the arbitrator is in many respects, but by no means with uniformity, allowed and even ordered by municipal legislators to accept the commands of the parties, this is because, and to the extent that, the local sovereign so provides [...] Is not every activity occurring on the territory of a State necessarily subject to its jurisdiction? Is it not for such State to say whether and in what manner arbitrators are assimilated to judges and, like them, subject to the law? Various States may give various answers to the questions, but that each of them has the right to, and does, answer it according to its own discretion cannot be doubted.'

[42] Generally on the theory of international arbitration and different theoretical considerations see, e.g. Gaillard (2010).

[43] Besson (2006), p. 402.

[44] Ibid.

However, there is an obvious difference between a mere *duty* as an arbitrator to observe certain fundamental human rights standards during arbitration proceedings and an actual obligation to comply with such standards under the ECHR. Undoubtedly, an arbitrator shall act according to the highest possible standards and observe national, international, and (if applicable) institutional requirements of fair proceedings and due process. At the same time, it is highly unlikely that arbitral tribunals can be held responsible for not giving effect to such rights, especially under the ECHR.[45]

The Convention's *ratione personae* requirement of applicability provides that individual claims can only be brought against alleged violations of the ECHR and its provisions by ECHR Member States. Similarly, Article 1 of the ECHR requires only ECHR Member States to 'secure to everyone within their jurisdiction the rights and freedoms defined in [...] this Convention'. There is no mention in the ECHR that privately established tribunals should give effect to the Convention's rights and freedoms, and, if they fail, be held responsible for that. The underlying question whether an arbitral tribunal can be considered being part of the State judicial machinery seems to be answered in negative indirectly by both the former Commission and the ECtHR.[46]

There is no question that the ECHR and its different rights and guarantees are directly applicable in compulsory or statutory arbitration. In arbitration that is provided by a legislative statute parties are obliged to settle their disputes before arbitral tribunals that are essentially created by a State through its organs. The submission to arbitration is neither voluntary nor is it based on party autonomy. Therefore, statutorily established arbitral tribunals are required to directly observe the Convention's human rights guarantees. The former Commission and the ECtHR have repeatedly established the direct applicability of the Convention's human rights standards in compulsory arbitration proceedings. For example, in *Bramelid and Malmström v. Sweden*, the former Commission held that:

> [a] distinction must be drawn between voluntary and compulsory arbitration. Normally Article 6 poses no problem where arbitration is entered into voluntarily [...] If, on the other hand, arbitration is compulsory in the sense of being required by law, as in this case, the parties have no option but to refer their dispute to an arbitration board, and the board must offer the guarantees set forth in [Article 6(1) ECHR] [...]'.[47]

A year later, the ECtHR would more elaborately establish the required method for guaranteeing the Convention's rights and freedoms before a quasi-judicial body to which a State has delegated and conferred powers to decide disputes:

---

[45] See, among others, Landrove (2006), p. 91.

[46] See, e.g. the already mentioned passage from *Firma Heinz Schiebler KG v. the Federal Republic of Germany*, App. No. 18805/91, ECmHR, 2 December 1991 where the Commission observed that 'the applicant company had voluntarily entered into an arbitration agreement and thereby renounced its right to have its civil rights determined in court proceedings for the conduct of which the State is responsible under the Convention'.

[47] *Bramelid and Malmström v. Sweden*, Apps. No. 8588/79 and 8589/79, ECmHR, 12 October 1982. See also *Suda v. Czech Republic*, App. No. 1643/06, ECtHR, 28 October 2010, para. 49; *Tabbane v. Switzerland*, App. No. 41069/12, ECtHR, 1 March 2016, para. 26.

> In many member States of the Council of Europe, the duty of adjudicating on disciplinary offences is conferred on jurisdictional organs of professional associations. Even in instances where [Article 6(1)] is applicable, conferring powers in this manner does not in itself infringe the Convention [...] Nonetheless, in such circumstances the Convention calls at least for one of the two following systems: either the jurisdictional organs themselves comply with the requirements of [Article 6(1)], or they do not so comply but are subject to subsequent control by a judicial body that has full jurisdiction and does provide the guarantees of [Article 6(1)].[48]

In case of a voluntary arbitration, however, it is not only the State that *permits* such a method for settling disputes, but, more importantly, the arbitrating parties who have voluntarily exercised their party autonomy and renounced their right to settle disputes before State courts. Also the former Commission has stressed that 'insofar as arbitration is based on agreements between parties to the dispute, it is a natural consequence of their right to regulate their mutual relations as they see fit.'[49]

The precedence given to party autonomy and their 'right to regulate their mutual relations as they see fit' is clearly visible also in more recent arbitration-related Court's judgments.[50] Moreover, an argument that the ECHR is directly applicable in arbitration proceedings and before arbitral tribunals, also goes against the general principle, as established by the former Commission and repeatedly confirmed by the ECtHR, that the signing of an arbitration agreement entails a *partial* renunciation of the exercise of the rights secured in the Convention, especially Article 6(1) of the ECHR.[51]

An additional argument against the direct applicability of the ECHR to arbitration is the fact that a final arbitral award is not necessarily *final*, at least for determining its compliance with fundamental procedural human rights. Arbitral tribunal is not the last instance in which parties may remedy violations of their Convention's rights and freedoms during arbitration proceedings. Generally, arbitral awards may still be subject to court control during setting-aside proceedings and recognition and enforcement proceedings before State courts. When an arbitral award reaches the domain of State courts, they have an obligation under the ECHR to apply the Convention's rights and freedoms and guarantee that arbitration proceedings were carried out in conformity with fundamental human rights.[52]

Of course, a completely different question is the availability of such *checks* in the applicable national arbitration law for ensuring that the Convention's rights and freedoms have been given due effect to by arbitral tribunals. If a State does not set aside or, on the opposite, recognizes and enforces an arbitral award that violates

---

[48] *Albert and Le Compte v. Belgium*, Apps. No. 7299/75 and 7496/76, ECtHR, 10 February 1983, para. 29.

[49] *Axelsson and others v. Sweden*, App. No. 11960/86, ECmHR, 13 July 1990.

[50] See, e.g. *Tabbane v. Switzerland*, App. No. 41069/12, ECtHR, 1 March 2016, para. 27.

[51] See, e.g. *R v. Switzerland*, App. No. 10881/84, ECmHR, 4 March 1987; *Suovaniemi and others v. Finland*, App. No. 31737/96, ECtHR, 23 February 1999. In more detail see Sect. 3.4.2.

[52] *Firma Heinz Schiebler KG v. the Federal Republic of Germany*, App. No. 18805/91, ECmHR, 2 December 1991; *Jakob Boss Söhn KG v. the Federal Republic of Germany*, App. No. 18479/91, ECmHR, 2 December 1991.

Convention's rights and freedoms, such a State incurs responsibility and can be held liable for the acts of an arbitral tribunal.

To conclude, arbitral tribunals are not required to directly observe the Convention's rights and freedoms during arbitration proceedings. Most national arbitration laws impose a duty on arbitral tribunals to act fairly and to observe the right to fair trial, however it is highly improbable that privately established arbitral tribunals could be considered being part of a State machinery, and thus required to directly observe the ECHR and its standards.[53] Since arbitral tribunals are not required to directly observe such standards, States in whose jurisdiction arbitration proceedings are conducted, are neither directly responsible for the acts or omissions of the arbitral tribunal. This, as seen, has been confirmed both by scholarly works and the Convention's controlling bodies.[54] Rather, the responsibility of States under the ECHR and thus the application of the ECHR to arbitration as such is engaged indirectly, i.e. through States' failure to exercise certain control over arbitration proceedings and to ensure that such proceedings observed parties' basic human rights.

3.2.3 Indirect Applicability

The most convincing approach to the applicability of the ECHR to arbitration is that the rights and freedoms guaranteed in the ECHR are indirectly applicable to arbitration proceedings. The indirect applicability of the ECHR to arbitration has been now broadly recognized by the Convention's controlling bodies[55] and the majority of scholars writing on the subject.[56] The still somewhat unanswered question, however, is to what extent exactly is the ECHR indirectly applicable to voluntary arbitration and when can ECHR Member States be held responsible for violations of human rights during arbitration proceedings.

ECHR Member States' obligations under the ECHR generally stem from Article 1 of the ECHR, taken together with a specific right or freedom that is provided in the Convention. For example, when speaking of a right to fair trial, Member States 'shall secure to everyone within their jurisdiction' (Article 1 of the ECHR) '[…] a

[53] See, e.g. Poudret and Besson (2006), p. 65.

[54] See, e.g. *R v. Switzerland*, App. No. 10881/84, ECmHR, 4 March 1987 where the Commission held that 'the State cannot be held responsible for the arbitrators' actions unless, and only insofar as, the national courts were required to intervene.'

[55] *Jakob Boss Söhn KG v. the Federal Republic of Germany*, App. No. 18479/91, ECmHR, 2 December 1991; *Firma Heinz Schiebler KG v. the Federal Republic of Germany*, App. No. 18805/91, ECmHR., 2 December 1991; *Stran Greek Refineries and Stratis Andreadis v. Greece*, App. No. 13427/87, ECtHR, 9 December 1994; *Regent Company v. Ukraine*, App. No. 773/03, ECtHR, 3 April 2008; *Kin-Stib and Majkić v. Serbia*, App. No. 12312/05, ECtHR, 20 April 2010.

[56] See, e.g. Jarrosson (1989), pp. 586–587, Kaufmann-Kohler and Schultz (2004), p. 198, Kurkela and Turunen (2010), p. 2, Landrove (2006) pp. 90–93, Poudret and Besson (2006), pp. 65–66, Petrochilos (2004), pp. 112–113 and 163–165, Briner and Von Schlabrendorff (2001), pp. 99–100, Jaksic (2007), p. 162, Samuel (2004), pp. 429–431.

fair and public hearing within a reasonable time by an independent and impartial tribunal established by law' (Article 6(1) of the ECHR). The obligation to *secure* entails both a negative and a positive aspect, and it has been argued that '[i]t would be an unnatural reading of those provisions to suggest that they require of a state only to organize its judiciary and court procedure so that court proceedings will comply with Article 6(1), but otherwise allow a state not to extend such guarantees to those persons who have chosen to arbitrate.'[57]

If States cannot be held directly responsible for the violations of the Convention's rights and freedoms by privately established arbitral tribunals, when is their responsibility under the Convention nevertheless engaged? Undoubtedly, the Convention's human rights standards apply before State courts. State courts may get involved in various matters that are ancillary to the main arbitration proceedings, e.g. in deciding on the challenge of jurisdiction of an arbitral tribunal, in deciding on the challenge of independence and impartiality of arbitrators, issuing of interim measures, hearing of witnesses, producing of evidence etc. Therefore, whenever State courts are convened by arbitrating parties to decide on matters ancillary to arbitration proceedings, State courts have an obligation to observe the Convention's human rights standards.[58]

The most common example of a State exercising, to put it in the former Commission's words, 'a certain control and guarantee as to the fairness and correctness of the arbitration proceedings',[59] is through a review of an arbitral award's conformity with fundamental rights during the setting-aside or recognition and enforcement proceedings. Whenever a State fails to remedy violations of the Convention's rights and freedoms by an arbitral tribunal during the setting-aside or recognition and enforcement proceedings, it essentially endorses such actions as its own and therefore may be held responsible both under the Convention and also internationally.[60] This, in turn, may be the result of a violation of both its ensuing negative and also positive obligations under the Convention.

For example, with regard to the recognition and enforcement proceedings, a State would be violating its negative obligation under Article 6(1) of the ECHR and Article 1 of Protocol 1 to the ECHR if it unlawfully interfered with a party's right to have an arbitral award be recognized and enforced in that State and failed to do so for a continuous period of time.[61] A positive action on behalf of a State, and therefore a violation of its negative obligation, would also be in case a State recognized and enforced an arbitral award that clearly violated the rights and freedoms set forth in

[57] Petrochilos (2004), p. 153.

[58] Poudret and Besson (2006), p. 66.

[59] *Jakob Boss Söhn KG v. the Federal Republic of Germany*, App. No. 18479/91, ECmHR, 2 December 1991.

[60] Petrochilos (2004), pp. 112–113 in referring to Article 11 of the United Nations (UN) International Law Commission (ILC) Draft Articles on Responsibility of States for Internationally Wrongful Acts (2001) which states that a '[c]onduct which is not attributable to a State under the preceding articles shall nevertheless be considered an act of that State under international law if and to the extent that the State acknowledges and adopts the conduct in question as its own.' See also Jaksic (2007), p. 162, Benedettelli (2015), p. 642.

[61] *Regent Company v. Ukraine*, App. No. 773/03, ECtHR, 3 April 2008, paras. 60-1.

the Convention.[62] On the other hand, a State would breach its positive obligation and similarly incur responsibility under the Convention if it failed 'to make use of all available legal means at its disposal in order to enforce a binding arbitration award providing it contains a sufficiently established claim amounting to a possession.'[63] The ECtHR has established that a 'State must make sure that the execution of [an arbitral] award is carried out without undue delay and that the overall system is effective both in law and in practice.'[64]

The same is true also if one looks in particular at the setting-aside mechanism—a State may be held responsible for violating both its negative and positive obligations in this regard. For example, if a State interfered with parties' rights and unjustifiably annulled an arbitral award, there would be a violation of the Convention's rights and freedoms.[65] Similarly, if a State, i.e. its judiciary, failed to set aside an arbitral award that clearly violated parties' rights under the Convention, such a State would be responsible for its failure to do so.[66]

The indirect applicability of the ECHR to arbitration is generally undisputed. On the other hand, the question of whether or not the ECHR is directly applicable before arbitral tribunals or arbitration institutions, or whether it is completely inapplicable to arbitration, is merely of a theoretical nature. Considering that the indirect applicability of the ECHR to arbitration has been also recognized by the Convention's controlling bodies, the search of the most ECHR-compatible legislative approach to excluding setting-aside proceedings naturally implies that such a search must be conducted through the prism of the intermediate approach to the applicability of the ECHR to arbitration.

3.3 ECHR Provisions and Their Applicability to Arbitration

As seen, one of the arguments against the applicability of the ECHR to arbitration is that neither the Convention's *travaux préparatoires*, nor the text of the ECHR itself contains an express reference to arbitration. At the same time, according to one of the Convention's principles of interpretation, 'the Convention is a living instrument which [...] must be interpreted in the light of present-day conditions.'[67] The various arbitration-related decisions of the Convention's controlling bodies evidence that also with regard to the Convention's application to arbitration it has been interpreted as such. The ECtHR takes 'account of evolving norms of national and international

---

[62] Jaksic (2007), p. 162, Petrochilos (2004), p. 154.

[63] *Kin-Stib and Majkić v. Serbia*, App. No. 12312/05, ECtHR, 20 April 2010, para. 83.

[64] *Marčić and others v. Serbia*, App. No. 17556/05, ECtHR, 30 October 2007 para. 56.

[65] See, e.g. *Stran Greek Refineries and Stratis Andreadis v. Greece*, App. No. 13427/87, ECtHR, 9 December 1994, paras. 66–75.

[66] Jaksic (2007), p. 162, Landrove (2006), p. 93.

[67] *Tyrer v. United Kingdom*, App. No. 5856/72, ECtHR, 25 April 1978, para. 31.

law'[68] and generally provides a broad and autonomous interpretation of the Convention. This also applies to the Court's interpretation of the most obvious provision of the ECHR that may have bearing on arbitration, namely Article 6(1) of the ECHR.

While this book limits itself to the analysis of the interplay between the ECHR and the setting-aside proceedings, this does not mean that the lack of other elements of court involvement during arbitration proceedings does not have any impact on arbitrating parties' rights and freedoms under the Convention. For example, it has been argued that a specific remedy to challenge the independence and impartiality of arbitrators 'should be considered as a guarantee protected by Article 6(1) of the ECHR' and that such a 'remedy should be separate from a general application to set an award aside.'[69] As argued by Petrochilos, 'parties should be able to have an arbitrator removed without having to go through the whole process of an arbitration which, at its conclusion, is likely to be a nullity.'[70] The lack of also other elements of court involvement in arbitration in the applicable *lex arbitri*, e.g. the availability of a mechanism to challenge validity of an arbitration agreement, may lead to a violation of the Convention's rights and freedoms.[71]

Although, as Petrochilos argues with regard to a right to challenge the impartiality and independence of arbitrators, the best solution would be to have a separate remedy in the applicable *lex arbitri* that would allow arbitrating parties to address national courts with various issues relating to parties' procedural human rights,[72] such objections can be also raised during the setting-aside proceedings. If, however, there was neither a specific remedy to address, e.g. the independence and impartiality of arbitrators, already during the arbitration proceedings nor a setting-aside mechanism that allowed to set aside an arbitral award on grounds of partiality or lack of independence of a tribunal, arbitrating parties, especially the award-debtor, would be left with no effective remedy to address potential violations of their basic procedural human rights. This is especially so in case of declaratory arbitral awards that do not require any recognition and enforcement proceedings where such violations could potentially be remedied by State courts.

Considering that the majority of arbitration-related cases heard by the Convention's controlling bodies, including those pertaining to setting-aside proceedings, have centered around alleged breaches of Article 6(1) of the ECHR and the right to a fair trial, the search for the most ECHR-compatible legislative approach to excluding setting-aside proceedings implies that the question must be generally looked at from

---

[68] See *Demir and Baykara*, App. No. 34503/97, ECtHR, 12 November 2008, para. 68.

[69] Petrochilos (2004), p. 136.

[70] Ibid.

[71] This, e.g. is illustrated by the Latvian Constitutional Court's judgment in the *Hiponia* case where it concluded that the strict interpretation of the *kompetenz—kompetenz* principle and a refusal by national courts to hear a claim for a challenge of the validity of an arbitration agreement, violated the right of access to a court. See Sect. 6.5.1.4.

[72] This indeed is the case in most of the countries, that provide in their arbitration laws access to court assistance in various different matters, e.g. in challenging the validity of arbitration agreement, in challenging the independence and impartiality of arbitration, gathering of evidence, hearing of witnesses or issuing of interim measures.

the perspective of the right to a fair trial under Article 6(1) of the ECHR and, in particular, the inherent right of access to a court without which other safeguards expressly established in Article 6(1) of the ECHR would be purely hypothetical.[73] The right of access to a court can be seen as a gatekeeper that, being present in the applicable *lex arbitri* in the form of a setting-aside mechanism, can remedy possible violations of other 'non-waivable' procedural human rights,[74] such as the broader right to a fair hearing or the right to an independent and impartial tribunal.

3.3.1 *Article 6(1) of the ECHR and the Right to a Fair Trial*

Article 6 of the ECHR is perhaps the most important provision in the whole Convention, guaranteeing a right to a fair trial in civil and criminal proceedings. Certainly, it has been the most frequently invoked provision of the ECHR by applicants before the Convention's controlling bodies.[75] This is true also for arbitration-related cases before the former Commission and the ECtHR. In its relevant parts, Article 6(1) of the ECHR provides:

> In the determination of his civil rights and obligations [...] everyone is entitled to a fair and public hearing within a reasonable time by an independent and impartial tribunal established by law.

Article 6(1) of the ECHR contains certain fundamental procedural guarantees that are deemed to constitute a fair administration of justice and taken as a whole (the right to fair trial) are considered to be basic elements of the notion of the rule of law.[76] The ECtHR has repeatedly stressed that 'the right to a fair trial, as guaranteed by [Article 6(1)] of the Convention, must be construed in the light of the principle of the rule of law […] which requires that all litigants should have an effective judicial remedy enabling them to assert their civil rights.'[77] Needless to say, the fundamental

---

[73] See, in particular, *Golder v. the United Kingdom*, App. No. 4451/70, ECtHR, 21 February 1975, para. 36; *Airey v. Ireland*, App. No. 6289/73, ECtHR, 9 October 1979, para. 26. See also Cranston (1997), p. 409.

[74] See Sect. 3.4.3.3.

[75] Rainey et al. (2014), p. 247.

[76] Ibid.

[77] *Běleš and Others v. the Czech Republic*, App. No. 47273/99, ECtHR, 12 November 2002, para. 49; *Cudak v. Lithuania*, App. No. 15869/02, ECtHR [GC], 23 March 2010, para. 54; See also, e.g. *Brumărescu v. Romania*, App. No. 28342/95, ECtHR [GC], 28 October 1999, para. 61 where the Court makes a reference also to the Convention's Preamble and stresses that '[t]he right to a fair hearing before a tribunal as guaranteed by Article 6 § 1 of the Convention must be interpreted in the light of the Preamble to the Convention, which declares, among other things, the rule of law to be part of the common heritage of the Contracting States.' See also *Stran Greek Refineries and Stratis Andreadis v. Greece*, App. No. 13427/87, ECtHR, 9 December 1994, para. 46 where the Court held that '[t]his principle [the rule of law], finds expression, inter alia, in Article 6 (art. 6) of the Convention.'

right to a fair trial is recognized not only in the ECHR, but also in other international human rights instruments,[78] as well as numerous national laws all over the world.

3.3.1.1 The Right of Access to a Court

Although not expressly stipulated in the text of Article 6(1) of the ECHR the right of access to a court has been impliedly recognized by the Court as constituting a vital and indispensable element for guaranteeing other expressly laid down rights in Article 6(1) of the ECHR. In 1975, the ECtHR ruled in the well-known *Golder* case that:

> It would be inconceivable [...] that [Article 6(1)] should describe in detail the procedural guarantees afforded to parties in a pending lawsuit and should not first protect that which alone makes it in fact possible to benefit from such guarantees, that is, access to a court. The fair, public and expeditious characteristics of judicial proceedings are of no value at all if there are no judicial proceedings.
>
> [I]t follows that the right of access constitutes an element which is inherent in the right stated by [Article 6(1)]. This is not an extensive interpretation forcing new obligations on the Contracting States: it is based on the very terms of the first sentence of [Article 6(1)] read in its context and having regard to the object and purpose of the Convention [...] and to general principles of law.
>
> [Article 6(1)] secures to everyone the right to have any claim relating to his civil rights and obligations brought before a court or tribunal. In this way the Article embodies the 'right to a court', of which the right of access, that is the right to institute proceedings before courts in civil matters, constitutes one aspect only. To this are added the guarantees laid down by [Article 6(1)] as regards both the organisation and composition of the court, and the conduct of the proceedings. In sum, the whole makes up the right to a fair hearing.[79]

Since then, the implied right of access to a court has been recognized and affirmed in countless other judgments by the ECtHR.[80] This is true also with regard to arbitration-related applications brought before the former Commission and the ECtHR. The majority of such applications have concerned alleged violations of the right of access to a court as stipulated in Article 6(1) of the ECHR.[81]

---

[78] See, e.g. art. 10 of the UDHR; art. 14(1) of the ICCPR; art. 7 of the ACHPR; art. 8(1) of the ACHR.

[79] *Golder v. United Kingdom*, App. No. 4451/70, ECtHR, 21 February 1975, paras. 35-6.

[80] See, e.g. *Kuzmenko v. Ukraine*, App. No. 49526/07, ECtHR, 9 March 2017, para. 25; *Baka v. Hungary*, App. No. 20261/12, ECtHR [GC], 23 June 2016, para. 120; *Cudak v. Lithuania*, App. No. 15869/02, ECtHR [GC], 23 March 2010, para. 54; *Markovic and others v. Italy*, App. No. 1398/03, ECtHR [GC], 14 December 2006, para. 92.

[81] See, e.g. *X. v. the Federal Republic of Germany*, App. No. 1197/61, ECmHR, 5 March 1962; *Deweer v. Belgium*, App. No. 6903/75, ECtHR, 27 February 1980; *Bramelid and Malmström v. Sweden*, Apps. No. 8588/79 and 8589/79, ECmHR, 12 October 1982; *Axelsson and others v. Sweden*, App. No. 11960/86, ECmHR, 13 July 1990; *Firma Heinz Schiebler KG v. the Federal Republic of Germany*, App. No. 18805/91, ECmHR., 2 December 1991; *Lundgren v. Sweden*, App. No. 22506/93, ECmHR, 17 May 1995; *Hedland v. Sweden*, App. No. 24118/94, ECmHR, 9 April 1997; *Pastore v. Italy*, App. No. 46483/99, ECtHR, 25 May 1999.

The right of access to a court is one of the most fundamental human rights through which individuals can assert their rights and obligations. Similarly as with the more general right to fair trial, also the right of access to a court 'must be construed in the light of the principle of the rule of law'.[82] The ECtHR held in the *Golder* case that:

> [I]n civil matters one can scarcely conceive of the rule of law without there being a possibility of access to the courts [...] The principle whereby a civil claim must be capable of being submitted to a judge ranks as one of the universally recognized fundamental principles of law; the same is true of the principle of international law which forbids the denial of justice. Article 6(1) must be read in the light of these principles.[83]

The dichotomy of State's negative and positive obligations is also applied when asserting State's obligations under the Convention in relation to the right of access to a court under Article 6(1) of the ECHR. It has been said that the right of access to a court requires States to refrain from imposing on individuals within their jurisdiction legal and factual impediments to access to justice.[84] Such impediments may be the result of both State's actions and the breach of negative obligations, e.g. by imposing unreasonable procedural bars to access to justice,[85] and also State's omissions and the breach of positive obligations, e.g. by not sufficiently legislating and regulating ways how individuals can have their civil rights and obligations determined by a court. The search for the most ECHR-compatible legislative approach to excluding setting-aside proceedings mandates that further analysis focuses more on ECHR Member States' positive obligations under Article 6(1) of the ECHR and the right of access to a court.

Like other human rights and freedoms of a more procedural nature in the Convention, also the right of access to a court 'by its very nature calls for regulation by the state, regulation which may vary in time and place according to the needs and resources of the community and of individuals'.[86] It is well established that the right of access to a court is not absolute and ECHR Member States enjoy a certain margin of appreciation and procedural discretion in how their national law guarantees the right

---

82 *Cudak v. Lithuania*, App. No. 15869/02, ECtHR [GC], 23 March 2010, para. 54; *Běleš and Others v. the Czech Republic*, App. No. 47273/99, ECtHR, 12 November 2002, para. 49.

83 *Golder v. United Kingdom*, App. No. 4451/70, ECtHR, 21 February 1975, paras. 34–35.

84 See, e.g. Akandji-Kombe (2007) *Positive obligations under the European Convention on Human Rights: A guide to the implementation of the European Convention on Human Rights*, Human rights handbooks, No. 7, p. 62. Council of Europe, Directorate General of Human Rights.

85 See, e.g. *Kreuz v. Poland*, App. No. 28249/95, ECtHR, 19 June 2001, paras 60–67; *Pérez de Rada Cavanilles v. Spain*, App. No. 28090/95, ECtHR, 28 October 1998, para. 49; *Běleš and Others v. the Czech Republic*, App. No. 47273/99, ECtHR, 12 November 2002, para. 50; *Stanev v. Bulgaria*, App. No. 36760/06, ECtHR [GC], 17 January 2012, paras. 241–245.

86 *Golder v. United Kingdom*, App. No. 4451/70, ECtHR, 21 February 1975, para. 38 quoting the so-called Belgian linguistics case, Apps. No. 1474/62; 1677/62; 1691/62; 1769/63; 1994/63; 2126/64, ECtHR, 23 July 1968, para. 5. See also, e.g. *Waite and Kennedy v. Germany*, 26083/94, ECtHR [GC], 18 February 1999, para. 59; *Jensen v. Denmark*, App. No. 8693/11, ECtHR, 13 December 2016, para. 34; *Dragomir v. Romania*, App. No. 43045/08, ECtHR, 14 June 2016, para. 43.

of access to a court.[87] Therefore, Member States may impose certain limitations on the right of access to a court. Similarly, and equally important for arbitration-related cases, individuals may, under certain well-defined conditions, also waive their right of access to a court. Analysis of the different conditions of a valid and permissible waiver and the scope of such a waiver will be carried out below when looking specifically at the Convention's controlling bodies' existing arbitration-related case law.[88]

Certainly, such a margin of appreciation and procedural discretion is not without limits. It would be against the whole purpose of the ECHR if its Member States could validly limit individuals' right of access to a court as they wish. Therefore, 'the ultimate decision as to the observance of the Convention's requirements rests with the Court'.[89] If limitations imposed on the right of access to a court 'restrict or reduce the access left to the individual in such a way or to such an extent that the very essence of the right is impaired'[90] the Court will find a violation of a State's obligations under the Convention.

In order to establish boundaries to the Member States' margin of appreciation and procedural discretion, the ECtHR applies a specific test and seeks to determine whether the restriction imposed by a Member States pursues a legitimate aim and whether there is a 'reasonable relationship of proportionality between the means employed and the aim sought to be achieved.'[91] If any of the requirements is not satisfied by the imposed restriction on the right of access to a court, such a restriction will not be compatible with the Convention and the respective Member State will therefore incur responsibility under the Convention. The said test has been applied in multiple arbitration-related cases, including that of the *Tabbane v. Switzerland* case.[92]

Additionally, in examining alleged violations of a right of access to a court under Article 6(1) of the ECHR the Court also looks whether such a right is *practical and effective*. The ECtHR has stressed that:

> [I]t should be remembered that the Convention is intended to guarantee not rights that are theoretical or illusory but rights that are practical and effective. This is particularly so of the

[87] See, e.g. *Dragomir v. Romania*, App. No. 43045/08, ECtHR, 14 June 2016, para. 43; *Cudak v. Lithuania*, App. No. 15869/02, ECtHR [GC], 23 March 2010, para. 55; *Kreuz v. Poland*, App. No. 28249/95, ECtHR, 19 June 2001, para. 53.

[88] See Sects. 3.4 and 3.5.

[89] *Golder v. United Kingdom*, App. No. 4451/70, ECtHR, 21 February 1975, paras. 35–6.

[90] *Ashingdane v. the United Kingdom*, App. No. 8225/78, ECtHR, 28 May 1985, para. 57. See also, e.g. *Philis v. Greece*, Apps. No. *12750/87; 13780/88; 14003/*88, ECtHR, 27 August 1991, para. 59; *De Geouffre de la Pradelle v. France*, App. No. 12964/87, ECtHR, 16 December 1992, para. 28; *Stanev v. Bulgaria*, App. No. 36760/06, ECtHR [GC], 17 January 2012, para. 229.

[91] See, e.g., *Fayed v. the United Kingdom*, App. No. 17101/90, ECtHR, 21 September 1994, para. 65; *Markovic and Others v. Italy*, App. No. 1398/03, ECtHR, 14 December 2006, para. 99; *Ashingdane v. the United Kingdom*, para. 57.

[92] See Sect. 5.2.4.

right of access to the courts in view of the prominent place held in a democratic society by the right to a fair trial.[93]

Taken together, these are the general principles applied by the ECtHR to claims alleging a Member State's violation of Article 6(1) of the ECHR and the right of access to a court. While for generally understanding the dichotomy between the ECHR and arbitration it is for now unnecessary to consider in detail the different aspects of the said principles and the corresponding case-law of the Convention's controlling bodies in more detail, their significance and nuanced details will prove to be pivotal in drawing a line between ECHR-compatible and non-compatible legislative approaches to excluding setting-aside proceedings.[94]

3.3.1.2 The Right to a Fair Hearing

The broader right to a fair trial as laid down in Article 6(1) of the ECHR includes also more specific requirements pertaining to the nature of civil proceedings per se. All democratic States governed by the rule of law recognize certain cornerstone principles that taken together constitute a 'fair hearing'. It is argued that in order to determine whether the requirements of 'fair hearing' have been met under Article 6(1) of the ECHR, each case must be considered individually and weighed 'in the context of the proceedings as a whole.'[95] Although the Court has not expressly provided a definition of what constitutes a *fair hearing* within the meaning of Article 6(1) of the ECHR, certain *fair hearing* components can be deduced from its ample case-law and doctrine. Among others, the most fundamental components of a *fair hearing* are the principle of procedural equality (equality of arms) and the right to adversarial proceedings.[96]

As regards the principle of procedural equality, the ECtHR has established that 'the requirement of equality of arms in the sense of a fair balance between the parties [in] litigation involving opposing private interests [...] implies that each party must be afforded a reasonable opportunity to present his case—under conditions that do not place him at a substantial disadvantage vis-à-vis his opponent'.[97]

As to the principle of adversarial proceedings, it is closely linked with the principle of equality of arms and similarly constitutes an indispensable and fundamental part

---

[93] *Cudak v. Lithuania*, App. No. 15869/02, ECtHR [GC], 23 March 2010, para. 58.

[94] See Chap. 7.

[95] See, e.g. *Talmane v. Latvia*, App. No. 47938/07, ECtHR, 13 October 2016, para. 20. See also Rainey et al. (2014), p. 263, Briner and Von Schlabrendorff (2001), p. 95.

[96] Rainey et al. (2014), pp. 263–265, Briner and Von Schlabrendorff (2001), pp. 95–96, Petrochilos (2004), pp. 144–149, Jaksic (2002), pp. 227–244. Generally on the difference between the two concepts see, e.g. *Krčmar and Others v. the Czech Republic*, App. No. 35376/97, ECtHR, 3 March 2000, paras. 38–46. See also Settem (2016).

[97] *Dombo Beheer B.V. v. the Netherlands*, App. No. 14448/88, ECtHR [GC], 27 October 1993, para. 33. See also, e.g. *Stran Greek Refineries and Stratis Andreadis v. Greece*, App. No. 13427/87, ECtHR, 9 December 1994, para. 46; *Avotiņš v. Latvia*, App. No. 17502/07, ECtHR [GC], 23 May 2016, para. 119.

of the requirement of a *fair hearing*,[98] guaranteeing 'the opportunity for the parties to have knowledge of and comment on the observations filed or evidenced adduced by the other party.'[99] In essence, the principle of adversarial proceedings guarantees everyone the right to be heard.

If put in perspective of the discussion of dichotomy between the ECHR and setting-aside proceedings, and in particular of the extent to which setting-aside mechanism should be available under national law, a question arises whether the right to a *fair hearing*, at least such core principles as the equality of arms and adversarial proceedings, can be validly excluded (or not provided in the first place in case of total lack of setting-aside proceedings under national law) by means of an exclusion agreement renouncing in full the right to setting-aside proceedings, i.e. a mechanism that, inter alia, verifies whether arbitrating parties' rights of due process were respected. The ECtHR has held that the conclusion of an arbitration agreement 'should not necessarily be considered to amount to a waiver of all the rights under Article 6' and that '[a] [w]aiver may be permissible with regard to certain rights but not with regard to certain others.'[100] At the same time, the ECtHR's judgment in the *Tabbane v. Switzerland* case suggests that through the principle of party autonomy parties are allowed to exclude the application of setting-aside proceedings, i.e. a mechanism that, inter alia, aims to ensure that the principle of a *fair hearing* has been duly observed during arbitration proceedings.[101]

Until now, neither the former Commission, nor the ECtHR has clearly determined which elements of Article 6(1) of the ECHR can be waived and which are the so-called *non-waivable* rights thereunder. Doctrine argues, and the case-law of the ECtHR indirectly confirms,[102] that the *non-waivable* rights include the right to an equal treatment, the right to an independent and impartial tribunal, and the right to be heard.[103] The unanswered question, however, is whether, by excluding the right to setting-aside proceedings as in the *Tabbane v. Switzerland* case, party autonomy also takes precedence over such seemingly non-waivable procedural human rights? Is it even possible to expressly renounce the application of the most fundamental procedural human rights that should be applicable to every human being?

Some authors argue that such fundamental principles as equality of arms and adversarial proceedings are directly applicable to arbitration proceedings and parties, by concluding an arbitration agreement, have no intention of excluding the applicability of basic principles; thus, a waiver of the right to a fair hearing under Article

---

[98] See, e.g. *Avotiņš v. Latvia*, App. No. 17502/07, ECtHR [GC], 23 May 2016, para. 119.

[99] See, e.g. *Sebahattin Evcimen v. Turkey*, App. No. 31792/06, ECtHR, 23 February 2010, para. 25; *K.S. v. Finland*, App. No. 29346/95, ECtHR, 31 May 2001, para. 21.

[100] *Suovaniemi and others v. Finland*, App. No. 31737/96, ECtHR, 23 February 1999.

[101] See Sect. 5.2.4.

[102] See, e.g. *Suovaniemi and others v. Finland*, App. No. 31737/96, ECtHR, 23 February 1999; See also *Albert and Le Compte v. Belgium*, Apps. No. 7299/75 and 7496/76, ECtHR, 10 February 1983, para. 35 where the Court stresses that 'the nature of some of the rights safeguarded by the Convention is such as to exclude a waiver of the entitlement to exercise them.'

[103] See, e.g., Briner and Von Schlabrendorff (2001), pp. 90–97, Petrochilos (2004), pp. 130–131, Jaksic (2007), pp. 165–166.

6(1) of the ECHR is inadmissible and has no binding force.[104] However, it is unclear if the same is true also if such a waiver impliedly stems from the broader exclusion of setting-aside proceedings.

3.3.1.3 The Right to an Independent and Impartial Tribunal Established by Law

Equally important to the guarantee of a fair hearing under Article 6(1) of the ECHR is everyone's right to have such a hearing before an independent and impartial tribunal established by law. What constitutes a 'tribunal' and when is such a 'tribunal' 'established by law' within the meaning of Article 6(1) of the ECHR is a topic that has been comprehensively covered both by the Convention's controlling bodies in their case law[105] and also in doctrine. However, of particular interest for the dichotomy between the ECHR and setting-aside proceedings is the seemingly *non-waivable* right that such a 'tribunal' is comprised of 'independent and impartial' adjudicators.

Without in detail addressing the different elements that constitute an 'independent and impartial' adjudicator as established by the former Commission and the ECtHR in their case-law,[106] it can be said that the right to an independent and impartial adjudicator is an essential part of the broader right to a fair trial and fair administration of justice, and thus is an equally important element of the rule of law.[107]

In short, the right to an *independent* adjudicator implies that such an adjudicator is independent vis-à-vis other powers of the State, i.e. the executive and the Parliament, and also vis-à-vis the involved parties.[108] When examining whether an adjudicatory body can be considered *independent* within the meaning of Article 6(1) of the ECHR, the Court will have regard, inter alia, 'to the manner of appointment of its members

---

104 Briner and Von Schlabrendorff (2001), p. 97.

105 For the notion of a 'tribunal' within the meaning of art. 6(1) of the ECHR please see, e.g. *Sramek v. Austria*, App. No. 8790/79, ECtHR, 22 October 1984; *Lithgow and others v. United Kingdom*, Apps. No. *9006/80; 9262/81; 9263/81; 9265/81; 9266/81; 9313/81; 9405/81*, ECtHR, 8 July 1986; *H. v. Belgium*, App. No. 8950/80, ECtHR, 30 November 1987; *Cyprus v. Turkey*, App. No. 25781/94, ECtHR [GC], 10 May 2001. For the notion of 'established by law' within the meaning of art. 6(1) of the ECHR please see, e.g. *Zand v. Austria*, App. No. 7360/76, ECmHR, 16 May 1977; *Lavents v. Latvia*, App. No. 58442/00, ECtHR, 28 November 2002, para. 81; *Sokurenko and Strygun v. Ukraine*, Apps. No. 29458/04 and 29465/04, ECtHR, 20 July 2006, para. 24; *DMD Group, A.S. v. Slovakia*, App. No. 19334/03, ECtHR, 5 October 2010, para. 61.

106 See generally, e.g. European Court of Human Rights (2019) Guide on Article 6 of the European Convention on Human Rights: Right to a fair trial (civil limb), pp. 26–32. http://www.echr.coe.int/Documents/Guide_Art_6_ENG.pdf. Accessed 28 May 2020.

107 See, e.g. *De Cubber v. Belgium*, App. No. 9186/80, ECtHR, 26 October 1984, para. 30; *Cocchiarella v. Italy*, App. No. 64886/01, ECtHR [GC], 29 March 2006, para. 83; *Stanev v. Bulgaria*, App. No. 36760/06, ECtHR, 17 January 2012, para. 231.

108 See, e.g. European Court of Human Rights (2019) Guide on Article 6 of the European Convention on Human Rights: Right to a fair trial (civil limb), pp. 27–28. http://www.echr.coe.int/Documents/Guide_Art_6_ENG.pdf. Accessed 28 May 2020.

and their term of office, to the existence of guarantees against outside pressures and to the question whether the body presents an appearance of independence [...]'.[109]

Commonly considered together with the notion of *independence* is the second aspect, namely, that of *impartiality* of an adjudicatory body. The aspect of *impartiality* 'normally denotes the absence of prejudice or bias and its existence or otherwise can be tested in various ways'.[110] The most common way in determining this is by the Court applying two tests: 'a subjective test seeking to determine the personal conviction and behavior of a particular judge; and an objective test seeking to ascertain whether the tribunal itself offered sufficient guarantees to exclude any legitimate doubt in respect of its impartiality.'[111] Under the subjective test 'the impartiality of a judge or a tribunal must be presumed until there is proof to the contrary', however, '[u]nder the second test it must be determined whether there are ascertainable facts which may raise doubts as to impartiality of a judge.'[112]

Similarly as with the right to a fair hearing, if the right to an independent and impartial adjudicator is put in perspective of the discussion of dichotomy between the ECHR and setting-aside proceedings, a question arises whether arbitrating parties when signing an arbitration agreement, in particular, when they by an express agreement exclude setting-aside proceedings, they also waive the right to an independent and impartial tribunal? To put it in the ECtHR's own terms—is such a waiver even *permissible*, considering that the right to an independent and impartial adjudicatory body is an essential part of the broader right to a fair trial and pertains to the rule of law? Even more so, if the setting-aside mechanism is absent from the respective national law altogether and arbitrating parties have no possibility to challenge an arbitral award, invoking lack of independence and impartiality of arbitrators, would not this result in a violation of their *non-waivable* right to independent and impartial tribunal within the meaning of Article 6(1) of the ECHR?

The question of the relationship between arbitration and the right to an independent and impartial tribunal within the meaning of Article 6(1) of the ECHR was considered in the *Suovaniemi and others v. Finland* case.[113] The case concerned arbitration proceedings in which parties had expressly approved certain arbitrators to decide their case despite being aware that there are certain issues pertaining to the arbitrators' independence and impartiality. After the award was issued, the dissatisfied party applied before the Finnish courts to have the award set aside on grounds of lack of independence and impartiality of certain members of the tribunal, however, due

---

[109] See, e.g. *Langborger v. Sweden*, App. No. 11179/84, ECtHR, 22 June 1989, para. 32; *Grieves v. United Kingdom*, App. No. 57067/00, ECtHR [GC], 16 December 2003, para. 69; *Sahiner v. Turkey*, App. No. 29279/95, ECtHR, 25 September 2001, para. 35.

[110] See, e.g. *Micallef v. Malta*, App. No. 17056/06, ECtHR [GC], 15 October 2009, para. 93; *Morice v. France*, App. No. 29369/10, ECtHR [GC], 23 April 2015, para. 73; *Upīte v. Latvia*, App. No. 7636/08, ECtHR, 1 September 2016, para. 30.

[111] *Upīte v. Latvia*, App. No. 7636/08, ECtHR, 1 September 2016, para. 30. See also *Micallef v. Malta*, App. No. 17056/06, ECtHR [GC], 15 October 2009, paras. 93–94; *Sahiner v. Turkey*, App. No. 29279/95, ECtHR, 25 September 2001, para. 36.

[112] *Upīte v. Latvia*, App. No. 7636/08, ECtHR, 1 September 2016, para. 30.

[113] *Suovaniemi and others v. Finland*, App. No. 31737/96, ECtHR, 23 February 1999.

to a collateral estoppel, i.e. a failure to raise such an issue during the arbitration proceedings and an express approval of the state of affairs, the Finnish courts argued that such a party had lost its right to invoke lack of independence and impartiality as a ground for setting aside an arbitral award.[114]

When the case reached the ECtHR, the Court pointed to the difference between the nature of certain rights of Article 6(1) of the ECHR and 'permissibility' to waive such rights:

> There is no doubt that a voluntary waiver of court proceedings in favour of arbitration is in principle acceptable from the point of view of Article 6 [...] Even so, such a waiver should not necessarily be considered to amount to a waiver of all the rights under Article 6 [...] [emphasis added] [A]n unequivocal waiver of Convention rights is valid only insofar as such waiver is 'permissible'. Waiver may be permissible with regard to certain rights but not with regard to certain others. A distinction may have to be made even between different rights guaranteed by Article 6.[115]

Although, by referring to its previous judgment in the *Pfeifer and Plankl v. Austria case*,[116] the ECtHR then went on to rhetorically question 'whether the fundamental right to an impartial judge can be waived at all',[117] it nevertheless concluded that parties had validly waived the right to an independent and impartial tribunal. The Court arrived at such a conclusion by limiting 'itself to the particular circumstances of the present case', i.e. a situation in which parties were aware of possible shortcomings of certain arbitrators in terms of their lack of independence and partiality, but nevertheless expressly approved such state of affairs.[118]

Taking into account that the Court's conclusion was confined to the very specific circumstances of the *Suovaniemi* case, a question that nevertheless remains unanswered is whether a waiver of the right to an independent and impartial tribunal would be *permissible* under Article 6(1) of the ECHR in other, less convincing circumstances. For example, would a mere exclusion of setting-aside proceedings at the time of signing an arbitration agreement, as opposed to an express confirmation as in the *Suovaniemi* case, also cover such a fundamental right as the right to an independent and impartial tribunal? Would such an exclusion be even *permissible* within the meaning of Article 6(1) of the ECHR, considering that the ECtHR has itself held that some of the rights in Article 6(1) of the ECHR are so fundamentally important in a democratic society that no individual should be deprived of their benefit, even if they have voluntarily waived such a right?[119]

---

[114] Generally on collateral estoppel or issue preclusion see Sect. 3.4.3.1.

[115] *Suovaniemi and others v. Finland*, App. No. 31737/96, ECtHR, 23 February 1999.

[116] *Pfeifer and Plankl v. Austria*, App. No. 10802/84, ECtHR, 25 February 1992.

[117] *Suovaniemi and others v. Finland*, App. No. 31737/96, ECtHR, 23 February 1999.

[118] Ibid.

[119] *Albert and Le Compte v. Belgium*, Apps. No. 7299/75 and 7496/76, ECtHR, 10 February 1983, para. 35. See also Petrochilos (2004), p. 122.

3.3.1.4 Public Hearing and Reasonable Time

The right to a public hearing and the right to such a hearing, as well as the resulting judgment, within a reasonable time are elements of Article 6(1) of the ECHR that, at least with regard to the dichotomy between the ECHR and arbitration, have slightly less weight than the right to a fair hearing or the right to an independent and impartial tribunal.

As regards the right to a public hearing, it suffices to state that the former Commission and the ECtHR have both found that, although the right to a public hearing is a fundamental principle enshrined in Article 6(1) of the ECHR, 'neither the letter nor the spirit of the provision prevents a person from waiving of his own free will, either tacitly or expressly, the entitlement to public hearing.'[120] Especially with regard to arbitration proceedings, it has been held that:

> the right to a public hearing can be validly waived even in court proceedings [...] The same applies, *a fortiori*, to arbitration proceedings, one of the very purposes of which is often to avoid publicity.[121]

Also in legal doctrine it is generally recognized that confidentiality and private nature is at the heart of arbitration proceedings, therefore the right to a public hearing is waived by concluding an agreement to arbitrate.[122]

Similar conclusions can be drawn with regard to the requirement of a reasonable time referred to in Article 6(1) of the ECHR. The right to a trial within reasonable time is validly waived at the moment when parties conclude an arbitration agreement and choose to arbitrate instead of submitting their dispute to state courts where such a requirement would have to be fully honoured. Party autonomy to opt out of State courts' jurisdiction is duly respected, however, by doing so, they are also required to face any difficulties concerning the expected length of proceedings.[123] It has been stressed that Member States will not be held responsible for violations of the reasonable time requirement by arbitral tribunals for the period prior to the engagement of State courts.[124] Their responsibility therefore is engaged upon application by parties to perform one of the supervisory functions ancillary to arbitration proceedings, e.g. when parties request the setting aside of an arbitral award.[125]

---

[120] *Axelsson and others v. Sweden*, App. No. 11960/86, ECmHR, 13 July 1990.

[121] *Suovaniemi and others v. Finland*, App. No. 31737/96, ECtHR. 23 February 1999. See also *Nordström-Janzon and Nordström-Lehtinen v. the Netherlands*, App. No. 28101/95, ECmHR, 27 November 1996 where the former Commission held that '[i]n some respects—in particular as regards publicity—it is clear that arbitral proceedings are often not even intended to be in conformity with [Article 6(1) ECHR].'

[122] See, e.g. Petrochilos (2004), p. 150, Briner and Von Schlabrendorff (2001), p. 98, Landrove (2006), p. 90.

[123] Briner and Von Schlabrendorff (2001), p. 97.

[124] *R v. Switzerland*, App. No. 10881/84, ECmHR, 4 March 1987. See also *Molin v. Turkey*, App. No. 23173/94, ECmHR, 22 October 1996.

[125] See, e.g. *Molin İnşaat v. Turkey*, App. No. 38424/97, ECtHR, 11 January 2005.

3.3.2 Other ECHR Provisions

Article 6(1) of the ECHR and the right to a fair trial, including its above-introduced constituent elements, is the most evident guarantee of the ECHR that could be interpreted to impliedly apply also to arbitration and certainly to court proceedings ancillary to arbitration. It is also Article 6(1) of the ECHR that has been most often invoked by parties in arbitration-related cases brought before the former Commission or the ECtHR. Nevertheless, over the years, it has become evident that besides Article 6(1) of the ECHR there are also other ECHR provisions that may have bearing upon arbitration proceedings and eventual State responsibility for actions or omissions related to arbitration.

Although there are numerous ECHR rights and freedoms that, according to some scholars, could be at least theoretically applicable to arbitration proceedings,[126] the most obvious are the right to an effective remedy (Article 13 of the ECHR) and the right to peaceful enjoyment of one's possessions (Article 1 of Protocol 1 to the ECHR).

3.3.2.1 Article 13 of the ECHR and the Right to an Effective Remedy

Article 13 of the ECHR provides for a right to an effective remedy and in its relevant parts states that '[e]veryone whose rights and freedoms as set forth in this Convention are violated shall have an effective remedy before a national authority [...]' Considered together with Article 1 of the ECHR, it obliges Member States to legislate and put in place effective remedies that would address alleged violations of the Convention's rights and freedoms already at a national level.[127]

Although Article 13 of the ECHR is a self-standing provision which could be violated even if there was no violation of other Convention's substantive provisions, there must be at least an arguable violation of another Convention right.[128]

---

[126] See, e.g. Benedettelli (2015), p. 642 where the author argues that the freedom of expression or the freedom of association or the right to respect one's home and correspondence might as well be of significance to arbitration proceedings. He even goes to state that '[s]hould the Convention be amended to cover also other human rights of the 'second' or 'third generation', then its relevance could extend also to investment arbitrations whenever a measure enacted by the host State for the protection of such rights is challenged by the investor under any applicable ground of the relevant bilateral or multilateral investment treaty'. See also Besson (2006), p. 397 where the author puts forward arguments for the applicability of art. 8 of the ECHR to arbitration. As to the application of art. 14 of the ECHR and the right to prohibition of discrimination to arbitration proceedings, in particular, the former art. 1704(4) of the BCCP (as amended on 27 March 1985) please see Jaksic (2002) pp. 301–309.

[127] Rainey et al. (2014), p. 129.

[128] Ibid., p. 130 in referring to *Klass and others v. Germany*, App. No. 5029/71, ECtHR, 6 September 1978, para. 63. See also *Boyle and Rice v. United Kingdom*, Apps. No. 9659/82 and 9658/92, ECtHR, 27 April 1988, para. 52 where the Court held that 'the existence of an actual breach of another provision of the Convention (a 'substantive' provision) is not a prerequisite for the application of the [Article 13] [...] Article 13 (art. 13) guarantees the availability of a remedy at national level

For the purposes of finding the most balanced approach to excluding setting-aside proceedings, the *other* right of the Convention that could be arguably violated if national law excessively limits the availability of setting-aside proceedings is the above-introduced Article 6(1) of the ECHR and the right of access to a court. In cases where there is generally no effective remedy in national law (as opposed to an appropriate remedy required by another provision of the ECHR),[129] the ECtHR has held that the application must be examined separately under Article 13 of the ECHR and the other provision of the Convention, which in the present case is Article 6(1) of the ECHR.[130]

Although, as the *Klass* case suggests, there does not have to be a violation of another Convention right for Article 13 of the ECHR to be applicable, the ECtHR requires that the complaint before it is at least *arguable*:

> [Article 13] cannot reasonably be interpreted so as to require a remedy in domestic law in respect of any supposed grievance under the Convention that an individual may have, no matter how unmeritorious his complaint may be: the grievance must be an arguable one in terms of the Convention [...].[131]

The notion of *arguability* under Article 13 of the ECHR has its parallels with the requirement that an application must not be 'manifestly ill-founded' within the meaning of Article 35(3)(a) of the ECHR.[132] The test applied by the ECtHR under both notions is in essence similar and requires a *prima facie* examination of the merits of the case and determination that the application concerns 'a Convention issue which merits further examination'.[133] In *Boyle and Rice v. United Kingdom* the ECtHR established that:

> The Court is thus competent to take cognisance of all questions of fact and of law arising in the context of the complaints before it under [Article 13], including the arguability or not of the claims of violation of the substantive provisions. In this connection, the Commission's decision on the admissibility of the underlying claims and the reasoning therein, whilst not being decisive, provide significant pointers as to the arguable character of the claims for the purposes of [Article 13]
>
> The Court does not think that it should give an abstract definition of the notion of arguability. Rather it must be determined, in the light of the particular facts and the nature of the legal issue or issues raised, whether each individual claim of violation forming the basis of a

to enforce—and hence to allege non-compliance with—the substance of the Convention rights and freedoms in whatever form they may happen to be secured in the domestic legal order [...]'.

[129] Ibid., p. 131 in referring to the so-called Vagrancy cases—*De Wilde, Ooms and Versyp v. Belgium*, App. Nos. 2832/66, 2835/66, 2899/66, ECtHR, 18 June 1977, paras. 74–80 and 95, and stating that if the principal complaint before the ECtHR is based on 'the absence of an appropriate remedy required by another provision of the Convention, it is unnecessary to consider Article 13'.

[130] Ibid. in referring to *Peck v. United Kingdom*, App. No. 44647/98, ECtHR, 28 January 2003.

[131] *Boyle and Rice v. United Kingdom*, Apps. No. 9659/82 and 9658/92, ECtHR, 27 April 1988, para. 52.

[132] *Powell and Rayner v. United Kingdom*, App. No. 9310/81, ECtHR, 21 February 1990, para. 33.

[133] Rainey et al. (2014), p. 132.

complaint under [Article 13] was arguable and, if so, whether the requirements of [Article 13] were met in relation thereto.[134]

Moreover, it is not sufficient that there is a mere remedy in national law providing for a possibility to address a potential violation of a Convention's right or freedom—such a remedy, as stressed by the text of Article 13 of the ECHR itself, must be *effective*. The ECtHR has held that:

> The scope of the Contracting States' obligations under Article 13 varies depending on the nature of the applicant's complaint; however, the remedy required by Article 13 must be 'effective' in practice as well as in law [...].
>
> The 'effectiveness' of a 'remedy' within the meaning of Article 13 does not depend on the certainty of a favourable outcome for the applicant. Nor does the 'authority' referred to in that provision necessarily have to be a judicial authority; but if it is not, its powers and the guarantees which it affords are relevant in determining whether the remedy before it is effective. Also, even if a single remedy does not by itself entirely satisfy the requirements of Article 13, the aggregate of remedies provided for under domestic law may do so [...].[135]

This, in turn, means that ECHR Member States are afforded a certain margin of appreciation 'as to the manner in which they conform to their Convention obligations under this provision'[136] and that the 'scope of the obligation under Article 13 varies depending on the nature of applicant's complaint under the Convention'.[137] What is nevertheless important is that such a remedy under Article 13 of the ECHR is *effective* in practice as well as in law.[138]

ECHR Member States' margin of appreciation is not, however, unlimited. It is argued that national procedural autonomy in satisfying obligations under Article 13 of the ECHR does not 'extend to the very existence of a remedy, since Article 13 of the ECHR requires that there is an effective remedy to enforce the substance of the Convention rights in the national legal order'.[139] The importance of Article 13 of the ECHR to the dichotomy between the ECHR and setting-aside proceedings depends therefore on the extent to which setting-aside mechanism is unavailable under national arbitration law. If, as in the case of Latvia, national law does not provide an effective remedy for challenging the validity of an arbitral award, national procedural autonomy cannot be invoked in justifying a complete absence of such a remedy.[140] The situation might, however, be different for exclusion agreements, where the remedy—setting-aside mechanism—itself exists in the respective national law, however, parties, through exercising their procedural autonomy, validly waive such a remedy.

---

[134] *Boyle and Rice v. United Kingdom*, Apps. No. 9659/82 and 9658/92, ECtHR, 27 April 1988, paras. 54–55.

[135] *Kudla v. Poland*, App. No, 30210/96, ECtHR [GC], 26 October 2000, para. 157. More recently see, e.g. *Ilias and Ahmed v. Turkey*, App. No. 47287/15, ECtHR, 14 March 2017, para. 98.

[136] See, e.g. *Rotaru v. Romania*, App. No. 28341/95, ECtHR [GC], 4 May 2000, para. 67; *Abuhmaid v. Ukraine*, App. No. 31183/13, ECtHR, 12 January 2017, para. 118.

[137] *Kudla v. Poland*, App. No, 30210/96, ECtHR [GC], 26 October 2000, para. 157.

[138] Ibid. See also, e.g. *Ilhan v. Turkey*, App. No. 22277/93, ECtHR [GC], 27 June 2000, para. 97.

[139] Rainey et al. (2014), p. 133.

[140] Ibid.

3.3.2.2 Protocol 1 to the ECHR and the Right to Protection of Property

Article 1 of Protocol 1 to the ECHR in its relevant parts provides that '[e]very natural or legal person is entitled to the peaceful enjoyment of his possessions' and that '[n]o one shall be deprived of his possessions except in the public interest and subject to the conditions provided for by law and by the general principles of international law'. To date, the ECtHR has heard a handful of arbitration-related applications in which, inter alia, it has been argued that the right to peaceful enjoyment of property within the meaning of Article 1 of Protocol 1 to the ECHR has been breached in one way or another.[141]

The very first in this regard was the *Stran Greek Refineries* case involving a dispute between Mr. Andreadis and a company owned by him, on the one hand, and the Greek State on the other hand.[142] After losing arbitration concerning the construction of a crude oil refinery, the Greek State enacted a decree that in essence declared the whole arbitration proceedings and the resulting arbitral award void and unenforceable. Mr. Andreadis and his company applied to the former Commission and argued, inter alia, that the Greek State, by enacting the said decree, had breached their right of property as guaranteed in Article 1 of Protocol 1 to the ECHR.

The *Stran Greek Refineries* case is important in establishing for the first time that an arbitral award can constitute a 'possession' within the meaning of Article 1 of Protocol 1 to the ECHR. The Court arrived at such a conclusion by ascertaining that 'the arbitration award had given rise to a debt in [the applicants'] favour that was sufficiently established to be enforceable'[143]:

> According to its wording, the award was final and binding; it did not require any further enforcement measure and no ordinary or special appeal lay against it [...] [T]he arbitration award [...] therefore conferred on the applicants a right in the sums awarded [...] Accordingly, in the Court's view, that right constituted a 'possession' within the meaning of [Article 1 of Protocol 1 to the ECHR].[144]

After establishing that the arbitral award constitutes a *possession*, the ECtHR continued in affirming that there was an interference with the applicants' *possession*[145] and that such an interference was not justified in the sense that a 'fair balance

---

[141] See, e.g. *Stran Greek Refineries and Stratis Andreadis v. Greece*, App. No. 13427/87, ECtHR, 9 December 1994; *Transado-Transportes Fluviais Do Sado, S.A. v. Portugal*, App. No. 35943/02, ECtHR, 16 December 2003; *Regent Company v. Ukraine*, App. No. 773/03, ECtHR, 3 April 2008; *Kin-Stib and Majkić v. Serbia*, App. No. 12312/05, ECtHR, 20 April 2010.

[142] *Stran Greek Refineries and Stratis Andreadis v. Greece*, App. No. 13427/87, ECtHR, 9 December 1994.

[143] Ibid., para. 59.

[144] Ibid., paras. 61–62.

[145] Ibid., para. 66 where the Court states that it 'find that there was an interference with the applicants' right of property as guaranteed by Article 1 of Protocol No. 1 (P1-1). Paragraph 2 of Article 12 of Law no. 1701/1987 declared the arbitration award void and unenforceable'.

was [not] struck between the demands of the general interest of the community and the requirements of the protection of the individual's fundamental rights'.[146]

The *Stran Greek Refineries* case concerned an unjustified interference by the State with one's lawful possession, i.e. an arbitral award, because of passing of a decree that essentially declared the arbitral award void and unenforceable. Later, the ECtHR witnessed other arbitration-related cases in which the interference with the right of property was manifested somewhat differently.

For example, the *Regent Company v. Ukraine* case concerned a continuing non-enforcement of an arbitral award by the Ukrainian courts. The applicants in this case argued that the Ukrainian State had breached its obligations under both Article 6 of the ECHR 'in that the arbitration award [...] had not been enforced within a reasonable time and in full',[147] and also Article 1 of Protocol 1 to the ECHR 'in that it had not ensured that the award was enforced in good time and had not taken necessary and adequate measures to ensure that the applicant company effectively enjoyed its property rights.'[148] The ECtHR confirmed that an excessively prolonged non-enforcement of an arbitral award indeed amount to a violation of both Article 6(1) of the ECHR and Article 1 of Protocol 1 to the ECHR.[149]

In another arbitration-related case—*Kin-Stib and Majkić v. Serbia*—the Court was repeatedly confronted with an application concerning non-enforcement of an arbitral award by State authorities and thus a potential violation of the right to peaceful enjoyment of property as provided in Article 1 of Protocol 1 to the ECHR.[150] In this case the Court more expressly stressed that:

> [I]t is the State's responsibility to make use of all available legal means at its disposal in order to enforce a binding arbitration award providing it contains a sufficiently established claim amounting to a possession [...] [T]he State must make sure that the execution of such an award is carried out without undue delay and that the overall system is effective both in law and in practice [...].[151]

From the above cases pertaining to the relationship between arbitration proceedings, in particular, an arbitral award, and the right to peaceful enjoyment of property, one can deduce that States may be potentially responsible for both—unjustified actions, such as passing of a decree that in essence declares the arbitral award void as in the *Stran Greek Refineries* case, and also omissions, such as continued non-enforcement of an arbitral award as in the *Regent Company v. Ukraine* and *Kin-Stib* cases. With regard to the latter, it is not hard to imagine that unavailability of a setting-aside mechanism in national arbitration law may as well lead to potential State liability under Article 1 of Protocol 1 to the ECHR. When recognizing and enforcing an arbitral award the State is 'stamping it with [its] seal of approval [and

---

[146] Ibid., para. 69 in referring to *Sporrong and Lönnroth v. Sweden*, Apps. No. 7151/75 and 7152/75, ECtHR, 18 December 1984, para. 69.

[147] *Regent Company v. Ukraine*, App. No. 773/03, ECtHR, 3 April 2008, para. 58.

[148] Ibid.

[149] Ibid., paras. 59–62.

[150] *Kin-Stib and Majkić v. Serbia*, App. No. 12312/05, ECtHR, 20 April 2010.

[151] Ibid., para. 83.

by] so doing, a state endorses the award and the process that led to it, and may as a result of such endorsement incur international responsibility.'[152] Recognition and enforcement of a procedurally defective arbitral award affecting the award-debtor's proprietary rights, on the one hand, and omission on behalf of a State by not providing an opportunity for the aggrieved party to challenge such a defective arbitral award, on the other hand, may equally lead to the violation of the Convention's rights and freedoms, especially the right of property as established in Article 1 of Protocol 1 to the ECHR.

3.4 Arbitration Agreement—A *Waiver* of the Convention's Rights?

To date, the relationship between arbitration and the ECHR has not been defined to the extent that every single question would have a clear and straightforward answer in the Court's case-law and principles established therein. Although over the years certain guidelines and closely-linked general principles pertaining to the dichotomy between the ECHR and arbitration have emerged from the Court's case-law, the picture, so to speak, is still rather blurry, at least with regard to some aspects of the said dichotomy. This blurriness, in turn, gives basis for the search of the most ECHR-compatible approach to excluding setting-aside proceedings in national law.

As argued, the ECHR and its applicability to compulsory (statutory) arbitration is not disputed. What, however, is disputed, is the exact extent of applicability of the ECHR to consensual arbitration, i.e. such that is the result of a voluntary agreement between parties to submit their dispute to arbitration instead of State courts. As seen when introducing the different approaches to the applicability of the ECHR to arbitration, questions with regard to the extent of such applicability have troubled the minds of many scholars. In addition to the ongoing debate in academia, the Convention's controlling bodies have considerably, albeit somewhat insufficiently, contributed to the understanding of the extent of the said relationship between the ECHR and consensual arbitration. Since most arbitration-related cases before the former Commission or the ECtHR have concerned an alleged violation of Article 6(1) of the ECHR, the principles established by the Convention's controlling bodies as to the applicability of the ECHR to arbitration have generally evolved from and in parallel to the various rights enshrined in Article 6(1) of the ECHR. Such principles are provided below and generally applied to every case that is brought before the Court and concerns consensual arbitration.

---

[152] Petrochilos (2004), pp. 112–113.

3.4.1 *Arbitral Tribunals and the ECHR*

The first principle is directly linked to the implied right of access to a court, its 'non-absolute' character and the requirement that a tribunal must be 'established by law' within the meaning of Article 6(1) of the ECHR. To date, it has been generally recognized that the setting up of arbitral tribunals is not per se contrary to the Convention and, especially, the right of access to a court as provided in Article 6(1) of the ECHR.[153]

By concluding an arbitration agreement parties exercise procedural autonomy to submit their dispute to an arbitral tribunal instead of a State court. This, in the view of the Convention's controlling bodies, is a consequence of their right to regulate their mutual relations as they deem appropriate.[154] In this context, however, a distinction must be made between the broader right of access to justice and the much narrower right of access to a court. While the former can in no way be validly waived, the latter may be waived in favour of another method of adjudication, e.g. consensual arbitration, without impairing the parties' right of access to justice in general.[155]

Similarly, when interpreting the Convention, the ECtHR takes 'account of evolving norms of national and international law'[156] and generally provides a broad and autonomous interpretation of the ECHR provisions. This also applies to the Court's interpretation of the term 'a tribunal established by law' within the meaning of Article 6(1) of the ECHR. The Court has concluded that when determining whether or not a judicial or non-judicial body can be considered as a tribunal established by law within the meaning of the Convention 'the authority which is invested with jurisdiction in the matter (ordinary court, administrative body, etc.) [is] of little consequence'.[157] Equally, a tribunal established by law 'is not necessarily to be understood as signifying a court of law of the classic kind, integrated within the standard judicial machinery'.[158] The jurisdictional authority invested in arbitral tribunals stems from both—an arbitration agreement and an underlying system of national law that provides for a possibility to arbitrate.[159] Having regard to the organizational,

---

[153] See, among others, *Transado-Transportes Fluviais Do Sado, S.A. v. Portugal*, App. No. 35943/02, ECtHR, 16 December 2003; *Zamet—Budowa Maszyn Spółka Akcyjna v. Poland*, App. No. 1485/11, ECtHR, 25 August 2015, para. 24.

[154] *Axelsson and Others v. Sweden*, App. No. 11960/86, ECmHR, 13 July 1990.

[155] Landrove (2006), p. 79.

[156] See *Demir and Baykara*, App. No. 34503/97, ECtHR, 12 November 2008, para. 68.

[157] *Ringeisen v. Austria*, App. No. 2614/65, ECtHR, 16 July 1971, para. 94.

[158] *Lithgow and Others v. the United Kingdom*, Apps. No. 9006/80; 9262/81; 9263/81; 9265/81; 9266/81; 9313/81; 9405/81, ECtHR, 8 July 1986, para. 201.

[159] On the relationship between arbitration and municipal law see, e.g. Mann (1967) in which the author asserts that '[n]o one has ever or anywhere been able to point to any provision or legal principle which would permit individuals to act outside the confines of a system of municipal law; even the idea of autonomy of the parties exists only by virtue of a given system of municipal law and in different systems may have different characteristics and effects. Similarly, every arbitration is necessarily subject to the law of a given State. No private person has the right or the power to act on any level other than that of municipal law. Every right or power a private person enjoys is

procedural and functional aspects[160] of arbitral tribunals as well as the case-law of the ECtHR,[161] arbitral tribunals can be considered as 'tribunals established by law' within the meaning of Article 6(1) of the ECHR.[162]

The fact that the establishing of arbitral tribunals is not per se contrary to the Convention and the right of access to a court is recognized also by the Convention's controlling bodies:

> In signing the arbitration agreement, the applicant waived his right to bring the dispute before an ordinary court. In addition, the right of access to a national court – a guarantee implicitly arising from [Article 6(1) ECHR] [...] – does not, in civil matters, entail an obligation to apply to a national court for settlement of a pecuniary dispute between private individuals.[163]

This conclusion, in turn, leads the discussion to the closely linked principle that, by concluding an arbitration agreement and thus submitting their dispute to arbitration, parties waive certain otherwise applicable Convention rights and freedoms. However, as already indicated when listing the different elements of Article 6(1) of the ECHR, the unanswered question is exactly which rights of Article 6(1) of the ECHR are waived by signing of an arbitration agreement. The more general question on the 'waiver' of the rights of Article 6(1) of the ECHR will therefore bring the discussion to the more specific question on 'permissibility' of such a waiver.

---

inexorably conferred by or derived from a system of municipal law which may conveniently and in accordance with tradition be called *lex fori*, though it would be more exact (but also less familiar) to speak of the *lex arbitri* or, in French, *la loi de l'arbitrage.*'

[160] Jaksic (2002), p. 187.

[161] *Bramelid and Malmsrtöm v. Sweden, Apps. No.8588/79, 8589/79,* ECmHR, 12 October 1982; *Ringeisen v. Austria*, App. No. 2614/65, ECtHR, 16 July 1971; *Lithgow and Others v. the United Kingdom*, Apps. No. 9006/80; 9262/81; 9263/81; 9265/81; 9266/81; 9313/81; 9405/81, ECtHR, 8 July 1986; *H v. Belgium*, App. No. 8950/80, ECtHR, 30 November 1989; *De Wilde, Ooms and Versyp v. Belgium*, Apps. No. 2832/66; 2835/66, 2899/66, ECtHR, 18 June 1971.

[162] Besson (2006), p. 397, Landrove (2006), pp. 79–82, Benedettelli (2015), p. 642, Jaksic (2002), p. 186, Petrochilos (2004), p. 153.

[163] *R v. Switzerland*, App. No. 10881/84, ECmHR, 4 March 1987. See also *Axelsson and Others v. Sweden*, App. No. 11960/86, ECmHR, 13 July 1990 where the Commission stresses that 'the right of access to the courts is not absolute. In the majority of the Contracting States, the right of access to courts is restricted or subject to special conditions in respect of [...] persons who are bound by an arbitration agreement. Such regulations are not in principle contrary to Article 6 (Art.6) of the Convention, where the aim pursued is legitimate and the means employed to achieve the aim is proportionate. [I]nsofar as arbitration is based on agreements between the parties to the dispute, it is a natural consequence of their right to regulate their mutual relations as they see fit. [A]rbitration procedures can also be said to pursue the legitimate aim of encouraging non-judicial settlements and of relieving the courts of an excessive burden of cases.' More recently see *Mutu and Pechstein v. Switzerland*, App. Nos. 40575/10 and 67474/10, 2 October 2018, para. 104.

3.4.2 *Arbitration Agreement as a* Waiver *of the Rights of Article 6(1) of the ECHR*

Article 6(1) of the ECHR obliges Member States to establish judicial institutions that satisfy the requirements of Article 6(1) of the ECHR and provide individuals with an effective access to such institutions whenever there has been an alleged interference with the exercise of one of their rights or freedoms.[164] Such an obligation, however, is not absolute and Member States may limit the right of access to a court, provided that certain fundamental prerequisites are fulfilled. Similarly, the ECtHR has repeatedly held that, in general, nowhere in the Convention it is said that parties could not waive the entitlement to the guarantees of a fair trial:

> Neither the letter nor the spirit of Article 6 of the Convention prevents a person from waiving of his own free will, either expressly or tacitly, the entitlement to the guarantees of a fair trial.[165]

There are, however, certain significant preconditions for a waiver to be valid and effective for Convention purposes. Article 6(1) of the ECHR contains the most fundamental procedural guarantees one may have in civil proceedings; therefore, it is only reasonable that there are strict conditions under which parties have the power to waive such rights. Moreover, one must keep in mind that there are certain *non-waivable* rights enshrined in Article 6(1) of the ECHR. These have already been indicated above and will be in more detail in relation to arbitration proceedings elaborated below.[166]

The fact that the so-called *waiver theory* also applies to consensual arbitration was established as early as in 1962 when the Commission was confronted with the very first case pertaining to the relationship between arbitration and the ECHR.

The case of *X v. the Federal Republic of Germany*[167] concerned an application by a German school teacher employed by a German school in Spain. Although the employment contract contained an arbitration clause, when the dispute arose the teacher applied to Spanish courts which declared the arbitration clause void and issued a judgment which, however, was not recognized in Germany (both Spanish and German laws prohibited arbitration clauses in employment contracts). The teacher applied to the Commission and argued that by not recognizing the Spanish judgment, the German courts had violated his right to an independent and impartial tribunal established by law as provided in Article 6(1) of the ECHR. When presented with the case, the Commission held that:

---

[164] See, e.g., *Sporrong and Lönnroth v. Sweden*, Apps. No. 7151/75; 7152/75, ECtHR, 23 September 1982, para. 80; *Bellet v. France*, App. No. 23805/94, ECtHR, 4 December 1995, paras. 36-38; *Skärby v. Sweden*, App. No. 12258/86, ECtHR, 28 June 1990.

[165] *Sejdovic v. Italy*, App. No. 56581/00, ECtHR, 1 March 2006, para. 86. See also *Salduz v. Turkey*, App. No. 36391/02, ECtHR [GC], 27 November 2008, para. 59; *Hermi v. Italy*, App. No. 18114/02, ECtHR [GC], 18 October 2006, para. 73; *Dvorski v. Croatia*, App. No. 25703/11, ECtHR, 20 October 2015, para. 100.

[166] See Sect. 3.4.3.3.

[167] *X. v. the Federal Republic of Germany*, App. No. 1197/61, ECmHR, 5 March 1962.

> [N]ational legislation quite frequently, particularly as regards labour law, restricts recourse to arbitration, but the Commission is not concerned with controlling the strict observation of such legislation except in so far as an infringement may involve any violation of the rights and freedoms protected by the Convention [...] [T]he inclusion of an arbitration clause in an agreement between individuals amounts legally to a partial renunciation of the exercise of those rights as defined by Article 6(1) [...] [N]othing in the text of that Article nor of any other Article of the Convention explicitly prohibits such renunciation [...] [T]he Commission is not entitled to assume that the Contracting States, in accepting the obligations arising under Article 6(1), intended to prevent persons coming under their jurisdiction from entrusting the settlement of certain matters to arbitrators.[168]

Since the Commission's admissibility decision in *X v. the Federal Republic of Germany*, the principles and general guidelines established therein have provided the foundation for further interpretation of the relationship between arbitration and the ECHR. However, at the same time, this foundation has proved to be somewhat troublesome, at least with regard to the passage where the Commission states that the conclusion of an arbitration agreement amounts legally to a *partial* renunciation of the exercise of those rights as defined by Article 6(1).'[169] To this day the Court has not established a clear border between the so-called *waivable* and *non-waivable* rights of Article 6(1) of the ECHR.

After the Commission's decision in *X v. the Federal Republic of Germany*, there was a considerable period of silence and no arbitration-related cases were brought before the Convention's controlling bodies. The debate on the relationship between arbitration and the ECHR resumed in early 1980s with the Court's judgment in *Deweer v. Belgium*—a case completely unrelated to arbitration and concerning criminal proceedings. The ECtHR in more detail, albeit still somewhat generally, elaborated on the nature of a valid waiver under Article 6(1) of the ECHR by giving an example:

> In the Contracting States' domestic legal systems a waiver of [a person's right to have his or her case heard by a court or tribunal] is frequently encountered [...] in civil matters, notably in the shape of arbitration clauses in contracts [...] The waiver, which has undeniable advantages for the individual concerned as well as for the administration of justice, does not in principle offend against the Convention [...].[170]

Generally, the so-called *waiver theory* is not disputed. As has become evident, many legal scholars affirm that by concluding an arbitration agreement, there is a waiver of at least some rights enshrined in Article 6(1) of the ECHR. However, there is a disagreement as to the specific rights of Article 6(1) of the ECHR that may be subjected to a waiver and this is exactly where the main problem of the dichotomy between arbitration and the ECHR begins to unfold.

The former Commission, and later also the Court, has not been entirely consistent in applying the *waiver theory* to arbitration-related cases. Almost every-arbitration related case before the former Commission or the Court has witnessed a different

---

[168] Ibid.

[169] Ibid.

[170] *Deweer v. Belgium*, App. No. 6903/75, ECtHR, 27 February 1980, para. 49. Similar conclusions are drawn also in other cases, e.g., *Pastore v. Italy*, App. No. 46483/99, ECtHR, 25 May 1999.

textual wording and interpretation of what the said institution at that time understood with a waiver of the rights of Article 6(1) of the ECHR by means of an arbitration agreement. As seen, in *X v. the Federal Republic of Germany*, the Commission stressed that the conclusion of an arbitration agreement amounts to a *partial* renunciation of Article 6(1) of the ECHR rights.[171] Later, in other Commission's admissibility decisions the Court's judgments, one can witness different wordings and interpretation of the extent of the waiver.

For example, in 1987 the Commission for the first time decided an application that concerned proper voluntary arbitration proceedings and their compliance with Article 6(1) of the ECHR.[172]

At first, by referring to the *Deweer v. Belgium* case, the Commission noted that 'in signing an arbitration agreement, the applicant waived his right to bring the dispute before an ordinary court.'[173] Few paragraphs below, by referring to the above-stated passage from the case of *X v. the Federal Republic of Germany* and omitting certain words thereof (i.e. 'partial'), the Commission concluded that 'an arbitration agreement entails a renunciation of the exercise of the rights secured by Article 6 para. 1 [...]'.[174] There is no indication as in the *X v. the Federal Republic of Germany* case that such a waiver only amounts to a partial renunciation of the rights of Article 6(1) of the ECHR. It is unknown whether the Commission had indeed intended to depart from its previous ruling in the *X v. the Federal Republic of Germany* case or such an interpretation and wording was a mere *faute d'inattention.*[175] Whatever the case may be, legal scholars have referred to this decision and, in particular, the above cited passage as meaning that 'the conclusion of an arbitration agreement had as a consequence the full and irrevocable waiver of all procedural guarantees enshrined in Article 6(1) of the ECHR.'[176]

Few years later, in two arbitration-related cases decided on the same date, i.e. the *Jakob Boss* and *Firma Heinz Schiebler* cases, the Commission, contrary to its previous conclusion in the *R. v. Switzerland* case, says nothing about a waiver of *all* the rights in Article 6(1) of the ECHR and simply states that by entering into a voluntary arbitration agreement the applicant 'renounced its right to have its civil rights determined in court proceedings [...]' Similar interpretation of the *waiver theory*, i.e. that by concluding an arbitration agreement parties waive solely their right to bring the case on merits before State courts, has been affirmed in later arbitration-related cases before the former Commission and the ECtHR.

For example, in *Lundgren v. Sweden* the Commission held that '[a]n individual may [...] waive his right to have his case dealt with by a tribunal [and] waivers of

---

171 *X. v. the Federal Republic of Germany*, App. No. 1197/61, ECmHR, 5 March 1962.

172 *R. v. Switzerland*, App. No. 10881/84, ECmHR, 4 March 1987.

173 Ibid.

174 Ibid.

175 Similar wording, however, appears also in other arbitration-related cases. See, e.g. *Molin v. Turkey*, App. No. 23173/94, ECmHR, 22 October 1996 ('La Commission rapelle qu'un compromise d'arbitrage comporte une renunciation à l'exercise des guaranties prévues par l'article 6 par. 1 [...]').

176 Jaksic (2007), p. 160, McDonald (2003), p. 533.

this kind are frequent, notably in the shape of arbitration clauses in contracts'.[177] Also in *Pastore v. Italy* the ECtHR held that '[i]n signing the arbitration clause, the applicant waived his right to bring the disputes [...] before an ordinary court.'[178] Similar conclusions have been drawn also in more recent cases, such as *Suda v. the Czech Republic*[179] and, in particular, *Tabbane v. Switzerland* where the Court held that the conclusion of arbitration agreement amounts to a waiver of only *certain* rights guaranteed by the ECHR.[180] Recently, the same interpretation has been confirmed by the Court in the *Pechstein* case.[181]

The Court's interpretation of the *waiver theory* in the *Tabbane v. Switzerland* case is in line with the Commission's interpretation of the *waiver theory* in the above-mentioned cases, especially that of *X v. the Federal Republic of Germany*. The decision in *R v. Switzerland*, on the other hand, where the former Commission omitted the use of the term *partial* when referring to the renunciation of the Convention's rights and freedoms by means of an arbitration agreement, stands out as the only ruling of this kind. As seen, all other rulings, especially the latest, i.e. the *Tabbane v. Switzerland* and *Pechstein* rulings, refer only to a *partial* waiver of the rights enshrined in Article 6(1) of the ECHR. This is also illustrated by the Court's case that most apparently stresses and evidences the partial nature of a waiver by means of arbitration agreement, i.e. the well-known *Suovaniemi and others v. Finland* case. This brings the analysis to the requirement of *permissibility* that a valid waiver must satisfy under Article 6(1) of the ECHR.

3.4.3 Permissibility *of a Waiver*

Closely linked with the issue of arbitration agreement as a waiver of the Convention's rights and freedoms is the question of a *permissibility* of such a waiver. It is said that not all rights under Article 6(1) of the ECHR are subject to a voluntary waiver by the parties. For a waiver to be valid within the scope of the Convention, such a waiver must be *permissible*.

Origins of the requirement that, in order to be valid under Article 6(1) of the ECHR, a waiver must be *permissible* can be traced back, at least impliedly, to the already mentioned case of *X v. the Federal Republic of Germany*, in which the Commission concluded that the signing of an arbitration agreement amounts legally

[177] *Lundgren v. Sweden*, App. No. 22506/93, ECmHR, 17 May 1995.

[178] *Pastore v. Italy*, App. No. 46483/99, ECtHR, 25 May 1999.

[179] *Suda v. the Czech Republic*, App. No. 1643/06, ECtHR, 28 October 2010, para. 48.

[180] *Tabbane v. Switzerland*, App. No. 41069/12, ECtHR, 1 March 2016 ('En effet, les parties à un litige sont libres de soustraire aux juridictions ordinaires certains différends pouvant naître de l'exécution d'un contrat. En souscrivant à une clause d'arbitrage, les parties renoncent volontairement à certains droits garantis par la Convention.').

[181] *Mutu and Pechstein v. Switzerland*, App. Nos. 40575/10 and 67474/10, 2 October 2018, para. 145 ('Les parties à un litige peuvent renoncer à certains droits garantis par l'article 6 § 1 pour autant que cette renonciation est libre, licite et sans équivoque.').

only to a *partial* waiver of the rights guaranteed by Article 6(1) of the ECHR. To date, however, the Convention's controlling bodies have not clearly clarified and defined the border between rights of Article 6(1) of the ECHR that are *waivable* and those rights which, on the other hand, are so fundamentally important that no one shall be entitled to waive them, even if done so voluntarily and freely.

One of few cases in which the Court expressly stressed the necessity that a waiver is *permissible* was the already-mentioned *Suovaniemi and others v. Finland* case in which the Court expressly stated that 'a waiver should not necessarily be considered to amount to a waiver of all the rights under Article 6 [...]' and a waiver of Convention's rights is valid 'only insofar as such waiver is 'permissible'.' As the Court stresses, 'waiver may be permissible with regard to certain rights but not with regard to certain others' and that a 'distinction may have to be made even between different rights guaranteed by Article 6.'[182]

But where lies the border between the different rights guaranteed by Article 6(1) of the ECHR? Which rights of Article 6(1) of the ECHR are more important than others and therefore it is not *permissible* to waive such rights? Unfortunately, the ECtHR has thus far not expressly elaborated further on the distinction between the different rights guaranteed by Article 6(1) of the ECHR from the viewpoint of their *waivability* by means of concluding an arbitration agreement. Although the former Commission's and the Court's case-law provides certain indications in this regard, a clear-cut and express distinction is still missing.

It is argued that by concluding an arbitration agreement parties have no intention to waive certain fundamental rights, such as the right to an independent and impartial tribunal or the right to a fair hearing.[183] When choosing to arbitrate parties are generally guided by other benefits that arbitration can offer over proceedings before State courts.[184] However, at the same time parties also believe that their most fundamental procedural rights will be duly respected.

The absence of a clear distinction between *waivable* and *non-waivable* Article 6(1) of the ECHR rights provides fertile ground for arguing that certain rights cannot be freely waived by means of an arbitration agreement. This book argues that such a conclusion stands true also in cases where the waiver of such rights indirectly stems from a broader a broader *waiver* (exclusion) of setting-aside proceedings, i.e. procedure wherein the observance of such *non-waivable* rights is guaranteed by State courts.

Before addressing the categorization of *waivable* and *non-waivable rights* within the scope of Article 6(1) of the ECHR, a short remark must be made as to the timing of a possible waiver and how such timing relates to the issue of permissibility.

---

[182] *Suovaniemi and others v. Finland*, App. No. 31737/96, ECtHR, 23 February 1999.

[183] See, e.g. Briner and Von Schlabrendorff (2001), pp. 94–96, Wedam-Lukic (1998), p. 17.

[184] It is established that arbitrating parties believe that arbitrating a dispute will be more neutral, flexible, efficient, confidential, speedier, cheaper and, most importantly, due to the New York Convention, it will be easier to eventually recognize and enforce the arbitral award in other countries. See Queen Mary University of London, White and Case (2018) 2018 International Arbitration Survey: The Evolution of International Arbitration, p. 7. http://www.arbitration.qmul.ac.uk/research/2018/. Accessed 29 May 2020.

3.4.3.1 Collateral Estoppel and the Timing of Waiver

In essence, the doctrine of collateral estoppel or issue preclusion generally recognizes that arbitrating parties are deemed to have waived their right to object a particular issue at a later stage in, e.g. the setting aside or recognition and enforcement proceedings, if they did not raise such an objection during arbitration proceedings.[185] Therefore, if a party is aware of certain procedural inconsistencies and fails to raise its objections during arbitration proceedings, it is considered that such a party is fully aware of the state of affairs and consciously renounces to exercise its right to object at a later moment.[186]

The doctrine of collateral estoppel is significant to the discussion of permissibility of a waiver because a distinction must be made between different rights of Article 6(1) of the ECHR and the timing of a waiver of such rights. Generally, it is said that parties may waive every right under Article 6(1) of the ECHR *after* a violation of such a right has occurred.[187] In such circumstances a party is fully aware of the committed violation, and by not objecting to it, it endorses and accepts such a violation and therefore is estopped from raising it at a later stage in either the setting aside or recognition and enforcement proceedings.[188] A good example in this regard is the German approach to permitting the exclusion of setting-aside proceedings. As will be explained in more detail below, in Germany only *ex ante* exclusion agreements are permissible.[189]

However, it is equally argued that it is not possible to waive in advance every right of Article 6(1) of the ECHR.[190] A mere signing of an arbitration agreement should not deprive parties of the most fundamental procedural rights, such as the right to an independent and impartial tribunal and the right to a fair hearing. The interrelation between the doctrine of collateral estoppel and permissibility of a waiver within the meaning of Article 6(1) of the ECHR is again best portrayed by the Court's arguing in the *Suovaniemi and others v. Finland* case.

As briefly introduced, the *Suovaniemi and others v. Finland* case concerned exactly a situation where one party to the arbitration proceedings was aware of a potential violation (alleged lack of independence and impartiality of an arbitrator),

---

[185] With regard to arbitration see, e.g. Landrove (2006), pp. 83–84, Petrochilos (2004), p. 112, Born (2014), pp. 3281–3284. Generally on the doctrine of collateral estoppel see, e.g. Article 4 of the UNCITRAL Model Law stating that '[a] party who knows that any provision of this Law from which the parties may derogate or any requirement under the arbitration agreement has not been complied with and yet proceeds with the arbitration without stating his objection to such non-compliance without undue delay or, if a time-limit is provided therefor, within such period of time, shall be deemed to have waived his right to object.' Similar provision can be found in many institutional arbitration rules. See, e.g. art. 40 of the ICC Arbitration Rules (2017); art. 32(1) of the LCIA Arbitration Rules (2014); art. 35 of the SCC Arbitration Rules (2017).

[186] Landrove (2006), pp. 84–89.

[187] Ibid. See also Benedettelli (2015), p. 646.

[188] Benedettelli (2015), p. 646.

[189] See Sect. 5.6.3.

[190] Landrove (2006), pp. 84–89, Benedettelli (2015), p. 646, Petrochilos (2004), pp. 122–123.

however, it nevertheless expressly confirmed such state of affairs and did not raise an objection during arbitration proceedings. Being faced with what can be described as a collateral estoppel the ECtHR held:

> [d]uring the proceedings before the arbitrators the applicants clearly abstained from pursuing their challenge against arbitrator M. In this respect the Court takes note of the decision of the Helsinki District Court of 26 July 1993 according to which, on the one hand, there were reasons to challenge the impartiality of M. under the Finnish Arbitration Act but, on the other hand, the applicant had lost their right to invoke his lack of impartiality as a ground for having the arbitral award quashed, since they had approved him as an arbitrator despite their being aware of the grounds for challenging him [...] [T]he impartiality of one of the arbitrators was open to doubt under domestic law but the applicants unequivocally accepted this state of affairs in the course of the arbitration proceedings.[191]

The Court eventually ruled that such a waiver 'should be regarded as effective for Convention purposes'[192] and that there is no violation of Article 6(1) of the ECHR. Very importantly, however, 'in deciding this question the Court limit[ed] itself to the particular circumstances of the present case',[193] i.e. a situation where one of the parties *expressly* confirmed violation of its rights and did not object to it. It is reasonable to argue that the Court would not arrive at the same conclusion in circumstances where, e.g. the lack of independence and impartiality of an arbitrator was not expressly confirmed by parties during arbitration proceedings. This interpretation is substantiated by the Court's repeated reference in the *Suovaniemi and others v. Finland* case that it only confines itself to the particular circumstances of the case. Moreover, the Court's rhetorical question as to 'whether the fundamental right to an impartial judge can be waived at all' strongly indicates the fundamental and generally *non-waivable* character of such a right, the collateral estoppel being a mere exception.

Although the Court has not clearly defined the *waivable* and *non-waivable* rights of Article 6(1) of the ECHR, its case-law gives certain indications. Such indications are further elaborated upon and affirmed by various legal writings. There seems to be a general consensus that Article 6(1) of the ECHR civil rights are generally divided in the following way.

3.4.3.2 *Waivable* Rights

By now it has become evident that it is *permissible* to waive certain rights of the Convention and, in particular, under Article 6(1) of the ECHR. The above overview and analysis of the different rights of Article 6(1) of the ECHR has already shed enough light to understand which rights of Article 6(1) of the ECHR are subject to a valid and *permissible* waiver and which, on the other hand, are the so-called *non-waivable* rights. As will be seen, a waiver of certain Article 6(1) of the ECHR rights

[191] *Suovaniemi and others v. Finland*, App. No. 31737/96, ECtHR, 23 February 1999.

[192] Ibid.

[193] Ibid.

will generally not conflict with the Convention, insofar it satisfies certain formal conditions.[194] Moreover, in order to be effective for Convention purposes, a waiver must be attended by 'minimum guarantees commensurate to its importance'[195] and 'it must not run counter to any important public interest.'[196]

As seen when analyzing both the right of access to a court[197] and the more specific issue of the compliance of arbitral tribunals with the ECHR as such,[198] by concluding an arbitration agreement parties waive the right to bring their case before State courts. In other words, due to the non-absolute character of the right of access to a court, it is *permissible* to waive such a right in favor of another method of adjudication, e.g. arbitration. A waiver of the right of access to a court of the *classic kind* will not be contrary to the Convention insofar it is made freely, licitly and unequivocally, and substantiated with certain minimum procedural safeguards and does not run counter to any important public interest.

Parties' procedural autonomy and their 'right to regulate their mutual relations as they see fit'[199] is not disputed. The former Commission and the Court has repeatedly held that parties are free to renounce their right to bring a dispute before an ordinary court and such a renunciation, provided that the afore mentioned conditions are satisfied, is not in principle contrary to the ECHR.[200] Similarly, there is no disagreement among legal scholars that by concluding an arbitration agreement parties waive their right of access to a court of the *classic kind*, an expression of party autonomy that is generally compatible with the aims of the Convention.[201]

In addition, the former Commission's and the Court's case-law evidences that by concluding an arbitration agreement parties are deemed to have waived also their right to a public hearing and the right to obtain a decision within a reasonable time.[202] Scholarly writings generally confirm such an interpretation of both the right

---

[194] More generally on the formal conditions of a valid waiver please see Sect. 3.5.

[195] See, e.g. *Pfeifer and Plankl v. Austria*, App. No. 10802/84, ECtHR, 25 February 1992, para. 37. More generally on the minimum safeguards that must accompany such a waiver please see Sect. 3.5.4.

[196] See, e.g. *Sejdovic v. Italy*, App. No. 56581/00, ECtHR, 1 March 2006, para. 86; *Håkansson and Sturesson v. Sweden*, App. No. 11855/85, ECtHR, 21 February 1990, para. 66.

[197] See Sect. 3.3.1.1.

[198] See Sect. 3.4.1.

[199] *Axelsson and others v. Sweden*, App. No. 11960/86, ECmHR, 13 July 1990.

[200] See, e.g. *X. v. the Federal Republic of Germany*, App. No. 1197/61, ECmHR, 5 March 1962; *Deweer v. Belgium*, App. No. 6903/75, ECtHR, 27 February 1980, para. 49; *R v. Switzerland*, App. No. 10881/84, ECmHR, 4 March 1987. See also *Axelsson and Others v. Sweden*, App. No. 11960/86, ECmHR, 13 July 1990; *Lundgren v. Sweden*, App. No. 22506/93, ECmHR, 17 May 1995; *Nordström-Janzon and Nordström-Lehtinen v. the Netherlands*, App. No. 28101/95, ECmHR, 27 November 1996; *Suovaniemi and others v. Finland*, App. No. 31737/96, ECtHR., 23 February 1999; *Pastore v. Italy*, App. No. 46483/99, ECtHR, 25 May 1999; *Tabbane v. Switzerland*, App. No. 41069/12, ECtHR, 1 March 2016 and others.

[201] See, e.g. Landrove (2006), pp. 79–82, Benedettelli (2015), p. 641, Briner and Von Schlabrendorff (2001), p. 91, Besson (2006), p. 400, Petrochilos (2004), p. 114, Wedam-Lukic (1998).

[202] See Sect. 3.3.1.4.

to a public hearing and the right to obtain a decision within a reasonable time.[203] Therefore, it is not disputed that the right to a public hearing and right to obtain a decision within a reasonable time are validly waived when concluding an arbitration agreement. Considering the existence of sufficient authority in this regard, proving the *waivable* character of these rights, the possibly adverse consequences of a waiver of the right to a public hearing and right to a decision within a reasonable time will not be considered further.

To sum up, it is generally established and agreed both by the Convention's controlling organs and academia that by concluding an arbitration agreement parties waive their right of (i) access to an ordinary state court; (ii) public hearing; and (iii) a decision within a reasonable time. The answer, however, is not as straightforward with the remaining civil rights of Article 6(1) of the ECHR.

3.4.3.3 *Non-waivable* Rights

To date, neither the former Commission, nor the ECtHR has provided an express clarification as to those Article 6(1) of the ECHR rights whose applicability and exercise does not depend solely on the will of the parties. Such Article 6(1) of the ECHR rights, however, can be indirectly deduced from the Convention's controlling bodies' case-law and legal doctrine.

As seen, the right of access to a court of the classic kind, the right to a public hearing and the right to a decision within a reasonable time can all be validly waived, provided that certain pre-conditions are satisfied. The same, however, cannot so assuredly be said about the remaining civil rights under Article 6(1) of the ECHR, i.e. the right to an independent and impartial tribunal and the right to a fair hearing. It is argued that 'the notions of an impartial and independent tribunal and party equality serve a wider purpose in the society than to protect the rights of the parties to any given dispute.'[204] Even more so, Petrochilos and also other authors[205] stress that it is arguable that 'those values should be protected regardless of the intentions of the parties to any given dispute, because they are part of (procedural) public policy.'[206]

The foundations for arguing that by concluding an arbitration agreement parties are not deemed to have waived all the rights of Article 6(1) of the ECHR can be found in the former Commission's and the ECtHR's case-law. The overwhelming majority of arbitration-related cases in which the former Commission or the Court has made a reference to a waiver of Article 6(1) of the ECHR rights by means of an arbitration agreement refers only to a *partial* waiver or waiver of *certain* Article

203 Ibid. See also Benedettelli (2015), p. 646. On the contrary, at least with regard to a right to obtain an award within a reasonable time, please see Besson (2006), p. 400.

204 Petrochilos (2004), p. 122.

205 See, e.g. Briner and Von Schlabrendorff (2001), pp. 92–93, Landrove (2006), pp. 86–90.

206 Petrochilos (2004), p. 122.

6(1) of the ECHR rights.[207] Among such cases the most convincing for arguing in favor of certain *non-waivable* Article 6(1) of the ECHR rights is the already introduced *Suovaniemi and others v. Finland* case[208] where the Court expressly stressed the difference between rights guaranteed by Article 6(1) of the ECHR in terms of permissibility of their waiver.[209] In the same *Suovaniemi and others v. Finland* case the Court also recognized that 'the right to a public hearing can be validly waived even in court proceedings [and] [t]he same applies, *a fortiori*, to arbitration proceedings, one of the very purposes of which is often to avoid publicity.'[210] However, the most important part, at least with regard to the *non-waivable* character of certain Article 6(1) of the ECHR rights, of the Court's reasoning comes right after where it, by referring to the *Pfeiffer and Plankl v. Austria* case questions 'whether the fundamental right to an impartial judge can be waived at all'.[211]

The outcome of the *Suovaniemi and others v. Finland* case has been already repeatedly stressed—the ECtHR, taking into account the particular circumstances of the case, concluded that the parties had validly waived their right to an independent and impartial tribunal. The emphasis, however, has to be put (as did the Court several times in its decision) on the particular circumstances of that particular case which concerned a collateral estoppel—a clear knowledge of and an express confirmation of the possible lack of impartiality of one of the arbitrators. However, one cannot deny that the distinction made by the Court between the *waivable* and *non-waivable* rights of Article 6(1) of the ECHR and reference to the non-waivable character of the right of an independent and impartial tribunal, suggests that generally this right cannot be subject to a waiver by parties.

As said, the Convention's controlling bodies have not expressly and unambiguously stressed that that the right to an independent and impartial tribunal or the right to a fair hearing is by no means subject to a waiver by parties. Such an interpretation, however, can be indirectly deduced from the Court's statements in not only arbitration-related cases, such as the *Suovaniemi and others v. Finland* case, but also other cases concerning the interpretation of an express or implied waiver of rights

---

[207] See, e.g. *X. v. the Federal Republic of Germany*, App. No. 1197/61, ECmHR, 5 March 1962 ('T]he inclusion of an arbitration clause in an agreement between individuals amounts legally to a *partial* [author's emphasis] renunciation of the exercise of those rights as defined by Article 6(1) [...]'); *Nordström-Janzon and Nordström-Lehtinen v. the Netherlands*, App. No. 28101/95, ECmHR, 27 November 1996 ('The arbitration was thus based on a voluntary agreement according to which disputes between the parties should not be settled by the ordinary courts but under a special arbitration system. Consequently, there was a renunciation by the parties of a procedure before the ordinary courts satisfying all the guarantees of Article 6 (Art. 6) of the Convention.'); *Tabbane v. Switzerland*, App. No. 41069/12, ECtHR, 1 March 2016, para. 27 ('En souscrivant à une clause d'arbitrage, les parties renoncent volontairement à certains droits garantis par la Convention.'). More recently see *Mutu and Pechstein v. Switzerland*, App. Nos. 40575/10 and 67474/10, 2 October 2018, para. 145.

[208] *Suovaniemi and others v. Finland*, App. No. 31737/96, ECtHR, 23 February 1999.

[209] Ibid.

[210] Ibid.

[211] Ibid.

enshrined in Article 6(1) of the ECHR. Thus, for example, the Court has repeatedly made a general statement that:

> [T]he nature of some of the rights safeguarded by the Convention is such as to exclude a waiver of the entitlement to exercise them [...] but the same cannot be said of certain other rights.[212]

The right to an independent and impartial tribunal is an essential component of the broader right to fair trial, which, according to the Court,[213] holds a prominent place in society. It is even argued that the right to an independent and impartial tribunal pertains to transnational procedural public policy, i.e. universal principles that should be respected by all civilized nations governed by the rule of law.[214] Therefore, considering the importance attached to the right of independent and impartial tribunal, it is unlikely that such a right can be validly waived also in advance, e.g. at the moment of conclusion of arbitration agreement. For example, in the *Pfeifer and Plankl v. Austria* case,[215] to which the Court refers in the *Suovaniemi and others v. Finland* case, the question whether the right to an independent and impartial tribunal within the meaning of Article 6(1) of the ECHR can be waived was unfortunately left somewhat open since in those circumstances the requirement of unequivocality was not satisfied. Nevertheless, the Court also noted that:

> [E]ven supposing that the rights in question can be waived by a defendant, the circumstances surrounding the applicant's decision deprived it of any validity from the point of view of the Convention.[216]

The Court's hypothetical statement *even supposing* that the right to an independent and impartial tribunal can be waived indicates exactly to the opposite. Moreover, even if one abstains from questioning whether the right to an independent and impartial tribunal can be waived or not, the ECtHR has made it clear that it will examine the issue of independence and impartiality irrespective of any alleged waiver:

> Regardless of whether a waiver was made or not, the Court has still to decide, from the standpoint of the Convention, whether the participation of Judge Schaumburger in the trial after taking part in the questioning of witnesses at the pre-trial stage could cast doubt on the impartiality of the trial court.[217]

---

[212] *Albert and Le Compte v. Belgium*, Apps. No. 7299/75 and 7496/76, ECtHR, 10 February 1983, para. 35. See also, e.g. *H. v. Belgium*, App. No. 8950/80, ECtHR, 30 November 1987, para. 54; *Galstyan v. Armenia*, App. No. 26986/03, ECtHR, 15 November 2007, para. 91.

[213] See, e.g. *De Cubber v. Belgium*, App. No. 9186/80, ECtHR, 26 October 1984, para. 30; *Lauko v. Slovakia*, App. No. 26138/95, ECtHR, 2 September 1998, para. 63; *Miroshnik v. Ukraine*, App. No. 75804/01, ECtHR, 21 November 2008, para. 61.

[214] See Sect. 7.2.2.1.

[215] *Pfeifer and Plankl v. Austria*, App. No. 10802/84, ECtHR, 25 February 1992.

[216] Ibid., para. 39.

[217] *Bulut v. Austria*, App. No. 17358/90, ECtHR, 22 February 1996, para. 30; *McGonnell v. the United Kingdom*, App. No. 28488/95, ECtHR, 8 February 2002; *Öcalan v. Turkey*, App. No. 46221/99, ECtHR, 15 May 2005. See also Power A (2012) Judicial Independence and the Democratic Process: Some Case Law of the European Court of Human Rights. International Bar Association Conference where the author, a former ECtHR judge, referring to the previously cited cases states that '[i]n view

The same *ex officio* Court's examination of independence and impartiality is also true with regard to arbitration-related cases. Although in the case of *Transado-Transportes Fluviais Do Sado, S.A. v. Portugal*[218] the applicant challenged the impartiality of an arbitral tribunal without providing any further information as to this complaint, the Court took up this issue and applied both the subjective and objective impartiality test to arbitrators[219]:

> [The Court] sees nothing capable of casting doubt on the subjective impartiality of the members of the arbitration tribunal nor the latter's objective impartiality. As to objective impartiality in particular, the procedure for setting up the arbitration tribunal, provided for in clause XXXIII, excludes any doubt in this area [...]'.[220]

All of the above speaks in favor of a conclusion that the right to an independent and impartial tribunal cannot be waived in advance, i.e. at the moment of conclusion of an arbitration agreement. Parties must have knowledge of the committed breach in order to decide for themselves whether such a breach will influence the decision of the allegedly partial arbitrator. Moreover, as will be seen,[221] even if a waiver is *permissible ex post*, it must satisfy certain formal conditions as well as must be accompanied by certain minimum safeguards commensurate to such waiver's gravity and importance. Many legal scholars affirm such an interpretation—the right to an independent and impartial tribunal is generally *non-waivable* and can be waived solely after arbitrating parties became aware of the alleged violation.[222] A question, however, arises

---

of their importance for public confidence in the judicial system, it is unlikely that the requirements of independence and impartiality can be waived. The Court considers itself bound to examine the impartiality of the tribunal irrespective of any alleged waiver by the applicant.'

218 *Transado-Transportes Fluviais Do Sado, S.A. v. Portugal*, App. No. 35943/02, ECtHR, 16 December 2003.

219 Jaksic (2007), p. 165.

220 *Transado-Transportes Fluviais Do Sado, S.A. v. Portugal*, App. No. 35943/02, ECtHR, 16 December 2003.

221 See Sect. 3.5.

222 See, e.g. Landrove (2006), pp. 89–90 stating that 'a party cannot waive, in advance, its right to challenge an arbitral tribunal (which represent its right to an independent and impartial tribunal) because such right pertains to public policy. But a waiver of the exercise of such right is admissible during the proceedings [...] Consequently, all due process rights are not equally waivable. In other words, there are levels among due process rights so that some of them are more fundamental than others and pertain to public policy. Those more fundamental rights are not waived by the mere signing of an arbitration agreement because at the time of the signing parties are not aware of all the consequences of a waiver. Subsequent conduct during the proceedings (once the facts are known) may affect those fundamental rights that could not have been waived beforehand (right to a fair hearing, and the right to an independent and impartial tribunal.' See also Benedettelli (2015), p. 646 stating that 'For the European Court other rights cannot be waived in advance, ie at the time of execution of an arbitration agreement (or of the terms of reference), but only after their beneficiary has become aware that a breach of them has been committed to his/her damage and is therefore best positioned to appreciate the impact of his/her decision [...] This applies to the right to a 'fair hearing, to the right 'to be heard' and to the right of 'equality of arms', as well as to the consequent rights to be judged by an independent and impartial tribunal [...] [T]he idea that parties to an arbitration agreement should be presumed having waived all the due process guarantees set out by Article 6.1. ECHR must be rejected as being at odds with the importance that the principle of fair

if the *non-waivable* character of the right to an independent and impartial tribunal may equally apply the dichotomy between the ECHR and setting-aside proceedings, in particular. If the right to an independent and impartial tribunal cannot be validly waived *prior* parties became aware of the potentially adverse consequences such a waiver may entail, does that not suggest that *ex ante* exclusion of setting-aside proceedings, excluding also the right to challenge an arbitral award on grounds of violations of arbitral tribunal's lack of independence or impartiality, are not compatible with the ECHR? During the annulment proceedings parties may object and raise, inter alia, questions relating to the composition of an arbitral tribunal,[223] however, in case there are no setting-aside proceedings either due to a total non-existence of such proceedings in the applicable *lex arbitri* or due to an exclusion agreement, possible violations of the independence and impartiality of an arbitral tribunal would remain unaddressed.

The same holds true for violations of the different constituent elements of the right to a fair hearing. The principles of equality of arms and adversarial proceedings are fundamental components of the right to a fair hearing within the meaning of Article 6(1) of the ECHR.[224] Moreover, as the Court stresses '[t]he right to a fair hearing before a tribunal [...] must be interpreted in the light of the Preamble to the Convention, which declares, among other things, the rule of law to be part of the common heritage of the Contracting States.'[225] Arguably the fundamentally significant right to a fair hearing and its constituent elements are even part of a broader procedural public policy.[226] As with the waiver of the right to an independent and impartial tribunal that is similarly considered as being part of procedural public policy it is equally argued for a waiver of the right to a fair hearing that:

> any waiver by the parties of compliance with the fundamental requirements of equal treatment of the parties, fair notice of the proceedings and a fair opportunity to present one's case, would have to be regarded as incompatible with human dignity, reducing the parties to mere pawns in the procedure. A waiver of the right to a fair trial under Article 6 ECHR, whether expressly agreed or implied, is therefore inadmissible and can have no binding effect.[227]

---

trial is granted by most contemporary laws of arbitration.' See also Briner and Von Schlabrendorff (2001), pp. 94–95, Jaksic (2007), pp. 165–166, Petrochilos (2004), pp. 122–123, Matscher (1999), pp. 282–283, Mourre (2000), p. 18.

[223] See Sect. 4.4.1.

[224] *Avotiņš v. Latvia*, App. No. 17502/07, ECtHR [GC], 23 May 2016, para. 119.

[225] *Brumărescu v. Romania*, App. No. 28342/95, ECtHR [GC], 28 October 1999, para. 61. See also *Ryabykh v. Russia*, App. No. 52854/99, ECtHR, 24 July 2003, para. 51; *Giuran v. Romania*, App. No. 24360/04, ECtHR, 21 June 2011, para. 28; *Driza v. Albania*, App. No. 33771/02, ECtHR, 13 November 2007, para. 63.

[226] See, e.g. Briner and Von Schlabrendorff (2001), pp. 93–99, Petrochilos (2004), pp. 122–123 (however, see also Petrochilos' brief analysis that, in his opinion, 'the fact that independence and impartiality, as well as party equality, are doubtless part of procedural public policy does not make them absolute standards.'). See also, e.g. Kreindler (2015), pp. 9–23, Mistelis (2010), pp. 960–961.

[227] Briner and Von Schlabrendorff (2001), p. 97, Landrove (2006), pp. 89–90 stating that 'a party cannot waive, in advance, its right to challenge an arbitral tribunal (which represent its right to an independent and impartial tribunal) because such right pertains to public policy. But a waiver of the

There is evidently greater importance attached to the two Article 6(1) of the ECHR rights, i.e. the right to an independent and impartial tribunal and the right to a fair hearing, than to other Article 6(1) of the ECHR rights that, as established earlier, can be validly waived by parties both in advance and also during arbitration proceedings. This is evidenced not only by the Court's own made distinction in the *Suovaniemi and others v. Finland* case 'even between different rights guaranteed by Article 6',[228] but also by its rhetorical questions about the validity of waivers of such rights, as well as repeated references in other judgments that the right to an independent and impartial tribunal and the right to a fair hearing must be interpreted in line with the principle of the rule of law. Although to date the ECtHR has not expressly indicated that these are the exact rights of Article 6(1) of the ECHR with regard to which a waiver is not *permissible*, taking into account the Court's case-law, impliedly suggesting this, as well as the vast number of scholarly writings confirming this, it follows that it is not possible to waive such rights *ex ante*, i.e. at the moment of concluding an arbitration agreement.

If an advance waiver is possible only of certain Article 6(1) of the ECHR rights (i.e. the right to a court, public hearing and decision within a reasonable time), there has to be a mechanism in the applicable *lex arbitri* through which the respective State in whose territory arbitration proceedings take place makes sure that the *non-waivable* Article 6(1) of the ECHR rights are properly observed during arbitration proceedings. This book argues that arbitrating parties should not be given an opportunity to exclude such a mechanism by means of an exclusion agreement to the extent that it is not possible to challenge an arbitral award on the basis of violations of the *non-waivable* rights under Article 6(1) of the ECHR. Analysis of the ECHR Member States' obligation to provide in their *leges arbitri* a non-waivable (at least to the extent of *non-waivable* rights of Article 6(1) of the ECHR) possibility for arbitrating parties to apply for setting-aside proceedings will be carried out in Chap. 7.

3.5 Formal Conditions of a Valid Waiver

For a waiver of certain Article 6(1) of the ECHR rights to be valid, it is not only required that such a waiver is in fact *permissible*—in order for a waiver to be effective for Convention purposes it must also satisfy certain formal conditions. To date, the formal requirements of a valid waiver have been broadly recognized in the Convention's controlling bodies' case-law and legal doctrine. Further insight into such requirements will be given solely from the perspective of the dichotomy between the ECHR and arbitration.

Due to the significant and potentially adverse consequences that a waiver of Article 6(1) of the ECHR rights may entail, parties choosing to waive certain rights under

---

exercise of such right is admissible during the proceedings. The same reasoning holds true for the right to a fair hearing.' See also Jaksic (2007), pp. 165–166.

[228] *Suovaniemi and others v. Finland*, App. No. 31737/96, ECtHR, 23 February 1999.

Article 6(1) of the ECHR should be doing it voluntarily. The conclusion of an arbitration agreement will result in a valid waiver of certain Article 6(1) of the ECHR insofar such an agreement (and the resulting waiver) is made freely and unequivocally. The exact wording and interpretation of these two intrinsically linked formal requirements have differed among the various arbitration-related cases brought before the former Commission and the ECtHR, however, the essence of such requirements has remained intact. In addition to the requirements of absence of constraint and equivocality, certain arbitration-related cases have witnessed also the mentioning and application of other formal conditions—the necessity that a waiver is accompanied by minimum safeguards commensurate to its importance and the requirement that it does not go against any public interest.

3.5.1 The Condition of **Absence of Constraint**

As regards the requirement of absence of constraint, the case of *X v. the Federal Republic of Germany* is the pioneer case in establishing that for a waiver to be valid, parties should have subjected themselves to such a waiver freely or, in the former Commission's words—without signing the underlying arbitration agreement under constraint:

> [T]he disputed arbitration clause might have been regarded as contrary to the Convention if X. had signed it under constraint, which was not the case.[229]

The requirement of *absence of constraint* has been at the heart of every arbitration-related case brought before the former Commission or the ECtHR and as such can be seen as stemming from the general voluntary character of arbitration. If persons through the exercise of their party autonomy decide to waive certain guarantees offered by the Convention's regime, they must do so freely and consciously—otherwise such a waiver will not be valid for the Convention purposes. Over the years, the requirement of *absence of constraint* has witnessed different interpretive wording in the Convention's controlling bodies' rulings, however, despite this, it is said that *absence of constraint* has been *at all events* one of the conditions to be satisfied if parties endeavour to validly waive the application of certain Article 6(1) of the ECHR guarantees.[230]

For example, in *R. v. Switzerland* the applicant claimed, inter alia, 'that arbitration was imposed on him by the opposing party by means of threats'.[231] After recalling what was already established in the cases of *X v. the Federal Republic of Germany* and *Deweer v. Belgium*, the Commission noted that:

> It follows that an arbitration agreement entails a renunciation of the exercise of the rights secured by Article 6 para. 1, provided that the agreement was not signed under duress. The

[229] *X. v. the Federal Republic of Germany*, App. No. 1197/61, ECmHR, 5 March 1962.

[230] *Deweer v. Belgium*, App. No. 6903/75, ECtHR, 27 February 1980, para. 49.

[231] *R. v. Switzerland*, App. No. 10881/84, ECmHR, 4 March 1987.

> applicant claims that arbitration was imposed on him by the opposing party by means of threats. This claim cannot be examined by the Commission because the domestic remedies were not exhausted on this point. The applicant did not make use of any remedies intended to establish that his consent was vitiated by duress.[232]

In the case of *Lundgren v. Sweden*, in addition to the previously used terms of *under constraint* and *under duress*, the Commission added another explanation to the said formal requirement:

> An individual may, for instance, waive his right to have his case dealt with by a tribunal. Waivers of this kind are frequent, notably in the shape of arbitration clauses in contracts. Waivers do not in principle offend against the Convention, provided that they are made without constraint [...] It has not been alleged by the applicant nor does the case-file show that the arbitration clause was imposed on him [...] by improper means.[233]

In the case of *Pastore v. Italy*, the ECtHR stressed that 'the right to court may be renounced in civil matters in favor of arbitration, provided this is done freely.'[234] Also more recent cases, such as the *Tabbane v. Switzerland* and the *Pechstein* cases, confirm that the requirement of *absence of constraint* is *at all events* one of the preconditions to be satisfied for a valid waiver.[235]

Despite the inconsistent wording, the former Commission's and the Court's *ratio* behind the requirement of *absence of constraint* is clear. If parties decide to waive certain Convention's guarantees, they must do so voluntarily and freely, i.e. without constraint and under no duress. The different cases in which such a requirement has been expressed indicate that the threshold will be rather high—arbitrating party's consent must be affected by real duress.[236] If that is so, all the Convention's guarantees, especially those under Article 6(1) of the ECHR, will remain intact and the

[232]Ibid. The term 'under duress' has been used also in other cases before the former Commission or the ECtHR. See, e.g. *Nordström-Janzon and Nordström-Lehtinen v. the Netherlands*, App. No. 28101/95, ECmHR, 27 November 1996 where the Commission states that 'the absence of constraint is one of the conditions to be satisfied (ibid.). The Commission notes that in the present case it has not been alleged that the arbitration agreement was concluded under duress.' See also *Molin v. Turkey*, App. No. 23173/94, ECmHR, 22 October 1996 where 'La Commission rappelle qu'un compromis d'arbitrage comporte une renonciation à l'exercice des garanties prévues par l'article 6 par. 1 (art. 6-1), sauf si le compromis a été signé sous la contrainte.'

[233]*Lundgren v. Sweden*, App. No. 22506/93, ECmHR, 17 May 1995.

[234]*Pastore v. Italy*, App. No. 46483/99, ECtHR, 25 May 1999.

[235]*Tabbane v. Switzerland*, App. No. 41069/12, ECtHR, 1 March 2016, para. 27 ('En souscrivant à une clause d'arbitrage, les parties renoncent volontairement à certains droits garantis par la Convention. Telle renonciation ne se heurte pas à la Convention pour autant qu'elle soit libre, licite et sans equivoque [...] En concluant ce compromis d'arbitrage, le requérant a expressément et librement renoncé à la possibilité de soumettre les litiges pouvant potentiellement surgir à l'avenir à un tribunal ordinaire qui lui aurait offert l'ensemble des garanties de l'article 6 de la Convention. Il n'existe aucune indication que le requérant ait agi sous la contrainte en signant la convention d'arbitrage. Par ailleurs, le requérant ne le prétend pas.'). See also *Mutu and Pechstein v. Switzerland*, App. Nos. 40575/10 and 67474/10, 2 October 2018, para. 96.

[236]Petrochilos (2004), p. 114.

arbitration agreement will not be given effect for the Convention purposes, thus allowing arbitrating parties to access courts of ordinary jurisdiction.[237]

3.5.2 *The Condition of* Unequivocality

In addition to the requirement of *absence of constraint*, it has been generally established that a waiver of the Convention's rights must be *unequivocal*. This applies also to a waiver of such rights by means of an arbitration agreement. A waiver will be *unequivocal* if it is clear and unambiguous, leaving no doubt as to its existence. The requirement of an *unequivocal* waiver has been confirmed in many cases before the former Commission and the Court.[238]

For example, in the case of *Axelsson and others v. Sweden* the applicants complained, inter alia, that they had been denied a public hearing before the Swedish Court of Appeal and the Supreme Court. After recalling that 'neither the letter nor spirit of the provision [Article 6(1) of the ECHR] prevents a person from waiving of his own free will, either tacitly or expressly, the entitlement to a public hearing' the Commission held that:

> A waiver must, however, be made in an unequivocal manner and not run counter to any public interest [...] By not requesting a hearing in the present case, the Commission finds that the applicants must be considered to have unequivocally waived their right under Article 6 (Art. 6) of the Convention to a public hearing before the Court of Appeal.[239]

The requirement of *unequivocality* was equally stressed in the case of *Suovaniemi and others v. Finland*:

> According to the Convention organs' established case-law, the waiver of a right guaranteed by the Convention – insofar as it is permissible – must be established in an unequivocal manner [...] [T]he Court considers that the waiver made during the arbitration proceedings was unequivocal [...] Not only was the submission to arbitration voluntary but, in addition, during the proceedings before the arbitrators the applicants clearly abstained from pursuing their challenge against arbitrator M.

In both cases the requirement of an *unequivocal* waiver was satisfied by a party expressly or impliedly agreeing to certain state of affairs that would later be challenged by the same party. Such an express or implied acceptance of certain circumstances is regarded as sufficient for the purposes of satisfying the requirement of *unequivocality*.

---

[237] Ibid., pp. 114–115.

[238] See, e.g. *Colozza v. Italy*, App. No. 9024/80, ECtHR, 12 February 1985, para. 28; *Barberà, Messegué and Jabardo v. Spain*, App. No. 10590, ECtHR, 6 December 1988, para. 82; *Oberschlick v. Austria*, App. No. 11662/85, ECtHR, 23 May 1991, para. 51; *Pfeiffer and Plankl v. Austria*, App. No. 10802/84, ECtHR, 25 February 1992, para. 37.

[239] *Axelsson and others v. Sweden*, App. No. 11960/86, ECmHR, 13 July 1990. See also *Eiffage SA and others v. Switzerland*, App. No. 1742/05, ECtHR, 15 September 2009.

In another case to be in more detailed analyzed below, i.e. the case of *Tabbane v. Switzerland*,[240] the requirement of *unequivocality* was satisfied by arbitrating parties including in their contract the following arbitration clause:

> Neither [party] shall be entitled to commence or maintain any action in a court of law upon any matter in dispute arising from or concerning this Agreement or a breach thereof except for the enforcement of any award rendered pursuant to arbitration under this Agreement. The decision of the arbitration shall be final and binding and neither party shall have any right to appeal such decision to any court of law.[241]

The implied reference to the finality of the decision of the arbitration and the fact that 'neither party shall have any right to appeal such decision to any court of law' satisfied, in the eyes of the Court, the requirement of *unequivocality*, to the extent necessary for determining whether or not parties validly excluded their right to setting-aside proceedings under Article 192(1) of the PILA.[242] Whether or not such an implied reference was indeed *unequivocal* for the purposes of a valid waiver under Article 6(1) of the ECHR (and not merely for the purposes of a valid waiver under Swiss law) will be scrutinized in Chap. 7.[243]

It can be deduced from the above examples of what constitutes an *unequivocal* waiver that as long as the circumstances of a case clearly and objectively justify parties' outward appearance and the resulting consequences thereof with regard to waiving certain Convention rights, such a waiver will be considered *unequivocal*. Although in most cases a waiver by means of an arbitration agreement will be concluded in writing, thus satisfying the requirement of *unequivocality*, a waiver generally need not be expressly indicated.[244] As seen, it can be also inferred from a particular conduct by the parties that impliedly indicates their acceptance of certain state of affairs.

When referring to the requirement of *unequivocality*, the case of *Suovaniemi and others v. Finland* also makes a reference to the other precondition for a valid waiver, i.e. absence of constraint that is inalienably linked with the requirement of

---

[240] In more detail see Sect. 5.2.4.

[241] *Tabbane v. Switzerland*, App. No. 41069/12, ECtHR, 1 March 2016, para. 5.

[242] Ibid., para. 30 where the Court states that: '[l]a renonciation au droit à un tribunal (ordinaire) en faveur d'un arbitrage doit être intervenue sans équivoque. En l'espèce, le Tribunal fédéral est arrivé à la conclusion, par voie d'interprétation des volontés des parties, que celles-ci, par l'inclusion d'une clause de renonciation dans l'article 8 b du compromis (paragraphe 4 ci–dessus) ont exclu tout recours contre la sentence arbitrale. A la lumière du texte de la clause («*neither party shall have any right to appeal such decision to any court of law*») et dans la mesure où elle est compétente pour trancher cette question, la Cour estime qu'une telle conclusion ne paraît ni arbitraire ni déraisonnable.'

[243] See Sect. 7.2.1.

[244] Harris et al. (2014), p. 411. See also cases, such as *Le Compte, Van Leuven and De Meyere v. Belgium*, Apps. No. 6878/75 and 7238/75, ECtHR, 23 June 1981, para. 59; *Pishchalnikov v. Russia*, App. No. 7025/04, ECtHR, 24 September 2009, para. 77.

unequivocality.[245] Their close interaction is best illustrated by the relatively recent ECtHR's arbitration-related judgment in the case of *Suda v. Czech Republic*.[246]

Suda v. Czech Republic concerned a claim by a third-party to arbitration proceedings alleging a violation of the right to a fair trial as provided by Article 6(1) of the ECHR. The applicant, a minority shareholder in a company, could not exercise his rights before the courts of ordinary jurisdiction due to an arbitration agreement concluded between the said company and another company which was the main shareholder of the former. In essence, the applicant argued that a waiver by means of an arbitration agreement was not voluntary—it was merely a third party affected by an arbitration agreement and arbitration proceedings between others.[247]

This was clearly not a case of compulsory or statutory arbitration, however, at the same time, the applicant was *forced* to submit its claims to an arbitral tribunal in arbitration proceedings to which it had not consented.[248] These particular circumstances, in the eyes of the ECtHR, meant that the requirements of *absence of constraint* and *unequivocality* were not satisfied and the applicant had not validly waived its right to a fair trial within the meaning of Article 6(1) ECHR.[249]

3.5.3 *The Condition of* Lawfulness

In addition to the formal requirements of *absence of constraint* and *unequivocality* when waiving certain rights of the Convention, the Convention's controlling bodies have occasionally stipulated that a waiver by means of an arbitration agreement must be also *lawful*.[250] Although the Court has not elaborated upon this particular requirement in detail, it seems that the requirement of *lawfulness* relates to the question of whether a particular dispute can be at all subjected to arbitration pursuant to the respective national law, namely that of arbitrability.

As seen, the Convention per se does not preclude persons from waiving certain Convention rights, therefore, for Convention purposes, generally such a waiver is considered *lawful*. However, it could be that a particular dispute, for example, regarding tax law, administrative law or criminal law, is not arbitrable according to the respective national law. If that is the case, a waiver of Convention rights, e.g.

[245] *Suovaniemi and others v. Finland*, App. No. 31737/96, ECtHR., 23 February 1999.

[246] *Suda v. Czech Republic*, App. No. 1643/06, ECtHR, 28 October 2010, para. 49.

[247] Ibid., paras. 38–39.

[248] Ibid., paras. 49–51.

[249] Ibid., paras. 52–55.

[250] See, e.g. *Suda v. Czech Republic*, App. No. 1643/06, ECtHR, 28 October 2010, para. 48 where the Court states that: '[r]ien n'empêche les justiciables de renoncer à leur droit à un tribunal en faveur d'un arbitrage, à condition qu'une telle renonciation soit libre, licite et sans equivoque [...]' See also *Tabbane v. Switzerland*, App. No. 41069/12, ECtHR, 1 March 2016, para. 30 where the Court stresses that '[e]n souscrivant à une clause d'arbitrage, les parties renoncent volontairement à certains droits garantis par la Convention. Telle renonciation ne se heurte pas à la Convention pour autant qu'elle soit libre, licite et sans equivoque [...]'.

the right of access to a court, by means of such an *unlawful* arbitration agreement would not be considered *lawful* within the meaning of the Convention's controlling bodies' case-law.

3.5.4 The Condition of Minimum Safeguards

A valid waiver of a right guaranteed by the ECHR must not only be *permissible* and manifested *unequivocally* without the presence of *duress* or *constraint*, but it also must be accompanied by certain *minimum safeguards*. Due to the potentially adverse consequences that such a waiver may entail, the Court has established that, at least in the case of procedural rights, such as Article 6(1) of the ECHR:

> a waiver, in order to be effective for Convention purposes, requires minimum guarantees commensurate to its importance.[251]

What exactly is meant by a valid waiver requiring 'minimum guarantees commensurate to its importance' is well illustrated by the Court's case-law.[252] This is best illustrated by two arbitration-related cases.

The first example is the case of *Suovaniemi and others v. Finland*. As seen, in this case a party to arbitration proceedings, although being aware of potential bias and partiality of one of the arbitrators to the arbitral proceedings, abstained from challenging such an arbitrator during arbitration proceedings and was later precluded to invoke this as a ground for setting aside the arbitral award before the Finnish courts. The underlying question was whether such a conduct constituted a valid waiver of a right to an independent and impartial tribunal for the purposes of Article 6(1) of the ECHR. After restating, inter alia, the established case-law that 'in the case of procedural rights a waiver, in order to be effective for Convention purposes, requires minimum guarantees commensurate to its importance', the Court stressed that:

> [C]onsidering that throughout the arbitration the applicants were represented by counsel, the waiver was accompanied by sufficient safeguards commensurate to its importance [...] [Furthermore] in the proceedings before the national courts the applicants had ample opportunity to advance their arguments, inter alia, concerning the circumstances in which the waiver took place during arbitration proceedings.[253]

Taking into account the particular circumstances of the case of *Suovaniemi and others v. Finland*, the Court considered that the existence of a counsel assisting the

---

[251] *Pfeiffer and Plankl v. Austria*, App. No. 10802/84, ECtHR, 25 February 1992, para. 37; *Richard v. France*, App. No. 33441/96, ECtHR, 22 April 1998, para. 49; *Frommelt v. Liechtenstein*, App. No. 49158/99, ECtHR, 24 June 2004, para. 33; *Litwin v. Germany*, App. No. 29090/06, ECtHR, 3 November 2011, para. 37.

[252] Ibid. See also, e.g. *Poitrimol v. France*, App. No. 14032/88, ECtHR, 23 November 1993; *Sigbatullin v. Russia*, App. No. 32165/02, ECtHR, 23 April 2009; *Sejdovic v. Italy*, App. No. 56581/00, ECtHR, 1 March 2006. More in particular with regard to arbitration see the recent Court's ruling in *Mutu and Pechstein v. Switzerland*, App. Nos. 40575/10 and 67474/10, 2 October 2018, para. 96.

[253] *Suovaniemi and others v. Finland*, App. No. 31737/96, ECtHR, 23 February 1999.

aggrieved party during arbitration proceedings and the party's entitlement to advance arguments relating to the issue before the Finnish courts were sufficient safeguards commensurate to the importance of an (implied) waiver of the right to an independent and impartial tribunal.

Examination of whether a waiver is accompanied by such *minimum safeguards* entails an all-encompassing analysis of all the circumstances of the case. A pre-condition that is somewhat related to the requirement of *minimum safeguards* is that a person who has waived the application of certain procedural Convention's rights 'could reasonably have foreseen what the consequences of his conduct would be.'[254] Apparently, in the eyes of the Court, the circumstances of the case of *Suovaniemi and others v. Finland* indicated that the applicant, being aware of the potential bias and partiality of one of the arbitrators, could indeed have reasonably foreseen that it would later be precluded from invoking such an issue if it failed to do it already during arbitration proceedings.

Another case illustrating that a waiver was accompanied by sufficient safeguards enabling parties to reasonably foresee its consequences is the case of *Tabbane v. Switzlerland*, which in more detail is addressed below.[255] In this case the applicant complained that Article 192(1) of the PILA, expressly permitting arbitrating parties in Switzerland to exclude the right to setting-aside proceedings, was contrary to Article 6(1) of the ECHR and the right to a fair trial. When analysing the case in detail, it will become apparent that such a waiver of the right of access to a court, as argued by the Court, was accompanied by *minimum safeguards*, i.e. parties were given a choice of arbitrators that chose Switzerland as the seat of arbitration; the Swiss Federal Tribunal duly heard the aggrieved party and its arguments; and the Swiss Federal Tribunal's judgment was sufficiently motivated.[256]

3.5.5 *The Condition of* Public Interest

Additionally, it has been also established that a waiver in order to be valid for Convention purposes 'must not run counter to any important public interest.'[257] However, this requirement is not entirely clear—what will constitute an *important public interest* in each given case will generally depend on all the circumstances of that particular case.

---

[254] See, e.g. *Sejdovic v. Italy*, App. No. 56581/00, ECtHR, 1 March 2006, para. 87; *Panovits v. Cyprus*, App. No. 4268/04, ECtHR, 11 December 2008, para. 68; *Lopata v. Russia*, App. No. 72250/01, ECtHR, 13 July 2010; *Yerokhina v. Ukraine*, App. No. 12167/04, ECtHR, 15 November 2012; para. 65; *Vanfuli v. Russia*, App. No. 24885/05, ECtHR, 3 November 2011, para. 96.

[255] *Tabbane v. Switzerland*, App. No. 41069/12, ECtHR, 1 March 2016. See Sect. 5.2.4.

[256] Ibid., para. 31.

[257] See, e.g. *Håkansson and Sturesson v. Sweden*, App. No. 11855/85, ECtHR, 21 February 1990, para. 66; *Sejdovic v. Italy*, App. No. 56581/00, ECtHR, 1 March 2006, para. 86; *Hermi v. Italy*, App. No. 18114/02, ECtHR [GC], 18 October 2006, para. 73; *Dvorski v. Croatia*, App. No. 25703/11, ECtHR, 20 October 2015, para. 100.

It has not become entirely evident which aspect of a particular case must be in conflict with an *important public interest*—is it the main subject matter of a case that must involve an *important public interest* so that a waiver can be considered ineffective for Convention purposes or is it the waiver itself of a particular right that must not run counter to an *important public interest*? Although the Convention's controlling bodies' case-law shows indications in favour of the former, to date no clear answer has been given as to the said distinction.

For example, if one tries to put this requirement in the context of arbitration-related cases, the case of *Axelsson and others v. Sweden* is one of the few arbitration-related submissions before the Convention's controlling bodies that expressly mentions the necessity to satisfy this requirement as a pre-condition for a valid waiver.[258] Although the issue of a waiver in this case was only impliedly linked to arbitration proceedings, it is nevertheless important to look how the Convention's controlling bodies interpret the requirement of such a waiver not being contrary to any *important public interest* in this regard.

The case of *Axelsson and others v. Sweden* concerned a dispute between certain taxi drivers and the Malmö Taxi Economic Association (MTEA) whose membership agreement provided that disputes between the MTEA and its members will be settled by means of arbitration. The issue of a waiver of a Convention right being potentially in conflict with an important public interest arose in connection with one of the claims before the former Commission that the taxi drivers raised, i.e. that they had not been given a public hearing before the Swedish Court of Appeal and the Supreme Court when they, despite the arbitration agreement, instituted proceedings before the Swedish courts. As seen,[259] the right to a public hearing may be subjected to a valid waiver, provided that it satisfies certain conditions. This was affirmed also by the Commission:

> Neither the letter nor spirit of [Article 6(1) of the ECHR] prevents a person from waiving of his own free will, either tacitly or expressly, the entitlement to a public hearing. A waiver must, however, be made in an unequivocal manner and not run counter to any important public interest [...][260]

The applicants to the former Commission had not exercised their statutory right and requested the Swedish courts to have a public hearing. Therefore '[b]y not requesting a hearing [...] the Commission [found] that the applicants must be considered to have unequivocally waived their right under [Article 6(1) of the ECHR] to a public hearing before the [Swedish courts].'[261] As to the potential conflict of the waiver to an *important public interest* in this case the Commission further noted that it:

> finds no indication that the litigation involved any issues of public interest which could have rendered a public hearing necessary irrespective of the applicants' request.[262]

---

[258] *Axelsson and others v. Sweden*, App. No. 11960/86, ECmHR, 13 July 1990.

[259] See Sect. 3.4.3.2.

[260] *Axelsson and others v. Sweden*, App. No. 11960/86, ECmHR, 13 July 1990.

[261] Ibid.

[262] Ibid.

This, in turn, indicates that it is the subject matter of a given case that must not run counter to any *important public interest* and not the waiver of a particular procedural right guaranteed by the Convention. This line of interpretation finds support also in other cases concerning a waiver of certain Convention rights and its potential conflict with an *important public interest*.[263] However, one cannot support such an interpretation in cases where parties, expressly or tacitly, are waiving the so-called *non-waivable* rights. In the author's opinion, if a waiver concerns, e.g. the right to an independent and impartial tribunal or the right to a fair hearing, the *public interest test* should apply not only to the main subject of the proceedings at stake, but also to the very nature of the waiver. Is it not an *important public interest* that every dispute settled within a particular jurisdiction is dealt with by an independent and impartial tribunal and that basic fair hearing principles, such as, e.g., the equality of arms, are duly respected? These fundamental rights are too important in a democratic society for them to be regarded as not serving *important public interests*.

Moreover, it is not entirely clear from the Court's case-law whose public interests must have been weighed against the waiver of Article 6(1) of the ECHR rights? If an arbitration agreement constitutes a waiver of Article 6(1) of the ECHR rights, whose public interests are at stake for determining whether or not such a waiver is valid for the purposes of Article 6(1) of the ECHR? Is it the public interests of the State of the seat of arbitration or perhaps the State where the resulting arbitral award is recognized or enforced? These and other questions pertaining to the requirements of public interest will be addressed in more detail in Chap. 7.

3.6 Summary

This book's search for the most ECHR-compatible legislative approach to excluding setting-aside proceedings mandates broader understanding of the contemporary relationship between arbitration and the ECHR per se. As must have become evident, determination of the said relationship and the particular extent to which the Convention has bearing upon arbitration proceedings, is a rather difficult task. Despite the somewhat relatively comprehensive Convention's controlling bodies' case-law on the dichotomy between arbitration and the ECHR, there are still certain grey areas, in particular when it comes to the Court's own-made difference between *waivable* and *non-waivable* rights of Article 6(1) of the ECHR.

The general applicability and impact of the ECHR on arbitration is no longer disputed. Notwithstanding the somewhat theoretical discussion on the absolute non-applicability of the ECHR to arbitration, and an equally theoretical discussion on the direct applicability thereof, the indirect applicability of the ECHR to arbitration is evidenced both by the Convention's controlling bodies' abundant case-law, as well as scholarly contributions to the matter. As explained, the most obvious provision of the

---

[263] See, e.g. *Schuler-Zgraggen v. Switzerland*, App. No. 14518/89, ECtHR, 24 June 1993, para. 58; *Håkansson and Sturesson v. Sweden*, App. No. 11855/85, ECtHR, 21 February 1990, paras. 66–67.

Convention evidencing the indirect applicability of the ECHR to arbitration is Article 6(1) of the ECHR and the right to a fair trial; however, the Convention's controlling bodies' case-law shows that also other Convention's provisions, e.g. Article 1 of Protocol 1 to the ECHR and the right to protection of property and Article 13 of the ECHR and the right to an effective remedy, may have an impact on arbitration proceedings.

The relationship between arbitration and the ECHR, in particular the right to a fair trial under Article 6(1) of the ECHR, is generally governed by the so-called *waiver theory*. Neither the letter nor the spirit of the Convention prevents a person from freely waiving his or her rights as enshrined in the Convention through the signing of an arbitration agreement. In that sense, the conclusion of an arbitration agreement and subjecting the dispute to arbitration, as opposed to ECHR Member States' ordinary jurisdiction courts, does not in principle offend against the Convention. However, before a *waiver* of Convention's rights and freedoms can be considered as valid and effective for the Convention's purposes, certain formal pre-conditions must be satisfied. As seen, nearly all arbitration-related cases before the Convention's controlling bodies have involved a scrupulous examination of each and every component of the so-called *waiver theory*. In that sense, the extent of applicability and impact of the ECHR, in particular the right to a fair trial under Article 6(1) of the ECHR, is ascertainable in a rather straightforward matter.

What, however, is not as straightforward is the closely linked issue of *permissibility* of a waiver of the Convention's rights and freedoms by means of an arbitration agreement. As the ECtHR famously held in the *Suovaniemi and others v. Finland* case 'a waiver should not necessarily be considered to amount to a waiver of all the rights under Article 6 [...]' and a waiver of Convention's rights is valid 'only insofar as such waiver is 'permissible'.' Moreover, as the Court stresses, a 'waiver may be permissible with regard to certain rights but not with regard to certain others' and that a 'distinction may have to be made even between different rights guaranteed by Article 6.'[264]

The Convention's controlling bodies' practice is rather clear as regards those rights of Article 6(1) of the ECHR that are *permissible* to waive, however, the same cannot be said of the 'non-waivable' rights, at least not with the same confidence. Although there are strong indications, both in the Convention's controlling bodies' case-law and scholarly contributions, that the right to an independent and impartial tribunal and the right to a fair hearing under Article 6(1) of the ECHR are both *non-waivable*, i.e. a waiver of these rights is not *permissible* within the meaning of the ECHR, a clear-cut answer in this regard is yet to be given.

It is exactly the said indefiniteness that leaves room for a normative discussion on the exact extent of applicability and impact of the ECHR, in particular the right to a fair trial under Article 6(1) of the ECHR, on arbitration. Although there may be many aspects of the interplay between arbitration and ordinary jurisdiction courts that could potentially raise issues of compatibility with the ECHR, this book's particular focus is on establishing the said extent of applicability solely vis-à-vis the annulment

[264] *Suovaniemi and others v. Finland*, App. No. 31737/96, ECtHR, 23 February 1999.

mechanism. The applicability and impact per se of the ECHR, in particular the right to a fair trial under Article 6(1) of the ECHR, on arbitration has been clearly evidenced by the above carried out analysis, however, determination of the exact extent, at least vis-à-vis setting-aside proceedings, requires a more thorough analysis of the concept of setting-aside proceedings in general, as well as the different legislative approaches to excluding setting-aside proceedings in national law.

References

Benedek W et al (eds) (2007) Economic globalisation and human rights. Cambridge University Press, Cambridge

Benedettelli MV (2015) Human rights as a litigation tool in international arbitration: reflecting on the ECHR experience. Arb Int'l 31(4):631–659

Besson S (2006) Arbitration and human rights. ASA Bull 24:395–416

Born G (2009) The principle of judicial non-interference in international arbitral proceedings. U Pa J Int'l L 30:999

Born G (2014) International commercial arbitration, 2nd edn. Kluwer Law International

Briner R, Von Schlabrendorff F (2001) Article 6 of the European convention on human rights and its bearing upon international arbitration. In: Briner R et al (eds) Law of international business and dispute settlement in the 21st century. Carl Heymanns Verlag KG, Liber Amicorum Karl-Heinz Bockstiegel

Cranston R (ed) (1997) Making commercial law: essays in honour of Roy Goode. Clarendon Press

Dupuy P et al (2009) Human rights in international investment law and arbitration. Oxford University Press, Oxford

Flauss J (1986) L'application de l'art. 6(1) de la Convention européenne des Droits de l'Homme aux procedures arbitrales. Gazete du Palais

Gaillard E (2010) Legal theory of international arbitration. Martinus Nijhoff

Garner BA (ed) (2014) Black's law dictionary, 10th edn. Thomson Reuters

Giunio M (2000) Right to a fair trial and efficiency of arbitral proceedings. Croat Arbit Yearb 7:31

Harris D et al (2014) Harris, O'Boyle & Warbrick: Law of the European convention on human rights, 3rd edn. Oxford University Press, United Kingdom

Jacot-Guillarmod O (1990) L'arbitrage privé face à l'Article 6(1) de la Convention européenne des Droits de l'Homme. In: Matscher F, Petzold H (eds) Protecting human rights: The European Dimension. Studies in Honour of Gérard J. Wiarda. C. Heymanns Verlag

Jaksic A (2002) Arbitration and human rights. Peter Lang, Frankfurt am Main

Jaksic A (2007) Procedural guarantees of human rights in arbitration proceedings: a still unsettled problem? J Int Arb 24(2):159

Jarrosson C (1989) L'arbitrage et la Convention européenne des droits de l'homme. Rev Arb 4:573–607

Kaufmann-Kohler G, Schultz T (2004) Online dispute resolution: challenges for contemporary justice. Kluwer Law International

Kreindler R (2015) Standards of procedural international public policy. In: Bray D, Bray HL (eds) International arbitration and public policy. JurisNet

Krings E, Matray L (1982) Le juge et l'arbitre. Rev. dr. int. et dr. comp. 227

Kurkela MS, Turunen S (2010) Due process in international commercial arbitration, 2nd edn. Oxford University Press, Oxford

Landrove JC (2006) European convention on human rights' impact on consensual arbitration. An État des Lieux of Strasbourg Case-Law and of a Problematic Swiss Law Feature In: Besson et al (eds) Human rights at the center. Schulthess

Lew JDM et al (2003) Comparative international commercial arbitration. Kluwer Law International
Mann F (1967) Lex Facit Arbitrum. In: Sanders P (ed) International Arbitration. Liver Amicorum for Martin Domke. Martinus Nijhoff, the Hague
Matscher F (1987) Schiedsgerichtsbarkeit und EMRK. In: Habscheid WJ, Schwab KH (eds) Beiträge zum internationalen Verfahrensrecht und zur Schiedsgerichtsbarkeit: Festschrift für Heinrich Nagel. Aschendorff
Matscher F (1999) L'arbitrage et la Convention. In: Pettiti LE et al (eds) La Convention européenne des droits de l'Homme. Commentaire article par article, Économica
McDonald N (2003) More harm than good? Human rights consideration in international commercial arbitration. J Int Arb 20(6):523–538
Mistelis L (2010) Concise international arbitration. Kluwer Law International
Moitry J (1989) Right to fair trial and the European convention on human rights: some remarks on the République de Guinée case. J Int'l Arb 6:115
Mourre A (2000) Le droit français de l'arbitrage international face à la Convention européenne des droits de l'Homme. Gazette du Palais 337:16
Mouyal LW (2016) International investment law and the right to regulate: a human rights perspective. Routledge
Park WW (2001) Why courts review arbitral awards. In: Briner R et al (eds) Law of international business and dispute settlement in the 21st Century, Liber Amicorum Karl-Heinz Bockstiegel. Carl Heymanns Verlag KG, Köln/Berlin/Bonn/München, pp 595–606
Petrochilos G (2004) Procedural law in international arbitration. Oxford University Press, Oxford
Poudret JF, Besson S (2006) Comparative law of international arbitration. Sweet & Maxwell, London
Rainey B et al (2014) Jacobs, White, and Ovey: The European convention on human rights, 6th edn. Oxford University Press, Oxford
Samuel A (2004) Arbitration, alternative dispute resolution generally and the European convention on human rights: an anglo-centric view. J Int Arb 21(5):413–438
Settem OJ (2016) Applications of the applications of the 'fair hearing' norm in ECHR article 6(1) to civil proceedings: with special emphasis on the balance between procedural safeguards and efficiency. Springer
Van den Berg AJ (1992) The efficacy of award in international commercial arbitration. Arbitration 58:267
Wedam-Lukic D (1998) Arbitration and article 6 of the European convention on human rights. Arb 64:16–21

Chapter 4
Setting-Aside Proceedings—Overview, Genesis and Grounds for Annulment

4.1 Overview and Genesis of Setting-Aside Proceedings

Arbitration as an alternative dispute settlement mechanism not only derives its existence and legitimacy from parties' agreement to arbitrate, but also from an underlying regulatory framework which 'controls the legal status and effectiveness of arbitration in a national and international legal environment [and also gives] effect to the agreement to arbitrate, the organization of the arbitration process and the finality and enforceability of the arbitration award.'[1] By concluding an arbitration agreement, parties seemingly wish to escape the constraints of ordinary jurisdiction courts, however, State courts play a significant complimentary role when it comes to assisting arbitral tribunals and parties with various procedural matters or guaranteeing the finality of arbitral awards by means of granting recognition and enforcement. The existence of judicial controls and court scrutiny over arbitration proceedings is yet another, perhaps the most widely debated function of State courts exercised in relation to arbitration proceedings.

Arbitration proceedings and, in particular, arbitral awards, have always been subject to some form of judicial supervision and scrutiny.[2] For example, already in Roman law, arbitration *ex compromisso* largely depended on the supervision of the State, in particular, the supervision of the praetor who 'kept an eye on the arbiter until he had discharged his duties by full performance.'[3] The praetor's edict legitimated the arbitral procedure and he had control over the arbiter and his duties, including the arbiter's appointment. The praetor also exercised control over the enforcement of a penalty in case one of the parties did not abide by the award and performed many other functions that to some extent are comparable to the functions of State courts in contemporary arbitration proceedings.[4]

---

[1] Lew et al. (2003), p. 16. See also Park (2001), p. 595 et seq.

[2] Van den Berg (2014), p. 3.

[3] Roebuck and De Loynes de Fumichon (2004), pp. 20 and 55.

[4] Ibid., pp. 96–97; 125–126; 145–146; 195–198.

© The Editor(s) (if applicable) and The Author(s), under exclusive license to Springer Nature Switzerland AG 2020

T. Krūmiņš, *Arbitration and Human Rights*,
https://doi.org/10.1007/978-3-030-54237-5_4

The origins of judicial review and scrutiny over arbitration naturally stem from the general hostility towards arbitration as an alternative dispute resolution mechanism—hostility that continued to be persistent until the middle of the twentieth century. For example, although England being one of the first to enact a statute governing arbitration in 1698, for quite some time local courts looked at arbitration with great hostility, holding as early as in 1746 that 'the [arbitration] agreement of the parties cannot oust [the jurisdiction of the courts].'[5] It is said that in subsequent centuries this doctrine 'provided ample support for [...] proponents of judicial hostility to arbitration.'[6] Although later legislative developments, such as the 1854 Common Law Procedure Act and the 1889 English Arbitration Act, saw a slightly more favourable attitude towards arbitration, strict court control, e.g. by means of extensive judicial review over the substance of arbitral awards (the 'case stated' procedure), remained a general practice until the adoption of the 1979 Arbitration Act.[7]

Similar historical developments regarding the somewhat sensitive relationship between arbitration and state can be witnessed elsewhere. For example, prior the French Revolution, arbitration was widely used by merchants in resolving their commercial disputes, however, after the French Revolution, it was considered 'a threat to the rule of law and the authority of the revolutionary state'.[8] Arbitration agreements that provided for the resolution of future disputes were unenforceable for most of the nineteenth century and it was only with France's ratification of the 1923 Geneva Protocol on Arbitration Clauses that 'agreements to arbitrate future international commercial disputes became fully enforceable in French courts.'[9] Also in the United States, similarly to England and France, judicial hostility and animosity obstructed the use of arbitration and only with the adoption of the Federal Arbitration Act in 1925 arbitration as a means of alternative dispute resolution gained more autonomy and recognition.[10]

For a long period of time therefore States and, in particular, their courts looked at arbitration with a degree of incredulity. They saw arbitration as a rival and, although in the beginning of the twentieth century States started to more and more recognize arbitration agreements and awards, they wanted to maintain close supervision over the arbitration process.[11] At the same time, the emergence of modern arbitration

[5] *Kill v. Hollister*, 95 Eng. Rep. 532 (K.B. 1746) (1746). See also Goode (2001), p. 20.

[6] Born (2015), pp. 17–18.

[7] Ibid., pp. 16–19. Generally on the most important changes regarding the relationship between court and arbitration brought by the 1979 Arbitration Act see, e.g. Kerr (1980), Park (1980), Hacking (1985).

[8] Born (2015), pp. 19–21.

[9] Ibid.

[10] See, e.g. decision of the Supreme Court of the United States in the case of *Hall Street Assoc. LLC v. Mattel, Inc.*, 128 S. Ct. 1396 (2008) ('Prior to the passage of the FAA, American courts were generally hostile to arbitration. They refused, with rare exceptions, to order specific enforcement of executory agreements to arbitrate. Section 2 of the FAA responded to this hostility by making written arbitration agreements 'valid, irrevocable, and enforceable."). See also Berger and Sun (2009), pp. 746–749, Born (2015), pp. 19–21.

[11] Lew et al. (2003), p. 17.

laws, establishment of international arbitration institutions and recognition of the importance of international arbitration per se all led to a greater autonomy being given to arbitration in the middle of the twentieth century. The increasing autonomy both regarding arbitration as a process and equally regarding all the actors in arbitration, on the one hand, and the continuing willingness of States to keep arbitration on a short leash, on the other hand, is what characterizes contemporary notion of judicial control and court scrutiny over arbitration.

It is said that 'legislators and courts must engage in a process of legal fine tuning that seeks a reasonable counterpoise between arbitral autonomy and judicial control mechanisms.'[12] The existence of judicial control and court scrutiny over arbitration's integrity by means of setting-aside proceedings can be said to be the result of this *legal fine tuning*. At the heart of the two competing issues, i.e. arbitral autonomy and judicial supervision, is also the delicate relationship between another two rival goals in arbitration—finality and fairness:

> Freeing awards from judicial challenge promotes finality, while enhancing fairness calls for some measure of court supervision. An arbitration's winner looks for finality, while the loser wants careful judicial scrutiny of doubtful decisions.[13]

The art of an effective arbitration system lies in reconciling these two rival goals of finality and fairness. A careful balance between party and arbitral autonomy,[14] on the one hand, and the guarantee of the most fundamental procedural standards during arbitration proceedings and in the final arbitral award, on the other hand, is what makes an arbitral seat truly pro-arbitration.

If party and arbitral autonomy is increased by a State less intervening in the arbitration process, how can one assure that the most basic fundamental principles of fairness are adhered to during arbitration? The most common method, adopted in most jurisdictions permitting and regulating arbitration, is to provide a degree of court supervision over arbitration proceedings. Judicial scrutiny is self-evident during the recognition and enforcement proceedings—a national judge recognizes the *res judicata* effect of an arbitral award and verifies, inter alia, whether the award is free from procedural irregularities and whether it conforms with certain overriding mandatory provisions, e.g. laws on arbitrability, and public policy of the enforcing state. There is, however, another form of judicial scrutiny, i.e. that of courts at the seat of arbitration by means of what is called the setting-aside proceedings.

Judicial review of an arbitral award by means of setting-aside proceedings is often expressed in different terms—recourse against an award, challenge, action for an annulment of award, application to set aside, vacatur of an arbitral award, and sometimes even an *appeal*.[15] What in essence the setting aside of an arbitral award

---

[12]Park (2001), p. 596.

[13]Ibid. See also Abedian (2011), p. 554 et seq.

[14]Generally on party and arbitral autonomy in international arbitration see, e.g. Born (2014a, b).

[15]For examples of the different expressions used in national arbitration legislations see, e.g. Poudret and Besson (2006), p. 703. Hereinafter in this book judicial review of an arbitral award by means of setting-aside proceedings will be interchangeably referred to as the 'challenging of an arbitral award', 'setting aside of an arbitral award' or 'the annulment of an arbitral award'.

entails is a decision of a national court at the seat of arbitration to the effect that the arbitral award has no legal force.[16] It is a review by a national court of an arbitral award in order to confirm that the arbitral award (and the underlying arbitration process) complies with, on the one hand, certain fundamental procedural principles and rules and, on the other hand, that State's overriding mandatory provisions and public policy. Generally, the setting aside of an arbitral award is understood as not entailing any review on the substance of an arbitral award.[17] This aspect of setting-aside proceedings, i.e. the fact that such proceedings are not an appeal to an arbitral award *stricto* sensu, must be stressed particularly since often the action for setting aside is wrongly mistaken with an action for an appeal. When introducing the grounds for setting aside an arbitral award, it will become apparent that the possibility of setting aside an arbitral award is very restrictive and generally aims to protect only the most fundamental parties' procedural rights and overriding mandatory provisions as well as public policy of the State at the seat of arbitration.

The setting aside of an arbitral award is considered as the mirror action of recognition and enforcement of an arbitral award. It is said that the setting aside of an arbitral award developed as a separate action due to two main factors—(i) the losing party's unwillingness to wait until the other party will bring an enforcement action and (ii) the growing internationalization of arbitration in a sense that enforcement of an arbitral award is no longer confined to the State where the arbitral award is made.[18] Since every State could decide on the recognition and enforcement of an arbitral award differently, the losing party had an incentive to obtain a declaration that the award is null and void from the State where such an award was made.[19]

As said, setting aside of an arbitral award is possible only on very limited grounds. It is seen as a form of risk management whereby courts remedy violations of fundamental procedural rights during arbitration proceedings.[20] Traditionally every national arbitration law contained different grounds upon which an arbitral award could be set aside. To some extent this is true also in contemporary arbitration world—each State can decide for itself on which grounds an arbitral award should be annulled.[21] Nevertheless, with the introduction of the UNCITRAL Model Law

---

[16] Jaksic (2002). p. 168. See also Born (2014a, b), p. 2905 ('The annulment or setting aside of an award has the effect of rendering the award null and void, at least under local law in the place where the annulment is effected [...] [T]he effects within the annulment forum are comparable to the vacatur of a lower court judgment.').

[17] See, e.g. Born (2014a, b), p. 3186. In some jurisdictions, for example, England, it is possible to also appeal the arbitral award *stricto* sensu. This is provided for in s. 69 of the 1996 English Arbitration Law ('Unless otherwise agreed by the parties, a party to arbitral proceedings may (upon notice to the other parties and to the tribunal) appeal to the court on a question of law arising out of an award made in the proceedings.').

[18] Van den Berg (2014), p. 3.

[19] Ibid.

[20] Park (2001), p. 595.

[21] See, e.g. Craig (1988). This diversity in approaches as regards setting-aside proceedings is confirmed also by the ECHR's enforcing bodies. See, e.g. *Nordström-Janzon and Nordström-Lehtinen v. the Netherlands*, App. No. 28101/95, ECmHR., 27 November 1996 ('The Commission observes that the grounds on which arbitral awards may be challenged before national courts differ

in 1985 the annulment grounds have been somewhat uniformed.[22] The UNCITRAL Model Law has been adopted in 83 States in a total of 116 jurisdictions.[23] Although it serves only as a *model* and interpretation of similarly or identically worded provisions may not be entirely uniform in all of the States, annulment grounds are substantially similar in every State whose legislation is based on the UNCITRAL Model Law. Even in those States that do not base their *leges arbitri* on the UNCITRAL Model Law the annulment grounds do not substantially differ from the grounds listed in the UNCITRAL Model Law.[24]

An exhaustive list of annulment grounds is provided in Article 34(2) of the UNCITRAL Model Law. Considering that these grounds generally represent a common consensus of the available means of recourse against arbitral awards, they serve as an illustration of the nature of setting-aside proceedings. More detailed analysis of each of the respective ground will be provided below.[25] For now, they can be summarized as follows:

(i) Incapacity of a party or invalidity of the arbitration agreement under the law chosen by the parties or the law of the seat of arbitration;
(ii) Violation of due process (improper notice of the appointment of arbitrator or the arbitral proceedings, inability to present one's case);
(iii) Excess of authority (the award deals with a dispute or contains decisions on matters beyond the scope of the submission to arbitration);
(iv) Irregularities in the arbitral procedure (composition of the tribunal or the arbitral procedure inconsistent with the agreement between the parties or with the applicable *lex arbitri*);
(v) Arbitrability (the subject-matter of the dispute is not capable of settlement by arbitration under the law of the seat of arbitration);
(vi) Public policy (the award violates the public policy of the seat of arbitration).

Since setting-aside proceedings are considered as the mirror action for recognition and enforcement of an arbitral award, the annulment grounds in Article 34(2) of the UNCITRAL Model Law essentially mirror the grounds for refusing recognition and enforcement under Article 36(1) of the UNCITRAL Model Law. The latter, in turn, were inspired by the New York Convention and virtually repeat the grounds for refusing recognition and enforcement of an arbitral award under Article V of the New York Convention.[26]

Judicial review of arbitration proceedings and the resulting arbitral award has been perhaps the most widely debated aspect of court involvement in arbitration

among the Contracting States [...] [E]ach Contracting State may in principle decide for itself on which grounds an arbitral award should be quashed.').

[22] The UNCITRAL Model Law, Explanatory note, para. 44.

[23] See Status of the Model Law. https://uncitral.un.org/en/texts/arbitration/modellaw/commercial_arbitration/status. Accessed 22 May 2020.

[24] States that have not based their arbitration law on the Model Law include, e.g., Switzerland, France, the Netherlands, Sweden, Finland, Italy and many others.

[25] See Sect. 4.4.1 below.

[26] The UNCITRAL Model Law, Explanatory note, para. 46. See also Born (2014a, b), p. 3187.

proceedings. Judicial review and the necessity of court involvement for the smooth and efficient functioning of arbitration per se is an accepted fact and not a matter of intellectual controversy.[27] What is, however, a matter of intellectual controversy and at the heart of the discussion regarding judicial review of arbitration in general is a question of the exact depth and extent of such a review.

The fact that States are free to 'apply whatever measures of judicial control'[28] of arbitration they deem necessary has generated various approaches and attitudes towards regulating arbitration. On the one hand, there are States that favour minimal court control over arbitration; on the other hand, there are States where arbitration is subjected to very strict State and judicial intervention, as opposed to mere support and control, thus undermining the whole essence of arbitration.[29]

It is said that 'an absence of any court scrutiny at the arbitral situs would adversely affect the victims of defective arbitration, and in some cases the interests of the reviewing State itself.'[30] At the other extreme, 'excessive judicial intervention [...] may undermine international arbitration as a private dispute settlement mechanism.'[31] What is necessary, however, for a truly efficient functioning of arbitration, is a careful legislative balance between the two opposing objectives of arbitration—finality and fairness.

4.2 Theoretical Considerations

A broader discussion on the necessity and exact degree of judicial control over arbitration by means of setting-aside proceedings is incomplete without also succinctly addressing the theoretical postulates behind judicial controls in arbitration, i.e. the legal foundations of arbitration and the legal order that governs arbitration.[32] Attitudes towards either more stringent or lenient judicial controls over arbitration, inter alia, also by means of setting-aside proceedings, find explanation in the different approaches that States employ with regard to provision and regulation of arbitration in their national law.

As explained, historically, there was a considerable judicial hostility towards arbitration as a means of alternative dispute settlement mechanism. Although the said hostility was not uniformly witnessed everywhere, it is said that only during the twentieth century the general mistrust of arbitration was eroded:

> The mistrust of the arbitral process which had arisen in some jurisdictions during the nineteenth century, was eroded, and then firmly repudiated, during the twentieth century. This

---

[27] Sattar (2010), p. 73.

[28] Craig (1988), p. 174.

[29] See, e.g. Sattar (2010) where the author discusses problems caused by illegal interference in arbitration by state courts and gives examples of such interference in India, Bangladesh and Pakistan.

[30] Park (2001), p. 599.

[31] Abedian (2011), p. 589.

[32] Paulsson (2013), p. 29.

> was accomplished by means of a panoply of related developments, including the adoption of international arbitration conventions, national arbitration legislation and institutional arbitration rules, and the supportive role of national courts in many jurisdictions. The driving force behind these various developments was the international business community, also the principal user of the arbitral process, which found ready audiences in national legislatures and judiciaries eager to promote international trade, investment and peace by providing workable, effective international dispute resolution mechanisms. It was the combination and active collaboration of these two communities – public and private – that produced the contemporary legal framework for international commercial arbitration.[33]

Contemporary legal framework of international arbitration was and still is characterized also by continuous judicial control over arbitration. Such a control naturally stems from the historic judicial hostility towards arbitration—it is only the degree and extent that has changed over the years. Explanation to the differing degrees of judicial controls in national arbitration laws can be found in the different theoretical considerations underpinning the existence and legal foundations of arbitration as a means for dispute resolution. The various legal theories of international arbitration can be very succinctly summarized as follows.

First and foremost, there is the school of ***territoriality***—perhaps the most well-recognized theory of arbitration that, at least currently, is perceived as somewhat outdated. At the same time, its influence still lingers and the plain fact that judicial controls still characterize contemporary arbitration can be to a great extent explained due to territoriality. The theory of territoriality assumes that not only parties' agreement to arbitrate is the source of arbitration, but, more importantly, arbitration as a means of dispute resolution is given effect by the law at the seat of arbitration. In other words, according to the school of territoriality, arbitration 'can have no foundation other than that of the legal order of the particular state where the arbitration takes place.'[34]

The territorialist thesis has its roots in one of its greatest proponents'—Francis Mann's—seminal work *Lex Facit Arbitrum* in which he famously noted:

> In the legal sense no international commercial arbitration exists. Just as, notwithstanding its notoriously misleading name, every system of private international law is a system of national law, every arbitration is a national arbitration, that is to say, subject to a specific system of national law [...] The *lex arbitri* cannot be the law of any country other than that of the arbitration tribunal's seat. No act of the parties can have any legal effect except as the result of the sanction given to it by a legal system. Hence, it is unavoidable to ascertain such system before the act of the parties can be upheld. When we say in the conflict of laws: 'contracts are governed by the law chosen by the parties', we do so, and can do so, only by reason of the fact that the rule is part of the law of a specific legal system. Similarly, the statement: 'arbitrations are subject to the law chosen by the parties as the *lex fori*' cannot have any validity in the absence of a legal rule to this effect.[35]

---

[33] Born (2014a, b), pp. 63–64.

[34] Paulsson (2013), p. 29.

[35] Mann (1967). Generally on the territorialist thesis with regard to arbitration see, e.g. Paulsson (2013), pp. 32–35, Gaillard (2010), pp. 15–24.

In effect, it is the general principle of territoriality applied to international arbitration, concluding that 'a state is sovereign within its own borders and that its law and its courts have the exclusive right to determine the legal effect of acts done (and consequently of arbitral awards made) within those borders.'[36] Applied to the present discussion on judicial controls by means of setting-aside proceedings, the territorialist thesis would presuppose that control of the effect of arbitral process and the resulting arbitral award is exercised solely at the seat of arbitration. It would equally presuppose a more stringent control over the whole arbitration process and the resulting arbitral award, i.e. an approach that is continuously predominant in certain jurisdictions.

However, in most national arbitration laws the setting aside of an arbitral award is possible only on very limited grounds. Although, the availability per se of an action for setting aside in the vast majority of national arbitration laws to a certain extent has its explanation in the territorialist thesis and willingness of States to exercise their sovereignty also by means of control over arbitration, by now the territorialist thesis in its purest form has been challenged and rebutted, and it can be indeed said that, taken in isolation, 'it simply does not fit the realities of an international society no longer constrained within national units [...]'.[37]

This, inter alia, is explained both due to the fact that, as will be demonstrated below, certain States allow parties to voluntarily exclude the application of setting-aside proceedings, as well as the fact that notwithstanding a decision of a court at the seat of arbitration to the effect that an arbitral award has no legal effect, i.e. it is set aside, certain States will nevertheless recognize and enforce such awards. This phenomenon has its explanation in a theory of arbitration representing the opposing end, namely delocalization.

It is said that the ***delocalization*** school has been in principle developed by leading French scholars, notably David, Goldman and Fouchard, and supported by certain other well-known scholars, such as Von Mehren and Lalive.[38] In essence, the theory of delocalization promotes 'the idea of international arbitration as something variously described as 'anational', 'stateless', 'delocalized' or 'detached',[39] i.e. arbitration not anchored in one single legal order.[40] In other words, a *delocalized*, *anational* or *detached* arbitration is considered as being free from the constraints of the applicable *lex loci arbitri* and deriving its legal effect 'from the agreement of the parties without a specific legal system serving as its foundation'.[41] Proponents of delocalization rebut the territorialist thesis and suggest for a very limited role of *lex loci arbitri* on the basis of various considerations, e.g. the fact that the seat of arbitration is

---

36 Goode (2001), p. 24.

37 Paulsson (2013), p. 35.

38 Goode (2001), p. 21. See also Lalive (1976).

39 Goode (2001), p. 21.

40 Generally see, e.g. Paulsson (1983).

41 Frick (2001), p. 276.

often chosen merely out of convenience, party desire to settle their disputes in a neutral third country, and the fact that the arbitral seat, in essence, has no necessary connection with the dispute.[42]

Applied to the present discussion on judicial controls by means of setting-aside proceedings, the delocalization theory would suggest that any court involvement at the seat of arbitration, unless requested by an arbitrator or the parties, should be kept to minimum.

The delocalization theory is embraced and best illustrated by the French court practice with regard to recognition and enforcement of awards that have been set aside at the seat of arbitration. This is a clear manifestation and echo of the delocalization thesis as primarily developed and promoted by the said French scholars. In a series of well-known cases, e.g. the *Norsolor*,[43] *Hilmarton*,[44] *Chromalloy*[45] and *Putrabali*,[46] the French courts, in particular the *Cour de Cassation*, despite an arbitral award being set aside by courts at the seat of arbitration, have nevertheless recognized and enforced such awards in France. In the *Hilmarton* case this was explained with the following famous passage:

> An international arbitral award, which is not anchored in any national legal order, is a decision of international justice whose validity must be ascertained with regard to the rules applicable in the country where its recognition and enforcement are sought.[47]

As recognized by Prof. Van den Berg, '[t]his is a purely French point of view that is shared by hardly any other country.'[48] Indeed, the French *anational* view on international arbitration is not shared by many countries. Although the French view is a good example demonstrating how different perception of the legal foundations of arbitration can lead to a diametrically opposed view on the extent of judicial controls in the arbitral process,[49] their excessive and particular view on the matter has neither been free from criticism.[50]

In addition to the pure forms of territoriality and delocalization and their sub-forms, such as, e.g. the jurisdictional and imputed choice approaches (territoriality) or

---

[42] See a comprehensive summary of these arguments and answers thereto in Goode (2001), pp. 32–33.

[43] *Société Pablak Ticaret Limited Sirketi v Norsolor S.A.*, Cour de cassation, 9 October 1984, 83-11.355.

[44] *Société Hilmarton Ltd v. Société Omnium de traitement et de valorisation (OTV)*, Cour de cassation, 23 March 1994, 92-15.137.

[45] *République arabe d'Egypte v Société Chromalloy Aero Services*, Cour d'appel de Paris, 14 January 1997, 95/23025.

[46] *Société PT Putrabali Adyamulia v Société Rena Holding et Société Moguntia Est Epices, Co*, Cour de cassation, 29 June 2007, 05-18.053.

[47] *Société Hilmarton Ltd v Société Omnium de traitement et de valorisation (OTV)*, Cour de cassation, 23 March 1994, 92-15.137.

[48] Van den Berg (2014), p. 20.

[49] To this, one must equally mention the exceptionally strong 'negative' aspect of the principle of *kompetenz-kompetenz* as characteristic to France.

[50] See, e.g. Paulsson (2013), p. 35.

transnational and contractual approaches (delocalization), there are also other recent theories of arbitration that add to the discussion, e.g. arbitration as an autonomous legal order as supported by Gaillard,[51] or the *hybrid* or *mixed* theories.[52] All of these different views on the theoretical foundations of international commercial arbitration are directly resembled also in the attitudes of States towards regulating setting-aside proceedings and either providing more stringent judicial controls or, on the other hand, more lenient controls over arbitration, e.g. by, inter alia, also permitting parties to contractually exclude the application of setting-aside proceedings—a phenomenon that, to a certain extent, can be seen as a fruit of the discussion on the theory and legal underpinnings of arbitration. Whatever view on the legal foundations of international commercial arbitration is preferred, the reality has been very well summarized by Lord Mustill:

> The old and sterile confrontation between the 'minimalists' and the 'maximalists' regarding the part to be played by the domestic courts has now given way to a recognition that the courts must recognize the essential role of arbitration in international commerce, and give it the maximum permissible support; and a converse recognition that arbitration cannot flourish without that support.[53]

Judicial control over arbitration, including by means of setting-aside proceedings, is an important part of contemporary international arbitration. No matter which theory of arbitration is supported, one can simply not deny the absolute fact that there exists judicial control over arbitration, to either greater or lesser extent, in almost every jurisdiction permitting arbitration as an alternative dispute resolution mechanism, and that setting-aside proceedings, in particular, are still a prevalent means for controlling arbitration. This, inter alia, is also confirmed by the relatively scarce practical use of the possibility to exclude application of setting-aside proceedings as provided in certain national arbitration laws.

4.3 Sources and Jurisdiction, Time-Limits and Decisions Subject to Annulment

The principle source of setting-aside proceedings is the national arbitration law applicable to arbitration proceedings.[54] Although each State is free to specify its own grounds for annulment, generally, such grounds to a large extent are very similar from one State to another. This is mainly due to the broad recognition and adoption of the UNCITRAL Model Law which, as seen above, provides in its Article 34(2) an exhaustive list of grounds pursuant on which an arbitral award may be annulled. Even in States whose national arbitration law is not based on the UNCITRAL Model

[51] See Gaillard (2010), pp. 35–67.

[52] Born (2014a, b), pp. 215–216.

[53] Mustill (1993), p. 118.

[54] For a general overview of setting-aside proceedings in international arbitration see, e.g. Born (2014a, b), pp. 3163–3393.

Law, annulment grounds generally mirror those of the UNCITRAL Model Law. Of course, there are also States whose arbitration laws provide for either more restrictive (e.g. France[55]) or more expansive (e.g. England[56]) annulment grounds, however, the general 'trend in recent years has been very decisively toward adopting or emulating the Model Law's limited lists of grounds for annulment [...]'.[57]

An arbitral award may be annulled only by a court at the place where arbitration proceedings are located, i.e. at the arbitral seat.[58] The annulment of an arbitral award is in the exclusive competence of courts at the seat of arbitration and therefore cannot be done anywhere else, e.g. at the State where recognition and enforcement of an arbitral award is sought. This *localization* of setting-aside proceedings stems, inter alia, also from the New York Convention, which impliedly limits jurisdictions in which an action for annulment may be brought to the 'country in which, or under the law of which, that award was made'.[59] The impossibility to challenge and possibly set aside an arbitral award in other States, such as the State of recognition and enforcement, is also one of the main reasons why the availability of a mechanism for setting aside arbitral awards at the seat of arbitration is of utmost importance both for arbitrating parties and the integrity of arbitration proceedings as such.

The specific court at the seat of arbitration to which an action for annulment must be filed and the procedure, including a possibility to appeal the decision on annulment, will differ from one State to another.[60] First, there are States where the annulment of an arbitral award can be potentially decided in three court instances.[61]

---

[55]Ibid., p. 3362 ('Under French law, the grounds for annulment of an international award made in France are identical to those available for non-recognition of a foreign award. In both instances, the showings that are required for annulment or non-recognition are more limited that those available for non-recognition under Article V of the New York Convention—reflecting a particularly pro-arbitration legislative approach.)'. See also Gharavi (2002), p. 33 et seq.

[56]The 1996 English Arbitration Law provides that an arbitral award may also be appealed on its merits. See sec. 69 ('Unless otherwise agreed by the parties, a party to arbitral proceedings may (upon notice to the other parties and to the tribunal) appeal to the court on a question of law arising out of an award made in the proceedings.').

[57]See, e.g. Born (2014a, b), p. 3340.

[58]Born (2014a, b), p. 2905, Gharavi (2002), pp. 11–17.

[59]See art. V(1)(e) of the New York Convention ('Recognition and enforcement of the award may be refused, at the request of the party against whom it is invoked, only if that party furnishes to the competent authority where the recognition and enforcement is sought, proof that: (e) The award has not yet become binding on the parties, or has been set aside or suspended by a competent authority of the country in which, or under the law of which, that award was made.').

[60]For example, under the UNCITRAL Model Law, each State is competent to specify the court or courts which will perform functions referred, inter alia, in art. 34(2) of the UNCITRAL Model Law. See art. 6 of the UNCITRAL Model Law ('The functions referred to in articles 11(3), 11(4), 13(3), 14, 16(3) and 34(2) shall be performed by… [Each State enacting this model law specifies the court, courts or, where referred to therein, other authority competent to perform these functions.]. Generally on the topic see, e.g. Poudret and Besson (2006), pp. 704–706.

[61]Until 2013, this was the case in Austria. In 2013 Austria reformed its arbitration law and now, similarly to Switzerland, provides only for one instance setting-aside proceedings. See sec. 615 of the Austrian Arbitration Act. Similarly, three-instance setting-aside proceedings were possible in Belgium and the Netherlands, however in these States recent amendments to their arbitration

Then there are also States where the action for annulment is submitted to and decided only in one instance, i.e. either before the respective Court of Appeal or the Supreme Court.[62] However, the most wide-spread approach is to provide a two-tier mechanism for reviewing arbitral awards by first submitting the application to an appellate court and then having a possibility to appeal that decision before the Supreme Court.[63]

Another aspect of setting-aside proceedings where States greatly differ is the available time-limit for parties to file for the annulment of an arbitral award.[64] The UNCITRAL Model Law provides that a such a request should be filed within 3 months from the date on which the party making that application had received the award. This is also the most common time limit required by many national arbitration laws.[65] There are, however, also States that specify a shorter period of time for filing an action for annulment, e.g. one month[66] or even shorter.[67]

Moreover, not all decisions of an arbitral tribunal or an arbitral institution may be challenged at the seat of arbitration. It is generally accepted that only arbitral *awards* (as opposed to procedural orders and mere decisions of either an arbitral tribunal or a supervising arbitral institution) issued by an arbitral tribunal may be subject to setting-aside proceedings at the seat of arbitration.[68] There is, however, divergence among States as to which arbitral awards may be challenged. For example, the UNCITRAL Model Law does not provide that the arbitral award must be 'final' before it can be submitted to State courts for challenge. Therefore, there is no express requirement of *finality*, meaning that under the UNCITRAL Model Law also interim awards may

laws do away with the cost and time-consuming three instance review of arbitral awards. See, e.g. Poudret and Besson (2006), p. 704.

[62]This is the case, e.g. in Switzerland, where actions for annulment of arbitral awards are submitted to and decided only by the Swiss Federal Tribunal (art. 191 of the Swiss PILA). Recently, other countries have followed the Swiss and amended their arbitration laws to make the setting-aside proceedings more effective. Such countries include, e.g. the Netherlands, Austria, Poland. See Orecki (2015) One Instance for Setting Aside and Enforcement Proceedings in Poland as of the Start of 2016. Kluwer Arbitration Blog, 3 November 2015. http://kluwerarbitrationblog.com/2015/11/03/one-instance-for-setting-aside-and-enforcement-proceedings-in-poland-as-of-the-start-of-2016/. Accessed 22 May 2020.

[63]See, e.g. art. 50(1) and (7) of the 2012 Lithuanian Law on Commercial Arbitration; sec. 43 of the 1999 Swedish Arbitration Act; art. 9 of the 2008 Slovenian Law on Arbitration; sec. 1065 of the German Code of Civil Procedure and other arbitration laws.

[64]Generally see, e.g. Poudret and Besson (2006), pp. 713–719, Born (2014a, b), pp. 3379–3385.

[65]See, e.g. sec. 1059(3) of the German Code of Civil Procedure; sec. 34 of the 1994 Czech Law on Arbitration; art. 37(4) of the 2005 Danish Arbitration Act; art. 1064(a)(2) of the 2015 Dutch Arbitration Act; sec. 41(3) of the 1999 Finnish Arbitration Act; art. 34(3) of the 1994 Ukrainian Law on Arbitration; art. 1717(4) of the BCCP and many others.

[66]See, e.g. art. 1519 of the FCCP ('An action to set aside shall be brought before the Court of Appeal of the place where the award was made. Such recourse can be had as soon as the award is rendered. If no application is made within one month following notification of the award, recourse shall no longer be admissible.').

[67]See sec. 70(3) of the 1996 English Arbitration Act ('Any application or appeal must be brought within 28 days of the date of the award or, if there has been any arbitral process of appeal or review, of the date when the applicant or appellant was notified of the result of that process.').

[68]Born (2014a, b), p. 3385.

be challenged.[69] On the other hand, there are States that only permit the challenging of *final* awards, either complete or partial, finally resolving only particular claims in arbitration. These States include, e.g. the Netherlands,[70] Spain,[71] the United States[72] and others.[73]

To sum up, States providing for judicial review of arbitration process and arbitral awards by means of setting-aside proceedings differ in terms of assigning jurisdiction to their State courts, providing time limits for parties to apply for the setting aside of an arbitral award, and also in prescribing which decisions of an arbitral tribunal can be submitted for challenge before state courts. Apart from these procedural divergences, States also differ as regards the available grounds pursuant to which an arbitral award can be challenged. For the purposes of further analysis, the UNCITRAL Model Law provides a good overview of such grounds, representing the common consensus of not only States that have implemented the UNCITRAL Model Law in their national arbitration law, but also other States that provide for generally similar grounds of annulment. This is explained by the fact that most contemporary legal systems 'all address the same international arbitral process and all generally share the same objectives (of facilitating that process).'[74]

4.4 The UNCITRAL Model Law

The UNCITRAL Model Law on International Commercial Arbitration is one of the most important international instruments in the field of international arbitration.[75] Adopted by the UNCITRAL Commission in 1985, it provides with, as the name suggests, a harmonized and unified 'model' law on international arbitration that States can implement in their national legislation. Together with the New York Convention and the 1976 UNCITRAL Arbitration Rules, it is said that the UNCITRAL Model Law 'significantly contributes to the establishment of a unified legal framework

69 Although there are exceptions, countries implementing the Model Law have generally adopted the same approach. For specific examples please see Born (2014a, b), p. 3387.

70 See arts. 1064 ('Only the legal remedies of setting aside and revocation based on the provisions in this Section shall be open against a final or a partial final arbitral award') and 1064a(3) ('The claim for setting aside an interim award may only be presented together with the claim for setting aside a final or partial final award') of the 2015 Dutch Arbitration Act.

71 Art. 40 of the 2003 Spanish Arbitration Act ('An application to set aside a final award may be made in the terms provided for under this Title.').

72 Born (2014a, b), p. 3385.

73 For a general overview please see Poudret and Besson (2006), pp. 706–713, Born (2014a, b), pp. 3385–3388.

74 Born (2014a, b), p. 3187.

75 By some described even as the 'single most important legislative instrument in the field of international commercial arbitration.' See Born (2014a, b), p. 134.

for the fair and efficient settlement of disputes arising in international commercial relations.'[76]

The UNCITRAL or the United Nations Commission on International Trade Law is a specialized commission of the United Nations that was created by the General Assembly in 1966 'in order to harmonize and unify international trade law.'[77] It has been described by the General Assembly as 'the core legal body within the United Nations systems in the field of international trade law, [with a mandate] to co-ordinate legal activities in this field in order to avoid duplication of effort and to promote efficiency, consistency and coherence in the unification and harmonization of international trade law.'[78]

During its existence, the UNCITRAL has been responsible for globally facilitating unification and harmonization of laws and regulations in different fields of international trade, such as international transport of goods, electronic commerce, insolvency, security interests and also international commercial arbitration and conciliation. The UNCITRAL has undertaken various noteworthy projects in the field of international arbitration, such as the drafting and adoption of the 1976 UNCITRAL Arbitration Rules and the development and adoption of the UNCITRAL Model Law.

At the end of 1970s certain inter-governmental bodies urged the UNCITRAL to 'explore ways to improve the overall framework of international commercial arbitration.'[79] The New York Convention started to gain increasing popularity (especially with the ratification of the United States in 1970) and it was feared that without appropriate steps (such as a new protocol to the New York Convention) national laws would prevent arbitrating parties from arbitrating in accordance with rules that they had chosen.[80] This issue was addressed in a consultative meeting in Paris in 1978 where arbitration experts decided that the most effective way how the UNCITRAL could strengthen the legal framework of international arbitration is by preparing a model law, as opposed to a protocol to the New York Convention or even a new convention.[81] It was believed that a model law (i) could be adopted by States throughout the world, thus leading to the establishment of uniform arbitration procedures; (ii) would achieve universal standards of fairness; (iii) could do away with the discrepancies between antiquated nationals laws and modern international arbitration rules; and (iv) could be also helpful in harmonizing and limiting the grounds for annulment of arbitral awards.[82] The form of a *model law*, as opposed to a protocol or a new convention, was seen as the most appropriate since a model law does not have

---

[76]United Nations General Assembly Resolution 40/72, A/RES/40/72, 11 December 1985. For a general overview of the UNCITRAL please see, e.g. United Nations (2013) A Guide to UNCITRAL Basic facts about the United Nations Commission on International Trade Law. http://www.uncitral.org/pdf/english/texts/general/12-57491-Guide-to-UNCITRAL-e.pdf. Accessed 22 May 2020.

[77]Holtzmann and Neuhaus (2015), p. 4.

[78]Ibid., p. 4 in citing United Nations General Assembly Resolution 40/71, A/RES/40/71, 11 December 1985.

[79]Ibid., p. 9.

[80]Ibid., pp. 9–10.

[81]Ibid., pp. 10–11.

[82]Ibid.

to be approved and ratified by States—it can easily be absorbed into the national arbitration law, thus having an immediate effect.[83]

The process of developing the final text of the UNCITRAL Model Law was rather challenging and time-consuming. A separate Working Group was set up to develop and draft the text of the Model Law. The Working Group met in total five times between 1982 and 1984 and after each two-week session draft texts of articles of the UNCITRAL Model Law were prepared. Each draft text was subsequently reviewed and refined in next sessions and with the final draft of the Working Group completed, the draft text was transmitted for comments to all governments within the United Nations system and also interested international organizations which generally welcomed and approved it. In its final session in 1985, the UNCITRAL reviewed the draft text and succeeded in adopting a final text of the UNCITRAL Model Law at the end of the session.[84]

Since 1985, the UNCITRAL Model Law has been adopted in 83 States in a total of 116 jurisdictions.[85] It has helped shaping the arbitration legislation of even more States. The UNCITRAL Model Law consists of 36 articles that relatively comprehensively deal with various arbitration-related issues that may arise in national courts. In short, the UNCITRAL Model Law contains, inter alia, provisions concerning the recognition and enforcement of arbitration agreements (Articles 7-9), composition of arbitral tribunals (Articles 10-15), jurisdiction of arbitral tribunals and the *kompetenz-kompetenz* principle (Article 16), provisional measures (Article 17), conduct of arbitral proceedings (Articles 18-27), the making of arbitral awards (Articles 28-33), recourse against arbitral awards (Article 34) and recognition and enforcement of arbitral awards (Articles 35-36).

This book's specific focus mandates further analysis of Article 34 UNCITRAL Model Law and the various grounds upon which an arbitral award may be set aside by courts at the seat of arbitration. The following brief overview is not intended as a comprehensive analysis of each and every ground for annulment specified in Article 34 of the UNCITRAL Model Law.[86] A succinct overview of the different annulment grounds will suffice for the present analysis.

---

[83] Ibid.

[84] For a more in-depth overview of the legislative history of the UNCITRAL Model Law see Holtzmann and Neuhaus (2015), pp. 9–15. See also Born (Born 2014a, b), pp. 134–141.

[85] For a list of States adopting the UNCITRAL Model Law see http://www.uncitral.org/uncitral/en/uncitral_texts/arbitration/1985Model_arbitration_status.html. Accessed 21 May 2020.

[86] For a general overview of setting-aside proceedings and the specific grounds for annulment see, e.g. Poudret and Besson (2006), pp. 719–773, Rubino-Sammartano (2014), pp. 1274–1337, Blackaby et al. (2015), pp. 569–604, Savage and Gaillard (1999), pp. 883–1002, Born (2015), pp. 1113–1187.

4.4.1 Article 34 of the UNCITRAL Model Law and Grounds for Annulment

One of the main aims during the development of the UNCITRAL Model Law was to unify the grounds for annulment of arbitral awards. Due to the sensitive nature of the issue, already at the outset of the drafting it was predicted that defining such grounds for annulment would be one of the most difficult tasks to be settled in the model law:

> [I]t will be one of the more delicate and complex problems of the preparation of a model law to strike a balance between the interest of the parties to freely determine the procedure to be followed and the interests of the legal system expected to give recognition and effect thereto. This involves, above all, a precise demarcation of the scope of possible intervention and supervision by courts and, in particular, of the substantive criteria for reviewing and reasons for setting aside an award. It is submitted that the result of this endeavour will have a considerable influence on the success of the whole project.[87]

Indeed, prior the adoption of the UNCITRAL Model Law (and, as seen above, to a much lesser extent also nowadays) there was a great diversity in national arbitration laws as regards the types of recourse available against an arbitral award.[88] In addition to the substantive aspect of the matter, there was also disparity in national arbitration laws regarding certain procedural aspects of judicial review, such as form, time-limits, competent authority entrusted with the matter etc.[89] The main aim of the UNCITRAL Model Law was therefore to reconcile both the substantive aspect of judicial review, i.e. the specific grounds upon which an arbitral award could be set aside, and also the above-mentioned procedural issues.

Already at the beginning of the drafting process of the UNCITRAL Model Law it was suggested that the grounds for setting aside of an arbitral award in the UNCITRAL Model Law be aligned with the grounds for refusal of recognition and enforcement of foreign arbitral awards in the New York Convention:

---

[87]Report of the Secretary-General: possible features of a model law on international commercial arbitration, A/CN.9/207, para. 21, 14 May 1981.

[88]Ibid. See also the UNCITRAL Model Law, Explanatory note, para. 44 ('The disparity found in national laws as regards the types of recourse against an arbitral award available to the parties presents a major difficulty in harmonizing international arbitration legislation. Some outdated laws on arbitration, by establishing parallel regimes for recourse against arbitral awards or against court decisions, provide various types of recourse, various (and often long) time periods for exercising the recourse, and extensive lists of grounds on which recourse may be based.').

[89]Report of the Secretary-General: possible features of a model law on international commercial arbitration, A/CN.9/207, para. 108, 14 May 1981 ('To start with the minor problem, i.e. the procedure, there is a great variety in national laws of different claims for 'attacking' an award, not only for setting aside or, sometimes treated separately, annulment of the award but also to other aims, e.g. suspension or reinstitution. The disparities extend to procedural particulars such as form, time-limits, and competent authority. For the sake of uniformity which would facilitate international practice as regards the post-award stage, an attempt should be made to establish commonly acceptable procedures, in particular, to provide for only one type of application and proceedings, probably to be called 'setting aside procedures').

> Ideally, one should aim at a list [...] that would contain only those reasons on which recognition and enforcement may be refused under the 1958 New York Convention, i.e. article V (1), (a)-(d) and (2) [...] It would help to prevent that an international award falls victim to local particularities of law although the case at hand bears no substantive connexion with that respective State.[90]

The proposal was generally welcomed by the Working Group. Although due to the importance of the issue, the Working Group during its meetings considered also numerous other possible grounds, each time 'the conclusion to adopt the New York Convention grounds, with some relatively minor modifications, was reaffirmed.'[91] Moreover, it was also generally agreed at the outset of negotiations that the grounds for annulment in the UNCITRAL Model Law must be exhaustive and that judicial recourse against an arbitral award by means of setting-aside proceedings will be the single and exclusive method of reviewing arbitral awards.[92]

Below is a very concise overview of the annulment grounds as provided in Article 34(2) of the UNCITRAL Model Law and available in numerous jurisdictions.

4.4.1.1 Incapacity of a Party or Invalidity of an Arbitration Agreement

The very first ground for annulment of an arbitral award recognized under the UNCITRAL Model Law and virtually under most national arbitration laws[93] is the incapacity of a party to conclude an arbitration agreement or the invalidity of an arbitration agreement.[94] Article 34(2)(a)(i) of the UNCITRAL Model Law provides that an arbitral award may be set aside by a court if the party making the application furnishes proof that:

> [A] party to the arbitration agreement [...] was under some incapacity; or the said agreement is not valid under the law to which the parties have subjected it or, failing any indication thereon, under the law of this State.[95]

---

[90] Ibid., para. 110.

[91] For a detailed overview of the negotiation process and the different other possibilities discussed at the meetings of the Working Group, please see Holtzmann and Neuhaus (2015), pp. 911–1006.

[92] Ibid., pp. 911–913.

[93] See, e.g. sec. 611(2)(1) of the 2013 Austrian Arbitration Act; art. 1717(3)(a)(i) of the BCCP; sec. 37(2)(1)(a) of the 2005 Danish Arbitration Act; art. 1065(1) of the 2015 Dutch Arbitration Act; art. 751(1)(i) and (ii) of the Estonian Code of Civil Procedure; art. 50(3)(i) of the 2012 Lithuanian Law on Commercial Arbitration; art. 43(1)(a) of the 2004 Norwegian Arbitration Act; sec. 34(1) of the SAA; art. 40(2)(1)(a) of the Slovenian Law on Arbitration; sec. 1059(2)(1)(a) of the ZPO and many others.

[94] For a detailed overview of this specific ground for annulment (and also for refusal of recognition and enforcement of a foreign arbitral award under the New York Convention) see, e.g. Born (2014a, b), pp. 3188, Van den Berg (1981), pp. 275–296, Nacimiento (2010). See also, e.g. United Nations (2012) UNCITRAL 2012 Digest of Case Law of the Model Law on International Commercial Arbitration, pp. 142–144. http://www.uncitral.org/pdf/english/clout/MAL-digest-2012-e.pdf. Accessed 22 May 2020. Generally on consent in international arbitration see Steingruber (2012).

[95] Since the UNCITRAL Model Law and its grounds for annulling an arbitral award were inspired by the New York Convention, a similar provision can be found in art. V(1)(a) of the New York

Annulment of an arbitral award based on incapacity of parties or invalidity of the underlying arbitration agreement is self-evident—it reflects the most fundamental postulate of international arbitration, i.e. a principle that the existence of arbitration depends on the consent of parties and a valid arbitration agreement, without which there is no basis for arbitration proceedings and the resulting arbitral award.[96] The burden of proof of showing that the other party lacked capacity to conclude the arbitration agreement or that there is no valid arbitration agreement at all lies on the party seeking the annulment.

The annulment ground under Article 34(2)(a)(i) of the UNCITRAL Model Law comprises two separate grounds, i.e. that of the incapacity of a party to the arbitration agreement and the invalidity of an arbitration agreement. As regards the former, it is generally accepted in most national arbitration laws that a party to an arbitration agreement must have legal capacity to conclude the arbitration agreement, which, as held by one court, must be assessed at the moment when parties conclude the arbitration agreement.[97] Concerning the latter, one must first keep in mind that the arbitration agreement is considered to be separate from the underlying contract (the so-called separability presumption or the principle of separability). Therefore, in order for this ground for annulment of an arbitral award to be applicable one must prove that the arbitration agreement (as opposed to the underlying contract) was invalid. The invalidity, in turn, comprises both formal validity (e.g. non-fulfilment of certain form requirements, such as the arbitration agreement being in writing[98]) and substantive validity of arbitration agreements (e.g. the so-called pathological arbitration clauses).[99]

Convention ('Recognition and enforcement of the award may be refused, at the request of the party against whom it is invoked, only if that party furnishes to the competent authority where the recognition and enforcement is sought, proof that: (a) The parties to the agreement referred to in article II were, under the law applicable to them, under some incapacity, or the said agreement is not valid under the law to which the parties have subjected it or, failing any indication thereon, under the law of the country where the award was made.').

[96] Born (2014a, b), p. 3188.

[97] United Nations (2012) UNCITRAL 2012 Digest of Case Law of the Model Law on International Commercial Arbitration, p. 142. http://www.uncitral.org/pdf/english/clout/MAL-digest-2012-e.pdf. Accessed 22 May 2020 in referring to *SDV. Transami Ltd. v. Agrimag Limited* et al., Kampala High Court, Commercial Division, Uganda, 19 June 2008, HCT-00-CC-AB-0002-2006.). See also Cordero-Moss (2010), Born (2014a, b), pp. 3219–3220, Van den Berg (1981), pp. 275–282.

[98] See, e.g. art. II of the New York Convention. See also, e.g. sec. 33(3) of the SAA ('An award is invalid: (3) if the award does not fulfil the requirements with regard to the written form and signature [...]').

[99] It is generally accepted that the substantive validity of an arbitration agreement should be assessed according to internationally recognized and accepted neutral contract law principles, as opposed to national discriminatory standards that impose stricter conditions. These internationally accepted general contract law standards can be found, e.g. in art. II(3) New York Convention ('[...] the said agreement is null and void, inoperative or incapable of being performed.'). See also United Nations (2012) UNCITRAL 2012 Digest of Case Law of the Model Law on International Commercial Arbitration, pp. 142–143. http://www.uncitral.org/pdf/english/clout/MAL-digest-2012-e.pdf. Accessed 22 May 2020.

4.4.1.2 Violation of Due Process

The second ground for annulment of an arbitral award under the UNCITRAL Model Law is violation of certain due process principles.[100] Article 34(2)(a)(ii) of the UNCITRAL Model Law provides that an arbitral award may be set aside if:

> [T]he party making the application was not given proper notice of the appointment of an arbitrator or of the arbitral proceedings or was otherwise unable to present his case.[101]

By concluding an arbitration agreement and thus subjecting themselves to a private dispute settlement mechanism parties have no intention to renounce the application of certain fundamental procedural rights.[102] The fact that arbitration proceedings should conform to particular due process standards and that both parties should be given an equal opportunity to present their case is recognized both in the UNCITRAL Model Law[103] and many national arbitration laws.[104] It is generally accepted that due process rights include, inter alia, such rights as the equality of the parties, the right to be heard, the right to fair and adversarial proceedings, non-arbitrary procedures and other fundamental procedural guarantees that must be observed in a fair and

---

[100] For a detailed overview of this specific ground for annulment (and also for refusal of recognition and enforcement of a foreign arbitral award under the New York Convention) please see, e.g. Born (2014a, b), pp. 3222–3260, Van den Berg (1981), pp. 296–311.

[101] Similarly to the first ground for annulment, also this ground is modelled closely on art. V(i)(b) of the New York Convention ('[...] the party against whom the award is invoked was not given proper notice of the appointment of the arbitrator or of the arbitration proceedings or was otherwise unable to present his case.'). Moreover, annulment of an arbitral award based on certain violations of due process is provided also in many national arbitration laws. See, e.g. sec. 611(2)(2) of the 2013 Austrian Arbitration Act; art. 1717(3)(a)(ii) of the BCCP; sec. 37(2)(1)(b) of the 2005 Danish Arbitration Act; art. 36(2)(1)(c) of the 2001 Croatian Law on Arbitration; art. 1520(4) of the FCCP; art. 751(1)(iii) of the Estonian Code of Civil Procedure; art. 50(3)(ii) of the 2012 Lithuanian Law on Commercial Arbitration; art. 43(1)(b) of the 2004 Norwegian Arbitration Act; art. 41(1)(b) of the 2003 Spanish Arbitration Act; art. 40(2)(1)(b) of the Slovenian Law on Arbitration; sec. 1059(2)(1)(b) of the ZPO and many others.

[102] See, e.g. Briner and Von Schlabrendorff (2001), pp. 94–96, Wedam-Lukic (1998), p. 517.

[103] Art. 18 of the UNCITRAL Model Law ('The parties shall be treated with equality and each party shall be given a full opportunity of presenting his case.'). See also art. 24(2) of the UNCITRAL Model Law ('The parties shall be given sufficient advance notice of any hearing and of any meeting of the arbitral tribunal for the purposes of inspection of goods, other property or documents.').

[104] See, e.g. art. 182 of the PILA ('[...] the arbitral tribunal shall ensure equal treatment of the parties and the right of both parties to be heard in adversarial proceedings.'); art. 1510 of the FCCP ('[...] the arbitral tribunal shall ensure that the parties are treated equally and shall uphold the principle of due process.'); art. 1036(2) of the 2015 Dutch Arbitration Act; sec. 18 of the 2005 Danish Arbitration Act ('The parties shall be treated with equality and each party shall be given a full opportunity of presenting his or her case.'); art. 1699 of the BCCP ('Notwithstanding any agreement to the contrary, the parties shall be treated with equality and each party shall be given a full opportunity of presenting his case, pleas in law and arguments in conformity with the principle of adversarial proceedings. The arbitral tribunal shall ensure that this requirement as well as the principle of fairness of the debates are respected.') and many other national arbitration laws. Importantly, such principles are also stipulated in the 2015 Latvian Arbitration Law. See arts. 19 and 20 of the 2015 Latvian Arbitration Law.

equitable procedure. These procedural safeguards generally apply to all stages and aspects of arbitration proceedings, such as the appointment of arbitrators, submission of evidence, opportunities to respond to the submissions of the other party etc.[105] Below is a brief overview of particular aspects of arbitral procedure in cases of which there would exist a possibility to annul the arbitral award on the basis of violation of due process.

For example, this would possibly happen if one party is denied a possibility by the arbitral tribunal to submit evidence or otherwise present its case (violation of the principle of equality of arms). Similarly, if a party is not provided with a notice of hearings or other procedural steps of the proceedings or the arbitral tribunal refuses to hold a hearing, this would possibly lead to the annulment of an arbitral award. Other potential grounds for annulment on the basis of violation of due process include, inter alia, improper service of documents, last-minute introduction of new claims without giving the other party sufficient time to respond, private fact-finding by arbitrators outside the record in the arbitration proceedings, *ex parte* communication between arbitrators and parties (or their counsel) etc.[106]

In addition, a successful challenge on the basis of violations of due process requires that the violation is material and substantial as opposed to trivial violations and mere mistakes by the arbitral tribunal. Some courts even require that 'alleged violation of the ability to present one's case have an effect on the content of the award to constitute a valid ground for setting aside an arbitral award.'[107] On the opposite, it is sometimes said that a violation of the right to be heard results in an automatic annulment of an arbitral award without the need of showing that the said violation had a causal connection to the arbitral tribunal's award.[108] The inability to object to violations of due process in case the application of setting-aside proceedings is contractually excluded or in case where there are no setting-aside proceedings available in the national arbitration law at all, is one of the greater concerns when arbitration is looked at from the perspective of the ECHR, especially the dichotomy between *waivable* and *non-waivable* Article 6(1) of the ECHR rights.

4.4.1.3 Excess of Authority

Article 34(2)(a)(iii) of the UNCITRAL Model Law further stipulates that an arbitral award may be set aside by a court at the seat of arbitration if:

---

[105] Born (2014a, b), p. 3225.

[106] See, e.g. United Nations (2012) UNCITRAL 2012 Digest of Case Law of the Model Law on International Commercial Arbitration, pp. 145–151. http://www.uncitral.org/pdf/english/clout/MAL-digest-2012-e.pdf. Accessed 22 May 2020. See also Born (2014a, b), pp. 3233–3255.

[107] United Nations (2012) UNCITRAL 2012 Digest of Case Law of the Model Law on International Commercial Arbitration, p. 146. http://www.uncitral.org/pdf/english/clout/MAL-digest-2012-e.pdf. Accessed 22 May 2020.

[108] Born (2014a, b), pp. 3233–3255, in referring to the Swiss Federal Tribunal's ruling of 31 January 2012, DFT 4A_360/2011.

> [T]he award deals with a dispute not contemplated by or not falling within the terms of the submission to arbitration, or contains decisions on matters beyond the scope of the submission to arbitration, provided that, if the decisions on matters submitted to arbitration can be separated from those not so submitted, only that part of the award which contains decisions on matters not submitted to arbitration may be set aside.[109]

A largely similar ground, though for refusing recognition and enforcement of a foreign arbitral award, is found in Article V(1)(c) of the New York Convention[110] and again—many national arbitration laws permitting the setting aside of arbitral awards on the basis of arbitral tribunal's excess of authority.[111]

Annulment claims relating to the excess of authority by the arbitral tribunal generally relate to claims of either *ultra petita* or *infra petita*. The former would cover situations in which an arbitral tribunal ruled on issues outside the parties' scope of submission or beyond the scope of arbitral tribunal's mandate. For example, a Spanish court held that an arbitral tribunal exceeded its mandate where it awarded interest on sums in arrears even though it was not claimed by the parties.[112] The latter, on the other hand, would cover situations whereby an arbitral tribunal failed to rule on certain issues submitted to them by the parties.[113] Other situations that could possibly raise questions of excess of authority include, e.g. cases where arbitral tribunal disproportionately exceeds time limit for rendering an arbitral award, where arbitral tribunal disregard parties' contract or the applicable law thereto or reclassifies issues submitted to it etc.[114]

---

[109] For a detailed overview of this specific ground for annulment (and also for refusal of recognition and enforcement of a foreign arbitral award under the New York Convention) see, e.g. Born (2014a, b), pp. 3287–3309, Van den Berg (1981), pp. 311–322.

[110] Art. V(1)(c) of the New York Convention ('[...] The award deals with a difference not contemplated by or not falling within the terms of the submission to arbitration, or it contains decisions on matters beyond the scope of the submission to arbitration, provided that, if the decisions on matters submitted to arbitration can be separated from those not so submitted, that part of the award which contains decisions on matters submitted to arbitration may be recognized and enforced.').

[111] See, e.g. sec. 611(2)(3) of the 2013 Austrian Arbitration Act; art. 1717(3)(a)(iii) of the BCCP; sec. 37(2)(1)(c) of the 2005 Danish Arbitration Act, sec. 41(1)(1) of the 1999 Finnish Arbitration Act; art. 1520(3) of the FCCP; art. 50(3)(iii) of the 2012 Lithuanian Law on Commercial Arbitration; art. 26(3) of the Organization for the Harmonization of Business Law in Africa (OHADA) Uniform Act on Arbitration; art. 41(1)(c) of the 2003 Spanish Arbitration Act; sec. 1059(2)(1)(c) of the ZPO; art. 190(2)(c) of the PILA and many others.

[112] *Jaral Decoración, S.L v. Peñasco Rodilla*, SL, Madrid Court of Appeal, Spain, 2 February 2007, case No. 94/2007—7/2005 (reported in United Nations (2012) UNCITRAL 2012 Digest of Case Law of the Model Law on International Commercial Arbitration, p. 152. http://www.uncitral.org/pdf/english/clout/MAL-digest-2012-e.pdf. Accessed 22 May 2020). See also Born (2014a, b), pp. 3289–3293.

[113] Generally on the discussion whether the UNCITRAL Model Law allows for *infra petita* annulment claims see Born (2014a, b), pp. 3293–3294.

[114] See United Nations (2012) UNCITRAL 2012 Digest of Case Law of the Model Law on International Commercial Arbitration, pp. 151–154. http://www.uncitral.org/pdf/english/clout/MAL-digest-2012-e.pdf. Accessed 22 May 2020.

4.4.1.4 Irregularities in the Arbitral Procedure

Article 34(2)(a)(iv) of the UNCITRAL Model Law provides that an arbitral award may be set aside at the seat of arbitration on the basis that:

> [T]he composition of the arbitral tribunal or the arbitral procedure was not in accordance with the agreement of the parties, unless such agreement was in conflict with a provision of this Law from which the parties cannot derogate, or, failing such agreement, was not in accordance with this Law.[115]

This ground for annulment can be divided into four parts—either (i) the composition of the arbitral tribunal or (ii) the arbitral procedure was not in accordance with the arbitration agreement; or (iii) the composition of the arbitral tribunal or (iv) the arbitral procedure was not in accordance with the applicable procedural law at the seat of arbitration.[116]

On the one hand, as regards the composition of the arbitral tribunal, arbitrating parties have the autonomy to stipulate in their arbitration agreement any preconditions they deem necessary for a valid constitution of a tribunal. These include, inter alia, the number of arbitrators, any professional qualifications, language, nationality, form of decision (e.g. only unanimity as opposed to mere majority) etc. A failure to obey the specific conditions stipulated by the arbitrating parties may lead to an annulment of an arbitral award due to irregular composition of the arbitral tribunal. In absence of any agreement by the parties as to the composition of the arbitral tribunal, an arbitral award may also be set aside if the composition did not conform with any applicable national default or mandatory rules on arbitral procedure.

The second limb of the present ground for annulment of an arbitral award relates to possible irregularities in the arbitral procedure as agreed either by the arbitrating parties or stipulated in the applicable national arbitration law. Thus, for example, arbitrating parties could agree on various procedural issues in their arbitration agreement (e.g. concerning disclosure, witness hearings, time limits for submissions and the award etc.). In case the arbitral tribunal failed to adhere to any of the procedural requirements, there would be a solid basis for arguing in favour of the annulment of the arbitral award. Moreover, certain procedural matters could be also imposed by the applicable national law, e.g. that the arbitral award must be reasoned.[117] Failure

---

[115] See also art. V(1)(d) of the New York Convention ('[...] The composition of the arbitral authority or the arbitral procedure was not in accordance with the agreement of the parties, or, failing such agreement, was not in accordance with the law of the country where the arbitration took place.'). Similar ground for annulment of an arbitral award can be found in many national arbitration laws. See, e.g. sec. 34(4) and (6) of the SAA; art. 34(2)(1)(d) of the Ukrainian Law on Arbitration; art. 1206(1)(4) of the Polish Code of Civil Procedure; art. 50(3)(iv) of the 2012 Lithuanian Law on Commercial Arbitration; sec. 1059(2)(d) of the ZPO; art. 37(2)(1)(d) of the 2005 Danish Arbitration Act; art. 1717(3)(a)(v) of the BCCP and many others.

[116] For a detailed overview of this specific ground for annulment (and also for refusal of recognition and enforcement of a foreign arbitral award under the New York Convention) please see, e.g. Born (2014a, b), pp. 3260–3376, Van den Berg (1981), pp. 322–331.

[117] Some national arbitration laws even provide for a specific ground for annulment in case of ill-reasoned arbitral award. See, e.g. art. 52(1)(e) of the 2010 Irish Arbitration Act. See also art. 26(6)

to satisfy such requirements may equally result in the annulment of an arbitral award by courts at the seat of arbitration on this specific ground.

4.4.1.5 Arbitrability

All of the above introduced grounds for annulment under Article 34 of the UNCITRAL Model Law must be raised by either of parties to the arbitration proceedings. Similarly, the party seeking annulment of an arbitral award on the basis of any of the first four grounds for annulment under Article 34(2) of the UNCITRAL Model Law bears also the burden of proof.[118] This is, however, different with the last two annulment grounds under Article 34(2) of the UNCITRAL Model Law, i.e. those of arbitrability and public policy that can be raised by courts at the seat of arbitration *ex officio*, i.e. on their own motion.[119]

Article 34(2)(b)(i) of the UNCITRAL Model Law provides that an arbitral award may additionally be set aside at the seat of arbitration if:

> [T]he subject-matter of the dispute is not capable of settlement by arbitration under the law of this State.

As with the previously introduced grounds for annulment in Article 34(2)(a) of the UNCITRAL Model Law, also the ground of non-arbitrability of a dispute is modelled on Article V(2)(a) of the New York Convention[120] and finds its counterparts in many national arbitration laws.[121]

The doctrine of arbitrability (or non-arbitrability) rests on the notion that certain categories of disputes are, as put by the New York Convention—'not capable of settlement by arbitration'.[122] This is due to the fact that 'some matters so pervasively involve 'public' rights and concerns, or interests of third parties, which are the subjects of uniquely governmental authority, that agreements to resolve such

---

of the Organization for the Harmonization of Business Law in Africa (OHADA) Uniform Act on Arbitration.

118 The UNCITRAL Model Law, Explanatory note, para. 46.

119 Ibid.

120 Art. V(2)(a) of the New York Convention ('Recognition and enforcement of an arbitral award may also be refused if the competent authority in the country where recognition and enforcement is sought finds that: (a) The subject matter of the difference is not capable of settlement by arbitration under the law of that country.').

121 See, e.g. sec. 611(2)(7) of the 2013 Austrian Arbitration Act; art. 1717(3)(b)(i) of the BCCP; art. 36(2)(2)(a) of the Croatian Law on Arbitration; sec. 37(2)(2)(a) of the 2005 Danish Arbitration Act; art. 751(2)(1) of the Estonian Code of Civil Procedure; art. 50(3)(v) of the 2012 Lithuanian Law on Commercial Arbitration; sec. 43(2)(a) of the 2004 Norwegian Arbitration Act; art. 46(3)(b)(i) of the Portuguese Arbitration Law; art. 41(1)(e) of the 2003 Spanish Arbitration Act; sec. 1059(2)(2)(a) of the ZPO and many others.

122 See art. II of the New York Convention. Generally on the doctrine of non-arbitrability in international arbitration please see, e.g. Born (2014a, b), pp. 943–1045, Mistelis and Brekoulakis (2009), Poudret and Besson (2006), pp. 326–366.

disputes by *private* arbitration should not be given effect.'[123] The notion of arbitrability therefore strongly concerns State sovereignty and its authority to limit categories of disputes that can be solved by means of private dispute settlement, such as arbitration. Generally, all nations impose some limits on the arbitrability of disputes, however, the particular types of claims that are non-arbitrable differ from State to State.[124] These may involve claims relating, inter alia, to competition law, intellectual property, employment and consumer law, criminal law, tax law, bankruptcy and insolvency etc.

In relation to the UNCITRAL Model Law, during negotiations there were heated debates concerning the inclusion of the non-arbitrability ground as a ground for annulment in the UNCITRAL Model Law. As seen, such a ground is present in the New York Convention, however, 'unlike in the context of recognition and enforcement, application of the forum's law for [the purpose of arbitrability] in a setting aside procedure gave that law 'global effect', since an award that had been set aside could not be enforced.'[125] Although this view attracted considerable support during negotiations,[126] the non-arbitrability ground of annulment in Article 34(2) of the UNCITRAL Model Law was nevertheless retained.

4.4.1.6 Public Policy

Lastly, Article 34(2)(b)(ii) of the UNCITRAL Model Law provides that an arbitral award may be set aside:

> [I]f the award is in conflict with the public policy of this State.[127]

As with the previous grounds for annulment, also this, rather exceptional public policy ground can be found in the New York Convention[128] and many national arbitration laws.[129] What in essence the public policy annulment ground entails is an annulment of an arbitral award on the basis of a violation of the most fundamental

---

[123] Born (2014a, b), p. 945.

[124] Born (2001), p. 245.

[125] Holtzmann and Neuhaus (2015), p. 918.

[126] Ibid., pp. 973–9 on the different positions of members of the Working Group and observers of the negotiations of the UNCITRAL Model Law.

[127] Generally on public policy as a ground for either annulment or refusal of recognition and enforcement of arbitral awards please see, e.g. Maurer (2013), Born (2014a, b), pp. 3312–339 and 3646–3694.

[128] Art. V(2)(b) of the New York Convention ('Recognition and enforcement of an arbitral award may also be refused if the competent authority in the country where recognition and enforcement is sought finds that: (b) The recognition or enforcement of the award would be contrary to the public policy of that country.').

[129] See, e.g. art. 34(2)(2)(b) of the 1994 Ukrainian Law on Arbitration; art. 190(2)(e) of the PILA; sec. 33(2) of the SAA; art. 40(1)(f) of the 2003 Spanish Arbitration Act; art. 40(2)(2)(b) of the Slovenian Law on Arbitration; art. 1206((2)(2) of the Polish Code of Civil Procedure; art. 43(2)(b) of the 2004 Norwegian Arbitration Act; art. 50(3)(6) of the 2012 Lithuanian Law on Commercial Arbitration; sec 55(2)(b) of the 1994 Hungarian Law on Arbitration; sec. 1059(2)(2)(b) of the ZPO;

public policies or mandatory laws of the state at the seat of arbitration.[130] Similarly to non-arbitrability, courts at the seat of arbitration may invoke the ground of public policy *ex officio*. Moreover, the public policy ground in annulment actions has an exceptional and limited nature and is applied very restrictively by national courts.[131]

Annulment of an arbitral award on the basis of the public policy ground would have to entail a very gross violation of the particular State's most fundamental and basic principles.[132] The standard of review is very high and only in exceptional cases an arbitral award will be annulled on grounds of public policy. Such cases include, inter alia, violations of fundamental principles of law, morality or justice, violations of the most basic principles of fairness as established by a particular State, incompatibility of an arbitral award with the very foundations of public and economic life and many others.[133] Generally, each claim that an arbitral award violates the public policy will differ from State to State pursuant to their particular notions of public policy.[134]

Public policy has been said to include both a substantive and also a procedural dimension. This, as explained by the UNCITRAL during negotiations of the UNCITRAL Model Law, is also true with regard to the interpretation of the notion of public policy under Article 34(2)(b)(ii) of the UNCITRAL Model Law.[135] A violation of a State's substantive public policy would include, e.g. as in the case of Switzerland, inter alia, 'the sanctity of contracts, compliance with the rules of good faith, the prohibition of abuse of rights, the prohibition of discriminatory and confiscatory measures,

sec. 40(1)(2) of the 1999 Finnish Arbitration Act; Art. 751(2)(2) of the Estonian Code of Civil Procedure; sec. 68(2)(g) of the 1996 English Arbitration Act; art. 1065(1)(e) of the 2015 Dutch Arbitration Act; art. 37(2)(2)(b) of the 205 Danish Arbitration Act; art. 1717(3)(b)(ii) of the BCCP and many other national arbitration laws.

[130] See, e.g. Born (2014a, b), p. 3312.

[131] United Nations (2012) UNCITRAL 2012 Digest of Case Law of the Model Law on International Commercial Arbitration, pp. 159–160. http://www.uncitral.org/pdf/english/clout/MAL-digest-2012-e.pdf. Accessed 22 May 2020.

[132] See, e.g. the Swiss Federal Tribunal's decision in case No. 4A_304/2013, 3 March 2014, at 5.1.1. ('An award is incompatible with public policy if it disregards the essential and broadly acknowledged values which, according to prevailing views in Switzerland, should be constitute the basis of any legal order [...]'). Similar definitions of the public policy notion have been established by many other courts. See, e.g. *SA Thales Air Defence v. GIE Euromissile and SA EADS France, Paris Cour d'appel*, 18 November 2004, Rev. arb. 751 (2005).

[133] See, e.g. United Nations (2012) UNCITRAL 2012 Digest of Case Law of the Model Law on International Commercial Arbitration, p.160. http://www.uncitral.org/pdf/english/clout/MAL-digest-2012-e.pdf. Accessed 22 May 2020.

[134] Ibid., pp. 160–161. For particular examples of what States consider as violations of their public policy see, e.g. Born (2014a, b), pp. 3321–3334.

[135] See Report of the UNCITRAL Commission, A/40/17, 21 August 1985, at 297 ('It was understood that the term 'public policy', which was used in the New York Convention and many other treaties, covered fundamental principles of law and justice in substantive as well as procedural respects. Thus, instances such as corruption, bribery or fraud and similar serious cases would constitute a ground for setting aside. It was noted, in that connection, that the wording 'the award is in conflict with the public policy of this State' was not to be interpreted as excluding instances or events relating to the manner in which an award was arrived at.').

as well as the protection of incapable persons.'[136] Violation of a procedural public policy, on the other hand, to some extent overlaps with the ground for annulment in Article 34(2)(a)(ii) of the UNCITRAL Model Law relating to violation of due process and similarly relates to fundamental violations of, e.g. the right to be heard and the right to equal treatment. It is suggested that only the most serious violations of fundamental procedural principles will lead to an annulment of an arbitral award on the basis of procedural public policy.[137]

European Public Policy

Additionally, the author would like to briefly stress the importance of European public policy that in the wake of recent jurisprudence of the Court of Justice of the European Union ('CJEU') has attracted considerable attention to, inter alia, also the discussion of court control over arbitration proceedings, especially when it comes to overseeing and guaranteeing correct and full application of EU law. Arguments in support of continuous availability of setting aside proceedings under national law (and limited possibility of exclusion thereof) gain additional weight when the necessity of setting-aside proceedings in national arbitration law is considered from the standpoint of EU public policy and EU law in general.

Interaction between EU law and international commercial arbitration has been a hot topic ever since the well-known *Eco Swiss* case[138] and even before that.[139] The subject-matter has already been extensively dealt with.[140] Nevertheless, certain recent developments pertaining to the relationship between arbitration and EU law, have sparked a new discussion on, inter alia, also the role of national courts in reviewing arbitral awards—a discussion that provides additional food for thought when looking

[136]The Swiss Federal Tribunal's decision in case No. 4A_304/2013, 3 March 2014, at 5.1.1. ('An award is contrary to substantive public policy when it violates some fundamental principles of the law applicable to the merits to such an extent as it is no longer consistent with the notions of justice and system of values; among such principles are, in particular, the sanctity of contracts, compliance with the rules of good faith, the prohibition of abuse of rights, the prohibition of discriminatory and confiscatory measures, as well as the protection of incapable persons.').

[137]For example, German courts have decided that 'a violation of a party's right to be heard could constitute a violation of procedural public policy, but only if there was a causal link between such violation of the right to be heard and the content of the award.' See United Nations (2012) UNCITRAL 2012 Digest of Case Law of the Model Law on International Commercial Arbitration, p. 160 in referring to a handful of decisions by German courts). http://www.uncitral.org/pdf/english/clout/MAL-digest-2012-e.pdf. Accessed 22 May 2020. Some States specifically include procedural public policy as a ground for setting aside an arbitral award. See, e.g. art. 628(2)(5) of the Liechtenstein Code of Civil Procedure ('An arbitral award shall be set aside if [...] the arbitral procedure was not carried out in accordance with the fundamentals of the Liechtenstein legal system (*ordre public*).').

[138]Case C-126/97 *Eco Swiss China Time Ltd v Benetton International BV*, CJEU, 1 June 1999.

[139]See, e.g. Case C-393/92 *Gemeente Almelo and Others v Energiebedrijf IJsselmij NV*, CJEU, 27 April 1994; Case C-102/81 *Nordsee Deutsche Hochseefischerei GmbH v Reederei Mond Hochseefischerei Nordstern AG & Co. KG and Reederei Friedrich Busse Hochseefischerei Nordstern AG & Co. KG,* CJEU, 23 March 1982.

[140]See, among many others, e.g. Bermann (2012), Von Mehren (2003), Van der Haegen (2009), Liebscher (2000). See generally also Ferrari (2017), Bermann (2011).

at the issue of necessity and importance of availability of setting-aside proceedings under national (especially in the EU) arbitration law.

It is, of course, the ruling of the CJEU in the *Achmea* case[141] that has recently attracted considerable attention and marked a new beginning for the relationship between investor-state dispute settlement ('ISDS') mechanisms and EU law. Considering its importance, the *Achmea* decision and its consequences have been considerably reflected by many.[142] That being the case, the present brief insight will focus only on those aspects of the *Achmea* case (and also other CJEU cases preceding the *Achmea* decision) that have broader relevance for judicial control over arbitration as a guarantee for the correct and full application of EU law.

In brief, without in detail examining the circumstances of the case,[143] the overarching issue in the *Achmea* case was whether an arbitral tribunal established by two EU Member States by means of a bilateral investment treaty ('BIT') can be regarded as a 'court or tribunal of a Member State' within the meaning of Article 267 Treaty on the Functioning of the European Union ('TFEU') and thus is able to refer questions to the CJEU for a preliminary ruling procedure—the object of which is to secure uniform interpretation of EU law, thereby ensuring its consistency, full affect and autonomy. Contrary to what Advocate-General (AG) Wathelet had previously suggested in his opinion,[144] the CJEU ruled that such an arbitral tribunal cannot be considered as a 'court or tribunal of a Member State' for the purposes of Article 267 of the TFEU and therefore cannot submit references to the CJEU for a preliminary ruling.[145] Even though disputes brought before such an arbitral tribunal might concern the interpretation and application of EU law, in such circumstances as in the *Achmea* case they might be prevented from being resolved in a manner that ensures the full effectiveness of EU law.[146] Consequently, ISDS mechanism contained in a BIT concluded between two EU Member States was considered as incompatible with EU law due to it having an adverse effect on its autonomy.[147]

The *Achmea* decision suggests for ISDS what previous decisions by the CJEU had already suggested and confirmed for international commercial arbitration—EU Member States must provide in their national law a mechanism through which the effectiveness and correct application of EU law can be guaranteed. The CJEU has made it clear in numerous cases pertaining to the dichotomy between international

---

[141] Case C-284/16 *Slowakische Republik (Slovak Republic) v Achmea BV*, CJEU, 6 March 2018.

[142] See, among many others, Pohl (2018), Basedow (2018), Sadowski (2018), Arp (2018).

[143] For an overview of the circumstances of the case see Case C-284/16 *Slowakische Republik (Slovak Republic) v Achmea BV*, CJEU, CJEU, 6 March 2018, paras. 1–22.

[144] Opinion of Advocate-General Wathelet in Case C-284/16 *Slowakische Republik v Achmea BV*, CJEU, 19 September 2017, paras. 126–131.

[145] Case C-284/16 *Slowakische Republik (Slovak Republic) v Achmea BV*, CJEU, 6 March 2018, para. 49.

[146] Ibid., para. 56.

[147] Ibid., paras. 59–60.

commercial arbitration and EU Law, e.g. the *Nordsee*,[148] *Almelo*,[149] *Eco Swiss*[150] and *Mostaza Claro*.[151] This was repeatedly stressed also in the *Achmea* case:

> It is true that, in relation to commercial arbitration, the Court has held that the requirements of efficient arbitration proceedings justify the review of arbitral awards by the courts of the Member States being limited in scope, provided that the fundamental provisions of EU law

---

[148]Case C-102/81 *Nordsee Deutsche Hochseefischerei GmbH v Reederei Mond Hochseefischerei Nordstern AG & Co. KG and Reederei Friedrich Busse Hochseefischerei Nordstern AG & Co. KG*, CJEU, 23 March 1982, paras. 14–15 ("[...] Community law must be observed in its entirety throughout the territory of all the Member States; parties to a contract are not, therefore, free to create exceptions to it. In that context attention must be drawn to the fact that if questions of Community law are raised in an arbitration resorted to by agreement the ordinary courts may be called upon to examine them either in the context of their collaboration with arbitration tribunals, in particular in order to assist them in certain procedural matters or to interpret the law applicable, or in the course of a review of an arbitration award—which may be more or less extensive depending on the circumstances—and which they may be required to effect in case of an appeal or objection, in proceedings for leave to issue execution or by any other method of recourse available under the relevant national legislation. is It is for those national courts and tribunals to ascertain whether it is necessary for them to make a reference to the Court under Article 177 of the Treaty in order to obtain the interpretation or assessment of the validity of provisions of Community law which they may need to apply when exercising such auxiliary or supervisory functions.").

[149]Case C-393/92 *Gemeente Almelo and Others v Energiebedrijf IJsselmij NV*, CJEU, 27 April 1994, para. 23 ("[...] It follows from the principles of the primacy of Community law and of its uniform application, in conjunction with Article 5 of the Treaty, that a court of a Member State to which an appeal against an arbitration award is made pursuant to national law must, even where it gives judgment having regard to fairness, observe the rules of Community law, in particular those relating to competition.").

[150]Case C-126/97 *Eco Swiss China Time Ltd v Benetton International BV*, CJEU, 1 June 1999, para. 32 et seq ("It is to be noted, first of all, that, where questions of Community law are raised in an arbitration resorted to by agreement, the ordinary courts may have to examine those questions, in particular during review of the arbitration award, which may be more or less extensive depending on the circumstances and which they are obliged to carry out in the event of an appeal, for setting aside, for leave to enforce an award or upon any other form of action or review available under the relevant national legislation [...]").

[151]Case C–168/05 *Elisa María Mostaza Claro v Centro Móvil Milenium SL.*, CJEU, 26 October 2006, paras. 34–35 ("[I]t is in the interest of efficient arbitration proceedings that review of arbitration awards should be limited in scope and that annulment of or refusal to recognise an award should be possible only in exceptional circumstances [...] However, the Court has already ruled that, where its domestic rules of procedure require a national court to grant an application for annulment of

> can be examined in the course of that review and, if necessary, be the subject of a reference to the Court for a preliminary ruling [...].[152]

Similarly to the CJEU's conclusion in the *Achmea* case with regard to arbitral tribunals created by two EU Member States through a BIT, it has been generally recognized that arbitral tribunals constituted pursuant to an arbitration agreement are neither courts of EU Member States within the meaning of Article 267 of the TFEU.[153] Advocate-General Wathalet, in arguing against the French *minimalist* approach to judicial review in the well-known *Genentech* case,[154] has aptly summarized EU Member States' obligations under the EU law from the standpoint of the dichotomy between international commercial arbitration and EU law:

> [L]imitations on the scope of the review of international arbitral awards such as those under French law [...] — namely the flagrant nature of the infringement of international public policy and the impossibility of reviewing an international arbitral award on the ground of such an infringement where the question of public policy was raised and debated before the arbitral tribunal — are contrary to the principle of effectiveness of EU law.
>
> Referring to the system for reviewing the compatibility of international arbitral awards with EU law through the public policy reservation, as established by the Court in its judgment in *Eco Swiss* [...], the Court has held that arbitral tribunals 'constituted pursuant to an agreement' are not courts of the Member States within the meaning of Article 267 TFEU. Consequently, they cannot refer questions for a preliminary ruling. It is therefore for the courts of the Member States, within the meaning of Article 267 TFEU, to examine, if necessary by referring a question for a preliminary ruling, the compatibility of (international or domestic) arbitral awards with EU law where an action is brought before them for annulment or enforcement, or where any other form of action or review is sought under the relevant national legislation.
>
> In other words, the system for reviewing the compatibility of international arbitral awards with substantive EU law through the public policy reservation, whether in the context of an action against recognition and enforcement or an action for annulment, shifts responsibility for the review downstream, namely to the courts of the Member States, rather than upstream, to arbitral tribunals.
>
> The task of arbitrators in international commercial arbitration is to interpret and apply the contract binding the parties correctly. In the performance of this task, arbitrators may naturally find it necessary to apply EU law, if it forms part of the law applicable to the contract (lex contractus) or the law applicable to the arbitration (lex arbitri). However, the responsibility for reviewing compliance with European public policy rules lies with the courts of the Member States and not with arbitrators, whether in the context of an action for annulment or proceedings for recognition and enforcement.[155]

---

an arbitration award where such an application is founded on failure to observe national rules of public policy, it must also grant such an application where it is founded on failure to comply with Community rules of this type [...]").

[152] Ibid., para. 54.

[153] Case C-126/97 *Eco Swiss China Time Ltd v Benetton International BV*, CJEU, 1 June 1999, para. 34; Case C-102/81 *Nordsee Deutsche Hochseefischerei GmbH v Reederei Mond Hochseefischerei Nordstern AG & Co. KG and Reederei Friedrich Busse Hochseefischerei Nordstern AG & Co. KG*, CJEU, 23 March 1982, paras. 10–12.

[154] Opinion of Advocate-General Wathelet in Case C-567/14 *Genentech Inc. v Hoechst GmbH, formerly Hoechst AG, Sanofi-Aventis Deutschland GmbH*, CJEU, 17 March 2017.

[155] Ibid., paras. 58–61.

How does the above then, including the implications of the recent *Achmea* ruling, help in shaping this book's more specific focus on the necessity and continuous availability of setting-aside proceedings in national law from the standpoint of the EU law? The CJEU case-law, from *Nordsee* and *Eco-Swiss* to *Genentech* and *Achmea*, is explicit that EU Member States bear ultimate responsibility for ensuring the uniform application of EU law and compliance with European public policy rules.[156] With regard to arbitration, this is done by means of review of arbitral awards:

> carried out in the context of an action to set aside the arbitral award before the courts of the seat of the arbitration or in the context of an objection to a request for recognition and enforcement of the award before the courts of the country in which recognition and enforcement of the award are sought [...][157]

Considering that arbitral tribunals are not viewed as courts of a Member State within the meaning of Article 267 of the TFEU and cannot refer to the CJEU for a preliminary ruling, setting-aside proceedings whereby national courts review arbitral awards and may, if necessary, refer to the CJEU, function as a gatekeeper for the guarantee of the effectiveness and correct application of EU law. If an EU Member State permits voluntarily exclusion of the application of setting-aside proceedings or, as in the case in Latvia (or formerly in Belgium), simply does not provide in its national law for the annulment of arbitral awards, a question arises whether such EU Member States can still be considered as complying with their obligation to ensure the uniform application of EU law and, in particular, compliance with European public policy rules.

When referring to EU Member States' obligations to ensure the full application of EU law, the above referred to case-law of the CJEU, additionally to the remedy of setting-aside proceedings, occasionally refers also to the recognition and enforcement proceedings through which EU Member States may guarantee the full application of EU law. At first sight, the existence of recognition and enforcement proceedings may seem as making the necessity of setting-aside proceedings redundant, at least from the standpoint of guaranteeing the effectiveness of EU law, thus suggesting that the present discussion is superfluous. However, there may be situations where recognition and enforcement of an arbitral award is not required, in particular, when the arbitral tribunal dismisses all claims or renders a declaratory award. One may not rule out that in such cases the fundamental provisions of EU law may be at stake, thus, in case there is no possibility to apply for setting-aside proceedings, leaving parties with no mechanism at the seat of arbitration through which the full effectiveness of EU law may be guaranteed.

The same applies, as stressed by the European Commission in the *Achmea* case, to cases where recognition and enforcement of arbitral awards incompatible with EU

---

[156] See Opinion of Advocate-General Wathelet in Case C-284/16 *Slowakische Republik v Achmea BV*, 19 September 2017, CJEU, para. 241.

[157] Ibid., para. 239. See also Opinion of Advocate-General Wathelet in Case C-567/14 *Genentech Inc. v Hoechst GmbH, formerly Hoechst AG, Sanofi-Aventis Deutschland GmbH*, CJEU, 17 March 2017, para. 60. Solely with regard to setting-aside proceedings see, e.g. Opinion of Advocate-General *Jääskinen* in Case C-352/13 *Cartel Damage Claims (CDC) Hydrogen Peroxide SA v Evonik Degussa GmbH and Others*, CJEU, 11 December 2014, para. 123.

law and issued by a tribunal in an EU Member State may be sought in a third State, as opposed to another EU Member State:

> [R]ecognition and enforcement of an arbitral award that was incompatible with EU law may be sought in a third country, in which cases the courts and tribunals of the European Union would not be involved and the Court of Justice would therefore never be requested to give a preliminary ruling.[158]

For example, if an arbitral tribunal fixes the seat of arbitration in Latvia, the ensuing arbitral award touches upon issues of EU public policy and the recognition and enforcement of such an award is sought in a third country, there is no possibility to challenge such an award's incompatibility with the EU law before a court of an EU Member State that is obliged to fulfil its obligations to effectively observe and guarantee the full effectiveness of EU law. The same is true in cases of exclusion agreements—if the arbitral seat is in an EU Member State and parties exclude the application of setting-aside proceedings, and recognition and enforcement of the ensuing arbitral award is sought in a third country, parties can technically circumvent the application of mandatory EU law provisions, whether it is the law on, e.g. competition, agency or consumer matters. Equally, by permitting the conclusion of exclusion agreements the particular EU Member State circumvents its obligation to guarantee the full effectiveness of EU law.

Similar argument is made by the European Commission in relation to intra-EU BITs which designate the ICSID as the institution acting as Registry in the arbitration:

> The same applies, in the Commission's submission, to the intra-EU BITS which designate the International Centre for Settlement of Investment Disputes (ICSID), established in Washington DC, as the institution acting as Registry in the arbitration. In such a case, the arbitral award would be binding on the parties and could not be subject to any appeal or any other remedy except those provided for in the ICSID Convention. It follows that there would be no legal means that would allow the courts and tribunals of the Member State to review the compatibility of ICSID arbitral award with EU law.[159]

Therefore, it is evident that the existence of setting-aside proceedings, at least when the seat of arbitration is fixed in an EU Member State, is of paramount significance for ensuring the full effectiveness of the rules of the EU, particularly those fundamental principles of EU law that pertain to European public policy. The existence of recognition and enforcement proceedings alone are not sufficient to fully observe EU Member States' obligation in this regard.

4.4.1.7 Other Grounds

In addition to the above-stated grounds for annulment as stipulated in the UNCITRAL Model Law and implemented in many States around the world, there are also States

---

158 Opinion of Advocate-General Wathelet in Case C-284/16 *Slowakische Republik v Achmea BV*, CJEU, 19 September 2017, para. 251.

159 Ibid., para. 252.

that provide for additional annulment grounds, i.e. grounds that have not found their way into the UNCITRAL Model Law.

Some national arbitration laws allow for the possibility to annul an arbitral award due to lack of reasoning in the arbitral award.[160] There are also States that permit the annulment of arbitral awards due to the non-fulfilment of certain formal requirements, such as the award being in writing and signed by all arbitrators.[161] Moreover, some national arbitration laws stipulate that an award may be set aside if it has been obtained by fraud[162] or there is a degree of corruption on the part of a member of the arbitral tribunal.[163] The margin of appreciation that States have in stipulating particular grounds for annulment in their arbitration laws is limitless—arbitral awards may be set aside on whatever grounds a particular State deem serious enough to strip an arbitral award from its binding force.

For example, Section 69 of the 1996 English Arbitration Act gives arbitrating parties possibility to either opt in (by default) or opt out of the appeal of an arbitral award on a question of law. This, in essence, permits arbitrating parties to appeal an arbitral award *stricto* sensu, unless, of course, parties agree to opt out of this possibility pursuant to Section 69(1) of the 1996 English Arbitration Act.[164] Similarly, in the United States, under the U.S. Federal Arbitration Act, it is possible to set aside an arbitral award pursuant to the doctrine of 'manifest disregard of law'.[165]

Another ground for annulment not *expressis verbis* addressed in the UNCITRAL Model Law, but of great importance to present analysis, is the annulment on the basis of violations of independence or impartiality on part of the members of an arbitral tribunal.

The independence or impartiality of the members of an arbitral tribunal is at the heart of effective, fair and just arbitration proceedings. The UNCITRAL Model Law,[166] many national arbitration laws (both those implementing the UNCITRAL

[160] Arts. 43(3)(6) and 42(3) of the Portuguese Arbitration Law; art. 52(1)(e) of the 2010 Irish Arbitration Act; art. 26(6) of the Organization for the Harmonization of Business Law in Africa (OHADA) Uniform Act on Arbitration; arts. 829(5) and 823(2)(3) of the Italian Code of Civil Procedure; art. 1065(d) of the 2015 Dutch Arbitration Act; art. 1717(3)(a)(iv) of the BCCP.

[161] Sec. 33(3) of the SAA ('An award is invalid [...] if the award does not fulfil the requirements with regard to the written form and signature in accordance with section 31, first paragraph.'); sec. 40(1)(4) of the Finnish Arbitration Act ('An award shall be null and void [...] if the arbitral award has not been made in writing or signed by arbitrators.'). See also arts. 43(3)(6) and 42(1) of the Portuguese Arbitration Law; arts. 829(5) and 823(2)(5) and (6) of the Italian Code of Civil Procedure; sec. 68(2)(h) of the 1996 English Arbitration Act; art. 1065(d) of the 2015 Dutch Arbitration Act.

[162] Art. 1206(1)(5) of the Polish Code of Civil Procedure; sec. 68(2)(g) of the 1996 English Arbitration Act.

[163] Art. 52(1)(c) of the 2010 Irish Arbitration Act.

[164] Generally on sec. 69 of the English Arbitration Act and the possibility to appeal an arbitral award on a point of law see, e.g. Dedezade (2006), Born (2014a, b), pp. 3348–3350. On statistics of sec. 69 appeals see Hirst (2018) *Do Arbitration Users Really Value Finality?*. Kluwer Arbitration Blog, 4 June 2018. http://arbitrationblog.kluwerarbitration.com/2018/06/04/arbitration-users-really-value-finality/. Accessed 22 May 2020.

[165] See, e.g. Born (2014a, b), pp. 3341–3348.

[166] See, e.g. art. 12 of the UNCITRAL Model Law.

Model Law[167] and also those that are not considered to be modelled on the basis of the UNCITRAL Model Law[168]), and also institutional arbitration rules[169] contain provisions on arbitrators' independence and impartiality as a necessary requirement that must be adhered to during all stages of arbitration proceedings. Nevertheless, as opposed to some national arbitration laws,[170] the UNCITRAL Model Law does not specify that the lack of independence or impartiality is a ground for annulment of an arbitral award.

The UNCITRAL Model Law and many national arbitration laws provide arbitrating parties with a possibility to challenge and replace a bias arbitrator already during the arbitration proceedings and, in fact, according to the doctrine of collateral estoppel, preclude challenging of an arbitral award on the basis of lack of independence or impartiality if the concerned party failed to raise this issue already during the arbitration proceedings. However, there are also States, such as the United States (and also Latvia) where 'it is not possible to challenge an arbitrator for lack of independence or impartiality during the course of the arbitration, and a party's only avenue for recourse is to preserve an objection and seek to annul the final award.'[171] In cases where national arbitration law does not provide for a possibility to challenge an arbitrator during arbitration proceedings before State courts, nor allows the setting aside of an arbitral award as such or permits the exclusion of setting-aside proceedings, arbitrating parties may be found in a deadlock situation with no possibility to

---

[167] See, e.g. art. 17(1) of the 2003 Spanish Arbitration Act ('An arbitrator shall be and remain independent and impartial during the arbitration. In no case shall he maintain any personal, professional or commercial relationship with any of the parties.'); art. 1174(1) of the Polish Code of Civil Procedure ('A person appointed to serve an arbitrator shall immediately disclose to the parties any circumstances which might raise doubts as to his or her impartiality or independence.'); art. 13 of the Norwegian Arbitration Act ('The arbitrators shall be impartial and independent of the parties, and shall be qualified for such office.'); art. 8(1) of the 2012 Lithuanian Law on Commercial Arbitration ('The arbitral tribunal, permanent arbitral institution and its chairman shall be independent while resolving the issues regulated in this Law.'). See also, e.g. sec. 11 of the Hungarian Law on Arbitration; sec. 1036(1) of the ZPO; sec. 12(1) of the 2005 Danish Arbitration Act and other arbitration laws.

[168] See, e.g. sec. 8 of the SAA ('An arbitrator shall be impartial.'); art. 1456(2) of the FCCP; sec. 9(1) of the Finnish Arbitration Act; secs 1(a) and 33(1) of the 1996 English Arbitration Act; art. 1033 of the 2015 Dutch Arbitration Act.

[169] See, e.g. art. 11(1) of the ICC Arbitration Rules (2017) ('Every arbitrator must be and remain impartial and independent of the parties involved in the arbitration.'); art. 18 of the SCC Arbitration Rules (2017) ('Every arbitrator must be impartial and independent.'); art. 5(3) of the LCIA Arbitration Rules (2014) ('All arbitrators shall be and remain at all times impartial and independent of the parties; and none shall act in the arbitration as advocate for or representative of any party. No arbitrator shall advise any party on the parties' dispute or the outcome of the arbitration.'); art. 24 of the CIETAC Arbitration Rules (2015) ('An arbitrator shall not represent either party, and shall be and remain independent of the parties and treat them equally.'); art. 13(1) of the SIAC Arbitration Rules (2016).

[170] Annulment of an arbitral award on the basis of arbitrator's lack of independence and impartiality is possible, e.g. in England (sec. 68(2)(a) of the 1996 English Arbitration Act); sec. 41(1)(3) of the 1999 Finnish Arbitration Act; art. 12(2) of the Icelandic Act on Contractual Arbitration; art. 829(2) of the Italian Code of Civil Procedure; sec. 34(5) of the SAA.

[171] Born (2014a, b), p. 3286.

challenge and replace biased arbitrators, or eventually set aside a defective arbitral award.

Although lack of independence or impartiality is not explicitly mentioned as a ground for setting aside an arbitral award in the UNCITRAL Model Law, authors have argued that the requirements of independent and impartial tribunal can be impliedly read into the text of other grounds expressly stipulated in Article 34(2) of the UNCITRAL Model Law.[172] For example, it is argued that claims for lack of independence or impartiality can be based on either Article 34(2)(a)(ii) of the UNCITRAL Model Law, arguing that in such cases an arbitrating party is denied an opportunity to present its case, or Article 34(2)(a)(iv) of the UNCITRAL Model Law, arguing that in such circumstances there is irregular composition of an arbitral tribunal. Moreover, a party could invoke Article 34(2)(b)(ii) of the UNCITRAL Model Law and arguments that a lack of independence or impartiality violates procedural public policy.[173] Therefore, it is generally established that despite absence in the UNCITRAL Model Law (and in many States' national arbitration laws) of explicit annulment ground on the basis of lack of independence or impartiality of arbitration, the said quintessential element of any arbitration proceedings is impliedly read into other annulment grounds, thus in practice raising no doubts as to possibility to annul an arbitral award on the basis of lack of arbitral tribunal's independence or impartiality.

4.5 Summary

This Chapter has succinctly introduced the remedy of setting-aside proceedings, including its genesis, the underlying theoretical considerations of judicial controls as such over arbitration and different technicalities pertaining to setting-aside proceedings. It in an equally succinct manner also introduced the various annulment grounds on the basis of which arbitrating parties may challenge arbitral awards at the seat of arbitration.

Although the remedy of setting-aside proceedings is of purely national character, the annulment grounds in most jurisdictions, either based on the UNCITRAL Model Law or not, are largely similar. The above introduced annulment grounds are internationally recognized exclusive means of recourse against an arbitral award in, as seen,

[172] Ibid., pp. 3277–3278 in referring to many national courts and commentators who have concluded the same way. For example, in absence of a specific ground for annulment, the Swiss courts have held that '[s]imilarly to a state judge, an arbitrator must present sufficient guarantees of independence and impartiality. Breaching that rules leads to irregular composition pursuant to Art. 190(2) [of the Swiss Private International Law Act].' See the Swiss Federal Tribunal's decision in case No. DFT 4A_234/2010, 29 October 2010, at 3.2.1.

[173] On the fact that the principle of independence and impartiality of arbitrators is part of procedural public policy see e.g. United Nations (2012) UNCITRAL Secretariat Guide on the Convention on the Recognition and Enforcement of Foreign Arbitral Awards (New York, 1958), 2016 edn., p. 252 et seq. http://www.uncitral.org/pdf/english/texts/arbitration/NY-conv/2016_Guide_on_the_Convention.pdf. Accessed 22 May 2020.

almost every State who has enacted a modern arbitration law. From an excessive court scrutiny over arbitration and possibility to appeal an arbitral award in a strict sense, the arbitration world has gone to a very limited, controlled, and most importantly, exclusive review of arbitration proceedings and the ensuing arbitral awards by State courts at the seat of arbitration. Setting-aside proceedings provide both the state where arbitration proceedings take place and also the arbitrating parties with a well-balanced possibility to challenge a potentially defective arbitration process and the resulting arbitral award on very fundamental, generally procedural grounds that are considered to be a cornerstone of every democratic society respecting the rule of law.

The necessity of judicial controls in arbitration proceedings, in particular by means of setting-aside proceedings, in recent years has been perhaps one of the most widely debated aspects of court involvement in arbitration proceedings. While generally setting-aside proceedings continue to serve as means of 'efficient control of aberrant arbitral behaviour, promoting confidence within the commercial community that arbitration will not be a lottery of erratic results',[174] recent discussions have also highlighted certain seemingly problematic aspects of the judicial controls system in contemporary framework of international arbitration.[175]

Undoubtedly, the present system of judicial controls system may be improved in order to tackle issues such as *double-control*, potential parallel proceedings and conflicting decisions, as well as the phenomena of enforcement of annulled arbitral awards. However, the aim of this book is not to address the somewhat perpetual discussion on the necessity of setting-aside proceedings from the standpoint of the said concerns and provide solutions on how to improve the judicial controls system in contemporary framework of international arbitration. Many prominent scholars have already attempted to address this issue.[176] Instead, this book embraces the continuous existence of setting-aside proceedings in contemporary framework of international arbitration and looks at the issue of necessity of such proceedings from a somewhat unusual perspective, i.e. the perspective of parties' procedural human rights under the ECHR.

References

Abedian H (2011) Judicial review of arbitral awards in international arbitration: a case for an efficient system of judicial review. J Int'l Arb 26(6):553

Arp B (2018) Slowakische Republik (Slovak Republic) v. Achmea B.V. Am J Int law 112(3):466–472

Basedow JR (2018) The achmea judgment and the applicability of the energy charter treaty in intra-eu investment arbitration. J Int Econ L 23(1):271–292

[174]Park (2001), p. 595.

[175]See, among others, Van den Berg (2014), Scherer (2016), Paulsson (2017).

[176]Ibid. See also, e.g. Reisman and Richardson (2012), Radicati Di Brozolo (2012).

Berger JE, Sun C (2009) The evolution of judicial review under the federal arbitration act. NYU J Law Bus 5:745

Bermann GA (2011) Reconciling European Union law demands with the demands of international arbitration. Fordham Int Law J 34(5):1193–1216

Bermann GA (2012) Navigating EU law and the law of international arbitration. Arb Int'l 28(3):397–446

Blackaby N et al. (2015) Redfern and hunter on international arbitration, 6th edn. Oxford University Press

Born G (2001) International commercial arbitration: commentary and materials, 2nd edn. Kluwer Law International

Born G (2014) International commercial arbitration, 2nd edn. Kluwer Law International

Born G (2014b) The Principle of judicial non-interference in international arbitral proceedings. U Pa J Int'l L 30(4):999

Born G (2015) International arbitration: cases and materials, 2nd edn. Kluwer Law International

Briner R, Von Schlabrendorff F (2001) Article 6 of the European convention on human rights and its bearing upon international arbitration. In: Briner R et al (eds) Law of international business and dispute settlement in the 21st century. Carl Heymanns Verlag KG, Liber Amicorum Karl-Heinz Bockstiegel

Cordero-Moss G (2010) Legal capacity, arbitration and private international law. In: Boele-Woelki K et al (eds) Convergence and divergence in private international law. Eleven International Publishing, Liber Amicorum Kurt Siehr

Craig WL (1988) Uses and abuses of appeal from awards. Arb Int'l 4:174

Dedezade T (2006) Are you in? Or are you out? An analysis of section 69 of the english arbitration act 1996: appeals on a question of law. Int A L R 2:56

Ferrari F (ed) (2017) The impact of eu law on international commercial arbitration. JurisNet

Frick J (2001) arbitration and complex international contracts. Schulthess Verlag

Gaillard E (2010) legal theory of international arbitration. Martinus Nijhoff

Gharavi HG (2002) The international effectiveness of the annulment of an arbitral award. Kluwer Law International

Goode R (2001) The role of the lex loci arbitri in international commercial arbitration. Arb Int'l 17(1):19–40

Hacking L (1985) Where we are now: trends and developments since the arbitration act (1979). J Int'l Arb 2:7

Holtzmann HM, Neuhaus JE (2015) A guide to the UNCITRAL model law on international commercial arbitration: legislative history and commentary. Kluwer Law International

Jaksic A (2002) Arbitration and human rights. Peter Lang, Frankfurt am Main

Kerr M (1980) The arbitration act 1979. Mod L Rev 43(1):45

Lalive P (1976) Les règles de conflits de lois appliquées au fond du litige par l'arbitre international siégeant en Suisse. Revue de l'arbitrage 155

Lew JDM et al. (2003) Comparative international commercial arbitration. Kluwer Law International

Liebscher C (2000) European public policy. J Int'l Arb 17(3):73–88

Mann F (1967) Lex facit arbitrum. In: Sanders P (ed) International arbitration. Liver Amicorum for Martin Domke. Martinus Nijhoff, the Hague

Maurer AG (2013) Public policy exception under the New York convention: history, interpretation, and application, revised edition. Juris

Mistelis L, Brekoulakis SL (eds) (2009) Arbitrability: international & comparative perspectives. Kluwer Law International

Mustill M (1993) Part III: Comments and conclusions. In: International Chamber of Commerce, 9th Joint Colloquium. Conservatory and Provisional Measures in International Arbitration, p 118

Nacimiento P (2010) Commentary on article V(1)(a). In: Kronke H et al. (eds) Recognition and enforcement of foreign arbitral awards: a global commentary on the New York convention. Kluwer Law International

Park WW (1980) Judicial supervision of transnational commercial arbitration: the english arbitration act of 1979. Harv Int'l L J 21:87

Park WW (2001) Why courts review arbitral awards. In: Briner R et al (eds) Law of international business and dispute settlement in the 21st century, liber amicorum karl-heinz bockstiegel. Carl Heymanns Verlag KG, Köln/Berlin/Bonn/München, pp 595–606

Paulsson J (1983) Delocalization of international commercial arbitration: when and why it matters. Int Comp L Q 32(1):53–61

Paulsson J (2013) The idea of arbitration. Oxford University Press

Paulsson MRP (2017) The 1958 New York convention on the recognition and enforcement of foreign arbitral Awards from an unusual perspective: moving forward by parting with it. Indian J Arb L 5(2):23

Pohl JH (2018) Intra-EU investment arbitration after the achmea case: legal autonomy bounded by mutual trust? Eur Const L Rev 14(4):767–791

Poudret JF, Besson S (2006) Comparative law of international arbitration. Sweet & Maxwell, United Kingdom

Radicati Di Brozolo LG (2012) The present—commercial arbitration as a transnational system of justice: the control system of arbitral awards: a pro-arbitration critique of Michael Reisman's "architecture of international commercial arbitration". In: Van den Berg AJ (ed) Arbitration: the next fifty years. ICCA Congress Series Volume. Kluwer Law International, pp 74–102

Reisman M, Richardson B (2012) The present—commercial arbitration as a transnational system of justice: an interpretation of the architecture of international commercial arbitration. In: Van den Berg AJ (ed) Arbitration: the next fifty years. ICCA Congress Series Volume. Kluwer Law International, pp 17–65

Roebuck D, De Loynes de Fumichon B (2004) Roman arbitration. Holo Books: The Arbitration Press, Oxford

Rubino-Sammartano M (2014) International arbitration: law and practice, 3rd edn. JurisNet

Sadowski W (2018) Protection of the rule of law in the European Union through investment treaty arbitration: is judicial monopolism the right response to illiberal tendencies in Europe? CML Rev 55(4):1025–1060

Sattar S (2010) National courts and international arbitration: a double-edged sword? J Int'l Arb 27(1):51

Savage J, Gaillard E (eds) (1999) Fouchard, gaillard, goldman on international commercial arbitration. Kluwer Law International

Scherer M (2016) The fate of parties' agreements on judicial review of awards: a comparative and normative analysis of party-autonomy at the post-award stage. Arb Int'l 32:437–457

Steingruber AM (2012) Consent in international arbitration. Oxford University Press

Van den Berg AJ (1981) The New York arbitration convention of 1958. Kluwer Law and Taxation Publishers

Van den Berg AJ (2014) Should the setting aside of the arbitral award be abolished? ICSID Rev 1–26. https://doi.org/10.1093/icsidreview/sit053

Van der Haegen O (2009) European public policy in commercial arbitration: bridge over troubled water. Maastricht J Eur Comp L 16:449

Von Mehren RB (2003) The Eco-Swiss case and international arbitration. Arb Int 19(4):465–470

Wedam-Lukic D (1998) Arbitration and article 6 of the European convention on human rights. Arbitration 64:16–21

Chapter 5
Approaches to Excluding the Annulment of Arbitral Awards—Exclusion Agreements

5.1 Introduction

The phenomenon of excluding setting-aside proceedings is commonly referred to as the *exclusion* of setting-aside proceedings or *waiver* of setting-aside proceedings or simply parties' right to conclude an *exclusion agreement*. In essence, exclusion of setting-aside proceedings is a statutorily provided possibility for arbitrating parties to exclude the applicability of setting-aside proceedings at the post-award stage. It must be distinguished from a collateral estoppel (or issue preclusion) by means of which a party to arbitration proceedings is deemed to have *waived* its right to object to an arbitral award (either in the annulment or recognition and enforcement proceedings) on a ground that it failed to raise during arbitration proceedings.[1] Provisions on a collateral estoppel can be found in the UNCITRAL Model Law,[2] various institutional arbitration rules[3] and also many national arbitration laws.[4] In order not to confuse

---

[1] Generally on a collateral estoppel regarding arbitration proceedings see, e.g. Petrochilos (2004), pp. 117–125, Born (2014), pp. 3269–3270 and 3281–3286.

[2] Art. 4 of the UNCITRAL Model Law ('A party who knows that any provision of this Law from which the parties may derogate or any requirement under the arbitration agreement has not been complied with and yet proceeds with the arbitration without stating his objection to such non-compliance without undue delay or, if a time-limit is provided therefor, within such period of time, shall be deemed to have waived his right to object.').

[3] See, e.g. art. 40 of the ICC Arbitration Rules (2017); art. 32(1) of the LCIA Arbitration Rules (2014); art. 36 of the SCC Arbitration Rules (2017).

[4] See, e.g. sec. 73(1) of the 1996 English Arbitration Act ('If a party to arbitral proceedings takes part, or continues to take part, in the proceedings without making, either forthwith or within such time as is allowed by the arbitration agreement or the tribunal or by any provision of this Part, any objection—(a) that the tribunal lacks substantive jurisdiction, (b) that the proceedings have been improperly conducted, (c) that there has been a failure to comply with the arbitration agreement or with any provision of this Part, or (d) that there has been any other irregularity affecting the tribunal or the proceedings, he may not raise that objection later, before the tribunal or the court, unless he shows that, at the time he took part or continued to take part in the proceedings, he did not know and could not with reasonable diligence have discovered the grounds for the objection.'); sec. 34 of the SAA ('A party shall not be entitled to rely upon a circumstance which, through participation in the proceedings without objection, or in any other manner, he may be deemed to have waived.'); sec. 3 of the 2005 Danish Arbitration Act ('A party who knows that any provision of this Act from which

© The Editor(s) (if applicable) and The Author(s), under exclusive license to Springer Nature Switzerland AG 2020

T. Krūmiņš, *Arbitration and Human Rights*,
https://doi.org/10.1007/978-3-030-54237-5_5

the exclusion of setting-aside proceedings with a collateral estoppel (that, similarly to *exclusion* or *waiver* of setting-aside proceedings is commonly also referred to as a *waiver*), further reference to the exclusion of setting-aside proceedings will omit the use of the term *waiver* and instead use either the term *exclusion of setting-aside proceedings* or simply *exclusion agreements*.[5]

Generally, while each jurisdiction permitting the exclusion of setting-aside proceedings has its own reasons behind doing so, the main reason in favour of providing a statutory possibility to exclude the annulment mechanism is to attract more arbitrating parties and thus international arbitrations to the particular jurisdiction. It is also said that the exclusion of setting-aside proceedings provides parties with an increased finality of an arbitral award, decreases costs and time associated with the filing of a claim for annulment of an arbitral award before State courts and possibly also avoids dilatory challenge requests. Moreover, when considering whether or not parties should be given the autonomy to exclude setting-aside proceedings, one can neither disregard the whole discussion of the necessity of setting-aside proceedings in the first place that in recent years have troubled the minds of arbitration scholars and also courts alike, at least in some jurisdictions. Overall, the exclusion of setting-aside proceedings therefore may seem as an attractive option that not only benefits the arbitral seat and arbitrating parties, but also fits well into the contemporary understanding of arbitration as an autonomous alternative dispute resolution mechanism.

However, even though a handful of jurisdictions have given parties the autonomy to exclude setting-aside proceedings, judicial control by means of setting-aside proceedings is still considered as one of the two most prevalent methods for exercising control over arbitration proceedings in most jurisdictions (the other being recognition and enforcement proceedings). It is said that setting-aside proceedings are seen as a form of risk management whereby courts remedy violations of fundamental procedural rights during arbitration proceedings.[6] In many countries, exclusion agreements are even unenforceable and considered to be incompatible with mandatory provisions of law and principles of public policy.[7]

Recently, the statutory possibility to exclude setting-aside proceedings provided in Article 192(1) of the PILA was challenged before the ECtHR in the case of *Tabbane v. Switzerland*. It was argued that the exclusion of setting-aside proceedings is incompatible with Article 6(1) of the ECHR and violates, inter alia, the right of

the parties may derogate or any requirement under the arbitration agreement has not been complied with and yet proceeds with the arbitration without stating an objection to such non-compliance without undue delay or, if a time-limit is provided therefor, within such period of time, shall be deemed to have waived the right to object.'), art. 1679 of the BCCP ('A party that, knowingly and for no legitimate reason refrains from raising, in due time, an irregularity before the arbitral tribunal is deemed to have waived its right to assert such irregularity.') and many others.

[5]Occasionally, e.g. when citing the relevant provisions of national arbitration law or passages of works of other others, the term 'waiver' will nevertheless be used, as it was used in the original source.

[6]Park (2001), p. 595.

[7]See Sect. 5.6.2.

access to a court. The ECtHR, however, concluded that the existence of such a right and the resulting exclusion of setting-aside proceedings is not contrary to the right of access to a court, provided that it satisfies the respective conditions of the *waiver theory*. Similarly, the ECtHR held that Article 192(1) of the PILA per se does not offend against the right of access to a court since it allegedly pursues a legitimate aim and is proportionate to the aim pursued.[8]

However, what if the exclusion agreement did not pursue a legitimate aim or was not proportionate? Would the judgment of the ECtHR be different if the exclusion of setting-aside proceedings was *mandatory*, i.e. it did not result from a voluntary exercise of statutory right to exclude setting-aside proceedings but there was no possibility in the applicable *lex arbitri* to challenge an arbitral award at all? Moreover, the Court's reasoning in the *Tabbane v. Switzerland* ruling per se raises certain questions as to the fulfillment of the different conditions of the 'waiver theory' under Article 6(1) of the ECHR,[9] as well as to the overall comprehensiveness and impact of the Court's conclusions on the phenomenon of exclusion agreements on the broader level. Additionally, the indefinite, albeit at the same time generally recognized distinction between *waivable* and *non-waivable* rights of Article 6(1) of the ECHR, raises a question whether it is *permissible* for the Convention purposes to exclude setting-aside proceedings to the extent that it is impossible to challenge an arbitral award on the basis of grounds that pertain to the *non-waivable* rights of Article 6(1) of the ECHR, i.e. the right to a fair hearing and the right to an independent and impartial tribunal.

Before in detail addressing the above raised issues, one must in an equal detail look at the different legislative approaches to permitting exclusion agreements. Only by understanding the underlying pre-conditions and effects of such agreements in different jurisdictions, it will be possible to identify the most balanced legislative approach from the standpoint of compatibility with the ECHR to providing a statutory possibility to opt-out of the application of setting-aside proceedings under national arbitration law.

Although a handful of States all over the world have liberalized their arbitration laws to provide with a possibility to exclude setting-aside proceedings, this book's more specific focus will generally lie at the most well-known Council of Europe jurisdictions in this regard, namely Switzerland, France, Sweden and Belgium. Each country has its own regulatory approach—there are different preconditions, effects and consequences that the exclusion of setting-aside proceedings entails in each particular jurisdiction. This, in turn, means that also from the perspective of compatibility of such exclusion agreements with the ECHR, the different legislative approaches may lead to diametrically opposed conclusions. Therefore, the aim of the below analysis is not only to introduce the legislative variety in this regard, but also to complement this book's search for the most ECHR-compatible legislative approach to permitting exclusion agreements. As will become apparent, the different legislative approaches to regulating exclusion of setting-aside proceedings may lead

---

[8] *Tabbane v. Switzerland*, App. No. 41069/12, ECtHR, 1 March 2016, para. 36.

[9] See Sect. 3.5.

to different conclusions when the compatibility of such approaches is viewed from the standpoint of the ECHR.

In order to have a more comprehensive overview of similarities and differences, further analysis of the said jurisdictions and their approaches to permitting exclusion agreements is structured as follows: first, an overview of the respective provision allowing for the exclusion of setting-aside proceedings is given; then the required prerequisites for a valid exclusion are set forth and; lastly, the respective provision's effects and consequences are scrutinized. The analysis of the Swiss approach additionally includes a separate reflection on the ECtHR's ruling in the *Tabbane v. Switzerland* case that is of particular significance for this work's more specific focus on the interplay between setting-aside proceedings and the ECHR. After a more detailed insight into the applicable regimes in this regard in Switzerland, France, Sweden and Belgium, a brief summary of other States' approaches will be given.

5.2 Switzerland

Switzerland is one of the very first countries that introduced in its arbitration law an express provision providing arbitrating parties with a possibility to exclude the application of setting-aside proceedings.[10] The PILA of 1989 in this regard can be considered as the pioneer and prototype legislation—an example and role model later followed by many other jurisdictions, such as France, Sweden, Belgium and others. Although Belgium had already in 1985 done away with the application of setting-aside proceedings for foreign nationals arbitrating in Belgium, its approach entailed no exercise of party autonomy in that respect—the non-application of setting-aside proceedings was automatic. The PILA, however, gave the final say to arbitrating parties. Therefore, the philosophy behind the Swiss and Belgian approaches is quite different.[11]

5.2.1 Overview of the Provision

Before the entry into force of the PILA in 1989,[12] both domestic and international arbitration in Switzerland was governed by the 1969 inter-cantonal Swiss Concordat

[10]Generally on exclusion of setting-aside proceedings in Switzerland see, among others, Gaillard (1988), pp. 25–31, Lalive (1988), pp. 2–24, Poudret (1988), pp. 278–299, Samuel (1991), Mayer (1999), Blessing (1988), Girsberg and Voser (2016), pp. 42–424, Geisinger and Mazuranic (2013), pp. 255–258, Krausz (2011), Baizeau (2013).

[11]Gaillard (1988), p. 30.

[12]PILA (Loi fédérale sur le droit international privé), 18 December 1987, RO 1988 1776. Generally on the 1989 PILA see, e.g., Blessing (1988), Tschanz (1990), Samuel (1991).

on Arbitration (*Concordat international sur l'arbitrage*)[13] under which the right to setting-aside proceedings was mandatory—it was not possible to exclude setting-aside proceedings, even in international cases where all parties were domiciled abroad.[14] When in 1973 a group of experts gathered to draft the PILA,[15] a proposal arose to reform this rigid approach and allow foreign parties 'to exclude by agreement the jurisdiction of Swiss courts to review the award.'[16] It is said that the previous rigid approach was often criticized by foreign parties as being 'unacceptable tutelage'[17] and that a possibility to exclude the application of setting-aside proceedings was 'a constant request of practitioners.'[18] Having recognized such criticism and with the aim to promote Switzerland as an arbitration-friendly jurisdiction, negotiations of the PILA led to the introduction of a new provision governing the so-called exclusion agreements—Article 192 of the PILA:

(1) If none of the parties have their domicile, their habitual residence, or a business establishment in Switzerland, they may, by an express statement in the arbitration agreement or by a subsequent written agreement, waive fully the action for annulment or they may limit to one or several of the grounds listed in Art. 190(2).

(2) If the parties have waived fully the action for annulment against the awards and if the awards are to be enforced in Switzerland, the New York Convention of 10 June 1958 on the Recognition and Enforcement of Foreign Arbitral Awards applies by analogy.[19]

In addition to the already mentioned criticism by parties and practitioners that seemingly influenced the drafting committee in reforming the then existing rigid application of setting-aside proceedings, the officially communicated reasons for

---

[13]Concordat sur l'arbitrage du 27 mars 1969 (Concordat on Arbitration of 27 March 1969), 27 mars 1969, RO 1969 1117. Until the entry into force of the Swiss Code on Civil Procedure on 1 January 2011 the 1969 Swiss Concordat on Arbitration continued to govern domestic arbitration and arbitration in which parties specifically excluded the application of the PILA. The PILA applies only to international arbitration (art. 176(1) of the PILA).

[14]Mayer (1999), p. 196 ('According to Article 36 paragraph f of the Concordat, the parties may not waive the recourse foreseen by this provision, even when all parties are domiciled abroad' in referring to the decision of the Federal Tribunal of October 15 1984, BGE 110 Ia 131. See also Poudret (1988), p. 282 in referring to ATF 110 1a 131, reported in Semaine Judiciaire ('SJ') 1985,296; ASA Bull 1985/1, at p. 19 and 1986/2, at p. 84; Journaux des Tribunaux ('JdT') 1981 III 104-105 No. 17, and 1988 III 43 No. 16. See also Blessing (1988), p. 75.

[15]Lalive (1988), p. 2.

[16]Ibid., p. 18.

[17]Blessing (1988), p. 75.

[18]Lalive (1988), p. 18.

[19]Translation. PILA (Loi fédérale sur le droit international privé), 18 December 1987, RO 1988 1776. Official text reads as follows:

'(1) Si deux parties n'ont ni domicile, ni résidence habituelle, ni établissement en Suisse, elles peuvent, par une déclaration expresse dans la convention d'arbitrage ou un accord écrit ultérieur, exclure tout recours contre les sentences du tribunal arbitral; elles peuvent aussi n'exclure le recours que pour l'un ou l'autre des motifs énumérés à l'art. 190, al. 2.

(2) Lorsque les parties ont exclu tout recours contre les sentences et que celles-ci doivent être exécutées en Suisse, la convention de New York du 10 juin 1958 pour la reconnaissance et l'exécution des sentences arbitrales étrangères s'applique par analogie.'

introducing Article 192 of the PILA were to (i) assure the efficacy of dispute resolution by means of arbitration; (ii) to promote the attractiveness of international arbitration in Switzerland, and (iii) to alleviate the Swiss Federal Tribunal of its workload.[20] Whether or not Article 192 of the PILA meets these objectives is subject to debate,[21] the most controversial aspects of which will be covered below.[22]

It is said that Article 192 of the PILA also targets the issues of potential *double control* and irreconcilable decisions that may arise if courts at the seat of arbitration and courts at the State of enforcement arrive at different conclusions as to the validity of arbitration agreement.[23] From parties' perspective, however, the main advantages of excluding the right to apply for setting aside of an arbitral award is increased finality and confidentiality of proceedings that is achieved by avoiding potentially lengthy and costly recourse to State courts.[24] Again, whether or not these objectives are achieved by excluding setting-aside proceedings is similarly subject to debate.[25]

Parties often choose Switzerland as the seat of arbitration due to its neutral and arbitration-friendly attitude and at first glance the possibility to exclude setting-aside proceedings may seem as a valuable tool to expedite the resolution of disputes and to increase finality of arbitral awards. However, as will be explained, the absence of setting-aside proceedings may not always prove beneficial. Generally, parties arbitrating in Switzerland are reluctant to exclude their right to setting-aside proceedings and such exclusions are more of a rarity than a common practice.[26] Moreover, not all parties will be able to benefit from the purported advantages of not having setting-aside proceedings in Switzerland since first certain conditions must be satisfied.

---

[20] Swiss Federal Council (1982) Message to the Federal Assembly on the Draft Bill for the PILA. 10 November 1982, FF 1983, at 451. See also Van den Berg (2014), p. 14 citing the same Swiss Federal Council Message of 10 November 1982 and noting that the reason of the said provision was to 'to assure the greatest possible efficacy for the obligation to resolve disputes through arbitration, [while avoiding] that the Swiss courts would be burdened with the task to decide on dilatory recourses regarding disputes which have no genuine connection with our country'. See also Girsberg and Voser (2016), p. 420, Krausz (2011) p. 138, Berger and Kellerhals (2015), para. 1840, Lalive (1988), p. 18 in referring to the Message of the Federal Council (Government) to Parliament, of 10 November 1982 No. 2101, in particular No. 2101, 27) ('This innovation had a dual purpose: on the one hand, 'to ensure the greatest possible effect to the obligation to settle disputes' by an arbitral award which should really be final and conclusive. At the same time, there was an increasing desire to diminish the burden of Swiss courts called upon, in a not inconsiderable number of cases, to adjudicate over (often dilatory) requests for setting aside an award in cases having no real connection with Switzerland.'). Affirmed also in, e.g. the decision of the Federal Tribunal in case No. 4P.114/2006, 7 September 2006, at 5.2, and the decision of the Swiss Federal Tribunal in case No. 4P.198.2005, 31 October 2005, at. 2.1 (cited by Krausz (2011), p. 138).

[21] Krausz (2011), p. 138.

[22] See Sect. 5.2.3.

[23] See Krausz (2011), p. 138.

[24] Baizeau (2005), p. 69.

[25] See Sect. 5.2.3.

[26] Van den Berg (2014), p. 15, Poudret and Besson (2006), p. 781.

5.2.2 *Prerequisites*

5.2.2.1 No Close Connection to Switzerland

First of all, Article 192(1) of the PILA provides that in order to be able to conclude an exclusion agreement none of the parties must have their domicile, habitual residence, or a business establishment in Switzerland.[27] Swiss law does not apply the nationality requirement and the reason for allowing non-Swiss parties to exclude setting-aside proceedings is solely their loose connection with Switzerland.[28] Therefore, only parties satisfying this criterion, i.e. parties with their domicile, habitual residence or a business establishment outside Switzerland, are allowed to exclude setting-aside proceedings before the Swiss Federal Tribunal.

The majority of legal commentators generally agree that if a foreign company has a branch or a business establishment in Switzerland, the conditions of Article 192(1) of the PILA are not fulfilled and, for example, the foreign mother company will not be able to conclude an exclusion agreement under Article 192(1) of the PILA.[29] Moreover, even if not expressly indicated, it is said that the requirement of no territorial connection to Switzerland must be met at the time the arbitration agreement or the express exclusion agreement of setting-aside proceedings is concluded.[30] Therefore, if a foreign party after concluding the arbitration agreement domiciles itself in Switzerland, the exclusion of setting-aside proceedings will remain intact. Similarly, if a Swiss party after concluding an arbitration agreement domiciles itself in a foreign country, it can then subsequently agree on the exclusion of setting-aside proceedings (provided that the other party is also domiciled abroad).[31] Some authors even argue for an extension of Article 192(1) of the PILA also to Swiss nationals—a solution adopted under French law[32] and possibly supported now also by the conclusions in the ECtHR case of *Tabbane v. Switzerland*.[33]

After determining that none of the arbitrating parties has its domicile, habitual residence, or a business establishment in Switzerland, a valid exclusion of setting-aside proceedings will further require that such an exclusion is explicit.

---

[27] Art. 192(1) of the PILA ('If none of the parties have their domicile, their habitual residence, or a business establishment in Switzerland [...]). See also arts. 20 and 21 of the PILA. 'Domicile' refers to the state in which a person resides with the intention to remain there permanently. 'Place of habitual residence' means a state in which a person lives for an extended period of time, even if this time period is initially limited. 'Place of business' refers to the state in which a person centers his or her business activities.

[28] Mayer (1999), p. 197.

[29] See, e.g. Baizeau (2013), p. 283, Girsberg and Voser (2016), p. 421, Geisinger and Mazuranic (2013), p. 255, Berger and Kellerhals (2010), p. 1673, Mayer (1999), pp. 197–198.

[30] Baizeau (2013), p. 283; Krausz (2011), p. 139, Girsberg and Voser (2016), p. 421.

[31] Girsberg and Voser (2016), p. 421.

[32] See Sect. 5.3.

[33] Mayer (1999), p. 198. See also Voser and George (2016).

5.2.2.2 Explicit Exclusion

Article 192(1) of the PILA provides that exclusion of setting-aside proceedings must be made by an express statement in the arbitration agreement or by a subsequent written agreement. Therefore, arbitrating parties do not necessarily have to stipulate their intention to exclude setting-aside proceedings in the arbitration agreement—it is also possible to conclude an exclusion agreement after the conclusion of the arbitration agreement and even after the issuing of the arbitral award.[34] Moreover, it is possible under Article 192(1) of the PILA to exclude setting-aside proceedings in full or limit such proceedings to one or more grounds listed in Article 190(2) of the PILA.[35] In case of a partial exclusion, parties must explicitly state the ground(s) that they wish to exclude.[36]

The requirement of an *express statement* has witnessed evolutionary changes since the entry into force of the PILA in 1989. Until 2005, the Swiss Federal Tribunal's interpretation of the notion *express statement* enshrined in Article 192(1) of the PILA was rather strict. Since '[t]he provision [was] intended to protect the parties from ill-considered waivers and their far-reaching consequences'[37] parties' will to exclude setting-aside proceedings had to be clearly and ambiguously expressed. This meant that the Swiss Federal Tribunal, when interpreting exclusion agreements under Article 192(1) of the PILA, required that parties refer to the specific legal remedy, i.e. either Article 190 or 192(1) of the PILA, and explicitly exclude it.[38] It was not sufficient to state in the arbitration agreement that, e.g. the award is 'final'[39] or 'application to State courts is excluded'.[40] Moreover, it was (and still is) generally recognized by legal scholars and also confirmed by the Swiss Federal Tribunal that

[34] Mayer (1999), p. 199.

[35] Art. 190(2) of the PILA ('The award may only be annulled: (a) if the sole arbitrator was not properly appointed or if the arbitral tribunal was not properly constituted; (b) if the arbitral tribunal wrongly accepted or declined jurisdiction; (c) if the arbitral tribunal's decision went beyond the claims submitted to it, or failed to decide one of the items of the claim; (d) if the principle of equal treatment of the parties or the right of the parties to be heard was violated; (e) if the award is incompatible with public policy.').

[36] Girsberg and Voser (2016), p. 421, Krausz (2011), pp. 148–149.

[37] Baizeau (2005), p. 71.

[38] Decision of the Swiss Federal Tribunal in case No. ATF 116 II 639, 19 December 1990 (1991) 9 ASA Bull 262. See also Krausz (2011), p. 141, Patocchi and Jermini (2000), p. 1790.

[39] See, e.g., decisions of the Swiss Federal Tribunal in case No. 4P.207/2002, 10 December 2002 (2003) 21 ASA Bull 585 and case No. 4P.64/2004, 2 June 2004 (2004) ASA Bull 782.

[40] Decision of the Swiss Federal Tribunal in case No. 4P.265/1996, 2 July 1997 (1997) 15 ASA Bull 494. Other insufficient references included, e.g. that the dispute will be 'definitively decided' by the arbitral tribunal (decision of the Swiss Federal Tribunal in case No. 4P.99/1993, 15 November 1993) or that the award shall be rendered without reasons (Baizeau (2005), p. 71 referring to many Swiss commentators). See also examples of invalid exclusion agreements listed by Baizeau (2013), p. 286 ('[a]greements containing the following language have been held not to suffice to constitute a valid waiver: (a) the award shall be 'final' *and* 'without appeal' ('*sans appel*' in French; 1990 decision; (b) the award shall be 'final and binding' and 'applications to the State courts are excluded' (1997 decision) […]').

reference to arbitration rules containing a provision excluding any recourse against an arbitral award would not amount to a valid exclusion under Article 192(1) of the PILA.[41] Nevertheless, if the arbitration agreement contains a specific reference to the exact provision of the particular institutional arbitration rules, parties are considered to have clearly expressed their will and this would generally suffice for a valid exclusion of setting-aside proceedings.[42]

However, in 2005 the Swiss Federal Tribunal departed from its previous strict interpretation of Article 192(1) of the PILA and ruled that an explicit reference in the exclusion agreement to Article 190 or 192(1) of the PILA is no longer necessary.[43] After acknowledging in the decision that a mere reference to arbitration rules or the arbitral award being 'final and binding' are not sufficient for a valid exclusion of setting-aside proceedings, it continued:

> No doubt the reference made to Art. 190 [of the PILA] and/or Art. 192 [of the PILA] in the arbitration clause itself constitutes the best way to cut short any discussion on the scope of the waiver, since it allows identifying with certainty the right which is being waived. For this reason, it is advisable. That is not to say that such a reference should be a sine qua non condition for any valid waiver of a right to challenge an international arbitration award.[44]

For the first time since the introduction of the PILA in 1989 the Swiss Federal Tribunal ruled in favour of a valid exclusion agreement and denied arbitrating party recourse to setting-aside proceedings.[45] It stressed that the exclusion agreement must show in a clear and distinct manner the common intention of the parties to exclude their right to setting-aside proceedings, yet it is not necessary that such an intention is expressed by citing the relevant provision[46]:

> [T]he express declaration referred to in Article 192(1) [of the PILA] must reveal in a clear and distinct manner the common intention of the parties to waive their right to challenge

---

[41] See, e.g., decision of the Swiss Federal Tribunal in case No. ATF 116 II 639, 19 December 1990 (1991) 9 ASA Bull 262. See also Baizeau (2013), p. 284.

[42] Decision of the Swiss Federal Tribunal in case No. ATF 116 II 639, 19 December 1990 (1991) 9 ASA Bull 262. See also Baizeau (2005), p. 71, Mayer (1999), pp. 201–202, Krausz (2011), p. 141. Provisions as regards the exclusion of any recourse against an arbitral award can be found, e.g., in art. 34(6) of the ICC Rules (2012)—'Every award shall be binding on the parties. By submitting the dispute to arbitration under the Rules, the parties undertake to carry out any award without delay and shall be deemed to have waived their right to any form of recourse insofar as such waiver can validly be made'. Similar provisions are also contained in art. 26.8 of the LCIA Arbitration Rules (2014), art. 40 of the SCC Arbitration Rules (2010) and other institutional arbitration rules.

[43] Decision of the Swiss Federal Tribunal in case No. 4P.236/2004, 4 February 2005. The Swiss Federal Tribunal considered the following provision as sufficient for a valid waiver under art. 192(1) of the PILA: '[a]ll and any awards or other decisions of the Arbitral Tribunal shall be made in accordance with the UNCITRAL Rules and shall be final and binding on the parties who exclude all and any rights of appeal from all and any awards insofar as such exclusion can validly be made'.

[44] Baizeau (2005), p. 71 in citing decision of the Swiss Federal Tribunal in case No. 4P.236/2004, 4 February 2005, para. 4.2.3.1.

[45] See, e.g. Baizeau (2013), p. 284 ('Indeed, where Art. 192 could apply, the parties have, by definition, no link with Switzerland and cannot thus be expected to include a reference to a provision in Swiss legislation, the existence of which they are most probably unaware […]').

[46] Ibid. See also Geisinger and Mazuranic (2013), p. 256.

> the decisions of the Arbitral Tribunal on the grounds provided for in Article 190(2) [of the PILA]. Yet, it is not essential in order to establish such an intention that the parties cite such or such provision or that they use such or such expression.[47]

By stipulating in the exclusion agreement that parties 'exclude all and any rights of appeal from all and any awards insofar as such exclusion can validly be made' the Swiss Federal Tribunal concluded that the term 'appeal' is used in its broader sense, i.e. including a challenge of the arbitral award in setting-aside proceedings, and the intention of parties was clear.[48] While some authors welcome the Swiss Federal Tribunal's shift to a more liberal approach in interpreting exclusion agreement under Article 192(1) of the PILA, others 'would still prefer to admit waivers only if they contain an explicit reference to PILA, Article 190 or Article 192 of the PILA, for the sake of protecting parties.'[49]

The 2005 decision paved the way to a much more liberal interpretation of Article 192(1) of the PILA and has since been followed in subsequent rulings, including a case which led to the ECtHR decision in *Tabbane v. Switzerland*.[50] However, despite the more permissive attitude towards exclusion agreements, it is argued that certain implied references will still be considered as insufficient for valid exclusion agreements.[51] Whether a particular exclusion agreement will be considered as valid or not will eventually be a matter of interpretation:

> It is necessary, but sufficient, that the express declaration of the parties reveals, indisputably, their common intention to waive their right to any challenge of the award. Whether this is the case is a matter of interpretation and will always remain so, which means that it is impossible to lay down rules that are applicable with respect to all conceivable situations.[52]

---

[47]Baizeau (2013), p. 286 in citing decision of the Federal Tribunal in case No. 4P.236/2004, 4 February 2005, para. 4.2.3.1.

[48]Decision of the Swiss Federal Tribunal in case No. 4P.236/2004, 4 February 2005, para. 4.2.3.2. The broader sense of the term 'appeal' refers to its generic character whereby it embraces the most diverse rights of recourse against an adjudicative decision, thus also an arbitral award. It is opposed to the much stricter sense that uses the term 'appeal' only in referring to an appeal on merits, namely an ordinary form of recourse.

[49]Krausz (2011), p. 144.

[50]Decision of the Swiss Federal Tribunal in case No. 4A_238/2011, 4 January 2012, 30 ASA Bull 369 (2012) which was later challenged before the ECtHR in the case of *Tabbane v. Switzerland*. Previously, the Federal Tribunal has also followed its liberal interpretation and stressed that an express reference to PILA is not necessary in the exclusion agreement. See, e.g., decision of the Swiss Federal Tribunal in case No. 4P.98/2005, 10 November 2005 (2006) 24 ASA Bull 92; decision of the Swiss Federal Tribunal in case No. 4A.500/2007, 6 March 2008, ATF 134 III 260. See also examples of valid waivers mentioned by Baizeau (2013), pp. 287–288.

[51]See Baizeau (2005), p. 74. Such insufficient references include, e.g., that the award shall be 'final' or 'final and binding', or that the award shall be 'without appeal', or that 'applications to the state courts are excluded'.

[52]Baizeau (2013), p. 284, in citing decision of the Swiss Federal Tribunal in case No. 4P.236/2004, 4 February 2005, para. 4.2.3.1. and other more recent cases.

5.2.3 *Effects and Consequences*

Effects of an exclusion agreement are self-explanatory. Parties who conclude such an agreement will not be able to challenge the arbitral award before the Swiss Federal Tribunal on the basis of grounds stipulated in Article 190(2) of the PILA. As seen, Article 192(1) of the PILA provides that an exclusion of setting-aside proceedings can either be made in full or be limited to some of the grounds listed in Article 190(2) of the PILA. If parties choose to limit the exclusion of setting-aside proceedings to certain grounds of Article 190(2) of the PILA, 'the award may only be challenged [...] on the grounds that have not been excluded by the parties.'[53]

Article 192(1) of the PILA concerns only the possibility to exclude the setting-aside proceedings and does not embrace renunciation of court assistance in general. Thus, parties can still benefit from the assistance of Swiss courts in, e.g. the taking of evidence (Article 184 of the PILA), challenge of arbitrators (Article 180 of the PILA) or issuing of interim measures (Article 183 of the PILA).[54] Moreover, '[d]espite a valid waiver, the [Federal Tribunal] will preliminarily examine the subjective scope of the arbitration agreement and that of the waiver agreement, if the award is challenged on the basis of lack of jurisdiction *ratione personae*.'[55]

Similarly, exclusion of the annulment mechanism does not mean that the arbitral award will not be subject to any court control in Switzerland. An important addition to the possibility of excluding setting-aside proceedings is Article 192(2) of the PILA which stipulates that in case parties have excluded the right to challenge an arbitral award and the enforcement takes place in Switzerland, the New York Convention applies *mutatis mutandis*.[56] Although the wording of Article 192(2) of the PILA suggests that the provision applies only in case of a full exclusion of setting-aside proceedings most legal scholars agree that this is rather a drafting error than the legislator's willingness to exclude the application of the New York Convention in cases of a partial exclusion of setting-aside proceedings.[57] In either way, the degree of protection offered to arbitrating parties that have concluded an exclusion agreement, but nevertheless seek enforcement of the arbitral award in Switzerland, is not the same as a challenge of an arbitral award under Article 190(2) of the PILA—even if enforcement is refused, the award still stands as *res judicata*.[58] The existence of Article 192(2) of the PILA also played a role in the outcome of the *Tabbane v. Switzerland* ruling by the ECtHR.[59]

---

[53] Girsberg and Voser (2016), p. 423.

[54] Krausz (2011), p. 150.

[55] Girsberg and Voser (2016), p. 423 in referring to decision of the Swiss Federal Tribunal in case No. 4A_631/2011, 9 December 2011, at 3.1. See also Geisinger and Mazuranic (2013), p. 257.

[56] Geisinger and Mazuranic (2013), p. 257, Baizeau (2013), pp. 290–291, Girsberg and Voser (2016), p. 423, Krausz (2011), pp. 153–154. For a more comprehensive overview of art. 192(2) of the PILA please see, e.g. Kaufmann-Kohler and Rigozzi (2015), pp. 508–535.

[57] See, e.g. Baizeau (2013), p. 290, Samuel (1991), pp. 52–53, Krausz (2011), p. 153.

[58] Baizeau (2013), p. 291.

[59] See Sect. 5.2.4.

Additionally, Swiss law provides for a possibility of revision of an arbitral award—an extraordinary remedy created by the well-known *Perrodo* case in 1992.[60] Grounds for a revision of an arbitral award are limited to very exceptional cases, e.g. when an arbitral award has been influenced by a crime or felony or if a party subsequently has discovered important facts or crucial evidence.[61] If the Swiss Federal Tribunal satisfies request for a revision,[62] the arbitral award is annulled and the case is referred back to the same or a new arbitral tribunal for reconsideration.[63] Generally, unlike setting-aside proceedings, the right to a revision of an arbitral award cannot be excluded.[64] Nevertheless, a recent decision suggests that, at least in part relating to irregularities in the proceedings which can be challenged with an annulment action, by excluding the right to setting-aside proceedings parties also exclude their right to request revision of an arbitral.[65] Recently, the Swiss Arbitration Association (ASA) has encouraged the Swiss legislator to consider extending the availability of exclusion agreements also to parties domiciled in Switzerland and to allow arbitrating parties to opt out of the remedy of revision.[66] To date, however, the PILA has not been amended to include the said encouragements.

Whether or not Article 192(1) of the PILA achieves enhanced efficacy in arbitration proceedings and decreases dilatory requests before the Swiss courts is debated. Although there are certain perceived advantages of excluding setting-aside proceedings (e.g. increased finality of arbitral awards, confidentiality, saving time and costs), most legal commentators doubt that parties would be better off when concluding an

[60]Decision of the Swiss Federal Tribunal in case No. ATF 118 II 199, 11 March 1992 (1993) Rev. Arb. 115, 1993 RSDIE 209. See also decision of the Swiss Federal Tribunal in case No. 4P.120/2002, 3 September 2002 (2003) 21 ASA Bull. 578. Generally on the revision of arbitral awards in Swiss law see, e.g. Girsberg and Voser (2016), pp. 424–430, Geisinger and Mazuranic (2013), pp. 258–274.

[61]Art. 123 of the Federal Tribunal Act. Similar 'revision' or 'revocation' of arbitral awards is possible in, e.g., Netherlands (art. 1068 of the 2015 Dutch Arbitration Act), Italy (art. 831 of the Italian Code of Civil Procedure) and other countries.

[62]To date, only a handful of requests for revision have been successful before the Swiss Federal Tribunal. See Dasser and Wójtowicz (2016), p. 291.

[63]Kaufmann-Kohler and Rigozzi (2015), p. 516.

[64]Krausz (2011), p. 151, Baizeau (2005), p. 75.

[65]See Decision of the Swiss Federal Tribunal in case No. 4A_53/2017, 17 October 2017.

[66]Association Suisse de l'Arbitrage (2017) Position Paper: Proposed Revision of Swiss International Arbitration Law (Chapter 12 of the Private International Law Act). https://www.arbitration-ch.org/asset/b8e06a96acaa7fccd3dd2262e4b5b31f/ASA%20Comments%20Chapter%2012%20PILA.pdf. Accessed 22 May 2020.

exclusion agreement of setting-aside proceedings.[67] Moreover, it also seems that parties rarely make use of the right to exclude setting-aside proceedings.[68]

Equally, commentators have long rebutted the above-stated perceived advantages of exclusion agreements. If parties strive for increased confidentiality, an exclusion of setting-aside proceedings does not necessarily achieve that—indeed, setting-aside proceedings before the Swiss Federal Tribunal are not confidential, however, the same is true if the arbitral award is subject to recognition and enforcement in Switzerland pursuant to Article 192(2) of the PILA or in any other jurisdiction in which the successful party attempts to recognize and enforce the award.[69] Moreover, post-award litigation is not entirely excluded also due to the fact that parties disappointed by an arbitral award will certainly attempt to question in court the validity, extent and effects of the exclusion agreement itself.[70] As to the alleged saving of time, it is also evident that setting-aside proceedings before the Swiss Federal Tribunal are very efficient (challenges of arbitral awards before the Swiss Federal Tribunal are on average decided in 6 months[71]) and generally would not result in a significant delay in arbitration proceedings.[72] Therefore, it is argued that in that context the recourse against the arbitral award 'is difficult to use for dilatory purposes.'[73]

Moreover, setting aside of arbitral awards under Article 190(2) of the PILA is possible only on very limited grounds pertaining to the most fundamental rights. It is not possible to review the award on merits and since the entry into force of the PILA in 1989 only very few challenges to arbitral awards have succeeded.[74] Due to the very pro-arbitration stance that Switzerland has adopted in the past decades,

---

67 See, e.g., Baizeau (2005), p. 76, Van den Berg (2014), p. 15, Geisinger and Mazuranic (2013), p. 257, Girsberg and Voser (2016), pp. 424–430 ('An exclusion agreement is generally not recommended [...] Firstly, the possibility of setting aside an award is an important control mechanism of the quality of the work performed by the arbitral tribunal. Secondly, Art. 192 [PILA] leaves a claimant who has been unjustly defeated (because arbitral tribunal declined jurisdiction and thus did not enter into the claim or because the claim was dismissed for other reasons) without any remedy because it cannot benefit, unlike the respondent, from a recognition procedure to try to cure the defect.'). See also Jermini and Arroyo (2009) arguing that 'the grounds for setting aside an award pursuant to Article 190 [PILA] are limited to such very basic guarantees (of due process and against the violation of public policy) that no party—given the unpredictability of the outcome of an arbitration—should be willing to waive them in advance'. Other commentators stress that some arbitral awards may not require any enforcing obligations, thus resulting with no control whatsoever if parties have concluded an exclusion agreement. See, in particular Berger and Kellerhals (2010), p. 1667.

68 Van den Berg (2014), p. 15.

69 See, e.g. Baizeau (2013), p. 292.

70 Van den Berg (1992), p. 273.

71 Dasser (2007), p. 457, Dasser and Wójtowicz (2016), pp. 287–288. See also Baizeau (2013), p. 292, Geisinger and Mazuranic (2013), p. 257.

72 Van den Berg (2014), p. 15, Baizeau (2005), p. 76.

73 Van den Berg (2014), p. 15 where the author indicates that 'it is rare to find in practice an agreement expressly excluding the action for setting aside the award. What it seems to show is that practice does not wish to abandon the action for setting aside the award in the country of origin as a universal bar to enforcement of a dubious award.'

74 Baizeau (2013), p. 292, Dasser and Wójtowicz (2016), pp. 280–284.

it is argued that 'Switzerland is arguably precisely a forum where it makes little sense to waive, at least entirely, the right to challenge an award before the courts.'[75] Moreover, due to the setting-aside proceedings functioning as a safety net and a guarantee of arbitrators' prudence in deciding the case it is equally argued that 'an exclusion agreement is also likely to decrease the degree of the pressure on the arbitrators which may to some extent be regarded as a guarantee for the quality of the arbitration proceedings.'[76] Therefore, before excluding the right to setting-aside proceedings parties should strictly consider whether, given the unpredictable outcome of arbitration, the purported benefits of not having setting-aside proceedings would outweigh the opposing benefits of maintaining the right to challenge and annul an arbitral award, especially in cases where such an arbitral award potentially violates fundamental procedural human rights guarantees.

5.2.4 Article 192(1) of the PILA and the ECHR

Before introducing other States' approaches to exclusion agreements, this book's search for the most ECHR-compatible approach to exclusion agreements mandates a more detailed look at the *Tabbane v. Switzerland* case—a case in which the ECtHR specifically addressed the issue of compatibility of exclusion agreements with the ECHR. The Court's judgment in *Tabbane v. Switzerland* is a landmark ruling in which the Court for the first time examined the legitimacy and compatibility of a party's right to exclude recourse against an arbitral award with the rights and freedoms enshrined in the ECHR. Although the ECtHR established that an exclusion of setting-aside proceedings under Article 192(1) of the PILA in the particular circumstances was not per se contrary to Article 6(1) of the ECHR, the author believes that the Court's conclusion is not set in stone, at least when looking generally at the issue of waiver of certain Article 6(1) ECHR rights and the manner in which the Court applied previously introduced formal requirements of the *waiver theory* to the particular circumstances of the case.

5.2.4.1 Facts of the Case

The facts of the *Tabbane v. Switzerland* case date back to late 1990s, when a French company Colgate-Palmolive Services SA ('Colgate') decided to market its goods in Tunisia and chose to cooperate locally with a Tunisian company owned by Mr Noureddine Tabbane ('Tabbane') and his sons. In this context, the parties concluded various agreements, all governed by the law of the state of New York, including a shareholders' agreement ('Shareholders' Agreement') and an option agreement ('Option Agreement') that under certain conditions granted Colgate the right to

---

[75] Baizeau (2013), p. 292.

[76] Patocchi and Jermini (2000), para. 57.

acquire the entire shareholding of Tabbane in exchange of a payment calculated on the basis of the profit made by the distribution company.

Following termination of a manufacturing contract in 2006 that the distribution company had concluded with a company controlled by Tabbane in 2000, Tabbane initiated arbitration proceedings ('First Arbitration') on the basis of the Shareholders' Agreement. In 2010 an arbitral tribunal issued an award dismissing the Tunisian party's claims, following which Tabbane filed a request before the Swiss Federal Tribunal to set aside that arbitral award. In a judgment of 21 March 2011 the Swiss Federal Tribunal ruled that due to a waiver contained in the Shareholders' Agreement,[77] it is not possible to subject the matter to the annulment proceedings.[78]

Meanwhile, after Tabbane refused to assign the entire shareholding to Colgate under the Option Agreement, the latter initiated arbitration proceedings against Tabbane and his sons before the ICC in 2008 ('Second Arbitration'). Pursuant to the applicable ICC Rules of Arbitration, each of the parties appointed one arbitrator and the ICC appointed the third arbitrator. In accordance with the Option Agreement, the three arbitrators had to determine the seat of arbitration—the arbitrators decided in favour of Geneva, Switzerland. Similarly to the Shareholders' Agreement, the Option Agreement contained an arbitration clause which in its relevant parts specifically provided the following:

> Neither [party] shall be entitled to commence or maintain any action in a court of law upon any matter in dispute arising from or concerning this Agreement or a breach thereof except for the enforcement of any award rendered pursuant to arbitration under this Agreement. The decision of the arbitration shall be final and binding and neither party shall have any right to appeal such decision to any court of law.[79]

---

[77] The Shareholders' Agreement contained the following arbitration clause: 'Neither party shall be entitled to commence or maintain any action in a court of law upon any matter in dispute arising from or concerning this Agreement or a breach thereof except for the enforcement of any award rendered pursuant to arbitration under this Agreement. The decision of the arbitration shall be final and binding and neither party shall have any right to appeal such decision to any court of law.'

[78] Decision of the Swiss Federal Tribunal in case No. 4A_486/2010, 21 March, 2011. English translation of the decision available at http://www.swissarbitrationdecisions.com/valid-clause-waiving-the-appeal-to-the-federal-tribunal/. Accessed 22 May 2020. In its relevant parts, the Swiss Federal Tribunal notated that 'clause certainly constitutes valid renunciation to the appeal. It expresses doubtlessly the common will of the parties to renounce any right of appeal against any decision of the Arbitral tribunal in front of any state court whatsoever. This intent to rule out any appeal against such a decision, clearly expressed in the emphasized sentence of the arbitral clause is reinforced and indirectly confirmed by the preceding sentence; it appears indeed that the state courts could not be seized by any party except to obtain the enforcement of an award issued by the Arbitral tribunal. Moreover, the renunciation at hand closely resembles that which was dealt with in the judgment published at ATF 131 III 173 at 4.2.3.2. Reference may accordingly be made mutatis mutandis to the reasons contained in that decision whilst pointing out that in this case as in the one which gave rise to the precedent quoted, the word 'appeal' must manifestly be understood in its general meaning. The Parties have therefore validly opted out of an appeal against any decision of the Arbitral tribunal.'

[79] See decision of the Swiss Federal Tribunal in case No. 4A_238/2011, 4 January 2012. English translation of the decision available at http://www.swissarbitrationdecisions.com/sites/default/files/4%20janvier%202012%204A%20238%202011.pdf. Accessed 22 May 2020.

On 9 March 2011, the arbitral tribunal issued a final award ordering Tabbane and his sons to assign all of their shares to Colgate. Similarly to the First Arbitration, not being satisfied with the ruling of the Second Arbitration, Tabbane filed a claim with the Swiss Federal Tribunal challenging the arbitral award and seeking its annulment. Tabbane argued that (i) the arbitral tribunal did not have jurisdiction to hear the dispute; (ii) his right to be heard was violated by rejecting his request to appoint a financial expert to conduct an audit in order to determine the price of the shares; (iii) the arbitral tribunal failed to consider several arguments raised by Tabbane; and (iv) the arbitral tribunal violated public policy.[80]

5.2.4.2 Ruling of the Swiss Federal Tribunal

In deciding the application to set aside the arbitral award, the Swiss Federal Tribunal first recalled the existing practice as regards exclusion agreements under Article 192(1) of the PILA. As was seen when analysing Article 192(1) of the PILA,[81] the Swiss Federal Tribunal's case-law in this regard has gradually developed from a very restrictive to a more permissive approach. Although it is no more required for a valid waiver to specifically refer in arbitration agreement to Articles 190 or 192 PILA, it has been repeatedly stressed that the intention of the parties to conclude a waiver of setting-aside proceedings still needs to be expressed clearly and directly.[82] This case was no different.

The starting point for the Swiss Federal Tribunal was its analysis carried out in the annulment proceedings following the First Arbitration.[83] The opting out clauses in arbitration agreements both in the Shareholders' Agreement and the Option Agreement (and the other two agreements between the parties) were identical, therefore the Swiss Federal Tribunal emphasised that the opting out clause in the Option Agreement cannot be interpreted differently from the one in the Shareholders' Agreement.[84] It had already held in the First Arbitration that:

> [The arbitration] clause certainly constitutes valid renunciation to the appeal. It expresses doubtlessly the common will of the parties to renounce any right of appeal against any decision of the Arbitral tribunal in front of any state court whatsoever.[85]

---

[80] Decision of the Swiss Federal Tribunal in case No. 4A_238/2011, 4 January 2012, para. C. For a more detailed overview of the facts of the case please see, e.g. decision of the Swiss Federal Tribunal in case No. 4A_238/2011, 4 January 2012, paras. A, B and C as well as decision of the Swiss Federal Tribunal in case No. 4A_486/2010, 21 March, 2011, paras. A, B and C.

[81] See Sect. 5.2.

[82] Decision of the Swiss Federal Tribunal in case No. 4A_238/2011, 4 January 2012, para. 2.1.

[83] See Decision of the Swiss Federal Tribunal in case No. 4A_486/2010, 21 March, 2011. English translation of the decision available at http://www.swissarbitrationdecisions.com/valid-clause-waiving-the-appeal-to-the-federal-tribunal/. Accessed 22 May 2020.

[84] Ibid., para. 2.2.2.

[85] Decision of the Swiss Federal Tribunal of 21 March 2011, para. 2.2.

The Swiss Federal Tribunal continued in its decision with addressing the appellant's arguments that the word 'appeal' in the opting out clause ('[…] neither party shall have any right to appeal such decision to any court of law') intended only ordinary appeals and did not affect setting-aside proceedings. Tabbane had submitted comparative analysis of the laws of civil procedure in the state of New York, Tunisia and France, arguing that all laws interpret 'appeal' *stricto* sensu, however, the Swiss Federal Tribunal observed that in all of the said countries, arbitration laws allow only for annulment action and not for an ordinary appeal of international arbitral awards.[86] Moreover, it delved into the distinction between 'right of appeal' and 'right to appeal' (as in the opting clause), concluding that parties used the latter 'with a view to excluding the possibility for each of them to challenge the award […]'[87]

Even more so, the Swiss Federal Tribunal referred to the fact that Article 78(6) of the Tunisian Code of Arbitration, similarly to Swiss law, provides parties with the possibility to renounce any recourse against an arbitral award, therefore Tabbane, who is a Tunisian national, should have been aware of the consequences that such an exclusion may entail.[88] It thus concluded that the requirements of Article 192(1) of the PILA are satisfied and the case is not capable of being subject to the setting-aside proceedings on the basis of that provision.[89]

Additionally, and what later also resulted in the case being brought before the ECtHR, Tabbane argued that Article 192(1) of the PILA is inconsistent with the ECHR, in particular, the right of fair trial guaranteed by Article 6(1) of the ECHR.[90] Prior the Swiss Federal Tribunal gave its own reasoning as to the alleged non-conformity of Article 192(1) of the PILA with Article 6(1) of the ECHR, it first turned to the opposing party's reasons why the Swiss Federal Tribunal should not even consider this issue.

First, Colgate argued that Article 190 of the Swiss Constitution, obliging the Swiss Federal Tribunal to apply federal laws and international law, prevents it from reviewing the compatibility of Article192(1) of the PILA with Article 6(1) of the ECHR. The Swiss Federal Tribunal, however, did not share this opinion, citing various cases in which the application of Swiss federal law was set aside in favour of an international treaty such as the ECHR.[91]

---

[86] See decision of the Swiss Federal Tribunal of 4 January 2012, para. 2.2.4.2. and the comparative discussion on the possibility of ordinary appeal against international arbitral award in the USA, France and Tunisia.

[87] Decision of the Swiss Federal Tribunal of 4 January 2012, para. 2.2.4.2.

[88] Ibid., para. 2.2.6. The Swiss Federal Tribunal noted that 'Article 78(6) of the [Tunisian] Arbitration Code indeed provides that the parties that have no domicile or principal residence or an establishment in Tunisia may expressly agree to exclude any recourse, total or partial, against any decision of the arbitral tribunal. There is therefore even less of a reason to disregard the exclusion clause that the party involved comes from a country where the possibility to renounce any recourse against an international arbitral award was codified in the same way as in Switzerland.'

[89] Ibid.

[90] Ibid., para. 3.

[91] Ibid., para. 3.1.1.

Second, Colgate relied upon case law pursuant to which violation of ECHR may not be invoked directly in the annulment proceedings before the Swiss courts.[92] While acknowledging that a direct reliance on the ECHR for violations of arbitrators in the arbitration proceedings is indeed not possible under Swiss law, the Federal Tribunal nevertheless asserted that in this case:

> [I]t is not whether the Arbitrators disregarded one or the other of these guarantees, interpreted in the light of Art. 6(1) EHRC if necessary, but rather to determine whether Art. 192 PILA [...] is consistent with Art. 6(1) EHRC (normative control in a specific case).[93]

Lastly, Colgate argued that the Swiss Federal Tribunal had already affirmatively decided the issue of compatibility of Article 192(1) of the PILA with the ECHR previously, namely in its decision following the First Arbitration. However, in those proceedings Tabbane had not raised the issue of compatibility of Article 192(1) of the PILA with the ECHR.[94] Until the case at hand, the Swiss Federal Tribunal had not had the chance to specifically address the said issue.[95] However, 'the time [had] come to give the issue a specific answer'.[96]

After recalling the essence of Article 6(1) of the ECHR and the well-known fact that this provision per se does not prohibit the creation of arbitral tribunals and the adjudication of disputes before such tribunals, the Swiss Federal Tribunal concluded that 'it is possible to renounce a recourse against a future arbitral award without violating Article 6(1) [of the ECHR]'.[97] The ECtHR has frequently held that the Convention does not prevent persons of their own free will from waiving the guarantees of fair trial stipulated in Article 6(1) of the ECHR, provided that such a renunciation is unequivocal.[98] Previous analysis of Article 192(1) of the PILA has

---

[92] Ibid., 3.1.2. In one of the cited cases, the Federal Tribunal states that 'only the grievances limitatively spelled out in art. 190 (2) PILA may be raised in an appeal against an international arbitral award and not a direct violation of the federal constitution, of the ECHR or of other international treaties […]'. See decision of the Swiss Federal Tribunal in case No. 4A_404/2010, 19 April 2011, para. 3.5.3.

[93] Ibid.

[94] Ibid., para. 3.1.3.

[95] The issue of the conformity of art. 192 of the PILA with the ECHR had been raised in a previous case before the Swiss Federal Tribunal, however it was not sufficiently formulated: '[a]s stated, the argument is not sufficiently reasoned to be acceptable. In fact, the Appellant did not explain why Art. 192 PILA would be incompatible with art. 6 ECHR, be it in general way or only in the case at hand'. See decision of the Swiss Federal Tribunal in case No. 4A_500/2007, 6 March 2008, para. 3.2.3. In another decision (decision ATF 133 III 137, 22 March 2007, para. 4.3.2.2) the Swiss Federal Tribunal dealt with the applicability of Art. 192 of the PILA to sportsmen and found it 'also questionable with regard to Art. 6(1) EHRC'. However, no specific answer by the Swiss Federal Tribunal had been given until the case brought by Tabbane.

[96] Decision of the Swiss Federal Tribunal of 4 January 2012, para. 3.1.3.

[97] Ibid., para. 3.2.

[98] The Swiss Federal Tribunal in this context makes reference to *Pauger v. Austria*, App. No. 1617/90, ECtHR, 28 May 1997, para. 58, where the Court held: 'neither the letter nor the spirit of [Art. 6(1) ECHR] prevents a person from waiving of his own free will, either expressly or tacitly, the entitlement to have his case heard in public. Any such waiver must be made in an unequivocal manner and must not run counter to any important public interest'.

shown that a valid waiver of setting-aside proceedings requires exactly this—the waiver has to be contained in an express agreement. The Swiss Federal Tribunal also substantiated its position with previous case-law pursuant to which a waiver entered into on the basis of vitiated consent could be invalidated.[99] Moreover, it stipulated that, given the contractual and private nature of arbitration, one does not see a priori which important public interest may be harmed by excluding in advance the application of setting-aside proceedings.[100]

Consequently, taking into account the strict conditions which parties have to satisfy if they wish to waive the right to challenge an arbitral award in Switzerland, the Swiss Federal Tribunal held that nothing in the wording and interpretation of Article 192(1) of the PILA would suggest that it is inconsistent with the procedural guarantees provided in Article 6(1) of the ECHR and as interpreted by the ECtHR.[101]

5.2.4.3 The ECtHR's Judgment

Upon lodging an application with the ECtHR Tabbane's main complaint was that due to the alleged waiver of setting-aside proceedings he had been denied access to a State court in Switzerland and he could not challenge an unfair arbitration award.[102] He argued that the Swiss Federal Tribunal's interpretation of Article 192(1) of the PILA was excessively restrictive and that the arbitrating parties had no intention to exclude any remedy against the award, but simply appeal in its ordinary sense, i.e. only on the merits of the case.[103] Tabbane invoked both Article 6(1) of the ECHR and Article 13 of the ECHR which guarantees everyone the right to an effective remedy. Relying on Article 6(1) of the ECHR Tabbane also complained that the arbitral tribunal's refusal to appoint a financial expert had violated the right to a fair trial, in particular the principle of equality of arms.[104]

The Court's decision begins with a recollection of the factual circumstances of the case and an overview of the relevant domestic law and practice, both covered above. Moreover, the Court also first devotes a few paragraphs as to the applicable principles in case the applicant has deceased.[105] Having dealt with the said preliminary issues,

---

[99] Decision of the Swiss Federal Tribunal of 4 January 2012, para. 3.2. The Federal Tribunal held: 'PILA meets these requirements as it requests an express renunciation, which must also be the object of an agreement between the parties, which excludes any unilateral renunciation. Moreover, a renunciation which a party would make not of its own free will but by vitiated consent could be invalidated on that ground (judgment 4A_514/201012 of March 1st, 2011 at 4.2).'

[100] Decision of the Swiss Federal Tribunal of 4 January 2012, para. 3.2.

[101] Ibid.

[102] *Tabbane v. Switzerland*, App. No. 41069/12, ECtHR, 1 March 2016, para. 16.

[103] Ibid.

[104] Ibid., para. 17.

[105] The applicant passed away on 28 March 2013, thus after the submission of the application. In such cases, the ECtHR has a long-established practice to allow close relatives or heirs to proceed with the application if they have sufficient interest in the matter. See, e.g. See, e.g., *Raimondo v. Italy*, App. No. 12954/87, ECtHR, 22 February 1994, para. 2; *Malhous v. Czech Republic*, App. No.

the Court then continues with a brief restatement of the main principles on the dichotomy between arbitration and the Convention.

The Applicable Principles The ECtHR first recalls the general principles pertaining to the right of access to a court as impliedly contained in Article 6(1) of the ECHR, i.e. the fact that such a right is not absolute and that States are granted certain margin of appreciation to limit it. Ultimately, however, it is the ECtHR that decides whether by limiting the right of access to a court a State does not restrict or reduce access 'in such a way or to such an extent that the very essence of the right is impaired'.[106] The Court also refers to the well-established tripartite test, namely that any limitation must established by law, have a legitimate aim and that such limitation has to be reasonably proportionate to the aim pursued.[107]

Next, the Court reiterates what has already become apparent—the ECHR does not in principle preclude resolution of disputes by means of arbitration since the right of access to a court does not imply the right to a court of the classic kind.[108] Moreover, the Court repeatedly stresses the distinction between statutory (compulsory) and voluntary (consensual) arbitration, whereby the former is being imposed by law and should provide all the guarantees of Article 6(1) of the ECHR.[109] The latter, on the other hand, is different since arbitrating parties conclude an arbitration agreement voluntarily.

As to the aspects of voluntary arbitration and its relationship with the ECHR, the Court expressly reaffirms its previous case law stating that by concluding an arbitration agreement, parties waive *certain* rights guaranteed by the Convention.[110] Equally, the Court recalls that before a waiver of certain rights of Article 6(1) of the ECHR can be considered valid, it has to satisfy certain formal conditions, meaning it must be 'free, licit and unequivocal'.[111] Lastly, by referring to the *Pfeiffer and Plankl*

33071/96, ECtHR [GC], 12 July 2001, para. 1; *Velikova v. Bulgaria*, App. No. 41488/98, ECtHR, 18 May 2000 and others. Having a legitimate interest, Tabbane's wife and three sons as the deceased's heirs decided to pursue the application on behalf of Tabbane.

[106] See, e.g. *Ashingdane v. the United Kingdom*, App. No. 8225/78, ECtHR, 28 May 1985, para. 57.

[107] *Tabbane v. Switzerland*, App. No. 41069/12, ECtHR, 1 March 2016, para. 24.

[108] See, e.g., *Ringeisen v. Austria*, App. No. 2614/65, ECtHR, 16 July 1971, at para. 94. See also *Lithgow and Others v. the United Kingdom*, Apps. No. 9006/80; 9262/81; 9263/81; 9265/81; 9266/81; 9313/81; 9405/81, ECtHR, 8 July 1986, at para. 201.

[109] *Tabbane v. Switzerland*, App. No. 41069/12, ECtHR, 1 March 2016, para. 26 ('En outre, il convient de distinguer entre arbitrage volontaire et arbitrage forcé. S'agissant d'un arbitrage forcé, en ce sens que l'arbitrage est imposé par la loi, les parties n'ont aucune possibilité de soustraire leur litige à la décision d'un tribunal arbitral. Celui-ci doit offrir les garanties prévues par l'article 6 § 1 de la Convention (Bramelid et Malmström c. Suède, nos 8588/79 et 8589/79, décision de la Commission du 12 octobre 1989, DR no 29).').

[110] Ibid., para. 27 ('En souscrivant à une clause d'arbitrage, les parties renoncent volontairement à certains droits garantis par la Convention.').

[111] Ibid., para. 27. The Court uses the expression '[t]elle renonciation ne se heurte pas à la Convention pour autant qu'elle soit libre, licite et sans équivoque' and refers to its previous case-law, including *Suda v. the Czech Republic*, App. No. 1643/06, ECtHR, 28 October 2010, para. 48; *Suovaniemi and*

v. Austria case,[112] the Court also notes that for a waiver of procedural rights to be effective for the Convention's purposes it 'must be attended by minimum safeguards commensurate to its importance'.[113] Notably, however, the Court omits any reference to the requirement that waiver must not run counter to any important public interest.

The Court's Reasoning In applying the established principles to the particular facts of the case the Court first stipulates that it will examine the complaint solely under Article 6(1) of the ECHR, and not under Article 13 of the ECHR since the latter is already absorbed by the first provision. As seen previously when introducing Article 13 of the ECHR,[114] if the principal complaint before the Court is based on the absence of an appropriate remedy required by another provision of the Convention, it is not necessary to consider it also under Article 13 of the ECHR.

The ECtHR then continues with the application of the *waiver theory*. As to the requirement of absence of constraint, the Court acknowledges that Tabbane, through expressly and freely signing the arbitration agreement, exercised his procedural autonomy, thus giving up the right to settle any future disputes before an ordinary court of law which would have had an obligation to observe all the guarantees enshrined in Article 6(1) of the ECHR. Tabbane did not argue that he concluded the arbitration agreement under duress.[115]

Moreover, the Court concurs with the Swiss Federal Tribunal's analysis that the exclusion agreement renouncing application of setting-aside proceedings was concluded unequivocally. As was explained,[116] Article 192(1) of the PILA requires that a waiver is contained in an express agreement. That requirement has not changed since the Swiss Federal Tribunal's departure from its previous strict interpretation of Article 192(1) of the PILA in 2005. Even though parties no longer have to specifically refer to Articles 190 and 192(1) of the PILA, their common intention is still the most important requirement for a valid waiver. In light of the respective arbitration clause that, inter alia, provided that 'neither party shall have any right to appeal such decision to any court of law', the ECtHR considered that the Swiss Federal Tribunal's conclusion was neither arbitrary nor unreasonable, thus satisfying the requirement of absence of unequivocality.[117]

As to the requirement of necessary minimum safeguards commensurate to the importance of the waiver, the Court notes that the *waiver* of setting-aside proceedings was attended by such minimum safeguards, i.e. Tabbane was able to select an

---

others v. Finland, App. No. 31737/96, ECtHR., 23 February 1999; *Transado-Transportes Fluviais Do Sado, S.A. v. Portugal*, App. No. 35943/02, ECtHR, 16 December 2003.

[112] *Pfeiffer and Plankl v. Austria*, App. No. 10802/84, ECtHR, 25 February 1992.

[113] *Tabbane v. Switzerland*, App. No. 41069/12, ECtHR, 1 March 2016, para. 27 ('De plus, pour entrer en ligne de compte sous l'angle de la Convention, la renonciation à certains droits garantis par la Convention doit s'entourer d'un minimum de garanties correspondant à sa gravité (Pfeifer et Plankl c. Autriche, 25 février 1992, § 37, série A no 227).').

[114] See Sect. 3.3.2.1.

[115] *Tabbane v. Switzerland*, App. No. 41069/12, ECtHR, 1 March 2016, para. 29.

[116] See Sect. 5.2.

[117] *Tabbane v. Switzerland*, App. No. 41069/12, ECtHR, 1 March 2016, para. 30.

arbitrator and participate in the arbitration proceedings, the Swiss Federal Tribunal respectively heard his arguments and considered all factual and legal elements that were relevant to the resolution of the dispute, and the resulting judgment was reasoned, therefore giving no appearance of arbitrariness.[118]

Despite concluding that the pre-conditions of the *waiver theory* were successfully fulfilled, the Court further continues with examining the compatibility of Article 192(1) of the PILA with Article 6(1) of the ECHR per se.

Regarding the legitimacy of Article 192(1) of the PILA, the ECtHR recalls that the possibility to conclude a waiver of setting-aside proceedings is the Swiss legislator's legislative policy aimed at (i) increasing the attractiveness and effectiveness of the respective seat of arbitration; (ii) avoiding *double-control*; and (iii) alleviating ordinary courts of case-load.[119] In that regard, Article 192(1) of the PILA, in the Court's opinion, serves a legitimate aim.

Moreover, the ECtHR noted that the waiver under Article 192(1) of the PILA is not mandatory. Unlike the former 1985 Law in Belgium, or the Latvian legislative approach providing no setting-aside proceedings at all, Article 192(1) of the PILA only gives foreign parties a *statutory right*, i.e. a possibility, to exclude setting-aside proceedings—parties are under no obligation to make use of such a right. This particularity, in the Court's opinion, was sufficient to satisfy the requirement of proportionality. Allowing foreign parties with no links to Switzerland to exclude setting-aside proceedings is proportionate to the aim of attracting international arbitration to Switzerland and it strengthens the principle of contractual freedom.[120]

Lastly, the Court also gives weight to Article 192(2) of the PILA. If an arbitral award, in respect of which setting-aside proceedings had been excluded, is subject to recognition and enforcement proceedings in Switzerland, parties may invoke the grounds of Article V of the New York Convention, even though the arbitral award per se is not 'foreign' within the meaning of the New York Convention. This, in the Court's opinion, adds additional review by the ordinary courts of arbitral tribunals.[121]

In light of these considerations, the ECtHR concludes that the limitation of the right of access to a court by means of Article 192(1) of the PILA pursues a legitimate aim, respects the principle of contractual freedom and cannot be regarded as disproportionate to the aim of enhancing Switzerland's arbitration environment.

---

[118] Ibid., para. 31.

[119] Ibid., para. 33 ('En ce qui concerne la présente affaire, la Cour note que l'article 192 LDIP reflète un choix de politique législative qui répond au souhait du législateur suisse d'augmenter l'attractivité et l'efficacité de l'arbitrage international en Suisse, en évitant que la sentence soit soumise au double contrôle de l'autorité de recours et du juge de l'exequatur, et de décharger le Tribunal fédéral (paragraphe 13 ci-dessus).').

[120] Ibid., para. 34 ('De plus, il convient de noter qu'une partie, n'ayant ni domicile, ni résidence habituelle, ni établissement en Suisse, n'est nullement obligée d'exclure tout recours; bien au contraire, elle peut librement choisir de saisir cette possibilité qu'offre la loi suisse en renonçant valablement à tout recours à un tribunal ordinaire. La Cour estime que ce moyen offert aux parties qui n'ont pas de liens avec la Suisse est proportionné au but de renforcer l'attractivité de la Suisse en matière d'arbitrage international et de renforcer le principe de la liberté contractuelle des parties.').

[121] Ibid., para. 35.

Therefore, the very essence of the right of access to a court is not impaired and there is no violation of Article 6(1) of the ECHR.[122]

The Court's ruling in the *Tabbane v. Switzerland* case is seemingly unequivocal, establishing that exclusion agreements concluded pursuant to Article 192(1) of the PILA and satisfying the necessary preconditions of a valid waiver under the Convention, are compatible with the Convention, in particular Article 6(1) of the ECHR and the right of access to a court. Nevertheless, as stressed, it equally leaves room for a broader discussion on the said decision's comprehensiveness and relevance for the phenomenon of exclusion agreements per se. Whether or not the Court's conclusions in the *Tabbane v. Switzerland* case are to be interpreted restrictively, i.e. as solely being applicable to the particular case and its factual and legal circumstances, or they have an overall impact on the phenomena of exclusion agreements more generally will be addressed in detail in Chap. 7.

5.3 France

5.3.1 Overview of the Provision

In France, a statutory possibility to exclude the annulment mechanism has been introduced relatively recently. Together with a number of other important innovations it was introduced in the new French Law on Arbitration, adopted on 13 January 2011 and being part of the French Code of Civil Procedure ('FCCP').[123] Before its entry into force the annulment mechanism was considered as being part of public policy and therefore could not be excluded.[124]

Reasons for the adoption of a new arbitration law were simple—the previously in force law on arbitration of 1981 had generated a vast amount of arbitration-related case-law that had evolved during the past 30 years, therefore, creating a pressing need to codify this case-law in order to make French law 'even more readily accessible to foreign practitioners.'[125] A new arbitration law was also seen as an opportunity to introduce certain innovations and refine French law on arbitration to reflect its pro-arbitration policy to the fullest extent.[126] Among other innovations, the new French

[122] Ibid., para. 36. The Court concludes its judgment by also dismissing Tabbane's complaint that the arbitral tribunal refused to appoint an expert, stating that the Convention does not provide for rules on evidence and that the matter of admissibility of evidence is a national competence. See, e.g., *Mantovanelli v. France*, App. No. 21497/93, ECtHR, 18 March 1997; *Garcia Ruiz v. Spain*, App. No. 30544/96, ECtHR, 21 January 1999.

[123] Decree No. 2011-48 of 13 January 2011, reforming the law governing arbitration. https://www.legifrance.gouv.fr/affichTexte.do?cidTexte=JORFTEXT000023417517&categorieLien=id. Accessed 22 May 2020. An unofficial translation in English is available at http://www.sccinstitute.com/media/37105/french_law_on_arbitration.pdf. Accessed 22 May 2020.

[124] Gaillard (2010b), p. 87.

[125] Gaillard (2011).

[126] Ibid.

law introduced also a possibility to exclude setting-aside proceedings. Influenced by the laws of other States,[127] Article 1522(1) of the FCCP now concisely provides:

> By way of a specific agreement the parties may, at any time, expressly waive their right to bring an action to set aside.[128]

Introduction of such a provision was driven merely by the persistent pro-arbitration policy present in France during the past decades. Both French legal scholars[129] and courts[130] have long supported a very particular view on arbitration which in their eyes must be considered as an autonomous legal order detached from the constraints of domestic law.[131] Considering that French courts have also repeatedly recognized and enforced arbitral awards that have been annulled at the seat of arbitration,[132] it comes as no surprise that excluding the right to challenge an arbitral award is now possible also in France. As in other States permitting exclusion of setting-aside proceedings, such agreements under Article 1522(1) of the FCCP require the fulfilment of certain preconditions.

5.3.2 *Prerequisites*

5.3.2.1 No Connection to France? Not Necessarily!

Generally, jurisdictions that permit exclusion of setting-aside proceedings do so only in case of international arbitration proceedings between two or more foreign parties having no connection with the particular jurisdiction. As seen, such an approach is adopted in Switzerland. However, the French approach goes a step further and does

---

[127] See the official report accompanying the new Law on Arbitration (Decree No. 2011-48 of 13 January 2011), Ministére de la Justice et des Libertés, Rapport au Premier ministre relatif au décret no 2011-48 du 13 janvier 2011 portant réforme de l'arbitrage, 14 January 2011, Journal Officiel de la République Fran*çaise*. ('Une telle disposition, qui préserve le droit des parties à un recours effectif, est inspirée de droits étrangers existant.') https://www.legifrance.gouv.fr/affichTexte.do?cidTexte=JORFTEXT000023417498. Accessed 22 May 2020. See also Cazenave (2011), p. 589.

[128] Art. 1522(1) of the FCCP. Author's translation. Official text reads as follows: 'Par convention spéciale, les parties peuvent à tout moment renoncer expressément au recours en annulation.'

[129] See, among others, Gaillard (2010a), pp. 38–39.

[130] See, e.g. the well-known decision of *Société PT Putrabali Adyamulia v Société Rena Holding et Société Moguntia Est Epices*, Cour de Cassation, 29 June 2007, 05-18.053 where the French Cour de Cassation concluded that '[a]n international arbitral award, which is not anchored in any national legal order, is a decision of international justice whose validity must be ascertained with regard to the rules applicable in the country where its recognition and enforcement are sought'.

[131] See Sect. 4.2. See also, e.g. Gaillard (2010a), pp. 35–66.

[132] See, e.g. *Société Pablak Ticaret Ltd. Sirketi v. Norsolor S.A.*, Cour de cassation, 9 October 1984, 83-11.355; *Société Hilmarton Ltd. v. Société Omnium de traitement et de valorisation (OTV)*, Cour de cassation, 23 March1994, 92-15.137; *République arabe d'Egypte v. Société Chromalloy Aero Services*, Cour d'appel de Paris, 14 January 1997, 95/23025.

not limit the applicability of the right to exclude setting-aside proceedings to foreign parties only.[133]

Article 1522(1) of the FCCP applies to any arbitration which qualifies as *international* within the meaning of the FCCP, regardless of parties' domicile, habitual residence or business establishment.[134] Article 1504 of the FCCP provides that '[a]n arbitration is international when international trade interests are at stake'.[135] This can be seen as economical rather than a legal precondition.[136] Therefore, the scope of Article 1522 of the FCCP is much wider since one French and one foreign party, or even two French parties, having a contract 'where international trade interests are at stake' would still be permitted under the FCCP to conclude an exclusion agreement ousting French courts' jurisdiction to hear parties' actions for annulment. Notably, however, in such cases French court control is not excluded entirely—upon enforcement of an arbitral award in France, the opposing party may still appeal the enforcement on the same grounds as those in setting-aside proceedings.[137]

The approach adopted in France is an unprecedented solution among States that provide in their *leges arbitri* a possibility to exclude setting-aside proceedings. It fully resembles the French pro-arbitration philosophy and gives arbitrating parties the most extensive party autonomy in deciding whether or not their arbitral award should benefit from a review by State courts. While other countries, e.g. Switzerland, especially after the ECtHR ruling in the case of *Tabbane v. Switzerland*,[138] are only considering to extend the application of exclusion agreements also to national parties, France is the first country to take the extra step. Whether or not it is a step in the right direction remains to be seen.

5.3.2.2 Explicit Exclusion

Article 1522 of the FCCP requires that parties conclude the exclusion agreement by a *specific agreement* (*convention spéciale*). This means that a general clause (e.g. arbitrating parties agreeing that 'the award shall be promptly executed' or that they

---

[133] See, e.g. Scherer (2016), p. 440, Gaillard and de Lapasse (2011), p. 117, Gaillard (2011).

[134] Strik (2012) Growing number of countries allowing exclusion agreement with respect to annulment warrants greater scrutiny of arbitration clauses. Kluwer Arbitration Blog, 11 January 2012. http://kluwerarbitrationblog.com/2012/01/11/growing-number-of-countries-allowing-exclusion-agreements-with-respect-to-annulment-warrants-greater-scrutiny-of-arbitration-clauses/. Accessed 22 May 2020.

[135] Art. 1504 of FCCP. Author's translation. Official text reads as follows: 'Est international l'arbitrage qui met en cause des intérêts du commerce international.'

[136] See, e.g. *Courrèges Designe v Sté André Courrèges*, Cour d'appel de Paris, 5 April 1990.

[137] See art. 1522(2) of FCCP that states: 'Dans ce cas, elles peuvent toujours faire appel de l'ordonnance d'exequatur pour l'un des motifs prévus à l'article 1520.' See also Cazenave (2011), p. 589.

[138] Voser and George (2016).

'waive any recourse against the award') will not suffice.[139] In order for an exclusion agreement under Article 1522 of the FCCP to be valid and effective, parties have to specifically refer to the action of setting aside an arbitral award. It will not be sufficient that parties impliedly exclude the annulment action, e.g. by referring to a particular set of institutional rules or express their intention through a general clause in their arbitration agreement.[140] Renunciation of setting-aside proceedings requires a *convention spéciale*, i.e. a manifestation of the will of the parties specifically directed at the action of annulment.[141]

Moreover, similarly to Switzerland, Article 1522 of the FCCP provides that an exclusion agreement under French law can be made at any time (*à tout moment*), thus also after the establishment of arbitral tribunal or presumably also after the issuing of the arbitral award. However, when it comes to the scope of an exclusion agreement, Article 1522 of the FCCP is more restrictive in this regard than its counterparts in other jurisdictions and does not allow a partial exclusion. An exclusion of setting-aside proceedings under French law is a complete renunciation of all the grounds listed in Article 1520 of the FCCP. It is not possible to limit the exclusion of setting-aside proceedings only to certain grounds of Article 1520 of the FCCP and not others.[142] As explained by the drafters of Article 1522 of the FCCP, 'the French legislature decided not to allow any *à la carte* waivers by which parties exclude certain grounds and maintain others.'[143]

5.3.3 *Effects and Consequences*

A valid exclusion agreement under Article 1522 of the FCCP will result in the inability of arbitrating parties to challenge the arbitral award before the French courts.[144] However, if the enforcement of the award takes place in France and parties

---

[139] Gaillard and de Lapasse (2011), p. 119. See also *SARL Farmex Technologies v République d'Arménie, Foreign Financing Projects Management Center of the Ministry of Finance (FFPMC)*, Cour d'appel de Paris, 3 April 2014, 13/22288.

[140] For example, art. 35(6) of the ICC Rules (2017) provides that: 'Every award shall be binding on the parties. By submitting the dispute to arbitration under the Rules, the parties undertake to carry out any award without delay and shall be deemed to have waived their right to any form of recourse insofar as such waiver can validly be made.' It is submitted that reference to ICC rules will not suffice for a valid waiver under art. 1522 of the FCCP. See, e.g. Gaillard and de Lapasse (2011), p. 119, Seraglini (2011), para. 32. See also Day (2011).

[141] Gaillard and de Lapasse (2011), p. 119. See also *SARL Farmex Tech. v Rep. Armenia, FFPMC*, Cour d'appel de Paris, 3 April 2014, No. 13/22288.

[142] Ibid. Art. 1520 of the FCCP provides that 'an award may only be set aside where (i) the arbitral tribunal wrongly upheld or declined jurisdiction; or (ii) the arbitral tribunal as not properly constituted; or (iii) the arbitral tribunal rules without complying with the mandate conferred upon it; or (iv) due process was violated; or (v) recognition or enforcement of the award is contrary to international public policy'.

[143] Scherer (2016), p. 440.

[144] Gaillard and de Lapasse (2011), p. 120.

have concluded a valid exclusion agreement, Article 1522(2) of the FCCP further provides that 'the parties nonetheless retain their right to appeal an enforcement order on one of the grounds set forth in Article 1520 [of the FCCP]'—a right that may not be excluded by the parties. In such a case, the five narrowly construed grounds listed in Article 1520 of the FCCP will apply to the review of an arbitral award by the French courts.[145] This is very similar to the practical effects of Article 192(2) of the PILA.

Exclusion of the annulment mechanism under Article 1522 of the FCCP has thus no effect in the context of the execution of an arbitral award in France.[146] The drafters of the new French Law on Arbitration considered the exclusion of setting-aside proceedings useful in cases where foreign parties having no assets in France choose France as their place of arbitration.[147] If, however, an arbitral award subject to a valid exclusion of setting-aside proceedings, requires recognition and enforcement in France, an effective remedy is nevertheless guaranteed by a right to appeal the exequatur, thereby compensating for the lack of an action to annul an arbitral award.[148] The effects of that extra possibility, however, are not exactly the same as those for the setting-aside of an arbitral award—an international arbitral award annulled at the seat of arbitration will generally[149] not be enforced in other Member States of the New York Convention (Article V(i)(e) of the New York Convention). However, if, as in the case of France, an international arbitral award is simply denied recognition and enforcement at the country of the seat of arbitration, it still has *res judicata* effect, thus barring parties from repeatedly deciding the case and enabling the winning party to seek recognition and enforcement in other countries.

Moreover, although Article 1518 of the FCCP expressly stipulates that 'the only means of recourse against an award made in France in an international arbitration is an action to set aside', a revision of an arbitral award is also possible in France. Until

---

[145] See the official report accompanying the new Law on Arbitration (Decree No. 2011-48 of 13 January 2011), Ministére de la Justice et des Libertés, Rapport au Premier ministre relatif au décret no 2011-48 du 13 janvier 2011 portant réforme de l'arbitrage, 14 January 2011, Journal Officiel de la République Franç*aise*. ('dans ce cas, elles pourront toujours interjeter appel de l'ordonnance d'exequatur, sur la base des mêmes motifs que ceux prévus pour le recours en annulation.'). https://www.legifrance.gouv.fr/affichTexte.do?cidTexte=JORFTEXT000023417498. Accessed 22 May 2020. See also Gaillard (2011).

[146] Gaillard and de Lapasse (2011), p. 120.

[147] Cazenave (2011), p. 589.

[148] Ibid. See also Gaillard and de Lapasse (2011), p. 120.

[149] There are, of course, notable exceptions—for example France itself which have long recognized and enforced foreign arbitral awards annulled at the seat of arbitration. See, e.g., *Société Pablak Ticaret Limited Sirketi v Norsolor S.A.*, Cour de cassation, 9 October 1984, 83-11.355; *Société Hilmarton Ltd v Société Omnium de traitement et de valorisation (OTV)*, Cour de cassation, 23 March 1994, 92-15.137; *République arabe d'Egypte v Société Chromalloy Aero Services*, Cour d'appel de Paris, 14 January 1997, 95/23025. Other States, e.g. the Netherlands, have also recognized and enforced arbitral awards that have been set aside at the seat. See, e.g., *Yukos Capital S.A.R.L. v OAO Rosneft*, Amsterdam Court of Appeal, 28 April 2009, 200.005.269/01. Generally on recognition and enforcement of annulled arbitral awards see, among others, Koch (2009), pp. 267–292, Gaillard (1999), p. 512, Chan (1999), p. 141.

recently revision was possible only for domestic arbitral awards, however, the new French Law on Arbitration has codified the existing French court practice and now provides for the remedy of revision also for international arbitral awards.[150] Article 1502 of the FCCP provides that an '[a]pplication for revision of an arbitral award may be made in the circumstances provided in Article 595 [of the FCCP] for court judgments [...]' Only in very limited circumstances, such as fraud, subsequently recovered decisive evidence and false documents, may a party apply for a revision of an arbitral award.[151] Application for revision is made directly to the arbitral tribunal (Article 1502(2) of the FCCP), however, if the arbitral tribunal cannot be reconvened, such an application shall be submitted to the Court of Appeal having jurisdiction over other forms of recourse against the award (Article 1502(3) of the FCCP).[152]

Exclusion of setting-aside proceedings in France is significantly different from its Swiss counterpart in some, but not all aspects. Unlike Switzerland, the exclusion in France is not limited to foreign parties only. Exclusion of the annulment mechanism without any limitations as to localization can be considered as a direct and clear manifestation of the French philosophy—the seat of arbitration, as opposed to the State of enforcement, is not the most relevant player in international arbitration proceedings.[153] Like in Switzerland, exclusion agreements in France may be concluded at any time, provided a specific agreement is concluded in that regard. Yet, unlike in Switzerland, it is not possible to exclude the annulment mechanism partially, i.e. to exclude certain annulment grounds while retaining others.

Despite the possibility to exclude setting-aside proceedings, parties in France are also provided with certain safeguards against possible violations of their procedural rights during arbitration proceedings. Such safeguards include the right to appeal enforcement of an arbitral award on the grounds listed in Article 1520 of the FCCP and the right to apply for revision under Article 1502 of the FCCP. In line with the conclusions of the *Tabbane v. Switzerland* case and the fact that such safeguards closely resemble their counterparts in Swiss law, from the Court's point of view they could be considered as sufficient for protecting parties against possible violations of due process during arbitration proceedings. Whether or not the same is true from the

[150] Voser and George (2011), p. 50. See also *Fougerolles v. Procofrance*, Cour de Cassation, 25 May 1992, Rev. Arb. 91 (1993); *Heresma SA v. société Granitalia SpA*, Cour d'appel de Paris, 15 February 2007, Rev. Arb. 159 (2009).

[151] Art. 595 of the FCCP reads as follows: 'An application for revision of a judgment may be made only where: (i) it comes to light, after the judgment is handed down, that it was obtained fraudulently by the party in whose favour it was rendered; (ii) decisive evidence that had been withheld by another party is recovered after the judgment was handed down; (iii) the judgment is based on documents that have since been proven or have been held by a court to be false; (iv) the judgment is based on affidavits, testimonies or oaths that have been held by a court to be false. In all four cases, an application for revision shall be admissible only where the applicant was not able, through no fault of his or her own, to raise such objection before the judgment became *res judicata*'.

[152] This provision, however, applies only in domestic arbitration, therefore, if in the case of international arbitration the initial tribunal cannot be reconvened, revision would not be possible. See Voser and George (2011), p. 51.

[153] Gaillard (2011).

broader point of view of the dichotomy between *waivable* and *non-waivable* Article 6(1) of the ECHR rights, will be addressed in Chap. 7.

By introducing the possibility to exclude setting-aside proceedings, France has reaffirmed its strong pro-arbitration policy and broadened the scope of party autonomy. Also in France the practical effects of the statutory availability to opt for exclusion of setting-aside proceedings is somewhat limited as such possibility appears to be seldom used.[154] As described in the Commentary to the French Law on Arbitration:

> this new rule would seem to be more of a symbolic reform than a change in practice, since, if foreign experiences are to be believed, the rule has been used only rarely, and is not likely to be used more frequently in France since, after all, it worries people.[155]

5.4 Sweden

5.4.1 Overview of the Provision

The right to exclude the application of setting-aside proceedings in Sweden was introduced with the adoption of the 1999 Swedish Arbitration Act ('SAA')[156] which replaced the outdated and previously applicable arbitration statutes of 1929.[157] Although, similarly to France and other States, the new Section 51 of the SAA providing for a possibility to conclude exclusion agreements was generally inspired by Swiss law,[158] Swedish courts had already recognized—albeit in an *obiter dictum*—the right of foreign parties to enter into agreements limiting the right to challenge an arbitral award in 1989.[159] Such a right dates back to the so-called *Uganda* case which

[154]Burda (2013), p. 653.

[155]Bratic (2018) The Parties Hereby Waive All Recourse ... But Not That One.' Why Parties Adopt Exclusion Agreements and Why Courts Hesitate in referring to Code de l'arbitrage commenté, CPC art. 1523, p. 227 (own translation) (original text: '*cette nouvelle règle relève certainement davantage du symbole que d'un changement des pratiques car, si l'on en croit les expériences étrangères, elle n'a été que peu utilisée, et ne devrais pas l'être tellement plus en France car, à juste titre, elle inquiète.*'). https://www.ibanet.org/Article/NewDetail.aspx?ArticleUid=c8d82ee3-cb34-4113-a63c-7fff919639ee). Accessed 22 May 2020.

[156]*Lag om skiljeförfarande* (1999:116) (Law on Arbitration), entry into force on 1 April 1999. Unofficial English translation. http://www.sccinstitute.com/media/37089/the-swedish-arbitration-act.pdf. Accessed 22 May 2020.

[157]The two statutes governing arbitration in Sweden prior the adoption of the 1999 Swedish Arbitration Act were the 1929 Arbitration Act and the 1929 Foreign Arbitration Agreements and Awards Act. They applied both to domestic and international arbitration. More on arbitration in Sweden prior the introduction of the 1999 Swedish Arbitration Act. See, e.g. Stockholm Chamber of Commerce (1984).

[158]Gaillard et al. (1999), p. 80.

[159]*Solel Boneh International Limited and Water Resources Development (International) Limited v. The Republic of Uganda and the National Housing and Construction Company of Uganda*, Svea Supreme Court, 18 April 1989, reported in Y.B. Comm. Arb 16:606 (1991). The Svea Supreme

paved the way to the introduction of a possibility to conclude exclusion agreements also in Sweden.[160] One of the most important new provisions of the SAA is now codified in Section 51 of the SAA providing:

> Where none of the parties is domiciled or has its place of business in Sweden, such parties may in a commercial relationship through an express written agreement exclude or limit the application of the grounds for setting aside an award as are set forth in section 34.
>
> An award which is subject to such an agreement shall be recognised and enforced in Sweden in accordance with the rules applicable to a foreign award.

Swedish courts have long been very liberal towards international arbitration,[161] therefore, Section 51 of the SAA is not merely seen as a codification of the principles established in the *Uganda* case, but also as a clear affirmation of the long-existing pro-arbitration attitude in Sweden. By allowing foreign parties to opt-out from the application of setting-aside proceedings, the SAA certainly competes with its rivals and endeavours to create more favourable environment for arbitration and to attract more international arbitrations to Sweden.[162]

5.4.2 *Prerequisites*

Section 51 of the SAA provides for a somewhat more limited option to exclude setting-aside proceedings if compared to its counterparts in Switzerland, France and other States. In addition to the fulfilment of certain preconditions, i.e. (i) none of the parties must have been domiciled or have their place of business in Sweden; (ii) the underlying relationship between the parties must be of a commercial nature; and (iii) the exclusion agreement must be documented expressly in writing, the SAA also distinguishes between grounds of invalidity of an arbitral award and grounds for challenge of an arbitral award. While the former can in no way be validly excluded, foreign parties are entitled to exclude fully or partially the grounds for challenge of an arbitral award. This distinction between the grounds of invalidity and a mere challenge is what makes the Swedish approach to excluding the annulment mechanism to stand out.

Court acknowledged that 'such parties [i.e. parties not having any contact with Sweden] must be considered entitled to agree—even before any dispute arises between them—to limit their right to challenge the award in a Swedish court on account of formal deficiencies'.

[160] Ibid. See also Paulsson (1989), p. 291.

[161] See, e.g., Gaillard et al. (1999), p. 80.

[162] Heuman and Jarvin (2006), p. 255. See also the *travaux préparatoires* to the SAA—*Ny lag om Skiljeförfarande* (New law on Arbitration) (1994:81), *Delbetänkande av Skiljedomsutredningen* (Interim Report of the Arbitration Commission), p. 191. http://weburn.kb.se/metadata/417/SOU_7265417.htm. Accessed 22 May 2020.

5.4.2.1 No Connection to Sweden

Similarly to Switzerland, only foreign parties not having their domicile or place of business in Sweden are be able to benefit from the possibility to conclude exclusion agreements.[163] Although the SAA applies to both domestic and international arbitration (Section 46 of the SAA), only foreign parties having no connection to Sweden are able to exclude the annulment mechanism.[164] This is affirmed also by the fact that Sections 47–51 of the SAA (and also Sections 52–60 of the SAA) are applicable only to international matters.

The *travaux préparatoires* to the SAA explain that the possibility of concluding exclusion agreements is provided only to foreign parties in international commercial disputes due to several reasons. Firstly, such disputes may have an inherent interest in limiting the instances in which the legal effect of arbitration is determined.[165] Secondly, foreign parties in international commercial disputes are more competent to independently assess the pros and cons of exclusion agreements.[166] Moreover, in such cases no Swedish legal interests are affected.[167] Therefore, there is no reason to restrict the ability of such parties to their right to challenge an arbitral award before Swedish courts.[168]

In determining whether or not a party is domiciled or has its place of business in Sweden, one should look at its status at the moment when the arbitration agreement (or a subsequent exclusion agreement) was concluded.[169] Moreover, the fact that a foreign company has a subsidiary in Sweden, or owns a property located in Sweden, should not disqualify such a party from the possibility of concluding an exclusion agreement under Section 51 of the SAA.[170] This interpretation of the territoriality requirement is different than, for example, in Switzerland where, as explained above,[171] the presence of a branch or even a business establishment alone in Switzerland would disqualify the abroad-located parent company from benefiting of the possibility to exclude setting-aside proceedings.

---

163 Madsen (2016), p. 454.

164 Hober (2001), p. 383, Knuts (2013), p. 264. See also *Solel Boneh International Limited and Water Resources Development (International) Limited v. The Republic of Uganda and the National Housing and Construction Company of Uganda*, Svea Supreme Court, 18 April 1989, reported in Y.B. Comm. Arb. 16:606 (1991).

165 *Ny lag om Skiljeförfarande* (New law on Arbitration) (1994:81), *Delbetänkande av Skiljedomsutredningen* (Interim Report of the Arbitration Commission), p. 191. http://weburn.kb.se/metadata/417/SOU_7265417.htm. Accessed 22 May 2020.

166 Ibid.

167 Ibid.

168 Ibid.

169 Ibid., p. 192.

170 Ibid.

171 See Sect. 5.2.2.

5.4.2.2 Commercial Relationship

In addition to allowing only foreign parties to conclude exclusion agreements under Section 51 of the SAA, it is also required that the relationship between the parties that subject themselves to an exclusion agreement is of commercial nature.[172] The *travaux préparatoires* to the SAA define the notion of 'commercial relationship' as being one between traders in their business activities.[173] Since disputes that are submitted to settlement by international arbitration proceedings are generally of a commercial nature, fulfillment of this requirement is not seen as problematic. To some extent it can be put on par with the requirement under French law that permits exclusion agreements only in international arbitrations, i.e. disputes that have international trade interests at stake.[174]

5.4.2.3 Explicit Agreement

As the provision suggests, exclusion of setting-aside proceedings under Section 51 of the SAA is only possible through an express written agreement. In other words, such exclusion must be unambiguous and explicit.[175] Parties have a choice—to include the exclusion clause in an arbitration agreement or sign a separate agreement when the dispute arises or even subsequently, i.e. after the arbitral award is issued.[176] This is very similar to the formal requirements in Switzerland and France. What matters most is that the agreement is in writing and that parties' intention to exclude the right to challenge an arbitral award pursuant to Section 34 of the SAA can be clearly established.

The *travaux préparatoires* to the SAA explain that it is important that a party does not lose its right to challenge an arbitral award simply by reference to arbitration rules that such a party might not be well aware of. Therefore, a general reference to institutional arbitration rules that provide for the finality of arbitral award will not

---

[172] See, e.g. Hober (2011), p. 383.

[173] *Ny lag om Skiljeförfarande* (New law on Arbitration) (1994:81), *Delbetänkande av Skiljedomsutredningen* (Interim Report of the Arbitration Commission), p. 308. http://weburn.kb.se/metadata/417/SOU_7265417.htm. Accessed 22 May 2020.

[174] See Sect. 5.3.2.

[175] Hober (2011), p. 383, Knuts (2013), p. 264. See also, e.g., case No. T 245-11, T 314-11, Svea Court of Appeal, 11 April 2014 ('A waiver of the right to review under Section 36 of the Swedish Arbitration Act must, just as waivers under Section 51 of the Swedish Arbitration Act of the right to review under Section 34, be unambiguous and explicit. Unofficial English translation. http://www.arbitration.sccinstitute.com/Views/Pages/GetFile.ashx?portalId=89&cat=79572&docId=2046506&propId=1578. Accessed 22 May 2020.

[176] Madsen (2016), p. 455.See also *Ny lag om Skiljeförfarande* (New law on Arbitration) (1994:81), *Delbetänkande av Skiljedomsutredningen* (Interim Report of the Arbitration Commission), p. 192. http://weburn.kb.se/metadata/417/SOU_7265417.htm. Accessed 22 May 2020.

suffice for a valid exclusion of the annulment mechanism.[177] Such a provision can be also found in the 2017 SCC Rules.[178]

The approach in Sweden is somewhat similar to the Swiss Federal Tribunal's interpretation of Article 192(1) of the PILA prior the ground-breaking ruling in 2005, i.e. it is required that parties specifically refer to the right to challenge an arbitral award under Section 34 of the SAA and exclude it:

> It is important to note that the exclusion agreement must be in *writing* [sic.] and that it must *specifically* [sic.] refer to the parties' waiver of the right to challenge an award pursuant to section 34 of the Act. This means, e.g. that it will not be sufficient for parties to refer to institutional rules, such as e.g. the ICC Rules, which may contain clauses similar to an exclusion agreement. Instead, under section 51, as mentioned, the parties must explicitly [sic.] state that they waive their rights pursuant to section 34.[179]

5.4.2.4 Grounds of Invalidity v. Grounds for Challenge

An interesting aspect of the SAA is that, unlike in Switzerland or France, the SAA differentiates between annulment grounds (Section 34 of the SAA) and grounds of invalidity (Section 33 of the SAA). Section 51 of the SAA permits exclusion of the annulment grounds only.[180] Exclusion agreements under Section 51 of the SAA will not affect the applicability of the grounds of invalidity provided in Section 33 of the SAA.[181]

The distinction between invalid and challengeable arbitral awards was made already in the previously applicable arbitration statutes of 1929:

> The first category includes awards which were invalid per se and which did not require any activity from any of the parties; if the award was invalid it was so ab initio and forever. The second category, challengeable awards, covers awards which could be set aside by a court of

---

[177] See, e.g. Madsen (2016), p. 455. See also *Solel Boneh International Limited and Water Resources Development (International) Limited v. The Republic of Uganda and the National Housing and Construction Company of Uganda*, Svea Supreme Court, 18 April 1989, reported in Y.B. Comm. Arb. 16:606 (1991).

[178] See art. 46 of the SCC Rules (2017) ('An award shall be final and binding on the parties when rendered. By agreeing to arbitration under these Rules, the parties undertake to carry out any award without delay.').

[179] Hober (2001), p. 383. See similar arguing in, e.g. Knuts (2013), p. 264.

[180] Heuman and Jarvin (2006), pp. 241–242, Hober (2001), p. 383, Knuts (2013), p. 264. Sec. 34 of the SAA provides that an award shall be set aside if (i) it is not covered by a valid arbitration agreement between the parties; (ii) the arbitrators have made the award after the expiration of the period decided on by the parties, or where the arbitrators have otherwise exceeded their mandate; (iii) arbitral proceedings, according to sec. 47, should not have taken place in Sweden; (iv) an arbitrator has been appointed contrary to the agreement between the parties or this Act; (v) if an arbitrator was unauthorized due to any circumstance set forth in secs. 7 or 8; or (vi) if, without fault of the party, there otherwise occurred an irregularity in the course of the proceedings which probably influenced the outcome of the case.

[181] Hober (2001), p. 383 ('Section 51 means that it is not possible to waive the invalidity grounds set out in section 33. Invalidity is beyond the control of the parties; it is beyond party autonomy.').

law at the request of a party under certain circumstances. The party had to make its request within a stipulated period of time.[182]

During the SAA's negotiations there were discussions 'whether or not it was necessary, or desirable, to maintain this distinction in Swedish law',[183] especially considering that neither the UNCITRAL Model Law or arbitration laws of other jurisdictions make such a distinction. The main justification for preserving this difference also in the SAA is that in case of an arbitral award being invalid, there are both third-party interests and also an element of public interest.[184]

The grounds of invalidity under Section 33 of the SAA include (i) non-arbitrability of a dispute under Swedish law; (ii) violation of Swedish public policy, and (iii) failure to fulfil certain formal requirements with regard to the written form and signature on the arbitral award.[185] The public policy ground in turn differentiates between substantive and procedural public policy, whereby '[i]nvalidity for breach of procedural public policy follows if the award is based on forged evidence or other procedural documents, and the forgery has affected the award.'[186] Violation of procedural public policy would also occur 'in situations where one of the parties has appointed all arbitrators, even if the appointment procedure is stipulated in the arbitration agreement.'[187]

The invalidity grounds in Section 33 of the SAA have been justified on grounds of public and third party interest, consequently being mandatory and not subject to exclusion by arbitrating parties.[188] Differentiation between the annulment grounds and grounds of invalidity is a particular characteristic of the Swedish arbitration law and appears in hardly any other *lex arbitri.*[189] Moreover, while action for the challenging of an arbitral award under Section 34 of the SAA must be brought within 3 months no such time limit exists for invalidity claims under Section 33 SAA.[190]

---

[182] Ibid., p. 378.

[183] Ibid.

[184] Hober (2001), p. 378. See also *Ny lag om Skiljeförfarande* (New law on Arbitration) (1994:81), *Delbetänkande av Skiljedomsutredningen* (Interim Report of the Arbitration Commission), p. 189. http://weburn.kb.se/metadata/417/SOU_7265417.htm. Accessed 22 May 2020.

[185] Sec. 33 of the SAA provides: 'An award is invalid: (i) if it includes determination of an issue which, in accordance with Swedish law, may not be decided by arbitrators; (ii) if the award, or the manner in which the award arose, is clearly incompatible with the basic principles of the Swedish legal system; or (iii) if the award does not fulfil the requirements with regard to the written form and signature in accordance with sec. 31, first paragraph […]'. More generally see, e.g., Hober (2011), pp. 301–309.

[186] Knuts (2013), p. 241.

[187] Ibid. in referring to Hober (2011), p. 306.

[188] Madsen (2016), p. 191.

[189] See secs. 40 and 41 of the Finnish Arbitration Act (1999). See also Report of the Parliamentary Committee on revision of the 1999 Swedish Arbitration Act, SOU 2015:37, p. 32. http://www.regeringen.se/rattsdokument/statens-offentliga-utredningar/2015/04/sou-201537. Accessed 22 May 2020.

[190] Knuts (2013), p. 240.

Although the Swedish arbitration law still differentiates between the two different notions of invalidity and challengeability, the current distinction has been perceived as unnecessary and problematic—until recently, it was proposed to move the public policy provision from Section 33 to Section 34 of the SAA and repeal Section 33 altogether.[191] Whether or not the proposed changes would find their way into the text of the revised SAA was unclear. Prior the adoption and entering into force of the revised SAA it was suggested that the distinction between the two different grounds, i.e. invalidity and challengeability, would remain intact.[192] Indeed, this is true also in the final version of the revised SAA as adopted by the Swedish legislature on 21 November 2018 and entered into force on 1 March 2019.[193]

5.4.3 *Effects and Consequences*

The effects of a valid exclusion agreement under Section 51 of the SAA are similar to the effects and consequences of such agreements in other States, such as France and Switzerland. By concluding an exclusion agreement, parties effectively can limit in part or exclude in full the otherwise applicable annulment grounds under Section 34 of the SAA. If a party brings annulment action notwithstanding the existing exclusion agreement, the court, upon the objection of the other party, will dismiss the action.[194]

Exclusion of the right to challenge an arbitral award, however, is much more limited in Sweden than in other States. This is particularly due to the untypical distinction between annulment grounds, on the one hand, and grounds of invalidity, on the other hand. Whereas the former may be subject to a partial or full exclusion by the parties pursuant to Section 51 of the SAA, it is not possible to exclude the invalidity grounds of Section 33 of the SAA. To some extent the non-waivable grounds of invalidity are comparable with grounds for revision in Swiss and French law, only much broader and with infinite time limit for application. In the author's opinion, the distinction made in Swedish arbitration law provides a sound balance between the interests of parties in limiting certain annulment grounds and the interests of the State to exercise certain control over arbitration proceedings. Apparently, since the distinction has been kept in the revised SAA, this is also the opinion of the Swedish legislator and arbitration community.

Moreover, Section 51(2) of the SAA provides that if an exclusion agreement is concluded and recognition and enforcement of the arbitral award takes place in Sweden, rules applicable to foreign awards are apply *mutatis mutandis*. Therefore,

[191] See Report of the Parliamentary Committee on revision of the 1999 Swedish Arbitration Act, SOU 2015:37, p. 32. http://www.regeringen.se/rattsdokument/statens-offentliga-utredningar/2015/04/sou-201537. Accessed 22 May 2020. See also Ipp (2015).

[192] Kotick (2018).

[193] Arbitration Institute of the Stockholm Chamber of Commerce (2019) Revised Swedish Arbitration Act in 2019. https://sccinstitute.com/about-the-scc/news/2018/revised-swedish-arbitration-act-in-2019/. Accessed 22 May 2020.

[194] Madsen (2016), p. 456.

similarly to Article 192(2) of the PILA or Article 1522(2) of the FCCP, parties are still afforded certain level of protection, even if they exclude the right to challenge the arbitral award and seek recognition and enforcement of an arbitral award in Sweden.[195]

In Sweden, like elsewhere, exclusion agreements are more a rarity rather than an every-day practice. Due to their infrequent use some authors have referred to exclusion agreements as white rhinoceros—'nice to see, could happen that it is seen, but it is extremely rare'[196]—while practitioners acknowledge that the exclusion of setting-aside proceedings is an 'extremely unattractive proposition to any contracting party'.[197]

5.5 Belgium

5.5.1 Overview of the Provision

A possibility to exclude the right to challenge an arbitral award is also provided in the recently amended Belgian law on arbitration, contained in Part VI of the Belgian Code of Civil Procedure ('BCCP').[198] Having realized the adverse consequences of the attempt to do away with the annulment mechanism altogether, introduced below when addressing States' approaches to total exclusion of setting-aside proceedings in national law,[199] the Belgian legislator drew inspiration from the Swiss PILA and amended its arbitration law in 1998 making the exclusion of setting-aside proceedings optional.[200] The Law of 19 May 1998 entered into force on 17 August 1998 and replaced the previously in place mandatorily applicable exclusion of setting-aside proceedings for foreign parties arbitrating in Belgium with a more lenient system of a possibility of opting-out.[201]

---

[195]Ibid., pp. 456–457, Hober (2001), p. 378, Heuman and Jarvin (2006), p. 255.

[196]Heuman and Jarvin (2006), p. 536.

[197]Ibid.

[198]The new Belgian arbitration law, amending Part VI of the Belgian Judicial Code, came into force on 1 September 2013. It is based on the Model Law (with 2006 amendments) and replaces the formerly applicable Belgian arbitration law, adopted on 4 July 1972 and amended on 27 March 1985 and 19 May 1998.

[199]See Sect. 6.2.

[200]Art. 1717(4) of the Arbitration Law 1998 (Belgium), amending the Judicial Code 1985 (Belgium), See also Jaksic (2002), p. 310. The old art. 1717(4) was replaced by the following new paragraph: 'Parties may, by an explicit declaration in the arbitration agreement or by a later agreement, exclude any application for the setting aside of an arbitral award, in case none of them is a physical person of Belgian nationality or a physical person having his normal residence in Belgium or a legal person having its principal seat or a branch office in Belgium'.

[201]Hanotiau and Block (1999), p. 98. Generally on the Law of 19 May 1998 see, e.g. Demeyere (1999), p. 308.

The new 2013 Belgian law on arbitration retains the same approach as in the Law of 19 May 1998 and almost identically to its predecessor provides parties with a mere possibility to opt-out of the setting-aside proceedings in Article 1718 of the BCCP:[202]

> By an explicit declaration in the arbitration agreement or by a later agreement, the parties may exclude any application for the setting aside of an arbitral award, where none of them is a natural person of Belgian nationality or a natural person having his domicile or normal residence in Belgium or a legal person having its registered office, its main place of business or a branch office in Belgium.

5.5.2 *Prerequisites*

Requirements for excluding setting-aside proceedings in Belgium are generally similar to the requirements under Swiss, French and Swedish law. Exclusion agreement will be considered valid and effective if two cumulative pre-conditions are fulfilled.

5.5.2.1 No Connection to Belgium

First of all, Article 1718 of the BCCP makes the conclusion of an exclusion agreement dependent upon the nationality, domicile or normal residence (in case of natural persons) or registered office, main place of business or a branch office (in case of legal persons) of the arbitrating parties. Thus, only foreign arbitrating parties with no actual link with Belgium, but for the seat of arbitration, will be able to exclude the setting-aside proceedings. If one of the parties to arbitration proceedings is of Belgian nationality or has its domicile or normal residence in Belgium, it will not be possible to benefit from the application of Article 1718 of the BCCP. The same is true in case one of the parties to the dispute has its registered office, main place of business or a branch office in Belgium.[203]

Save for the nationality requirement, the Belgian provision is very similar to its Swiss counterpart in Article 192 of the PILA. As the Belgian legislator provides, the main rationale for allowing only foreign parties to enter into exclusion agreements is the fact that the enforcement and thus also judicial control of arbitral awards between such persons will take place before the courts of another State.[204]

---

[202] Art. 1718 of the BCCP is almost identical to its predecessor—art. 1717(4) of the former BCCP, except for minor formal clarifications. Generally on the new 2013 Belgian law on arbitration see, e.g. Verbist (2013), pp. 597–618.

[203] Verbruggen (2016), p. 491. See also Verbist (2013), p. 606.

[204] Verbruggen (2016), p. 491.

5.5.2.2 Explicit Exclusion

Second of all, it is equally necessary that parties renounce their right to challenge an arbitral award explicitly, i.e. by an explicit declaration (*par une déclaration expresse*; *door een uitdrukkelijke verklaring*). An exclusion agreement will be considered valid if parties' decision to exclude setting-aside proceedings is sufficiently clear and unambiguous.[205]

When the opting-out possibility was introduced in the Law of 19 May 1998, there was a discussion what exactly amounts to an *explicit declaration*—a similar discussion as seen in Switzerland. However, while in Switzerland the position changed in 2005, Belgian law adopts the previously prevalent interpretation that a general reference to the finality of an arbitral award in, e.g. arbitration agreement, the applicable arbitration rules or terms of reference will not constitute an explicit declaration within the meaning of Article 1718 of the BCCP.[206] Belgian courts have affirmed that generally vague exclusion agreements (e.g. that 'the award is shall be final') and a mere reference to institutional rules[207] will not satisfy the requirement of explicitness.[208] Therefore, when considering the exclusion of setting-aside proceedings in Belgium, parties are advised to state explicitly that they wish to exclude setting-aside proceedings.

Moreover, Article 1718 of the BCCP provides that an exclusion of setting-aside proceedings can either be made in the arbitration agreement or by a later agreement, e.g. during the arbitration proceedings (in the terms of reference, for instance) or after the final arbitral award is rendered.[209] As seen, discretion as to the moment of conclusion of an exclusion agreement and similar requirements of explicitness are provided also in Swiss, French and Swedish law.

5.5.3 *Effects and Consequences*

By concluding a valid exclusion agreement parties renounce their statutory right to have the arbitral award set aside by Belgian courts on grounds stipulated in Article

[205] Ibid., p. 490.

[206] Demeyere (1999), p. 308 stating that '[s]ince it was expressly stated in the *travaux préparatoires* that the intention was to adopt the rule applied in Switzerland, it is most probable that the same interpretation will also prevail. Moreover, it conforms to the case law of the Belgian Supreme Court, according to which the waiver of a right cannot be presumed but may only be deduced from facts which are not susceptible of another interpretation.'

[207] See, e.g. art. 32(2) of the CEPANI Arbitration Rules (2013) or art. 34(6) of the ICC Arbitration Rules (2012).

[208] *Cytec Industrie BV v. SNF SAS*, Brussels Court of Appeal. Rev. Arb. 3:574 (2009). General references include, e.g. a reference in the arbitration agreement that 'the award is final' or that 'the parties waive their right to any form of recourse insofar as such a waiver can be validly made'. See Verbruggen (2016), p. 490.

[209] Philippe (2014).

1717 of the BCCP. Although Article 1718 of the BCCP is silent upon the possibility to exclude the annulment mechanism partially, it is generally accepted that parties may do so, i.e. to partially exclude certain grounds of Article 1717 of the BCCP while at the same time retaining others.[210] In contrast to Swiss and French law, the BCCP does not provide for an option to revoke an arbitral award, however, fraudulently obtained award is listed as an additional and self-standing ground for the annulment of arbitral awards under Article 1717 of the BCCP and can be invoked by the Belgian courts *ex officio*.[211] Moreover, Article 1716 of the BCCP also gives parties an opportunity to agree on appeal against the arbitral award that, if agreed, has to be filed within one month of the notification of the arbitral award.

In practice, even though the possibility to exclude setting-aside proceedings is expressly provided in the BCCP, it is said that foreign parties very rarely make use of such a right.[212] Also legal commentators consider that due to the severe consequences that renunciation of setting-aside proceedings entail parties should be cautious with excluding such a right before the issuing of the final award and are advised to conclude exclusion agreements only in exceptional circumstances.[213]

5.6 Other States

Although Switzerland, France, Sweden and Belgium are the most common examples of jurisdictions that under certain circumstances permit parties to exclude their right to file for the annulment of an arbitral award, they are not the only ones that provide arbitrating parties with such a possibility. While a handful of other jurisdictions around the globe have adopted an equally liberal approach to permitting exclusion of setting-aside proceedings, other States take a much more restrictive approach in that regard. Certain others, somewhat similarly to the Swedish approach, find themselves in the middle, adopting an intermediate approach to providing arbitrating parties with a possibility to exclude setting-aside proceedings. While the below brief overview will not witness the same amount of detail as the above introduced jurisdictions and is not an exhaustive list of States adopting either liberal, restrictive or intermediate approaches to regulating exclusion of setting aside proceedings (in particular consid ering that some of the below States are not Council of Europe Member States, thus not subject to the ECHR regime), it nevertheless provides a useful glimpse at the various different legislative approaches that States take in this regard.

---

210 Verbruggen (2016), p. 491.

211 Art. 1717(3)(b)(iii) of the BCCP.

212 Verbruggen (2016), p. 492.

213 Ibid., p. 491.

5.6.1 The Liberal Approach

In addition to Switzerland, France and Belgium, there are a handful of other States that adopt a rather liberal approach to regulating exclusion of setting-aside proceedings in their *leges arbitri.* A non-exhaustive overview of such States is provided below.

5.6.1.1 Columbia

Both domestic and international arbitration in Columbia is governed by the Law 1563 of 12 July 2012, i.e. the Columbian Arbitration Act, which entered into force in October 2012.[214] Article 107 of the Columbian Arbitration Act provides for a similarly liberal approach to excluding setting-aside proceedings as, e.g. Switzerland. In case neither party is domiciled or resident in Columbia, parties may exercise a right to exclude their right to bring an action for annulment at the post-award stage, or limit such action to one or more of the grounds exhaustively listed in Article 108 of the Columbian Arbitration Act. In its relevant part Article 107 of the Columbian Arbitration Act provides:

> When neither party has its domicile or residence in Colombia, the parties may, by express declaration in the arbitration agreement or by a subsequent written agreement, completely exclude the action for annulment, or limit it to one or more of the grounds contemplated exhaustively in this section.[215]

Columbian approach is very much similar to the Swiss approach—exclusion of setting-aside proceedings is possible only with respect to international arbitration where all parties to the arbitration are domiciled and reside outside Colombia. Equally, an express declaration in the arbitration agreement, or a subsequent written agreement is required. Exclusion is possible of either all of the annulment grounds provided for in Article 108 of the Columbian Arbitration Act or only some. In domestic arbitration exclusion of setting-aside proceedings is not possible.

---

[214] Law 1563 of 2012, Columbian Arbitration Act. http://www.secretariasenado.gov.co/senado/basedoc/ley_1563_2012.html. Accessed 22 May 2020.

[215] Ibid., art. 107, second part (own translation). The original reads as follows: 'Cuando ninguna de las partes tenga su domicilio o residencia en Colombia, las partes podrán, mediante declaración expresa en el acuerdo de arbitraje o mediante un acuerdo posterior por escrito, excluir completamente el recurso de anulación, o limitarlo a una o varias de las causales contempladas taxativamente en la presente sección.'

5.6.1.2 Mauritania

Domestic and international arbitration in Mauritania is governed by Law No. 2000-06 of 18 January 2000, i.e. the Code of Arbitration[216] which in its Article 59(4)(b) provides:

> Parties which are neither Mauritanian, nor domiciled, having principal residence or establishment in Mauritania, may agree to expressly exclude any recourse, total or partial, against any decision of the arbitral tribunal.[217]

Mauritanian Code of Arbitration is slightly more explicit as to the international character of exclusion agreements, providing that exclusion of setting-aside proceedings is possible only when none of the arbitrating parties are Mauritanian, have no domicile, principal residence or establishment in Mauritania. The remaining requirements are largely comparable to the Swiss approach, requiring express exclusion of the respective remedy and permitting to exclude either all of only some of the annulment grounds listed in Article 59 of the Mauritanian Code of Arbitration.

5.6.1.3 Peru

Domestic and international arbitration in Peru is governed by the legislative decree No. 1017 of 4 June 2004, i.e. Peruvian Arbitration Act which is based on the UNCITRAL Model Law. Article 63(8) of the Peruvian Arbitration Act provides:

> When none of the parties to the arbitration is Peruvian or has his domicile, habitual residence or place of main activities in Peruvian territory, an express agreement may be concluded to waive any application to set aside or to limit such application to one or more grounds set out in this Article. If the parties have waived any application to set aside and enforcement of the award is sought in the Peruvian territory, the provisions in Title VIII [Recognition and Enforcement of Foreign Awards] shall apply.[218]

A similar pattern to providing possibility to exclude the application of setting-aside proceedings can be witnessed also under the Peruvian Arbitration Act. Exclusion is only possible in international arbitration proceedings, i.e. 'when none of the parties to the arbitration is Peruvian or has his domicile, habitual residence or place of

---

[216] Mauritanian Code of Arbitration, Law No. 2000-06 of 18 January 2000. http://www.newyorkconvention.org/national+arbitration+law+-+mauritania. Accessed 22 May 2020.

[217] Ibid., art. 59(4)(b) of the Code of Arbitration (own translation). The original reads as follows: 'les parties qui n'ont en Mauritanie ni domicile, ni résidence principale, ni établissement, peuvent convenir expressément d'exclure tout recours, total ou partiel, contre toute décision du tribunal arbitral.'

[218] Peruvian Arbitration Act, decree No. 1017 of 4 June 2004, art. 63(8) (own translation). The original reads as follows: 'Cuando ninguna de las partes en el arbitraje sea de nacionalidad peruana o tenga su domicilio, residencia habitual o lugar de actividades principales en territorio peruano, se podrá acordar expresamente la renuncia al recurso de anulación o la limitación de dicho recurso a una o más causales establecidas en este artículo. Si las partes han hecho renuncia al recurso de anulación y el laudo se pretende ejecutar en territorio peruano, será de aplicación lo previsto en el título VIII.'

main activities in Peruvian territory'. Equally, a valid exclusion agreement mandates express agreement of all or only some of the annulment grounds provided for in Article 63 of the Peruvian Arbitration Act. As in Switzerland, for arbitral awards with respect to which an exclusion agreement has been concluded, but whose enforcement is sought in Peru, the applicable provisions on recognition and enforcement of foreign arbitral awards will apply.

5.6.1.4 Tunisia

Domestic and international arbitration in Tunisia is governed by Law No. 93-42 of 26 April 1993, i.e. the Code of Arbitration, which in its Article 78(6) provides:

> The parties who have neither domicile, principal residence, nor business establishment in Tunisia, may expressly agree to exclude totally or partially all recourse against an arbitral award.[219]

The wording of the above provision is very similar to that in the Swiss PILA, permitting exclusion agreements only to foreign parties with no domicile, principal residence or business establishment in Tunisia. Such an agreement moreover has to be made expressly with regard to either the recourse as a whole or only some of the annulment grounds listed in Article 78(2) of the Tunisian Code of Arbitration. As seen above, the fact that Article 78(6) of the Tunisian Code of Arbitration provides for largely similar opportunity of foreign parties in international arbitration to renounce the application of setting-aside proceedings played important factor also in the Swiss Federal Tribunal's decision preceding the *Tabbane v. Switzerland* case. As the Swiss Federal Tribunal noted:

> Article 78(6) of the [Tunisian] Arbitration Code indeed provides that the parties that have no domicile or principal residence or an establishment in Tunisia may expressly agree to exclude any recourse, total or partial, against any decision of the arbitral tribunal. There is therefore even less of a reason to disregard the exclusion clause that the party involved comes from a country where the possibility to renounce any recourse against an international arbitral award was codified in the same way as in Switzerland.[220]

5.6.1.5 Turkey

International arbitration in Turkey is generally governed by the International Arbitration Law No. 4686 of 21 June 2001, which in its relevant parts of Article 15 provides:

---

[219] Art. 78(6) of the Tunisian Code of Arbitration, Law No. 93-42, Art. 78(6). The original reads as follows: 'Les parties qui n'ont en Tunisie, ni domicile, ni résidence principal ni établissement, peuvent convenir expressément d'exclure tout recours, total ou partiel, contre toute décision du tribunal arbitral.' For more details see, e.g. Knoll (2012), Kallel (1992).

[220] Decision of the Federal Tribunal of 4 January 2012, para. 2.2.4.2.

> The parties may, in part or in full, renounce the right to initiate an action for setting aside the award. A party whose domicile or habitual residence is not in Turkey may renounce that right completely in an express clause in the arbitration agreement or in writing, following the signature of the arbitration agreement. Alternatively, in the same manner, the parties may renounce the above right for one or more of the reasons as set forth above for setting aside the award [see Article 15A(2)(1), above].[221]

Article 15 of the Turkish International Arbitration Law similarly to its counterparts in other States' laws introduced above provides that parties by an express agreement may fully or partially renounce their right to initiate setting-aside proceedings. Such a possibility is granted only to parties whose domicile or habitual residence is not in Turkey.[222]

Generally, States adopting a liberal approach towards permitting exclusion of setting-aside proceedings follow a similar pattern, built on the pioneering Swiss PILA. Interestingly, Turkey, as well as Tunisia and Peru, are considered to be UNCITRAL Model Law countries, i.e. countries that have based their arbitration laws on the UNCITRAL Model Law, and yet they permit arbitrating parties to renounce their right to setting-aside proceedings—a mechanism that is provided for in Article 34 of the UNCITRAL Model Law.

An explanation to this rather considerable deviation has been given in 1998 by the Ontario Court (General Division) in Canada (now the Ontario Superior Court of Justice) in the case of *Noble China Inc v Lei Kat Cheong*.[223] The case concerned a dispute on the basis of an arbitration agreement that provided: 'No matter which is to be arbitrated is to be the subject matter of any court proceeding other than a proceeding to enforce the arbitration award.'[224] Arbitration proceedings were governed by the Ontario International Commercial Arbitration Act (ICAA)—UNCITRAL Model Law statute—and when the respondent tried to apply for the setting aside of an arbitral award, the Court in essence concluded that the UNCITRAL Model Law permits parties to agree on the procedure to be followed by the arbitral tribunal in conducting the proceedings and that Article 34 of the UNCITRAL Model Law is not a mandatory provision of the UNCITRAL Model Law.[225] Therefore, parties may exclude setting-aside proceedings, as long as their agreement is not contrary to

[221] International Arbitration Law No. 4686, art. 15. Unofficial English translation. http://www.camera-arbitrale.it/Documenti/tial_turkey.pdf. Accessed 22 May 2020. The original reads as follows: 'Taraflar, iptal davası açma hakkından kısmen veya tamamen feragat edebilirler. Yerleşim yerleri veya olağan oturma yerleri Türkiye dışında bulunan taraflar, tahkim anlaşmasına koyacakları açık bir beyanla veya sonradan yazılı şekilde anlaşmak suretiyle iptal davası açma hakkından tamamen feragat edebilecekleri gibi; yukarıda sayılan bir veya bir kaç sebepten dolayı iptal davası açmak hakkından da feragat edebilirler.'

[222] For more details on art. 15 of the Turkish International Arbitration Law see, e.g. Tiryakioğlu and Bayata Canyaş (2015), pp. 186–189.

[223] *Noble China Inc. v. Lei Kat Cheong*, (1998), 42 O.R. (3d) 69, (Ont. Gen. Div. Nov. 4, 1998).

[224] Ibid., at 73.

[225] Leon and Karimi (2007), pp. 7–8 in referring to *Noble China Inc. v. Lei Kat Cheong*, (1998), 42 O.R. (3d) 69, 87 (Ont. Gen. Div. Nov. 4, 1998) at 87, 90, 92 and 93-4).

mandatory provisions of law or principles of public policy.[226] Argumentation of the Ontario Court was based on the fact that Article 34 of the UNCITRAL Model Law did not contain the familiar mandatory language of *shall*, but instead used the more permissive language of *may*.[227] This, in the eyes of the Ontario Court, permitted parties to exclude the application of setting-aside proceedings.

Notwithstanding the above and irrespective of the increasing autonomy that arbitration as a dispute settlement mechanism has gained in the past few decades, States permitting the exclusion of setting-aside proceedings are still considered more as the odd ones out rather than jurisdictions whose particular legislative choice in allowing parties to renounce the application of setting-aside proceedings would constitute a general trend in contemporary international arbitration. Apart from the above few jurisdictions, other States are more restrictive in regulating arbitration and do not give up their right to exercise certain control over arbitration proceedings.

5.6.2 *The Restrictive Approach*

States adopting a restrictive approach in this regard can be put in two categories—on the one hand there are those States that are silent upon whether or not they permit arbitrating parties to renounce their right to apply for the setting-aside of an arbitral award, albeit at the same time in practice it is recognized that such exclusion is not permissible; on the other hand, an increasing number of States around the globe expressly stipulate in their *leges arbitri* that arbitrating parties cannot exclude the possibility to apply for the setting-aside of an arbitral award at the post-award stage. Irrespective of the adopted approach, the main reason behind such a restrictive attitude towards permitting exclusion of setting-aside proceedings is the fact that the annulment mechanism is being considered either as a mandatory provision of law or part of the particular States broader public policy. A non-exhaustive overview of States adopting restrictive approach to excluding setting-aside proceedings is provided below.

5.6.2.1 Argentina

International arbitration in Argentina is governed by the International Commercial Arbitration Law No. 27.449 of 4 July 2018 (ICAL), which is based on the UNCITRAL Model Law.[228] While the law itself is silent upon the possibility to exclude

---

[226]Interestingly, no similar possibility of contracting out of the application of setting-aside proceedings exist under the Ontario domestic arbitration statute. See *Noble China Inc. v. Lei Kat Cheong*, (1998), 42 O.R. (3d) 69, 87 (Ont. Gen. Div. Nov. 4, 1998), at 88-9.

[227]*Noble China Inc. v. Lei Kat Cheong*, (1998), 42 O.R. (3d) 69, 87 (Ont. Gen. Div. Nov. 4, 1998), at 90.

[228]International Commercial Arbitration Law No. 27.449, 4 July 2018. http://www.senado.gov.ar/parlamentario/comisiones/verExp/228.16/PE/PL. Accessed 22 May 2020.

the application of setting-aside proceedings in international arbitration cases, it is said that the ICAL does not provide the parties with the right to exclude grounds of challenge against an arbitral award.[229] The law governing national arbitration is more explicit in this regard—Article 1656 of Argentinian Civil and Commercial Code expressly provides that the annulment action cannot be waived by means of an arbitration agreement as that would be contrary to the legal order.[230]

5.6.2.2 Brazil

Arbitration in Brazil is governed by Law 9.307,[231] i.e. the Brazilian Arbitration Act, which entered into force in 1996 and is said to be partially based on the UNCITRAL Model Law and the 1998 Spanish Arbitration Act.[232] Although the Brazilian Arbitration Act is silent upon possibility to renounce the right to apply for setting-aside of an arbitral award, it is recognized that such a right cannot be validly waived as it would be contrary to the right of access to a court under the Constitution of Brazil.[233]

5.6.2.3 Croatia

Arbitration in Croatia is governed by the Croatian Arbitration Act of 2001 which is based on the UNCITRAL Model Law.[234] Croatia is one of the handful of jurisdictions expressly providing in its arbitration law that parties are not permitted to exclude the application of setting-aside proceedings. Article 36(6) of the Croatian Arbitration Act succinctly provides:

> The parties cannot derogate in advance their right to contest the award by an application for setting aside.

The fact that the right to request the annulment of an arbitral award cannot be validly excluded under the Croatian Arbitration Act is equally recognized in practice.[235]

---

229 Corra and Peña (2019).

230 Codigo Civily Comercial de la Nacion, Law No. 26.994 of 1 October 2014, Art. 1656 (own translation). http://www.newyorkconvention.org/national+arbitration+law+-+argentina. Accessed 22 May 2020. The original reads as follows: 'En el contrato de arbitraje no se puede renunciar a la impugnación judicial del laudo definitivo que fuera contrario al ordenamiento jurídico.'

231 Brazilian Arbitration Act, Law 9.307. http://www.planalto.gov.br/ccivil_03/LEIS/L9307.htm. Accessed 22 May 2020.

232 Monteiro et al. (2009).

233 Ramos and Salomão (2016).

234 Croatian Arbitration Act of 2001. http://www.vsrh.hr/CustomPages/Static/HRV/Files/Legislation__Law-Arbitration-RC.pdf. Accessed 22 May 2020.

235 Močibob et al. (2018).

5.6.2.4 Egypt

International arbitration in Egypt is governed by Law No. 27/1994 Promulgating the Law Concerning Arbitration in Civil and Commercial Matters, i.e. the Egyptian Arbitration Act, which is based on the UNCITRAL Model Law.[236] Similarly to Croatian Arbitration Act, the Egyptian Arbitration Act in its Article 54(1) explicitly provides that exclusion of setting-aside proceedings is not possible:

> The action for annulment of the arbitral award must be brought within ninety days of the date of the notification of the arbitral award to the party against whom it was made. The admissibility of the action for annulment shall not be prevented by the applicant's renouncement of its right to request the annulment of the award prior to the making of the arbitral award.

The Egyptian Arbitration Act differs between exclusion of annulment action either before or after the arbitral award is made. It is said that an agreement to exclude any form of recourse against an award is valid and enforceable only if such agreement was concluded after the award was rendered and notified to the parties.[237] This impliedly follows from the wording of Article 54(1) of the Egyptian Arbitration Act. Therefore, exclusion of the right of recourse against an arbitral award is not valid if concluded prior to issuing the arbitral award.

5.6.2.5 England

In England, arbitration is governed by the 1996 Arbitration Act.[238] The English approach to judicial controls over arbitration in itself is rather untypical since in addition to the traditional annulment grounds, Section 69 of the 1996 Arbitration Act provides that, in absence of an agreement to the contrary, a party to arbitral proceedings may (upon notice to the other parties and to the tribunal) also appeal to the court on a question of law arising out of an award made in the proceedings. Thus, in essence, English law provides for the possibility to appeal an arbitral award *stricto* sensu, i.e. on a question of law. The classic action for annulment, however, cannot be excluded since Sections 67 and 68, providing for the challenge of an arbitral award for lack of jurisdiction or irregularity affecting the tribunal, the proceedings, or the award, are considered mandatory provisions of law that have effect notwithstanding any agreement to the contrary (Section 4(1) of the 1996 Arbitration Act).

---

[236] Law No. 27/1994 Promulgating the Law Concerning Arbitration in Civil and Commercial Matters. https://www.wipo.int/edocs/lexdocs/laws/en/eg/eg020en.pdf. Accessed 22 May 2020. See Abbas and Matouk (2019).

[237] Wahad (2019).

[238] 1996 English Arbitration Act. http://www.legislation.gov.uk/ukpga/1996/23/section/68. Accessed 22 May 2020.

5.6.2.6 India

Domestic and international arbitration in India is governed by the Arbitration and Conciliation Act of 1996 (as amended in 2019).[239] While the 1996 Arbitration And Conciliation Act is silent upon exclusion of annulment action, it is generally recognized that judicial review as such cannot be excluded as that would be contrary to the public policy of India and would be considered to be a restraint on legal proceedings, prohibited by Indian law.[240]

5.6.2.7 Italy

Domestic and international arbitration in Italy is governed by the Italian Code of Civil Procedure, in particular Sections 806 to 840.[241] Section 829(1) of the Italian Code of Civil Procedure lists the available annulment grounds and expressly provides that a recourse for setting aside may be filed on the basis of such grounds notwithstanding any waiver.

5.6.2.8 Jordan

Domestic and international arbitration in Jordan is governed by Law No. 31 of 2001, i.e. the Jordan Arbitration Law, which is said to be mainly derived from the Egyptian Arbitration Act of 1994, that is based on the UNCITRAL Model Law.[242] Article 50 of the Jordan Arbitration Law provides:

> An action for nullity of the arbitral award must be raised within thirty days following the date on which the arbitral award was notified to the party against whom it was rendered; and such action is admissible even if the party invoking nullity had waived his right to do so before the issuance of the arbitral award.

Therefore, an action for annulment under the Jordan Arbitration Law is admissible even if an arbitrating party waived its right to annulment proceedings prior the issuing of the arbitral award. Therefore, similarly as in Egypt, exclusion of setting-aside proceedings *ex post* would still be admissible in Jordan.

---

[239] 1996 Arbitration and Conciliation Act. http://legislative.gov.in/sites/default/files/A1996-26.pdf. Accessed 22 May 2020.

[240] Kachwaha and Rautray (2019).

[241] Italian Code of Civil Procedure. Translation of relevant parts applicable to arbitration. https://www.jus.uio.no/lm/italy.arbitration/doc.html. Accessed 22 May 2020.

[242] Jordan Arbitration Law, Law No. 31 of 2001. Unofficial English translation. http://www.ilo.org/dyn/natlex/natlex4.detail?p_lang=en&p_isn=63091&p_country=JOR&p_count=146. Accessed 22 May 2020.

5.6.2.9 Greece

Domestic arbitration in Greece is regulated under Articles 867-903 of the Greek Code of Civil Procedure,[243] while Greek Law No. 2735/1999 on International Commercial Arbitration provides the framework for international commercial arbitration.[244] Article 900 of the Greek Code of Civil Procedure explicitly provides that a renunciation of the right to file an action for setting aside of an arbitral award before such award was rendered shall be null. Therefore, while *ex ante* exclusion of setting aside proceedings is impermissible under Greek law, *ex post* exclusion agreements, i.e. such that are concluded after the issuance of an arbitral award, are admissible and effective under Greek law.

5.6.2.10 Lebanon

Arbitration proceedings in Lebanon are governed by the Lebanese Code of Civil Procedure, that draws a distinction between domestic arbitration (Articles 762 to 808) and international arbitration (Articles 809 to 821). It is said that in both domestic and international arbitration proceedings the annulment action is considered to be part of public order and therefore cannot be excluded by parties' agreement.[245]

5.6.2.11 New Zealand

Both domestic and international arbitration in New Zealand is governed by the 1996 Arbitration Act, which is based on the UNCITRAL Model Law.[246] Although the law is silent upon the possibility to exclude the annulment action, it is generally recognized that the right to apply for the setting aside of an arbitral award under Article 34 of Schedule 1 of the Arbitration Act is part of the irreducible mandatory core of arbitration law that may not be waived by the parties.[247] An interesting example in this regard is the case of *Methanex Motonui Ltd v Joseph Spellman and Ors*[248] decided by the Court of Appeal in New Zealand where in similar circumstances as in the Ontario Superior Court of Justice's case of *Noble China Inc*, a completely

---

[243] Greek Code of Civil Procedure. Translation of the relevant parts applicable to domestic arbitration. https://www.uv.es/medarb/observatorio/leyes-arbitraje/europa-resto/grecia-ccp-domestic-arbitration.pdf. Accessed 22 May 2020.

[244] Law No. 2735/1999 on International Commercial Arbitration. https://www.hellenicparliament.gr/Nomothetiko-Ergo/Anazitisi-Nomothetikou-Ergou?law_id=8f3088f5-99d6-4223-b97a-1c9016d2fb53. Accessed 22 May 2020.

[245] Comair-Obeid (2019).

[246] New Zealand Arbitration Act of 1996. http://www.legislation.govt.nz/act/public/1996/0099/latest/DLM403277.html. Accessed 22 May 2020.

[247] Kalderimis (2018).

[248] *Methanex Motonui Ltd v Joseph Spellman and Ors, Court of Appeal of New Zealand*, CA 171/03, 17 June 2004.

opposite outcome in interpreting Article 34 of the UNCITRAL Model Law was reached. As the Court of Appeal in New Zealand ruled:

> A reading of the *travaux préparatoires* associated with the UNCITRAL Model Law suggests that there was no contemplation that parties to arbitral proceedings could seek to limit further the rights of review contemplated by Article 34 [...] Looking at the issue from a purely common law perspective, the UNCITRAL Model Law was finalised in 1985 at a time when the prevailing orthodoxy [...] was that exclusion of curial review was not possible.[249]

Therefore, in New Zealand the impermissibility of exclusion of setting-aside proceedings is explained not only due to the annulment action being a mandatory core of arbitration law, but also with regard to the aim behind the UNCITRAL Model Law.

5.6.2.12 Oman

Both domestic and international arbitration in Oman is governed by the Law of Arbitration in Civil and Commercial Disputes, Royal Decree 47/1997 (as amended),[250] which in its Article 54(1) explicitly provides that exclusion of setting-aside proceedings prior the issuing of an arbitral award will have no effect on arbitrating parties' right to nevertheless apply for the setting aside action:

> The suit seeking nullification of the arbitration award shall be filed within ninety days following the date of notification of the arbitration award to the party against whom the award is passed. Waiver of the right to submit the nullification suit prior to the passing of the award shall not prevent the aggrieved party from submitting his suit thereafter.

Impermissibility of *ex ante* exclusion agreements is also recognized in practice.[251] However, *ex post* exclusion of setting-aside proceedings will be admissible under the Omanis arbitration law. In this respect, the law in Oman is very much similar to the above introduced laws in Egypt and Jordan.

5.6.2.13 Panama

Panama is a very interesting example that has transitioned from a liberal to restrictive approach permitting exclusion agreements. Until 2013 Panamian arbitration law

---

[249] Ibid., at 109. See also para. 110 where the Court refers to the Law Commission's explanation in its report that '[t]he matters upon which an award may be challenged under article 34 must be taken to be fundamental to the procedure which the Model Law establishes.'

[250] Law of Arbitration in Civil and Commercial Disputes, Royal Decree 47/1997. English translation. http://www.newyorkconvention.org/11165/web/files/document/2/1/21103.pdf. Accessed 22 May 2020.

[251] Malik and Penz (2019).

permitted the exclusion of setting-aside proceedings.[252] Article 36 of the Panamian decree-law no. 5, 8 July 1999[253] provided that:

> If the arbitration is an international commercial arbitration in the meaning of this decree-law, the parties can decide, or the arbitration rules can allow, to waive the annulment action provided for in the article above.[254]

However, by a decision of 7 October 2005, the Panama Supreme Court held that Article 36 of the Panamian decree-law no. 5 permitting parties to renounce the application of setting-aside proceedings is unconstitutional as it violates parties' rights of due process.[255] Consequently, when the Panamian arbitration law was reformed in 2013, Article 36 was deleted and currently arbitrating parties in Panama are not permitted to exclude setting-aside proceedings.[256]

5.6.2.14 Portugal

Both domestic and international arbitration in Portugal is governed, inter alia, by the Voluntary Arbitration Law, as stipulated by Law No. 62/2011 of 14 December 2011, which is based on the UNCTRAL Model Law.[257] Article 46(5) of the Voluntary Arbitration Law expressly provides that an action for annulment of an arbitral award cannot be excluded by arbitrating parties:

> Without prejudice to the provisions of the preceding paragraph, the right to apply for the setting aside of an arbitral award cannot be waived.

Therefore, the right to apply for the setting-aside of an arbitral award cannot be excluded in Portugal.

5.6.2.15 Romania

The primary source for both domestic and international arbitration in Romania is the New Civil Procedure Code, in force as of 15 February 2013.[258] Article 609 of the New Civil Procedure Code provides that *ex ante* exclusion of setting-aside proceedings is not permissible in Romania:

---

[252]See art. 36 of the Panamian decree-law no. 5, 8 July 1999 ('If the arbitration is an international commercial arbitration in the meaning of this decree-law, the parties can decide, or the arbitration rules can allow, to waive the annulment action provided for in the article above'.

[253]Panamian decree-law no. 5, 8 July 1999. http://biblioteca.cejamericas.org/bitstream/handle/2015/4389/pan_decley5.pdf?sequence=1&isAllowed=y. Accessed 22 May 2020.

[254]Panamian decree-law no. 5, 8 July 1999, art. 36. Translation taken from Scherer (2016), p. 442.

[255]See Scherer (2016), p. 442.

[256]Ibid.

[257]Voluntary Arbitration Law, Law No. 62/2011 of 14 December 2011. http://www.newyorkconvention.org/11165/web/files/document/1/6/16314.pdf. Accessed 22 May 2020.

[258]New Civil Procedure Code, part IV, On Arbitration. http://www.newyorkconvention.org/11165/web/files/document/2/1/21368.pdf. Accessed 22 May 2020.

Article 609. Waiver of the action for annulment

(1) The parties cannot waive their right to file an action for annulment of the arbitral award in their arbitration agreement.
(2) This right can be waived only after the award is made.[259]

Therefore, exclusion of setting aside proceedings in Romania is only permissible after the issuing of the arbitral, however, not prior.

5.6.2.16 Saudi Arabia

The main law governing arbitration in Saudi Arabia is the Royal Decree No. M/34 (24/5/1433H), dated 16 April 2012[260] which in its Article 51(1) provides:

> An action for nullification of the arbitration award shall be filed by either party within sixty days following the date of notification of said party of the award; and such action is admissible even if the party invoking nullification waives his right to do so prior to the issuance of the arbitration award

The Saudi approach to exclusion of setting-aside proceedings is very much inspired by its counterparts in, e.g. Egypt and Jordan. While exclusion of setting-aside proceedings per se is possible under the Saudi arbitration law, arbitrating parties will be entitled to apply for the annulment of an arbitral award even if a valid exclusion agreement has been concluded before the award is made. *Ex post* exclusion agreements, however, are admissible under the Saudi arbitration law.

5.6.2.17 Serbia

Both domestic and international arbitration in Serbia is governed by the Serbian Arbitration Act, Law No. 46/2006,[261] which is based on the UNCITRAL Model Law. Article 62 of the Serbian Arbitration Act *expressis verbis* provides that exclusion of setting-aside proceedings is not permissible under Serbian law:

> The parties may not waive in advance their right to apply for setting aside of the arbitral award.

To sum up, States adopting a restrictive approach to permitting exclusion agreements are still in the majority when compared to those handful of States that allow arbitrating parties to exclude the annulment action *ex ante*, i.e. at the time of conclusion of an arbitration agreement. Setting-aside proceedings are viewed as an important mechanism of judicial controls over arbitration that not only

---

[259] New Civil Procedure Code, Article 609.

[260] Royal Decree No. M/34 (24/5/1433H), dated 16 April 2012. http://www.newyorkconvention.org/11165/web/files/document/2/1/21112.pdf. Accessed 22 May 2020.

[261] Serbian Arbitration Act, Official Journal of the Republic of Serbia, No. 46/2006. http://www.newyorkconvention.org/11165/web/files/document/2/1/21113.pdf. Accessed 22 May 2020.

protects parties' procedural rights of due process, but also functions as a safety net for the respective States to guarantee that their mandatory provisions of law and public policy is duly observed during arbitration proceedings. The above briefly introduced States adopting a restrictive approach towards exclusion of setting-aside proceedings are not necessarily the only such examples—other States, e.g. Austria,[262] Bulgaria,[263] the Czech Republic,[264] Japan,[265] Lithuania,[266] the Netherlands,[267] Poland,[268] Spain,[269] Vietnam[270] and others[271] adopt an equally restrictive approach in this regard and consider the annulment mechanism being either a mandatory provision of law or part of public policy, and thus not subject to exclusion by parties.

5.6.3 The Intermediate Approach

In addition to States adopting liberal and restrictive approaches to regulating exclusion agreements in their national arbitration laws, there are also a few States that try to balance the interests of increased party and arbitral autonomy, on the one hand, and protection of parties' due process rights and the interests of the respective State, on the other hand.

As it has become evident, one such example is Sweden that differs between grounds of invalidity (Section 33 of the SAA) and grounds for challenge of an arbitral award (Section 34 of the SAA)—while the former can in no way be validly excluded, foreign parties are entitled to exclude fully or partially the grounds for challenge of an arbitral award. A similar distinction between grounds of invalidity and grounds for challenge of an arbitral award appears to made also in Finland.[272]

---

[262] Zeiler (2018).

[263] Chuturkova (2018).

[264] Kudrna (2018).

[265] Tezuka and Kawabata (2018).

[266] Pavan and Aukstuoliene (2018), p. 19 where the authors stress that as a matter of public policy the right to apply for the setting aside of an arbitral award cannot be waived as it would be considered to be a restraint on the constitutional right to apply to court. https://www.ibanet.org/Document/Default.aspx?DocumentUid=E8DF3800-DB62-44C7-8F32-C40967BCBE36. Accessed 22 May 2020.

[267] Schellaars and Marsman (2018).

[268] Krużewski B, Diehl M, IBA Arbitration Committee Arbitration Guide, Poland. International Bar Association, p. 19. https://www.ibanet.org/Document/Default.aspx?DocumentUid=DE8F3274-8525-432D-9118-88300110F445. Accessed 22 May 2020.

[269] Santos (2018).

[270] Dzung and Ha (2018).

[271] Please see the IBA Arbitration Committee Arbitration Guide (2019) in which the majority of States represented do not permit parties to waive the right to initiate an action for annulment of an arbitral award. https://www.ibanet.org/LPD/Dispute_Resolution_Section/Arbitration/Arbcountryguides.aspx. Accessed 22 May 2020.

[272] Section 40(1) of the Finnish Arbitration Act provides: 'An award shall be null and void (1) to the extent that the arbitrators have in the award decided an issue not capable for settlement by

However, the distinction between the Swedish and Finnish approaches to differentiating between grounds of invalidity and grounds for challenge lies in the fact that, unlike in Sweden, the grounds for challenge cannot be excluded in advance under the Finnish Arbitration Act.[273] *Ex post* exclusion agreements, however, seem admissible under Finnish law.[274] As seen, a similar approach to permitting also *ex post* exclusion agreements is adopted also in a handful of States that generally view exclusion agreements impermissible under their law. This can be explained by the fact that after the issuing of an arbitral award arbitrating parties must have been already aware of any possible inconsistencies in the arbitral procedure that may lead to the challenging of the award. Therefore, in case after the issuing of an arbitral award both parties wish to agree on the exclusion of annulment mechanism, States generally tend to make way for such unequivocal expressions of party autonomy. At the same time, it is somewhat hard to imagine a situation where an arbitrating party, being aware of potentially defective arbitral proceedings or an arbitral award after its issuing, would nevertheless agree on the exclusion of setting-aside proceedings. This possibility seems more of a theoretical rather than of a practical nature.

Another noteworthy example is Germany that, somewhat similarly to Sweden, adopts an intermediate approach to permitting the exclusion of setting-aside proceedings and divides the grounds for setting aside of an arbitral award between waivable and non-waivable grounds.

On the one hand, Section 1059(2)(1) of the German Code of Civil Procedure ('ZPO') lists grounds that 'are deemed to be in the interest of the parties, and thus can be waived by them under certain conditions.'[275] The grounds listed in Section 1059(2)(1) of the ZPO essentially mirror those of Article 34(2)(a) of the UNCITRAL Model Law. However, on the other hand, Section 1059(2)(2) of the ZPO contains grounds (non-arbitrability and public policy) that are considered to be in the public interest and consequently cannot be excluded by arbitrating parties under any condition.[276] This is due to them being based on notions of non-derogable public policy.[277] However, even in the case of the waivable grounds for setting aside an arbitral award, the parties are permitted to exclude such grounds only if they have knowledge of the potential defect of the arbitral award.[278] In essence this means that the exclusion of grounds for setting aside an arbitral award under Section 1059(2)(1)

arbitration under Finnish law; (2) to the extent that the recognition of the award is to be deemed contrary to the public policy of Finland; (3) if the arbitration award is so obscure or incomplete that it does not indicate how the dispute has been decided; or (3) if the arbitration award has not been made in writing or signed by the arbitrators.' https://www.finlex.fi/fi/laki/kaannokset/1992/en19920967.pdf. Accessed 22 May 2020.

273 Hentunen et al. (2018).

274 Ibid.

275 Scherer (2016), p. 444.

276 Ibid.

277 Kreindler et al. (2018).

278 Ibid. See also Kröll and Kraft (2015), sec. 1059 at 7. It is said that exclusion of setting-aside proceedings in advance, i.e. prior the award being made, is violating the constitutionally required minimum control. See Cordero-Moss (2013), p. 182.

of the ZPO can be made only after the award is issued (or in rare circumstances also before if the particular facts underlying the excluded defect are known to the parties).[279]

In the author's opinion, this division of different grounds for setting aside an arbitral award, and more importantly the imposed limitation regarding time of the exclusion of such grounds, creates a healthy balance between the needs of party autonomy and the interests of the State to maintain the review mechanism of possibly defective arbitral awards. Moreover, by stipulating that the waivable grounds of setting aside an arbitral award can be excluded only *after* the relevant facts pertaining to the defectiveness of an arbitral award have become known to the parties, due process, and, in particular, the balance of the parties, is maintained on an equal level. Whether or not the German approach is a sensible solution to permitting exclusion agreements also from the Convention's standpoint will be assessed in Chap. 7.

5.7 Summary

Requirements for a valid and effective exclusion of setting-aside proceedings in Switzerland, France, Sweden, Belgium and other States permitting such exclusion are generally similar, although there exist certain and—as will become apparent in Chap. 7, at least from the perspective of such approaches' compatibility with the ECHR—crucial differences.

States that allow parties the option to exclude the annulment action position themselves as very arbitration friendly and give parties the greatest autonomy to tailor arbitration proceedings to their particular needs. After all, party autonomy is one of the most profound characteristics of contemporary international commercial arbitration.[280] However, it is also evident, especially considering the somewhat scarce practical use of exclusion agreements, that parties nevertheless want to retain certain judicial oversight of arbitration proceedings, even if it results in giving up a share of their party autonomy. Setting-aside proceedings function as a safety net, giving parties an opportunity to challenge and set aside a defective arbitral award at the seat of arbitration.[281] Therefore, before opting for an exclusion of setting-aside proceedings, parties should carefully consider whether their particular relationship and the potential future dispute would benefit from alleged rapidity and economy in case of no setting-aside proceedings or, on the other hand, legal certainty that the setting aside of a defective arbitral award can achieve.

---

[279] Kröll and Kraft (2015), sec. 1059 at 7.

[280] Born (2009), p. 1004.

[281] A former Lord Justice of Appeal in England Sir Michael Kerr has aptly put that judicial review is a 'bulwark against corruption, arbitrariness, bias, improper conduct and—where necessary—sheer incompetence, in relation to acts and decisions with binding legal effect for others. No one having the power to make legally binding decisions in this country should be altogether outside and immune from this system. No one below the highest tribunals should have unreviewable legal powers over others'. See Kerr (1985), p. 706.

All the more, since the introduction of a possibility to exclude setting-aside proceedings in various arbitration laws, many authors have questioned compatibility of such exclusion agreements with fundamental rights of due process, including the right of access to a court inherently provided in Article 6(1) of the ECHR.[282] Concerns that exclusion of setting-aside proceedings may inevitably impact arbitrating parties' procedural rights of due process, are equally behind many States' restrictive approaches to permitting such agreements. Indeed, the idea of excluding in advance ones right to challenge a decision of a private tribunal before State courts does seem to raise questions as to its legitimacy, especially with regard to such seemingly non-waivable fundamental rights as the right to an independent and impartial tribunal and the right to a fair hearing. The *Tabbane v. Switzerland* case seems to provide an answer to the said concerns, or does it?

Leaving a more detailed discussion and analysis of the comprehensiveness of the Court's reasoning in the *Tabbane v. Switzerland* case for Chap. 7, it can be said that the Court's ruling in the *Tabbane v. Switzerland* case is undoubtedly a landmark decision—the Court for the first time examined compatibility of exclusion agreements with the guarantees of Article 6(1) of the ECHR. Having received *carte blanche* from the ECtHR, other States having similar provisions in their *leges arbitri*, can now seemingly breathe a sigh of relief. As long as the respective provisions providing for exclusion of setting-aside proceedings require an express, unequivocal and most importantly voluntary waiver, there seems to be no violation of the right of access to a court as guaranteed in Article 6(1) of the ECHR. At the same time, considering that the said conditions for a valid waiver under Article 6(1) of the ECHR must be weighed against all the particular factual circumstances and applicable legal framework in a specific case, one cannot rule out a possibility that a similar application challenging the compatibility of provisions permitting exclusion agreements in, e.g. Belgium, France or elsewhere, would result in a violation of Article 6(1) of the ECHR.

With the *Tabbane v. Switzerland* ruling the ECtHR affirms its previous case-law and gives arbitrating parties full procedural freedom to regulate their private relations as they see fit, even if that requires the renunciation of a possibility to challenge potentially defective award.[283] The Court's consistent recognition of the principle of party autonomy indicates that, as long as certain basic preconditions are fulfilled, freedom to contract out of the applicability of ECHR rights is one of the most important elements of the ECHR. However, there also seems to be an essential contradiction between the Court's ruling in the *Tabbane v. Switzerland* case and its

---

[282] See, e.g. Jaksic (2002), pp. 277–318, Petrochilos (2004), pp. 124–125, Landrove (2006), p. 93, Asouzu (1995), pp. 94–95. See also Park (1989), p. 650 where the author stresses that 'the arbitral situs bears a duty to provide the loser of an arbitration with a non-waivable right to challenge an award for an arbitrator's disregard either of his mission or of fundamental due process in the proceedings. This obligation springs from the active and passive support that the country of proceedings gives to the arbitration. Elimination of any and all grounds for challenge of awards is an intriguing but misguided experiment, likely to do more harm than good to fair and efficient international dispute resolution.'

[283] *Axelsson and others v. Sweden*, App. No. 11960/86, ECmHR, 13 July 1990.

previous rulings establishing that it is not *permissible* to subject certain Article 6(1) of the ECHR rights to a waiver, even if such a waiver is free and unequivocal.

As seen, there exists considerable consensus both in the Court's case-law and scholarly writings that certain rights of Article 6(1) of the ECHR carry more weight than others, in terms of their significance. It is not argued that the right to access to an ordinary court, the right to a public hearing and the right to a decision within a reasonable time could not be validly waived by parties. Their *waivable* character has been confirmed also by the Court.[284] However, the *non-waivable* rights, i.e. the right to an independent and impartial tribunal and the right to a fair hearing (and its constituent elements thereof), are considered to be part of the rule of law and no democratic state should be permitted to allow persons to waive the right to challenge a private arbitral tribunal's decision on the basis of violations of these fundamental rights. This suggests that exclusion of setting-aside proceedings should be permitted only as regards the validly *waivable* rights of Article 6(1) of the ECHR or, alternatively, solely *ex post*. The Court-made difference between the *waivable* and *non-waivable* rights confirms this understanding.

The Court's conclusions in the *Tabbane v. Switzerland* case not only raise the above issue of whether parties are indeed entitled to voluntarily waive the application of all rights of Article 6(1) of the ECHR, but also raise questions as to the Court's application of the formal conditions of a valid waiver to the particular circumstances in the case. For example, can the particular arbitration agreement and opt out clause indeed be considered an unequivocal and voluntary waiver within the meaning of the Convention, considering that parties themselves did not choose Switzerland as the seat of arbitration, but arbitrators did? Do arguments, such as Switzerland's economic interests, willingness to promote Switzerland as an attractive seat of arbitration and Swiss Federal Tribunal's alleged case overload indeed justify the resulting inability of parties to challenge a possibly defective arbitral award on grounds of violations of independence and impartiality or equality of arms?

Moreover, a distinction must be made between a mere possibility to contract out of the application of setting-aside proceedings (as in the case of *Tabbane v. Switzerland*), on the one hand, and having no possibility to challenge an arbitral award in the first place. As the ECtHR submits, the former is fully consistent and proportionate to the aim of enhancing the attractiveness of the particular seat of arbitration. This reasoning, however, does not seem to take into account the Court's own made distinction between *waivable* and *non-waivable* rights of Article 6(1) of the ECHR. The issue becomes even more problematic when looking at the issue of total lack of setting-aside proceedings in the applicable *lex arbitri*.

In addition to States adopting either liberal, restrictive or intermediate approach to permitting exclusion of setting-aside proceedings, there are certain *exotic* jurisdictions that do not regulate the annulment of arbitral awards in their national laws at all. The most well-known example is the former Belgian approach, in particular

[284] See Sect. 3.4.3.2.

its law of 27 March 1985 that introduced an 'absolutely unique'[285] and unprecedented[286] solution to limiting judicial review of arbitral awards and under certain conditions excluded the application of setting-aside proceedings altogether. In 1998 Belgium amended its excessively restrictive approach in this regard and, as introduced above, currently the law in Belgium very much resembles that of the Swiss PILA. Apart from the former example of Belgium, there are very few other jurisdictions that rather uniquely omit regulation of setting-aside proceedings altogether. This is not only the author's home country Latvia, but also formerly in Malaysia and currently in Kyrgyzstan. At a time when the necessity of setting-aside proceedings in the contemporary framework of international arbitration is questioned by many, the said somewhat exotic approaches serve as a cautious reminder of the continuous importance of judicial review by means of setting-aside proceedings.

References

Abbas A, Matouk J (2019) The Middle Eastern and African arbitration review 2019: Egypt. Global Arbitration Review. https://globalarbitrationreview.com/insight/the-middle-eastern-and-african-arbitration-review-2019/1190120/egypt. Accessed 22 May 2020

Asouzu AA (1995) The national arbitration law and international commercial arbitration: the indispensability of the national court and the setting aside procedure. RADIC 7:68

Baizeau D (2005) Waiving the right to challenge an arbitral award rendered in Switzerland: caveats and drafting considerations for foreign parties. Int Arab Law Rev 3:69

Baizeau D (2013) Chapter 2, Part II: Commentary on Chapter 12 PILS, Article 192 [Waiver of annulment]. In: Arroto M (ed) Arbitration in Switzerland: the practitioner's guide. Kluwer Law International

Berger B, Kellerhals F (2010) International and domestic arbitration in Switzerland. Sweet & Maxwell

Berger B, Kellerhals F (2015) International and domestic arbitration in Switzerland, 3rd edn. Bloomsbury Publishing

Blessing M (1988) The new international arbitration law in Switzerland—a significant step towards liberalism. J Int Arbitr 5:9

Born G (2009) International litigation & arbitration—the principle of judicial non-interference in international arbitral proceedings. Univ Pennsylvania J Int Law 30(4):999

Born G (2014) International commercial arbitration, 2nd edn. Kluwer Law International

Burda J (2013) La renunciation au recours en annulation dans le nouveau droit français de l'arbitrage. RTD Com. 653

Cazenave A (2011) Le nouveau droit de l'arbitrage français (à propos du décret 2011-48 du 13 janvier 2011). Rev droit des Affaires Int 2011:577

Chan R (1999) The enforceability of annulled foreign arbitral awards in the United States: a critique of chromalloy. Boston Univ Int Law J 17:141

---

285 Gaillard (1986), p. 725.

286 Apart from Belgium there seems to be only one country—Malaysia—that until the entry into force of the 2005 Arbitration Act adopted a similar approach and for certain matters mandatorily excluded recourse to state courts through set-aside proceedings. See, e.g., Gharavi (2002), pp. 27–28, Shütze (2013), pp. 678–680.

Chuturkova K (2018) IBA arbitration committee arbitration guide, Bulgaria. International Bar Association, p 19. https://www.ibanet.org/Document/Default.aspx?DocumentUid=CF178C40-0C14-4AFA-988E-99B61EBC471E. Accessed 22 May 2020
Comair-Obeid N (2019) The Middle Eastern and African arbitration review 2019: Lebanon. Global Arbitration Review. https://globalarbitrationreview.com/insight/the-middle-eastern-and-african-arbitration-review-2019/1190121/lebanon. Accessed 22 May 2020
Cordero-Moss G (2013) International commercial arbitration: different forms and their features. Cambridge University Press
Corra MI, Peña SL (2019) Argentina: international arbitration 2019. International and comparative legal guide to international arbitration 2019 (Global Legal Group 2019). https://iclg.com/practice-areas/international-arbitration-laws-and-regulations/argentina. Accessed 22 May 2020
Dasser F (2007) International arbitration and setting-aside proceedings in Switzerland: a statistical analysis. ASA Bull 25:444
Dasser F, Wójtowicz P (2016) Challenges of Swiss arbitral awards—updated and extended statistical data as of 2015. ASA Bull 34(2):280
Day J (2011) Commentary—arbitration in France: the 2011 reform (June 2011), at 4. http://www.jonesday.com/files/Publication/b9ce7786-7e7e-47b9-a628-bc2a9361e704/Presentation/PublicationAttachment/d609618d-63cc-43e9-a0e7-bc6ae3b7663e/Arbitration%20in%20France.pdf. Accessed 22 May 2020
Demeyere L (1999) 1998 Amendments to Belgian arbitration law: an overview. Arbitr Int 15(3):295
Dzung NM, Ha DVM (2018) IBA arbitration committee arbitration guide, Vietnam. International Bar Association, p 23. https://www.ibanet.org/Document/Default.aspx?DocumentUid=4DCE3539-D1B4-4251-B850-0B6C61DC0105. Accessed 22 May 2020
Gaillard E (1986) Belgium: statute on the setting aside of arbitral awards (introductory note). Int Legal Mater 25:725
Gaillard E (1988) A foreign view of the new Swiss law on international arbitration. Arbitr Int 4(1):25–31
Gaillard E (1999) Enforcement of awards set aside in the country of origin: the French experience. In: Van den Berg AJ (ed) Improving efficiency of arbitration agreements and awards: 40 years of application of the new york convention. Kluwer Law International
Gaillard E et al (eds) (1999) Fouchard Gaillard Goldman on international commercial arbitration. Kluwer International Law
Gaillard E (2010a) Legal theory of international arbitration. Martinus Nijhoff Publishers
Gaillard E (ed) (2010b) The review of international arbitral awards. JurisNet
Gaillard E (2011) France adopts new law on arbitration. New York Law J 245(15)
Gaillard E, De Lapasse P (2011) Commentaire analytique du décret du 13 janvier 2011 portant réforme du droit français de l'arbitrage. Cahier de l'arbitrage 2:263
Geisinger E, Mazuranic A (2013) Chapter 11: Challenge and revision of the award. In: Geisinger E, Voser N (eds) International arbitration in Switzerland: a handbook for practitioners, 2nd edn. Kluwer Law International
Gharavi HG (2002) The international effectiveness of the annulment of an arbitral award. Kluwer Law International
Girsberg D, Voser N (2016) International arbitration: comparative and Swiss perspectives, 3rd edn. Kluwer Law International, Schulthess Juristische Medien AG
Hanotiau B, Block G (1999) Note on the law of 19 May 1998 amending Belgian arbitration legislation. Arbitr Int 15(1):97
Hentunen M et al (2018) IBA arbitration committee arbitration guide, Finland. International Bar Association, p 22. https://www.ibanet.org/Document/Default.aspx?DocumentUid=74DDFD18-657A-4373-9F32-03A602C5160B. Accessed 22 May 2020
Heuman L, Jarvin S (eds) (2006) The Swedish arbitration act of 1999 five years on: a critical review of strengths and weaknesses. JurisNet
Hober K (2001) Arbitration reform in Sweden. Arbitr Int 17(4):351
Hober K (2011) International commercial arbitration in Sweden. Oxford University Press

Ipp AH (2015) Time to upgrade: review of the Swedish arbitration act. Kluwer Arbitration Blog, 17 October 2015. http://kluwerarbitrationblog.com/2015/10/17/time-to-upgrade-review-of-the-swedish-arbitration-act/. Accessed 22 May 2020

Jaksic A (2002) Arbitration and human rights. Peter Lang, Frankfurt am Main

Jermini C, Arroyo M (2009) Pitfalls of Waiver Agreements under Article 192 PILS in multi-contract settings: some remarks on Swiss Federal Court Decision 134 III 260. ASA Bull 27:103

Kachwaha S, Rautray D (2019) India: international arbitration 2019. International and comparative legal guide to international arbitration. Global Legal Group. https://iclg.com/practice-areas/international-arbitration-laws-and-regulations/india. Accessed 22 May 2020

Kalderimis D (2018) IBA arbitration committee arbitration guide, New Zealand. International Bar Association, p 23. https://www.ibanet.org/Document/Default.aspx?DocumentUid=278729D0-AAA9-4D8B-A7D8-A27F2E3F711D. Accessed 22 May 2020

Kallel S (1992) The Tunisian Draft law on international arbitration. Arab Law Q 7(3):175–196

Kaufmann-Kohler G, Rigozzi A (2015) International arbitration: law and practice in Switzerland. Oxford University Press

Kerr M (1985) Arbitration and the courts: the UNCITRAL model law. Int Comp Law Q 34:647

Knoll J (2012) Waivers of recourse in international arbitration—where Switzerland and Tunisia meet. Int J Arab Arbitr 4(4)

Knuts G (2013) Chapter 9 Recourse to the courts against an arbitral award. In: Franke U et al (eds) International arbitration in Sweden: a practitioner's guide. Kluwer Law International

Koch C (2009) The enforcement of awards annulled in their place of origin—the French and U.S. experience. J Int Arb 26(2):267–292

Kotick B (2018) The Swedish Government revives efforts to modernise the arbitration act. Kluwer Arbitration Blog, 9 May 2018. http://arbitrationblog.kluwerarbitration.com/2018/04/09/the-swedish-government-revives-efforts-to-modernise-the-arbitration-act/. Accessed 22 May 2020

Krausz N (2011) Waiver of appeal to the Swiss Federal tribunal: recent evolution of the case law and compatibility with ECHR, Article 6. J Int Arbitr 28(2):137–162

Kreindler R et al (2018) IBA arbitration committee arbitration guide, Germany. International Bar Association, p 20. https://www.ibanet.org/Document/Default.aspx?DocumentUid=72111D60-6585-412C-B239-189ABF22108F. Accessed 22 May 2020

Kröll S, Kraft P (2015) Recourse against the award. In: Böckstiegel KH et al (eds) Arbitration in Germany: the model law in practice, 2nd edn. Kluwer Law International

Kudrna J (2018) IBA arbitration committee arbitration guide, Czech Republic, International Bar Association, p 16. https://www.ibanet.org/Document/Default.aspx?DocumentUid=04296388-C288-4A09-BA82-EC543F49F3EF. Accessed 22 May 2020

Lalive P (1988) The new Swiss law on international arbitration. Arbitr Int 4(1):2–24

Landrove JC (2006) European convention on human rights' impact on consensual arbitration. An État des Lieux of Strasbourg Case-Law and of a Problematic Swiss Law feature. In: Besson S et al (eds) Human rights at the center. Schulthess

Leon B, Karimi L (2007) The Canadian position: can parties to an arbitration agreement vary the statutory scope of judicial review of the award? ILSA J Int Comp Law 14(1):1

Madsen F (2016) Commercial arbitration in Sweden: a commentary on the arbitration act (1999:116) and the arbitration rules of the arbitration institute of the Stockholm Chamber of Commerce, 4th edn. Jure Forlag

Malik M, Penz E (2019) Oman: international arbitration 2019. International and comparative legal guide to international arbitration 2019. Global Legal Group. https://iclg.com/practice-areas/international-arbitration-laws-and-regulations/oman. Accessed 22 May 2020

Mayer CU (1999) Exclusion agreements according to article 192 of the Swiss Private International Law Act. ASA Bull 17(1):191

Močibob L et al (2018) IBA arbitration committee arbitration guide, Croatia, p 16. International Bar Association. https://www.ibanet.org/Document/Default.aspx?DocumentUid=73D95EA2-BAAA-4162-B882-09892B2FC13A. Accessed 22 May 2020

Monteiro AL et al (2009) Is Brazil an arbitration-friendly jurisdiction? Kluwer Arbitration Blog, 6 Jan 2009. http://arbitrationblog.kluwerarbitration.com/2019/01/06/is-brazil-an-arbitration-friendly-jurisdiction/. Accessed 22 May 2020

Park WW (1989) National law and commercial justice: safeguarding procedural integrity in international arbitration. Tulane Law Rev 63(3):647–709

Park WW (2001) Why courts review arbitral awards. In: Briner R et al (eds) Law of international business and dispute settlement in the 21st Century, Liber Amicorum Karl-Heinz Bockstiegel. Carl Heymanns Verlag KG, Köln, pp 595–606

Patocchi PM, Jermini C (2000) Art. 192 of the Swiss federal private international law act. In: Berti SV et al (eds) International arbitration in Switzerland. Kluwer Law International

Paulsson J (1989) Rights of recourse in Sweden. Arbitr Int 5(3):291

Pavan VV, Aukstuoliene G (2018) IBA arbitration committee arbitration guide. International Bar Association, Lithuania, p 19

Petrochilos G (2004) Procedural law in international arbitration. Oxford University Press

Philippe D (2014) Modernisation of the Belgian law on arbitration. DAOR 109:5–20

Poudret JF (1988) Challenge and enforcement of arbitral awards in Switzerland. Arbitr Int 4(4):278–299

Poudret JF, Besson S (2006) Comparative law of international arbitration. Sweet & Maxwell, United Kingdom

Ramos LG, Salomão MS (2016) Arbitration procedures and practice in Brazil: overview. Thompson Reuters Practical Law. https://uk.practicallaw.thomsonreuters.com/3-520-5274?transitionType=Default&contextData=(sc.Default)&firstPage=true&bhcp=1#co_anchor_a464671. Accessed 22 May 2020

Samuel A (1991) A critical look at the reform of Swiss arbitration law. Arbitr Int 7(1):27–56

Santos C (2018) IBA arbitration committee arbitration guide, Spain. International Bar Association, p 22. https://www.ibanet.org/Document/Default.aspx?DocumentUid=E5431E65-E56C-4866-8E48-FF9996CF1AC5. Accessed 22 May 2020

Schellaars R, Marsman A (2018) IBA arbitration committee arbitration guide, the Netherlands. International Bar Association, p 18. https://www.ibanet.org/Document/Default.aspx?DocumentUid=771279FD-6BA6-4A4B-8A5B-7A0A3D9FC62C. Accessed 22 May 2020

Scherer M (2016) The fate of parties' agreements on judicial review of awards: a comparative and normative analysis of party-autonomy at the post-award stage. Arbitr Int 32:437–457

Seraglini C (2011) L'efficacité et l'autorité renforcées des sentences arbitrales en France après le décret n° 2011-48 du 13 janvier 2011. Cahiers de l'Arbitrage 2:375

Shütze RA (2013) Institutional arbitration: a commentary. Verlag

Tezuka H, Kawabata Y (2018) IBA arbitration committee arbitration guide, Japan. International Bar Association, p 21. https://www.ibanet.org/Document/Default.aspx?DocumentUid=DBCF3CAB-E985-4A9B-BBA1-D8D9D191EF5E. Accessed 22 May 2020

Tiryakioğlu B, Bayata Canyaş A (2015), Chapter 7: Challenges to arbitral awards. In: Esin I, Yesilirmak A (eds) Arbitration in Turkey. Kluwer Law International

Tschanz P (1990) A breakthrough in international arbitration: Switzerland's New Act. Int Law 24:1107

Van den Berg AJ (1992) The efficacy of award in international commercial arbitration. Arbitration 58:267

Van den Berg AJ (2014) Should the setting aside of the arbitral award be abolished? ICSID Rev 1–26. https://doi.org/10.1093/icsidreview/sit053

Verbist H (2013) New Belgian arbitration law of 24 June 2013 and new CEPANI arbitration rules of 1 January 2013. J Int Arbitr 30(5):597–618

Verbruggen C (2016) Commentary on Part VI of the Belgian Judicial Code, Chapter VII: Article 1718. In: Bassiri N, Draye M (eds) Arbitration in Belgium. Kluwer Law International

Voser N, George A (2011) Revision of arbitral awards. In: Tercier P (ed) Post award issues. Huntington

Voser N, George A (2016) ECtHR: Waiver of recourse against international arbitral award not incompatible with ECHR. Kluwer Arbitration Blog, 31 Mar 2016. http://kluwerarbitrationblog.com/2016/03/31/ecthr-waiver-of-recourse-against-international-arbitral-award-not-incompatible-with-echr/. Accessed 22 May 2020

Wahad MA (2019) Commercial arbitration: Egypt. Global Arbitration Review. https://globalarbitrationreview.com/jurisdiction/1005756/egypt. Accessed 22 May 2020

Zeiler G (2018) IBA arbitration committee arbitration guide, Austria. International Bar Association, p 18. https://www.ibanet.org/Document/Default.aspx?DocumentUid=53134AEA-7488-4A8D-8C9B-A2E2ECAA0396. Accessed 22 May 2020

Chapter 6
Approaches to Excluding the Annulment of Arbitral Awards—Total Exclusion

6.1 Introduction

As Prof. William W. Park has aptly put some 30 years ago:

> [T]he arbitral situs bears a duty to provide the loser of an arbitration with a non-waivable right to challenge an award for an arbitrator's disregard either of his mission or of fundamental due process in the proceedings. This obligation springs from the active and passive support that the country of the proceedings gives to the arbitration. Elimination of any and all grounds for challenge of awards is an intriguing but misguided experiment, likely to do more harm than good to fair and efficient international dispute resolution.[1]

At the time, elimination of grounds for challenge of awards in national arbitration was indeed an intriguing experiment. Belgium had recently amended its BCCP, doing away with the application of setting-aside proceedings for arbitral awards issued in Belgium unless one of the parties to arbitration proceedings was Belgian. Also Switzerland, albeit in a somewhat not as drastic manner as in Belgium, in its 1989 PILA provided arbitrating parties with an opportunity to voluntary exclude the application of setting-aside proceedings at the post-award stage. Both approaches drew much attention from the wider arbitration community. The former was criticized as going a bit too far; the latter, on the other hand, served as an example and role model for a handful of other jurisdictions, such as France, Sweden, and, indeed, also the same Belgium that in 1998 amended the BCCP to align it with the Swiss example.

It has become evident that different States around the globe adopt different approaches to excluding the annulment of arbitral awards. While some provide rather great party autonomy in this regard, permitting advance exclusion of setting-aside proceedings if certain preconditions are satisfied, the great majority are still rather restrictive and either provide explicitly in their national arbitration laws that the annulment mechanism cannot be excluded beforehand, or such a conclusion follows impliedly from the relevant States' practice. Whereas the previous Chapter addressed

[1] Park (1989a), pp. 231–232.

© The Editor(s) (if applicable) and The Author(s), under exclusive license to Springer Nature Switzerland AG 2020

T. Krūmiņš, *Arbitration and Human Rights*,
https://doi.org/10.1007/978-3-030-54237-5_6

the different approaches to permitting (or not) the exclusion of setting-aside proceedings, the following Chapter will address a somewhat more exotic issue, namely that of total lack of setting-aside proceedings in national arbitration law.

The author's interest into the relationship between setting-aside proceedings and procedural human rights under the ECHR partially stems from the non-availability of such a mechanism in the Latvian arbitration law. At first, it may seem that a discussion on total lack of setting-aside proceedings in national arbitration law is therefore of purely local and territorially limited interest, i.e. relevant solely for Latvia as its national procedural peculiarity not having bearing on a more international level. Indeed, at least currently, Latvia, to the author's knowledge, is the only Member State of the Council of Europe that does not provide in its national arbitration law a mechanism for challenging arbitral awards. However, considering certain historical as well as contemporary developments in international arbitration, a more in-depth discussion on this seemingly national phenomenon can be relevant not only to Latvia, but also on a more international level.

Thus, for example, in 1980s a similar, albeit not as blatantly categorical, procedural *innovation* was introduced in Belgium. Belgian legislator's choice at that time provoked not merely a vivid national discussion on the necessity and legitimacy of an automatic statutory exclusion of setting-aside proceedings, but also attracted reflections on the subject by many international scholars, particularly on the compatibility of Belgian arbitral awards with the New York Convention. Therefore, the phenomenon of total lack of setting-aside proceedings per se can be of great interest also to the general international arbitration community.

Moreover, as already briefly introduced, contemporary framework of international arbitration is also characterized by what may seem as a perpetual discussion on the rivalry between the so-called *maximalist* and *minimalist* approaches to international arbitration, in particular, State control over arbitration. In fact, the whole issue of exclusion agreements and the broader discussion on the necessity of setting-aside proceedings as a control mechanism may be seen, inter alia, as a direct consequence of this *maximalist* versus *minimalist* rivalry. It is well-known that certain States (the best example being France) have long defended and promoted minimal court involvement and control over arbitration proceedings. France's (and certain other States') *a-national* view on international arbitration and, in particular, the resulting arbitral award, arguing that the enforcement court is best situated to oversee the legitimacy of arbitration proceedings and recognizing and enforcing annulled arbitral awards, raises certain fundamental questions that are at the heart of the discussion on the future of setting-aside proceedings.

Is it only France with its long-established particular view on international arbitration and certain other few States or international arbitration community in general that is moving towards a system where setting-aside proceedings will play less and less important role, perhaps even be abandoned in their entirety? Seeing that States that permit exclusion agreements are nevertheless not yet ready to do away with the annulment mechanism *in toto* suggests that it continuously serves as an important mechanism for exercising control over arbitration proceedings.

All this evidences that a discussion on total lack of setting-aside proceedings is not merely relevant nationally, but also internationally. This is even more so since Latvia is not the only State that omits regulation of setting-aside proceedings altogether. For example, in addition to the former Belgian example, previously also Malaysia and currently Kyrgyzstan serve as examples that in one way or another have omitted or still omit statutory regulation of the annulment mechanism. While the present Chapter will also succinctly introduce the relevant approaches in this regard in Belgium, Malaysia and also Kyrgyzstan, the main focus will be on the author's home country Latvia. As stressed, Latvia is currently the only Member State of the Council of Europe, i.e. a State bound by the Convention's regime, that omits regulation of setting-aside proceedings altogether. The more in-depth insight into Latvia's approach will therefore serve as an example demonstrating the continuous significance of the annulment mechanism both for the smooth functioning and efficacy of arbitration proceedings and, somewhat more importantly, for the protection of parties' legitimate interests and fundamental procedural human rights in arbitration proceedings.

Additional support for the relevance of a broader discussion of total lack of setting-aside proceedings may be found in recent developments pertaining to the relationship between arbitration and EU law. The CJEU decided in the *Achmea* case that investor-state dispute settlement clauses in intra-EU bilateral investment treaties violate EU law due to the fact that such clauses 'prevent those disputes from being resolved in a manner that ensures the full effectiveness of EU law [...]'[2] Similarly, with regard to commercial arbitration the CJEU noted the following:

> It is true that, in relation to commercial arbitration, the Court has held that the requirements of efficient arbitration proceedings justify the review of arbitral awards by the courts of the Member States being limited in scope, provided that the fundamental provisions of EU law can be examined in the course of that review and, if necessary, be the subject of a reference to the Court for a preliminary ruling [...].[3]

Therefore, total lack of setting-aside proceedings in national arbitration law not only raises questions of compatibility of such a legal vacuum with certain procedural human rights under the ECHR, but also with the defaulting EU Member State's obligations under EU law to guarantee the full effectiveness and application of EU law.

The following Chapter will proceed by first briefly introducing the examples of Belgium, Malaysia and Kyrgyzstan as States that either formerly (in the case of Belgium and Malaysia) or currently (Kyrgyzstan) exclude from their national arbitration laws the annulment mechanism altogether. This brief overview will be followed by a more detailed insight into Latvia's approach, serving as a contemporary example of how insufficient judicial involvement in arbitration proceedings, in particular by means of setting-aside proceedings, may lead to a violation of parties' procedural human rights under the ECHR. This exposition will include a brief general overview of arbitration in Latvia and a more *in concreto* analysis of the issue of setting-aside proceedings in Latvian arbitration law from both a historical perspective, e.g.

---

[2] Case C-284/16 *Slowakische Republik 'v Achmea BV*, CJEU, 6 March 2018, para. 56.

[3] Ibid. para. 54.

analysing the applicable annulment mechanism in Latvian arbitration law between 1918 and 1940, and a contemporary perspective, seeking to find reasons for the continuous non-availability of the annulment mechanism under Latvian law.

6.2 Belgium

Belgium is perhaps the most notoriously known example that, with a view to attract more international arbitrations to Belgium, introduced an absolutely unique and unprecedent solution to limiting judicial review of arbitral awards. By the law of 27 March 1985 on the setting aside of arbitral awards (the '1985 Law') it amended its BCCP and under certain circumstances excluded the application of setting-aside proceedings altogether.

The reform leading to the adoption of the 1985 Law was introduced in the Belgian Senate in 1981 and 'appeared to be a single person action […] much to the surprise of the arbitration community in Belgium.'[4] That 'single person' was senator Marcel Storme—described as 'the main promoter' of the 1985 Law.[5] The amendments introduced in the Belgian Senate and later also adopted and included in the BCCP provided that Article 1717 of the BCCP shall be completed with the following paragraph:

> Belgian Courts have jurisdiction on an action to set aside only when at least one of the parties to the dispute settled by an arbitral award is either an individual of Belgian nationality or a Belgian resident or a legal entity which is incorporated in Belgium or which has a branch or any establishment in Belgium.[6]

Consequently, where both parties to the arbitral proceedings were not of Belgian nationality or did not have residence in Belgium, setting-aside proceedings were excluded altogether and such parties had no possibility to challenge the arbitral award in Belgium at all. In essence, the new provision meant that there was 'simply no way for the dissatisfied party to bring a challenge to an award rendered in Belgium.'[7] It was not even possible for parties to 'opt-in', i.e. to conclude an agreement that the Belgian courts would nevertheless have jurisdiction to set aside an arbitral award.[8] It was an utterly novel approach that immediately resonated in significant amount of legal writings concerning its usefulness and efficacy.[9]

---

[4] Van den Berg (2014), p. 14.

[5] Storme and Demeulenaere (1989), p. 3.

[6] The official French text of paragraph 4 of art. 1717 of the BCCP read as follows:
'Les tribunaux belges ne peuvent connaître d'une demande en annulation que lorsqu'au moins une partie au différend tranché par la sentence arbitrale est soit une personne physique ayant la nationalité belge ou une résidence en Belgique, soit une personne morale constituée en Belgique ou y ayant une succursale ou un siège quelconque d'opération.'

[7] Paulsson (1986), p. 69.

[8] Van den Berg (1994), p. 141.

[9] See, e.g., Van Houtte (1986), Matray (1986), Paulsson (1986), Hampton (1985), Storme (1986), Vanderelst (1986), Gaillard (1986).

Reportedly inspired by the English Arbitration Act of 1979,[10] the 1985 Law intended to achieve two main goals—(i) to establish and promote Belgium as an attractive seat of arbitration and (ii) to exclude judicial review of arbitral awards that have no connection with Belgium.[11] The Belgian legislator argued that the exclusion of setting-aside proceedings would target those proceedings where challenges are often brought for dilatory purposes and arbitral awards are enforced abroad.[12] As explained, arguments of enhanced arbitral proceedings and perceived dilatoriness were later also advanced by other legislators (e.g. the Swiss) that introduced in their arbitration laws a mere *right* to exclude setting-aside proceedings, as opposed to automatic exclusion of the right to bring a challenge to an arbitral award.

With minor exceptions,[13] the 1985 Law generally witnessed severe criticism labelling it as 'radical'[14] and 'too extreme'.[15] Commentators, and more importantly also arbitrating parties, were worried about the practical consequences of not having setting-aside proceedings at the seat of arbitration. In this context, the following objections were advanced.

Firstly, it was argued that in the absence of any judicial review at the seat of arbitration, the awards issued in Belgium would be considered as *stateless*, i.e. not having Belgian nationality, and for this purpose they would not benefit from the New York Convention regime.[16] These purported fears, however, never really resulted in the non-enforcement of 'Belgian' arbitral awards in other States since Article V of

---

[10]The English Arbitration Act of 1979 in certain limited circumstances allowed foreign parties to conclude exclusion agreements. The 1985 Law, however, went a step further and excluded the set-aside proceedings altogether. See, e.g., Storme (1986), Vanderelst (1986), Gaillard (1986). The situation created in Belgium after introducing the 1985 Law more resembled the state of affairs created by the *Gotaverken* case in France in 1980 whereby the Court of Appeal of Paris refused to hear a challenge of an arbitral award rendered in ICC international arbitration proceedings with their seat in Paris. A year later in 1981, however, this approach was overturned by a Decree stipulating that all awards rendered in France are subject to challenge on a restricted number of grounds. See Paulsson (1986), p. 69. Generally on the *Gotaverken* case see, e.g. Paulsson (1980), p. 364 et seq.

[11]Jaksic (2002), p. 289, Vanderelst (1986), p. 78, Gaillard (1986), p. 725, Gaillard et al. (eds) (1999), pp. 73–74.

[12]Legislative history of the 1985 Law (cited by Vanderelst (1986), p. 86). The legislator argued that '[i]n fact, the proposal will lead to the exclusion of judicial review of arbitral awards which do not at all concern out country, and which at present are often used for purely dilatory purposes, since the enforcement of the award takes place abroad. It appears normal therefore that possible objections against the award also be formulated abroad during the enforcement proceedings.'

[13]See, e.g., Storme (1986). Marcel Storme was a member of the Belgian Senate who introduced the amendment and was the main driving force behind the proposed amendments, thus it is no surprise that after the adoption of the 1985 Law he labelled Belgium as the 'paradise for international commercial arbitration'. Moreover, it is argued that possibly the non-existence of set-aside proceedings influenced the choice of Brussels as the seat of arbitration in the well-known *Channel Tunnel* case. See, e.g., Hanotiau (1997), p. 327, Gaillard et al. (eds.) (1999), p. 911.

[14]Vanderelst (1986), p. 84.

[15]Van den Berg (1992), p. 269. See also Piers (2006), p. 156 et seq. More recently see, e.g. Verbruggen (2016), p. 489.

[16]Vanderelst (1986), p. 85, Gaillard (1986), p. 726. See also on the opposite Storme (1986).

the New York Convention simply does not provide 'the non-existence of setting-aside proceedings' as one of the grounds for refusing recognition and enforcement of foreign arbitral awards.[17]

Secondly, since arbitral awards could no longer be annulled by the Belgian courts, the winning party would have a considerably stronger upper hand against the defendant in the enforcement proceedings. It was argued that the exclusion of setting-aside proceedings would lead to *enforcement shopping* whereby the winning party would institute enforcement proceedings in as many States as possible even despite the existence of possible legal flaws in the arbitral award.[18] Although the *enforcement shopping* would be limited by the number of States in which the award debtor has assets, there still remained a risk that one State would nonetheless grant enforcement of a questionable award.[19] This concern is very much alive also nowadays in the case of arbitral awards issued in Latvia.

Thirdly, the non-existence of setting-aside proceedings would put the losing party in the unenviable position of having no forum to challenge the arbitral award.[20] Such a party would have no remedy against a defective arbitral award rendered in breach of fundamental procedural guarantees, such as due process or objectivity and impartiality of arbitrators.[21] While the winning party would be able to exercise its procedural rights through the enforcement proceedings, the losing party would have to wait and rebut every enforcement action without having the right to annul the arbitral award at the seat of arbitration and put an end to theoretically infinite enforcement proceedings.[22] Again, also this concern stands ground in the case of Latvia.

Fourthly, since the losing party would be deprived of the right to adjudicate the status of questionable awards in courts at the seat of arbitration it was argued that this would create the so-called *ghost awards*.[23] Arbitral awards continue to produce legal effects until the moment they are annulled by courts at the seat of arbitration. However, if no annulment takes place, such awards infinitely remain in force and principles of *res judicata* would preclude the initiation of new proceedings and thus also prevent the losing party from obtaining redress.[24] Also this objection applies to the current situation in Latvia.

By adopting the 1985 Law the intention of the Belgian legislator was that Belgium becomes an attractive seat of arbitration. However, it did not envisage that no judicial

[17] Vanderelst (1986), p. 85, Gaillard (1986), p. 726.

[18] Van den Berg (1994), p. 160, Vanderelst (1986), p. 85.

[19] Ibid.

[20] Park (1989b), p. 23, Jaksic (2002), p. 289, Van den Berg (1994), p. 160. See also Park (1989a), pp. 694–695.

[21] For a more detailed analysis of the former art. 1714(4) of the BCCP and its bearing upon human rights, in particular art. 13 of the ECHR (right to an effective remedy) and art. 14 of the ECHR (prohibition of discrimination), please see Jaksic (2002), pp. 293–309.

[22] See, e.g., Jaksic (2002), p. 292.

[23] Van den Berg (1994), p. 160.

[24] Vanderelst (1986), p. 86.

control at all over arbitration proceedings would achieve exactly the opposite effect. Parties were not eager to choose a State as their seat of arbitration where court control by way of the setting aside of an arbitral award was automatically excluded.[25] Reportedly, with the 1985 Law in force the number of arbitrations in Belgium even decreased.[26] It is said that, for example, the ICC avoided Belgium as a seat for arbitration whenever the task of choosing a seat for arbitration proceedings was in the hands of the ICC International Court of Arbitration.[27]

Formal legal infrastructure, including the applicable *lex arbitri*, is one of the most important factors that influence parties' choice of the seat of arbitration.[28] As much as arbitrating parties want to escape the jurisdiction and interference of national courts, they also wish to retain certain degree of healthy judicial assistance and court supervision as a safety net.[29] Avoidance of Belgium as a seat of arbitration evidently indicates such a desire. This, to some extent notorious example of statutorily automatic exclusion of setting-aside proceedings, not only echoes the current situation in Latvia, but formerly also in Malaysia.

6.3 Malaysia

Belgium, although the most notorious and widely discussed example in this regard, is not the only State that has attempted to innovate its national arbitration law and, under certain circumstances, ousted the jurisdiction of its courts to hear arbitrating parties' annulment requests. In 1980 a similar approach was adopted in Malaysia.

The year 1978 saw the establishment of the Asian International Arbitration Centre ('AIAC'), then known as the Regional Centre for Arbitration, Kuala Lumpur ("RCAKL"). It was established under the auspices of the Asian-African Legal Consultative Organization ("AALCO") and was the first regional centre established

---

[25] Verbruggen (2016), p. 489. See also Demeyere (1999), p. 308.

[26] Hanotiau and Block (1999), p. 99, Correll and Szczepanik (2012), p. 595, 565, Van den Berg (1992), p. 273. See also Van den Berg (2014), p. 14 where the author indicates that '[p]arties turned away from Belgium as place of arbitration. Belgium was also black listed by arbitral institutions as place of arbitration'. See also Poudret and Besson (2006), p. 30.

[27] Demeyere (1999), p. 308. On the opposite see, e.g. Paulsson (1986), p. 71 where the author argues that whenever arbitral institutions or arbitral tribunals would be given a power to select a seat of arbitration, they will be tempted to choose Belgium, knowing that their awards could not be set aside.).

[28] Queen Mary University of London, White & Case (2010) 2010 International Arbitration Survey: Choices in International Arbitration, pp. 17–19. http://www.arbitration.qmul.ac.uk/docs/123290.pdf. Accessed 29 May 2020. See also Queen Mary University of London, White & Case (2015) 2015 International Arbitration Survey: Improvements and Innovations in International Commercial Arbitration, p. 14. http://www.arbitration.qmul.ac.uk/docs/164761.pdf. Accessed 29 May 2020.

[29] Park (2001), pp. 599–600 ('[p]erhaps the best evidence of business community desire for court scrutiny at the arbitration situs lies in Belgium's failed experiment in mandatory 'non-review' of awards.'). See also Van den Berg (1992), p. 273 ('the number of [arbitrations] has decreased as parties appear to be reluctant to give up the right to challenge an award in the courts').

by AALCO in the Asia Pacific Region with the aim to serve as a neutral and independent venue for the conduct of both domestic, as well as international arbitration proceedings.[30] RCKAL was established pursuant to an agreement with the Government of Malaysia and was the first arbitral centre in the world to adopt the 1976 UNCITRAL Arbitration Rules.[31]

Following the establishment of the RCKAL, in 1980 the Malaysian Arbitration Act of 1952 was amended to introduce a new Section 34, creating 'an odd divide based on the choice of regime dictated by the arbitration agreement'.[32] The newly introduced Section 34 provided:

> (1) Notwithstanding anything to the contrary in this Act or in any other written law but subject to subsect. (2) insofar it relates to the enforcement of an award, the provisions of this Act or other written law shall not apply to any arbitration held under the Convention on the Settlement of Investment Disputes Between States and Nationals of the States 1965 or under the United Nations Commission on International Trade law Arbitration Rules 1976 and the Rules of the Regional Centre for Arbitration at Kuala Lumpur.
>
> (2) Where an award made in an arbitration held in conformity with the Convention or the Rules specified in subsect. (1) is sought to be enforced in Malaysia, the enforcement proceedings in respect thereof shall be taken in accordance with the provisions of the Convention specified in subsect. (1) or the Convention on the Recognition and Enforcement of Foreign Arbitral Awards 1958, as may be appropriate.
>
> (3) The competent court for the purposes of such enforcement shall be the High Court.[33]

In essence, Section 34 excluded application of the Malaysian Arbitration Act of 1952 not only to any arbitration held under the Convention on the Settlement of Investment Disputes Between States and Nationals of the States 1965 (ICSID Convention), but also under the 1976 UNCITRAL Arbitral Rules and the Rules of the RCKAL. It thus excluded also all applications, including annulment actions, before Malaysian courts relating to such arbitration proceedings.[34]

Excluding the application of the Malaysian Arbitration Act of 1952, including the possibility to file an annulment action, for any arbitration held under the ICSID Convention is not surprising—the ICSID Convention itself provides for a self-contained annulment mechanism;[35] awards made under the auspices of the International Centre the International Centre for Settlement of Investment Disputes (ICSID) are not subject to annulment proceedings before the courts at the arbitral seat. However, for the other two categories of arbitration proceedings mentioned under Section 34, i.e. those under the 1976 UNCITRAL Arbitration Rules and the Rules of the RCKAL, this meant that Malaysian courts' jurisdiction to arbitration-related submissions, including annulment actions, was ousted altogether. Arbitration proceedings under the auspices of other arbitral institutions such as HKIAC,

[30]Rajoo (2019), p. 27.

[31]Ibid.

[32]Ibid.

[33]Shütze (2013), p. 678.

[34]Gharavi (2002), pp. 27–28.

[35]See Article 52 of the ICSID Convention.

SIAC, LCIA, ICC or SCC remained subject to the full supervisory jurisdiction of the Malaysian courts under the Malaysian Arbitration Act of 1952.[36]

Reportedly, the purpose behind the 1980 amendments to the Malaysian Arbitration Act of 1952 was to encourage the use of the RCKAL by arbitrating parties who did not wish the involvement of the Malaysian courts in any form before, during or after arbitration proceedings, except for the recognition and enforcement proceedings.[37] Other sources note that, similarly to the Belgian example where its legislator by means of the 1985 Law wished to promote Belgium as attractive seat of arbitration, also in Malaysia the 1980 amendments were adopted with a view to promote Malaysia as future centre of international arbitration proceedings.[38]

However, contrary to the Belgian approach, Section 34 of the Malaysian Arbitration Act of 1952 did not make the ousting of the Malaysian courts' jurisdiction conditional upon the absence of any type of connections with Malaysia to trigger the exclusion—it only required the application of the 1976 UNCITRAL Arbitration Rules or the Rules of the RCKAL.[39] Thus, it did not follow the divide between domestic and international arbitration proceedings (or arbitrating parties), but simply the choice of the applicable arbitration regime in the arbitration agreement.[40] Moreover, it was not only the Malaysian Arbitration Act of 1952 that was not to apply in such cases, but, as the provision suggests, also 'other written law'. The jurisdiction of the Malaysian courts for the said type of arbitration proceedings was ousted altogether—Malaysian courts could neither intervene in arbitration proceedings, nor assist such arbitration proceedings.

Section 34 of the Malaysian Arbitration Act of 1952 created a lacuna that, as expected by such a regime, was highlighted by situations where arbitral tribunals did not always posses the necessary coercive powers to ensure that arbitration proceedings were conducted properly and resulted with the issuing of a fair and just arbitral award.[41] The said provision led to a series of court cases,[42] and overall, similarly to its counterpart in Belgium, was seen as anomalous dichotomy not finding equivalent in arbitral regimes in other developed jurisdictions, providing nothing more than a fertile ground of a wholesale reform of the Malaysian arbitration law. Such reform saw its light on 30 December 2005 with the adoption of the 2005 Arbitration Act that is based on the UNCITRAL Model Law, and repealed and replaced the Malaysian Arbitration Act of 1952.[43] Unsurprisingly, the 2005 Arbitration Act did not

---

[36] Rajoo (2019), p. 27.

[37] Ibid.

[38] Shütze (2013), p. 678.

[39] Gharavi (2002), p. 28.

[40] See the decision in *Jati Erat Sdn Bhd v City Land Sdn Bhd*, [2002] 1 CLJ 346 that confirmed that the exclusion applied to any arbitration held under the then Rules of the RCKAL irrespective of whether the parties were local or international. Reported in Rajoo (2019), p. 28.

[41] Rajoo (2019), p. 28.

[42] See Shütze (2013), p. 678. Referring to multiple decisions by the Malaysian courts applying Section 34 of the Malaysian Arbitration Act of 1952.

[43] See generally Baskaran (2019).

continue its predecessor's notorious legacy in excluding altogether the involvement of Malaysian courts in arbitration proceedings governed by the 1976 UNCITRAL Arbitration Rules or the Rules of the RCKAL.

The Malaysian example in excluding the application of setting-aside proceedings altogether follows a somewhat different route than its counterpart in Belgium. Malaysian law neither made the exclusion optional, nor subject to parties' connection with Malaysia. The exclusion was triggered by parties' simple choice of the applicable arbitration regime, either that of the ICSID Convention, the 1976 UNCITRAL Arbitration Rules or the Rules of the RCKAL. The underlying purpose of the 1980 amendment and its adverse consequences, however, can be put on par with the former Belgian example. It is especially due to the latter that the former Section 34 of the Malaysian Arbitration Act of 1952 has lost its importance for the future.[44]

6.4 Kyrgyzstan

Contrary to the above introduced examples of Belgium and Malaysia where total exclusion of setting aside proceedings is a creature of the past, the Kyrgyz Republic, in addition to Latvia (see Sect. 6.5), serves as a contemporary example of a State not providing for the setting-aside of arbitral awards at all. In Kyrgyzstan, similarly as in Latvia, it is simply impossible for arbitrating parties to apply before the Kyrgyz courts with an action to set aside an arbitral award issued by an arbitral tribunal seated in Kyrgyzstan.

Arbitration in Kyrgyzstan is generally governed by the Law on Arbitration Courts of 30 July 2002. In addition, the relatively newly adopted Code of Civil Procedure of the Kyrgyz Republic of 25 January 2017 provides, inter alia, provisions for recognition and enforcement of arbitral awards.[45] Although reportedly the 2002 Law on Arbitration Courts is *mostly* based on the UNCITRAL Model Law,[46] Kyrgyzstan is not considered to be UNCITRAL Model Law country.[47]

As said, in Kyrgyzstan, there is no procedure for challenging arbitral awards before the Kyrgyz courts whose competence is limited to refusing recognition and enforcement of arbitral awards. Kyrgyz courts have no competence to decide on the annulment of arbitral awards, following such application by a party to arbitration proceedings.[48] Prof. Van den Berg has described such awards as *ghost awards*.[49]

---

[44] Shütze (2013), p. 678.

[45] Generally on arbitration in Kyrgyzstan see, e.g., Korobeinikov and Inshakova (2019). See also Taychayev and Alenkina (2019), Sabirov (2020).

[46] Korobeinikov and Inshakova (2019).

[47] Status: UNCITRAL Model Law on International Commercial Arbitration (1985), with amendments as adopted in 2006. https://uncitral.un.org/en/texts/arbitration/modellaw/commercial_arbitration/status. Accessed 29 May 2020.

[48] Sabirov (2020), p. 201.

[49] Van den Berg (1994), p. 160.

The losing party to arbitration proceedings has no other option than to wait until the award creditor files for recognition and enforcement proceedings and then try to oppose such recognition and enforcement. There is no separate remedy pursuant to which an arbitral award may be annulled. As such, it continues to produce *res judicata* effects indefinitely.

Reportedly, during the adoption process of the 2017 Code of Civil Procedure of the Kyrgyz Republic, the Kyrgyz government proposed to introduce provisions providing for the challenging of arbitral awards issued in Kyrgyzstan.[50] It is said that the proposal was based on concerns that, even if arbitral awards issued in Kyrgyzstan contradict the Kyrgyz public policy, such awards could not be set aside by the Kyrgyz courts. Although the Kyrgyz government's proposal was seen as a positive step, it was nevertheless rejected and not included in the adopted final version of the 2017 Code of Civil Procedure.[51]

The very unusual approach in Kyrgyzstan with regard to regulation of setting-aside proceedings (or absence thereof) has its commonalities with the approach (and reasons thereof) in Latvia. Both relatively newly (re)established States share common history as to their ties with the Soviet Union that, as will be explained below (Sect. 6.5.), did not provide for arbitration as an alternative dispute resolution mechanism as it was and still is understood in the rest of the world. Although *arbitration* as such existed in the Soviet Union, the term *arbitration* had a totally different understanding and meaning—it referred to and encompassed the so-called *arbitration courts*, i.e. specialized commercial courts that were an inherent part of the judicial system and still continue to exist in Russia nowadays. Notably, parties *arbitrating* before these *arbitration courts* had no remedy to apply for the setting aside of arbitral awards. In the author's opinion, the former Soviet legacy in this regard and the said States' inexperience and understanding (or rather lack thereof) of arbitration as an alternative dispute resolution mechanism is one of the reasons why the annulment mechanism is simply absent from their national laws. The said premise will be further developed by a more in detail look at the case of Latvia.

6.5 Latvia

Court involvement in arbitration proceedings is axiomatic. There are many internationally well recognized ways how national courts may get involved in arbitration proceedings and, as once famously put by a prominent English judge, national courts are the only ones 'possessing coercive powers which could rescue the arbitration if it is in danger of foundering'.[52]

---

[50] Korobeinikov and Inshakova (2019a), p. 2.

[51] Ibid.

[52] Lord Mustill in *Copee Levalin NV v Ken-Ren Fertilisers and Chemicals* [1994] 2 Lloyd's Rep. 109 at 116, HL acknowledging that: '[t]here is plainly a tension here. On the one hand the concept of arbitration as a consensual process reinforced by the ideas of transnationalism leans against the

Ideally, arbitration proceedings commence, take place and result in a voluntarily performed arbitral award, therefore not requiring the involvement of national courts. If, however, for any reasons, the smooth functioning and effectiveness of arbitration proceedings is endangered, national courts are the ones carrying out various ancillary tasks intended to preserve the status quo of arbitration proceedings and protect parties' legitimate interests and rights.

If the applicable national arbitration law provides for insufficient court involvement, when such an involvement is truly necessary for maintaining the integrity and effectiveness of arbitration proceedings or protecting persons from violations of their most fundamental rights, the whole concept of arbitration as an alternative venue for dispute resolution becomes, to put it mildly, less appealing in the eyes of its potential users. This is brilliantly illustrated by foreign parties shying away from Belgium as the seat of arbitration when such parties, by operation of the 1985 Law, were statutorily prohibited from challenging arbitral awards issued by arbitral tribunals in Belgium. Therefore, arbitrating parties, perhaps contrary to what they initially intend to achieve by concluding an arbitration agreement, nevertheless are eager to maintain a healthy and balanced involvement of national courts when such involvement is indispensable for the effectiveness of arbitration and protection of parties' fundamental rights.[53]

Latvia is perhaps one of the *best* examples of how insufficient national court involvement can not only result in arbitration as a mechanism of dispute settlement losing its appeal in the eyes of its potential users, but, more importantly, also in the violation of certain fundamental party procedural human rights, such as the right of access to a court. The Latvian *lex arbitri* is simply silent upon the possibility to challenge arbitral awards before State courts. Latvian law is not only silent in this regard, but also regarding several other aspects of court involvement in arbitration proceedings, such as the appointment and challenging of arbitrators, hearing of witnesses, production of evidence, issuing of interim measures during arbitration proceedings etc. Notably, in 2014, one of such *legislative gaps* in the Latvian *lex arbitri*, namely the strict interpretation of the *kompetenz-kompetenz* principle and the impossibility to challenge the validity of arbitration agreements before national courts, resulted in a case before the Latvian Constitutional Court, which concluded that such a legal vacuum violates arbitrating parties' right of access to a court under the Latvian Constitution.

involvement of the mechanisms of state through the medium of a municipal court. On the other side there is the plain fact, palatable or not, that it is only a Court possessing coercive powers which could rescue the arbitration if it is in danger of foundering'.

[53] See, e.g. Van den Berg (1992), p. 273.

6.5.1 Arbitration in Latvia—A Brief Summary

Since the proclamation of the Republic of Latvia as an independent State in 1918, arbitration has existed and been used alongside other dispute resolution mechanisms. Until the outset of the World War II, domestic arbitration in Latvia was governed by the former Russian Civil Procedure Law of 1864 (as amended and modified between 1918 and 1940).[54] It is reported that only few domestic (and no international) arbitration proceedings took place under the auspices of the two permanent arbitral institutions at that time, the Latvian Chamber of Commerce and Industry ('LCCI') and the Latvian Craftsman Chamber.[55]

There were no permanent arbitral institutions in Latvia during the Soviet occupation (1944–1991)[56] and the term *arbitration* acquired a totally different meaning by means of the so-called *arbitration courts*, i.e. specialized commercial courts that were an inherent part of the judicial system and still continue to exist in Russia nowadays.[57] Since these *arbitration courts* were not an alternative mechanism for the resolution of disputes they had very little or nothing to do with the concept of arbitration as it was, and still is, known in the rest of the world.[58]

After Latvia re-established its independence in 1991, there was a profound need to thoroughly reform the Latvian legal system in its entirety. This included also the regulation on arbitration. As with any newly (re)established State, the Latvian legal system faced many practical and legal challenges both domestically and internationally—drafting of a new arbitration law and ratification of international arbitration conventions was one of them.

Shortly after 1991, Latvia signed and ratified both the New York Convention and also the ICSID Convention.[59] Latvia soon also witnessed the rise of new arbitration

---

[54]During the 1920s and 1930s civil procedural rights in Latvia, including the applicable civil procedural regulations, developed on the basis of the former Russian Civil Procedure law of 1864. It was amended, supplemented and developed according to the needs of the newly established independent State. For more information see, e.g. Blūzma et al. (2000), pp. 256–258 and 277–279.

[55]Ūdris and Kačevska (2004). More generally on arbitration in Latvia between 1918 and 1940 see, e.g., Bukovskis (1933), pp. 568–579.

[56]Ūdris and Kačevska (2004), p. 211.

[57]See, e.g. Žukova (2008), p. 2.

[58]Ibid.

[59]The New York Convention was ratified by Latvia in 1992, Estonia in 1993, and Lithuania in 1995. The ICSID Convention was ratified by Latvia in 1997, Estonia in 1992, and Lithuania in 1992. Moreover, Latvia later (in 2003) also succeeded to the 1961 European Convention on International Commercial Arbitration.

law. Although the Latvian judiciary was reformed already in 1993, the new arbitration law ('1999 Arbitration Law')[60] came into force only in 1999—much later than arbitration laws in the neighbouring Lithuania and Estonia.[61]

It was not only the timing of introduction of new arbitration laws that differed among the three Baltic States—it was also the substance and approach that each legislator employed in drafting its new arbitration law. Although all three states drew inspiration from the UNCITRAL Model Law and the 1976 UNCITRAL Arbitration Rules, neither the 1991 Law on the Arbitration Court of the Estonian Chamber of Commerce and Industry (ECCI),[62] nor the Lithuanian 1996 Law on Commercial Arbitration,[63] or the Latvian 1999 Arbitration Law resembled the UNCITRAL Model Law to the extent that the respective States could be labelled as 'Model Law countries.'[64] In Estonia and Lithuania that, however, changed in 2005 and 2012, respectively, when both States enacted new arbitration laws based on the UNCITRAL Model Law. This, however, is still not the case in Latvia.

6.5.1.1 Reasons for Distrust in Arbitration

Contemporary Latvian arbitration environment is characterized by a relatively high degree of distrust—the reasons for this can be traced back to a seemingly unreasoned choice to include a provision in the 1999 Arbitration Law that allowed any legal person to establish a permanent arbitral institution.[65] In other States, permanent arbitral institutions are generally linked to chambers of commerce and professional

[60]It was included as a separate section in the Latvian Code of Civil Procedure (LCCP). Until the entry into force of the 2015 Arbitration Law, arbitration was regulated by Part D of the Latvian LCCP. Further references in this book to the 1999 Arbitration Law is a general reference to Part D of the LCCP previously in force.

[61]New arbitration laws were introduced in Estonia and Lithuania in 1991 and 1996, respectively.

[62]The 1991 Law on the Arbitration Court of the ECCI (in an amended version still applicable as the ECCI institutional rules. www.koda.ee/public/Reglement_2013-inglise_keelne.pdf. Accessed 29 May 2020) was replaced by the 2005 Estonian Code of Civil Procedure, secs. 712–757 of which are now the applicable law on arbitration in Estonia. www.riigiteataja.ee/en/eli/513122013001/consolide. Accessed 29 May 2020.

[63]The 1996 Law on Commercial Arbitration (www3.lrs.lt/pls/inter3/dokpaieska.showdoc_e?p_id=56461. Accessed 29 April 2020) was replaced by a new Law on Commercial Arbitration in 2012. www.newyorkconvention.org/11165/web/files/document/2/1/21090.pdf. Accessed 29 May 2020.

[64]It is said that initially the draft of the 1999 Arbitration Law was based on the UNCITRAL Model Law, however, during negotiations certain provisions, especially in relation to court assistance to arbitration proceedings, were deleted and not included in the final version. See Ūdris and Kačevska (2004), p. 212. The Lithuanian 1996 Law on Arbitration was drafted in accordance with the UNCITRAL Model Law, however, only the 2012 Law on Arbitration is considered as being based on the UNCITRAL Model Law. www.uncitral.org/uncitral/en/uncitral_texts/arbitration/1985Model_arbitration_status.html. Accessed 29 May 2020.

[65]Kačevska (2004). Art. 486(3) of the LCCP (1999 version) stated that 'a permanent arbitration institution may be established by legal persons that notify the Ministry of Justice of such an establishment'.

trade associations, however, in Latvia, until the entry into force of the 2015 Arbitration Law, any legal person could establish a permanent arbitral institution and settle disputes therein.

Such an unreasoned decision opened a floodgate of permanent arbitral institutions and is seen as the main reason for the disproportionately high number of such institutions in Latvia.[66] Latvia witnessed the establishing of a staggering 214(!) permanent arbitral institutions by the end of 2014.[67] Due to the fact that establishing a permanent arbitration institution was so effortless, the whole concept of arbitration became, and to a large extent still is, a dangerous tool in the hands of the dishonest. The term *pocket arbitration courts*, as known not only in relation to Latvia, but also other countries, e.g. Russia,[68] best characterizes the problem at hand whereby seemingly *permanent* arbitral institutions are created by arbitrating parties (or their counsel) themselves, thus taking justice into their own hands.[69]

Despite certain hesitant attempts to decrease the number of permanent arbitral institutions, currently there are still 69 *permanent* arbitral institutions in Latvia.[70] Their high number has been one of the main reasons why the Latvian legislator has continuously refrained from introducing the much-needed court assistance in support of arbitration. The situation is quite paradoxical—one the one hand, the disproportionately high amount of permanent arbitral institutions has relieved courts of, on average, at least 9 percent of their annual case-load,[71] however, on the other hand, the majority of arbitral awards issued by such *permanent* arbitral institutions are of questionable nature. This can be mainly explained due to the almost non-existent court control that Latvian courts exercise over arbitration proceedings.

---

[66] Ibid.

[67] Kačevska (2014), pp. 23–24.

[68] See, e.g. Philippov (2015) The Problem of 'Pocket Arbitration Courts' in Russia: Finally Resolved? CIS Arbitration Forum, 7 April 2015. http://www.cisarbitration.com/2015/04/07/the-problem-of-pocket-arbitration-courts-in-russia-finally-resolved/. Accessed 29 May 2020.

[69] See, e.g. *Aero-lukss v. Latvijas finieris* (2002), reported in Ūdris and Kačevska (2004), p. 220.

[70] Commercial Register of the Republic of Latvia (2020) List of permanent arbitral institutions in Latvia. https://www.ur.gov.lv/lv/registre/organizaciju/skirejtiesas/skirejtiesu-saraksts/. Accessed 29 May 2020.

[71] For example, in 2004 the total number of applications for the enforcement of arbitral awards was 7,379; in 2005, 6,960 applications; however, in 2008, 8,433 applications (i.e. 25%) in comparison with a total of 34,010 civil applications in the courts of first instance. This is mainly due to the fact that it was also possible to settle consumer disputes in arbitration. Since 2007 the number of applications for enforcement of arbitral awards has decreased every year and in 2015 'only' 979 applications for the enforcement of arbitral awards were received. These numbers represent only the submitted applications for recognition and enforcement of arbitral awards and do not reflect the total number of cases decided by means of arbitration in Latvia. See the Court Information System (2020) Statistics. http://tis.ta.gov.lv/tisreal?FORM=TIS_STaT_O. Accessed 29 May 2020.

6.5.1.2 Failed Attempts to Remedy the Adverse Consequences

In 2005, minor amendments to the 1999 Arbitration Law were adopted, creating a specific register of permanent arbitral institutions.[72] However, there were still hardly any restrictions on the establishment of such institutions. Thus, the 2005 amendments did not solve the most worrying issue—their high number that at the beginning of 2005 had already reached 110.[73]

In order to address the considerable amount of criticism[74] of the 1999 Arbitration Law and the resulting adverse consequences thereof, the Ministry of Justice attempted to develop a completely new draft arbitration law in 2007. Unfortunately, it was a failure. Reportedly the drafting committee had only minor knowledge of arbitration and could not draft a modern arbitration law reflecting international arbitration standards and principles.[75] The possibility of implementing the UNCITRAL Model Law was repeatedly ignored. The new draft law contained provisions utterly hostile to the nature of arbitration[76] and it received another round of criticism.[77] Consequently, the legislative process was put on hold until 2008 when the Ministry of Justice came up with an updated version of the first draft.

Even though the 2008 version differed from the initial draft, it was still not based on the UNCITRAL Model Law and equally considerably departed from generally accepted principles of arbitration. For example, it did not contain any provisions on court assistance in arbitration; it stripped arbitral tribunals of the right to rule on their own jurisdiction pursuant to the *kompetenz–kompetenz* principle and it also ignored the principle of separability of an arbitration agreement from the underlying contract.

Having learned that the Ministry of Justice had prepared the two drafts without any input from international arbitration experts, the LCCI and various other interested parties took the initiative and invited distinguished international arbitration experts to comment on the updated draft arbitration law. Opinions were received from various notable authorities in the field of international arbitration: Gary Born, Prof. Loukas Mistelis, Prof. Dr. Rolf Knieper and Carl F. Salans, Their opinions were translated and published in the local weekly periodical *Jurista Vārds*.[78] They all shared an alarming impression that the draft arbitration law was a very serious departure from broadly recognized international arbitration principles and that it in many aspects deviated from the UNCITRAL Model Law. For example, Carl F. Salans indicated that:

---

[72] The so-called 'Arbitration Register' is still in existence and operates under the auspices of the Commercial Register of the Republic of Latvia. https://www.ur.gov.lv/lv/registre/organizaciju/skirejtiesas/skirejtiesu-saraksts/. Accessed 29 May 2020.

[73] Torgāns (2005).

[74] See, e.g., Kačevska (2004), Ūdris and Kačevska (2004), Rozenbergs (2005).

[75] Tipaine (2014).

[76] Ibid. See also Volkova (2007).

[77] See, e.g., Repšs (2014), Lapsa (2007), Kačevska (2008), p. 32.

[78] See Born (2008), Salans (2008), Mistelis (2008), Knieper (2008).

> In many respects, the Latvian Draft Law on Arbitration departs from the text of the Model Law. I understand the unique situation in the Latvian Republic where the large number of small arbitration courts whose work is subject to major criticism, undermines confidence in arbitration proceedings. [It] appears from reading the Draft Law that several of its provisions go against the core principles of arbitration. The legislators cannot promote successfully a system of arbitration which guarantee the fair and impartial resolution of disputes, while disregarding the bedrock principles of arbitration.[79]

Regretfully, their valuable independent critique and input into the development of arbitration in Latvia in the right direction was disregarded. In the beginning of 2009, the Ministry of Justice organized a meeting regarding possible improvements of the draft arbitration law, and its further legislative development thereof, however, due to the differing opinions and conceptual visions in the committee, the draft arbitration law was withdrawn from further legislative consideration.[80]

In 2012, the legislative process finally resumed, however, although the LCCI in cooperation with various stakeholders had developed a new, modern draft arbitration law based on the UNCITRAL Model Law, the poor-quality 2007 draft, despite its condemnation by international arbitration experts, again found its way into the Parliament's corridors, and regrettably so, prevailed in further negotiations. At the same time, the number of permanent arbitral institutions had reached its peak (214 permanent arbitral institutions in 2014) and it seemed that the only focus during the negotiations of the new arbitration law was simply to reduce the disproportionately high number of such institutions. Other issues, such as introduction of UNCITRAL Model Law-type court control and setting-aside proceedings, were not even considered.

The currently in-force 2015 Arbitration Law is another failure: it is still not based on the UNCITRAL Model Law and contains serious anomalies that go against the core principles of arbitration.[81] Although the number of permanent arbitral institutions is reduced by more than one-half, their number is still very high. However, the most worrying issue is the still-prevalent misconception of the whole idea of arbitration—its effectiveness continues to be undermined by very strict qualification

[79]Salans (2008). Similar observations were made by other experts. For example, Prof. Mistelis, surprised by the large number of permanent arbitral institutions concluded that '[t]his is a rather bizarre phenomenon [...] If the motivation is to regulate arbitral institutions, you perhaps need a different law or a system of accreditation rather than a new arbitration law.' See Mistelis (2008). Gary Born concluded that '[his] main concerns with regard to the Latvian Draft Law are a lack of court assistance in support of arbitral proceedings, and the uncertainties contained therein. These entail the risk of unnecessarily lengthy and costly arbitral proceedings, invalidity of the arbitration agreement and consequently frustration of the parties' expectations.' See Born (2008). He also noted that 'the UNCITRAL Model Law provides for a sound approach to resolving the problems raised below. The Model Law has been adopted by more than 50 jurisdictions around the world, including specifically in Europe, and in my view it can provide the Latvian legislature with a basis to solve problems and improve the Latvian Draft Law without preventing Latvia from addressing domestic particularities such as the large number of arbitral institutions currently existing in Latvia. As such, the Model Law can help ensure that international parties will feel secure in choosing Latvia as the seat of arbitration.' Introductory note to the opinion. Unpublished.

[80]Lapsa (2010).

[81]For a brief general overview see Tipaine and Fjodorova (2016).

requirements for arbitrators, almost no court assistance prior, during, and after arbitration proceedings, and other peculiarities, such as non-existence of setting-aside proceedings.

6.5.1.3 Lack of Court Involvement in Latvian Arbitration Law

It is true that by loosening the *lex arbitri* and decreasing judicial control over arbitration proceedings, on the one hand, and giving more procedural autonomy to arbitrating parties, on the other hand, many States strive for more attractiveness when it comes to choosing a venue and the *lex arbitri* applicable to arbitration proceedings. Undoubtedly, an arbitration-friendly legal environment is one of the most important prerequisites that parties consider when choosing an arbitral seat.[82]

However, a total hands-off approach to judicial control over arbitration may achieve exactly the opposite—being apprehensive that potential violations of vital procedural guarantees during arbitration proceedings will not be addressed and remedied by ordinary courts, parties may look at arbitration with a degree of suspicion. This is exactly what happened in Belgium.[83] A more contemporary example in this regard is Latvian arbitration law that allows arbitration to proceed in a relative legal vacuum. However, arbitration does not and cannot exist in a legal vacuum[84]—it is not only regulated by *lex arbitri* and the rules of procedure chosen by the parties, but its success also heavily depends on court assistance during the life-cycle of arbitration.

In Latvia, courts assist arbitral tribunals only in referring parties to arbitration, issuing interim measures (solely prior to the establishment of an arbitral tribunal), and in recognizing and enforcing arbitral awards. Following the Latvian Constitutional Court's ruling in 2014, Latvian courts are now also required to hear claims regarding the existence and validity of arbitration agreements. As per other generally accepted roles of national courts, e.g. the appointment and challenges of arbitrators, issuing of interim measures during arbitration proceedings, taking of evidence, or the hearing of witnesses, neither the formerly applicable 1999 Arbitration Law, nor the currently in force 2015 Arbitration Law provides any court support in these matters. There is neither any mechanism for challenging arbitral awards before Latvian courts.

Since the adoption of the 1999 Arbitration Law court assistance in support of arbitration has been one of the most broadly debated topics among legal practitioners in Latvia. Although initially the draft 1999 Arbitration Law was based on the UNCITRAL Model Law and its draft provisions provided for court involvement, the final version omitted almost all provisions on court assistance in support of arbitration.[85] It has been said that the 1999 Arbitration Law was adopted 'at a time when Latvia

[82] See, e.g., Queen Mary University of London, White & Case (2015) 2015 International Arbitration Survey: Improvements and Innovations in International Commercial Arbitration, p. 14. www.arbitration.qmul.ac.uk/docs/164761.pdf. Accessed 29 May 2020.

[83] See Sect. 6.2.

[84] Redfern et al. (2004), p. 77, Kaufmann-Kohler and Rigozzi (2015), p. 16.

[85] Ūdris and Kačevska (2004), p. 212.

did not have a strong tradition of settling disputes by arbitration, the judiciary did not want to deal with arbitral matters and supporters of the former State arbitration [i.e. the 'arbitration courts' as in place during the Soviet occupation] were lobbying for minimal court control and interference.'[86] Taken together with the unreasoned choice to permit any legal person to establish a permanent arbitration institution, the lack of proper and much needed court assistance has been at the heart of problems underlying the whole arbitration system in Latvia.

The main argument against the introduction of court assistance is that with the high number of permanent arbitral institutions and disputes settled therein, court assistance would disproportionately overburden courts with various legitimate and also dilatory requests by arbitrating parties.[87] At the same time, simply ignoring the necessity of court assistance in support of arbitration is not an answer. This is best illustrated by the Latvian Constitutional Court's ruling of 2014, confirming that an argument of increased court workload cannot justify disproportionate limitations on parties' right of access to a court. Court assistance, as opposed to unreasonable interference, is not only a crucial element for the smooth and effective functioning of any arbitration system,[88] but needed for the protection of parties' fundamental procedural human rights.

6.5.1.4 The Latvian Constitutional Court's Ruling in the *Hiponia* Case

In 2014, the refusal of Latvian courts to hear a claim challenging the validity of an arbitration agreement, resulted in the second arbitration-related case before the Latvian Constitutional Court. The first case was decided in 2005 and established that a court's duty to refer parties to arbitration was consistent with the right of access to a court.[89] Although the 2005 case is considered as the pioneering arbitration-related case before the Latvian Constitutional Court, it is the second case that provides a valuable lesson with respect to the adverse consequences that lack of adequate court involvement in arbitration can cause to arbitrating parties.

The 2014 *Hiponia* case concerned the interpretation of the well-known principle of *kompetenz–kompetenz*, i.e. an arbitral tribunal's competence to decide on its own

---

[86] Ibid.

[87] See the draft 2015 Arbitration Law, Preliminary impact assessment report (Explanatory report), Section 2. http://titania.saeima.lv/LIVS11/saeimalivs11.nsf/0/A182DD228B4DAF6CC2257C4E003D7B1B?OpenDocument#b. Accessed 29 April 2020. See also Kačevska (2014), Kucina (2014), Repšs (2014), Tipaine and Fjodorova (2016).

[88] In the context of Latvian arbitration law, see, e.g., Born (2008) where the author states that 'in order to ensure the effective resolution of disputes a modern arbitration law should provide for court assistance in support of the arbitral process. Indeed, national courts' assistance is indisputedly helpful, and even required, in many cases'.

[89] *Asmers* case, No. 2004-10-01, the Constitutional Court of the Republic of Latvia, 17 January 2005. www.satv.tiesa.gov.lv/wp-content/uploads/2004/05/2004-10-01_Spriedums_ENG.pdf. Accessed 29 May 2020.

jurisdiction. Before the entry into force of the 2015 Arbitration Law, the *kompetenz–kompetenz* principle was enshrined in Article 495(1) of the LCCP providing that 'an arbitral tribunal shall decide on its own jurisdiction, also in cases when one of the parties challenges the existence or validity of the arbitration agreement.'[90]

However, unlike, e.g., Article 16(3) of the UNCITRAL Model Law or provisions of various national arbitration laws,[91] the LCCP did not contain any further reference to subsequent court involvement in finally determining the existence or validity of an arbitration agreement and thus also the jurisdiction of an arbitral tribunal. Moreover, the Latvian Supreme Court had consistently interpreted Article 495(1) of the LCCP very restrictively and refused to hear applications regarding the existence or validity of arbitration agreements.[92]

Taking into account that the 1999 Arbitration Law hardly provided any court assistance in support of arbitration, there was no possibility to challenge an arbitral award, and the fact that courts *controlled* arbitration proceedings only formally during the enforcement proceedings,[93] arbitrating parties had no effective remedy to challenge the jurisdiction of an arbitral tribunal. The majority of the then existing 214 *permanent* arbitral institutions assumed jurisdiction over arbitration disputes with no hesitation. Courts, on the other hand, denied applications for the challenge of validity of arbitration agreements and, by strictly interpreting the *kompetenz–kompetenz* principle, stressed that challenges to arbitral jurisdiction must be submitted to and heard solely by arbitral tribunals.

This inability to challenge the jurisdiction of arbitral tribunals before State courts resulted in a case before the Latvian Constitutional Court. In the 2005 case, the Constitutional Court put that 'control [over arbitration proceedings] during the enforcement stage is considered a sufficient mean, at least to guarantee the compliance of fundamental rights.'[94] Later, this statement was also invoked when arguing against the introduction of setting-aside proceedings.[95] However, the 2014 *Hiponia* case proved

[90] Currently, the *kompetenz–kompetenz* principle is contained in art. 24(1) of the 2015 Arbitration Law.

[91] See, e.g., art. 11(2) of the 2012 Lithuanian Law on Commercial Arbitration; art. 730(6) of the Estonian Code of Civil Procedure; sec. 2 of the SAA; sec. 1040(3) of the ZPO; sec. 32 of the 1996 English Arbitration Act.

[92] See, e.g., Case No. SKC-213, the Supreme Court of the Republic of Latvia, 14 May 2008; Case No. SKC-1037, the Supreme Court of the Republic of Latvia, 13 October 2010; Case No. SKC-514, the Supreme Court of the Republic of Latvia, 26 September 2012; Case No. SKC-20, the Supreme Court of the Republic of Latvia, 30 January 2013. Although courts of first instance and courts of appeal had occasionally heard applications regarding the existence or validity of arbitration agreements (see, e.g., Case No. C29526804/C21C10, the Latgale City Court, 23 February 2010; Case No. C40108906, the Kurzeme Court of Appeal, 10 June 2011) their judgments were subsequently overturned by the Supreme Court of the Republic of Latvia.

[93] See *Asmers* case, No. 2004-10-01, the Constitutional Court of the Republic of Latvia, 17 January 2005. www.satv.tiesa.gov.lv/wp-content/uploads/2004/05/2004-10-01_Spriedums_ENG.pdf. Accessed 29 May 2020.

[94] Ibid. at 9.1.

[95] See, e.g. Kucina (2014).

that control over arbitration solely at the stage of enforcement proceedings is insufficient for the guarantee of parties' fundamental procedural rights, such as the right of access to a court.

In brief, the *Hiponia* case[96] examined the compatibility of Article 495(1) of the LCCP (insofar it did not provide a right to challenge the invalidity of an arbitration agreement in ordinary jurisdiction courts) with Article 92 of the Latvian Constitution and the right of access to a court. Proceedings before the Latvian Constitutional Court involved various parties, each having diametrically opposed views as to the interpretation of Article 495(1) of the LCCP and the principle of *kompetenz–kompetenz* as well as its compatibility with the right of access to a court.

Representatives of the Latvian Parliament and the Ministry of Justice referred, inter alia, to the perennial argument of court overload and argued that arbitrating parties should not be given an opportunity to challenge the jurisdiction of an arbitral tribunal in ordinary jurisdiction courts.[97] Others, on the contrary, referred, inter alia, to the UNCITRAL Model Law, and stressed that the current control over arbitration proceedings is ineffective, and that the *kompetenz–kompetenz* principle is internationally interpreted as giving 'the last say' over the validity of arbitration agreements to State courts.[98]

In its analysis, the Latvian Constitutional Court first briefly recalled its 2005 ruling and various arbitration-related ECtHR cases and principles established therein,[99] reaffirming the obvious—conclusion of an arbitration agreement, provided that it is made freely and unequivocally, does not per se violate Article 6(1) of the ECHR.[100] However, by referring to the ECtHR's *Jakob Boss* case, the Latvian Constitutional Court also noted that a State has a duty to create a mechanism for determining whether a person has voluntarily waived his or her right to a fair trial, including the right of access to a court.[101]

It then went on to analyze the reach of the *kompetenz–kompetenz* principle to determine whether it should be interpreted as giving the power to rule on its jurisdiction solely to an arbitral tribunal, or entails also the involvement of State courts. After referring to the parties' differing opinions, the Latvian Constitutional Court examined provisions of the 1961 European Convention on International Commercial Arbitration and the New York Convention (both binding on Latvia), and also the UNCITRAL Model Law.[102] With great emphasis on the latter, it stressed that the

[96] *Hiponia* case, No. 2014-09-01, the Constitutional Court of the Republic of Latvia, 28 November 2014. www.satv.tiesa.gov.lv/wp-content/uploads/2014/03/2014-09-01_Spriedums_ENG.pdf. Accessed 29 May 2020.

[97] Ibid. paras. 3 and 4.

[98] Ibid. paras. 5, 8, 10, and 11.

[99] *Suda v. Czech Republic*, App. No. 1643/06, ECtHR, 28 October 2010; *Suovaniemi and others v. Finland* (1999); *Jakob Boss Söhne v. Federal Republic of Germany* (1991).

[100] *Hiponia* case, No. 2014-09-01, the Constitutional Court of the Republic of Latvia, 28 November 2014, para. 14.2. www.satv.tiesa.gov.lv/wp-content/uploads/2014/03/2014-09-01_Spriedums_ENG.pdf. Accessed 29 May 2020.

[101] Ibid.

[102] Ibid. paras. 15.1–15.4.

kompetenz–kompetenz doctrine does not in principle exclude the possibility of court involvement in determining the jurisdiction of an arbitral tribunal.[103]

The Latvian Constitutional Court also considered the importance of the Latvian Supreme Court's consistently strict interpretation of Article 495(1) of the LCCP in refraining to hear applications on the validity of arbitration agreements. Limitation of the fundamental right of access to a court is obvious in the Latvian Supreme Court's interpretation of Article 495(1) of the LCCP, however, that does not entail an automatic violation of the right of access to a court. The right of access to a court may be subject to limitations, provided that such limitations (i) are stipulated by law; (ii) have a legitimate aim; and (iii) are proportionate to the aim pursued.[104]

There was no dispute that the limitation had been provided by law, i.e. Article 495(1) of the LCCP and the consistently restrictive Latvian Supreme Court's interpretation in this regard. It seemingly also had a legitimate aim—to decrease court workload and provide for a speedy and fast resolution of disputes. The purported benefits of arbitration had already been previously recognized in the case of 2005.[105] As seen, similar *legitimate aims* were advanced in the *Tabbane v. Switzerland* case.[106]

The most relevant issue, however, was whether such a limitation was proportionate to the legitimate aim pursued. Certainly, the legislator's chosen means were suitable to decrease court workload—if an application challenging the validity of an arbitration agreement was submitted to a court, it would simply be dismissed and courts would not hear the case. Nevertheless, the Latvian Constitutional Court indicated that there were alternative, more flexible, and less restrictive means to address this issue.[107] The increase of court workload per se, in the Latvian Constitutional Court's opinion, could not justify restrictions on a person's right of access to a court to the extent that the essence of such a right would be impaired.[108] In a situation where interests of national courts' procedural efficiency collide with a need to protect persons' fundamental rights, the latter must be given precedence.[109]

---

[103] Ibid. para. 15.5, holding that "[i]f, by systematically analysing the applicable law of other countries in a particular matter, one may establish a sufficiently unequivocal and general conclusion regarding the harmonization of national laws or a uniform standard in this matter, the results of compiling the applicable law and practice in other countries may serve as a recommendation for solving a particular problem or as a general principle of law. This applies also to legal regulation in the field of arbitration and its application in practice thereof […]".

[104] See, e.g., *Fayed v. the United Kingdom*, App. No. 17101/90, ECtHR, 21 September 1994, para. 65; *Markovic and Others v. Italy*, App. No. 1398/03, ECtHR, 14 December 2006, para. 99; *Ashingdane v. the United Kingdom*, para. 57. Generally, see Sect. 3.3.1.1.

[105] *Asmers* case, No. 2004-10-01, the Constitutional Court of the Republic of Latvia, 17 January 2005. www.satv.tiesa.gov.lv/wp-content/uploads/2004/05/2004-10-01_Spriedums_ENG.pdf. Accessed 29 May 2020.

[106] See Sect. 5.2.4.

[107] *Hiponia* case, No. 2014-09-01, the Constitutional Court of the Republic of Latvia, 28 November 2014, para. 20.2.1. www.satv.tiesa.gov.lv/wp-content/uploads/2014/03/2014-09-01_Spriedums_ENG.pdf. Accessed 29 May 2020.

[108] Ibid.

[109] Ibid.

The Latvian Constitutional Court ruled that Article 495(1) of the LCCP, insofar it did not provide for a right to challenge the jurisdiction of an arbitral tribunal before ordinary jurisdiction courts, was incompatible with Article 92 of the Latvian Constitution and the right of access to a court. Since the now applicable 2015 Arbitration Law was already passed by the Latvian Parliament (however not yet entered into force), Article 24(1) of the 2015 Arbitration Law was also declared incompatible with Article 92 of the Latvian Constitution.

While other States are trying to attract more arbitrations with a truly arbitration friendly formal legal infrastructure, the Latvian arbitration environment is still in its infancy and rather scares away than attracts investors and arbitrating parties. The current, somewhat defective legal framework of arbitration in Latvia is the result of years long inability to cut ties with the Soviet-minded understanding of arbitration as an alternative dispute resolution mechanism and to finally introduce an effective and well-functioning arbitration framework. Not only the Latvian legislator has itself created the main cause of the current ill-functioning arbitration framework (the cause being the unreasoned choice to permit any legal person to establish a permanent arbitral institution), but, regrettably so, it has continuously been unable to remedy adverse consequences thereof.

The remainder of this Chapter will in detail and chronologically address the phenomenon of setting-aside proceedings and its place in the Latvian legal system, beginning the analysis of the applicable legal framework in the pre-war Latvia, leading to the adoption of the currently in force 2015 Arbitration Law.

6.5.2 *Total Lack of Setting-Aside Proceedings in the Latvian Arbitration Law*

6.5.2.1 Not Always the Case—A Glimpse of History

Total lack of setting-aside proceedings characterizes only contemporary Latvian arbitration law, i.e. the previously in force 1999 Arbitration Law and the currently applicable 2015 Arbitration Law. Interestingly, in the period from the establishment of the Republic of Latvia as an independent state in 1918 until 1940 and the occupation of Latvia as a result of the World War II, the possibility of challenging arbitral awards was explicitly regulated by the then applicable procedural law in Latvia. Until 1940 domestic arbitration was governed by the Russian Civil Procedure Law of 1864 ('Pre-war CPL') that in an amended and modified form continued to be used as the main source of civil procedural law in Latvia during the 1920s and 1930s.[110] Under

[110] After the establishment of the Republic of Latvia as an independent State in 1918, a temporary decree issued by the People's Council of Latvia [a predecessor of the Latvian Provisional Government (1918–1920)] on 6 December 19 stipulated that all previously in force laws (i.e. those in force until the October Revolution of 24 October 1917) shall be recognized as sources of procedural law. These 'previously in force laws' included also the Russian Civil Procedure Law of 1864 that during

the heading 'Arbitration', its Articles 1488–1521[111] regulated domestic arbitration proceedings in Latvia. Although only a handful of domestic arbitrations took place in Latvia at that time, Articles 1488–1521 of the Pre-war CPL and their brief commentaries[112] provide a very insightful overview of the understanding of arbitration and its principles in Latvia at that time.

In particular, when looking at whether there were any grounds in the Pre-war CPL upon which arbitral awards could be challenged, one comes across Articles 1518–1521 of the Pre-war CPL that explicitly regulated the annulment of arbitral awards. Generally, the Pre-war CPL did not permit the appeal of arbitral awards *stricto* sensu (Article 1514 of the Pre-war CPL),[113] however it nevertheless permitted the challenging of arbitral awards on the basis of certain formal violations.

To some extent, the grounds for challenge in the Pre-war CPL were similar and can be compared to grounds for challenge found in contemporary national and international arbitration instruments, e.g. the previously introduced UNCITRAL Model Law. The Pre-war CPL distinguished between grounds that could be invoked by any of the arbitrating parties and grounds that could be invoked by State courts *ex officio*. Article 1518 of the Pre-war CPL provided for the former:

> Arbitral awards, upon a party's motion, are considered invalid and may be annulled only in cases where they have been issued after the expiry of the said term, or on the basis of an agreement that has not been signed by all persons taking part in its drafting, or the terms of the agreement are not adhered to at all.[114]

The first ground for annulment referred to arbitrators' obligation to observe a time-limit for issuing an arbitral award, as stipulated in the arbitration agreement or laid down in the Pre-war CPL. Article 1493 of the Pre-war CPL stated that unless the term for issuing an arbitral award is agreed by the parties, arbitrators shall decide the case within 4 months from the date of verification of the arbitration agreement.[115] Reportedly, the legislator's justification behind this ground for annulment was that:

---

the 1920s and 1930s was locally referred to simply as the Civil Procedure Law. See e.g. Blūzma (2000), pp. 209, 256 and 277.

[111] In the amended numbering as referred to in the very first official issue of the then applicable Civil Procedure Law in Latvian in 1932. Supplemented by brief commentaries of the Civil Cassation Department of the Latvian Senate, i.e. the Supreme Court of the Republic of Latvia at that time, it provided a very comprehensive overview of the Civil Procedure Law itself and its interpretation by the Civil Cassation Department of the Latvian Senate. See Konradi and Walter (1933).

[112] See Konradi and Walter (1933). See also Konradi and Zvejnieks (1939).

[113] Art. 1514 of the Pre-war CPL stated that 'An appeal of an arbitral award is not permissible'. See also Bukovskis (1933), pp. 574–575.

[114] Art. 1518 of the Pre-war CPL. Author's translation. The text is translated *sic erat scriptum*, trying to depict the somewhat historic original text as close as possible. Original reads as follows: 'Šķīrējtiesas spriedumi, uz prāvnieku sūdzībām, atzīstami par spēkā neesošiem un ir anulējami tikai tajos gadījumos, kad tie taisīti pēc noteiktā termiņa notecējuma, vai pēc līguma, kuru nav parakstījušas visas tā sastādīšanā piedalījušās personas, vai vispār neievērojot līgumā noteiktos nosacījumus'.

[115] Generally on the first ground of annulment see, e.g. Pommers (1938), pp. 23–26. At that time, the submission of a dispute to arbitration was possible only *ex post*, i.e. after the dispute had arisen. In order to convene an arbitral tribunal it was required to sign two agreements: (i) *compromissum*

> [A]n arbitral award cannot be considered valid if arbitrators had failed to issue it in the said term, because, pursuant to the arbitration agreement, the arbitrators' jurisdiction is limited to a certain time, beyond which it shall not extend [...][116]

The second ground referred to the invalidity of an arbitration agreement and addressed a situation where the statutorily required *ex post* arbitration agreement was not signed by all future arbitrating parties. Thus, it can be generally compared to the ground of invalidity of arbitration agreement contained in, e.g. Article 34(2)(a)(i) of the UNCITRAL Model Law and many national arbitration laws. In such cases, i.e. where an arbitration agreement lacked signatures of all or only one of the arbitrating parties, an arbitral award could have been subject to challenge on the basis of Article 1518 of the Pre-war CPL. It is reported that the legislator's justification behind this ground for annulment was that:

> [A] voluntary agreement that is essentially required for the establishing of an arbitral tribunal, can solely arise from the signatures of arbitrating parties and arbitrators, in the absence of which the arbitration agreement and the arbitration process cannot be considered to have happened, as well as the arbitral awards to be valid.[117]

The third annulment ground referred to irregularities in the arbitral procedure and can be compared to Article 34(2)(a)(iv) of the UNCITRAL Model Law. It in essence addressed all those cases where arbitrators did not adhere to the terms of the arbitration agreement. However, not all cases of non-compliance of certain terms of an arbitration agreement led to a valid challenge of an arbitral award on the basis of this ground. It was generally agreed that only non-compliance of significant terms of an arbitration agreement, due to which the interests of an arbitrating party were violated, would lead to the annulment of an arbitral award on the basis of this ground. Whether or not a term of the arbitration agreement was significant enough to trigger the application of this ground for annulment was for the State court hearing the annulment action to decide.[118]

(an agreement between the parties regarding the submission of a specific dispute to arbitration); and (ii) *receptum arbitri* (agreement by the parties and arbitrators). Both agreements formed one single 'arbitration agreement' that had to be signed before a notary public. This signing of the agreement and verification by the notary public was thus the starting point of the 4 month term for arbitrators to decide the dispute. See Bukovskis (1933), p. 571. Nevertheless, arts. 1506 and 1507 of the Pre-war CPL also permitted parties to contractually extend the agreed term for arbitrators to decide the case. Whether this additional extension could happen multiple times was subject to debate. See Pommers (1938), pp. 24–25.

[116]The legislator's aim behind the first ground for annulment as reported by Pommers (1938), p. 23. Author's translation. The original reads as follows: '[...] spriedums nevar tikt atzīts par spēkā esošu, ja starpnieki to nav taisijuši noteiktā laikā, jo ar šķīrējtiesas līgumu starpnieku pilnvarojums tiek aprobežots ar noteiktu laiku, par kuru tālāk tas nevar sniegties [...]'.

[117]The legislator's justification behind the second ground for annulment as reported by Pommers (1938), p. 27. Author's translation. The original reads as follows: '[...] labprātīga vienošanās, kas būtiski nepieciešama šķīrējtiesas nodibināšanai, var vienīgi izpausties pušu un starpnieku parakstos, bez kuriem šķīrējtiesas līgums un šķīrējtiesa nevar tikt atzīti par notikušiem, kā arī šķīrējtiesas spriedumi par spēkā esošiem'.

[118]Pommers (1938), p. 29.

There was a debate whether the above annulment grounds were exhaustive—on the one hand, according to certain scholars and a judgment of the Russian Senate of 1902,[119] the said annulment grounds were not exhaustive, however, later in 1927 the Latvian Senate arrived at an opposite conclusion, stipulating that such grounds are exhaustive and sufficient for the protection of parties' interests.[120] At the same time, it was also recognized that the annulment of an arbitral award on the basis of grounds stipulated in Article 1518 of the Pre-war CPL is not possible when the violation has indecisive character not affecting the party petitioning the annulment.[121] Moreover, annulment of an arbitral award on the basis of grounds in Article 1518 of the Pre-war CPL led to the annulment of an arbitral award solely in full—it was not possible to annul an arbitral award only in part.[122]

In addition, Article 1519 of the Pre-war CPL provided certain annulment grounds that could have been invoked by State courts *ex officio*:

> Arbitral awards shall be considered non-existent and they have no force and effect as regards: (i) such persons that have not taken part in the drafting of the arbitration agreement; (ii) such matters that fall outside the scope of submission on the basis of the arbitral agreement; and (iii) the matters stipulated in Article 1489.[123]

The first ground concerned the also nowadays well-recognized issue of third-party non-signatories in arbitration proceedings and protected such parties from consequences of the arbitral award. The second ground referred to another well-recognized matter, i.e. the excess of arbitrators' authority (*arbiter nihil extra compromissum facere potest*).[124] Such a ground is also provided for in the UNCITRAL Model Law and many national arbitration laws. Lastly, the Pre-war CPL also permitted the annulment of an arbitral award if it violated the applicable norms of arbitrability, i.e. Article

[119]The *Calki* case (No. 66), Russian Senate (1902) reported in Konradi and Walter (1933), p. 485. Since the Pre-war CPL was largely based on the 1864 Russian Civil Procedure Law the Latvian Senate regularly referred to and cited pre-First World War judgments of the Russian Senate.

[120]See Bukovskis (1933), pp. 575–576, Konradi and Walter (1933), p. 485–486, Konradi and Zvejnieks (1939), p. 442. See also the *Rojaks* case, Latvian Senate (Civil Cassation Department), 28 April 1927 reported in Senāta Civilā Kasācijas Departamenta spriedumi (1927) In: Tieslietu Ministrijas Izdevums (1932) Tieslietu Ministrijas Vēstnesis, No. 11/12, pp. 48–50. Generally on the discussion of interpretation of both art. 1518 and art. 1519 see, e.g. Pommers (1938), pp. 31–43.

[121]Konradi and Walter (1933), p. 486. Similarly, it had been recognized that, e.g. a violation of art. 1510 of the Pre-war CPL ('An arbitral award shall contain the names and surnames of parties and arbitrators, claims and evidence, and grounds on which the case has been decided') was not considered as a valid ground for annulling the arbitral award. See Konradi and Zvejnieks(1939), p. 442.

[122]Pommers (1938), pp. 29–30.

[123]Art. 1519 of the Pre-war CPL. Author's translation. The text is translated *sic erat scriptum*, trying to depict the somewhat historic original text as close as possible. Original reads as follows: 'Šķīrējtiesas spriedumi atzīstami par neesošiem un tiem nav nekāda spēka un ietekmes: (i) attiecībā uz personām, kas nav piedalijušās šķīrējtiesas līguma sastādīšanā; (ii) attiecībā uz tādiem priekšmetiem, kas nav bijuši nodot šķīrējtiesas izšķiršanai uz līguma pamata, un (iii) attiecībā uz 1489. pantā norādītām lietām.'

[124]Bukovskis (1933), p. 576. More specifically on the excess of authority in this regard see Konradi and Walter (1933), pp. 486–487.

1489 of the Pre-war CPL that laid down specific rules on non-arbitrability of certain matters, such as matters pertaining to public law, family law, criminal law etc.[125] As opposed to Article 1518 of the Pre-war CPL, violation of any of the annulment grounds in Article 1519 of the Pre-war CPL led only to a partial annulment of an arbitral award, annulling solely that part of an arbitral award that led to a violation of Article 1519 of the Pre-war CPL.[126] As explained by the legislator and affirmed by the Latvian Senate at that time, an opposite scenario (i.e. where an arbitral award would be annulled in full) would be unjust.[127]

An application for setting aside of an arbitral award had to be submitted to State courts within one month from the issuing of an arbitral award (Article 1520 of the Pre-war CPL).[128] If a State court annulled the arbitral award, parties were back to *status quo ante*, meaning that they had a right to repeatedly submit their dispute to an arbitral tribunal on the basis of a new arbitration agreement or to a state court.[129] Until the amendments of the Pre-war CPL of 11 May 1939, the annulment decision of the court of first instance could have been appealed to the Court of Appeal and subsequently to the Supreme Court, i.e. the Latvian Senate. However, the said amendments simplified this procedure to only two instances—the court of first instance whose judgment was subject to appeal before the Latvian Senate.[130]

To sum up, the Pre-war CPL provided for several grounds of challenge that were deemed sufficient for the protection of arbitrating parties' rights during arbitration proceedings. The procedure for annulment was not entirely different from the challenge procedure in, e.g. the UNCITRAL Model Law or contemporary national arbitration laws. There were certain grounds for challenge that could be invoked by either one of the arbitrating parties or State courts *ex officio*. Moreover, the possibility of applying for the setting aside of arbitral award was not merely theoretical—case-law of the former Latvian Senate and several commentaries on the subject matter evidence that such a possibility was often used by arbitrating parties. Therefore, it comes as a surprise how well the annulment action was regulated and functioned during the 1920s and 1930s. Unfortunately, it is equally surprising that, considering the existence of the annulment action in the pre-war Latvia per se and the relatively extensive scholarly reflections on the subject, the annulment mechanism did not find its way into the drafting process of the 1999 Arbitration Law after Latvia regained its independence in the 1990s.

[125] More in detail see, e.g. Pommers (1938), pp. 13, 15–17.

[126] Ibid. p. 31.

[127] Ibid.

[128] Art. 1520 of the Pre-war CPL: 'Applications for annulling arbitral awards shall be submitted within one month from the date of their issuing'. Author's translation. Original reads as follows: 'Lūgumi anullēt šķīrējtiesas spriedumus iesniedzami mēneša laikā no to pasludināšanas dienas.'

[129] Bukovskis (1933), p. 576.

[130] Konradi and Zvejnieks (1939), p. 443. See also Blūzma (2000), p. 277.

6.5.2.2 Total Lack of Setting-Aside Proceedings in Contemporary Latvian Arbitration Law

The concept of setting-aside proceedings was not alien to pre-war Latvia and the legal environment of that time—not only the Pre-war CPL explicitly regulated the annulment of arbitral awards, but the former Latvian Senate decided several annulment cases and the matter per se was considerably reflected in scholarly writings. The question, however, is why all this extensive *know-how* did not find its way into the negotiations of the 1999 Arbitration Law when Latvia regained its independence in 1991? Finding an answer to this question is a challenging task that requires looking at the issue from the very start, i.e. the drafting process of the 1999 Arbitration Law.

The 1999 Arbitration Law and its *Travaux Preparatoires.*

The official *travaux preparatoires* of the 1999 Arbitration Law do not contain any references to setting-aside proceedings. There is no discussion in preparatory acts of the 1999 Arbitration Law of whether or not the possibility of challenging arbitral awards should be included in the text of the 1999 Arbitration Law. Interestingly, however, the *travaux preparatoires* do contain, references to the Pre-war CPL and its provisions on, e.g. the formalities of arbitral procedure.[131] This, in turn, suggests that the drafting committee was well aware of the existence of the Pre-war CPL and its provisions on arbitration and ought to have been aware also of its Articles 1518 and 1519 providing for the annulment of arbitral awards.

Equally and to some extent also ironically, considering that the finally adopted 1999 Arbitration Law was a severe departure from the UNCITRAL Model Law, the *travaux preparatoires* contain also multiple references to the UNCITRAL Model Law and the need of the draft 1999 Arbitration Law to comply with and reflect the general principles of arbitration established therein. For example, an explanatory letter accompanying the first draft 1999 Arbitration Law provided:

> The model law as developed by the UNCITRAL (United Nations Commission on International Trade Law) and affirmed in 1985 by the United Nations General Assembly (hereinafter–UNCITRAL Model Law) has been taken as a basis for the draft *Arbitration Law*. Regulation of arbitration in the Model Law is based upon well-established principles of arbitration that have been established since the second decade of this century and are adhered to when drafting both international conventions and also laws regulating arbitration in a particular state. Suggestion to use the UNCITRAL Model Law stemmed from the experience of leading arbitration organizations. 17 countries have developed their laws on the basis of the UNCITRAL Model Law, including Australia, Bulgaria, Canada, Finland, Hong Kong, Mexico, Russia, Scotland, Ukraine, 4 States of USA, however Sweden, where arbitration law was in force even prior the of the Model Law, currently amends its law in accordance with the UNCITRAL Model Law.[132]

[131] Letter from the chairman of the committee for the development of the draft 1999 Arbitration Law, Mr. Z. Špengelis, addressed to the Legal Affairs Committee of the Latvian Parliament, 15 December 1997. Unpublished.

[132] Explanatory letter No. 4–2/119 accompanying the first draft 1999 Arbitration Law, the Ministry of Justice of the Republic of Latvia, 8 January 1997. Signed by the State Secretary A. Maldups. Author's translation. Original reads as follows: 'Par pamatu Šķīrējtiesu likuma projektam ņemts

References to the UNCITRAL Model Law can be found also in later preparatory documents, e.g. the drafting committee's suggestions for amendments of the draft 1999 Arbitration Law as addressed to the Legal Affairs Committee of the Latvian Parliament. These letters refer, inter alia, to many different provisions of the UNCITRAL Model Law (e.g. Articles 5, 7 and 16 of the UNCTIRAL Model Law), proposing suggestions to amend the draft 1999 Arbitration Law in accordance with the UNCITRAL Model Law.[133]

Despite the repeated references to the UNCITRAL Model Law during the drafting process of the 1999 Arbitration Law, the first draft of the 1999 Arbitration Law resembled the UNCITRAL Model Law only to a very limited extent and could not as such be considered to be 'based' on the UNCITRAL Model Law.[134] The same is true also for later drafts adopted by the Latvian Parliament.[135] If looking only at the aspect of court assistance, neither of the drafts contained provisions on court involvement in the appointment and challenge of arbitrators, summoning and hearing of witnesses, taking of evidence, issuing interim measures (except prior the establishment of an arbitral tribunal) and, most importantly, the setting aside of arbitral awards. In order to understand why exactly this was the case, one has to take a step back and look at the issue from a broader perspective, in particular considering the historical underpinnings underlying the development of the 1999 Arbitration Law after the re-establishment of Latvia's independence in 1991.

Generally, the 1999 Arbitration Law can be seen as an unfortunate continuation of the former State arbitration, i.e. State *arbitration courts* that existed as part of the judicial system in the Latvian Soviet Socialist Republic ('LSSR') during the Soviet occupation.

The so-called LSSR State arbitration was initially established on 10 April 1941 with a decision of the LSSR People's Council of Commissioners (*Tautas Komisāru Padome*) ('LSSR PCC')—the government of the LSSR created on 26 August 1940 after the occupation and incorporation of Latvia into the Soviet Union two months earlier. The established LSSR State arbitration had jurisdiction over economic and

---

UNCITRAL (ANO Starptautiskās tirdzniecības tiesību komiteja) izstrādātais un 1985. gadā ANO Ģenerālajā Asamblejā apstiprinātais parauglikums (turpmāk—UNCITRAL parauglikums). Parauglikumā šķīrējtiesu darbības reglamentācija balstās uz vispāratzītiem šķīrējtiesas darbības principiem, kuri apkopoti kopš šā gadsimta divdesmitajiem gadiem un tiek ievēroti, izstrādājot gan starptautiskās konvencijas, gan atsevišķas valsts šķīrējtiesu darbību reglamentējošo likumdošanu. UNCITRAL parauglikuma izmantošanas priekšlikums radās, pamatojoties uz vadošo šķīrējtiesas organizāciju pieredzi. Balstoties uz UNCITRAL parauglikumu, nacionālo likumdošanu izstrādājušas 17 valsts, to skaitā Austrāija, Bulgārija, Kanāda, Somija, Honkonga, Meksika, Krievija, Skotija, Ukraina un 4 ASV štati, bet Zviedrija, kurā likums par šķīrējtiesu biju spēkā vēl pirms parauglikuma apstiprināšanas, pašlaik pārstrādā savu likumdošanu atbilstoši UNCITRAL parauglikumam.' Unpublished.

133 Letters from the chairman of the committee for the development of the draft 1999 Arbitration Law, Mr. Z. Špengelis, addressed to the Legal Affairs Committee of the Latvian Parliament, dated 1 December 1997, 15 December 1997 and 18 December 1997. Unpublished.

134 Draft 1999 Arbitration Law, adopted by the Cabinet of Ministers on 8 July 1997. Unpublished.

135 Draft 1999 Arbitration Law, adopted by the Latvian Parliament (2nd reading), 10 June 1998. Unpublished. Draft 1999 Arbitration Law, submitted for approval by the Latvian Parliament (3rd reading), 6 October 1998. Unpublished.

commercial disputes between institutions of public sector, companies and organizations. The LSSR PCC appointed the staff of LSSR State arbitration, including *arbitrators*.[136] After the World War II, the LSSR State arbitration was included in the general state arbitration system of the Soviet Union, comprised of the Union of Soviet Socialist Republics ('USSR') State arbitration and State arbitrations of the different republics and districts of the USSR.[137] As such, the LSSR State arbitration was subordinate to the USSR Council of Ministers and the LSSR Council of Ministers.

Organization and procedure of the LSSR State arbitration was regulated by the LSSR Civil Procedural Codex, Annex 3 'Regulation on arbitration' ('LSSR Regulation on Arbitration'). The LSSR Regulation on Arbitration contained only 20 brief Articles and the procedure was relatively straightforward. There was no involvement of courts of ordinary jurisdiction whatsoever, apart from the recognition and enforcement stage. The main idea behind State arbitration was to provide swift resolution of disputes and speedy enforcement. It was not possible to either appeal *stricto* sensu or request annulment of arbitral awards issued by an arbitral tribunal under the LSSR State arbitration.

In 1990, the transitional parliament—the Supreme Council of the Republic of Latvia—issued a decision by means of which, inter alia, a two-tier procedure was introduced—awards of the State arbitration were subject to appeal to the State's main *arbitrator* or his deputy; it was additionally stipulated that 'the involvement of other bodies, organizations or state officials in the proceedings before the State arbitration, when it decides commercial disputes, is inadmissible.'[138] A year later, the State arbitration was replaced altogether by the Commercial court (*Saimnieciskā tiesa*) whose organization and procedure was governed by two laws—the Law on the Commercial Court[139] and the law on the Procedure of the Commercial Court.[140]

Generally, knowledge of principles of arbitration as they were known in the rest of the world was very poor at that time in Latvia. The LSSR and its legal environment, including academia and practice, was even more isolated and distanced from the Western world than the Soviet State itself. Legal practitioners and scholars for almost 50 years lived and worked according to perception of law and the general organization of society utterly alien to the Western world. There was very little or no scholarly literature at all available on international law, let alone on international arbitration,

[136] Blūzma (2000), pp. 256–258, 345.

[137] Ibid. pp. 256–258, 407.

Generally on state arbitration in the USSR see, e.g. Van den Berg (1985), p. 169, Feldbrugge et al. (1985), pp. 54–55.

[138] Supreme Council of the Republic of Latvia, On the resolution of disputes in the State arbitration of the Republic of Latvia (*Par strīdu izskatīšanu Latvijas Republikas Valsts arbitrāžā*), 23 October 1990. https://m.likumi.lv/doc.php?id=72740. Accessed 29 May 2020.

[139] Law on the Commercial Court (*Latvijas Republikas likums 'Par Saimniecisko tiesu'*), 27 November 1991. https://m.likumi.lv/doc.php?id=70520. Accessed 29 May 2020.

[140] Law on the Procedure in the Commercial Court (*Latvijas Republikas likums 'Par Saimnieciskās tiesas procesu'*), 27 November 1991. https://m.likumi.lv/doc.php?id=70521. Accessed 29 May 2020.

wherefrom one could learn how law, in particular arbitration law, was organized outside the Soviet Union.

When Latvia's independence was restored in 1991, the State apparatus and the general society witnessed considerable reforms—as regards the judicial system, it had to be rebuilt almost anew. At the same time, persons who were in charge of rebuilding the new State's judicial system, were the same that had lived and worked according to the distorted 'old' system in the LSSR. Alternative dispute resolution by means of arbitration was seen as a somewhat logical continuation of the former State arbitration, including all its drawbacks and inconsistencies that it had when compared with the understanding of arbitration in the Western world. Arbitration after 1991, just like its predecessor State arbitration in the former LSSR, needed to provide swift resolution of commercial disputes, exclude any court involvement and guarantee quick enforcement. Considering it was alien to the former State arbitration, the annulment mechanism neither had place in the 1999 Arbitration Law.

Exceptionally, however, the very first draft of the 1999 Arbitration Law, dated January 1994, was a very modern reflection of the UNCITRAL Model Law and principles of arbitration provided therein.[141] If looking solely at the issue of court involvement, it not only provided provisions on challenging an arbitral tribunal's jurisdiction, appointment of arbitrators, issuing of provisional measures, recognition and enforcement of arbitral awards, but also on the annulment of arbitral awards:

Article 422 Grounds for setting aside an arbitral award

A party may file a claim requesting the setting aside of an arbitral award in the respective district (city) court in the following cases:

(i) The arbitration agreement was entered into by a person lacking capacity;
(ii) The arbitration agreement is not valid;
(iii) The party against whom the award is invoked was not given proper notice of the appointment of the arbitrator or of the arbitration proceedings or was otherwise unable to present his case;
(iv) The award deals with a difference not contemplated by or not falling within the terms of the submission to arbitration, or it contains decisions on matters beyond the scope of the submission to arbitration, provided that the award may be set aside only in part that is not covered by the arbitration agreement, only if matters submitted to arbitration can be separated from those not so submitted;
(v) The composition of the arbitral authority or the arbitral procedure was not in accordance with the arbitration agreement;
(vi) If a party has intentionally hidden documents that could have considerably affect the arbitral award, and the other party has obtained such documents only after the issuing of the arbitral award;
(vii) If a lawfully enforceable court judgment in a criminal case establishes facts pertaining to fraud, deceit, bribery or other facts pertaining to criminal activities that could have affected the arbitral award.

[141] Draft 1999 Arbitration Law, January 1994. Unpublished.

Article 423 Procedure for setting aside an arbitral award

(1) In case of any of the grounds listed in Article 422(1)–(5) a claim requesting the setting aside of an arbitral award may be submitted within 3 months of the receipt of the award, or after the rejection date of request submitted in accordance with Article 420; in case of any of the grounds listed in Article 422(6)–(7) within 3 months of the date when the party obtained documents stipulated in Article 422(6) or when it became aware of the court decision in a criminal case stipulated in Article 422(7).

(2) A court that has received a claim for the setting aside of an arbitral award, at the request of a party or on its own initiative, may stay the proceedings in order to give the arbitral tribunal a possibility to remedy deficiencies stipulated in the claim.

Article 424 Consequences for submitting a claim for setting aside an arbitral award

(1) Submission of a claim to set aside an arbitral award does not stay the enforcement of an arbitral award.

(2) However, if the court deems necessary, it may stay the enforcement proceedings until the claim is decided on merits.[142]

The faith of the very first draft of the 1999 Arbitration Law, dated January 1994, is unclear. When the draft 1999 Arbitration Law was forwarded from the Ministry of Justice to the Parliament on 9 July 1997, its provisions were a very remote reflection of the original 1994 draft and excluded nearly all provisions providing for court involvement in arbitration proceedings, including those prescribing the annulment mechanism.

Despite the *travaux preparatoires* of the 1999 Arbitration Law containing multiple references to the UNCITRAL Model Law and stipulating that the 1999 Arbitration Law was based on the UNCITRAL Model Law, in reality the various versions of the draft 1999 Arbitration Law as adopted by the Parliament between 1997 and 1999 were a severe disregard of the UNCITRAL Model Law. Such references were only artificial—relatively very little had the draft 1999 Arbitration Law in common with the UNCITRAL Model Law. This was also confirmed by well-known international arbitration experts that in 1997 were asked to comment on the draft 1999 Arbitration Law. Reportedly, it was indicated that:

> Provided that Latvia does not base its arbitration law on the UNCITRAL Model Law, it will not be considered a 'Model Law country'; therefore, one may anticipate that the majority of international arbitration specialists will not suggest Latvia as a seat for international arbitration.[143]

It is striking that already in 1997 international arbitration experts urged Latvia to adopt the UNCITRAL Model Law in its entirety in order to be considered a

---

[142] Draft 1999 Arbitration Law, January 1994. Unpublished.

[143] Hacher et al. (1997) Comments on the Draft law on Arbitration of the Republic of Latvia, Strasbourg, 10 July 1997. Unpublished (reported in Kačevska I (2010) *Starptautiskās komerciālās arbitrāžas tiesības* [*International Commercial Arbitration Law*]. Doctoral thesis at the University of Latvia, p. 84).

'Model Law country'. Ten year later, similar suggestions followed from international arbitration experts when they were asked to reflect on the 2008 draft arbitration law. Equally striking is the fact that more than 20 years later the currently in force 2015 Arbitration Law is still not based on the UNCITRAL Model Law.

To sum up, non-inclusion of the annulment mechanism in the 1999 Arbitration Law (and the more general hesitation to provide for court involvement in arbitration proceedings per se), can be seen as a *logical* result of various interlinked factors—the unfortunate legacy of the former LSSR State arbitration, general lack of knowledge of international law, in particular, international arbitration law at that time, strong lobbying from various interested parties, including large companies and banks, to minimize court involvement and provide for quick enforcement of arbitral awards, and the fact that some of the very same *arbitrators* who sat in the former LSSR State arbitration were now in charge of developing and adopting the draft 1999 Arbitration Law. Taken together, these factors seemingly explain why the final text of 1999 Arbitration Law contained almost no provisions on court involvement in arbitration proceedings, including provisions on setting-aside proceedings.

First Criticism

After the entry into force of the 1999 Arbitration Law, the arbitration environment in Latvia embarked on a very thorny road. Due to the unreasoned choice to allow any legal person to establish permanent arbitral institutions, the so-called *pocket arbitration courts* emerged rapidly. There was very little court supervision of arbitration—only at the enforcement stage did national courts superficially verified whether arbitration proceedings satisfied certain basic procedural principles.

The 1999 Arbitration Law as a whole and, in particular, the non-existence of setting-aside proceedings, witnessed severe criticism from arbitration practitioners and scholars soon after the adverse effects of the distorted 1999 Arbitration Law were felt in practice.[144] Only few years after entry into force, the 1999 Arbitration

[144] See, e.g. Ūdris and Kačevska (2004), p. 220 recognizing that "The award cannot be appealed [sic.]. This provision has created a dangerous situation because the law does not provide any way to have the arbitral award set aside. Thus, even if enforcement is not granted by the court, the arbitral award remains in force and can serve as res judicata in other proceedings […] [T]he law does not contain important provisions concerning court assistance in forming the arbitral tribunal, in applying interim and protection measures, in discovery, and in possible deadlock cases. As a result of the Latvian judiciary's desire to stay away from arbitral proceedings and the government's policy of not spending money to exert control over arbitration in order to ensure a fair process, distrust of arbitration as a means of settling commercial disputes is rapidly growing. Accordingly, only speedy and substantial changes in the statutory regulation of arbitration can rectify this situation in Latvia.' See also Kačevska (2004) noting that: 'One of the most worrying issues, in particular in Latvia, is a process that is provided in Article 34 [UNCITRAL] Model Law, namely, the setting aside of an arbitral award. A particular institution may set aside an arbitral award if a party proves that certain generally recognized procedural norms have not been observed. Such a claim may be submitted to the institution within 3 months from the date of receipt of arbitral award. Such norms have been

Law had started to produce its adverse consequences—the number of *arbitration courts* in less than 5 years had reached 110 and in 2004 more than 5000 requests for recognition and enforcement of arbitral awards were received by State courts.[145] Certain amendments to the 1999 Arbitration Law were underway, however, introduction of more court assistance, including the annulment mechanism, unfortunately was not part of them. Requests for recognition and enforcement of arbitral awards were growing by day and the drafting committee of amendments to the 1999 Arbitration Law was afraid that similar number of requests would follow after introducing possibility to challenge arbitral awards. The already considerably high number of *arbitration courts* had created a perception that any additional court involvement in arbitration proceedings, whether in the form of assistance in appointment or challenging of arbitrators, hearing of witnesses or setting aside arbitral awards, would require additional human resources and be a disproportionate financial burden.

The Latvian Constitutional Court's Judgment of 2005

The year of 2005 witnessed a very important development for arbitration in Latvia. The Latvian Constitutional Court delivered a judgment in the very first arbitration-related case before it. The so-called *Asmers* case concerned a challenge of the constitutionality of the then in force Articles 132(1)(3) and 223(6) of the LCCP, providing that a judge refuses to accept a statement of claim if parties have agreed to settle their dispute by means of arbitration.[146] Essentially, the constitutional complaint sought to determine whether State courts' duty to refer parties to arbitration was consistent with the right of access to a court. Apart from being the first arbitration case before the Latvian Constitutional Court, the *Asmers* case did not per se add any additional value to the topic of dichotomy between arbitration and human rights. The Latvian Constitutional Court generally reflected and referred to the arbitration-related practice established by the ECtHR and the former ECmHR, as introduced before in Chap. 3, and found that the conclusion of arbitration agreement as such does not violate parties' rights of access to a court.

included in the arbitration laws of Hungary, Sweden, Austria. Also in Lithuania, parties may turn to the Lithuanian Court of Appeal, and in Estonia–Tallinn Court of Appeal, in order to set aside an arbitral award pursuant to the same grounds as provided for in Article 34 of the UNCITRAL Model Law. These grounds, upon which an arbitral award may be set aside, are grounds for refusing a writ of execution under Article 536 of the LCCP. The challenging of arbitral awards has been recently one of the most discussed topics in Latvia; however, this idea was not supported in the drafting committee of the LCCP amendments, because additional resources are necessary for courts to hear such cases. Possibly, by sticking to such a scheme, Latvia could nonetheless provide a possibility to appeal decision on the issuing of a writ of execution [...]'. For more criticism on the 1999 Arbitration Law see also Torgāns (2005).

[145] Torgāns (2005).

[146] A somewhat 'national' version of the generally recognized passage of art. II(3) of the New York Convention ('The court of a Contracting State, when seized of an action in a matter in respect of which the parties have made an agreement within the meaning of this article, shall, at the request of one of the parties, refer the parties to arbitration [...]').

However, as regards the annulment mechanism in particular, the *Asmers* case marks a very important, albeit somewhat two-folded, development of understanding of the need for setting-aside proceedings in national arbitration law. On the one hand, it was the Latvian Constitutional Court that as early as in 2005 *expressis verbis* pointed to the possible adverse effects that the lack of setting-aside proceedings in Latvian arbitration law might have. On the other hand, it was also the Latvian Constitutional Court that nevertheless stressed that control over arbitration proceedings solely at the recognition and enforcement stage is *sufficient* for guaranteeing the protection of the so-called 'non-waivable' human rights:

> Pursuant to a general principle, a state is not responsible for violations of fundamental rights in arbitration proceedings. Deciding on the admissibility of such complaints that are related to arbitration, the European Commission of Human Rights has several times indicated that 'the State cannot be held responsible for the arbitrator's actions unless, and only insofar as, the national courts were required to intervene' (*R c. la Suisse*; *Jakob Boss Söhne KG v. Germany*, No. 18479/91; see also, e.g. *Heinz Schiebler KG v. Germany*, No. 18805/91). However, the State has a duty to, first of all, provide means for protection against violations of the said procedural rights in arbitration proceedings and, second of all, to refuse to recognize the result of such arbitration proceedings.
>
> In Latvia, contrary to the majority of other countries, both of the said duties converge, due to the law not providing for the possibility to challenge an arbitrator or to set aside an arbitral award in a state court. Therefore, the control over arbitration is concentrated at the enforcement stage. One may doubt whether such a solution is optimal and whether it is necessary to refrain from an internationally known and recognized model of controlling arbitration, however the state has a wide margin of appreciation in determining regulation of arbitration proceedings. A control during the enforcement stage is considered a sufficient mean, at least to guarantee the compliance of fundamental rights.[147]

Despite recognizing that control over arbitration solely at the recognition and enforcement stage is sufficient, the Latvian Constitutional Court also indicated to certain deficiencies in the then in force regime and in an *obiter dicta* suggested the Latvian legislator to amend the arbitration law in order to provide for the annulment mechanism:

> At the same time, the Constitutional Court sees certain existing problems pertaining to arbitration proceedings that recently have been emphasized in Latvian legal doctrine and practice

---

[147] *Asmers* case, No. 2004-10-01, the Constitutional Court of the Republic of Latvia, 17 January 2005, para. 9.1. Author's translation. The original reads as follows: 'Saskaņā ar vispārējo principu valsts nav atbildīga par šķīrējtiesas procesā pieļautiem pamattiesību pārkāpumiem. Lemjot par tādu sūdzību pieņemamību, kuras saistītas ar šķīrējtiesām, Eiropas Cilvēktiesību komisija ne reizi vien norādījusi, ka „šķīrējtiesnešu darbības nevar izraisīt valsts atbildību, kamēr vien valsts tiesas netiek aicinātas šajās darbībās iejaukties" (R c. la Suisse; Jakob Boss Söhne KG v. Germany, No 18479/91; sk. arī, piem: Heinz Schiebler KG v. Germany, No 18805/91). Taču valstij ir pienākums, pirmkārt, nodrošināt līdzekļus aizsardzībai pret minēto procesuālo tiesību pārkāpumiem šķīrējtiesas procesā un, otrkārt, neatzīt šāda šķīrējtiesas procesa rezultātu. Latvijā, atšķirībā no lielākās daļas citu valstu, abi minētie pienākumi saplūst, jo likums neparedz iespēju valsts tiesā pieprasīt šķīrējtiesneša noraidīšanu vai šķīrējtiesas sprieduma atcelšanu. Tādēļ šķīrējtiesu kontrole ir koncentrēta izpildu raksta izsniegšanas stadijā. Var šaubīties par to, vai šāds risinājums ir optimāls, kā arī par to, vai nepieciešams atteikties no pasaulē pazīstama un pieņemta šķīrējtiesu kontroles modeļa, taču valstij ir plaša rīcības brīvība šķīrējtiesas procesa regulējuma noteikšanā. Kontrole izpildu raksta izsniegšanas stadijā ir uzskatāma par pietiekamu līdzekli vismaz pamattiesību ievērošanas nodrošināšanai.'

[…] Currently in the LCCP and its draft amendments there are no provisions that would provide a mechanism for challenging an arbitral award even if no enforcement request is submitted. Considering the often-expressed critique as to the work of arbitral institutions and the prima facie flaws in regulating the enforcement proceedings, the internationally recognized mechanism for setting aside arbitral awards would be of particularly great significance in Latvia.[148]

The *Asmers* case, in particular the Latvian Constitutional Court's reference to the necessity of setting-aside proceedings in Latvian arbitration law, was an important step towards understanding reasons behind the need of introducing setting-aside proceedings. However, since the Latvian Constitutional Court's suggestion to introduce the annulment mechanism was merely an *obiter dicta*, its first conclusion, i.e. that control over arbitration during recognition and enforcement stage is sufficient to guarantee protection of the 'non-waivable' human rights, was emphasised more in further attempts to finally introduce setting-aside proceedings also in Latvian arbitration law.

The 2007 and 2008 Draft Arbitration Laws

The immediate aftermath of the *Asmers* case saw little, albeit short-lived, positive developments and attempts to introduce setting-aside proceedings in Latvian arbitration law. In 2007 the Ministry of Justice introduced a new draft arbitration law. Generally, the new draft law contained provisions utterly hostile to the nature of arbitration[149] and it received severe criticism,[150] however, at least with regard to setting-aside proceedings, the 2007 draft arbitration law perhaps is the closest that Latvian arbitration environment has been to seeing introduction of the annulment mechanism.

The initiative to introduce it came from within the Ministry of Justice itself, supposedly as a response to the criticism of the 1999 Arbitration Law and its adverse consequences, as well as the Latvian Constitutional Court's ruling of 2005. The 2007 draft arbitration law was adopted on 18 October 2007, however, already at the end of November 2007, provisions on setting-aside proceedings were deleted due to the unfortunate use of terminology—provisions permitting *setting-aside proceedings* in the 2007 draft arbitration law referred to *appeal* rather than setting-aside, annulling or challenging of arbitral awards. As announced by the Ministry of Justice:

In order to strengthen the society's confidence in arbitration and its lawfulness, and to create a possibility to protect rights violated during arbitration proceedings, prevent mistakes and

[148] Ibid. para. 10. Author's translation. The original reads as follows: 'Vienlaikus Satversmes tiesa saskata atsevišķas šķīrējtiesas procesa problēmas, kuras pastāv un pēdējā laikā īpaši uzsvērtas Latvijas tiesību zinātnē un praksē […] Šobrīd Civilprocesa likumā un tā grozījumu projektā nav arī normu, kas noteiktu procedūru šķīrējtiesas sprieduma apstrīdēšanai, pat ja netiek pieprasīta izpildu raksta izsniegšana. Ņemot vērā bieži pausto kritiku par šķīrējtiesu darbu un prima facie saskatāmos trūkumus izpildu raksta izsniegšanas regulējumā, pasaulē akceptētajam šķīrējtiesas sprieduma apstrīdēšanas institūtam Latvijā būtu jo sevišķi liela nozīme.'

[149] Tipaine (2014), Volkova (2007).

[150] See, e.g., Repšs (2007), Lapsa (2007), Kačevska (2008), p. 32.

> violations of the law, the draft [arbitration] law contains a right to appeal an arbitral award, more in detail regulated by the Civil Procedure Law. An arbitral award may be subject to appeal through ordinary claim proceedings before the district (city) court at the seat of arbitration.[151]

The true intention behind the unfortunate wording is unclear. Allegedly, the drafting committee mistook setting-aside proceedings for an appeal of arbitral awards *stricto* sensu.[152] As noted by Ms. Baiba Broka, a Parliamentary Secretary of the Ministry of Justice at that time:

> Only at the end of November this year the permanent drafting committee arrived at an essential agreement to delete from the draft arbitration law the possibility to appeal an arbitral award. One must add that pursuant to international law and conception of arbitration, arbitral awards are not subject to appeal.[153]

It seems that what was a sound initiative, i.e. to adhere to the Constitutional Court's *obiter dicta* to introduce setting-aside proceedings in Latvian arbitration law, eventually turned into another fiasco simply due to lack of knowledge and understanding of the distinction between the appeal *stricto* sensu and a mere challenge of arbitral awards. After deleting from the 2007 draft arbitration law provisions on the unfortunately worded *setting-aside proceedings*, a broader discussion on the introduction of setting-aside proceedings resumed only in 2012 when the 2015 Arbitration Law witnessed its first draft. The 2008 draft arbitration law which substituted the 2007 draft arbitration law did not contain any provisions on setting-aside proceedings. As explained above, in 2009 discussions on the need of a separate arbitration law, let alone introduction of setting-aside proceedings, were abandoned altogether.

The Legislative Development of the 2015 Arbitration Law

The legislative development of the currently in force 2015 Arbitration Law dates back to 2012 when discussions on the need to nevertheless develop a new arbitration law finally resumed.

The outset of discussions was again promising—a working group composed of academics, members from the largest law firms in Latvia, arbitral institutions and the LCCI, developed a new draft arbitration law. The working group managed to take

[151] The Ministry of Justice of the Republic of Latvia (2007) Izstrādāts Šķīrējtiesu likums [Arbitration law has been developed], 18 October 2007. https://www.tm.gov.lv/lv/aktualitates/tm-informacija-presei/izstradats-skirejtiesu-likums. Accessed 29 May 2020. Author's translation. The original reads as follows: 'Lai veicinātu sabiedrības uzticību šķīrējtiesu institūtam un to darbības tiesiskumam un radītu iespēju aizsargāt šķīrējtiesas procesā aizskartās tiesības, novērstu pieļautās kļūdas vai likuma pārkāpumus, likumprojektā iekļautas tiesības pārsūdzēt šķīrējtiesas spriedumu, ko sīkāk regulēs Civilprocesa likums. Šķīrējtiesas spriedumu varēs pārsūdzēt prasības kārtībā rajona (pilsētas) tiesā pēc šķīrējtiesas atrašanās vietas.'

[152] The Constitutional Court in its 2005 judgment referred to 'challenging' as opposed to 'appeal' of arbitral awards. The unfortunate use of terminology was pointed out also by a leading Latvian scholar shortly after the adoption of the 2007 draft arbitration law. See Torgāns (2007). See also Torgāns (2008), pp. 41–51.

[153] Broka (2007).

into account the peculiarities of the Latvian arbitration environment and still come up with a draft law that was based on the UNCITRAL Model Law providing, inter alia, also for the annulment of arbitral awards. Article 59 of the 2012 draft arbitration law stipulated:

Article 59 Annulment of an arbitral award

(1) If a ground for refusing issuing of writ of execution as stipulated in the LCCP exists, an interested party may, pursuant to the procedure laid down in the LCCP, file an application before the district (city) court for the annulment of an arbitral award.

(2) Application for the annulment of an arbitral award may be filed within 3 months from the date on which the party making that application had received the award or, if a request had been made under Article 56 [correction of arbitral award], from the date on which that request had been disposed of by the arbitral tribunal.

(3) If an arbitral award is annulled, arbitration agreement becomes valid, provided that parties have not agreed to the contrary or it is not contrary to the judgment on the annulment of arbitral award by the district (city) court judge.[154]

When the 2012 draft arbitration law was forwarded to the Ministry of Justice for further consideration, it *disappeared* in the corridors of the Ministry of Justice and unfortunately was not subject to further negotiations during the legislative process. Instead, the Ministry of Justice developed its own draft arbitration law on the basis of the poorly drafted 2007 and 2008 versions that, as explained previously, had been subject to heavy criticism from local and international arbitration experts.[155]

The draft arbitration law developed by the Ministry of Justice (eventually being the draft 2015 Arbitration Law) was again a severe disregard of generally recognized arbitration practices and failed to contain principles vital for the smooth functioning of arbitration, most notably—provisions on court assistance, including the annulment action. Ironically, and here again parallels can be drawn with the legislative process of the 1999 Arbitration Law, the Explanatory report accompanying the draft 2015 Arbitration Law contained multiple references to the UNCITRAL Model Law and the fact that allegedly the UNCITRAL Model Law has been taken into account when developing the draft 2015 Arbitration Law.[156] In reality, however, despite certain aspects of the UNCITRAL Model Law were indeed *taken into account*, the draft 2015 Arbitration Law as a whole was very far from being in conformity with the UNCITRAL Model Law and as such could not have been considered to be based on it.

---

[154] 2012 Draft Arbitration Law. Unpublished. Author's translation.

[155] See Tipaine (2014), Born (2008), Mistelis (2008), Salans (2008), Knieper (2008).

[156] The Draft 2015 Arbitration Law, Preliminary impact assessment report (Explanatory report), sec. 2. http://titania.saeima.lv/LIVS11/saeimalivs11.nsf/0/A182DD228B4DAF6CC2257C4E003D7B1B?OpenDocument#b. Accessed 29 May 2020. ('In developing the normative regulation [the 2013 draft arbitration law] the following international normative acts have been taken into account—the UNCITRAL Model Law on International Commercial Arbitration of 21 June 1985 (in relation to the conduct of arbitral process), the New York Convention on the Recognition and Enforcement of Foreign Arbitral Awards of 10 June 1985 [sic.]');.

For someone distant from the particularities of the arbitration environment in Latvia it must be very hard to understand why the Latvian legislator, in particular the Ministry of Justice, has consistently drifted away from the simple act of adopting the UNCITRAL Model Law and instead tried to develop its own arbitration law from scratch—an arbitration law that almost fully excludes any court assistance to arbitration proceedings, lacks provisions on setting-aside proceedings and contains other anomalies. It is certainly clear why this was the case when developing the 1999 Arbitration Law—the Latvian State, including its legislature, academia and practitioners had little, if any, knowledge of arbitration, not in the sense of the former State *arbitration*, but arbitration as a mechanism of alternative dispute resolution known in the rest of the world. As explained, echoes of the former State *arbitration* materialized into the finally adopted 1999 Arbitration Law.

The aftermath of the 1999 Arbitration Law, leading mainly to efforts to deal with its adverse consequences and eagerly denying the need for court assistance in arbitration proceedings, can be best explained by the fact that the 1999 Arbitration Law allowed any legal person to establish a *permanent arbitral institution*,[157] thus leading to a skyrocketing of the so-called *pocket arbitration courts*. When the draft 2015 Arbitration Law was being developed, the number of these *pocket arbitration courts* had reached its peak—214(!). Every time the legislator had to consider improvements in the defectively functioning arbitration system, including the introduction of increased court assistance and setting-aside proceedings, one could not possibly shy away from the fact that if there are 214 arbitral institutions and more than 8000 enforcement requests per year, then introduction of the UNCITRAL Model Law-type court assistance in arbitration proceedings and statutory provision of setting-aside proceedings would possibly indeed overburden national courts with various requests from arbitral institutions and arbitral tribunals. This reasoning is well illustrated by the Explanatory report to the draft 2015 Arbitration Law:

> The draft 'Law on Arbitration' does not provide court involvement of ordinary jurisdiction courts in, for example, the taking and securing of evidence, appointing arbitrators, challenging of arbitrators. One must note that currently there 214 arbitral institutions established and permanently operating in Latvia, a large part of which are operating in Riga city or Riga region. One must additionally note that the draft 'Law on Arbitration' permits also the establishment of ad hoc arbitral tribunals. At the same time, there are only 34 first instance courts of ordinary jurisdiction in Latvia, 5 of which are Riga city courts.
>
> Considering the current overload of ordinary jurisdiction courts and the terms for deciding cases, imposing additional obligations on part of ordinary jurisdiction courts is not supported. Moreover, we draw the attention to one of the most important qualities of arbitration proceedings—speed of proceedings and thus also the effectiveness of arbitration proceedings in general.[158]

---

[157] Kačevska (2004). Art. 486(3) of the LCCP (1999 version) stated that 'a permanent arbitration institution may be established by legal persons that notify the Ministry of Justice of such an establishment.'

[158] The Draft 2015 Arbitration Law, Preliminary impact assessment report (Explanatory report), sec. 2. http://titania.saeima.lv/LIVS11/saeimalivs11.nsf/0/A182DD228B4DAF6CC2257C4E003D7B1B?OpenDocument#b. Accessed 29 May 2020.

The Explanatory report to the 2015 Arbitration Law explains *black on white* that the sole reason for not adopting the UNCTRAL Model Law in full, thus introducing also court assistance and setting-aside proceedings, is due to the legislator's own mistake to allow any legal person to establish permanent arbitral institutions—a mistake that eventually lead to an enormous amount of *pocket arbitration courts*. The main, if not the sole, goal during deliberations of the 2015 Arbitration Law, was not to accept and remedy the said mistake, but to aim to improve the damaged reputation of the already existing arbitration system (e.g. by introducing strict qualification requirements for arbitrators) and to find a compromise solution with regard to the high number of arbitral institutions, rather than a complete overhaul.

The initial draft 2015 Arbitration Law contained drastic conditions for the establishment of permanent arbitral institutions, meaning that out of the existing 214 *arbitral institutions* only two would survive.[159] Being a measure at the other extreme, the initiative received criticism. During the legislative process it was substituted with a less severe limitation.[160] The legal community was seemingly not ready to decrease the number of arbitral institutions so drastically, i.e. from 214 to only 2, partially due to the fact that the settling of disputes in these *arbitral institutions*, despite their somewhat dubious character, greatly alleviated court workload. However, in order to fully adopt the UNCITRAL Model Law, such a severe cut was exactly what was inevitably necessary. On the other hand, these *arbitral institutions* were strongly lobbying against such a drastic cut. It seems that the reforming of the Latvian arbitration system and the negotiation process of the 2015 Arbitration Law entailed a scrupulous cost-benefit analysis—whether to keep the *old* system with the high number of arbitral institutions that alleviate court workload or to create a major overhaul by decreasing the number of *arbitral institutions* to minimum and introduce proper court assistance, including setting-aside proceedings, thus guaranteeing more quality, but fewer arbitration proceedings. Unfortunately, the first option eventually prevailed.

[159] Art. 2 of the initial Draft 2015 Arbitration Law stipulated that 'A permanent arbitration institution can be established by an association that corresponds to the following criteria: (a) an association who is comprised of at least 10 members—legal persons registered in the commercial register; (b) association whose total annual net turnover is no less than 50 million lats [c. 70 million EUR]; (c) association is registered in the association and register for at least three years before submitting an application for the registration of a permanent arbitration institution'. Author's translation. http://tap.mk.gov.lv/doc/2005/TMLik_111113_skirejties.1311.doc. Accessed 29 May 2020.

[160] Tipaine (2014), Repšs (2014).

The draft 2015 Arbitration Law received considerable criticism from local arbitration practitioners. Among other deficiencies, many pointed to the continuous non-availability of the annulment action in the draft 2015 Arbitration Law.[161] Nevertheless, none of them were eventually taken into account. The 2015 Arbitration Law was adopted on 11 September 2014 as it was, i.e. with all its deficiencies and still not being based on the UNCITRAL Model Law. Before the entry into force of 2015 Arbitration Law on 1 January 2015, certain other significant developments took place, adding more weight, albeit somewhat too late, to the discussion on the necessity of inclusion of setting-aside proceedings in the 2015 Arbitration Law.

Recent Attempts to Introduce the Annulment Mechanism and the Current State of Affairs

The need to finally introduce setting-aside proceedings in Latvian arbitration law was repeatedly stressed also by the Latvian Constitutional Court in the already briefly introduced *Hiponia* ruling in late November 2014. Notably, the Latvian Constitutional Court, similarly as in the 2005 *Asmers* case, repeatedly urged, albeit again

[161] See, e.g. Ūdris (2014) noting that '[I]f in other countries the applicable legal framework allows the affected party to file a claim in a court regarding an unlawful arbitral award that has been based, e.g. on forged documents, in Latvia such a right is not granted by the applicable legal framework and the draft arbitration law. The draft developed by the LCCI [the 2012 draft arbitration law] that was forwarded to the Ministry of Justice, included a mechanism for challenging arbitral awards, however, in the current version of the draft law the said mechanism is excluded. This means that also in future we will be faced with arbitral awards that formally satisfy the requirements of law, but in fact are based on legally invalid, fictitious and forged documents, and such arbitral awards will remain valid even if the court will refuse issuing of writ of execution.' Author's translation. See also Kačevska (2014) recognizing that 'It is of utmost significance to introduce a mechanism for challenging arbitral awards. Currently, if an [arbitral] award is not granted an exequatur, the award remains in force; therefore, one may try to enforce the award elsewhere, or it can be used by one of the parties as evidence in another case. If an [arbitral] award is issued unlawfully, there is no mechanism to challenge such an award. One could introduce a mechanism, such as in Germany, where an [arbitral] award on procedural grounds can be challenged at the moment when it is subjected to exequatur proceedings. Also in case no exequatur is needed, there must be a mechanism by means of which an [arbitral] award can be challenged in a court. Understandably, in Latvia courts are afraid the a mechanism for challenging arbitral awards would significantly overburden them due to the fact that in Latvia there are many enforcement cases. However, one must consider not only the workload of courts. A mechanism for challenging [arbitral] awards, possibly, may serve as means through which we could improve arbitration environment in Latvia, because courts would then have statistics as to those arbitral institutions whose arbitral awards are annulled as unlawful. This may be an effective mechanism how to eliminate procedural irregularities'. Author's translation. Similar conclusions were drawn by other authors. See, e.g. Tipaine (2014) ('Yes, such a mechanism is necessary. Already now in practice we can see situations where such a mechanism would be very useful. For example, in a situation where the arbitral award is declaratory and no enforcement is needed, the losing party has no option to object to it and must simply accept all the resulting consequences. Also during the enforcement stage the losing party has limited possibilities to object to the recognition and enforcement of an arbitral award, i.e. no right to file an ancillary claim against the decision recognizing and enforcing an arbitral award is provided; moreover, the whole process is written, preventing parties from orally stating their position.'). Author's translation.

in an *obiter dicta*, the Latvian Parliament to take legislative steps and introduce a mechanism for challenging arbitral awards in Latvian arbitration law:

> The Constitutional Court already in the judgment of 17 January 2005 in case No. 2004-10-01 indicated that the LCCP omits provisions that would determine procedure for challenging an arbitral award, even if no enforcement request is submitted (see the Constitutional Court's judgment of 17 January 2005 in case No. 2004-10-01, para. 10).
>
> The said regulation [regulation of setting-aside proceedings] has been incorporated neither in the LCCP, nor in the [2015] Arbitration Law.
>
> In certain cases, in order to have an arbitral award enforced, there is no need to turn to a national court and seek a writ of execution; and there may be such situations where an arbitral award is to be recognized or enforced in a foreign state. Similarly, the LCCP does not stipulate what happens with an arbitral award if a national court has refused the issuing of a writ of execution for its compulsory enforcement. In such a case, a person has no legal remedies against a possibly defective arbitral award; it, in fact, remains in force and a party to the proceedings may try to repeatedly seek its enforcement, for example, in a foreign state.
>
> Considering also, inter alia, the deficiencies, as indicated by the summoned persons, in both the functioning of arbitral institutions and the legal framework for issuing writs of execution, the internationally recognized mechanism for challenging arbitral awards would be of particularly great importance in Latvia. Therefore, the Constitutional Court repeatedly draws the Saeima's [the Latvian Parliament's] attention to the necessity of stipulating the grounds and procedure for challenging arbitral awards.[162]

Nearly 10 years had passed since the initial Latvian Constitution Court's *obiter dicta* observation in the *Asmers* case, however, nothing, apart from several discussions and short-lived initiatives, had changed in this regard. In 2014, the Latvian Constitutional Court repeatedly urged the Latvian Parliament to introduce the annulment mechanism in Latvian arbitration law, however, the Latvian Constitutional Court's repeated *obiter dicta* suggestions have been left without further consideration by the Latvian Parliament. The 2015 Arbitration Law as it currently stands, and Latvian arbitration law more generally, is still silent upon the possibility of challenging arbitral awards before State courts. Latvia uniquely remains as the only Member State of the Council of Europe that omits regulation of setting-aside proceedings in its national law. Presently, nothing suggests that reforming of the Latvian arbitration system would be in the Latvian legislator's current legislative and working schedule.

---

[162] *Hiponia* case, No. 2014-09-01, the Constitutional Court of the Republic of Latvia, 28 November 2014, para. 22. www.satv.tiesa.gov.lv/wp-content/uploads/2014/03/2014-09-01_Spriedums_ENG.pdf. Accessed 29 May 2020. Author's translation.

6.6 Summary

The phenomenon of total lack of setting-aside proceedings in national arbitration law is rather unusual. Although many States provide arbitrating parties with a possibility to exclude the application of setting-aside proceedings by means of the so-called exclusion agreements, only few States have taken the extra step to statutorily exclude the annulment mechanism altogether. This chapter introduced 4 such States—Belgium, Malaysia, Kyrgyzstan and, in more detail, Latvia.

The most notoriously known example in this regard is that of Belgium. As seen (Sect. 6.2), Belgium's innovation in the year 1985 brought considerable attention from arbitration practitioners all over the world. In Belgium, total exclusion of setting-aside proceedings was made conditional upon parties' not having any connection with Belgium. Malaysia's approach (Sect. 6.3), on the other hand, was somewhat different since the statutory exclusion of setting-aside proceedings was conditioned upon mere choice of the applicable arbitration regime. In both Belgium and Malaysia, total exclusion of setting-aside proceedings is a creature of past. The same cannot be said of the other of the two addressed States, namely Kyrgyzstan and Latvia, where it is still impossible to apply for the setting aside of arbitral awards.

As has become evident, there have been multiple attempts to introduce setting-aside proceedings in Latvian arbitration law, however, every time the legislative roller-coaster of such attempts has resulted in fiasco. The currently in force 2015 Arbitration Law is still silent upon challenging arbitral awards and, at least among the Member States of the Council of Europe, Latvia remains the only State where it is simply impossible to challenge arbitral awards before State courts.

To some extent the current Latvian approach echoes the innovative (albeit severely criticized and later also abandoned) Belgium's approach that abolished setting-aside proceedings for arbitral awards issued in Belgium unless one of the parties to the arbitration proceedings was Belgian. As seen in Chap. 4, the Swiss PILA and a number of other national arbitration laws expressly provide, under certain conditions, a possibility to conclude the so-called exclusion agreements. However, the Latvian arbitration law goes a step further and ignores the concept of setting-aside proceedings *in toto*.

Although international arbitration community, at least on a theoretical level, has long expressed concerns about the necessity of setting-aside proceedings as such,[163] setting-aside proceedings are still a prevalent method of judicial control over arbitration proceedings in the vast majority of States permitting arbitration as an alternative method of dispute resolution. The challenge procedure is seen as a form of risk management whereby courts remedy violations of fundamental procedural rights during arbitration proceedings.[164] Moreover, even though some States provide for

[163]For the issue of 'double control', see, e.g. Gerald W. Ghikas (2006), p. 53, Weigand (2009), p. 1119, Van den Berg (2014), p. 3. For the issue of irreconcilability of decisions, see, e.g. the well-known case of *Dallah Real Estate and Tourism Holding Co. v. Ministry of Religious Affairs, Government of Pakistan* [2010] UKSC 46.

[164]Park (2001), pp. 90–97.

the option to voluntarily exclude the application of setting-aside proceedings, arbitrating parties are generally reluctant to exercise such a possibility due to the severe consequences that such waivers entail.

As was seen in Chap. 4, the ECtHR examined compatibility of exclusion agreements with Article 6(1) of the ECHR in the case of *Tabbane v. Switzerland*. It concluded that the existence of such a right and the resulting waiver is not per se contrary to the right of access to a court, provided that the waiver is made freely, licitly and unequivocally, pursues a legitimate aim, and is proportionate to the aim pursued. However, what if the waiver was not made freely or unequivocally, or perhaps did not pursue a legitimate aim or was not proportionate? Would the judgment of the ECtHR in *Tabbane v. Switzerland* be different if the waiver was *mandatory*, i.e. it did not result from a voluntary exercise of statutory right to exclude setting-aside proceedings but there was no possibility in the applicable *lex arbitri* to challenge an arbitral award at all? Although the former Article 1717(4) of the BCCP was considerably criticized, no one had raised the issue of its compatibility with Article 6(1) of the ECHR and the right of access to a court.[165]

Non-existence of the annulment mechanism in *lex arbitri* not only discourages parties from choosing such a State as the seat of arbitration proceedings, but it also raises questions of such legislative approach's compatibility with the ECHR. The ECtHR's ruling in *Tabbane v. Switzerland* may suggest the opposite—in such cases there is no violation of the right of access to a court. However, there is an obvious difference between a voluntary and deliberate exclusion of setting-aside proceedings through the exercise of party autonomy and complete non-existence of such proceedings in the applicable arbitration law at all.

If an arbitral tribunal has issued a declaratory award or an award dismissing all claims, no enforcement is required and the affected party is left with no effective remedy to challenge the possibly defective arbitral award.[166] In addition, if no forum enjoys an *erga omnes* power to nullify an arbitral award, the winner of a defective award can repeatedly seek enforcement in other countries, hoping that somewhere the award will nevertheless be recognized and enforced.[167] The fact that in case of a declaratory award the losing party has no effective remedy to defend its interests against a possibly defective award was also stressed by the Latvian Constitutional Court in the *Hiponia* case.[168] Similarly, the adverse consequences of not having a

[165] Some authors have argued, for example, that 'the German Constitution does not oblige the legislator to provide for an action for the annulment of an arbitral award.' See Geimer (1994), p. 186, Sonnauer (1992), p. 45.

[166] Jaksic (2002), p. 313.

[167] See, e.g., Reisman and Richardson (2012), p. 28, Park (2001), p. 599 et seq.

[168] *Hiponia* case, No. 2014-09-01, the Constitutional Court of the Republic of Latvia, 28 November 2014, para. 22. www.satv.tiesa.gov.lv/wp-content/uploads/2014/03/2014-09-01_Spriedums_ENG.pdf. Accessed 29 May 2020.

procedure for challenging an arbitral award were already pointed out by the Latvian Constitutional Court in the *Asmers* case in 2005.[169]

It is not only the Latvian Constitutional Court that has continuously tried to address this issue and urged the Latvian Parliament to exercise its legislative power and take steps in providing arbitrating parties in Latvia with a possibility to apply for the setting aside of an arbitral award. Also the Latvian arbitration community has repeatedly stressed that a mechanism for challenging arbitral awards is of utmost significance for an effective arbitration framework.[170] The Latvian legislator, on the other hand, has continuously ignored such a necessity, under the pretext of court overload if court assistance and control over arbitration, including the provision of setting-aside proceedings, is finally introduced in Latvian arbitration law.

Recent developments, such as the ECtHR's ruling in the *Tabbane v. Switzerland* case, give rise to a broader discussion and analysis of whether such a legislative approach, i.e. not providing for setting-aside proceedings in national arbitration law altogether, is in conformity with the ECHR, in particular the right of access to a court under Article 6(1) of the ECHR. Whether or not the Court's *Tabbane v. Switzerland* ruling is set in stone with regard to exclusion agreements and whether or not a total lack of setting-aside proceedings in the applicable national arbitration law can indeed lead to a violation of parties' right of access to a court under Article 6(1) of the ECHR will be scrutinized below in Chap. 7.

References

Baskaran T (2019) Arbitration in Malaysia: a commentary on the Malaysian Arbitration Act. Kluwer Law International, Kluwer

Blūzma V et al. (2000) Latvijas tiesību vēsture (1914–2000). Fonds Latvijas Vēsture

Born G (2008) Vai nacionālais regulējums atbilst starptautiskajiem principiem [Does the National Law Complies with International Principles]. Jurista Vārds 47(542)

Broka B (2007) Šķīrējtiesu reglamentācija jaunajā likumprojektā [Regulation of arbitration in the new draft law], Jurista Vārds 51(504)

Bukovskis V (1933) Civīlprocesa mācības grāmata. Autora izdevums

Correll CC Jr, Szczepanik RJ (2012) No arbitration is an Island: the role of courts in aid of international arbitration. WAMR 6:565

Demeyere L (1999) 1998 Amendments to Belgian Arbitration law: an Overview. Arb Int l 15(3):295

Feldbrugge FJM et al. (eds) (1985) Encyclopedia of soviet law, 2nd edn. Martinus Nijhoff, Leiden

Gaillard E (1986) Belgium: statute on the setting aside of arbitral awards (Introductory Note). I.L.M. 25:725

Gaillard E et al. (eds) Fouchard Gaillard Goldman on International Commercial Arbitration. Kluwer International Law

169 See *Asmers* case, No. 2004-10-01, the Constitutional Court of the Republic of Latvia, 17 January 2005, para. 10. www.satv.tiesa.gov.lv/wp-content/uploads/2004/05/2004-10-01_Spriedums_ENG.pdf. Accessed 29 May 2020. Author's translation.

170 Rajoo (2019), p. 27. https://journal.arbitration.ru/upload/medialibrary/ff2/Arbitration.ru_N5_9_2019_stranitsy_25_35.pdf. Accessed 29 May 2020.

Geimer R (1994) Schiedsgerichtsbarkeit un Verfassung (Deutschland). In: Schlosser P (ed) Integritätsprobleme im Umfeld der Justiz. Bielefeld
Gharavi HG (2002) The International Effectiveness of the Annulment of An Arbitral Award. Kluwer Law International, Leiden
Ghikas GW (2006) Principled approach to adjourning the decision to enforce under the model law and the New York convention. Arb Intl 22:53
Hampton C (1985) Belgium's radical move on arbitration. financial times
Hanotiau B (1997) Survey of a new statute amending belgian legislation on arbitration. Am Rev Int'l Arb 8:327
Hanotiau B, Block G (1999) Note on the Law of 19 May 1998 amending belgian arbitration legislation. Arb. Int'l. 15(1):97
Jaksic A (2002) Arbitration and human rights. Peter Lang
Kačevska I (2004) Šķīrējtiesu attīstība: līdz šim un nākotnē [The Development of Arbitration until Now and in the Future]. Jurista Vārds 48(353)
Kačevska I (2008) Arbitration agreements in the Latvian arbitration environment. Baltic Yearbook Int Law 8:32
Kačevska I (2014) Ir normāla situācija, un ir Latvijas situācija [There is a Normal Situation, and There is a Latvian Situation]. Jurista Vārds 22 (824)
Kaufmann-Kohler G, Rigozzi A (2015) International arbitration: law and practice in Switzerland. Oxford University Press, Oxford
Knieper R (2008) Komentāri par Latvijas Šķīrējtiesu likumprojektu [Comments on the Latvian Draft Arbitration Law]. Jurista Vārds 47(542)
Konradi F, Walter A (1933) Civīlprocesa nolikums, 1932. gada izdevums ar Latvijas Senāta Civīlā Kasācijas Departamenta paskaidrojumiem. Jurist
Konradi F, Zvejnieks T (1939) Civilprocesa likums (1938. g. izd. 1939. g. iespied.) ar paskaidrojumiem–izvilkumiem no Latvijas Senata un Tiesu palatas spriedumiem un no attiecīgās zinātniskās literaturas, kā arī dažiem aizrādijumiem uz likumdošanas motiviem. Valsts tipografijas izdevums
Korobeinikov A, Inshakova A (2019) Chapter on Kyrgyzstan. In: The Baker McKenzie International Arbitration Yearbook. 12th edn, 2018–2019, p. 2. https://globalarbitrationnews.com/wp-content/uploads/2019/04/Kyrgyzstan.pdf. Accessed 29 May 2020
Kucina I (2014) Par šķīrējtiesu regulējumu un tā pilnveidi [On the Arbitration Regulation and Its Perfection], Jurista Vārds 22(824)
Lapsa J (2007) Šķīrējtiesu darbības pārmaiņas gaidot [Waiting for the Changes for Arbitration]. Jurista Vārds 51(504)
Lapsa J (2010) Šķīrējtiesas process: aktualitātes un nepieciešamās izmaiņas [Arbitration Process: Topicalities and the Required Changes]. Jurista Vārds 28(623)
Matray L (1986) La loi belge du 27 mars 1985 et ses repercussions sur l'arbitrage international. Rev. dr. Int. et comp. 24
Mistelis L (2008) Galvenais risks—tieksme pārāk stingri regulēt šķīrējtiesu [The Main Risk—Willingness to Regulate Arbitration Too Strictly]. Jurista Vārds 47(542)
Park WW (1989a) Judicial controls in the arbitral process. Arb Int Law 5(3):230
Park WW (1989b) National law and commercial justice: safeguarding procedural integrity in international arbitration. Tulane L. Rev 63(3):647–709
Park WW (2001) Why courts review arbitral awards. In: Briner R et al (eds) Law of International Business and Dispute Settlement in the 21st Century, Liber Amicorum Karl-Heinz Bockstiegel. Carl Heymanns Verlag KG, Köln/Berlin/Bonn/München, pp 595–606
Paulsson J (1980) Arbitration unbound: award detached from the law of its country of origin. Int Comp Law Q 30:358
Paulsson J (1986) Arbitration unbound in Belgium. Arb Int Law 2:68
Piers M (2006) Setting aside an arbitral award: a topical discussion. In: Keutgen G (ed) La sentence arbitrale/De arbitale uitspraak. Bruylant
Pommers A (1938) Šķīrējtiesas spriedumu nozīme un spēks pēc Civilprocesa likuma (CPL 1518. un 1519. panti). Rota

Poudret JF, Besson S (2006) Comparative Law of International Arbitration. Sweet and Maxwell, United Kingdom

Rajoo S (2019) Arbitration in Malaysia. Arbitration.ru 2019(5), p 27. https://journal.arbitration.ru/upload/medialibrary/ff2/Arbitration.ru_N5_9_2019_stranitsy_25_35.pdf. Accessed 29 May 2020

Redfern A et al. (2004) Law and practice of international commercial arbitration, 4th edn. Sweet and Maxwell, United Kingdom

Reisman M, Richardson B (2012) The present—commercial arbitration as a transnational system of justice: an interpretation of the architecture of international commercial arbitration. In: Van den Berg AJ (ed) : The next fifty years. ICCA Congress Series Volume, Kluwer Law International, pp 17–65

Repšs A (2007) Piezīmes par jauno šķīrējtiesas nolēmumu regulējumu [Remarks on the New Regulation for Arbitral Awards]. Jurista Vārds 51(504)

Repšs A (2014) Nav pamata neizdot izpildrakstu ad hoc šķīrējtiesu spriedumiem [There is No Justification Not to Issue an Enforcing Order for Ad Hoc Arbitral Awards]. Jurista Vārds 22(824)

Rozenbergs J (2005) Satversmes tiesa: būt šķīrējtiesām Latvijā [The Constitutional Court: 'Yes' for Arbitration Courts in Latvia]. Jurista Vārds 4(359)

Salans CF (2008) Valsts tiesu atbalsts ir vēlams, nevis izskaužams [Court Assistance is Preferable, and not Subject to Eradication]. Jurista Vārds 47(542)

Sabirov N (2020) Chapter on Kyrgyzstan. In: International Arbitration. Global Legal Insights, p. 201. http://www.k-a.kg/sites/default/files/gli_ia_kyrgyzstan.pdf. Accessed 29 may 2020

Shütze RA (2013) Institutional arbitration: a commentary. verlag

Sonnauer H (1992) Die Kontrolle der Schiedsgerichte durch die staatlichen Gerichte. Heymanns

Storme M (1986) Belgium: a paradise for international commercial arbitration. IBL 14(8):294

Storme M, Demeulenaere B (1989) International commercial arbitration in belgium: a handbook. Kluwer Law and Taxation, Leiden

Taychayev H, Alenkina N (2019) Arbitration in Kyrgyzstan: evolution and next steps ahead. Kluwer Arbitration Blog. 22 Feb 2019. http://arbitrationblog.kluwerarbitration.com/2019/02/22/arbitration-in-kyrgyzstan-evolution-and-next-steps-ahead/?doing_wp_cron=1590499793.2892630100250244140625. Accessed 29 May 2020

Tipaine M (2014) Šķīrējtiesu reputāciju grauj neitralitātes trūkums [The Reputation of Arbitration Courts is Undermined by Lack of Neutrality]. Jurista Vārds 22(824)

Tipaine M, Fjodorova L (2016) Arbitration in Latvia: Was a Restart a Failure? Kluwer Arbitration Blog. http://kluwerarbitrationblog.com/2016/01/25/arbitration-in-latvia-was-a-restart-a-failure/. Accessed 29 May 2020

Torgāns K (2005) Šķīrējtiesas Latvijā: vajadzīgas radikālas pārmaiņas [Arbitration Courts in Latvia: Need for Radical Changes]. Jurista Vārds 1(356)

Torgāns K (2007) Šķīrējtiesas sprieduma apstrīdēšanai der sevišķās tiesāšanās kārtība [The specific litigation order suits the challenging of arbitral awards]. Jurista Vārds 51(504)

Torgāns K (2008) Possible solutions to challenges of arbitral awards in Latvia. Balt Yearb Int Law 8:41

Ūdris Z (2014) Uzticību šķīrējtiesām var nodrošināt ar tiesas kontroli pār to nolēmumiem [Trust in Arbitration Courts may be Achieved with Court Control over Arbitral Awards]. Jurista Vārds 22(824)

Ūdris Z, Kačevska I (2004) Arbitration in Latvia: urgent need for statutory reform. J Int Law Arb 21(2):211

Van den Berg AJ (1994) Annulment of awards in international arbitration. In: Lillich RB, Brower CN (eds) International arbitration in the 21st century: towards 'judicialization' and uniformity?. Transnational Publishers, Twelfth Sokol Colloquium

Van den Berg AJ (1992) The Efficacy of Award in International Commercial Arbitration. Arbitration 58:267

Van den Berg AJ (2014) Should the setting aside of the arbitral award be abolished? ICSID Rev 1–26. https://doi.org/10.1093/icsidreview/sit053

Van den Berg GP (1985) The soviet system of justice: figures and policy. Springer-Science + Business Media, B.V, Berlin
Van Houtte H (1986) La loi belge du 27 mars 1985 sur l'arbitrage international. Rev arb 1:29
Vanderelst A (1986) Increasing the appeal of Belgium as an international arbitration forum?—the Belgian law of march 27, 1985 concerning the annulment of arbitral awards. J Int Law Arb 3:77
Verbruggen C (2016) Commentary on Part VI of the Belgian judicial code, Chapter VII: Article 1718. In: Bassiri N, Draye M (eds) Arbitration in Belgium. Kluwer Law International
Volkova M (2007) Valsts un šķīrējtiesa [The State and Arbitration]. Jurista Vārds 51(504)
Weigand F (ed) Practitioner's handbook on international commercial arbitration, 2nd edn. Oxford University Press, Oxford
Žukova G (2008) Arbitration in three baltic states: a thorny path of learning. Balt Yearb Int Law 8:2

Chapter 7
Approaches to Excluding the Annulment of Arbitral Awards and Their Compatibility with the ECHR

7.1 Introduction

The indefinite relationship between arbitration and the ECHR, especially the somewhat obscure distinction between *waivable* and *non-waivable* rights of Article 6(1) of the ECHR, and the different legislative approaches to excluding the annulment of arbitral awards, leave this book with the last final question—to what extent exclusion of annulment of arbitral awards in national arbitration law may lead to a violation of the procedural human rights guarantees enshrined in the ECHR? The reader has been generally introduced to two different, albeit at the same time interlinked approaches to excluding the annulment of arbitral awards, i.e. by means of a voluntary exclusion (Chap. 5) and by means of a legal vacuum in this regard (Chap. 6). The present Chapter will aim to answer the said question with regard to both approaches.

As to the latter, currently, at least within the reach of the ECHR, it is the rather unique Latvian legislator's choice of not statutorily regulating the annulment of arbitral awards. Undoubtedly, ECHR Members States enjoy a certain margin of appreciation in this regard and the right of access to a court can be also validly limited. However, it is equally known that such limitations are valid only insofar persons' rights and freedoms have not been restricted and reduced in a way that the very essence of their rights under the ECHR is impaired. Could it be argued that total lack of setting-aside proceedings in the applicable *lex arbitri* disproportionately restricts and violates parties' rights and freedoms, and that a State that has chosen such a legislative approach violates its obligations under the ECHR?

As to the former, i.e. voluntary exclusion of the annulment mechanism, this book's focus in this regard has been shaped by the Court's ruling in the *Tabbane v. Switzerland* case where the Court affirmed the compatibility of exclusion agreements with the ECHR. Nevertheless, the Court's ruling has equally left open certain questions pertaining to the limits of party autonomy and the relationship between arbitration and the ECHR.

© The Editor(s) (if applicable) and The Author(s), under exclusive license to Springer Nature Switzerland AG 2020

T. Krūmiņš, *Arbitration and Human Rights*,
https://doi.org/10.1007/978-3-030-54237-5_7

Since the ECtHR's reasoning in the *Tabbane v. Switzerland* case already suggests that a lack of setting-aside proceedings, provided it results from a voluntary exclusion agreement, is not contrary to parties' rights and freedoms under the ECHR, the answering of the question on the extent to which non-availability of the annulment mechanism may lead to a violation of the ECHR, must naturally begin with a critical analysis of the *Tabbane v. Switzerland* ruling. In the author's view, the Court's conclusions in the *Tabbane v. Switzerland* case cannot be interpreted as meaning that the issue of exclusion agreements will consequently never give rise to a potential violation of the Convention's rights and freedoms. Having first critically addressed the Court's ruling in the *Tabbane v. Switzerland* case, the author will then move on with an equally critical analysis of a legislative approach that omits regulation of setting-aside proceedings altogether. Although both approaches to excluding the annulment of arbitral awards share certain commonalities, in particular when they are considered from the perspective of interplay between arbitration and the ECHR, the somewhat more restrictive approach of total exclusion of setting-aside proceedings raises a number of additional issues from the viewpoint of its compatibility with the ECHR. After in detail analysis of the compatibility of both approaches to excluding the annulment action with the ECHR, the author will reflect on the *status quo* of setting-aside proceedings in contemporary framework of international arbitration and provide certain *de lege ferenda* recommendations on how to best regulate exclusion of the annulment mechanism from the perspective of the ECHR.

7.2 Exclusion Agreements and Their Compatibility with the ECHR

The first part of the broader question on the extent to which non-availability of the annulment mechanism in national law is permissible for a State to comply with its obligations under the ECHR relates to the phenomenon of exclusion agreements. As seen, a number of States have introduced in their national arbitration law explicit provisions permitting, under certain circumstances, an advance exclusion of setting-aside proceedings.

In the 2016 *Tabbane v. Switzerland* ruling the ECtHR concluded that Article 192(1) of the PILA is not contrary to the ECHR and that exclusion agreements, provided they satisfy certain conditions, do not generally infringe upon parties' procedural human rights, such as the right of access to a court. As a result, scholars have already suggested that other States' provisions permitting the exclusion of setting-aside proceedings, such as Article 1522(1) of the FCCP and Section 51 of the SAA, are therefore also compatible with the ECHR.[1]

However, as has become evident, the relationship between voluntary arbitration and the ECHR is not as clear cut as to conclude with utmost certainty that exclusion agreements will never give rise to potential violations of the ECHR. The ECtHR's

[1] Voser and George (2016).

considerable reliance on and weight given to both the underlying national framework governing arbitration proceedings and the particular circumstances of each case before it suggests that the Court's conclusion in the *Tabbane v. Switzerland* case is limited only to those particular factual and legal circumstances. This therefore means that another case concerning the compatibility of an exclusion agreement with the ECHR could nevertheless result in a violation of parties' rights and freedoms under the ECHR, depending how the particular circumstances of a case are weighed by the ECtHR against the different requirements of a valid waiver of the Convention's rights by means of an arbitration agreement.

Moreover, it is not only the ECtHR's interpretation that could and certainly will differ when analyzing whether or not an exclusion agreement in particular circumstances would result in a valid and lawful waiver of, e.g. rights enshrined in Article 6(1) of the ECHR. Perhaps even more significant is the still rather volatile ECtHR-made distinction between rights of Article 6(1) of the ECHR that can be validly waived by parties, on the one hand, and the so-called *non-waivable* rights, i.e. rights that are so fundamentally important in a democratic society that no individual should be deprived of their benefit, on the other hand.

Certain universally recognized grounds for challenging arbitral awards relate exactly to the Court's distinctively differed *non-waivable* rights of Article 6(1) of the ECHR. If, by concluding an exclusion agreement, parties fully waive their right to setting-aside proceedings, i.e. a mechanism by means of which, inter alia, the protection of their *non-waivable* rights can be guaranteed, a question arises whether such exclusion agreements are indeed unconditionally and fully compliant with the ECHR and the Court's established distinction between the *waivable* and *non-waivable* rights of Article 6(1) of the ECHR.

On the other hand, it also follows from the Convention controlling bodies' case-law that States are given considerable discretion when it comes to regulating the issue on which grounds an arbitral award can be set aside. For example, in *Nordström-Janzon and Nordström-Lehtinen v. the Netherlands* the former Commission stated that:

> [T]he grounds on which arbitral awards may be challenged before national courts differ among the Contracting States and [...] each Contracting State may in principle decide itself on which grounds an arbitral award should be quashed.[2]

Notably, however, this line of reasoning relates to the particular circumstances of the case in which one of the parties to arbitration challenged the actual scope (as opposed to the very existence of setting-aside proceedings) of the public policy ground for setting aside arbitral awards as provided in the Dutch arbitration law.[3] The question, however, that interests the present book is whether there are any limits

---

[2]*Nordström-Janzon and Nordström-Lehtinen v. the Netherlands*, App. No. 28101/95, ECmHR, 27 November 1996.

[3]Ibid. To stress the relevance of the Commission's conclusions solely with regard to the scope of setting-aside proceedings (as opposed to existence in the first place), one most note that the Commission in its conclusions gave weight to the fact that the applicants had actual access to a court by means of setting-aside proceedings ('The Commission furthermore notes that in the proceedings

to State discretion regarding the regulation of setting-aside proceedings and what is the extent of such a discretion? Previous analysis showed that State responsibility for violations of the ECHR during arbitration proceedings is engaged, inter alia, indirectly whenever the dispute reaches the domain of State courts, e.g. during the setting-aside or recognition and enforcement proceedings.[4] However, the *Tabbane v. Switzerland* case equally suggests that States, by statutorily permitting exclusion of setting-aside proceedings, can circumvent their obligations and no longer be held responsible for potential violations occurring during arbitration proceedings.[5] If parties have concluded an exclusion agreement, courts at the seat of arbitration are simply unable to set aside a possibly defective arbitral award, e.g. violating any of the annulment grounds that pertain to the Court's own made category of *non-waivable* rights under Article 6(1) of the ECHR.

Analysis of the extent to which voluntary exclusion agreement are compatible with the ECHR will naturally proceed by first analyzing the ECtHR's conclusions in the *Tabbane v. Switzerland* case and weighing such conclusions against the different requirements of a valid waiver of the Convention's rights by means of an arbitration agreement. Each requirement of the *waiver theory* will be considered in particular both against the factual circumstances of the *Tabbane v. Switzerland* case as well as the practice of other States permitting exclusion of agreements. Thereafter, the author will cross into the no-man's land and argue why such voluntary exclusion of setting aside proceedings should not be compatible with the ECHR insofar it limits parties' right to challenge possibly defective arbitral awards on grounds that pertain to the category of *non-waivable* rights under Article 6(1) of the ECHR.

---

before the national courts themselves the applicants were provided with ample opportunity to state their case and to challenge the arguments of the adverse party.').

[4]See, e.g. Petrochilos (2004), pp. 112–113 arguing that when recognizing and enforcing an arbitral award the State is 'stamping it with [its] seal of approval [and by] so doing, a state endorses the award and the process that led to it, and may as a result of such endorsement incur international responsibility.' For the ECHR controlling bodies' case-law, see, e.g. *Jakob Boss Söhn KG v. the Federal Republic of Germany*, App. No. 18479/91, ECmHR, 2 December 1991 ('This does not mean, however, that the respondent State's responsibility is completely excluded […] as the arbitration award had to be recognised by […] courts and be given executory effect by them. The courts thereby exercised a certain control and guarantee as to the fairness and correctness of the arbitration proceedings which they considered to have been carried out in conformity with fundamental rights and in particular with the right of the applicant company to be heard.'). Generally, see Chap. 3.

[5]This additionally raises issues of international state responsibility, considering that art. 27 of the Vienna Convention on the Law of the Treaties states that '[a] party may not invoke the provisions of its internal law as justification for its failure to perform a treaty.'

7.2.1 *Exclusion Agreements and the* Waiver Theory—*Is the ECtHR's Decision in* Tabbane v. Switzerland *Set in Stone?*

The relationship between arbitration and the ECHR is predominantly governed by what is known as the *waiver theory*. In the words of the ECtHR, 'neither the letter nor the spirit of Article 6 of the Convention prevents a person from waiving of his own free will, either expressly or tacitly, the entitlement to the guarantees of a fair trial.'[6]

More in particular with regard to arbitration, the ECtHR has repeatedly stressed that the conclusion of an arbitration agreement amounts legally to a partial renunciation of the exercise of rights as defined by Article 6(1) of the ECHR.[7] However, it has been equally established that a *waiver* of the Convention rights, in particular the procedural rights guaranteed by Article 6(1) of the ECHR, must satisfy certain conditions to be considered valid and effective for Convention purposes. A waiver will not conflict with the ECHR insofar it is free, lawful and unequivocal.[8] It must be also accompanied by certain minimum safeguards commensurate to its importance and must not run counter to any important public interest.[9] Additionally, not all rights of the Convention may subject to a waiver—in other words, a waiver of Convention rights must in fact be *permissible*.[10]

The *waiver theory*, and the various conditions thereof, was applied by the ECtHR also in the *Tabbane v. Switzerland* case in order to determine whether an exclusion agreement, as permitted under Article 192(1) of the PILA, in the particular circumstances was compatible with the right of access to a court implicitly provided under Article 6(1) of the ECHR. As seen, the ECtHR concluded that exclusion of setting-aside proceedings is not per se contrary to Article 6(1) of the ECHR, provided the said conditions are met.[11]

In the assessment whether or not a waiver is legally valid and effective for the Convention purposes, the ECtHR considers also the underlying national arbitration law framework. This is not only evidenced by the *Tabbane v. Switzerland* case where the Court in its reasoning took into account various particularities of the applicable Swiss law, but also other arbitration-related cases.[12] The ECtHR, in essence, carries

[6] *Sejdovic v. Italy*, App. No. 56581/00, ECtHR, 1 March 2006, para. 86. See also *Salduz v. Turkey*, App. No. 36391/02, ECtHR [GC], 27 November 2008, para. 59; *Hermi v. Italy*, App. No. 18114/02, ECtHR [GC], 18 October 2006, para. 73; *Dvorski v. Croatia*, App. No. 25703/11, ECtHR, 20 October 2015, para. 100.

[7] See Sect. 3.4.2.

[8] See Sect. 3.5.

[9] Ibid.

[10] See Sect. 3.4.3.

[11] See Sect. 5.2.4.

[12] See, e.g. *Suovaniemi and others v. Finland*, App. No. 31737/96, ECtHR, 23 February 1999, where the ECtHR took into account the respective framework of arbitration proceedings under Finnish law. See also, inter alia, *Axelsson and others v. Sweden*, App. No. 11960/86, ECmHR, 13 July 1990

out a cross-analysis, weighing the particular circumstances of the case and the applicable national legal framework against the principles and conditions of a valid waiver developed by the ECtHR in its case-law. This, in turn, suggests that the ECtHR's ruling in the *Tabbane v. Switzerland* case is not absolute, at least not in the sense that exclusion agreements in other circumstances and (or) stemming from a different national legal framework would not lead to a violation of the Convention's rights and freedoms. What matters is whether or not the particular circumstances, including the applicable national legal framework, satisfy the conditions of a valid waiver under the ECHR.

In the *Tabbane v. Switzerland* case the ECtHR established that a waiver in those circumstances, taken together with the applicable Swiss legal framework, was valid and effective for the Convention purposes. However, the Court's reasoning, as concise as it stands, is not entirely convincing—it leaves many unanswered questions not only with regard to the various conditions of a valid waiver and the degree of reliance put by the ECtHR on the underlying legal framework in establishing whether or not such conditions have been satisfied, but also with regard to the Court's own made distinction between *waivable* and *non-waivable* rights of Article 6(1) of the ECHR.

7.2.1.1 The Condition of *Absence of Constraint*

The requirement of *absence of constraint* is at all events one of the conditions to be satisfied for a waiver to be valid and effective for the Convention purposes.[13] As a necessary pre-condition the absence of constraint requirement was set forth in the very first arbitration-related case before the former Commission[14] and since then has been the Court's most emphasized criterion, and as such can be considered as a *conditio sine qua non* for a valid and effective parties' waiver of the Convention's rights and freedoms.[15]

The *Tabbane v. Switzerland* case was no exception in this regard. In its decision the ECtHR argued that an arbitration agreement was signed through the exercise of freedom of contract, and that by concluding the arbitration agreement parties

and *Nordström-Janzon and Nordström-Lehtinen v. the Netherlands*, App. No. 28101/95, ECmHR, 27 November 1996.

[13]*Deweer v. Belgium*, App. No. 6903/75, ECtHR, 27 February 1980, para. 49.

[14]*X. v. the Federal Republic of Germany*, App. No. 1197/61, ECmHR, 5 March 1962.

[15]To the author's knowledge, the ECtHR has referred to the requirement of 'absence of constraint' in almost every arbitration-related case. See, inter alia, *Deweer v. Belgium*, App. No. 6903/75, ECtHR, 27 February 1980; *R. v. Switzerland*, App. No. 10881/84, ECmHR, 4 March 1987; *Jakob Boss Söhn KG v. the Federal Republic of Germany*, App. No. 18479/91, ECmHR, 2 December 1991; *Firma Heinz Schiebler KG v. the Federal Republic of Germany*, App. No. 18805/91, ECmHR, 2 December 1991; *Lundgren v. Sweden*, App. No. 22506/93, ECmHR, 17 May 1995; *Molin v. Turkey*, App. No. 23173/94, ECmHR, 22 October 1996; *Pastore v. Italy*, App. No. 46483/99, ECtHR, 25 May 1999; *Axelsson and others v. Sweden*, App. No. 11960/86, ECmHR, 13 July 1990; *Suda v. Czech Republic*, App. No. 1643/06, ECtHR, 28 October 2010; *Nordström-Janzon and Nordström-Lehtinen v. the Netherlands*, App. No. 28101/95, ECmHR, 27 November 1996; *Tabbane v. Switzerland*, App. No. 41069/12, ECtHR, 1 March 2016.

expressly and voluntarily renounced the possibility to submit disputes that may potentially arise in the future to an ordinary court that would provide all the guarantees of Article 6(1) of the ECHR. Moreover, in the ECtHR's opinion, there were no indications whatsoever that the applicant was under duress when signing the arbitration agreement. Neither the opposite was argued.[16]

However, despite the Court's often referenced necessity to satisfy the requirement of absence of constraint at all events, neither the former Commission, nor the ECtHR has provided any concrete examples of elements needed for establishing that a consent to a waiver of the Convention's rights and freedoms was vitiated. The different cases in which such a requirement has been expressed indicate that the threshold will be rather high—arbitrating party's consent must be affected by real duress.[17] Nevertheless, lack of constraint is in itself not sufficient for a valid waiver of the Convention's rights and freedoms—a waiver must in fact follow out of someone's own free will.[18] Moreover, a waiver can only be considered as stemming from one's own free will if the respective person is fully aware of the rights that he or she waives.[19]

The particular circumstances of the *Tabbane v. Switzerland* case, at least when considered solely from the viewpoint of whether or not parties voluntarily entered into an arbitration agreement as opposed to, e.g. exclusive jurisdiction agreement, do not pose particular difficulties. Neither of the parties in the *Tabbane v. Switzerland* case seemed to object to the conclusion of the arbitration agreement. Moreover, both parties had equal bargaining power when it comes to agreeing on a certain method

---

[16] *Tabbane v. Switzerland*, App. No. 41069/12, ECtHR, 1 March 2016, para. 29 ('Dans la présente affaire, la Cour observe d'emblée que le requérant était un homme d'affaires tunisien domicilié à El Menzah en Tunisie qui entrait en collaboration avec la société Colgate, société de droit français ayant son siège en France. Il ne prétend pas que l'arbitrage était imposé par la loi. Bien au contraire, en exerçant sa liberté contractuelle, il a signé une convention d'arbitrage avec la société Colgate contenant une clause compromissoire pour résoudre des litiges qui pourraient naître entre eux [...] En concluant ce compromis d'arbitrage, le requérant a expressément et librement renoncé à la possibilité de soumettre les litiges pouvant potentiellement surgir à l'avenir à un tribunal ordinaire qui lui aurait offert l'ensemble des garanties de l'article 6 de la Convention. Il n'existe aucune indication que le requérant ait agi sous la contrainte en signant la convention d'arbitrage. Par ailleurs, le requérant ne le prétend pas.')

[17] Petrochilos (2004), p. 114. Any form of economic duress does not per se imply that a waiver is invalid. See, e.g. *Axelsson and others v. Sweden*, App. No. 11960/86, ECmHR, 13 July 1990; *Hedland v. Sweden*, App. No. 24118/94, ECmHR, 9 April 1997.

[18] See, e.g. *Albert and Le Compte v. Belgium*, Apps. No. 7299/75 and 7496/76, ECtHR, 10 February 1983, para. 35 ('if [...] this is in accordance with the will of the person concerned.'). See also *Pauger v. Austria*, App. No. 1617/90, ECtHR, 28 May 1997, para. 58; *Sejdovic v. Italy*, App. No. 56581/00, ECtHR, 1 March 2006, para. 86. See also *Salduz v. Turkey*, App. No. 36391/02, ECtHR [GC], 27 November 2008, para. 59; *Hermi v. Italy*, App. No. 18114/02, ECtHR [GC], 18 October 2006, para. 73; *Dvorski v. Croatia*, App. No. 25703/11, ECtHR, 20 October 2015, para. 100.

[19] See Lawson (1996), p. 159 in referring to *T v. Italy*, App. No. 14104/88, ECtHR, 12 October 1992. See also *Talat Tunç v. Turkey*, App. No. 32432/96, ECtHR, 27 March 2007, para. 59; *Jones v. the United Kingdom*, App. No. 30900/03, ECtHR, 9 September 2003; *Aleksandr Zaichenko v. Russia*, App. No. 39660/02, ECtHR, 18 February 2010, para. 40. Implicitly on this requirement applied by the ECtHR in an arbitration-related case see, e.g. *Suovaniemi and others v. Finland*, App. No. 31737/96, ECtHR, 23 February 1999.

of dispute resolution in their agreement. This, in particular, may be the reason why the ECtHR in its decision did not pay greater attention to the question of whether or not the requirement of *absence of constraint* was satisfied.

The same, however, cannot so assuredly be said of other forms of arbitration, e.g. sports arbitration or consumer arbitration where one of the parties is in a weaker position. A contract containing an exclusion agreement in procedural regulations of a sports association or a business to consumer (B2C) agreements, raises a question whether or not it satisfies the requirement of *absence of constraint* for a valid waiver of the Convention's rights and freedoms.

At least with regard to the former, i.e. sports arbitration, this has been answered by the Swiss Federal Tribunal in the well-known *Cañas* case.[20] In the case at hand, a tennis player, in order to become a member of the Association of Tennis Professionals (ATP), had to consent to the ATP's procedural rules, containing an arbitration agreement and an exclusion agreement, stipulating that the decision of the Court of Arbitration for Sport (CAS) shall be final, non-reviewable, non-appealable and enforceable.[21] After unsuccessful arbitration proceedings before the CAS, *Cañas* challenged the arbitral award before the Swiss Federal Tribunal. Although the ATP invoked the exclusion agreement, the Swiss Federal Tribunal rejected it and concluded that *Cañas* had not consented to the exclusion agreement of his own free will. Professional sports is characterized by a hierarchical structure, comprised of sports federations and associations on a national and international level. An athlete, wishing to excel professionally has no other option but to become a member of particular sports association and accept the arbitration agreement, and in this case also the exclusion agreement. In other words, an athlete does not have an equal bargaining power when compared to a sports association.[22] For these reasons, the Swiss Federal Tribunal considered

[20] Decision of the Swiss Federal Tribunal in case No. ATF 133 III 235, 22 March 2007.

[21] Ibid. See also Rigozzi (2010), p. 227.

[22] The relevant part of the Swiss Federal Tribunal's decision explains the specificity of sports arbitration as follows ('Th[e exclusion] agreement, as any other contract, comes into existence only provided that the parties have expressed their mutual intention to waive setting-aside proceedings. As a constituent element of party autonomy, freedom of contract requires that such a declaration should not rest on an intent which has been coerced in any way whatsoever. It is all the more important that the intent to waive setting-aside proceedings should not be tainted by any form of duress or undue influence because such waiver will deprive its author of the ability to challenge any future award, whether the award disregards fundamental principles in force in any state based on the rule of law, such as public policy, or fundamental procedural guarantees such as the proper constitution of the arbitral tribunal, arbitral jurisdiction, equal treatment for the parties as well as the parties' right to present their case before the arbitrator. Sports competition is characterized by a highly hierarchical structure, as much on the international as on the national level. Vertically integrated, the relationships between athletes and organisations in charge of the various sports disciplines are distinct from the horizontal relationship represented by a contractual relationship between two parties […]. This structural difference between the two types of relationships is not without influence on the volitional process driving the formation of every agreement. In principle, when two parties are on equal footing, each party expresses its intention without being dependent on the other. This is the usual structure in the case of international commercial relations. However, the situation is very different in the sports arena. Aside from the (theoretical) case of a famous athlete who, due to his notoriety, would be in a position to dictate his requirements to the international federation in

that an exclusion agreement, as permitted under Article 192(1) of the PILA, is not enforceable against an athlete.

Given the reasons put forward by the Swiss Federal Tribunal and despite the lack of specific indications by ECtHR as to the necessary elements of *constraint*, it can be argued that an exclusion agreement in such circumstances would be considered being concluded under duress, or at least not *freely* within the meaning of the relevant conditions for a valid waiver under the Convention, and therefore would be contrary to the Convention.

On 2 October 2018, the non-voluntary character of sports arbitration was confirmed by the ECtHR in the *Pechstein* ruling, examining, inter alia, the issue of whether or not an athlete waives rights under Article 6(1) of the ECHR by agreeing to arbitrate disputes under the auspices of the CAS.[23] After recalling the generally established principles pertaining to the dichotomy between arbitration and the ECHR,[24] the Court compared the characteristics of sports arbitration with those of commercial arbitration in three previous cases before the Court, i.e. *Tabbane v. Switzerland*,[25] *Eiffage*[26] and *Transado-Transportes*[27] concluding, by referring, inter alia, also to the *Cañas* case, that athletes are not considered to accept arbitration in a free and unambiguous manner.[28] Therefore, the Court established that sports arbitration is in fact *forced* and thus should offer all the guarantees of Article 6(1) of the ECHR.[29]

The same conclusion could be drawn in relation to B2C arbitration agreements. Pursuant to Directive 93/13/EEC of 5 April 1993 on unfair terms in consumer contracts, an arbitration agreement in consumer contracts is an unfair contract term, provided parties did not negotiate it *ex post*. However, even if a B2C arbitration agreement was negotiated after the dispute arose, express exclusion of a right to

charge of the sport concerned, experience has shown that, by and large, athletes will often not have the bargaining power required and would therefore have to submit to the federation's requirements, whether they like it or not. Accordingly, any athlete wishing to participate in organised competition under the control of a sports federation whose rules provide for recourse to arbitration will not have any choice but to accept the arbitral clause, in particular by subscribing to the articles of association of the sports federation in question in which the arbitration clause was inserted, all the more so if the athlete in question is a professional athlete. Such an athlete will face the following alternative: to consent to arbitration or to practice his sport merely non-professionally […] Put before the alternative of submitting to arbitral jurisdiction or else practice his sport just 'in his own garden' […] and watch competition 'on the television' […] any athlete wishing to engage in true competition or having to do so as his sport is his only source of income (financial or in kind, advertising income, etc.) will in fact, *nolens volens*, have to opt for submitting to arbitral jurisdiction.'). Translation of the excerpt of the Swiss Federal Tribunal's decision is taken from Rigozzi (2010), p. 227.

[23] *Mutu and Pechstein v. Switzerland*, App. Nos. 40575/10 and 67474/10, 2 October 2018.

[24] Ibid., paras. 94–96.

[25] *Tabbane v. Switzerland*, App. No. 41069/12, ECtHR, 1 March 2016.

[26] *Eiffage SA and others v. Switzerland*, App. No. 1742/05, ECtHR, 15 September 2009.

[27] *Transado-Transportes Fluviais Do Sado, S.A. v. Portugal*, App. No. 35943/02, ECtHR, 16 December 2003.

[28] *Mutu and Pechstein v. Switzerland*, App. Nos. 40575/10 and 67474/10, 2 October 2018, paras. 103–114.

[29] Ibid., para. 115.

challenge the arbitral award could possibly result in the arbitration agreement being unreasonable and unfair, thus not satisfying the requirement of *absence of constraint*. This is especially the case considering the *mandatory* character of EU consumer law within the realm of EU law and the fact that EU Member States' courts are required to exercise judicial control over arbitration in order to guarantee the full effectiveness of EU law.[30]

Moreover, in the *Tabbane v. Switzerland* decision the ECtHR puts great emphasis on the voluntary character of an exclusion agreement under Article 192(1) of the PILA. The ECtHR asserts that parties were under no obligation to exclude any recourse against the award—on the contrary, they could freely choose whether or not to take *advantage* of this possibility offered by Swiss law.[31] This voluntary character appears to have a significant impact on the Court's conclusion that the particular exclusion agreement was compatible with the Convention. However, a notable fact that characterizes the *Tabbane v. Switzerland* case is that the relevant seat of arbitration—Switzerland, was chosen by the arbitral tribunal, as opposed to arbitrating parties in their agreement. In such circumstances it is debatable whether the requirement of full awareness of the rights that a person waives is satisfied. In the *Tabbane v. Switzerland* case the parties had agreed that the seat of arbitration shall be determined by the arbitral tribunal. Is such an indirect choice of the respective forum providing for the exclusion of setting-aside proceedings sufficient for satisfying the Court's stressed *voluntariness*? The ECtHR's own line of reasoning in the *Tabbane v. Switzerland* case implies that such an *implicit* choice would not be sufficient.[32]

Alternatively, in the circumstances leading to the *Tabbane v. Switzerland* case, pursuant to the applicable ICC Arbitration Rules the seat of arbitration would have been fixed by the ICC, unless parties had agreed on it in their arbitration agreement. Considering that there are still generally more States that do not permit exclusion agreements than States that allow such agreements (let alone do away with setting-aside proceedings altogether), it is arguable whether the requirement of *absence of constraint* would be fulfilled due to the fact that parties could not have reasonably foreseen that the arbitral tribunal or the relevant arbitral institution would choose an arbitral seat that permits exclusion of setting-aside proceedings or even excludes setting-aside proceedings altogether.

---

[30]See Sect. 4.4.1.6. Generally on the particular requirements of consumer arbitration see, e.g. Piers (2011).

[31]*Tabbane v. Switzerland*, App. No. 41069/12, ECtHR, 1 March 2016, para. 34 ('De plus, il convient de noter qu'une partie, n'ayant ni domicile, ni résidence habituelle, ni établissement en Suisse, n'est nullement obligée d'exclure tout recours; bien au contraire, elle peut librement choisir de saisir cette possibilité qu'offre la loi suisse en renonçant valablement à tout recours à un tribunal ordinaire. La Cour estime que ce moyen offert aux parties qui n'ont pas de liens avec la Suisse est proportionné au but de renforcer l'attractivité de la Suisse en matière d'arbitrage international et de renforcer le principe de la liberté contractuelle des parties.').

[32]It appears that an express choice in favour of an exclusion agreement is needed. *Tabbane v. Switzerland*, App. No. 41069/12, ECtHR, 1 March 2016, para. 29 ('En concluant ce compromis d'arbitrage, le requérant a *expressément* et librement renoncé à la possibilité de soumettre les litiges pouvant potentiellement surgir à l'avenir à un tribunal ordinaire qui lui aurait offert l'ensemble des garanties de l'article 6 de la Convention.' [emphasis added]).

The discussion on *implicit* waiver and the required wording of an arbitration agreement in order to conclude with certainty that parties indeed agreed upon the exclusion of setting-aside proceedings, is closely linked with the next requirement for a valid and effective *waiver* under the Convention, namely that of *unequivocality*.[33]

7.2.1.2 The Condition of *Unequivocality*

The requirement that a waiver of the exercise of a right guaranteed by the Convention must be expressed *unequivocally* has been affirmed by the former Commission and the ECtHR in numerous cases,[34] including arbitration-related cases.[35] A waiver of the exercise of a right guaranteed by the Convention may be either express or tacit,[36] however the condition of *unequivocality* requires that there should be no doubt as to its existence and scope.[37]

In the *Tabbane v. Switzerland* case, the ECtHR appears to link the requirement of *unequivocality* with the applicable national law and the Swiss Federal Tribunal's interpretation of the specific arbitration agreement, stipulating in its relevant part that '[t]he decision of the arbitration shall be final and binding and neither party shall have any right to appeal such decision to any court of law.' As to the fulfilment of the requirement of *unequivocality* the ECtHR stresses that the Swiss Federal Tribunal has concluded, by interpretation of the will of the parties, that by means of the exclusion agreement in their arbitration agreement they ruled out any recourse against the award. Such a conclusion, considering the wording of the clause, in the Court's eyes was neither arbitrary nor unreasonable.[38]

---

[33] See *Suda v. Czech Republic*, App. No. 1643/06, ECtHR, 28 October 2010.

[34] See, e.g. *Colozza v. Italy*, App. No. 9024/80, ECtHR, 12 February 1985, para. 28; *Barberà, Messegué and Jabardo v. Spain*, App. No. 10590, ECtHR, 6 December 1988, para. 82; *Oberschlick v. Austria*, App. No. 11662/85, ECtHR, 23 May 1991, para. 51; *Pfeiffer and Plankl v. Austria*, App. No. 10802/84, ECtHR, 25 February 1992, para. 37; *Håkansson and Sturesson v. Sweden*, App. No. 11855/85, ECtHR, 21 February 1990, para. 66.

[35] See, e.g. *Axelsson and others v. Sweden*, App. No. 11960/86, ECmHR, 13 July 1990; *Suda v. Czech Republic*, App. No. 1643/06, ECtHR, 28 October 2010; *Suovaniemi and others v. Finland*, App. No. 31737/96, ECtHR, 23 February 1999; *Transado-Transportes Fluviais Do Sado, S.A. v. Portugal*, App. No. 35943/02, ECtHR, 16 December 2003; *Eiffage SA and others v. Switzerland*, App. No. 1742/05, ECtHR, 15 September 2009.

[36] See, e.g. *Håkansson and Sturesson v. Sweden*, App. No. 11855/85, ECtHR, 21 February 1990, para. 66. See also *Suovaniemi and others v. Finland*, App. No. 31737/96, ECtHR, 23 February 1999.

[37] Vitkauskas and Dikov (2012) Protecting the right to a fair trial under the European Convention on Human Rights Council of Europe human rights handbooks. Council of Europe, p. 10.

[38] *Tabbane v. Switzerland*, App. No. 41069/12, ECtHR, 1 March 2016, para. 30 ('La renonciation au droit à un tribunal (ordinaire) en faveur d'un arbitrage doit être intervenue sans équivoque. En l'espèce, le Tribunal fédéral est arrivé à la conclusion, par voie d'interprétation des volontés des parties, que celles-ci, par l'inclusion d'une clause de renonciation dans l'article 8 b du compromis (paragraphe 4 ci–dessus) ont exclu tout recours contre la sentence arbitrale. A la lumière du texte de la clause («neither party shall have any right to appeal such decision to any court of law») et dans la mesure où elle est compétente pour trancher cette question, la Cour estime qu'une telle conclusion ne paraît ni arbitraire ni déraisonnable.').

As seen when analyzing the state of exclusion agreements under Swiss law,[39] the requirement of an *express statement* under Article 192(1) of the PILA has witnessed certain evolutionary changes. Until 2005 parties' will to exclude setting-aside proceedings had to be clearly and unambiguously stated by referring to the specific remedy, i.e. setting-aside proceedings, and its exclusion thereof. However, by means of the Swiss Federal Tribunal's decision of 2005, the strict requirement of express reference was recognized as not being an indispensable condition for a valid waiver of a right to challenge an arbitral award.[40] While the waiver must still show in a clear and distinct manner the common intention of parties to exclude setting-aside proceedings, express reference or citation of the relevant remedy is no longer required. As a result, seemingly broad exclusion clauses, such as in the case of *Tabbane v. Switzerland*, are considered to amount to a valid exclusion of setting-aside proceedings under Article 192(1) of the PILA. However, implied references to, e.g. arbitration rules containing a provision excluding any recourse against an arbitral award, would still not amount to a valid exclusion agreement under Article 192(1) of the PILA.[41]

At the same time, the comparative analysis carried out in Chap. 5, evidences that Switzerland is the only State where such broad exclusion agreements would be considered valid. In France, exclusion of setting-aside proceedings requires a *convention spéciale*, i.e. a manifestation of the will of the parties specifically directed at the action of annulment.[42] The same is true in Belgium[43] and also in Sweden where parties are required to specifically refer to the right to challenge an arbitral award under Section 34 of the SAA and exclude it.[44]

The ECtHR's strong reliance in the *Tabbane v. Switzerland* case on the interpretation of the respective exclusion agreement given by the Swiss Federal Tribunal, considered together with the fact that arbitrating parties in the said case did not themselves choose Switzerland as the seat of arbitration and the fact that only a handful of States permit exclusion of setting-aside proceedings, raises a question whether or not such a broad reference in the arbitration agreement excluding *any right to appeal* is indeed *unequivocal* enough to be considered as leaving no doubt as to its existence and scope and thus being considered as a valid waiver of the exercise of the rights guaranteed by the Convention.

In its decision,[45] the Swiss Federal Tribunal rather extensively analyzed the particular wording in the arbitration agreement excluding *any right to appeal* and the ECtHR appears to simply embrace the findings of the Swiss Federal Tribunal that such a reference, for the purposes Article 192(1) of the PILA and its interpretation

---

[39] See Sect. 5.2.

[40] Baizeau (2005), p. 71 in citing decision of the Swiss Federal Tribunal in case No. 4P.236/2004, 4 February 2005, para. 4.2.3.1.

[41] See Sect. 5.2.2.

[42] See Sect. 5.3.2.

[43] See Sect. 5.5.2.

[44] See Sect. 5.4.2.

[45] See Sect. 5.2.4.2.

thereof, amounted to an *unequivocal* exclusion of a right to challenge an arbitral award. However, in other of the previously analyzed States permitting exclusion of setting-aside proceedings, such a broad reference excluding *any right to appeal* would not be sufficient for a valid exclusion. Provided that the arbitral tribunal had chosen the arbitral seat in e.g. Belgium or Sweden[46] the respective reference in the arbitration agreement to exclusion of *any right to appeal* would not amount to a valid exclusion agreement under the respective national laws. Therefore, considering the particular circumstances, it is difficult to see how such a broad reference, in the eyes of the ECtHR, could have satisfied the requirement of *unequivocality* and leave no doubts as to the existence and scope of a waiver.

The choice of the arbitral seat in favor of Switzerland is seemingly the only scenario according to which the particular arbitration agreement would amount to a valid exclusion of setting-aside proceedings.[47] This, in turn, is exactly what leaves reasonable doubts as to the existence and scope of the waiver in such circumstances. Depending on the arbitral institution's or the arbitral tribunal's choice of the arbitral seat, interpretation of the exact same arbitration agreement could result in diametrically opposed outcomes from the perspective of compatibility of such exclusion agreements with the ECHR. It is arguable whether, absent an express and specific reference to the respective remedy, i.e. setting-aside proceedings, and its exclusion thereof, parties could have or should have foreseen in such circumstances that, depending on where the arbitral seat is located, they would be stripped of a possibility to challenge an arbitral award. Therefore, the requirement that one must reasonably foresee the consequences of the waiver and be fully aware of the rights he or she waives, is arguably not satisfied. The ECtHR fails to consider this aspect in its *Tabbane v. Switzerland* decision.

7.2.1.3 The Condition of *Minimum Safeguards*

A waiver of a right guaranteed by the Convention must be accompanied by certain *minimum safeguards* commensurate to its importance. The requirement stems from the criminal limb of Article 6(1) of the ECHR and, as seen in previous analysis,[48] has been equally applied by the ECtHR also in arbitration-related cases.

In the *Suovaniemi and others v. Finland* case, a waiver of the right to an independent and impartial tribunal in the particular circumstances was considered to be accompanied by *minimum safeguards* due to the fact that the respective party in arbitration was represented by a counsel and that later in court proceedings ample opportunity was given to advance arguments pertaining to the exact circumstances

[46] In the particular circumstances, the seat of arbitration could not be located in France since one of the parties, i.e. Colgate, was French and the arbitration agreement expressly stipulated that a seat of arbitration, other than the country of either party, must be chosen by arbitrators.

[47] This is true not only among the various States that permit exclusion agreements, but also when considered more generally—the majority of States do not permit exclusion of setting-aside proceedings at all.

[48] See Sect. 3.5.4.

in which the waiver occurred during arbitration proceedings.[49] In the *Tabbane v. Switzerland* case, the ECtHR saw no doubt that the waiver was surrounded by *minimums safeguards* commensurate to such waiver's importance—parties were able to elect arbitrators of their choice who, in turn, agreed on the seat of arbitration to be in Geneva, thus making Swiss law the applicable law to arbitration. Moreover, the ECtHR asserted that parties were duly heard by the Swiss Federal Tribunal that took into account all the factual and legal elements objectively relevant for the resolution of case at hand, and that the Swiss Federal Tribunal's judgment was duly motivated, showing no appearance of arbitrariness.[50] Additionally, although not expressly mentioned by the ECtHR when verifying fulfilment of the requirement of *minimum safeguards*, the Court also emphasizes the fact that when parties exclude setting-aside proceedings pursuant to Article 192(1) of the PILA and the arbitral award is to be executed in Switzerland, the New York Convention applies by analogy, thus adding an additional review by ordinary courts of arbitral tribunals.[51] This may also be seen as a supplementary safeguard commensurate to the importance of the consequences of an exclusion agreement.

In order to establish whether or not a waiver of a right guaranteed by the ECHR has been accompanied by certain *minimum safeguards*, in both decisions, i.e. the *Suovaniemi and others v. Finland* and *Tabbane v. Switzerland* cases, the ECtHR carried out a factual check of not only the relevant circumstances of the case, but also the underlying legislative framework. In multiple other arbitration-related cases, the ECtHR has stressed that the underlying legislative framework is of paramount importance when determining whether or not a waiver was attained by *minimum*

[49] See Ibid. and the discussion on *Suovaniemi and others v. Finland*, App. No. 31737/96, ECtHR, 23 February 1999.

[50] *Tabbane v. Switzerland*, App. No. 41069/12, ECtHR, 1 March 2016, para. 31 ('De plus, rien ne permet de douter que cette renonciation n'était pas entourée du minimum de garanties correspondant à son importance. La Cour note, à cet égard, que le requérant a pu élire un arbitre de son choix. Celui-ci, agissant de concert avec les deux autres arbitres, a été d'accord de choisir le lieu du siège de l'arbitrage à Genève de sorte que le droit suisse est devenu la loi applicable à l'arbitrage, c'est-à-dire la loi qui régit l'arbitrage. Par ailleurs, la Cour observe que le Tribunal fédéral a dûment entendu les arguments du requérant et a pris en compte tous les éléments factuels et juridiques qui étaient objectivement pertinents pour la résolution du litige. L'arrêt du Tribunal fédéral s'avère par ailleurs dûment motivé de sorte qu'aucune apparence d'arbitraire ne puisse être décelée dans le cas d'espèce.').

[51] *Tabbane v. Switzerland*, App. No. 41069/12, ECtHR, 1 March 2016, para. 35 ('De surcroît, la Cour constate que, si les parties optent pour l'exclusion de tout recours contre une sentence conformément à l'article 192 alinéa 1 LDIP, l'alinéa 2 de cette disposition prévoit que, si celle-ci doit être exécutée en Suisse, la Convention de New York pour la reconnaissance et l'exécution des sentences arbitrales étrangères s'applique par analogie, ce qui ajoute un contrôle supplémentaire exercé par les tribunaux ordinaires sur les tribunaux arbitraux (voir, dans ce sens, *Zamet – Budowa Maszyn Spółka Akcyjna c. Pologne* (déc.), no 1485/11, 25 août 2015). En effet, la reconnaissance et l'exécution d'une sentence peuvent exceptionnellement être refusées pour les motifs énumérés à l'article V de ladite convention (paragraphe 15 ci-dessus).').

safeguards and whether national courts still retained some measure of control over the arbitration proceedings.[52]

The validity of exclusion agreements for the purposes of the Convention will therefore depend, inter alia, on the existence of additional safeguards in the applicable national legislative framework and how such safeguards interplay with the relevant factual circumstances. In the *Tabbane v. Switzerland* decision the ECtHR predominantly focused on the existence of such safeguards *ex post*, i.e. when the exclusion agreement was already concluded. However, the Court's reference to Article 192(2) of the PILA evidences that particular safeguards inherent in the applicable legislative framework also prior the conclusion of exclusion agreement will be of equal importance in the Court's analysis of whether or not the conditions of a valid waiver are met.

Additional safeguards provided for by Article 192(2) of the PILA are not the only statutory stipulated guarantees that parties can nevertheless make use of despite the conclusion of an exclusion agreement. Although not mentioned by the Court in its analysis, parties excluding setting-aside proceedings can also benefit from the possibility of *révision*.[53] Although a recent decision by the Swiss Federal Tribunal suggests that by excluding the right to setting-aside proceedings parties also exclude their right to request revision of an arbitral, at least to the extent that the respective irregularity on the basis of which revision is requested could have been brought by means of an annulment action,[54] revision of an arbitral award may still be requested in other cases.[55] Equally, exclusion of setting-aside proceedings pursuant to Article 192(1) of the PILA does not embrace renunciation of court assistance in general—parties can still benefit from the assistance of Swiss courts in challenging arbitrators, issuing interim measures and taking of evidence.[56] Moreover, under certain circumstances and despite allegedly valid exclusion agreement, the Swiss Federal Tribunal will also preliminary examine the subjective scope of the arbitration agreement and that of the exclusion agreement.[57]

---

[52] See, e.g. *R v. Switzerland*, App. No. 10881/84, ECmHR, 4 March 1987 ('The Commission nevertheless considers that, in order to answer the question of whether the guarantees secured by Article 6 apply, account must be taken not only of the arbitration agreement between the parties and the nature of the private arbitration proceedings, but also of the legislative framework providing for such proceedings.'). See also *Nordström-Janzon and Nordström-Lehtinen v. the Netherlands*, App. No. 28101/95, ECmHR, 27 November 1996 ('However, the Commission considers that account must be taken not only of the arbitration agreement between the parties and the nature of the private arbitration proceedings, but also of the legislative framework providing for such proceedings in order to determine whether the domestic courts retained some measure of control of the arbitration proceedings and whether this control has been properly exercised in the concrete case [...]').

[53] See Sect. 5.2.3.

[54] See Decision of the Swiss Federal Tribunal in case No. 4A_53/2017, 17 October 2017.

[55] See Sect. 5.2.3. The PILA does not contain any express provisions on revision, however, it has been recognized by the Federal Tribunal that provisions of the Federal Tribunal Act (FTA) on the revision of decision by the Federal Tribunal (see Article 123 FTA) apply by analogy also to arbitral awards. See Voser and George (2011).

[56] See Sect. 5.2.3.

[57] Girsberg and Voser (2016), p. 423. See also Geisinger and Mazuranic (2013), p. 257.

As seen previously in Chap. 5, also other States statutorily permitting exclusion agreements nevertheless provide certain minimum safeguards that at least partially reduce the possibility of gross procedural violations during arbitration proceedings. For example, in France, a similar action of revision is possible notwithstanding the conclusion of exclusion agreement.[58] In Sweden, parties may benefit from the continuously existing distinction between grounds of invalidity and grounds for challenge, whereby exclusion agreements will not affect the applicability of the grounds of invalidity under Section 33 of the SAA.[59] Similarly, in all of the States subject to detailed analysis in Chap. 5, ordinary jurisdiction courts may be summoned to assist arbitral tribunals and arbitrating parties with various procedural issues.

Therefore, whether the necessary *minimum safeguards* accompanying an exclusion agreement in particular circumstances are established *ex post* on a case-by-case basis, or a priori by looking solely at the relevant national legislative framework, States permitting exclusion agreements appear to nevertheless offer parties wishing to exclude setting-aside proceedings certain safety net when it comes to possible violations of their procedural rights during arbitration proceedings. Whether or not an exclusion agreement has been accompanied by certain minimum safeguards will depend on the particular factual circumstances and the underlying national legislative framework. In other cases the combination of the said two aspects could fall short of the requirement of adequate *minimum safeguards*, especially if the respective national legislative framework is very scarce in providing court assistance to arbitration proceedings, at the same time permitting exclusion agreements, or as the case may be, not providing for the possibility to challenge arbitral awards at all.

7.2.1.4 The Condition of *Public Interest*

Lastly, it is well established that a waiver to be valid for the Convention purposes must not run counter to any important *public interest*.[60] The former Commission and the ECtHR have referred to and examined this condition in many cases pertaining to the validity of an alleged waiver of the Convention's rights and freedoms,[61] including, albeit in a much more limited number of matters, also arbitration-related cases.[62] The question of whether or not a waiver of a particular right under the Convention

[58] See Sect. 5.3.3.

[59] See Sect. 5.4.2.4.

[60] See Sect. 3.5.5.

[61] See, inter alia, *Håkansson and Sturesson v. Sweden*, App. No. 11855/85, ECtHR, 21 February 1990, para. 66; *Sejdovic v. Italy*, App. No. 56581/00, ECtHR, 1 March 2006, para. 86; *Hermi v. Italy*, App. No. 18114/02, ECtHR [GC], 18 October 2006, para. 73; *Dvorski v. Croatia*, App. No. 25703/11, ECtHR, 20 October 2015, para. 100. More recently see, e.g. *Leuska and Others v. Estonia*, App. No. 64734/11, ECtHR, 7 November 2017, para. 74; *Sadkov v. Ukraine*, App. No. 21987/05, ECtHR, 6 July 2017, para. 128; *Goran Kovačević v. Croatia*, App. No. 34804/14, ECtHR, 12 April 2018, para. 70.

[62] See *Axelsson and others v. Sweden*, App. No. 11960/86, ECmHR, 13 July.

runs counter to any important public interest is inseparably linked to the concerned right and the context in which it operates.[63]

Interestingly, in the *Tabbane v. Switzerland* case the ECtHR did not explicitly address the condition that a waiver under the Convention must not run counter to any important *public interest*. The Court's analysis limited itself to addressing the requirements of *absence of constraint*, *unequivocality* and *minimum safeguards*.[64] However, after concluding that the said conditions of a valid waiver were satisfied in the particular circumstances, the ECtHR continued with examining compatibility of the possibility of excluding setting-aside proceedings under Article 192(1) of the PILA with Article 6(1) of the ECHR and the impliedly guaranteed right of access to a court. Since the applicant argued that Article 192(1) of the PILA violated his right of access to a court under Article 6(1) of the ECHR the Court's analysis did not stop with verifying fulfillment of the said pre-conditions of a valid waiver. The ECtHR continued with establishing whether the respective limitation, i.e. consequences created by an exclusion agreement under Article 192(1) of the PILA, on the right of access to a court pursued a legitimate aim and whether there was a reasonable degree of proportionality between the means employed and the aim sought to be achieved. Although not per se constituting a separate and thorough check on whether a waiver in the particular circumstances ran counter to any important *public interests*, the Court's applied test on the validity of limitation on the right of access to a court nevertheless indirectly sheds some light on aspects and interests taken into account by the Court in its conclusions.

The Court in its analysis was very concise. The Swiss legislator's desire to increase the attractiveness and effectiveness of international arbitration proceedings in Switzerland, avoidance of double-control at the seat of arbitration and at the place of enforcement, as well as decrease of the Swiss Federal Tribunal's work-load were all seen by the Court as sound legitimate aims for permitting exclusion agreements under Article 192(1) of the PILA.[65] As to proportionality, the Court emphasised party autonomy and the voluntary character of exclusion agreements under Article 192(1) of the PILA, and also the additional review by ordinary courts provided by Article 192(2) of the PILA in case the arbitral award, in respect of which an exclusion agreement is concluded, is subject to enforcement in Switzerland.[66] Regrettably, emphasis in the Court's analysis is placed solely on the interests and policy considerations served by Article 192(1) of the PILA—the Court omits any analysis to the opposite, i.e. interests and policy considerations that may possibly be against exclusion of setting-aside proceedings. The Court's failure to properly balance the two opposing ends therefore warrants a brief discussion on the interests and policy considerations behind exclusion agreements.

---

[63] Aall (2010), p. 358.

[64] *Tabbane v. Switzerland*, App. No. 41069/12, ECtHR, 1 March 2016, paras. 29–31.

[65] Ibid., para. 33. The Court recently confirmed in the *Pechstein* case that such reasons constitute a legitimate aim. See *Mutu and Pechstein v. Switzerland*, App. Nos. 40575/10 and 67474/10, 2 October 2018, para. 97.

[66] *Tabbane v. Switzerland*, App. No. 41069/12, ECtHR, 1 March 2016, paras. 34–35.

7.2.1.5 Interests and Policy Considerations in Favor of Exclusion Agreements

Reasons, or in the Court's terminology—legitimate aims, behind and seemingly in favor of the introduction of a statutory possibility to exclude setting-aside proceedings had been put forward by the Court in its analysis. The Court's invoked reasons generally correspond to the Swiss legislator's officially communicated reasons for introducing Article 192(1) of the PILA, i.e. to promote the attractiveness of international arbitration in Switzerland and assure the efficacy of dispute resolution by means of arbitration and to alleviate the Swiss Federal Tribunal of its workload.[67] With the adoption of the amendments to the BCPP in 1985 the Belgian legislator sought to achieve similar aims—to establish and promote Belgium as an attractive seat of arbitration and to exclude judicial review of arbitral awards that have no connection with Belgium. Introduction of exclusion agreements in Sweden and, more recently, also in France has been driven by similar reasons, generally aiming to establish themselves as attractive seats of arbitration.[68] Additionally, other perceived advantages of exclusion agreements include, e.g. increased finality of arbitral awards, confidentiality (i.e. absence of need to subject an arbitral award to scrutiny by public state courts), lower costs and saving of time.[69]

Putting aside the various more or less similarly tailored policy considerations behind the introduction of a possibility to limit or, as the case may be, exclude in full the available means of judicial review over arbitral awards in the respective national arbitration laws, the overarching argument in favor of exclusion agreements is the fact that arbitration is based on party autonomy, and parties should be free to determine not only the particularities of the arbitration proceedings, but also the scope of judicial review of the resulting arbitral award.[70] Arbitration is a creature of contract—it cannot exist without a prior agreement between parties to submit their controversies for final resolution before an arbitral tribunal. Party autonomy undoubtedly is the guiding principle, endorsed both by national laws and international instruments, for determining the procedure to be followed in international commercial arbitration.[71]

However, the argument of party autonomy and contractual freedom to, as the ECtHR has put, 'regulate their mutual relations as they see fit'[72] as the source of their power to exclude judicial review of arbitral awards is intrinsically linked to the more broader and theoretical discussion on the source of not only party autonomy in arbitration, but arbitration as a means of alternative dispute resolution itself.[73] The different views on the very legal basis of international commercial arbitration

[67] See Sect. 5.2.1.

[68] See Sects. 5.3.1 and 5.4.1.

[69] See Chap. 5.

[70] See, e.g. Scherer (2016), pp. 447–448. See also decision of the Swiss Federal Tribunal in case No. 4A_238/2011, 4 January 2012, para. 3.2.

[71] Redfern et al. (2004), p. 265.

[72] *Axelsson and others v. Sweden*, App. No. 11960/86, ECmHR, 13 July 1990.

[73] See Sect. 4.2.

are directly resembled also in the attitudes of States towards regulating setting-aside proceedings, including the issue of whether or not parties should be provided a possibility to exclude setting-aside proceedings.

Arbitration does not derive its legitimacy solely from party autonomy and contractual freedom, despite the fact it undoubtedly plays significant aspect. In other words, party autonomy is not unlimited. Party autonomy and the freedom to establish private justice has limits.[74] It is said that the self-sufficiency of arbitration as a system of dispute resolution may seem a realistic goal, provided the legal relationship remains within the borders of the closed circuit.[75] However, this may not always be the case. Arbitration is heavily dependent on and, at the same time, derives its legitimate force from the underlying system of law that explicitly provides for the possibility to arbitrate, regulates and also provides the necessary court support to arbitration proceedings. Arbitration is therefore characterized by a relative party autonomy that, depending on various circumstances, is limited to a greater or lesser extent both by external and also internal considerations.[76] The same is true for an argument that the power to limit or exclude the right to judicial control over an arbitral award altogether has its roots in the party autonomy. Parties' freedom to exercise their autonomy over the fate of setting-aside proceedings must be balanced against other interests and policy considerations that limit parties' autonomy to fully regulate their relations as they deem fit.[77]

7.2.1.6 Interests and Policy Considerations Against Exclusion Agreements

A discussion on the interests and policy considerations behind less permissive attitude towards unrestricted party autonomy in relation to judicial controls over arbitration proceedings, can be looked at, as Prof. Scherer has done, from two perspectives—protection of arbitrating parties' interests and the interests of third parties and the general public.[78]

First, as to the former, setting-aside proceedings generally serve to guarantee the solution of disputes in fair and just arbitration proceedings and to protect arbitrating parties from unreasonable interferences with their fundamental procedural rights. Party autonomy and freedom of contract is therefore limited by matters of fundamental law reflecting the basic values of a society, such as the right to a fair hearing and the right to an independent and impartial tribunal.[79] The majority of grounds on the basis of which an arbitral award may be set aside relate to procedural rights that are in the interests of arbitrating parties.

---

[74] Paulsson (2013), p. 105.

[75] Cordero-Moss (2015), p. 186.

[76] Ibid.

[77] Scherer (2016), pp. 448–449.

[78] Ibid.

[79] Paulsson (2013), p. 105.

If arbitration as an alternative means of dispute resolution is made available by a State, it is in the interests of that State to guarantee that the provided means are subject to certain minimum safeguards protecting the very fundamental rights of arbitrating parties. Also for the purposes of State's obligations under the ECHR the former Commission has established that State's responsibility will be certainly engaged whenever a State exercises control and guarantee as to the fairness and correctness of the arbitration proceedings through recognizing and enforcing an arbitral award.[80] Generally, States guarantee this by both (i) regulating arbitration proceedings and statutorily setting certain general requirements for arbitration proceedings, as well as providing court assistance to arbitration proceedings, on the one hand, and (ii) providing for the possibility to eventually invalidate a defective arbitral award, on the other hand. Arbitration laws of most States contain explicit provisions on, inter alia, party equality, fairness of arbitration proceedings and independence and impartiality of arbitrators. The same can be said of the availability of setting-aside proceedings—a continuously prevalent means of judicial control over arbitration proceedings and the resulting arbitral awards in most States.

Parties are generally not advised to exclude the possibility of challenging an arbitral award exactly for these reasons.[81] The automatic exclusion of setting-aside proceedings formerly in Belgium reportedly even decreased the number of arbitrations in Belgium because parties simply did not wish to exclude their possibility to attack an arbitral award at a post-award stage on grounds that are at the heart of their fundamental rights and freedoms.[82] The Swiss Federal Tribunal summarized in the *Cañas* case that exclusion of setting-aside proceedings under Article 192(1) of the PILA deprives a party from the possibility of attacking a future arbitral award, even if it violates fundamental principles pertaining to the rule of law, such as public policy, or essential procedural safeguards, such as the regular composition of the arbitral tribunal, its jurisdiction, the equality of the parties or the right of those parties to be heard in adversarial proceedings.[83] Therefore, parties should be fully aware and understand the significant consequences that exclusion of setting-aside proceedings entails for the protection of their fundamental interests.

As to the latter perspective, i.e. interests of third parties and the general public, judicial review by means of setting-aside proceedings acts as also as a guardian for the protection of interests of third parties and those of the public. States have an equal interest to limit party autonomy and contractual freedom due to considerations of

---

[80] *Jakob Boss Söhn KG v. the Federal Republic of Germany*, App. No. 18479/91, ECmHR, 2 December 1991 ('This does not mean, however, that the respondent State's responsibility is completely excluded […] as the arbitration award had to be recognised by […] courts and be given executory effect by them. The courts thereby exercised a certain control and guarantee as to the fairness and correctness of the arbitration proceedings which they considered to have been carried out in conformity with fundamental rights and in particular with the right of the applicant company to be heard.'). See also *Firma Heinz Schiebler KG v. the Federal Republic of Germany*, App. No. 18805/91, ECmHR, 2 December 1991.

[81] See, e.g. Sect. 5.2.3 for Switzerland, Sect. 5.5.3 for Belgium and Sect. 5.4.3 for Sweden.

[82] See Sect. 6.2.

[83] Decision of the Swiss Federal Tribunal in case No. ATF 133 III 235, 22 March 2007, para. 4.3.2.2.

public policy and the need to protect third parties. On a practical level, the protection of the interests of third parties and the general public may only be reflected in the minority of grounds of review, i.e. the non-arbitrability and public policy exceptions.[84] Generally, States have an *ex officio* right to set aside an arbitral award if the subject-matter of arbitration proceedings is considered by the relevant State as non-arbitrable due to considerations of third parties, public rights or governmental authority.[85] Similarly, as seen, States have an *ex officio* right to invalidate an arbitral award on the basis of public policy considerations if the arbitral award entails a gross violation of that State's, or as the case may be if the State is an EU Member State—also the EU's, most fundamental principles.[86]

It is argued that the importance of the need to protect the interests of third parties and those of the public by means of setting-aside proceedings is somewhat diminished due to the fact that States permitting exclusion agreements still exercise certain control over arbitration (including issues of arbitrability and public policy) if the respective arbitral award is recognized and enforced in that State.[87] A State permitting exclusion agreements will nevertheless verify compatibility of the arbitral award with the interests of third parties and those of the public if the arbitral award is submitted for recognition and enforcement in that State. However, in case recognition and enforcement is sought in another State, the arbitral seat simply shifts the required check to the State of enforcement.

The issue of whether or not, in addition to recognition and enforcement proceedings, judicial control is also required by setting-aside proceedings at the arbitral seat boils down to the difference between the two set of judicial proceedings.[88] Generally, a court's judgment on the validity of an arbitral award has an *erga omnes* effect—if an arbitral award is set aside at the arbitral seat it will be barred from recognition and enforcement in other States.[89] A court's judgment on the recognition and enforcement of an arbitral award, on the other hand, has no such *erga omnes* effect—if refused, parties may seek recognition and enforcement of an arbitral award in other States.[90] Lack of setting-aside proceedings in national arbitration law therefore creates imbalance between arbitrating parties—while the winning party may seek recognition and enforcement of allegedly defective arbitral award in as many States it wishes, the losing party is stripped of its right to defend against a defective arbitral award, independently of the other party's intentions to recognize and enforce the arbitral award. Lack of a possibility to invalidate a defective arbitral award at the seat of arbitration

[84] Scherer (2016), p. 452.

[85] See Sect. 4.4.1.5.

[86] See Sect. 4.4.1.6.

[87] Scherer (2016), p. 452. As seen, art. 192(2) of the PILA and, e.g. its counterpart in French law—art. 1522(2) of the FCCP, provide that arbitral awards, in respect of which an exclusion agreement is concluded, are still subject to review by courts at the recognition and enforcement stage if so requested by parties in that state.

[88] Ibid.

[89] Art. V(1)(e) of the New York Convention.

[90] See, e.g. Van den Berg (2010), p. 182.

becomes particularly problematic in cases where the arbitral tribunal issues a declaratory award or an award dismissing all claims. The aggrieved party that believes that its rights to a fair hearing or to an independent and impartial tribunal have been violated by such an award, has no effective remedy since there is nothing to be subjected to exequatur procedure.

Another aspect at the heart of the necessity to have setting-aside proceedings at the seat of arbitration, at least within the borders of the EU, relates to the obligation of EU Member States to guarantee the full effectiveness of EU law. Questions on the interpretation of EU law should be open to examination by national courts during the setting-aside proceedings and, if needed, it should be possible for those questions to be referred to the CJEU for a preliminary ruling.[91] As explained by AG Wathelet in his opinion in the *Genentech* case, overturning the French *minimalist* approach to review of arbitral awards:

> [L]imitations on the scope of the review of international arbitral awards such as those under French law […] namely the flagrant nature of the infringement of international public policy and the impossibility of reviewing an international arbitral award on the ground of such an infringement where the question of public policy was raised and debated before the arbitral tribunal — are contrary to the principle of effectiveness of EU law.
>
> Referring to the system for reviewing the compatibility of international arbitral awards with EU law through the public policy reservation, as established by the Court in its judgment in Eco Swiss […] — which concerned, as in this case, an action for annulment of an international arbitral award based on an infringement of public policy and was confirmed by the judgment in Gazprom […], involving an application for the recognition and enforcement of an international arbitral award disputed on public policy grounds — the Court has held that arbitral tribunals 'constituted pursuant to an agreement' are not courts of the Member States within the meaning of Article 267 TFEU. Consequently, they cannot refer questions for a preliminary ruling. It is therefore for the courts of the Member States, within the meaning of Article 267 TFEU, to examine, if necessary by referring a question for a preliminary ruling, the compatibility of (international or domestic) arbitral awards with EU law where an action is brought before them for annulment or enforcement, or where any other form of action or review is sought under the relevant national legislation.
>
> [T]he responsibility for reviewing compliance with European public policy rules lies with the courts of the Member States and not with arbitrators, whether in the context of an action for annulment or proceedings for recognition and enforcement.[92]

EU Member States' courts therefore have an obligation to verify the compatibility of arbitral awards with EU Law. If an EU Member State permits exclusion of setting-aside proceedings, it in effect waives its obligation to guarantee full effectiveness of EU law. This may cause particular difficulties if the recognition and enforcement of an arbitral award that is incompatible with EU law is sought in a third country—in such a case the courts of EU Member States are not involved and the effectiveness

---

[91] Opinion of AG Jääskinen in Case C-352/13 *Cartel Damage Claims (CDC) Hydrogen Peroxide SA v Evonik Degussa GmbH and Others*, CJEU, 11 December 2014, para. 123.

[92] Opinion of AG Wathelet in Case C-567/14 *Genentech Inc. v Hoechst GmbH and Sanofi-Aventis Deutschland GmbH*, CJEU, 17 March 2016, paras. 58–61.

of EU law cannot be guaranteed, e.g. by requesting the CJEU to give a preliminary ruling on point of EU law.[93]

7.2.1.7 Balancing of Interests and Interim Conclusion

Regrettably, the ECtHR in its *Tabbane v. Switzerland* decision fails to properly counter-balance the different interests behind the availability of the annulment mechanism at the arbitral seat. In fact, the ECtHR even fails to explicitly address the requirement that a valid waiver for the Convention purposes must not run counter to any important public interests. The Court only refers to several seemingly *legitimate aims* in favor of policy permitting exclusion agreements as communicated also by the Swiss legislator. However, the Court's referred to *legitimate aims* are not genuinely balanced against the interests that setting-aside proceedings actually serve, both from the perspective of arbitrating parties and those of the seat of arbitration.

As seen, whether or not the aims of Article 192(1) of the PILA are indeed achieved in practice is subject to debate.[94] The former Belgian example evidences that parties do not view a seat of arbitration as more attractive and effective simply because it excludes (or provides a possibility thereto) the right to challenge an arbitral award before State courts. On the opposite—parties shied away from Belgium as a seat of arbitration due to this exact reason, i.e. that setting-aside proceedings were excluded automatically.[95] Nevertheless, despite this empirical evidence, the ECtHR has recently confirmed in the *Pechstein* case that a legislative policy aimed at increasing the attractiveness and effectiveness of international arbitration could constitute a legitimate aim.[96] At the same time, the *Tabbane v. Switzerland* decision provides very limited analysis on the aspect of proportionality, failing to genuinely weigh the *legitimate aims* behind introducing Article 192(1) of the PILA, on the one hand, and the broader interests of arbitrating parties, third parties and the general public in having the possibility to apply for the setting aside of arbitral awards.

As seen, the Latvian Constitutional Court's *Hiponia* case was characterized by a similar scenario, whereby the Latvian Constitutional Court had to weigh the proportionality between the *legitimate aims* as put forward by the Latvian legislator and the fundamental right of access to a court of arbitrating parties in order to challenge the validity of an arbitration agreement.[97] Similarly to the *Tabbane v. Switzerland* case, also in the *Hiponia* case the Latvian legislator invoked an argument of increased court work-load, however, the Latvian Constitutional Court held that the increase of court workload per se cannot justify restrictions on a person's right of access to a court to the extent that the very essence of such a right would be impaired. When interests of

[93] See, e.g. Opinion of AG Wathelet in Case C-284/16 *Slowakische Republik v Achmea BV*, CJEU, 19 September 2017, para. 251.

[94] See Sect. 5.2.3.

[95] See Sect. 6.2.

[96] *Mutu and Pechstein v. Switzerland*, App. Nos. 40575/10 and 67474/10, 2 October 2018, para. 97.

[97] See Sect. 6.5.1.4.

increased procedural efficiency of national courts collide with the need to guarantee protection of persons' fundamental rights, the latter, in the Latvian Constitutional Court's opinion, must be given precedence. The *Tabbane v. Switzerland* decision, however, suggests that seemingly economic aims of the seat of arbitration prevail over arbitrating parties' restrictions on the right of access to a court under Article 6(1) of the ECHR. Considering the lack of explicit weighing of interests by the Court and doubts surrounding the fulfillment of the formal requirements of a valid waiver for the Convention purposes, such a conclusion is certainly subject to debate.

To preliminary conclude, the above analysis evidences that that the faith of exclusion agreements is not set in stone. Not only the ECtHR's decision in the *Tabbane v. Switzerland* case itself somewhat fails to genuinely weigh the pros and cons behind a legislative policy of permitting exclusion agreements, but the different conditions of a valid waiver for the Convention purposes certainly suggest that exclusion agreements in other circumstances may lead to a violation of the Convention's rights and freedoms. The extent to which a voluntary exclusion of setting-aside proceedings may lead to a violation of the procedural human rights guarantees enshrined in the ECHR, at least from the perspective of the various conditions of a valid waiver under the Convention, will therefore depend on the particular circumstances of the case. The *Pechstein* case suggests that, provided Article 192(1) of the PILA was at stake, exclusion agreement by a weaker party would not satisfy the requirements of *absence of constraint* and *unequivocality*.[98] In other circumstances, e.g. whereby the relevant national arbitration law lacks provisions on sufficient court support to arbitration proceedings, exclusion agreement may be considered as not accompanied by certain *minimum safeguards*.

The *Tabbane v. Switzerland* case equally fails to take into account the Court's own established difference between *waivable* and *non-waivable* rights of Article 6(1) of the ECHR. If certain rights of Article 6(1) of the ECHR are so fundamentally important for the fair administration of justice in a democratic society that no individual should be deprived of their benefit, is a full advance waiver of all annulment grounds of arbitral awards even compatible with this very basic notion underlying the Convention?

7.2.2 *Permissibility of Exclusion Agreements—*Non-waivable *Rights of Article 6(1) of the ECHR and Their Relation to Setting-Aside Proceedings*

The issue of *permissibility* of a waiver and the difference between *waivable* and *non-waivable* rights under Article 6(1) of the ECHR was addressed in Chap. 3.[99] As

[98] *Mutu and Pechstein v. Switzerland*, App. Nos. 40575/10 and 67474/10, 2 October 2018, paras. 103–115.

[99] See Sect. 3.4.3.

regards the different rights of the Convention, the ECtHR held in the *Albert and Le Compte* case that 'the nature of some of the rights safeguarded by the Convention is such as to exclude a waiver of the entitlement to exercise them […] but the same cannot be said of certain other rights.'[100] By now the *non-waivability* of certain Convention rights and freedoms has been generally established and confirmed—when examining whether or not a person in particular circumstances has made a waiver of otherwise applicable Convention right or freedom, the ECtHR often refers to the 'insofar as it is permissible' pre-condition.[101] This book's particular focus relates not to the somewhat broader question of *non-waivability* of different rights of the Convention, but to the much narrower question of potential *non-waivability* of certain rights under Article 6(1) of the ECHR and their interrelation with arbitration and, in particular, the setting-aside mechanism.

It has become evident that it is permissible to waive certain rights of Article 6(1) of the ECHR, provided such a waiver satisfies the various conditions of a valid waiver for the Convention purposes. These rights include, e.g. the right to bring a dispute before an ordinary court, the right to a public hearing and the right to obtain a decision within a reasonable time. However, the answer is not as straightforward with regard to other rights of Article 6(1) of the ECHR, in particular, the right to an independent and impartial tribunal and the right to a fair hearing. The ECtHR has repeatedly stressed that the signing of an arbitration agreement amounts legally only to a *partial* waiver or a waiver of only *certain* rights guaranteed by Article 6(1) of the ECHR. The ECtHR's decision in the *Tabbane v. Switzerland* case,[102] as well as the recent ECtHR decision in the *Pechstein* case, confirms such an interpretation:

> […] Article 6 of the Convention does not preclude the establishment of arbitral tribunals to try certain disputes of a financial nature between individuals […], contractual arbitration agreements present undeniable advantages for the individuals concerned as well as for the administration of justice […] Parties to a dispute may waive *certain* rights guaranteed by Article 6(1) provided such a waiver is free, lawful and unequivocal [emphasis added]. In the opposite case, an arbitral tribunal must offer the guarantees provided for in Article 6(1) of the Convention […][103]

---

[100] *Albert and Le Compte v. Belgium*, Apps. No. 7299/75 and 7496/76, ECtHR, 10 February 1983, para. 35 in referring to the Belgian vagrancy cases, i.e. *De Wilde, Ooms and Versyp ('Vagrancy') v. Belgium*, App. Nos. 2832/66, 2835/66; 2899/66, ECtHR, 18 June 1971, para. 65.

[101] See, among others, *Oberschlick v. Austria*, App. No. 11662/85, ECtHR, 23 May 1991, para. 51; *Pfeiffer and Plankl v. Austria*, App. No. 10802/84, ECtHR, 25 February 1992, para. 37; *Frommelt v. Liechtenstein*, App. No. 49158/99, ECtHR, 24 June 2004, para. 33; *Galstyan v. Armenia*, App. No. 26986/03, ECtHR, 15 February 2008, para. 90; *Zakshevskiy v. Ukraine*, App. No. 7193/04, ECtHR, 17 June 2016, para. 112; *Rostovtsev v. Ukraine*, App. No. 2728/12, ECtHR, 25 October 2017, para. 29.

[102] *Tabbane v. Switzerland*, App. No. 41069/12, ECtHR, 1 March 2016, para. 27 ('En souscrivant à une clause d'arbitrage, les parties renoncent volontairement à certains droits garantis par la Convention.').

[103] *Mutu and Pechstein v. Switzerland*, App. Nos. 40575/10 and 67474/10, 2 October 2018, para. 145 ('l'article 6 de la Convention ne s'oppose pas à ce que des tribunaux arbitraux soient créés afin de juger certains différends de nature patrimoniale opposant des […], les clauses contractuelles d'arbitrage présentant pour les intéressés comme pour l'administration de la justice des avantages indéniables […] Les parties à un litige peuvent renoncer à certains droits garantis par l'article 6

Nevertheless, as has become equally evident, the ECtHR has generally limited its guidance on the issue by simply referring to the *permissibility* of a *partial* waiver or waiver of only *certain* rights of Article 6(1) of the ECHR when concluding an arbitration agreement and has not given a clear-cut answer which Article 6(1) of the ECHR rights are considered *non-waivable*. As noted, the ECtHR explicitly recognized the narrower distinction between the different rights of Article 6(1) of the ECHR in the *Suovaniemi* case:

> There is no doubt that a voluntary waiver of court proceedings in favour of arbitration is in principle acceptable from the point of view of Article 6 […] Even so, such a waiver should not necessarily be considered to amount to a waiver of all the rights under Article 6 […] [A]n unequivocal waiver of Convention rights is valid only insofar as such waiver is 'permissible'. Waiver may be permissible with regard to certain rights but not with regard to certain others. A distinction may have to be made even between different rights guaranteed by Article 6.[104]

The ECtHR's analysis and conclusions in the *Suovaniemi* case suggest that it is *permissible* to waive the right to an independent and impartial tribunal *ex post*, i.e. after one became aware of the potential irregularity and did not object to it. This corresponds to the requirement that a waiver can only be valid for the Convention purposes if a person is fully aware of the respective right he or she waives. Also legal doctrine reflects consensus that parties may waive every right under Article 6(1) of the ECHR *after* a violation of such a right has occurred.[105] Conversely, a waiver before the fact is only permissible with regard to the *waivable* rights of Article 6(1) of the ECHR.

When concluding a contract containing an exclusion agreement, parties not only are not aware of any possible future disputes associated with their relationship, but even more so—have no knowledge whatsoever of possible irregularities in the potential future arbitration proceedings that may violate their fundamental procedural rights. If a waiver of *non-waivable* Article 6(1) of the ECHR rights is permissible only *ex post*, it is arguable that parties should not be permitted to fully exclude in advance the possibility to challenge an arbitral award before State courts on grounds that pertain to the *non-waivable* rights of Article 6(1) of the ECHR, i.e. the independence and impartiality of an arbitral tribunal and the right to a fair hearing.

The ECtHR is not unambiguously clear on the exact difference between *waivable* and *non-waivable* rights of Article 6(1) of the ECHR. It is neither unambiguously clear that it is permissible (or impermissible) for the Convention purposes to waive in advance certain guarantees that have been considered as *non-waivable* rights of Article 6(1) of the ECHR, i.e. the right to an independent and impartial tribunal and the right to a fair hearing. This normative vacuum, considered together with the available principles established by the Convention's controlling bodies in this regard, therefore makes it possible to argue that an advance exclusion of all grounds for

§ 1 pour autant que cette renonciation est libre, licite et sans équivoque. Dans le cas contraire, le tribunal arbitral doit offrir les garanties prévues par l'article 6 § 1 de la Convention […]'). Author's translation.

[104] *Suovaniemi and others v. Finland*, App. No. 31737/96, ECtHR, 23 February 1999.

[105] See, e.g. Landrove (2006), pp. 84–89, Benedettelli (2015), p. 646.

setting aside an arbitral award is incompatible with Article 6(1) of the ECHR, insofar parties are precluded from challenging the arbitral award on grounds pertaining to the *non-waivable* rights of Article 6(1) of the ECHR.

The timing of a waiver is of paramount importance for determining the extent to which the exclusion of setting-aside mechanism may lead to a violation of Article 6(1) of the ECHR, at least from the perspective of *non-waivable* Article 6(1) of the ECHR rights. Parties should not be able to fully exclude in advance all grounds for challenging an arbitral award without being aware of the exact repercussions of such an exclusion. As seen,[106] this concern underlies the German approach to permitting exclusion agreements and differentiating between *waivable* grounds for challenge and *non-waivable* grounds for challenge. Parties are permitted to exclude the *waivable* grounds for challenge, i.e. those considered to be in their interests, however only *ex post*.[107]

Whether or not the German solution provides a healthy compromise between the needs of party autonomy and the interests (and also obligations under the ECHR) of States to maintain a review mechanism of possibly defective awards violating parties' *non-waivable* rights under Article 6(1) of the ECHR will be addressed below when concluding the findings. Next, the author would like to briefly focus on each of the procedural guarantees considered to possess the character of *non-waivable* rights under Article 6(1) of the ECHR and seek for arguments that support their alleged *non-waivable* character and thus also the impossibility to waive such rights *ex ante* at the time of concluding an advance exclusion agreement of setting-aside proceedings.

7.2.2.1 Independence and Impartiality

The principle that arbitrators shall be independent and impartial is recognized in the UNCITRAL Model Law,[108] most national arbitration laws (both those implementing the UNCITRAL Model Law[109] and those that are not considered to be based on the

---

[106] See Sect. 5.6.3.

[107] Ibid.

[108] Arts. 11(5) and 12 of the UNCITRAL Model Law.

[109] See, e.g. art. 17(1) of the 2003 Spanish Arbitration Act ('An arbitrator shall be and remain independent and impartial during the arbitration. In no case shall he maintain any personal, professional or commercial relationship with any of the parties.'); art. 1174(1) of the Polish Code of Civil Procedure ('A person appointed to serve an arbitrator shall immediately disclose to the parties any circumstances which might raise doubts as to his or her impartiality or independence.'); art. 13 of the Norwegian Arbitration Act ('The arbitrators shall be impartial and independent of the parties, and shall be qualified for such office.'); art. 8(1) of the 2012 Lithuanian Law on Commercial Arbitration ('The arbitral tribunal, permanent arbitral institution and its chairman shall be independent while resolving the issues regulated in this Law.'). See also, e.g. sec. 11 of the Hungarian Law on Arbitration; sec. 1036(1) of the ZPO; sec. 12(1) of the 2005 Danish Arbitration Act and other arbitration laws.

UNCITRAL Model Law[110]), and also institutional arbitration rules.[111] Therefore, there is no doubt that the independence and impartiality of arbitrators is a necessary requirement that must be adhered to during all stages of arbitration proceedings. As such, it constitutes a fundamental and indispensable principle of every arbitration[112] and, as will shortly be provided below, is even considered to be part of (transnational) procedural public policy.

The possibility to challenge an arbitral award on the basis of lack of independence and/or impartiality of the arbitral tribunal is not *expressis verbis* provided for under the UNCITRAL Model Law. In fact, only a handful of States explicitly include such an annulment ground in their national arbitration laws.[113] Annulment grounds under the UNCITRAL Model Law were inspired from and those of Article V of the New York Convention, therefore unsurprisingly the lack of independence and impartiality is neither expressly provided as a ground for refusing recognition and enforcement of arbitral awards under Article V of the New York Convention. This, however, does not mean that an arbitral award cannot be challenged or refused recognition and enforcement on the basis of lack of independence and impartiality of the arbitral tribunal.

Despite an express basis, the requirements of independent and impartial tribunal can be impliedly read into the text of other, seemingly universally accepted annulment grounds (and also grounds for refusing recognition and enforcement under the New York Convention). These include, e.g. Article 34(2)(a)(ii) of the UNCITRAL Model Law and Article V(1)(b) of the New York Convention—party's inability to present its case; Article 34(2)(a)(iv) of the UNCITRAL Model Law and Article V(1)(d) of the New York Convention—irregular composition of an arbitral tribunal; or even Article

[110]See, e.g. sec. 8 of the SAA ('An arbitrator shall be impartial.'); art. 1456(2) of the FCCP; sec. 9(1) of the Finnish Arbitration Act; secs 1(a) and 33(1) of the 1996 English Arbitration Act; art. 1033 of the 2015 Dutch Arbitration Act; art. 14(5) of the Latvian 2015 Arbitration Law and many others.

[111]See, e.g. art. 11(1) of the 2017 ICC Arbitration Rules ('Every arbitrator must be and remain impartial and independent of the parties involved in the arbitration.'); art. 18 of the 2017 SCC Arbitration Rules ('Every arbitrator must be impartial and independent.'); art. 5(3) of the 2014 LCIA Arbitration Rules ('All arbitrators shall be and remain at all times impartial and independent of the parties; and none shall act in the arbitration as advocate for or representative of any party. No arbitrator shall advise any party on the parties' dispute or the outcome of the arbitration.'); art. 24 of the 2015 CIETAC Arbitration Rules ('An arbitrator shall not represent either party, and shall be and remain independent of the parties and treat them equally.'); art. 13(1) of the 2016 SIAC Arbitration Rules; art. 9 of the 2018 DIS Arbitration Rules ('Every arbitrator shall be impartial and independent of the parties throughout the entire arbitration […]'); art. 11(1) of the 2013 HKIAC Administered Arbitration Rules ('An arbitral tribunal confirmed under these Rules shall be and remain at all times impartial and independent of the parties.') and many others.

[112]See, e.g. Van den Berg (2014), p. 377. Generally on the principle of independence and impartially of the arbitral tribunal in arbitration proceedings see, e.g. Born (2014), pp. 1760–1911.

[113]Setting-aside of an arbitral award on the basis of arbitrator's lack of independence and impartiality is explicitly provided for in, e.g. England (sec. 68(2)(a) of the 1996 English Arbitration Act); Finland (sec. 41(1)(3) of the 1999 Finnish Arbitration Act); Iceland (art. 12(2) of the Icelandic Act on Contractual Arbitration); Italy (art. 829(2) of the Italian Code of Civil Procedure); and Sweden (sec. 34(5) of the SAA).

34(2)(b)(ii) of the UNCITRAL Model Law and Article V(2)(b) of the New York Convention—violation of (procedural) public policy. It is not therefore disputed that the lack of independence and/or impartiality is generally considered as a valid basis for both the annulment and also refusal of recognition and enforcement of an arbitral award.[114] The question, however, is whether, from the standpoint of the Convention, it is permissible for arbitrating parties to exclude in advance setting-aside proceedings, to the extent that it is impossible to challenge an arbitral award on the basis of lack of independence and/or impartiality of the arbitral tribunal. Before considering express and implied indications in this regard, as developed by the Convention's controlling bodies, one must briefly stress such right's character as a principle of (transnational) procedural public policy.

Independence and Impartiality as a Principle of (Transnational) Procedural Public Policy

A party may challenge an arbitral award on grounds of lack of independence and impartiality of an arbitral tribunal also by availing itself to the much broader ground of public policy. As regards the New York Convention, it has been said that nothing in Article V prevents a party from raising an argument under Article V(2)(b) if the same argument could have been raised under any of the grounds of Article V(1)—parties should be free to argue that their procedural rights have been violated on the basis of the public policy exception.[115] The same reasoning should apply *mutatis mutandis* to the annulment mechanism.

Public policy, at least when considered from the perspective of setting-aside proceedings or a State's right to refuse recognition and enforcement of an arbitral award under the New York Convention, entails two aspects—substantive and procedural. The substantive aspect is concerned with the merits of an arbitral award,

---

[114]See, e.g. Born (2014), pp. 3277–3278 in referring to many national courts and commentators who have concluded the same way.

[115]United Nations Commission on International Trade Law (2016) UNCITRAL Secretariat Guide on the Convention on the Recognition and Enforcement of Foreign Arbitral Awards (New York, 1958), 2016 Edition, pp. 255–256. http://www.uncitral.org/pdf/english/texts/arbitration/NY-conv/2016_Guide_on_the_Convention.pdf. Accessed 29 May 2020 ('Indeed, nothing in article V prevents a party from putting forward an argument under article V (2)(b) that could also properly be brought under one of the grounds of article V(1). To the contrary, there is some support in the *travaux préparatoires* for the proposition that parties wishing to argue that their procedural rights had been violated should be free do so on the basis of a violation of public policy.').

while the procedural one with how an arbitral tribunal reached the decision.[116] As summarized by the Swiss Federal Tribunal:

> [t]here is a difference between substantive and procedural public policy […] procedural public policy guarantees parties the right to an independent judgment on their submissions and the facts submitted to the arbitral tribunal, in accordance with the applicable procedural law; substantive public policy is breached when fundamental and generally recognized principles are breached, leading to an untenable contradiction with the notion of justice, so that the decision appears incompatible with the values recognized in a state governed by the rule of law.[117]

By now it has been generally established that the requirement that an arbitral tribunal is independent and impartial throughout the arbitration proceedings pertains to the latter, i.e. the principle of procedural public policy.[118] The International Law Association (ILA) in its Final Report on public policy as a bar to enforcement of international arbitral awards has explicitly recognized that the independence and impartiality of arbitrators is an issue of procedural public policy.[119] The importance of independence and impartiality of adjudicators, in the present case—arbitrators, as a fundamental value common to all civilized nations governed by the rule of law is therefore not disputed. It is even argued that the independence and impartiality of arbitrators pertains to a transnational procedural public policy, i.e. those universal standards and accepted norms of conduct that represent an international consensus and must therefore always apply irrespective of the localization of arbitration proceedings.[120]

---

[116]Mantilla-Serrano (2005), p. 166. Generally on the 'substantive' and 'procedural' aspects of public policy see, e.g. United Nations Commission on International Trade Law (2016) UNCITRAL Secretariat Guide on the Convention on the Recognition and Enforcement of Foreign Arbitral Awards (New York, 1958), 2016 Edition, pp. 247–256. http://www.uncitral.org/pdf/english/texts/arbitration/NY-conv/2016_Guide_on_the_Convention.pdf. Accessed 29 May 2020, Rubino-Sammartano (2001), pp. 507–531, Bray et al. (2014), pp. 9–49, Kaufmann-Kohler and Rigozzi (2015), pp. 489–501.

[117]United Nations Commission on International Trade Law (2016) UNCITRAL Secretariat Guide on the Convention on the Recognition and Enforcement of Foreign Arbitral Awards (New York, 1958), 2016 Edition, p. 247. http://www.uncitral.org/pdf/english/texts/arbitration/NY-conv/2016_Guide_on_the_Convention.pdf. Accessed 29 May 2020.

[118]See, e.g. United Nations Commission on International Trade Law (2016) UNCITRAL Secretariat Guide on the Convention on the Recognition and Enforcement of Foreign Arbitral Awards (New York, 1958), 2016 Edition, pp. 252–254. http://www.uncitral.org/pdf/english/texts/arbitration/NY-conv/2016_Guide_on_the_Convention.pdf. Accessed 29 May 2020) and cases cited therein. See also Luttrell (2009), p. 13.

[119]See recommendation 1(e) of the Final Report on public policy as a bar to enforcement of international arbitral awards, International Law Association (ILA), Committee on International Commercial Arbitration, ILA New Delhi Conference, 2002 (reported in Mayer and Sheppard (2003), pp. 249–263).

[120]On the independence and impartiality of arbitrators as part of transnational procedural public policy see Mantilla-Serrano (2005). See also Conde e Silva GJ (2007) Transnational Public Policy in International Arbitration, PhD thesis, pp. 183 and 193–197. Queen Mary Collage, University of London. Generally on the notion of transnational public policy see, e.g. Lalive (1987), pp. 258–318, Kessedjian (2007), pp. 857–870, Sheppard (2004), p. 3 defining transnational public policy

Whether the principle of independence and impartiality in international arbitration is considered as pertaining to national, international or transnational (truly international) public policy, the said right's categorization as such evidences that, contrary to certain *waivable* rights within the meaning of Article 6(1) of the ECHR, the right to an independent and impartial tribunal, at least in the context of international arbitration, is viewed as somewhat more superior and perceived as a fundamental and universal standard common to all civilized nations that are governed by the rule of law and permit arbitration as a means of alternative dispute resolution. Therefore, the undeniable fact that the violation of the right to an independent and impartial tribunal is perceived as a violation of, depending on one's perception, national, international or transnational procedural public policy, certainly supports an argument in favor of the right to an independent and impartial tribunal under Article 6(1) of the ECHR being considered as generally *non-waivable*.

Non-waivability of the Right to an Independent and Impartial Tribunal Under Article 6(1) of the ECHR

When the right to an independent and impartial tribunal is considered from the perspective of Article 6(1) of the ECHR and the Court's own analysis, it is equally arguable that such a right is *non-waivable* within the meaning of Article 6(1) of the ECHR and that parties, by excluding in advance and in full the right to challenge an arbitral award, should not be precluded from nevertheless challenging an arbitral award on grounds of lack of independence and/or impartiality of an arbitral tribunal. In other words, exclusion of all grounds for challenging an arbitral award should be permissible only *ex post*, i.e. after the relevant violation became known to the parties. This is due to the reason that the right to an independent and impartial tribunal within the meaning of Article 6(1) of the ECHR serves a 'wider purpose in the society than to protect the rights of the parties to any given dispute [...] and those values should be protected regardless of the intentions of the parties to any given dispute, because they are part of (procedural) public policy.'[121] Or to put it in the words of another legal scholar:

> [T]he idea that parties to an arbitration agreement should be presumed having waived all the due process guarantees set out by Article 6.1. ECHR must be rejected as being at odds with the importance that the principle of fair trial is granted by most contemporary laws of arbitration.[122]

---

as '[...] those principles that represent an international consensus as to universal standards and accepted norms of conduct that must always apply. The concept of "transnational public policy", is said to comprise fundamental rules of natural law, principles of universal justice, *jus cogens* in public international law, and the general principles of morality accepted by what are referred to as "civilized nations".'

[121] Petrochilos (2004), p. 122.

[122] Benedettelli (2015), pp. 646–647.

The author, similarly to Petrochilos, does not argue that the right to an independent and impartial tribunal should be absolute and under no circumstances be subject to a waiver by the arbitrating parties.[123] This line of reasoning has been supported also by the ECtHR in the *Suovaniemi* case whereby it considered an *ex post* waiver of the right to an independent and impartial tribunal valid for the Convention purposes. However, it equally follows from the same ECtHR's reasoning in the *Suovaniemi* case that *ex ante* waiver of the right to an independent and impartial tribunal under Article 6(1) of the ECHR is not *permissible.* This conclusion is supported by the following considerations.

The Court-Made Notion of Permissibility

The existence per se of the Court-made notion of *permissibility* applied in the context of waiver of rights under the Convention, primarily adds to the credibility of the conclusion that it is not *permissible* for the Convention purposes to waive the right to an independent and impartial tribunal, at least not *ex ante*, i.e. before the person waiving such a right became fully aware of the rights subject to a waiver and the significant consequences that such a waiver entails for the protection of such person's fundamental interests.

As seen, the *insofar it is permissible* requirement in relation to a waiver of Convention rights and freedoms has been applied by the Court not only when distinguishing between the different rights under the Convention, but, more specifically, also under Article 6(1) of the ECHR.[124] The leading authority confirming this is the ECtHR's decision in the *Suovaniemi* case.[125] The different rights of Article 6(1) of the ECHR are therefore divided into those rights with regard to which a waiver may be *permissible* and those with regard to which a waiver is not *permissible.* The Court has explicitly recognized that the right to access to a court of the *classic* kind, the right to a public hearing and the right to obtain a decision within a reasonable time fall under the former. The latter category of the civil limb of Article 6(1) of the ECHR is therefore not left with many other rights but for the right to an independent and impartial tribunal (and also the right to a fair hearing). The Court's hypothetical question as to 'whether the fundamental right to an impartial judge can be waived at all'[126] and the fact that to date there is no case-law of the Court that would suggest the opposite, strengthens the premise that the right to an independent and impartial tribunal is generally *non-waivable.* At the same time, the Court's final conclusion in the *Suovaniemi* case also suggests that *ex post* waiver of the right to an independent and impartial tribunal is *permissible* for the Convention purposes and is not seen as incompatible with Article 6(1) of the ECHR. If put in the context of exclusion agreements, this would translate into a hypothesis that parties may exclude the possibility

[123] Petrochilos (2004), pp. 122–123.

[124] See Sect. 3.4.3.

[125] *Suovaniemi and others v. Finland*, App. No. 31737/96, ECtHR, 23 February 1999.

[126] Ibid.

to challenge an arbitral award on the basis of lack of independence and impartiality of arbitral tribunal, but only *ex post*.

Arbitration Agreement—A Partial Waiver or a Waiver of Only Certain Rights of Article 6(1) of the ECHR

Closely linked with the issue of *permissibility*, the generally *non-waivable* character of the right to an independent and impartial tribunal is equally supported by the Court's often made reference to a *partial* waiver or waiver of only *certain* rights of Article 6(1) of the ECHR in case parties conclude an arbitration agreement. As seen, this was firmly established by the Court already in the first arbitration-related case before it—the case of *X. v. the Federal Republic of Germany*, and since then has been affirmed in almost every arbitration-related case, including the recent *Pechstein* case.[127]

Again, to date the Court has not answered *in concreto* which are those *certain* rights of Article 6(1) of the ECHR that parties are deemed to have waived when concluding an arbitration agreement and those that they have not. However, the Court's often-made reference to only *certain* rights per se, taken together with the notion of *permissibility*, confirms that not all rights of Article 6(1) of the ECHR are automatically excluded from application upon signing an arbitration agreement. Considering the much more certain answer as to the *waivable* rights of Article 6(1) of the ECHR and the somewhat more significant character of the right to an independent and impartial tribunal in a democratic society, it can be reasonably argued that such a right falls outside the category of *certain* rights that parties are deemed to have waived when concluding an arbitration agreement. As recognized, '[i]t certainly cannot be assumed that when parties agree on arbitration as a means of dispute settlement they thereby waive any requirement as to the impartiality and/or independence of the arbitrators.'[128]

Verification of Violation Irrespective of a Waiver

The *non-waivable* character of the right to an independent and impartial tribunal within the meaning of Article 6(1) of the ECHR additionally finds support in the ECtHR's case-law, recognizing that regardless of whether or not parties have waived the right to an independent and impartial tribunal, the ECtHR will examine the issue

[127] See Sect. 3.4.2.

[128] Briner and Von Schlabrendorff (2001), p. 94. A former ECtHR judge Ann Power-Forde has similarly concluded that '[i]n view of their importance for public confidence in the judicial system, it is unlikely that the requirements of independence and impartiality can be waived. The Court considers itself bound to examine the impartiality of the tribunal irrespective of any alleged waiver by the applicant.' See Power A (2012) *Judicial* Independence and the Democratic Process: Some Case Law of the European Court of Human Rights, p. 14. International Bar Association Conference 2012. https://www.ibanet.org/Document/Default.aspx?DocumentUid=F0C95268-A24E-40CE-B0CC-45A531B552D9. Accessed 29 May 2020.

of independence and impartiality on its own motion. Therefore, in effect, generally a waiver of the right to an independent and impartial tribunal is *non-waivable* and the ECtHR will examine the issue of independence and impartiality irrespective of any alleged waiver.

In *Bulut v. Austria*,[129] the ECtHR was faced with a question of impartiality and participation in the trial of a judge who had previously participated in the preliminary investigation. Although, as recognized by the Court, the legal counsel in the case had unequivocally waived the opportunity to challenge an allegedly impartial judge, the ECtHR considered itself nevertheless bound to review the impartiality of the particular judge from the standpoint of the Convention:

> Regardless of whether a waiver was made or not, the Court has still to decide, from the standpoint of the Convention, whether the participation of Judge Schaumburger in the trial after taking part in the questioning of witnesses at the pre-trial stage could cast doubt on the impartiality of the trial court.[130]

As suggested, the reason for Court's *ex officio* examination of the requirements of an independent and impartial tribunal from the standpoint of the Convention, irrespective of an alleged waiver, is due to the importance of such requirements for public confidence in the judicial system. In other words, '[the right to an independent and impartial tribunal] is of essential importance and its exercise cannot depend on the parties alone.'[131]

The fact that the ECtHR will examine requirements of independence and impartiality of the tribunal within the meaning of Article 6(1) of the ECHR irrespective of an allegedly valid waiver has been also confirmed in arbitration-related cases. In the *Transado-Transportes* case the ECtHR *ex officio* examined the subjective and objective impartiality of arbitrators, despite an alleged waiver in the form of an arbitration agreement and despite the applicant's failure to provide elaborate reasons for its assertion as to the lack impartiality of the arbitral tribunal:

> As to the tribunal's partiality, the Court notes firstly that the applicant company provided no information about this complaint and limited itself to challenging the tribunal's "impartiality". Further, it sees nothing capable of casting doubt on the subjective impartiality of the members of the arbitration tribunal nor the latter's objective impartiality. As to objective impartiality in particular, the procedure for setting up the arbitration tribunal, provided for in clause XXXIII, excludes any doubt in this area [...][132]

On the other hand, the Court's approach in the *Suovaniemi* case suggests that the requirements of independence and impartiality will not be examined by the ECtHR *ex officio* in all cases concerning an alleged waiver in the form of an arbitration agreement. The different approaches taken by the Court regarding the *waivability*

---

[129] *Bulut v. Austria*, App. No. 17358/90, ECtHR, 22 February 1996.

[130] Ibid., para. 30; *McGonnell v. the United Kingdom*, App. No. 28488/95, ECtHR, 8 February 2002; *Öcalan v. Turkey*, App. No. 46221/99, ECtHR, 15 May 2005.

[131] *Pfeiffer and Plankl v. Austria*, App. No. 10802/84, ECtHR, 25 February 1992, para. 38.

[132] *Transado-Transportes Fluviais Do Sado, S.A. v. Portugal*, App. No. 35943/02, ECtHR, 16 December 2003.

and *ex officio* examination of the right to an independent and impartial tribunal may be explained by the different factual circumstances characterizing each case. For example, although the factual underpinnings in *Bulut v. Austria* are comparable to those in the *Suovaniemi*, i.e. both cases concerned actual knowledge and express confirmation of the relevant circumstances eventually leading to alleged violation of the right to an independent and impartial tribunal, the *Bulut v. Austria* case, as opposed to the *Suovaniemi* case, did not concern arbitration. This may explain why the ECtHR nevertheless *ex officio* examined the requirements of independence and impartiality in the *Bulut v. Austria* case, and refused to do so in the *Suovaniemi* case.[133] The facts of the *Transado-Transportes* case, however, suggest that in case the waiver of the right to an independent and impartial tribunal was not as unequivocal as in the *Suovaniemi* case, the ECtHR still considers itself bound to examine the independence and impartiality of the arbitral tribunal. Therefore, apparently the Court will carry *ex officio* examination of the requirements of independence and impartiality in case parties simply concluded an arbitration agreement, but not if parties were aware of lack of independence and impartiality and failed to raise such an issue already during arbitration proceedings. The timing therefore again proves to be of particular significance not only with regard to the scope of the waiver, but also with regard to whether or not the Court will eventually examine the issue on its own motion.

7.2.2.2 Interim Conclusion

The ECtHR has always emphasised the prominent place of the right to a fair trial held in a democratic society and that the right to an independent and impartial tribunal is an indispensable part of that right. The particular significance of the principle of independence and impartiality of the arbitral tribunal is enshrined and equally stressed in most national arbitration laws, arbitration rules of major arbitral institutions and international instruments, such as the UNCITRAL Model Law. As such, it has been established to pertain to procedural public policy and even has been said to constitute a principle of transnational procedural public policy, i.e. a universal standard that represents an international consensus and must therefore always apply irrespective of national legislative standards and rules of arbitral procedure as may be agreed by the parties.[134]

Despite clear-cut indications by the Convention's controlling bodies, there exists a reasonable basis, stemming from both the Court's own made case-law and principles established therein, as well as the generally recognized character of the right to an independent and impartial tribunal in a democratic society, to argue that it is generally not permissible for the Convention purposes to waive the right to an independent and impartial tribunal under Article 6(1) of the ECHR. In turn, the fact that the right to an

---

[133] The idea that the Convention's controlling bodies do not apply the same strict standards to arbitration as required to court proceedings is also reflected in legal literature. See, e.g. Briner and Von Schlabrendorff (2001), p. 92.

[134] See, inter alia, Briner and Von Schlabrendorff (2001), p. 92, Landrove (2006), p. 89.

independent and impartial tribunal is generally *non-waivable* leads to the conclusion that parties, at least from the Convention's standpoint, should not be permitted to exclude in advance their right to challenge an arbitral award on the ground of lack of independence and impartiality of the arbitral tribunal. Such an exclusion could only be valid for the Convention purposes if done *ex post*, i.e. after parties became aware of the relevant facts leading to a possible violation of the right to an independent and impartial tribunal. The *Suovaniemi* case provides a good illustration in this regard.

The somewhat problematic aspect in the hypothesis that arbitrating parties should not be permitted to conclude advance exclusion agreements to the extent that they exclude the *non-waivable* right to an independent and impartial tribunal is in the fact that, as seen, only a handful of States expressly provide the lack of independence and impartiality of the arbitral tribunal as a ground for challenge of an arbitral award. In those States, the relevant annulment ground could simply not be subject voluntary exclusion, provided exclusion agreements are permitted at all under the respective national arbitration law. However, most *leges arbitri* do not expressly provide for such a specific annulment ground. As seen, the requirement of independence and impartiality of the arbitral tribunal, is generally read into other annulment grounds, thereby making it more difficult to reconcile the *non-waivable* character of the right to an independent and impartial tribunal with the scope of validity of exclusion agreements in this regard.

A possible solution may be found in the compromise approach provided for under the German law, generally permitting exclusion agreements only *ex post*, and not *ex ante*. Another solution could be to interpret the lack of independence and impartiality as falling solely under the *inability to present its case* ground for review and permit exclusion agreements *ex ante*, to the extent that the *inability to present its case* ground for review remains intact. In such a way, it would be guaranteed that the right to an independent and impartial tribunal is not subject to exclusion agreements. Although, considering the broad discretion that States have in regulating arbitration on a national level, it is evident that such a uniform solution is not universally practicable, at least from the Convention perspective, the said approaches seem as the ideal solution for reconciling the increasing acceptance of exclusion agreements with the requirements of the Convention. The same is true with regard to other *non-waivable* right of Article 6(1) of the ECHR, i.e. the right to a fair hearing.

7.2.2.3 Fair Hearing

The right to a fair hearing is at the core of the procedural guarantees provided for under the Convention, in particular Article 6(1) of the ECHR. It encompasses a variety of guarantees aimed at the protection of parties' most fundamental procedural rights in legal proceedings, essentially allowing to pursue their procedural position under the same conditions.[135] Although the ECtHR has avoided giving an enumeration of

[135] Grabenwarter (2014), p. 134.

the elements of the right to a fair hearing in abstract, it is said that the most fundamental components of the right to a fair hearing within the meaning of Article 6(1) of the ECHR are the principle of procedural equality (equality of arms) and the right to adversarial proceedings.[136] These principles are considered fundamental cornerstones of not only court proceedings, but also arbitration proceedings.[137] Therefore, a question arises—to what extent arbitrating parties are permitted for the Convention purposes to exclude their right to a fair hearing, in particular its most fundamental components, such as the equality of parties and the right to adversarial proceedings? Is it even *permissible* under the Convention to exclude such rights?

Similarly to the principle of independent and impartial tribunal, the most fundamental aspects of the right to a fair hearing, such as the aforementioned principles of equality of arms and the right to adversarial proceedings, are enshrined in most national arbitration laws,[138] arbitration rules of major arbitral institutions[139] and international instruments, e.g. the UNCITRAL Model Law.[140] Therefore, also the most fundamental guarantees of a fair hearing constitute fundamental and indispensable elements of every arbitration and as such must be adhered to during all stages

---

136 See, e.g. Van Dijk et al. (2006), p. 579. In *Avotiņš v. Latvia*, App. No. 17502/07, ECtHR, 23 May 2016, para. 119 the ECtHR recognized that 'the adversarial principle and the principle of equality of arms, which are closely linked, are fundamental components of the concept of a "fair hearing" within the meaning of Article 6 § 1 of the Convention.' Other constituent elements of the right to a fair hearing include, inter alia, the right to access to a court, the right to inspection of files, the right to be heard, the right to a reasoned decision, the right to have the assistance of a lawyer, the right to a public hearing, the right to a decision within a reasonable time and many others.

137 Briner and Von Schlabrendorff (2001), p. 96.

138 See, inter alia, art. 182(3) of the PILA; art. 1699 of the BCCP; art. 1510 of the FCCP; sec. 1042(1) of the ZPO; sec. 33 of the English Arbitration Act (1996); sec. 22 of the Finnish Arbitration Act (1999); art. 732 of the Estonian Civil Procedural Law; art. 8 of the Lithuanian Law on Commercial Arbitration (2012); art. 1036(2) of the Dutch Arbitration Act (2015); sec. 18 of the Danish Arbitration Act (2005); arts. 19 and 20 of the Latvian 2015 Arbitration Law and many others.

139 See, e.g. art. 22(4) of the 2017 ICC Arbitration Rules ('In all cases, the arbitral tribunal shall act fairly and impartially and ensure that each party has a reasonable opportunity to present its case.'); art. 23(2) of the 2017 SCC Arbitration Rules ('In all cases, the Arbitral Tribunal shall conduct the arbitration in an impartial, efficient and expeditious manner, giving each party an equal and reasonable opportunity to present its case.'); art. 14(4) of the 2014 LCIA Arbitration Rules ('[…]the Arbitral Tribunal's general duties at all times during the arbitration shall include: (i) a duty to act fairly and impartially as between all parties, giving each a reasonable opportunity of putting its case and dealing with that of its opponent(s) […]'); art. 35(1) of the 2015 CIETAC Arbitration Rules ('[…]the arbitral tribunal shall act impartially and fairly and shall afford a reasonable opportunity to both parties to present their case.'); art. 21(1) of the 2018 DIS Arbitration Rules ('The parties shall be treated equally. Each party shall have a right to be heard in adversarial proceedings.'); art. 13(1) of the 2013 HKIAC Administered Arbitration Rules ('[…] the arbitral tribunal shall adopt suitable procedures for the conduct of the arbitration in order to avoid unnecessary delay or expense, having regard to the complexity of the issues and the amount in dispute, and provided that such procedures ensure equal treatment of the parties and afford the parties a reasonable opportunity to present their case.') and many others.

140 Art. 18 of the UNCITRAL Model Law ('The parties shall be treated with equality and each party shall be given a full opportunity of presenting his case.'). See also, e.g. art. 9 of the Uniform Arbitration Act of the Organization for the Harmonization of Business Law in Africa (OHADA)

of arbitration.[141] As will be provided below, it is said that also these guarantees are considered to be part of (transnational) procedural public policy.

Contrary to the principle of independent and impartial tribunal whose lack constitutes an express ground for setting aside an arbitral award only in a handful of States, violation of parties' due process guarantees (of which the right to a fair hearing is an inherent part) is a self-standing annulment ground in most *leges arbitri*,[142] and also under the UNCITRAL Model Law.[143] Violation of due process guarantees will also be a valid ground for refusal of recognition and enforcement under the New York Convention.[144] The fact that the principle of a fair hearing, in particular, its most fundamental elements of equality of arms and the right to adversarial proceedings, is of paramount significance at all stages of arbitration proceedings is therefore not disputed.[145] This is evidenced both by the emphasis put on adherence to such principles in national arbitration laws, arbitration rules of major arbitral institutions, as well as international instruments, and also the fact that generally violation of parties' due process guarantees will constitute both a valid ground for annulment of an arbitral award under the UNCITRAL Model law and a valid ground for refusal of recognition and enforcement of an arbitral award under the New York Convention.

Similarly as with the right to an independent and impartial tribunal under Article 6(1) of the ECHR, the question is whether, from the standpoint of the Convention, it is *permissible* for arbitrating parties to exclude in advance setting-aside proceedings, to the extent that it is impossible to challenge an arbitral award on the basis of violations of the most fundamental due process guarantees, i.e. the equality of arms and the right to adversarial proceedings. As recognized:

> There is every reason to assume that parties who agree to arbitration as a means of dispute resolution wish these basic rights [i.e. equality of arms and the right to adversarial proceedings] to be observed in the arbitral proceedings. Parties refer to international commercial arbitration as an alternative to court proceedings and it would therefore be a mistake to think they had any intention of waiving their fundamental right to a fair trial.[146]

('The parties shall be treated with equality and each party shall be given a full opportunity to present is case.').

[141] Born (2014), p. 3225.

[142] See, inter alia, art. 190(2)(d) of the PILA; art. 117(3)(2) of the BCCP; art. 1520(4) of the FCCP; sec. 1059(2)(1)(b) of the ZPO; sec. 41(1)(4) of the Finnish Arbitration Act (1999); art. 751(1)(3) of the Estonian Civil Procedural Law; sec. 68(2)(a) of the English Arbitration Act (1996); sec. 37(2)(b) of the Danish Arbitration Act (2005); art. 43(b) of the Norwegian Arbitration Act (2004); art. 50(3)(2) of the Lithuanian Law on Commercial Arbitration (2012) and many others.

[143] Art. 34(2)(a)(ii) of the UNCITRAL Model Law.

[144] Art. V(1)(b) of the New York Convention.

[145] Generally on mandatory procedural requirements in international arbitration see, e.g. Born (2014), pp. 2154–2189.

[146] Briner and Von Schlabrendorff (2001), p. 96. See also Benedettelli (2015), pp. 646–647 ('[T]he idea that parties to an arbitration agreement should be presumed having waived all the due process guarantees set out by Article 6.1 ECHR must be rejected as being at odds with the importance that the principle of fair trial is granted by most contemporary laws of arbitration.').

Can it be reasonably argued that the same conclusions as applicable to the principle of independent and impartial tribunal should also apply to the right to a fair hearing, at least to the cornerstone aspects of such a right, i.e. the equality of arms and the right to adversarial proceedings? Considering the significance of the right to a fair hearing in a democratic society together with the Court-made notion of *permissibility* of a waiver and ever present references to only a *partial* waiver or waiver of only *certain* Article 6(1) of the ECHR rights, it is arguable that parties should only be permitted to exclude the right to challenge an arbitral award on grounds of violation of their due process guarantees only *ex post*, and not *ex ante*.

Fair Hearing as a Principle of (Transnational) Procedural Public Policy

The most fundamental aspects of the right to a fair hearing, i.e. the equality of arms and the right to adversarial proceedings, are said to pertain to procedural public policy, be it national, international or even transnational, as suggested by some authors.[147]

Whether the principles of equality of arms and adversarial proceedings in international arbitration are considered as pertaining to national, international or transnational (truly international) public policy, the said rights' categorization as such evidences that, contrary to certain *waivable* rights within the meaning of Article 6(1) of the ECHR, the principles of equality of arms and adversarial proceedings, at least in the context of international arbitration and similarly to the right to and independent and impartial tribunal, are viewed as somewhat more superior and perceived as fundamental and universal standards common to all civilized nations that are governed by the rule of law and permit arbitration as a means of alternative dispute resolution.

Thus, for example, despite the existence of an express ground for both the annulment of an arbitral award under the UNCITRAL Model Law or the refusal of recognition and enforcement of an arbitral award under the New York Convention, it is generally recognized that a violation of parties' due process guarantees during arbitration proceedings may also lead to a violation of procedural public policy and accordingly either annulment[148] or refusal of recognition and enforcement of an arbitral award.[149] In that sense, it is considered that there exists a certain overlap between the express ground for either annulment or refusal of recognition and enforcement of an arbitral award on the basis of due process violations and the implied safeguard of the same principles under the public policy exception.[150]

---

[147] Generally on the equality of arms and the right to adversarial proceedings being part of procedural public policy see, e.g. Luttrell (2009), p. 1. On the aspects of transnational procedural public policy see, e.g. Mantilla-Serrano (2005), Bray et al. (2014), pp. 10–22. See also Kreindler (2013), pp. 299–302.

[148] Generally on the interrelation between due process guarantees and procedural public policy in the context of setting-aside proceedings see, e.g. Born (2014), pp. 3332–3333.

[149] Generally see, e.g. Born (2014), pp. 3683–3688.

[150] Born (2014), p. 3332.

National courts around the world have invoked their procedural public policy as a bar to recognition and enforcement under Article V(2)(b) of the New York Convention of arbitral awards that contain very serious procedural unfairness or irregularities, among others, violations of parties' right to an equal treatment and right to adversarial proceedings.[151] Moreover, in the famous *Dutco* case,[152] the French *Cour de Cassation* held that the principle of equal treatment of arbitrating parties is part of the French understanding of *international public policy* and thus the right to equal treatment can only be waived *ex post*. It must be mentioned, however, that in most States only the core aspects of due process will constitute a violation of procedural public policy.[153] In Germany, for example, the German Federal Supreme Court (*Bundesgerichtshof*) has held that Article V(1)(b) of the New York Convention has to be read in conjunction with the constitutional due process requirement under Article 103(1) of the German Constitution (*Grundgesetz*) and also Article V(2)(b) of the New York Convention, and that an arbitral award will be refused recognition and enforcement only if violation of the due process requirement or any other principle of procedural public policy affected, or could have affected, the outcome of the dispute.[154]

Some legal scholars even argue that the most basic aspects of the right to a fair hearing, such as the equality of parties, adversarial proceedings and the right to have reasonable opportunity to be heard, constitute transnational procedural public policy, i.e. similarly to the right to an independent and impartial tribunal, such rights are universal standards and accepted norms of conduct that represent an international consensus and must therefore always apply irrespective of the localization of arbitration proceedings.[155]

Therefore, similarly to the right to an independent and impartial tribunal, the fact that the violation of the core elements of the right to a fair hearing is perceived as a violation of, depending on one's perception, national, international or transnational procedural public policy, certainly supports argument in favor of the right to a fair hearing under Article 6(1) of the ECHR, or at least the most fundamental elements thereof, being considered as generally *non-waivable*.

---

[151] Ibid., pp. 3683–3884 and cases of national courts referred therein.

[152] *Societes BKMI et Siemens c. societe Dutco*, Cour de cassation, 7 January 1992, Rev.arb. 470 (1992).

[153] See Born (2014), pp. 3685–3687 in referring to examples of matters that have not been considered by national courts as issues of procedural public policy.

[154] Decision of the German Federal Supreme Court in Case III ZB 83/07, 15 January 2009, SchiedsVZ 2009, 126.

[155] See, e.g. Mantilla-Serrano (2005), Bray et al. (2014), pp. 10–22, Kreindler (2013), pp. 299–302. Generally on transnational public policy, including its definition see Lalive (1987), pp. 258–318, Kessedjian (2007), pp. 857–870, Sheppard (2004), p. 1.

Non-waivability of the Right to Fair Hearing Under Article 6(1) of the ECHR

When the right to a fair hearing is considered from the perspective of Article 6(1) of the ECHR and the Court's own analysis, it is equally arguable that the most core elements of the right to a fair hearing, i.e. the principle of equality of parties and the right to adversarial proceedings, are generally *non-waivable* within the meaning of Article 6(1) of the ECHR and that parties, by excluding in advance and in full the right to challenge an arbitral award, should not be precluded from nevertheless challenging an arbitral award on grounds of violation of such fundamental principles. In other words, exclusion of all annulment grounds should be permissible only *ex post*, i.e. after the relevant violation became known to the parties. Arguably, the *non-waivable* character shall apply only to the most fundamental and significant elements, i.e. the principle of equality of parties and the right to adversarial proceedings. As explained, such principles are generally considered to be part of procedural public policy—national, international or even transnational procedural public policy.

The *non-waivable* character of the principles of equality of parties and adversarial proceedings is recognized by many legal scholars. For example, Briner and Von Schlabrendorff have stressed that:

> [A]ny waiver by the parties of compliance with the fundamental requirements of equal treatment of the parties, fair notice of the proceedings and a fair opportunity to present one's case, would have to be regarded as incompatible with human dignity, reducing the parties to mere pawns in the procedure. A waiver of the right to a fair trial under Article 6 ECHR, whether expressly agreed or implied, is therefore inadmissible and can have no binding force.[156]

Similarly, also Landrove has argued that:

> [A]ll due process rights are not equally waivable. In other words, there are levels among due process rights so that some of them are more fundamental than others and pertain to public policy. Those more fundamental rights are not waived by the mere signing of an arbitration agreement because at the time of the signing parties are not aware of all the consequences of a waiver. Subsequent conduct during the proceedings (once the facts are known) may affect those fundamental rights that could not have been waived beforehand (right to a fair hearing, and right to an independent and impartial tribunal).
>
> Then the signing of an arbitration agreement merely waives the right to a State's tribunal, and the right to a public hearing within a reasonable time, but does not affect fair hearing aspects (such as equality of arms, right to be heard, etc.) nor the right to an independent and impartial tribunal.[157]

[156] Briner and Von Schlabrendorff (2001), p. 97.

[157] Landrove (2006), p. 89. See also, e.g. Hörnle (2009), p. 108 recognizing that '[t]he absolute waiver theory is not supported by the jurisprudence of the Strasbourg institutions. It is also to be rejected on the grounds of principle in that it ignores the courts' involvement in arbitration and it illogically confuses the parties' waiver not to go to the court with a waiver of all due process rights. Hence the fundamental principles of due process—such as equality of arms between the parties in the hearing, giving every party a reasonable opportunity to present their case under conditions that do not place that party at a significant disadvantage towards its opponent, and the impartiality and independence of the arbitrator—must be guaranteed despite the existence of a general agreement

Also Jaksic has maintained that:

> No one can presume that parties intended to waive fundamental procedural guarantees by their conclusion of an arbitration agreement. It would be unreasonable to argue that litigants have it in mind to agree to bring their cases before arbitrators who would be biased and in proceedings in which they would be deprived of due process of law. Any adjudicatory proceedings which infringe these fundamental procedural principles would be contrary to the principle of the rule of law.[158]

Therefore, at least from a scholarly point of view, there seems to exist a general consensus as to those Article 6(1) of the ECHR rights that are considered *waivable* and those with regard to which a waiver is not *permissible* within the meaning of Article 6(1) of the ECHR. What makes, however, arguing in favour of the general *non-waivability* of the core elements of the right to a fair hearing somewhat more abstract, is the lack of adequate, or at least comparable to that for the right to an independent and impartial tribunal, support in the Convention's controlling bodies case-law. As seen, the general *non-waivability* of the right to an independent and impartial tribunal under Article 6(1) of the ECHR is supported by ample case-law—*Suovaniemi, Transado-Transportes, Bulut v. Austria, Pfeiffer and Plankl v. Austria* to mention just a few. The same, however, cannot be said with regard to the waiver of the most fundamental aspects of the right to a fair hearing, i.e. the principle of equality of parties and/or the right to adversarial proceedings in either court proceedings or arbitration proceedings. Despite this, the general principles as established by the Convention's controlling bodies provide sufficient basis for arguing that it is *permissible* to waive the said fundamental principles, but only *ex post*. To put it in the perspective of this book' specific focus—it is arguable that *ex ante* exclusion of setting-aside proceedings should not be permissible from the Convention's point of view to the extent that parties are precluded from challenging an arbitral award on the basis of violations of the most fundamental elements of their right to a fair hearing, i.e. the principle of equality of parties and the right to adversarial proceedings. In other words, similarly as for the right to an independent and impartial tribunal, such voluntary exclusions should be valid only if concluded *ex post*. This conclusion is supported by the following considerations.

The Court-made Notion of Permissibility

First, it is the Court-made notion of *permissibility* that evidences that a waiver may not be *permissible* with regard to certain rights of the ECHR. The above considerations in this regard vis-à-vis the right to an independent and impartial tribunal[159] apply *mutatis mutandis* also to the right to a fair hearing. If a distinction as regards *permissibility* of certain ECHR rights 'may have to be made even between different rights guaranteed

---

to arbitrate. By contrast, other due process rights, such as publicity or the right to appeal, may be modified under the ECHR in voluntary, private dispute-resolution process, simply because of the inherent nature of the particular private dispute-resolution process (general waiver).'

[158] Jaksic (2007), p. 165.

[159] Sect. 7.2.2.1.

by Article 6',[160] then the most fundamental aspects of the right to a fair hearing arguably fall within the category of those Article 6(1) of the ECHR rights as to which a waiver is generally not *permissible.*

This line of reasoning is supported not only by the fact that, as established afore, the core elements of the right to a fair hearing pertain to procedural public policy, but also by the ample scholarly writings that, in referring to the Court-made notion of *permissibility*, have recognized that, despite the absence of clear-cut indications by the Court, the right to an independent and impartial tribunal and the right a fair hearing, in particular the principle of equality of arms and the right to adversarial proceedings, should fall within the category of those rights with regard to which a waiver is not be *permissible.*[161] The distinguishing between the different rights under Article 6(1) of the ECHR for the purposes of the *permissibility* of a waiver and the somewhat more superior character of the right to an independent and impartial tribunal and the afore-stipulated core elements of the right to a fair hearing, evidences the generally *non-waivable* character of such rights.

Arbitration Agreement—A Partial Waiver or a Waiver of Only Certain Rights of Article 6(1) of the ECHR

Equally, closely linked with the issue of *permissibility* is the Court's often made reference to a *partial* waiver or waiver of only *certain* rights of Article 6(1) of the ECHR in case parties conclude an arbitration agreement. The above considerations in this regard vis-à-vis the right to an independent and impartial tribunal[162] apply

[160] *Suovaniemi and others v. Finland*, App. No. 31737/96, ECtHR, 23 February 1999.

[161] See, among many others, Benedettelli (2015), pp. 646–647 ('So far, the European Court has held that the execution of an arbitration agreement triggers a valid waiver to the right to a public hearing within the arbitral proceedings [...] For the European Court other rights cannot be waived in advance, ie at the time of execution of an arbitration agreement (or of the terms of reference), but only after their beneficiary has become aware that a breach of them has been committed to his/her damage and is therefore best positioned to appreciate the impact of his/her decision [...] In addition, according to the European Court certain due process rights may not be waived in any circumstances. Of course, the idea that parties to an arbitration agreement should be presumed having waived all the due process guarantees set out by Article 6.1 ECHR must be rejected as being at odds with the importance that the principle of fair trial is granted by most contemporary laws of arbitration.'); Mourre (2000), p. 22 arguing that the right to adversarial proceedings, the principle of equality of parties and the right to an independent and impartial tribunal cannot be validly waived by the parties; Besson (2006), p. 400 ('Today, however, it is well-established that a complete waiver is not permissible. The arbitration agreement only amounts to a partial waiver of the rights under article 6(1). I would even say that it is a very partial waiver because the only rights which undisputedly are waived are the right of access to a state court in order to obtain a decision on the merits - this task is for the arbitral tribunal - and the right to a public hearing.'); Krausz (2011), p. 137 ('[...] the submission to arbitration is only a partial waiver of the rights guaranteed by ECHR, Article 6. However, the applicability of this provision must be determined on a case-by-case basis. Finally, the inalienable rights under Article 6 coincide with the contents of international procedural public policy, as understood in international arbitration: equal treatment of the parties, independent tribunal, and fair opportunity to present one's case.').

[162] Sect. 7.2.2.1.

mutatis mutandis also to the right to a fair hearing. The generally *non-waivable* character of the right to a fair hearing, at least its constituent core elements—the principle of equality of arms and the right to adversarial proceedings, is additionally supported by the theory of only a *partial* waiver of Article 6(1) of the ECHR when concluding an arbitration agreement.

Verification of Violation Irrespective of a Waiver

As to the ECtHR's *ex officio* verification of alleged violation of the right to fair hearing, the *Tabbane v. Switzerland* case provides a good illustration. After holding that both the *waiver theory* is satisfied and Article 192(1) of the PILA per se does not violate the right of access to a court under Article 6(1) of the ECHR, the Court nevertheless continued with *ex officio* examining the applicant's second complaint, i.e. that the refusal of the arbitral tribunal to appoint an expert violated his right to a fair hearing, in particular the principle of equality of arms.[163] Despite the ECtHR eventually concluding that the principle of equality of arms was not violated, the fact alone that it nevertheless examined the complaint and provided arguments why it considers that the principle of equality of arms was duly respect by the arbitral tribunal and the Swiss Federal Tribunal, evidences that the ECtHR, similarly to the right to an independent and impartial tribunal, will also verify *ex officio* any alleged violation of the right to a fair hearing irrespective of a seemingly valid waiver.

Additionally, the ECtHR will verify the existence of guarantees pertaining to the right to fair hearing as part of examination of the *minimum safeguards* criterion. It has become evident that a waiver of the Convention's guarantees in the form of an arbitration agreement, in order to be effective for Convention purposes, requires certain minimum guarantees commensurate to its importance.[164] Whether or not a waiver is attended by such *minimum safeguards* will depend both on the factual circumstances of the case and also the underlying legislative framework.[165] In the *Suovaniemi* case, *ex post* waiver of the right to an independent and impartial tribunal was accompanied by sufficient guarantees commensurate to its importance in that 'in the proceedings before the national courts the applicants had ample opportunity to advance their arguments, inter alia, concerning the circumstances in which the waiver took place during arbitration proceedings.'[166] Similarly, in the *Tabbane v.*

[163] *Tabbane v. Switzerland*, App. No. 41069/12, ECtHR, 1 March 2016, paras. 37–39.

[164] See Sect. 3.5.4. See also Sect. 7.2.1.3.

[165] To put it in the words of the former Commission—'to answer the question of whether the guarantees secured by Article 6 apply, account must be taken not only of the arbitration agreement between the parties and the nature of the private arbitration proceedings but also of the legislative framework providing for such proceeding'. See *R v. Switzerland*, App. No. 10881/84, ECmHR, 4 March 1987.

[166] *Suovaniemi and others v. Finland*, App. No. 31737/96, ECtHR, 23 February 1999.

Switzerland case a waiver was accompanied by *minimum safeguards* because, inter alia, the Swiss Federal Tribunal duly heard parties' arguments.[167]

Therefore, in essence, by verifying that a waiver is accompanied by minimum safeguards commensurate to such waiver's importance, the Court will make sure that the most fundamental aspects of the right to a fair hearing, i.e. the principle of equality of arms and the right to adversarial proceedings, have been nevertheless observed. At least this is what the ECtHR has done in both the *Suovaniemi* and the *Tabbane v. Switzerland* cases, in addition, at least in the latter, to the *ex officio* examination of an alleged violation of the principle of equality in the first place. If such safeguards were not present, a waiver would not be effective for Convention purposes.

7.2.2.4 Interim Conclusion

The principles of equality of arms and adversarial proceedings are fundamental components of the right to a fair hearing within the meaning of Article 6(1) of the ECHR.[168] The right to a fair hearing, in turn, 'must be interpreted in the light of the Preamble to the Convention, which declares, among other things, the rule of law to be part of the common heritage of the Contracting States.'[169] The particular significance of the principles of equality of arms and adversarial proceedings in arbitration proceedings has been equally stressed in most national arbitration laws, arbitration rules of major arbitral institutions and international instruments, such as the UNCITRAL Model Law. Similarly to the right to an independent and impartial tribunal, also the said components of the right to a fair hearing have been generally recognized as pertaining to procedural public policy and even said to constitute principles of transnational procedural public policy—those universal standards that represent an international consensus and must therefore always apply.[170] The question, however, is to what extent, considering the importance of such principles for the fair administration of justice in a democratic State and taking into account the Court's established principles pertaining to the dichotomy between arbitration and the ECHR, it is *permissible* for the Convention purposes to exclude setting-aside proceedings—a mechanism that verifies, inter alia, adherence to the principles of equality of arms and adversarial proceedings?

Arguably, the starting point, similarly to the right to an independent and impartial tribunal, is to conclude that generally, the most fundamental components of the right

[167] *Tabbane v. Switzerland*, App. No. 41069/12, ECtHR, 1 March 2016, para. 31 ('Par ailleurs, la Cour observe que le Tribunal fédéral a dûment entendu les arguments du requérant et a pris en compte tous les éléments factuels et juridiques qui étaient objectivement pertinents pour la résolution du litige. L'arrêt du Tribunal fédéral s'avère par ailleurs dûment motivé de sorte qu'aucune apparence d'arbitraire ne puisse être décelée dans le cas d'espèce.').

[168] *Avotiņš v. Latvia*, App. No. 17502/07, ECtHR, 23 May 2016, para. 119.

[169] See, e.g. *Brumarescu v. Romania*, App. No. 28342/95, ECtHR, 28 October 1999, para. 61; *Sovtransavto Holding v. Ukraine*, App. No. 48553/99, ECtHR, 25 July 2002, para. 72.

[170] See Sect. 7.2.2.3.

to a fair hearing—the principles of equality of arms and adversarial proceedings, should be regarded as *non-waivable* for the Convention purposes. Their generally *non-waivable* character is evidenced, inter alia, by (i) the Court's-established notion of *permissibility* of waiver, differentiating even between specific rights of Article 6(1) of the ECHR; (ii) the reference in nearly all arbitration-related decisions to only a *partial* waiver or a waiver of *certain* rights of Article 6(1) of the ECHR; the fact that (iii) other components of the right to a fair trial have been *expressis verbis* considered by the Court as *waivable*; (iv) even in case of a waiver, the Court will *ex officio* verify adherence to such principles; (v) the principles of equality of arms and adversarial proceedings have been established to pertain to procedural public policy (national, international and even transnational). Despite the generally *non-waivable* character of such principles, upon careful consideration of the Court's existing practice in this regard, in particular the rulings in the *Suovaniemi* and *Tabbane v. Switzerland* cases, the following general conclusions can be drawn both with regard to the *non-waivability* of the right to a fair hearing, particular the principles of equality of arms and adversarial proceedings, as well as to the *non-waivability* of the right to an independent and impartial tribunal.

First, *ex post* waiver of both the right to an independent and impartial tribunal and the core elements of the right to a fair hearing should be *permissible* from the Convention's stand point. This is evidenced by the Court's ruling in the *Suovaniemi* case and generally is in line with the requirement that the person waiving his rights under the Convention must reasonably foresee the consequences of the waiver and be fully aware of the rights he or she waives.[171] In this sense, the German approach to exclusion agreements—differentiating between *waivable* and *non-waivable* grounds for challenge and even for the *waivable* grounds requiring that parties have knowledge of the potential irregularity—provides the most sensible solution that can be deemed as being fully compatible with the ECHR, reflecting also the practice of the ECtHR. The principle of party autonomy and the 'right to regulate their mutual relations as they [arbitrating parties] see fit'[172] has been at the forefront of the Court's reasoning in every arbitration-related decision. The private nature of arbitration proceedings and the fact that, by concluding an arbitration agreement, parties, at least to a certain extent, express their willingness to escape the constraints and strict procedures of State courts, therefore justifies the applicability of a more lenient standard towards permissibility of *ex post* waivers of Convention guarantees. As seen when analyzing the different approaches to exclusion agreements, *ex post* exclusion of setting-aside proceedings is also permissible in Switzerland, France, Sweden, Belgium and other States generally permitting exclusion agreements, therefore, as long as arbitrating parties reasonably foresee the consequences of an exclusion agreement and are aware of the rights they waive, exclusion agreements should be compatible with the ECHR.

Secondly, the same, however, cannot be said of *ex ante* exclusion agreements, at least to the extent the annulment mechanism is excluded in full and parties are

[171] As seen, also legal scholars generally support the validity of *ex post* waivers of all Article 6(1) ECHR rights for the purposes of the Convention.

[172] *Axelsson and others v. Sweden*, App. No. 11960/86, ECmHR, 13 July 1990.

precluded from subsequently challenging an arbitral award on the basis of grounds pertaining to the *non-waivable* rights within the meaning of Article 6(1) of the ECHR. Despite clear-cut indications by the Court as to the specific rights falling in the category of *non-waivable* rights of Article of the 6(1) ECHR, the above discussion has evidenced with reasonable certainty that the right to an independent and impartial tribunal and the most fundamental principles of the right to a fair hearing are so fundamental for fair administration of justice in a democratic society that no one should be permitted to waive them before actually being aware of the consequences of such a waiver.

To put the said conclusion in the perspective of the more specific focus of this book, one would require distinguishing between the different annulment grounds and permit *ex ante* exclusion solely of those grounds that do not strip arbitrating parties of their right to challenge an arbitral award on the basis of violations of the principles of an independent and impartial tribunal, equality of arms and that of adversarial proceedings. Considering that in most cases violation of the said principles may be tailored as a violation of simultaneously multiple annulment grounds, therefore making it more difficult to distinguish between grounds that may be subject to *ex ante* exclusion agreements, the most reasonable solution from the standpoint of the Convention would be to permit only *ex post* exclusion agreements.

Abstaining from the somewhat categorical and impracticable argument solely in favor of *ex post* exclusion agreements, one may nevertheless see room for a debate, from the Convention's perspective, of the compatibility of *ex ante* exclusion agreements of all grounds for challenge, however, only under certain circumstances.

First, no such potential compatibility can be imagined without requiring arbitrating parties to refer expressly in their exclusion agreements to the remedy of setting aside proceedings. In France, Belgium and Sweden, exclusion agreements will only be considered valid if parties specifically refer to the relevant remedy—the annulment mechanism—and unambiguously exclude the application of it in their arbitration agreement. If parties are fully conscious of excluding setting-aside proceedings (as opposed to vague exclusions of e.g. *all rights to appeal*), they should be deemed to reasonably foresee and understand that no recourse will lie against the arbitral award, including on the basis of violations of such fundamental principles as the independence and impartiality of the arbitral tribunal, equality of arms and adversarial proceedings. In this sense, the requirement in France, Belgium and Sweden of an express reference to setting-aside proceedings, would preliminary be in line with the corresponding requirement under the ECHR that parties, in case of a waiver of their rights under the Convention, should be aware of the rights they waive and consequences thereof.

This, however, is not the case under Swiss law that since 2005 no more requires express reference to the remedy of setting-aside proceedings for an exclusion agreement to be valid. This raises a question whether in such circumstances, as in the *Tabbane v. Switzerland* case, parties are fully aware of the consequences that a generally broad clause in their arbitration agreement, e.g. excluding *all rights to appeal* or *any recourse against the award*, may have on the protection of their fundamental procedural human rights at the post-award stage. From the Convention's standpoint therefore *ex ante* exclusion agreements not requiring a specific reference to the remedy of setting-aside proceedings, should not be deemed *permissible*.

Second, the *permissibility* of *ex ante* exclusion agreements for the Convention purposes will also greatly depend on *minimum safeguards* commensurate to the importance of exclusion of the annulment mechanism. When evaluating the *minimum safeguards* requirement the ECtHR has put great emphasis both on the factual circumstances of the case and also the underlying national legal framework.[173] If the national arbitration framework provides sufficient guarantees, e.g. in the form of adequate court assistance to arbitration proceedings where parties' most fundamental rights may effectively be protected, and, in addition, parties expressly refer in their exclusion agreement to exclusion of the annulment mechanism (as opposed to a generally framed exclusion of *all rights to appeal* etc.), party autonomy may prevail. In such cases parties could be considered to be fully aware of their actions and consequences thereof. If, on the other hand, the applicable national arbitration law does not provide for adequate court involvement in, e.g. the appointment and challenging of arbitrators, and arbitrating parties are deemed to have excluded the application of setting-aside proceedings through a rather broad reference in their arbitration agreement (e.g. excluding *all rights to appeal*), there is no possibility to ascertain possible violations of parties' fundamental procedural rights, such as the *non-waivable* rights of Article 6(1) of the ECHR. Whether or not an *ex ante* exclusion agreement will be considered as *permissible* from the standpoint of the Convention, will therefore depend on the particular circumstances of the case and the underlying national arbitration framework.

7.3 Total Exclusion of Setting-Aside Proceedings—*Permissible* Under the ECHR?

Having discussed the interplay between exclusion agreements and the ECHR, in particular under Article 6(1) of the ECHR, and concluded that the ECtHR's decision in the *Tabbane v. Switzerland* case seemingly fails to take into account various significant aspects associated with both the *waiver theory* and the *non-waivable* rights of Article 6(1) of the ECHR, and that therefore its implications may not be

[173]The importance of the underlying national legal framework has played a significant role not only with regard to the requirement of 'minimum safeguards', but in arbitration-related cases in general. See, e.g. *Nordström-Janzon and Nordström-Lehtinen v. the Netherlands*, App. No. 28101/95, ECmHR, 27 November 1996 ('However, the Commission considers that account must be taken not only of the arbitration agreement between the parties and the nature of the private arbitration proceedings, but also of the legislative framework providing for such proceedings in order to determine whether the domestic courts retained some measure of control of the arbitration proceedings and whether this control has been properly exercised in the concrete case […]'); *R v. Switzerland*, App. No. 10881/84, ECmHR, 4 March 1987 ('[…] to answer the question of whether the guarantees secured by Article 6 apply, account must be taken not only of the arbitration agreement between the parties and the nature of the private arbitration proceedings but also of the legislative framework providing for such proceedings […]').

as far-reaching as initially expected, this book's more specific focus also on the phenomenon of total exclusion of setting-aside proceedings mandates subjecting the said phenomenon to similar scrutiny. In other words, one must question whether such a legislative choice, i.e. not providing for a possibility in national law to apply for the setting-aside of arbitral awards altogether, is in conformity with both the *waiver theory* and certain fundamental guarantees provided for in the Convention, in particular, the right of access to a court under Article 6(1) of the ECHR.

As seen when addressing the continuous necessity of the annulment mechanism from the viewpoint of EU law and European public policy,[174] although the CJEU has repeatedly stressed that the requirements of efficient arbitration proceedings justify the review of arbitral awards by the EU Member States' courts being limited in scope, the EU law still requires that the most fundamental provisions of EU law can be examined and reviewed by the EU Member States' courts. The author is of the opinion that a similar maxim follows when the necessity of the annulment mechanism is considered from the viewpoint of the ECHR and the ECtHR's case-law pertaining to the dichotomy of arbitration and the ECHR.

The ECHR controlling bodies have stressed that the ECHR Member States enjoy wide discretion in deciding on which grounds arbitral awards should be set aside. For example, in the *Nordström* case the former Commission observed that:

> [T]he grounds on which arbitral awards may be challenged before national courts differ among the Contracting States […] [E]ach Contracting State may in principle decide itself on which grounds an arbitral award should be quashed.[175]

Also in the *Suovaniemi* case the ECtHR considered that:

> [T]he Contracting States enjoy considerable discretion in regulating the question on which grounds an arbitral award should be quashed, since the quashing of an already rendered award will often mean that a long and costly arbitral procedure will become useless and that considerable work and expense must be invested in new proceedings […][176]

However, although it has been stressed that the ECHR Member States' enjoy considerable discretion in this regard, it does not follow that such a discretion is unlimited, i.e. that the ECHR Member States could exclude the annulment mechanism altogether.

Recent developments imply that party autonomy plays a quintessential role in determining the applicability of the ECHR to arbitration-related cases. As seen, the ECtHR has recently confirmed in the *Pechstein* case that there are limits to the *waiver theory* and its application to sports arbitration, concluding that sports arbitration fails to satisfy the conditions of *absence of constraint* and *unequivocality* and in fact possesses the characteristics of compulsory arbitration and thus must offer all the guarantees of the ECHR. Similarly, in the *Tabbane v. Switzerland* case the Court put great emphasis on the fact that parties under Article 192(1) of the PILA

---

[174] See Sect. 4.4.1.6.

[175] *Nordström-Janzon and Nordström-Lehtinen v. the Netherlands*, App. No. 28101/95, ECmHR, 27 November 1996.

[176] *Suovaniemi and others v. Finland*, App. No. 31737/96, ECtHR, 23 February 1999.

are under no obligation to exclude the annulment mechanism, thus cementing the prevalence of party autonomy in this regard. These recent developments suggest that, although ECHR Member States indeed enjoy considerable discretion with regard to regulating arbitration and, in particular, setting-aside proceedings, such a discretion is not without limits.

Both the previous discussion on compatibility of exclusion agreements with the *waiver theory* and the Court-made distinction between *waivable* and *non-waivable* rights of Article 6(1) of the ECHR, as well as the Court's heavy reliance on party autonomy in the *Tabbane v. Switzerland* case, provides reasonable basis for arguing that total exclusion (non-availability) of the annulment mechanism in national law may fail to satisfy the respective requirements of the *waiver theory* when looked at from the perspective of a waiver of the right of access to a court in the narrow sense, i.e. the entitlement to have the arbitral award subject to the annulment mechanism. Equally, such a legislative vacuum may exceed the margin of appreciation granted to ECHR Contracting States in limiting the right of access to a court under Article 6(1) of the ECHR in the broader sense. Further discussion will therefore look at the compatibility of such a legislative approach from the said two perspectives—the *waiver theory*, analysing the respective requirements thereof similarly to analysis carried out above with regard to exclusion agreements, and the right of access to a court under Article 6(1) of the ECHR. As seen previously, a similar two-tier approach was applied by the ECtHR in the *Tabbane v. Switzerland* case.

7.3.1 Total Exclusion of Setting-Aside Proceedings and the Waiver Theory

As has become apparent, the relationship between arbitration and the Convention is characterized by the so-called *waiver theory*, permitting under certain conditions individuals to waive of their own free will the entitlement to the guarantees of a fair trial. A waiver will not be contrary to the ECHR as long as it is free, lawful and unequivocal. It must be also accompanied by certain minimum safeguards commensurate to its importance and must not run counter to any important public interest. Similarly, it has become evident that not all rights of the ECHR may be subject to a waiver—a waiver must in fact be *permissible*.

Although the general *permissibility* of a waiver of the right of access to a court of the classic kind by means of an arbitration agreement is not disputed, such a waiver must satisfy the relevant requirements, i.e. be free, lawful, unequivocal and accompanied with certain minimum procedural safeguards. As seen, the relevant test has been applied by the Convention controlling bodies in all arbitration-related cases when determining whether arbitrating parties waived their right of access to a court in favor of another method of adjudication—arbitration. Equally, in the much narrower sense, the same test was applied by the ECtHR in the *Tabbane v. Switzerland* case in determining whether the specific exclusion agreement in the particular circumstances could have been considered as an effective waiver of the right of access to a court by means of setting-aside proceedings.

Theoretically, one may argue that by concluding an arbitration agreement and choosing as a seat of arbitration a State that does provide in its national law a mechanism for challenging arbitral awards, parties voluntarily waive both the possibility to have the matter referred to courts of the classic kind in favor of another method of adjudication—arbitration (the broader waiver) and the entitlement to the possibility to have an arbitral award set aside by national courts (the narrower waiver). The effectiveness of the broader waiver, provided it is free, lawful and unequivocal, is not disputed from the standpoint of the Convention. Therefore, further discussion will focus only on the narrower waiver, i.e. ascertaining whether the choice of a particular arbitral seat can satisfy the *waiver theory* so as to argue that through the choice of a specific arbitral seat parties also *exclude* (or *waive*) the right to apply for the setting-aside of an arbitral award.

7.3.1.1 The Condition of *Absence of Constraint*

The condition of *absence of constraint* is at all events one of the requirements to be satisfied for a waiver to be valid and effective for the Convention purposes.[177] The said condition has been at the forefront of the ECtHR's analysis in arbitration-related cases, including the latest *Tabbane v. Switzerland* and the *Pechstein* cases. In the former, the Court recognized that the arbitration agreement (and the exclusion agreement contained therein) was not signed under duress while in the latter, although the arbitration proceedings before the CAS were not imposed by law, the acceptance of the CAS's jurisdiction by signing an arbitration agreement had not been free from constraint due to the particular nature of sports arbitration.[178] Since in both cases the signing of the particular arbitration agreement was closely interlinked with the consequential exclusion of setting-aside proceedings,[179] the requirement of *absence of constraint* may be considered as a necessary precondition also exclusively in relation to an exclusion agreement, irrespective of the underlying arbitration agreement. This would certainly be the case if an exclusion agreement is concluded by means of a subsequent written agreement, and not initially included in the arbitration agreement.

[177] See, e.g., *Deweer v. Belgium*, App. No. 6903/75, ECtHR, 27 February 1980, para. 49.

[178] *Mutu and Pechstein v. Switzerland*, App. Nos. 40575/10 and 67474/10, 2 October 2018, paras. 113–115.

[179] In the *Tabbane v. Switzerland* case this is evidenced by the 'exclusion agreement' itself being read into the arbitration agreement. In the *Pechstein* case, the issue of exclusion agreements and art. 192(1) PILA was only marginal, therefore more valuable example in this regard could be the previously mentioned *Cañas* case whereby the exclusion of setting-aside proceedings resulted from consent to ATP procedural rules which, in turn, contained an arbitration agreement and an exclusion agreement, stipulating that the decision of the CAS shall be final, non-reviewable, non-appealable and enforceable. Due to the particular nature of sports arbitration, arguments regarding the condition of 'absence of constraint' for the purposes of present analysis stem from both the ECtHR *Pechstein* judgment and the Swiss Federal Tribunal's *Cañas* case.

An argument that total exclusion of setting-aside proceedings in national law violates the right of access to a court from the standpoint of the *waiver theory*, in particular, the non-fulfillment of the criterion of *absence of constraint*, requires to look at the issue not so much from the formal subjective perspective, ascertaining whether arbitrating party's consent to arbitrate in the particular State not providing for the annulment mechanism, was vitiated by real duress,[180] but, more importantly, from the broader perspective, analyzing whether, to put it in the words of the ECtHR, parties have been under an obligation to exclude any recourse against an arbitral award.[181] The voluntariness of the exclusion agreement, as emphasized by the Court in the *Tabbane v. Switzerland* case,[182] was stressed against the requirement of *absence of constraint* already above and the same conclusions apply *mutatis mutandis* also here.[183]

If arbitrating parties voluntarily choose an arbitral seat where no annulment is possible, they should foresee that their right to have an arbitral award set aside will in effect be non-existent. However, if, as in the *Tabbane v. Switzerland* case, parties merely stipulate that the seat of arbitration shall be determined by the arbitral tribunal, certainly arbitrating parties' *choice* of a seat of arbitration not providing for the annulment mechanism is not entirely free. A waiver under the Convention must follow from one's own free will, demonstrating that a person is fully aware of the rights that he or she waives.[184] Evidently, by simply stipulating that the arbitral tribunal (or, in alternative, the respective arbitral institution) shall determine the seat of arbitration, one cannot be fully aware of the particular seat, let alone the relevant arbitration legislation and whether or not the particular State permits the annulment of arbitral awards or not.

Alternatively, a national regime not providing for setting-aside proceedings arguably fails to satisfy the requirement that parties should not be under an obligation to exclude setting aside proceedings. As seen, the ECtHR put considerable emphasis on the aspect of voluntariness in the *Tabbane v. Switzerland* case. If parties (or an arbitral tribunal) chose an arbitral seat where the annulment of arbitral awards

---

[180] Petrochilos (2004), p. 114. Any form of economic duress does not per se imply that a waiver is invalid. See, e.g. *Axelsson and others v. Sweden*, App. No. 11960/86, ECmHR, 13 July 1990; *Hedland v. Sweden*, App. No. 24118/94, ECmHR, 9 April 1997. In any event, provided such a consent was indeed vitiated by real duress, the requirement of 'absence of constraint' would not be fulfilled.

[181] *Tabbane v. Switzerland*, App. No. 41069/12, ECtHR, 1 March 2016, para. 34 ('[…] il convient de noter qu'une partie, n'ayant ni domicile, ni résidence habituelle, ni établissement en Suisse, n'est nullement obligée d'exclure tout recours; bien au contraire, elle peut librement choisir de saisir cette possibilité qu'offre la loi suisse en renonçant valablement à tout recours à un tribunal ordinaire.').

[182] Ibid.

[183] See Sect. 7.2.1.1.

[184] See Lawson (1996), p. 159 in referring to *T v. Italy*, App. No. 14104/88, ECtHR, 12 October 1992). See also *Talat Tunç v. Turkey*, App. No. 32432/96, ECtHR, 27 March 2007, para. 59; *Jones v. the United Kingdom*, App. No. 30900/03, ECtHR, 9 September 2003; *Aleksandr Zaichenko v. Russia*, App. No. 39660/02, ECtHR, 18 February 2010, para. 40. Implicitly on this requirement applied by the ECtHR in an arbitration-related case see, e.g. *Suovaniemi and others v. Finland*, App. No. 31737/96, ECtHR, 23 February 1999.

is not possible, they would effectively be under an obligation to exclude setting-aside proceedings simply due to the reason that such a remedy is non-existent under the relevant law. Generally, States permitting exclusion agreements provide this as an option—parties are free to explicitly agree on the exclusion of setting-aside proceedings. On the opposite, the much-criticized former Belgian law and the current Latvian approach leaves parties with no choice but to accept the legislative state of affairs if they choose to arbitrate in that particular country. In Belgium, the 1998 amendments to the BCCP saw this mandatory non-applicability of setting-aside proceedings reversed, however, in Latvia this is still the case. Arbitrating parties in Latvia have neither a choice to opt in and include in their arbitration agreement a remedy, allowing national courts to decide on challenges of arbitral awards. In essence, even though parties' choice in favour of arbitration may be entirely free, it can be said that their *choice* vis-à-vis setting-aside proceedings is constrained. This, in turn raises a question of proportionality of such a legislative approach, addressed in more detail below.

Moreover, the obligatory character of a legislative regime not providing for the annulment mechanism (and neither providing option to opt-in) to some extent resembles sports arbitration briefly addressed above, at least insofar parties in both situations are left with no choice but to accept the relevant state of affairs. The ECtHR has recently concluded in the *Pechstein* case that athletes are not acting freely in their acceptance of arbitration clauses, therefore sports arbitration before the CAS must in fact be regarded as 'forced' and thus should offer all the guarantees of Article 6(1) of the ECHR.[185] More in particular with regard to exclusion agreements, the Swiss Federal Tribunal recognized in *Cañas* case that an exclusion agreement, notwithstanding its technical validity, cannot, in principle, be used as a defense against an athlete due to the athlete's consent to an exclusion agreement not being the result of a freely expressed desire.[186] Equally, one may argue that arbitrating parties' acceptance of a legislative vacuum with regard to setting-aside proceedings, is merely something that parties cannot influence upon choosing to arbitrate in the particular State not providing the relevant remedy.

Clearly, the said reasoning may seem a bit far-fetched—by choosing a particular arbitral seat parties inevitably accept also that seat's *lex arbitri* with all its benefits and possible drawbacks. Therefore, although there are indications in favor of considering total exclusion of setting-aside proceedings as not satisfying the *waiver theory* due to the failure to adhere to the condition of *absence of constraint*, one must not view the issue in isolation from the closely linked requirement of *unequivocality*.

[185] *Mutu and Pechstein v. Switzerland*, App. Nos. 40575/10 and 67474/10, 2 October 2018, para. 115.

[186] Decision of the Swiss Federal Tribunal in case No. ATF 133 III 235, 22 March 2007.

7.3.1.2 The Condition of *Unequivocality*

A waiver of the exercise of a right guaranteed by the Convention must be expressed *unequivocally*, leaving no doubt as to its existence and scope. Although in the *Tabbane v. Switzerland* case the Court initially refers to this requirement from the broader perspective (i.e. waiver of the right of access to a court in favor of arbitration)[187] the Court's further reference explicitly to the relevant arbitration agreement constituting an alleged exclusion agreement suggests that the condition of *unequivocality* is in fact considered from the much narrower perspective,[188] scrutinizing not only the *unequivocality* of parties' choice in favor of arbitration, but, in particular, also such *unequivocality* with regard to their choice to exclude the annulment mechanism.

As stressed when addressing the issue of exclusion agreements, it is arguable whether in the *Tabbane v. Switzerland* case the parties' choice in favor of an exclusion agreement was indeed *unequivocal*—not only they did not themselves choose Switzerland as the seat of arbitration, but the wording of their alleged exclusion agreement was ambiguous, Switzerland being seemingly the only State permitting exclusion agreements where such a vague wording could lead to an effective exclusion agreement.

Arguably, a waiver of the right to access to a court through setting-aside proceedings simply through the choice of a particular State as the arbitral seat even more so fails to satisfy the requirement of *unequivocality*. The *Tabbane v. Switzerland* decision implies that the Convention requires an explicit exclusion of setting-aside proceedings, in turn leaving a certain margin of appreciation for the particular State with regard to the particular wording of an exclusion agreement and the required standard of *explicitness*. In circumstances where parties simply choose an arbitral seat, as opposed to explicitly renouncing their right to setting-aside proceedings, the waiver of the right of access to a court through setting-aside proceedings may be considered as equivocal, certainly leaving room for doubts as to its scope (being interpreted so broadly) and existence it the first place.

7.3.1.3 The Condition of *Minimum Safeguards*

In order to be effective for the Convention purposes a waiver of the right of access to a court under Article 6(1) ECHR must be also attended by certain *minimum safeguards* commensurate to the importance of such a waiver. Determination of whether or not a waiver is accompanied by *minimums safeguards* commensurate to

[187] *Tabbane v. Switzerland*, App. No. 41069/12, ECtHR, 1 March 2016, para. 30 ('La renonciation au droit à un tribunal (ordinaire) en faveur d'un arbitrage doit être intervenue sans équivoque.').

[188] Ibid. ('En l'espèce, le Tribunal fédéral est arrivé à la conclusion, par voie d'interprétation des volontés des parties, que celles-ci, par l'inclusion d'une clause de renonciation dans l'article 8 b du compromis (paragraphe 4 ci–dessus) ont exclu tout recours contre la sentence arbitrale. A la lumière du texte de la clause («neither party shall have any right to appeal such decision to any court of law») et dans la mesure où elle est compétente pour trancher cette question, la Cour estime qu'une telle conclusion ne paraît ni arbitraire ni déraisonnable.').

its importance will depend on both the particular factual circumstances of the case and also the underlying national legislative framework.[189] While the former aspect is rather subjective, the latter aspect is purely objective—the existence of *minimum safeguards* in the relevant *lex arbitri* is ascertainable a priori.

Generally, States permitting exclusion agreements nevertheless provide in their national arbitration laws certain *minimum safeguards* that at least partially reduce the possibility of gross procedural violations during arbitration proceedings. This is evidenced not only by certain peculiarities of each *lex arbitri* in this regard (e.g. the availability of *révision* in Switzerland and comparable action in France; distinction between grounds of invalidity and grounds for challenge in Sweden etc.), but also generally by the overall quality of the formal legal infrastructure at those seats. Therefore, even if parties decide to voluntarily exclude the annulment mechanism, observance of their fundamental rights may be guaranteed through other means, among which the most notable being the possibility, in certain well-defined circumstances, of access to national courts already during arbitration proceedings. The in-detail discussed States permitting arbitrating parties to exclude setting-aside proceedings equally provide them with various additional remedies, such as a separate action for challenging the independence and impartiality of arbitrators[190] and assistance of national courts in the taking of evidence,[191] by means of which arbitrating parties are afforded certain *minimum safeguards*. These safeguards, at least to a certain extent, can be considered as commensurating to the importance of excluding the annulment mechanism at the post award stage.

In Latvia, however, not only arbitrating parties are not provided with a possibility to apply for the setting aside of an arbitral award, but the Latvian *lex arbitri* per se cannot be considered as an adequate source providing parties with necessary remedies needed for the protection of their fundamental rights both during and after the arbitration proceedings. Court involvement in arbitration proceedings in Latvia is limited to a bare minimum—courts interact with arbitration only by referring, if necessary, parties to arbitration, issuing of interim measures prior to the establishment of an arbitral tribunal, and in recognizing and enforcing arbitral awards. As a result of

---

[189] The importance of the latter, in particular, has been stressed by the Convention controlling bodies in multiple arbitration-related cases. See, e.g. See, e.g. *R v. Switzerland*, App. No. 10881/84, ECmHR, 4 March 1987 ('The Commission nevertheless considers that, in order to answer the question of whether the guarantees secured by Article 6 apply, account must be taken not only of the arbitration agreement between the parties and the nature of the private arbitration proceedings, but also of the legislative framework providing for such proceedings.') and *Nordström-Janzon and Nordström-Lehtinen v. the Netherlands*, App. No. 28101/95, ECmHR, 27 November 1996 ('However, the Commission considers that account must be taken not only of the arbitration agreement between the parties and the nature of the private arbitration proceedings, but also of the legislative framework providing for such proceedings in order to determine whether the domestic courts retained some measure of control of the arbitration proceedings and whether this control has been properly exercised in the concrete case […]').

[190] See, e.g. art. 180 of the PILA; art. 1680(2) of the BCCP; sec. 10 of the SAA; art. 1454 of the FCCP.

[191] See, e.g. art. 184 of the PILA; art. 1680(4) of the BCCP; sec. 26 of the SAA; art. 1469 of the FCCP.

the Latvian Constitutional Court's *Hiponia* ruling national courts must now also hear claims regarding the existence and validity of arbitration agreements. However, the 2015 Arbitration Law and the LCCP are silent upon other generally accepted roles of national courts vis-à-vis arbitration. The non-existence of adequate court assistance to arbitration proceedings raises reasonable doubts as to whether the already unique *waiver*, i.e. a legislative approach of excluding setting-aside proceedings altogether, is accompanied by sufficient *minimum safeguards* that commensurate to the significance of not having a possibility to apply for the setting aside of an arbitral award.

For example, with regard to one of the *non-waivable* rights of Article 6(1) of the ECHR, i.e. the right to an independent and impartial tribunal, it has been argued that 'parties should be able to have an arbitrator removed without having to go through the whole process of an arbitration which, at its conclusion, is likely to be a nullity.'[192] Indeed, the best solution would be to have a separate remedy in the applicable *lex arbitri* that would allow arbitrating parties to address national courts already during arbitration proceedings with various issues relating to parties' procedural human rights, including that of challenging arbitrators on grounds of lack of independence and impartiality. This, as was explained above, is the case in all of the in-detail discussed States permitting exclusion agreements[193] and can be seen as a *minimum safeguard* available for arbitrating parties even if they decide to exclude setting-aside proceedings.

If, however, there is neither a specific remedy allowing to challenge the independence and impartiality of arbitrators before national courts already during the arbitration proceedings, nor an annulment mechanism available at the post award stage, arbitrating parties are left with no effective remedy to address violations of their *non-waivable* right to independent and impartial arbitral tribunal within the meaning of Article 6(1) of the ECHR. In Latvia, this translates into a situation where, despite the 2015 Arbitration Law containing references to certain qualities of arbitrators,[194] in reality there is no effective mechanism for challenging arbitrators or applying for the annulment of an arbitral award on the basis of lack of independence or impartiality of the arbitral tribunal. Therefore, even if arbitrating parties' choice of Latvia as an arbitral seat could hypothetically be considered as an implied waiver of the right of access to a court through the setting-aside proceedings, such a waiver would arguably be ineffective for the Convention purposes as it is not accompanied by certain *minimum safeguards* commensurate to the importance of such a waiver.

---

[192] Petrochilos (2004), p. 136.

[193] See, e.g. art. 180 of the PILA; art. 1680(2) of the BCCP; sec. 10 SAA; art. 1454 of the FCCP.

[194] See arts. 14–17 of the 2015 Arbitration Law.

7.3.1.4 The Condition of *Public Interest*

The required condition that a waiver must not run counter to any important *public interest* has been introduced above.[195] The reader has been also introduced to the relevant interests and policy considerations in favour of and against exclusion agreements (or generally the existence of setting-aside proceedings in national arbitration law per se).[196] The above discussion *mutatis mutandis* applies also when considering whether a *waiver* of the annulment mechanism through a simple choice of an arbitral seat runs counter to any important *public interest*. As discussed, there are numerous interests and policy considerations behind the continuous existence of setting-aside proceedings in contemporary framework of international arbitration.[197]

As in the *Tabbane v. Switzerland* ruling where the ECtHR did not expressly address the condition of *public interest* when examining the requirements of the *waiver theory*, but continued with directly addressing the issue of whether Article 192(1) of the PILA is compatible with the right of access to a court under Article 6(1) of the ECHR, discussion of the relevant interests behind total exclusion of setting-aside proceedings equally mandates that the said phenomenon is looked not only from the perspective of the *waiver theory*, but, somewhat more generally, from the perspective of its compatibility with the right of access to a court under Article 6(1) of the ECHR.

7.3.2 *Total Exclusion of Setting-Aside Proceedings and the Right of Access to a Court*

The Court's analysis in the *Tabbane v. Switzerland* case represents a two-fold approach to the issue of validity of exclusion agreements in the particular circumstances with the right of access to a court under Article 6(1) of the ECHR. Firstly, the Court analyzes the matter from the perspective of the *waiver theory*, impliedly concluding that the relevant arbitrating party waived the right of access to a court. Secondly, despite concluding that a waiver in such circumstances was valid and effective for the Convention purposes, the Court continuous with considering the matter from the perspective of the consistency of Article 192(1) of the PILA with Article 6(1) of the ECHR. Namely, the Court considers whether the possibility of excluding setting-aside proceedings as provided by the Swiss legislator can be seen as a limitation to the right of access to a court under Article 6(1) of the ECHR.[198]

---

[195] See Sect. 3.5.5 and Sect. 7.2.1.4.

[196] See Sect. 7.2.1.5 and Sect. 7.2.1.6.

[197] Ibid.

[198] *Tabbane v. Switzerland*, App. No. 41069/12, ECtHR, 1 March 2016, para. 32 ('Concernant la question de savoir si l'article 192 alinéa 1 LDIP est compatible avec l'art. 6 § 1 de la Convention, à savoir si la possibilité de renoncer à recourir contre une sentence arbitrale ne viole pas l'article 6 § 1 de la Convention […]').

The right of access to a court under Article 6(1) of the ECHR is not absolute—the ECHR Member States are afforded a certain margin of appreciation and procedural discretion in guaranteeing individuals the right of access to a court.[199] The pioneering *Golder* case suggests that the right of access to a court 'by its very nature calls for regulation by the state, regulation which may vary in time and place according to the needs and resources of the community and of individuals'.[200] At the same time, it is equally established that limitations to the right of access to a court must not 'restrict or reduce the access left to the individual in such a way or to such an extent that the very essence of the right is impaired'.[201] The boundaries to the ECHR Member States' margin of appreciation in this regard are determined by the Court—a limitation on the right of access to a court will be compatible with Article 6(1) of the ECHR insofar it pursues a legitimate aim and there is a reasonable relationship of proportionality between the means employed and the aim sought to be achieved. Therefore, in order to determine whether total exclusion of setting-aside proceedings may lead to a violation of the right of access to a court under Article 6(1) of the ECHR, the phenomenon of total exclusion, similarly to the Swiss legislator's choice of providing arbitrating parties with a possibility to voluntarily exclude setting-aside proceedings, must be considered against the required preconditions for a valid and effective limitation of an individual's right of access to a court under Article 6(1) of the ECHR. Namely, one must ask whether such a legislative approach pursues a legitimate aim and whether there is a reasonable relationship of proportionality between the means employed and the aim sought to be achieved.

7.3.2.1 Legitimate Aim

The non-absolute character of the right of access to a court is evidenced not only by the fact that, as seen, it can be validly waived under certain conditions but also by the fact that it can also be validly restricted through procedural limitations, such as time-limits,[202] court fees,[203] security for costs and other limitations. In other words,

---

[199]The ECtHR has recently recognized that despite the right to bring a civil claim before a court is one of the universally recognised fundamental principles of law, the Court does not consider these guarantees to be among the norms of *jus cogens* in the current state of international law. See *Al-Dulimi and Montana Management Inc. v. Switzerland*, App. No. 5809/08, ECtHR [GC], 21 June 2016, para. 136.

[200]*Golder v. United Kingdom*, App. No. 4451/70, ECtHR, 21 February 1975, para. 38 quoting the so-called Belgian linguistics case, Apps. No. 1474/62; 1677/62; 1691/62; 1769/63; 1994/63; 2126/64, ECtHR, 23 July 1968, para. 5. More recently see, e.g. *Jureša v. Croatia*, App. No. 24079/11, ECtHR, 22 May 2018, para. 41; *Dimitras v. Greece*, App. No. 11946/11, ECtHR, 19 April 2018, para. 38.

[201]*Ashingdane v. the United Kingdom*, App. No. 8225/78, ECtHR, 28 May 1985, para. 57. See also, e.g. *Philis v. Greece*, Apps. No. *12750/87; 13780/88; 14003/*88, ECtHR, 27 August 1991, para. 59; *De Geouffre de la Pradelle v. France*, App. No. 12964/87, ECtHR, 16 December 1992, para. 28; *Stanev v. Bulgaria*, App. No. 36760/06, ECtHR [GC], 17 January 2012, para. 229.

[202]See, e.g. *Stubbings and Others v. the United Kingdom*, App. Nos. 22083/93 and 22095/93, ECtHR, 22 October 1996, paras. 51–57.

[203]See, e.g. *Kreuz v. Poland*, App. No. 28249/95, ECtHR, 19 June 2001, paras. 58–66.

the ECHR Member States enjoy a certain margin of appreciation in regulating the right of access to a court. The margin of appreciation in this regard has been also recognized by the Convention's controlling bodies with regard to regulation of setting aside-proceedings and the grounds on which an arbitral award may be set aside by national courts.[204] At the same time, although in cases such as the *Nordström-Janzon and Nordström-Lehtinen v. the Netherlands, Suovaniemi and others v. Finland* and the recent *Tabbane v. Switzerland*, the Convention controlling bodies have addressed the issue of availability of setting-aside proceedings, their conclusions, in particular with regard to States' discretion to decide for themselves on which grounds arbitral awards should be set aside, related to the scope of such a mechanism, and not to its very existence under national law.

In *Nordström-Janzon and Nordström-Lehtinen v. the Netherlands* the scope of the Dutch annulment ground of public policy was at stake; the *Suovaniemi and others v. Finland* concerned a collateral estoppel as a bar to setting-aside proceedings while the *Tabbane v. Switzerland* case related to parties' voluntary exclusion of setting-aside proceedings. To date, the Convention controlling bodies have not ruled on a case pertaining to total exclusion (non-availability) of the annulment mechanism under national law and such approach's compatibility with the right of access to a court under Article 6(1) of the ECHR.

When looking at the requirement of a *legitimate aim* as a *conditio sine qua non* for a valid limitation of a right of access to a court under Article 6(1) of the ECHR, the Convention controlling bodies' case-law is rather extensive in this respect—the following, inter alia, have been considered as *legitimate aims* limiting the right of access to a court: proper functioning of the judiciary,[205] proper administration of justice,[206] legal certainty,[207] good international relations requiring State immunity,[208] and also restrictions aimed at preventing court overload so as to avoid that courts become overloaded with cases of lesser importance.[209]

[204] See, e.g. *Nordström-Janzon and Nordström-Lehtinen v. the Netherlands*, App. No. 28101/95, ECmHR, 27 November 1996 ('the grounds on which arbitral awards may be challenged before national courts differ among the Contracting States and […] each Contracting State may in principle decide itself on which grounds an arbitral award should be quashed.'). See also *Suovaniemi and others v. Finland*, App. No. 31737/96, ECtHR, 23 February 1999 ('[T]he Contracting States enjoy considerable discretion in regulating the question on which grounds an arbitral award should be quashed, since the quashing of an already rendered award will often mean that a long and costly arbitral procedure will become useless and that considerable work and expense must be invested in new proceedings […]').

[205] *Ernst and Others v. Belgium*, App. No. 33400/96, ECtHR, 15 July 2003, para. 50.

[206] *Harrison Mckee v. Hungary*, App. No. 22840/07, ECtHR, 3 June 2014, para. 27. See also *Tolstoy Miloslavsky v. the United Kingdom*, App. No. 18139/91, ECtHR, para. 61; *Annoni di Gussola and Others v. France*, App. Nos. 31819/96 and 33293/96, ECtHR, 14 November 2000, para. 51; *Stone Court Shipping Company, S.A. v. Spain*, App. No. 55524/00, ECtHR, 28 October 2003, para. 34.

[207] *Tricard v. France*, App. No. 40472/98, ECtHR, 10 July 2001, para. 29.

[208] *Prince Hans-Adam II of Liechtenstein v. Germany*, App. No. 42527/98, ECtHR [GC], 12 July 2001, para. 69.

[209] *Brualla Gómez de la Torre v. Spain*, App. No. 26737/95, ECtHR, 19 December 1997, para. 36.

More in particular with regard to alleged *legitimate aims* behind the limitation of the right of access to a court through regulation of setting-aside proceedings, helpful guidance as to what could constitute a *legitimate aim* in such circumstances is found in the former Commission's reasoning in the *Nordström-Janzon and Nordström-Lehtinen v. the Netherlands* case where it held that:

> It finds it reasonable that in this respect [in determining whether or not to quash an arbitral award] Dutch law requires strong reasons for quashing an already rendered award, since the quashing will often mean that a long and costly arbitral procedure will become useless and that considerable work and expense must be invested in new proceedings.[210]

The same argument was used by the ECtHR in the *Suovaniemi and others v. Finland* case.[211] Moreover, as seen with regard to the alleged *legitimate aims* behind exclusion agreements, the ECtHR noted in the *Tabbane v. Switzerland* case that:

> [...] Article 192 PILA reflects a legislative policy choice that meets the desire of the Swiss legislator to increase the attractiveness and effectiveness of international arbitration in Switzerland by removing awards from the double control of the appeals body and the exequatur judge, and to lighten the workload of the Federal Tribunal [...][212]

Concluding its findings in the *Tabbane v. Switzerland* case, the ECtHR similarly found that:

> In light of the foregoing, the restriction of the right of access to a court pursued a legitimate aim, namely the development of Swiss arbitral seat by flexible and speedy procedures, while respecting the freedom of contract of the applicant and cannot be regarded as disproportionate.[213]

Also in the recent *Pechstein* ruling the Court recalled that:

> [...] it has already pointed out that the PILA reflected a choice of legislative policy which responded to the Swiss legislator's wish to increase the attractiveness and effectiveness of

---

[210] *Nordström-Janzon and Nordström-Lehtinen v. the Netherlands*, App. No. 28101/95, ECmHR, 27 November 1996.

[211] See also *Suovaniemi and others v. Finland*, App. No. 31737/96, ECtHR, 23 February 1999 ('[T]he Contracting States enjoy considerable discretion in regulating the question on which grounds an arbitral award should be quashed, since the quashing of an already rendered award will often mean that a long and costly arbitral procedure will become useless and that considerable work and expense must be invested in new proceedings [...]').

[212] *Tabbane v. Switzerland*, App. No. 41069/12, ECtHR, 1 March 2016, para. 33. Author's translation. The original reads as follows: '[...] l'article 192 LDIP reflète un choix de politique législative qui répond au souhait du législateur suisse d'augmenter l'attractivité et l'efficacité de l'arbitrage international en Suisse, en évitant que la sentence soit soumise au double contrôle de l'autorité de recours et du juge de l'*exequatur*, et de décharger le Tribunal fédéral [...]'.

[213] *Tabbane v. Switzerland*, App. No. 41069/12, ECtHR, 1 March 2016, para. 36. Author's translation. The original reads as follows: 'Compte tenu de ce qui précède, la restriction du droit d'accès à un tribunal a poursuivi un but légitime, à savoir la mise en valeur de la place arbitrale suisse, par des procédures souples et rapides, tout en respectant la liberté contractuelle du requérant, et ne saurait être considérée comme disproportionnée.'

> international arbitration in Switzerland […] and that the development of the Swiss place of arbitration could constitute a legitimate aim […][214]

All of the above suggests that, in the eyes of the Convention controlling bodies, the following aspects constitute *legitimate aims* for restrictively regulating setting-aside proceedings and providing arbitrating parties with a possibility to voluntary exclude the application of setting-aside proceedings: cost and time efficiency; alleged increased attractiveness and effectiveness of a particular seat of arbitration; development of an arbitral seat by introducing flexible and speedy procedures; avoidance of *double-control*; and prevention of increase of court overload.

Although it is disputed whether or not, at least in Switzerland, the particular aims behind PILA are indeed achieved, they could, in the eyes of the ECtHR, constitute *legitimate aims* for such a legislative policy. The question, however, is what *legitimate aims*, if any, are behind a legislative choice of excluding the annulment mechanisms in national law altogether.

Strive for increased attractiveness of Belgium as a seat of arbitration was also behind the Belgian legislator's policy to introduce amendments to the BCCP in 1985, excluding setting-aside proceedings automatically where both arbitrating parties were not of Belgian nationality or did not have residence in Belgium. However, despite the Belgian legislator's *good* intentions, the said legislative *innovation* achieved exactly the opposite—arbitrating parties and arbitral institutions shied away from designating Belgium as a seat of arbitration. Evidently, therefore, an argument of increased attractiveness exists as a seeming *legitimate aim* only in theory. Moreover, considering the somewhat hesitant use by arbitrating parties of the possibility to exclude setting-aside proceedings in States permitting such a possibility, it is arguable whether the availability of such a possibility in national arbitration law is indeed what attracts arbitrating parties to a particular arbitral seat. Recent studies show that the availability of a possibility to exclude setting-aside proceedings is not among the most important reasons for preferring certain arbitral seats over others.[215]

The Convention controlling bodies' observations regarding alleged *legitimate aims* behind limiting arbitrating parties' right of access to a court by means of setting aside proceedings, whether this is due to cost and time efficiency, increased attractiveness and effectiveness of a particular arbitral seat, decrease of court workload or otherwise, seem to be concerned not so much with the actual achievement of these aims, but rather with the fact that such *aims* are pursued by the relevant legislator in the first place. Thus, a limitation of a right of access to a court will be effective for the Convention purposes if it solely, in the terminology used by the Convention controlling bodies, *pursues* a legitimate aim, notwithstanding whether or not such an

---

214 *Mutu and Pechstein v. Switzerland*, App. Nos. 40575/10 and 67474/10, 2 October 2018, para. 97 ('la Cour rappelle avoir déjà relevé que la LDIP reflétait un choix de politique législative qui répondait au souhait du législateur suisse d'augmenter l'attractivité et l'efficacité de l'arbitrage international en Suisse (*Tabbane*, décision précitée, § 33) et que la mise en valeur de la place arbitrale suisse pouvait constituer un but légitime (*ibidem*, § 36).').

215 With regard to arbitral seats see, e.g. Queen Mary University of London, White & Case (2018) 2018 International Arbitration Survey: The Evolution of International Arbitration, p. 9. http://www.arbitration.qmul.ac.uk/research/2018/. Accessed 29 May 2020.

aim is in fact achieved. Otherwise, the Court's analysis in the *Tabbane v. Switzerland* case would go much further than simply repeating what the Swiss legislator has put forward as alleged aims behind permitting exclusion agreements.

In all of the in-depth discussed legislative approaches to exclusion agreements, the respective legislators had stipulated certain aims that in their eyes would be achieved by allowing parties to exclude application of the annulment mechanism. Even the Belgian legislator had put forward certain alleged aims behind the total exclusion of setting-aside proceedings with the 1985 amendments to the BCCP. However, when looking at the example of Latvia and its policy considerations behind the legislative roller coaster vis-à-vis introduction of increased court assistance in arbitration, including setting-aside proceedings, it is difficult to identify what, if any, aims have been behind the continued non-introduction of the annulment mechanism in Latvia.

Contrary to States permitting exclusion agreements, the Latvian legislator in its choice for a legislative vacuum in this regard has not been guided by concerns of effectiveness or attractiveness of Latvia as a seat of arbitration, or cost and time saving, increased confidentiality or finality of arbitral awards. Seemingly the only reasonable explanation behind the continued non-availability of the annulment mechanism in Latvian law is found in the adverse consequences of the 1999 Arbitration Law, in particular the fact that it allowed any legal person to establish an arbitral institution. As explained, this led to a skyrocketing of arbitral institutions, the number of which in 2014 reached its peak—214. Currently, there are still 69 permanent arbitral institutions in Latvia.

The Explanatory report accompanying the draft 2015 Arbitration Law confirms that the main concern behind the Latvian legislator's unwillingness to introduce the UNCITRAL Model-Law-type court assistance to arbitration is the fact that with such a disproportionately high number of arbitral institutions, there is a high probability that ordinary jurisdiction courts would become overburdened with various legitimate and dilatory requests:

> The draft 'Law on Arbitration' does not provide court involvement of ordinary jurisdiction courts in, for example, the taking and securing of evidence, appointing arbitrators, challenging of arbitrators. One must note that currently there 214 arbitral institutions established and permanently operating in Latvia, a large part of which are operating in Riga city or Riga region. One must additionally note that the draft 'Law on Arbitration' permits also the establishment of ad hoc arbitral tribunals. At the same time, there are only 34 first instance courts of ordinary jurisdiction in Latvia, 5 of which are Riga city courts.
>
> Considering the current overload of ordinary jurisdiction courts and the terms for deciding cases, imposing additional obligations on part of ordinary jurisdiction courts is not supported […][216]

The above being the only account when the Latvian legislator has put forward plausible policy considerations behind adhering to minimal court involvement in

[216] See the draft 2015 Arbitration Law, Preliminary impact assessment report (Explanatory report), Section 2. http://titania.saeima.lv/LIVS11/saeimalivs11.nsf/0/A182DD228B4DAF6CC2257C4E003D7B1B?OpenDocument#b. Accessed 29 May 2020.

arbitration, and supposedly also non-provision of the annulment mechanism, it is questionable whether the legislator's concern of increased court workload can be seen as a *legitimate aim* for limiting arbitrating parties' right of access to a court by means of setting-aside proceedings.

The ECtHR has recognized that restrictions aimed at preventing court overload in order to avoid that courts become overloaded with cases of lesser importance may constitute a *legitimate aim* for the purposes of limiting the right of access to a court.[217] Also in the *Tabbane v. Switzerland* case the Court held that the lightening of the Swiss Federal Tribunal's workload may constitute a *legitimate aim*.[218] As seen, also the Latvian Constitutional Court recognized in the *Hiponia* case that limitation of arbitrating party's right of access to a court to challenge the validity of an arbitration agreement might pursue *legitimate aims*, such as decrease of court workload and provision of speedy and fast resolution of disputes.[219]

However, despite the fact that decrease in court workload can be seen as a *legitimate aim in abstracto*, it is questionable whether the same is true when looking at the actual reasons why the increase in court workload might be a potential issue in the first place. The Latvian legislator's argument regarding increased workload is not, as in the case of Switzerland, a pro-active defense of an already exceptionally well-functioning formal legal infrastructure that potentially, at least in the Swiss legislator's eyes, would only benefit from a reasoned legislative choice to permit exclusion agreements. The Latvian legislator's concerns of increased workload echo its own past mistakes, in particular, the already mentioned legislative choice to permit any legal person to establish an arbitral institution. It is exactly because of this that Latvia witnessed a boom of *pocket arbitral institutions* which, in turn, during the negotiations of the 2015 Arbitration Law led to concerns of excessive court overload if increased court assistance to arbitration is introduced. It is arguable that the defense of court overload can serve as a *legitimate aim* for limiting parties' right of access to a court by means of setting-aside proceedings in case the legislator itself has created an ill-functioning arbitration environment whose adverse consequences require that interests of court overload should seemingly take precedence over the protection of arbitrating parties' fundamental rights.

At the same time, considering that the ECtHR seemingly does not go as far as to inquire whether an alleged *legitimate aim* is in fact achieved by the respective limitation of an individual's right under the Convention, it is arguable that the Court would not in detail consider the actual reasons behind the need for such a *legitimate aim*. Therefore, notwithstanding the Latvian legislator's own past mistakes that eventually led to stipulating possible court overload as a reason against introduction

[217] *Brualla Gómez de la Torre v. Spain*, App. No. 26737/95, ECtHR, 19 December 1997, para. 36.

[218] *Tabbane v. Switzerland*, App. No. 41069/12, ECtHR, 1 March 2016, para. 33 ('[…] l'article 192 LDIP reflète un choix de politique législative qui répond au souhait du législateur suisse d'augmenter l'attractivité et l'efficacité de l'arbitrage international en Suisse, en évitant que la sentence soit soumise au double contrôle de l'autorité de recours et du juge de l'*exequatur*, et de décharger le Tribunal fédéral […]').

[219] *Hiponia* case, No. 2014-09-01, the Constitutional Court of the Republic of Latvia (2014), para. 19.

of increased court assistance in arbitration, including setting-aside proceedings, the aim to prevent court overload per se and *in abstracto* may be potentially viewed as a sound *legitimate aim* for the purposes of the Convention. However, even if a legislative regime omitting *in toto* the annulment mechanism may be seen as pursuing a *legitimate aim*, such as the prevention of court overload, it is arguable the degree of proportionality between the means chosen to achieve such *legitimate aims* is not reasonable. In such circumstances the right of access to a court is restricted in such a way or to such an extent that the very essence of the right is impaired'.[220]

7.3.2.2 Proportionality

It is established case-law that even if a limitation on the right of access to a court under Article 6(1) of the ECHR pursues a legitimate aim, there must be also a reasonable relationship of proportionality between the means employed and the aim sought to be achieved.[221]

As seen when analyzing the *Tabbane v. Switzerland* case, Article 192(1) of the PILA and the possibility of excluding setting-aside proceedings as provided therein was seen by the Court as not only pursuing a *legitimate aim*, as explained above, but also as being *proportionate* to that aim.[222] This was not only due to the aspect of voluntariness that characterizes the Swiss approach to exclusion agreements, but also due the consequences of Article 192(2) of the PILA, i.e. the fact that even if arbitrating parties exclude the action for annulment, provided such an award is to enforced in Switzerland, the New York Convention applies by analogy. This, in the Court's opinion, adds additional scrutiny by ordinary courts to arbitral tribunals.[223]

However, at least in the case of Latvia, it is certainly not voluntariness that characterizes total exclusion of setting-aside proceedings in national arbitration law. The non-availability of the annulment mechanism at the post award stage does not follow from parties' contractual freedom. If the ECtHR put seemingly decisive emphasis on the aspect of party autonomy in concluding that Article 192(1) of the PILA is consistent with Article 6(1) of the ECHR and the right of access to a court, naturally, the Latvian approach may seem as a disproportionate limitation to parties' right of access to a court under Article 6(1) of the ECHR.

---

[220] *Ashingdane v. the United Kingdom*, App. No. 8225/78, ECtHR, 28 May 1985, para. 57. See also, e.g. *Philis v. Greece*, Apps. No. *12750/87; 13780/88; 14003/*88, ECtHR, 27 August 1991, para. 59; *De Geouffre de la Pradelle v. France*, App. No. 12964/87, ECtHR, 16 December 1992, para. 28; *Stanev v. Bulgaria*, App. No. 36760/06, ECtHR [GC], 17 January 2012, para. 229.

[221] See, e.g. *Waite and Kennedy v. Germany*, 26083/94, ECtHR [GC], 18 February 1999, para. 59; *Fogarty v. United Kingdom*, App. No. 37112/97, ECtHR [GC], 21 November 2001, para. 33; *Cudak v. Lithuania*, App. No. 15869/02, ECtHR [GC], 23 March 2010, para. 55. See more recently, e.g. *Kamenova v. Bulgaria*, App. No. 62784/09, ECtHR, 12 July 2018, para. 43; *Zubac v. Croatia*, App. No. 40160/12, ECtHR [GC], 12 April 2018, para. 78.

[222] *Tabbane v. Switzerland*, App. No. 41069/12, ECtHR, 1 March 2016, paras 34; 35 and 36.

[223] The ECtHR in this regard refers to *Zamet - Budowa Maszyn Spółka Akcyjna v. Poland*, App. No. 1485/11, ECtHR, 25 August 2015, para. 28.

In 2005 the Latvian Constitutional Court, despite its *obiter dicta* regarding the necessity to introduce setting-aside proceedings, nevertheless found that 'control [over arbitration proceedings] during the enforcement stage is considered a sufficient mean, at least to guarantee the compliance of fundamental rights.'[224] Similarly, the ECtHR in the *Tabbane v. Switzerland*, albeit solely in addition to the main aspect of voluntariness, emphasized the availability of court scrutiny at the enforcement stage. At the same time, the Latvian Constitutional Court's 2014 *Hiponia* ruling suggests that in certain circumstances court scrutiny of arbitration only at the enforcement stage may not be sufficient to guarantee the protection of parties' fundamental human rights. Also in the *Zamet—Budowa Maszyn Spółka Akcyjna v. Poland* case, to which the ECtHR refers to in support of its argument in the *Tabbane v. Switzerland* case, stipulates control at the enforcement stage only as a supplementary remedy to the availability of setting-aside proceedings:

> The Court further notes that the parties have remedies which enable them to contest the judgments of the courts of arbitration in case of qualified violations of the law; a judgment given by the court of arbitration may be quashed, among other things, if in the proceedings before the court of arbitration the rules of fair trial, including the right to defense, were not respected […] Furthermore, any judgment of the court of arbitration, before it is enforced, needs to be recognized by the domestic court. The requirement of recognition is a further institution by which the courts exercise control over the jurisprudence of the courts of arbitration.[225]

The question with regard to total exclusion of setting-aside proceedings in national arbitration law, however, is whether, considering the absence of voluntariness and party autonomy in this respect, court scrutiny solely at the enforcement stage can guarantee parties the protection of their fundamental procedural human rights. In order to determine this one must weigh the *proportionality* of a legislative regime omitting setting-aside proceedings *in toto* against the aims that such a legislative regime allegedly pursues.

The *classic* proportionality test, as developed and utilized by the German Federal Constitutional Court (*Bundesverfassungsgericht*)[226] and also other courts, including the Latvian Constitutional Court, is much more detailed than the proportionality test applied by the ECtHR. While the ECtHR appears to generally focus on the balance between the means employed and the aim sought to be achieved, the *classic* proportionality test subjects limitations of fundamental rights to a three-pronged test, cumulatively requiring (i) *suitability* (measures affecting and limiting fundamental rights must be suitable for the purpose of attaining the pursued aim; (ii) *necessity* (a suitable measure must also be necessary in a sense the aim pursued cannot be achieved by other equally suitable measures that are less restrictive to the protected rights; and (iii) *balance*—(requiring that a reasonable balance is achieved by the

[224] See *Asmers* case, No. 2004-10-01, the Constitutional Court of the Republic of Latvia, 17 January 2005, para. 9.1. www.satv.tiesa.gov.lv/wp-content/uploads/2004/05/2004-10-01_Spriedums_ENG.pdf. Accessed 29 April 2020.

[225] *Zamet - Budowa Maszyn Spółka Akcyjna v. Poland*, App. No. 1485/11, ECtHR, 25 August 2015, para. 28.

[226] See generally Hirschberg (1981), Schlink (1976), Alexy (2002).

interests served by the measure and the interests that are harmed by introducing it).[227] Notably, the Court's utilized proportionality test is reflected in the third prong of the *classic* proportionality test.

Suitability

Despite the fact that the Latvian legislator has not formally *expressis verbis* formulated which legitimate aims or policy considerations are behind its continuous reluctance to introduce the annulment mechanism in Latvian arbitration law, the above discussion has shown that this is mainly due to concerns of increased court overload.

Certainly, statutory non-provision of the annulment mechanism achieves the alleged legitimate aim of preventing increased court overload in case Latvian law would introduce the UNCITRAL Model Law-type court assistance to arbitration, including the annulment mechanism. Since there is no remedy to this effect available under national law, State courts are not called upon to decide on the annulment of arbitral awards and therefore no increase in court workload is seen. In that sense, the legislative vacuum in this regard is *perfectly* suitable for achieving the alleged legitimate aim of prevention of court overload.

Necessity

The condition of necessity requires that the respective measure limiting individual's fundamental rights is necessary, i.e. the aim pursued by such a limitation cannot be achieved by other equally suitable measures that are less restrictive to the protected rights.[228] As regards total exclusion of setting-aside proceedings in the case of Latvia, this would require that such a legislative choice was necessary for the purposes of achieving its alleged *legitimate aims*, i.e. prevention of increase of court workload, leaving no room for other, less restrictive measures that could achieve such an aim.

The increase of court workload alone cannot justify an argument in favor of total exclusion of setting-aside proceedings. The Latvian Constitutional Court explained this reasoning well in the *Hiponia* case when it examined the requirement of necessity vis-à-vis the strict application of the *kompetenz-komptenez* principle:

> One can agree with the *Saeima's* [the Latvian Parliament] and the Ministry of Justice's argument that by granting an individual a right to turn to ordinary jurisdiction courts and to challenge the competence of an arbitral tribunal, court overload may be increased. However, such an argument per se cannot serve as a justification for depriving an individual from its rights on the substance. Namely, the legislator's chosen aim – to decrease the workload of ordinary jurisdiction courts and thus to expedite other court proceedings – shall not jeopardize the protection of person's fundamental rights which it has not freely waived. In the present

---

[227] Ibid. See generally also Christoffersen (2009), pp. 68–76. See also Gerards (2013), pp. 466–490, Möller (2012), pp. 709–731.

[228] See generally, e.g. Gerards (2013), pp. 466–490.

> case, where the necessity of facilitating the speed of court proceedings collides with the necessity of protecting fundamental rights of a person, the protection of fundamental rights of a person in particular should take precedence.
>
> […]
>
> Therefore, the Constitutional Court acknowledges that the increase of ordinary jurisdiction courts' workload cannot justify a total prohibition to challenge the competence of an arbitral tribunal in a court [of ordinary jurisdiction].[229]

The above reasoning applies *mutatis mutandis* also to a situation of total exclusion of setting-aside proceedings. It inherently reflects some of the most basic principles as established by the ECtHR, in particular that the right of access to a court cannot be reduced in such a way or to such an extent that the very essence of the right is impaired.[230] The Latvian Constitutional Court's reference that 'the legislator's chosen aim […] shall not jeopardize the protection of person's fundamental rights which it has not freely waived' correlates with the ECtHR's emphasis on party autonomy in the *Tabbane v. Switzerland* case. It was argued previously with regard to the fulfillment of the requirements of the *waiver theory* that when choosing to arbitrate in Latvia parties can be deemed to have waived only the possibility to have the matter referred to courts of the classic kind in favor of another method of adjudication—arbitration (the broader waiver). The Latvian Constitutional Court's *Hiponia* and the ECtHR's *Tabbane v. Switzerland* rulings confirm that an equal test of adherence to the *waiver theory* shall be carried out also with regard to the annulment mechanism.

Another noteworthy aspect of the Latvian Constitutional Court's ruling in the *Hiponia* case deals with the fact that, as argued by the Latvian legislator in those proceedings, the validity of an arbitration agreement and the competence of an arbitral tribunal is subject to review already at the enforcement stage, thus it would

---

[229] *Hiponia* case, No. 2014-09-01, the Constitutional Court of the Republic of Latvia, 28 November 2014, para. 20.2.1. www.satv.tiesa.gov.lv/wp-content/uploads/2014/03/2014-09-01_Spriedums_ENG.pdf. Accessed 29 May 2020.

[230] See, among other notable cases, *Cudak v. Lithuania*, App. No. 15869/02, ECtHR [GC], 23 March 2010, paras. 54–55 ('The Court reiterates that the right to a fair hearing, as guaranteed by Article 6 § 1 of the Convention, must be construed in the light of the principle of the rule of law, which requires that all litigants should have an effective judicial remedy enabling them to assert their civil rights […] Everyone has the right to have any claim relating to his civil rights and obligations brought before a court or tribunal […] However, the right of access to a court secured by Article 6 § 1 of the Convention is not absolute, but may be subject to limitations; these are permitted by implication since the right of access by its very nature calls for regulation by the State. In this respect, the Contracting States enjoy a certain margin of appreciation, although the final decision as to the observance of the Convention's requirements rests with the Court. It must be satisfied that the limitations applied do not restrict or reduce the access left to the individual in such a way or to such an extent that the very essence of the right is impaired. Furthermore, a limitation of the right of access to a court will not be compatible with Article 6 § 1 if it does not pursue a legitimate aim and if there is not a reasonable relationship of proportionality between the means employed and the aim sought to be achieved […]'). See also *Aït-Mouhoub v. France*, App. No. 22924/93, ECtHR, 28 October 1998, para. 52 and *Fayed v. the United Kingdom*, App. No. 17101/90, ECtHR, 21 September 1994, para. 65.

only be repetitive to permit a separate remedy in this regard prior to enforcement proceedings.[231] Although the Latvian Constitutional Court did not support the said reasoning, noting that the review at the enforcement stage is rather limited both in its scope and also in terms of filing evidence,[232] a similar argument may nevertheless be put forward when arguing regarding the necessity of setting-aside proceedings.

This, in fact, has already been done by advancing the argument of *double-control*, i.e. having a judicial review of an arbitral award on similar grounds both in the enforcement proceedings and setting-aside proceedings.[233] Although the *double-control* of arbitral awards may seem as somewhat unnecessary, it can be remedied by similar provisions to that of Section 1060 of the ZPO or cumulatively ensuring that the setting-aside of arbitral awards (i) takes place in the State of origin and (ii) prior to a decision of enforcement in a foreign State; and (iii) is respected by applying the ground for refusal of enforcement under Article V(1)(e) of the New York Convention.[234] At the same time, one must keep in mind that the consequences of an arbitral award being annulled are diametrically different from those of a mere refusal of recognition and enforcement. While the latter has effect only in the particular State, annulment of an arbitral award at the seat of arbitration has *erga omnes* effect—at least this is the prevailing opinion, the French, predominately, being the odd ones out. Setting-aside proceedings and enforcement proceedings, while serving a somewhat similar purpose—control of arbitration proceedings, have entirely different legal effects. Therefore, at least in the current legal framework of contemporary arbitration, the *double-control* of arbitration seems to be an inevitability.

Moreover, the prevailing view, as argued by Prof. Van den Berg, is that the courts at the arbitral seat should have the last word with universal effect about the validity of an international arbitral award.[235] In that regard, Prof. Van den Berg believes that a passage he wrote more than 30 years ago still stands as *good law* also in contemporary environment of international arbitration:

> […] A losing party must be afforded the right to have the validity of the award finally adjudicated in one jurisdiction. If that were not the case, in the event of a questionable award a losing party could be pursued by a claimant with enforcement actions from country to country until a court is found, if any, which grants the enforcement. A claimant would

[231] *Hiponia* case, No. 2014-09-01, the Constitutional Court of the Republic of Latvia, 28 November 2014, para. 20.2.2. www.satv.tiesa.gov.lv/wp-content/uploads/2014/03/2014-09-01_Spriedums_ENG.pdf. Accessed 29 May 2020. The argument in essence advocates for a French-style minimalistic court involvement in arbitration proceedings. However, while in France courts may still be called upon to decide on the competence of arbitral tribunals where the arbitration agreement is "manifestly void" or "manifestly not applicable", the Latvian strict approach at that time did not provide any possibility whatsoever in this regard.

[232] Ibid., paras. 20.2.3, 20.2.4 and 20.2.5.

[233] See, among others, Van den Berg (2014), p. 3. For an insightful challenge to the existing New York Convention, proposing to do away with national setting-aside proceedings see Paulsson MRP (2018) The Future of the New York Convention in Its Most Extreme Sense: A Dual Convention that Disposes of National Setting Aside Regimes, Kluwer Arbitration Blog. http://arbitrationblog.kluwerarbitration.com/2018/08/15/the-future-of-the-new-york-convention/. Accessed 29 May 2020.

[234] Van den Berg (2014), p. 23.

[235] Ibid., p. 24.

obviously refrain from doing this if the award has been set aside in the country of origin and this is a ground for refusal of enforcement in other Contracting States.[236]

The Latvian Constitutional Court in the *Hiponia* case made a similar observation regarding the necessity of the annulment mechanism:

> […] a party interested in the enforcement of an arbitral award has a right to turn to the district (city) court with an application for the issuing of an exequatur. However, the law, in relation to arbitration proceedings, does not provide any rights to turn to a court for a person that is bound by an enforceable obligation arising out of an arbitral award. This person may only raise its observations against an already submitted application for the issuing of an exequatur. Therefore, this person's rights to court protection, for example in case a fundamental procedural violation occurred during the arbitration proceedings, are dependent on the fact of whether and when the interested party will decide to turn to a court with an application for the issuing of an exequatur.
>
> Moreover, in such situations where the enforcement of an arbitral award is not necessary, a person, that is bound by certain obligations arising out of an arbitral award or is deprived of certain rights thereof, has no possibility whatsoever to request a court of ordinary jurisdiction to remedy violations committed during arbitration proceedings. Nevertheless, such arbitral awards may have significant impact on a person's rights […][237]

Undoubtedly, therefore, the recognition and enforcement mechanism cannot be put on par with and substitute the annulment mechanism, at least not in the current legal framework of international arbitration. The annulment mechanism per se and the various fundamental procedural guarantees it protects arguably outweigh the alleged need of preventing increased court workload. In any event, the said alleged *legitimate aim* could be achieved by other, equally suitable measures that are less restrictive to the protected rights, namely the right of access to a court under Article 6(1) of the ECHR.

In the case of Latvia this certainly could be achieved by adopting a modern arbitration law and, inter alia, by statutorily limiting the number of permanent arbitral institutions. Despite the decrease of such institutions as a result of the 2015 Arbitration Law, their number is still very high and should be limited to a bare minimum. The existence of only a handful of permanent arbitral institutions would provide a healthy environment for introducing the UNCITRAL Model Law-type court assistance, including the annulment mechanism. Inevitably this would also increase the overall quality and effectiveness of arbitration as an alternative dispute resolution mechanism. In turn, effective arbitration environment would in fact lead to decrease of court workload. Therefore, somewhat ironically, it is not the lack of court involvement in arbitration proceedings, including the annulment mechanism, that achieves the Latvian legislator's alleged *legitimate aim* behind its reluctance to introduce balanced court assistance in arbitration proceedings, including the annulment mechanism; it is, in fact, the opposite thereof. Arguably, therefore, the prevention of court

---

[236] Ibid., p. 25.

[237] *Hiponia* case, No. 2014-09-01, the Constitutional Court of the Republic of Latvia, 28 November 2014, para. 20.2.4. www.satv.tiesa.gov.lv/wp-content/uploads/2014/03/2014-09-01_Spriedums_ENG.pdf. Accessed 29 May 2020.

workload as alleged policy consideration can be achieved by other suitable means that are less restrictive to parties' fundamental rights, in particular, the right of access to a court under Article 6(1) of the ECHR.

Balance

The test of proportionality *stricto* sensu requires the balancing of the allegedly impaired right, i.e. in this case the right of access to a court under Article 6(1) of the ECHR, and the other interest at stake allegedly impairing the said right, determining which of the values takes precedence. In other words, the balancing entails determination whether the interference with the relevant right is justified when compared to the gain in the protection for the competing interest or right.[238] The ECtHR frequently applies the proportionality test *stricto* sensu in determining whether there has been a violation of a person's right of access to a court.[239]

As has become evident, this was also the case in the *Tabbane v. Switzerland* case whereby the Court found that limitation of the right of access to a court through Article 192(1) of the PILA cannot be regarded as disproportionate to the Swiss legislator's pursued legitimate aim, namely the development of Switzerland as an attractive and effective seat of arbitration.[240] As has equally become evident, the Court arrived at such a conclusion by balancing the two values and, inter alia, putting great emphasis on the aspect of party autonomy, i.e. parties' choice to exclude the application of setting aside proceedings, and the supplementary protection provided by Article 192(2) of the PILA.[241] The question, however, is whether the same conclusion with regard to the proportionality of the restriction of the right of access to a court may be drawn vis-à-vis a situation of total exclusion of setting-aside proceedings in *lex arbitri*. Arguments in favor of answering the said question in negative have been put forward, at least impliedly, already previously.

First of all, it is the much-stressed aspect of party autonomy that predominately influenced the ECtHR's reasoning in favor of Article 192(1) of the PILA being considered proportionate to the said Swiss legislator's aims of enhancing the attractiveness and effectiveness of Switzerland as a seat of arbitration.[242] In the eyes of

[238] See Möller (2012), p. 715.

[239] For examples where the ECtHR has found the right of access to a court disproportionately limited see, e.g. *Kreuz v. Poland*, App. No. 28249/95, ECtHR, 19 June 2001; *Hadjianastassiou v. Greece*, App. No. 12945/87, ECtHR, 16 December 1992; *Vacher v. France*, App. No. 20368/92, ECtHR, 17 December 1996; *Kulikowski v. Poland*, App. No. 18353/03, ECtHR, 19 May 2009; *Atanasova v. Bulgaria*, App. No. 72001/01, ECtHR, 2 October 2008. On the opposite see, e.g. *Stubbings and Others v. the United Kingdom*, App. Nos. 22083/93, 22095/93, ECtHR, 22 October 1996; *Urbanek v. Austria*, App. No. 35123/05, ECtHR, 9 December 2012.

[240] *Tabbane v. Switzerland*, App. No. 41069/12, ECtHR, 1 March 2016, paras. 33–36.

[241] Ibid.

[242] Ibid., para. 34 ('[…] il convient de noter qu'une partie, n'ayant ni domicile, ni résidence habituelle, ni établissement en Suisse, n'est nullement obligée d'exclure tout recours; bien au contraire, elle peut librement choisir de saisir cette possibilité qu'offre la loi suisse en renonçant

the Court, providing only a possibility of excluding the application of setting-aside proceedings (as opposed to, in the Court's own wording, 'obligation to exclude any recourse')[243] is proportionate to the said *legitimate aims*. The Court-made comparison, in turn, between being either under an obligation to exclude any recourse against an arbitral award and having a possibility to freely make such a decision, in itself suggests that the former approach would not be considered proportionate to the said Swiss legislator's pursued *legitimate aims*. By analogy, the same shall hold true for the Latvian legislator's stipulated *legitimate aim* behind continuously failing to introduce the annulment mechanism. In case of total exclusion of setting-aside proceedings the legislator's fears of increased court workload cannot and do not outweigh the arbitrating parties' interests in having proper access to State courts, especially by means of setting-aside proceedings, i.e. a mechanism that serves to protect arbitrating parties' most fundamental human rights, including rights that arguably are even *non-waivable*. The current Latvian approach can be seen as restricting the right of access to a court in a way that the very essence of such a right is impaired.

Secondly, it is the aspect of court control during the recognition and enforcement stage that, in the eyes of the Court, functions as an additional safety net for arbitrating parties that have chosen to exclude the application of setting-aside proceedings.[244] Indeed, by now it has been generally established that the ECHR Member States' responsibility under the ECHR may be engaged whenever they exercise control and guarantee as to the fairness and correctness of the arbitration proceedings at the recognition and enforcement stage.[245] However, it follows from the Court's reasoning in the *Tabbane v. Switzerland* case that the existence of court control at the recognition and enforcement stage functions solely as an additional safeguard—the emphasis is nevertheless on arbitrating parties' freely expressed choice to exclude setting-aside proceedings. Also in the Court's cited *Zamet—Budowa Maszyn Spółka Akcyjna v. Poland* case the existence of recognition and enforcement proceedings functioned solely as an additional safeguard (additional to the existence of setting-aside proceedings) for protecting arbitrating parties from violations of their fundamental rights during arbitration proceedings.[246] Court control over arbitration proceedings at the

valablement à tout recours à un tribunal ordinaire. La Cour estime que ce moyen offert aux parties qui n'ont pas de liens avec la Suisse est proportionné au but de renforcer l'attractivité de la Suisse en matière d'arbitrage international et de renforcer le principe de la liberté contractuelle des parties.').

[243] Ibid. ('[…] n'est nullement obligée d'exclure tout recours […]').

[244] *Tabbane v. Switzerland*, App. No. 41069/12, ECtHR, 1 March 2016, para. 35.

[245] See, e.g. *Jakob Boss Söhn KG v. the Federal Republic of Germany*, App. No. 18479/91, ECmHR, 2 December 1991; *Firma Heinz Schiebler KG v. the Federal Republic of Germany*, App. No. 18805/91, ECmHR, 2 December 1991. See also Petrochilos (2004), pp. 112–113.

[246] *Zamet - Budowa Maszyn Spółka Akcyjna v. Poland*, App. No. 1485/11, ECtHR, 25 August 2015, para. 28 ('The Court further notes that the parties have remedies which enable them to contest the judgments of the courts of arbitration in case of qualified violations of the law; a judgment given by the court of arbitration may be quashed, among other things, if in the proceedings before the court of arbitration the rules of fair trial, including the right to defense, were not respected […] Furthermore, any judgment of the court of arbitration, before it is enforced, needs to be recognized by the domestic court. The requirement of recognition is a further institution by which the courts exercise control over the jurisprudence of the courts of arbitration.').

recognition and enforcement stage alone would evidently amount to insufficient and ineffective protection of arbitrating parties' fundamental procedural human rights. This follows also from the Latvian Constitutional Court's reasoning in the *Hiponia* case.

Moreover, the discussion on proportionality and court control at the recognition and enforcement stage as an additional safeguard for the non-existence of setting-aside proceedings (either due to a mere exclusion agreement or a regulatory vacuum as in the case of Latvia) correlates with previous discussion on *minimum safeguards* and the *waiver theory*. For example, the availability of a possibility to challenge arbitrators on grounds of lack of independence or impartiality already during arbitration proceedings would certainly, albeit not solely in isolation, add to the proportionality of not having the annulment mechanism at the post award stage. This, however, is not the case in Latvia where State courts do not hear challenges to arbitral tribunal's independence or impartiality. In such circumstances, the necessity of the annulment mechanism at the post award stage carries even more significance from the viewpoint of the requirement of proportionality. Arguably, the said observations suggest that total exclusion of setting-aside proceedings disproportionately limits parties' right of access to a court under Article 6(1) of the ECHR.

In addition, a discussion on the proportionality *stricto* sensu is incomplete without also looking at the aspect of margin of appreciation and other principles of interpretation of the Convention. On the one hand, the Convention controlling bodies have repeatedly recognized that the annulment grounds differ among the ECHR Member States and that each State may in principle decide for itself on which grounds an arbitral award should be annulled.[247] In other words—'the Contracting States enjoy considerable discretion in regulating the question on which grounds an arbitral award should be quashed […]'[248] At the same time, the said conclusions were drawn in cases that concerned the actual scope of national annulment grounds, and not the very existence of the annulment mechanism. Although the ECHR Member States' discretion or margin appreciation in this regard may be viewed as *considerable*, such a conclusion shall apply only to the scope of an already existing remedy of setting-aside proceedings, and not to its very existence. Namely, the margin of appreciation afforded to the Contracting States is not without limits.

The scope of the margin of appreciation varies according to circumstances, subject matter, context and the background of the case.[249] An important element for determining the scope of the margin of appreciation is another interpretation method applied by the Court, i.e. the common standards technique. As the Court has stressed, a wide margin of appreciation will exist when 'there is no consensus within the member States of the Council of Europe, either as to the relative importance of the interest at stake or as to the best means of protecting it […]'.[250] The Court has also

[247] See, e.g. *Nordström-Janzon and Nordström-Lehtinen v. the Netherlands*, App. No. 28101/95, ECmHR, 27 November 1996.

[248] *Suovaniemi and others v. Finland*, App. No. 31737/96, ECtHR, 23 February 1999.

[249] *Hämäläinen v. Finland*, App. No. 37359/09, ECtHR [GC], 16 July 2014, para.109.

[250] *Evans v. United Kingdom*, App. No. 6339/05, ECtHR [GC], 10 April 2007, para. 77.

stressed that, in cases involving issues that are subject to constant developments, the Court may examine the situation in other ECHR Member States in respect of the issues at stake in order to assess whether there exists a *European consensus* or at least a certain trend among the ECHR Member States.[251] If the above considerations are put in the context of setting-aside proceedings, the following conclusions can be drawn.

Despite being to a large extent similar in many ways, the national annulment mechanisms also greatly differ among the ECHR Member States. This is evidenced, inter alia, also by the fact that, certain ECHR Member States provide for a possibility to exclude setting-aside proceedings. In this sense, it can be said that the remedy of setting-aside proceedings per se is subject to constant developments and therefore a wide margin of appreciation shall be afforded with regard to regulating the scope of setting-aside proceedings. This conforms also with the Convention controlling bodies' observations that ECHR Member States 'enjoy considerable discretion in regulating the question on which grounds an arbitral award should be quashed […]'.[252] However, when the *very existence* of the annulment mechanism in ECHR Member States' national laws is considered, it is apparent that not only the very existence of the annulment mechanism represents a certain trend among the ECHR Member States, but that, in fact, there exists an overall *European consensus* in this regard. Latvia is the *only* ECHR Member State that does not regulate the annulment of arbitral awards in its national law. Therefore, it can be said that while ECHR Member States enjoy a wide margin of appreciation with regard to regulating the *scope* and *extent* of setting-aside proceedings (subject to the guarantee of the protection of the *non-waivable* rights), their margin of appreciation vis-à-vis the *very existence* of such a remedy in national law shall be rather narrow.

7.3.3 Interim Conclusion

Arguably, the balance between the Latvian legislator's concerns of increased court workload, on the one hand, and limitation of the right of access to a court caused by total exclusion (non availability) of setting-aside proceedings, on the other hand, does not represent a reasonable degree of proportionality. Moreover, absent explicitly communicated policy considerations behind such a legislative choice, it is equally arguable whether there are any legitimate aims at all behind the Latvian legislator's continuous reluctance to regulate setting-aside proceedings in national law. Even if such were to exist, e.g. in the form of prevention of increase court workload, it would be similarly arguable whether such an aim could not be achieved by other equally

[251] *Naït-Liman v. Switzerland*, App. No. 51357/07, ECtHR [GC], 15 March 2018, para. 175 in referring to *Bayatyan v. Armenia*, App. No. 23459/03, ECtHR [GC], 7 July 2011, para. 122; *Hämäläinen v. Finland*, App. No. 37359/09, ECtHR [GC], 16 July 2014, paras. 72–75; *Magyar Helsinki Bizottság v. Hungary*, App. No. 18030/11, ECtHR [GC], 8 November 2016, para. 138.

[252] *Suovaniemi and others v. Finland*, App. No. 31737/96, ECtHR, 23 February 1999.

suitable measures that are less restrictive to the protected right, i.e. the right of access to a court under Article 6(1) of the ECHR.

As such, other, equally suitable measure that would achieve the same aim would be to statutorily limit the number of permanent arbitral institutions and to provide for an UNCITRAL Model Law-type court assistance in arbitration proceedings, including the annulment mechanism. Alternatively, and somewhat less drastically, another possibility would be to introduce a similar mechanism as in the German ZPO whereby arbitral awards may be annulled during the recognition and enforcement stage, thus doing away with the issue of *double-control* and allowing 'two bites at the same cherry in the country of origin.'[253]

The current Latvian approach, however, not only balances on the edge of being considered incompatible with the right of access to a court, but in fact, can arguably be seen as violating arbitrating parties' right of access to a court under Article 6(1) of the ECHR. Being statutorily stripped of the possibility to apply for the setting-aside of arbitral awards, parties are equally stripped of their right of access to a court under Article 6(1) of the ECHR. Such a limitation not only fails to pursue a legitimate aim and be reasonably proportionate, but also restricts the right of access to a court to the extent that the very essence of it is impaired. The question of interest, however, is to what extent total exclusion of setting-aside proceedings in the national arbitration law may lead to a violation of the ECHR?

The absolute non-existence of the annulment mechanism in national law in itself strongly speaks in favor of a conclusion that such an approach violates, first and foremost, the right of access to a court under Article 6(1) of the ECHR. In other words, the very non-existence per se of the annulment mechanism as a tool for guaranteeing the protection of parties' fundamental procedural rights limits arbitrating parties' right of access to a court to the extent that the very essence of such a right is impaired. Violation of the Convention, in particular the right of access to a court, therefore is inherent in the very fact that the remedy of setting-aside proceedings is non-existent under national law. This is true both from the perspective of such a legislative choice being considered from the standpoint of compatibility with the *waiver theory* and also from the standpoint of a violation of the right of access to a court under Article 6(1) of the ECHR per se. The extent of a violation of the Convention in this sense is rather self-explanatory. Although, as recognized by the Convention controlling bodies, ECHR Member States enjoy a wide discretion in regulating setting-aside proceedings, such a discretion is not without limits and it does not extend to the *very existence* of the annulment mechanism in national law. The necessity and relevance of setting-aside proceedings in contemporary legal framework of international arbitration is

[253] Van den Berg (2014), p. 23. Sec. 1060(2) of the ZPO provides that '[t]he petition for a declaration of enforceability to be issued is to be denied, while annulling the arbitration award, if one of the grounds for annulment designated in section 1059 (2) is given. Such grounds for annulment shall not be taken into account insofar as a petition for annulment based on these grounds has been denied, in a final and binding judgment, at the time the petition for declaration of enforceability is received. Grounds for annulment pursuant to section 1059 (2) number 1 also shall not be taken into account if the periods determined in section 1059 (3) have expired, without the respondent having filed a petition for annulment of the arbitration award.'

evidenced not only by a *European consensus*, but a much more general consensus and awareness in this regard.[254]

The somewhat consequential aspect on the extent of a violation of the Convention relates to the issue of *non-waivable* rights of Article 6(1) of the ECHR, i.e. the right to a fair hearing and the right to an independent and impartial tribunal. Providing that the *very existence* of the annulment mechanism is not at stake, the question is whether the considerable discretion afforded to the ECHR Member States in regulating the question on which grounds an arbitral award should be annulled extends also to annulment grounds pertaining to the *non-waivable* rights under Article 6(1) of the ECHR. In other words, provided that the annulment mechanism per se is in place in the relevant national law, does the said discretion pertains also to the (non-)provision of annulment grounds addressing issues inherent in the *non-waivable* rights of Article 6(1) of the ECHR? The answer should be in negative.

Although it is not disputed that, by concluding an arbitration agreement, parties waive the application of *certain* rights of Article 6(1) of the ECHR, this book has argued that such a waiver shall not apply to the *non-waivable* rights of Article 6(1) of the ECHR, i.e. the right to a fair hearing and the right to an independent and impartial tribunal. In that sense, one may question whether a very narrow annulment mechanism, i.e. a mechanism by means of which an arbitral award cannot be challenged on grounds that pertain to the *non-waivable* rights of Article 6(1) of the ECHR, is *permissible* from the standpoint of the Convention. Considering the *non-waivable* character of the right to a fair hearing and the right to an independent and impartial tribunal, the premise should be that generally ECHR Member States' discretion in regulating the scope of setting-aside proceedings should be limited to the extent that it is possible for arbitrating parties to challenge arbitral awards on the basis of at least the annulment grounds pertaining to their *non-waivable* rights under Article 6(1) of the ECHR.

Certainly, the indefinite relationship between arbitration and the ECHR, especially considering the somewhat obscure distinction between *waivable* and *non-waivable* rights of Article 6(1) of the ECHR, leaves room for a discussion on the most appropriate approach with regard to regulating setting-aside proceedings; an approach that would most correspond with the Court's own established principles and recent conclusions in cases such as the *Tabbane v. Switzerland* or *Pechstein*. Whatever view on the issue is taken, one cannot deny that the somewhat open-ended normative vacuum in this regard allows for arguing and advocating in favor of many different possibilities. It is exactly the said indefiniteness and relative obscurity characterizing the relationship between arbitration and the ECHR that allows concluding that both issues, i.e. exclusion agreements and total exclusion of setting-aside proceedings, do raise questions as to their compatibility with the ECHR. Before concluding this book's findings, one must look at how this conclusion sits into the contemporary legal

[254]Consider, for example, the fact that the UNCITRAL Model Law (providing, inter alia, for setting-aside proceedings) has been currently adopted in 83 States in a total of 113 jurisdictions. Similarly, the New York Convention, providing as one of the grounds for refusal of recognition and enforcement of an arbitral award a ground that an arbitral award has been set aside at the seat of arbitration, has currently 159 Contracting States.

framework of international arbitration and whether there are any *de lege ferenda* recommendations for ECHR Member States to regulate the annulment of arbitral awards in a manner that would most conform with the Convention's standards.

7.4 Summary

The plain, irrefutable truth is that judicial review by means of setting-aside proceedings still constitutes a prevalent method for States to exercise control over arbitration proceedings. The present conclusory discussion neither searches for causes, nor aims to provide solutions to the somewhat perpetual dialogue on the seeming *malfunctioning* of the contemporary system of judicial control of arbitration and the necessity of setting-aside proceedings per se. Many notable scholars have already attempted to do this.[255] Absent a general overhaul of what has been described as an *unsatisfactory* present legal framework,[256] the annulment mechanism will continue to play a paramount role both from the standpoint of the interests of a Sate at the arbitral seat and also those of arbitrating parties. What the present brief conclusory discussion aims to provide, however, is some *de lege ferenda* recommendations on how to best approach the *status quo* of setting-aside proceedings in the contemporary framework of international arbitration from the perspective of compatibility of the different judicial control regimes with the ECHR.

To a certain extent, the above interim conclusions for both the issue of exclusion agreements and the phenomenon of total exclusion of setting-aside proceedings have already attempted to hypothetically construct an annulment mechanism that would fully conform with the Court's own established general principles pertaining to the relationship between arbitration and the ECHR. The *constructing* of such a mechanism would have to start bottom-up, by first addressing the issue of total exclusion of setting-aside proceedings, and then trying to seek the most appropriate solution to exclusion agreements from the standpoint of the Convention.

As to the former, i.e. total exclusion of setting-aside proceedings, the hypothesis is rather straightforward—a legislative approach failing to provide for the annulment mechanism arguably violates arbitrating parties' right of access to a court under Article 6(1) of the ECHR. The non-compatibility of such an approach with the Convention stems from both the failure to accord to the necessary requirements of the *waiver theory* and, more importantly, the violation of the right of access to a court under Article 6(1) of the ECHR per se. A rather simple solution to the adverse consequences of a legal system not providing for a possibility to apply for the annulment of arbitral awards would be to introduce a mechanism similar to that provided in Germany, namely Section 1060 of the ZPO, that kills two birds with one stone. The same straightforward conclusion, however, does not apply to regulating

[255] See, among many others, Van den Berg (2014), Scherer (2016), Reisman and Richardson (2012), Radicati Di Brozolo (2012), Gharavi (2002), Paulsson (2017).
[256] Van den Berg (2014), p. 23.

the extent of the annulment mechanism, including by means of providing a possibility to exclude application of the annulment mechanism.

Despite the Court's ruling in the *Tabbane v. Switzerland* case that *expressis verbis* addresses the compatibility of exclusion agreements with the ECHR, in particular, the right of access to a court under Article 6(1) of the ECHR, the overall picture, so to say, is still rather blurry, especially when taking into account the Court's indefinitely made distinction between *waivable* and *non-waivable* rights of Article 6(1) of the ECHR. Not only the ECtHR's conclusions in the *Tabbane v. Switzerland* case are not set in stone from the perspective of the different requirements of the *waiver theory*, but the issue of compatibility of exclusion agreements with the ECHR raises even more questions when the said difference between *waivable* and *non-waivable* rights of Article 6(1) of the ECHR is put to test.

The necessity to fulfil the different requirements of the *waiver theory* in all respects evidences that the Court's conclusions in the *Tabbane v. Switzerland* case as to the compatibility of Article 192(1) of the PILA with the right of access to a court under Article 6(1) of the ECHR will not be applicable to all cases pertaining to the compatibility of exclusion agreements with the ECHR. Exclusion agreements in other circumstances, e.g. resulting from an arbitration agreement or an exclusion agreement influenced by constraint, or from a choice not being unequivocal, or not accompanied by certain minimum safeguards, may as well result in such exclusion agreements being considered contrary to arbitrating parties' right of access to a court under Article 6(1) of the ECHR. Therefore, at least from the standpoint of the *waiver theory*, the compatibility of such agreements with the ECHR must be assessed on a case-by-case basis, making it difficult to draw all-encompassing conclusions applying to the phenomenon of exclusion agreements in general.

Moreover, in searching for the most ECHR-compatible approach to regulating exclusion agreements, one must conclude that from the Convention's perspective *ex post* exclusion agreements, i.e. exclusion agreements concluded after arbitrating parties became aware of the relevant circumstances potentially having an effect on the validity of an arbitral award, shall be *permissible*. Such a conclusion is not only based on the Court's reasoning in, *inter alia*, the *Suovaniemi* and the *Tabbane v. Switzerland* cases, but is also in line with the generally established principle that the person waiving his rights under the Convention must reasonably foresee the consequences of the waiver and be fully aware of the rights he or she waives. Similar observations follow from many scholarly writings on the topic.[257] Therefore, even if a *non-waivable* right, e.g. the right to an independent an impartial tribunal, is at stake, arbitrating parties are free to exclude setting-aside proceedings, including the possibility to challenge an arbitral award on grounds of lack of independence and/or impartiality, *ex post*. As seen, generally, States permitting exclusion agreements also permit *ex post* exclusion agreements, therefore, at least in this regard, no ECHR-compatibility issues arise.

[257] See, e.g. Benedettelli (2015), p. 646, Landrove (2006), pp. 89–90, Briner and Von Schlabrendorff (2001), pp. 94–95, Jaksic (2007), pp. 165–6, Petrochilos (2004), pp. 122–123, Matscher (1999), pp. 282–3, Mourre (2000), p. 18.

However, it is obvious that, although permitting solely *ex post* exclusion agreements would be the most appropriate approach from the standpoint of compatibility with the Convention, the reality is that if and when such exclusion agreements are concluded, the conclusion in most cases takes place together with the arbitration agreement inserted in the underlying contract, and not *ex post*. Therefore, the most challenging aspect from the perspective of the Convention is not the compatibility of *ex post*, but *ex ante* exclusion agreements.

Ex ante exclusion of setting-aside proceedings not only raises questions as to compatibility with the requirements of the *waiver theory* that, as seen, will depend on a case-by-case basis, but, more significantly, touches also upon the issue of difference between *waivable* and *non-waivable* rights of Article 6(1) of the ECHR. Despite the Court's own-made distinction in this regard being not entirely definitive, it has been shown that considerably more support can be found in favor of concluding that the right to a fair hearing and the right to an independent and impartial tribunal under Article 6(1) of the ECHR possess *non-waivable* character. As noted by a leading arbitration scholar:

> [A]ccording to the European Court certain due process rights may not be waived in any circumstances. Of course, the idea that parties to an arbitration agreement should be presumed having waived all the due process guarantees set out by Article 6.1 ECHR must be rejected as being at odds with the importance that the principle of fair trial is granted by most contemporary laws of arbitration.[258]

If, to repeatedly put it in the Court's words a '[w]aiver may be permissible with regard to certain rights but not with regard to certain others' and '[a] distinction may have to be made even between different rights guaranteed by Article 6',[259] *ex ante* exclusion agreements, excluding, in particular, annulment grounds pertaining to the right to a fair hearing and the right to an independent and impartial tribunal, are at odds with the Court's own-made notions of *permissibility* and *non-waivability* of certain rights of Article 6(1) of the ECHR.

However, the most challenging task, is to reconcile the above conclusion with the variety of annulment grounds existing under national *leges arbitri*. In other words, elements of the right to a fair hearing and the right to an independent and impartial tribunal may be simultaneously read into multiple of the most common annulment grounds. Only a handful of States provide lack of independence and/or impartiality of an arbitral tribunal as an explicit annulment ground in their arbitration laws. However, in States not expressly providing for such an annulment ground, challenges to arbitral awards on the basis of lack of independence and/or impartiality of arbitrators has to be done via different routes, e.g. arguing for a denial of an opportunity to present the case, irregular composition of the tribunal or a violation of procedural public policy. The same holds true for the right to a fair hearing whose fundamental elements, i.e. adversarial proceedings and equality of arms, may be read into multiple annulment grounds. Consequently, if distinguishing between *waivable* and *non-waivable* rights of Article 6(1) of the ECHR is rather straightforward, a comparable distinguishing

---

[258] Benedettelli (2015), pp. 646–647.

[259] *Suovaniemi and others v. Finland*, App. No. 31737/96, ECtHR, 23 February 1999.

between annulment grounds that parties should be permitted to exclude *ex ante*, and those that they shall not, is not that simple. In fact, it is not even feasible, considering the variety of annulment grounds provided for in the ECHR Member States' national arbitration laws and the fact that elements of the *non-waivable* rights of Article 6(1) of the ECHR may be read into multiple annulment grounds.

A sensible *de lege ferenda* solution to tackle the said issue may yet again be found in the German approach to setting-aside proceedings and, in particular, exclusion agreements. As seen, not only the German ZPO distinguishes between *waivable* and *non-waivable* annulment grounds (the latter being arbitrability and public policy),[260] but even for the *waivable* grounds (Section 1059(2)(1) of the ZPO, largely corresponding those of Article 34(2)(a) of the UNCITRAL Model Law) it is required that parties are aware of the issue potentially affecting the validity of the arbitral award, thus understanding the extent of the waiver.[261] Such an approach, in essence, redirects the discussion back to permitting only *ex post* exclusion agreements—a solution that is the most sensible from the standpoint of the Convention, in particular, the Court-made distinction between *waivable* and *non-waivable* rights of Article 6(1) of the ECHR. It not only parallels the Court's own established general principle that a waiver of the Convention's right is considered as stemming from one's own free will if the respective person is fully aware of the right it waives, but generally also provides a healthy balance between the needs of party autonomy, on the one hand, and continuous protection of the most fundamental procedural rights, on the other hand. Whether or not such a uniform solution in all ECHR Member States is practicable and desirable, is another question.

The golden mean, at least from the perspective of the ECHR, for regulating the annulment mechanism in national law may therefore be summarized as follows.

Total exclusion of setting-aside proceedings—such as in Latvia—is at odds with both the *waiver theory* and the required degree of proportionality for limiting the right of access to a court under Article 6(1) of the ECHR. Therefore, such a legislative approach should be considered as incompatible with the Convention, in particular the right of access to a court under Article 6(1) of the ECHR. The same arguably holds true for exclusion agreements, however, only to the extent arbitrating parties are precluded from challenging arbitral awards on the basis of annulment grounds pertaining to the *non-waivable* rights of Article 6(1) of the ECHR, i.e. the right to a fair hearing and the right to an independent and impartial tribunal. The ECtHR-made distinction between *waivable* and *non-waivable* rights of Article 6(1) of the ECHR implies that arbitrating parties should be permitted to exclude such annulment grounds only *ex post*, i.e. after they became aware of the relevant circumstances potentially affecting the validity of an arbitral award.

Apart from the German approach that, as argued, provides a sensible solution to regulating setting-aside proceedings and exclusion agreements, fully reflecting also concerns for parties' *non-waivable* procedural human rights under the ECHR,

---

[260] These grounds are considered to be in the public interest and thus cannot be excluded by arbitrating parties under any condition. See Scherer (2016), p. 444.

[261] Scherer (2016), p. 444.

the above suggested golden mean, unfortunately, in the author's opinion, is generally unattainable in contemporary legal framework for international arbitration. Although the first aspect, i.e. total exclusion of setting-aside proceedings, similarly as with the *Hiponia* case before the Latvian Constitutional Court and the strict interpretation of the *kompetenz-kompetenz* principle, may indeed at a certain point result in a case before the Latvian Constitutional Court or the ECtHR and in all probability be considered as incompatible with the ECHR, the variety of annulment grounds provided for in national *leges arbitri* and the relative margin of appreciation given to ECHR Member States in this regard prevents the drawing of more specific conclusions with regard to the general compatibility of exclusion agreements with the ECHR.

Undoubtedly, the German approach endeavors to please both the arbitrating parties and their autonomy as well as the State at the seat of arbitration and its role as a supervisor of arbitration proceedings. As evidenced, it can also be considered to be fully compliant with the ECHR and its established principles with regard to arbitration. However, without a general overhaul of the whole judicial controls system in contemporary international arbitration (and a subsequent uniform acceptance of such an overhaul by all ECHR Member States),[262] the said German formula cannot be simply imposed on the rest of the ECHR Member States, in particular those permitting exclusion agreements. The reality is that the variety of different national annulment mechanisms, including approaches to exclusion agreements, will continue to co-exist together. In turn, evaluation of compatibility of such mechanisms with the ECHR will be ascertained on a case-by-case basis if and when the issue of alleged incompatibility of such mechanisms is raised before the ECtHR. The question, however, is whether arbitrating parties in the contemporary legal framework of international arbitration can be sure that their *non-waivable* rights will nevertheless be protected, notwithstanding a concluded *ex ante* exclusion agreement.

In the author's opinion, that question is answered in affirmative, mainly due to the reason that the Court, notwithstanding an alleged waiver, will nevertheless *ex officio* verify alleged violations of parties' *non-waivable* rights of Article 6(1) of the ECHR. The same *ex officio* verification of an alleged violation of the principle of equality of arms was carried out in the *Tabbane v. Switzerland* case, whereby the Court, even after recognizing that Article 192(1) of the PILA is compatible with the right of access to a court, nevertheless went on to consider whether the arbitral tribunal's refusal to appoint a financial expert in that case violated the principle of equality of arms.[263] Although one may doubt whether such an *ultima ratio* approach to ascertaining potential violation of parties' *non-waivable* rights under Article 6(1) of the ECHR is effective, in the current fragmented framework of national arbitration laws, including their annulment mechanisms and approaches to exclusion agreements, it seems as the only feasible way (apart from the German approach) of how to continue protecting parties' *non-waivable* rights under Article 6(1) of the ECHR, notwithstanding allegedly concluded *ex ante* exclusion agreements.

---

[262] This, at least theoretically, may be achieved by a new dual convention, replacing the New York Convention. On the (non)prospects of such a vision see, e.g. Paulsson (2017).

[263] *Tabbane v. Switzerland*, App. No. 41069/12, ECtHR, 1 March 2016, paras. 37–40.

References

Aall J (2010) Waiver of human rights: setting the scene (Part I/III). Nordic J Hum Rts 28:300

Alexy R (2002) A theory of constitutional rights (trans: Rivers J). Oxford University Press, Oxford

Baizeau D (2005) Waiving the right to challenge an arbitral award rendered in Switzerland: caveats and drafting considerations for foreign parties. Int ALR 3:69

Benedettelli MV (2015) Human rights as a litigation tool in international arbitration: reflecting on the ECHR experience. Arb Int 31(4):631–659

Besson S (2006) Arbitration and human rights. ASA Bull 24:395–416

Born G (2014) International commercial arbitration, 2nd edn. Kluwer Law International, Alphen aan den Rijn

Bray D et al (eds) (2014) International arbitration and public policy. JurisNet

Briner R, Von Schlabrendorff F (2001) Article 6 of the European Convention on Human Rights and its bearing upon international arbitration. In: Briner R et al (eds) Law of international business and dispute settlement in the 21st century. Liber Amicorum Karl-Heinz Bockstiegel. Carl Heymanns Verlag KG

Christoffersen J (2009) Fair balance: a study of proportionality, subsidiarity and primarity in the European Convention on Human Rights. Martinus Nijhoff Publishers, Boston

Cordero-Moss G (2015) Limits on party autonomy in international commercial arbitration. Penn St J Law Int Aff 4:186

Geisinger E, Mazuranic A (2013) Chapter 11: Challenge and revision of the award. In: Geisinger E, Voser N (eds) International arbitration in Switzerland: a handbook for practitioners, 2nd edn. Kluwer Law International, Alphen aan den Rijn

Gerards J (2013) How to improve the necessity test of the European Court of Human Rights. Int J Const Law 11(2):466–490

Gharavi HG (2002) The international effectiveness of the annulment of an arbitral award. Kluwer Law International, Alphen aan den Rijn

Girsberg D, Voser N (2016) International arbitration: comparative and Swiss perspectives, 3rd edn. Kluwer Law International, Schulthess Juristische Medien AG

Grabenwarter C (2014) European Convention on Human Rights: commentary. C.H. Beck, Hart, Nomos Helbing Lichtenhahn Verlag

Hirschberg L (1981) Der Grundsatz der Verhältnismässigkeit. Schwartz

Hörnle J (2009) Cross-border internet dispute resolution. Cambridge University Press, Cambridge

Jaksic A (2007) Procedural guarantees of Human Rights in arbitration proceedings: a still unsettled problem? J Int Arb 24(2):159

Kaufmann-Kohler G, Rigozzi A (2015) International arbitration: law and practice in Switzerland. Oxford University Press, Oxford

Kessedjian C (2007) Transnational public policy. In: Van den Berg AJ (ed) International arbitration 2006: back to basics? ICCA international arbitration congress series, vol 13. Kluwer Law International, Alphen aan den Rijn, pp 857–870

Krausz N (2011) Waiver of appeal to the Swiss Federal Tribunal: recent evolution of the case law and compatibility with ECHR, Article 6. J Int Arb 28(2):137–162

Kreindler RH (2013) Competence-competence in the face of illegality in contracts and arbitration agreements. Brill, Nijhoff

Lalive P (1987) Transnational (or truly international) public policy and international arbitration. In: Sander P (ed) Comparative arbitration practice and public policy in arbitration. ICCA congress series, vol 1986. Kluwer Law International, New York, pp 258–318

Landrove JC (2006) European Convention on Human Rights' impact on consensual arbitration. An État des Lieux of Strasbourg Case-Law and of a problematic Swiss Law Feature. In: Besson et al (eds) Human rights at the center. Schulthess

Lawson RA (1996) Arbitrage en artikel 6 EVRM: vrijheid in gebondenheid. Tijdschrift voor Arbitrage 96(4):157

Luttrell S (2009) Bias challenges in international commercial arbitration: the need for a 'real danger' test. Kluwer Law International, Alphen aan den Rijn
Mantilla-Serrano F (2005) Towards a transnational procedural public policy. In: Gaillard E (ed) Towards a uniform international arbitration law. Juris Publishing, New York
Matscher F (1999) L'arbitrage et la Convention. In: Pettiti LE et al (eds) La Convention européenne des droits de l'Homme. Commentaire article par article. Économica
Mayer P, Sheppard A (2003) Final ILA report on public policy as a bar to enforcement of international arbitral awards. Arbitr Int 19(2):249–263
Möller K (2012) Proportionality: challenging the critics. Int J Const Law 10(3):709–731
Mourre A (2000) Le droit français de l'arbitrage international face à la Convention européenne des droits de l'Homme. Gazette du Palais 337:16
Paulsson J (2013) The idea of arbitration. Oxford University Press, Oxford
Paulsson MRP (2017) The 1958 New York Convention on the Recognition and Enforcement of Foreign Arbitral Awards from an unusual perspective: moving forward by parting with it. Indian J Arb Law 5(2):23
Petrochilos G (2004) Procedural law in international arbitration. Oxford University Press, Oxford
Piers M (2011) Consumer arbitration in the EU: a forced marriage with incompatible expectations. J Int Dispute Settl 2(1):209–230
Radicati Di Brozolo LG (2012) The present—commercial arbitration as a transnational system of justice: the control system of arbitral awards: a pro-arbitration critique of Michael Reisman's "Architecture of International Commercial Arbitration". In: Van den Berg AJ (ed) Arbitration: the next fifty years. ICCA congress series. Kluwer Law International, Alphen aan den Rijn, pp 74–102
Redfern A et al (2004) Law and practice of international commercial arbitration, 4th edn. Sweet & Maxwell, London
Reisman M, Richardson B (2012) The present—commercial arbitration as a transnational system of justice: an interpretation of the architecture of international commercial arbitration. In: Van den Berg AJ (ed) Arbitration: the next fifty years. ICCA congress series. Kluwer Law International, Alphen aan den Rijn, pp 17–65
Rigozzi A (2010) Challenging awards of the court of arbitration for sport. J Int Dispute Settl 1(1):217–265
Rubino-Sammartano M (2001) International arbitration law. Kluwer Law International, Alphen aan den Rijn
Scherer M (2016) The fate of parties' agreements on judicial review of awards: a comparative and normative analysis of party-autonomy at the post-award stage. Arb Int 32:437–457
Schlink B (1976) Abwägung im Verfassungsrecht. Duncker & Humblot
Sheppard A (2004) Public policy and the enforcement of arbitral awards: should there be a global standard? Transnatl Dispute Manag 2004(1):1
Van den Berg AJ (2010) Enforcement of arbitral awards annulled in Russia: case comment on court of appeal of Amsterdam, April 28, 2009. J Int Arb 27(2):179
Van den Berg AJ (2014) Should the setting aside of the arbitral award be abolished? ICSID Rev 29:263–288. https://doi.org/10.1093/icsidreview/sit053
Van Dijk P et al (eds) (2006) Theory and practice of the European Convention on Human Rights. Intersentia
Vitkauskas D, Dikov G (2012) Protecting the right to a fair trial under the European Convention on Human Rights Council of Europe human rights handbooks. Council of Europe, p 10
Voser N, George A (2011) Revision of arbitral awards. In: Tercier P (ed) Post-award issues. ASA special series, vol 38. JurisNet, pp 43–74
Voser N, George A (2016) ECtHR: waiver of recourse against international arbitral award not incompatible with ECHR. Kluwer Arbitration Blog. http://kluwerarbitrationblog.com/2016/03/31/ecthr-waiver-of-recourse-against-international-arbitral-award-not-incompatible-with-echr/. Accessed 29 May 2020

Chapter 8
Conclusion

This book began by stating that the necessity of court involvement in arbitration proceedings is axiomatic. Indeed, in this sense, Jan Paulsson's *great paradox* of international arbitration is still *good law*. Only the most adamant proponents of arbitration as *delocalized* or *anational* form of alternative dispute resolution would still argue that court involvement in arbitration proceedings at the seat of arbitration, let alone control (as opposed to mere assistance) over arbitration proceedings, should be limited to a bare minimum. The reality, however, is different from this somewhat utopian view on international arbitration. Most international instruments regulating international arbitration, such as the UNCITRAL Model Law, and national *leges arbitri* provide various forms of court involvement during the life-cycle of arbitration proceedings with the aim to enhance the effectiveness of arbitration as an alternative dispute resolution mechanism. This is true also with regard to what has been the main point of focus in the present book, i.e. setting-aside proceedings.

As has become evident, the necessity of judicial controls in arbitration proceedings, in particular by means of setting-aside proceedings, in recent years has been perhaps one of the most widely debated aspects of court involvement in arbitration proceedings. The issue of *double-control*, potential parallel proceedings, conflicting decisions, enforcement of annulled arbitral awards etc.—the list of seeming or actual concerns behind the somewhat perpetual discussion on the necessity of a general overhaul of the judicial controls system over arbitration proceedings goes on and on. Despite the said concerns, the annulment mechanism continues to serve as a globally recognized and established form of judicial control over arbitration, available to the users of arbitration in nearly all jurisdictions permitting arbitration as an alternative method of dispute resolution.

The present book has not attempted to contribute to the said somewhat perpetual dialogue regarding the overall necessity and desirability of the annulment mechanism in the contemporary framework of international arbitration.[1] Instead, it has

[1] This, as argued previously, has already been done by many prominent arbitration scholars. See, e.g., among many others, Van den Berg (2014), Scherer (2016), Reisman and Richardson (2012), Radicati Di Brozolo (2012) Gharavi (2002), Paulsson (2017).

© The Editor(s) (if applicable) and The Author(s), under exclusive license to Springer Nature Switzerland AG 2020

T. Krūmiņš, *Arbitration and Human Rights*,
https://doi.org/10.1007/978-3-030-54237-5_8

embraced the fact that setting-aside proceedings as a mechanism of judicial control over arbitration proceedings still characterizes, and at least in the author's opinion, will continue to characterize contemporary framework of international arbitration in the coming years, and tried to look at the issue of necessity of setting-aside proceedings from a somewhat unusual perspective—that of parties' procedural human rights under the ECHR.

The specific focus of the present book and the emphasis put on two distinct, albeit at the same time symbiotic issues, namely voluntary exclusion of setting-aside proceedings, on the one hand, and total lack of setting-aside proceedings, on the other hand, and the issue of their relationship and compatibility with the ECHR, finds its explanation in various interlinked developments.

First and foremost, it is the said seemingly perpetual dialogue regarding the necessity of setting-aside proceedings per se in the contemporary framework of international arbitration. The *great paradox* of arbitration, namely the synergetic dichotomy between the private and the public—arbitration and State courts, is a fascinating area of research in itself, however, it is in particular the said dichotomy at the post-award stage, that has recently attracted substantially more attention among arbitration scholars and caught also the author's eye.

Undoubtedly, the referred to dichotomy on a national level and its thorny development in the author's home country, i.e. Latvia, has also played a noticeable role in shaping this book's specific focus on the interplay between setting-aside proceedings and the ECHR. The rather unique state of affairs in this regard in Latvia, i.e. the fact that the Latvian arbitration law simply does not provide arbitrating parties with a possibility to challenge arbitral awards before State courts, is a largely unprecedented phenomenon that requires a closer look as to such legislative approach's underlying reasons and, in turn, its compatibility with arbitrating parties' fundamental procedural human rights, in particular under the ECHR. The former Belgium's approach in doing away with the annulment mechanism was very much criticized. At the same time, in recent years more and more States have adopted less restrictive attitudes towards judicial controls, inter alia, by also permitting arbitrating parties to voluntarily exclude the application of the annulment mechanism at the post-award stage. However, only a few States have gone as far to exclude judicial controls by setting-aside proceedings altogether. As explained, at least to certain extent this was formerly the case in Belgium (Sect. 6.2) and Malaysia (Sect. 6.3), and currently is the practice in Kyrgyzstan (Sect. 6.4) and Latvia (Sect. 6.5).

Moreover, in early 2016 the ECtHR delivered a judgment in the *Tabbane v. Switzerland* case, finding that Article 192(1) of the PILA—a provision by means of which arbitrating parties in Switzerland could (and still may) under certain conditions voluntarily exclude the application of the annulment action at the post-award stage—was compatible with Article 6(1) of the ECHR and the right of access to a court. Following the Court's decision in the *Tabbane v. Switzerland* case, scholars have suggested that other States' approaches permitting exclusion of setting-aside proceedings, such as provided for in Article 1522(1) of the FCCP (in the case of France) or Section 51 of the SAA (in the case of Sweden), are therefore also compatible with the ECHR.[2] But is this truly, unconditionally, the case in reality? Is party autonomy in international arbitration unlimited? Is it even permissible to exclude in advance such seemingly *non-waivable* rights as the right to a fair hearing and the right to an independent and impartial tribunal, both embodied in Article 6(1) of the ECHR and reflected in the annulment grounds available in most jurisdictions? Answers to these questions have been seemingly left open after the Court's *Tabbane v. Switzerland* ruling. Considered together with the *exotic* Latvian approach to setting-aside proceedings that in itself casts doubts as to such approach's compatibility with the ECHR, the Court's ruling in the *Tabbane v. Switzerland* raises a broader question on the required extent (from the perspective of the ECHR) to which the annulment mechanism shall be at all times available to parties under the *lex arbitri*. Hence, this book's dual structure, focusing on both the issue of voluntary exclusion of setting-aside proceedings, one the one hand, and the somewhat more specific phenomenon of total lack of setting-aside proceedings in national law, on the other hand, and the potential implications of both approaches on parties' procedural human rights under the ECHR, in particular the right to a fair trial under Article 6(1) of the ECHR.

So what has this book been all about? Does it add anything new to the discussion on arbitration and human rights, in particular under the ECHR? The present book has linked two seemingly disparate issues—arbitration and human rights, in particular the annulment action, on the one hand, and procedural human rights guarantees under the ECHR, in particular the right to a fair trial under Article 6(1) of the ECHR, on the other hand. The issue of human rights implications on international arbitration and the overall applicability of the ECHR to arbitration has been widely covered by many prominent scholars whose work very much influenced also the present contribution.[3] At the same time, the more specific issue of the relationship between the annulment mechanism and the ECHR, in particular the relationship and compatibility with the ECHR of both voluntary exclusion agreements and total lack of setting-aside proceedings in national arbitration law, has not enjoyed the same scholarly attention. The issue of potential implications of the ECHR on the extent of availability of the annulment mechanism at the seat of arbitration has not been addressed by many and the issue largely remains a grey area that the present book has sought to make clearer, at least to a certain extent.

The first major point of focus of this contribution, i.e. exclusion agreements and their compatibility with the ECHR, has attempted to answer the question on the extent to which a voluntary exclusion of the annulment mechanism may lead to a violation of the procedural human rights guarantees enshrined in the ECHR. At first sight, the ECtHR's ruling in the *Tabbane v. Switzerland* seemingly provides a

---

[2] Voser N, George A (2016) ECtHR: Waiver of Recourse Against International Arbitral Award Not Incompatible with ECHR. Kluwer Arbitration Blog. http://kluwerarbitrationblog.com/2016/03/31/ecthr-waiver-of-recourse-against-international-arbitral-award-not-incompatible-with-echr/. Accessed 29 May 2020.

[3] Just to repeatedly mention a few—Jaksic (2002, 2007), Benedettelli (2015), Besson (2006), Jarrosson (1989), Briner and Von Schlabrendorff (2001), Petrochilos (2004), Landrove (2006), Matscher (1999), Mourre (2000).

straightforward answer to this question—party autonomy prevails and, provided the constituent elements of the *waiver theory* are fulfilled, voluntary exclusion agreements raise no compatibility issues with the ECHR. However, on a closer look, it becomes evident that the said ruling's implications on the phenomenon of exclusion agreements on a broader scale may not be as far-reaching as it seems at first sight. Throughout this book the author has demonstrated that, despite the Court's ruling in *Tabbane v. Switzerland*, exclusion agreements may still raise compatibility issues with the ECHR.

This is due to both—the necessity for a valid waiver of the Convention's rights to satisfy all the constituent elements of the *waiver theory*, on the one hand, and the Court's own-made, albeit still somewhat ambiguous, distinction between *waivable* and *non-waivable* rights of Article 6(1) of the ECHR, one the other hand. As to the former, exclusion agreements in different circumstances may, as well, fail to satisfy the required elements of the *waiver theory*, thus equally failing to constitute a valid and effective *waiver* of the rights guaranteed by the ECHR. Arguably, as this book has argumented, even the Court's reasoning in the *Tabbane v. Switzerland* case casts doubts as to the fulfilment of the said elements—absence of constraint, unequivocality, the presence of minimum safeguards and absence of any important public interest. With regard to the latter—it is exactly the indefiniteness in the Court-made distinction between *waivable* and *non-waivable* rights of Article 6(1) of the ECHR that has allowed the present book to conclude that the extent of compatibility of exclusion agreements with the ECHR depends not only on the fulfilment of the different constituent elements of the *waiver theory*, but also on the eventual availability of a possibility to challenge an arbitral award on grounds that pertain to the *non-waivable* rights of Article 6(1) of the ECHR, namely the right to a fair hearing and the right to an independent and impartial tribunal.

The more difficult issue, however, lies in how to reconcile the said conclusion with the characteristics of the annulment mechanism and its place in the contemporary framework of international arbitration. A sensible *de lege ferenda* solution in the current framework of international arbitration lies in the German approach to permitting exclusion agreements. At least from the Convention's perspective, allowing only *ex post* exclusion agreements, is the most appropriate and ECHR-compatible way in respecting party autonomy while still making sure that their *non-waivable* rights of Article 6(1) of the ECHR are nevertheless protected. If and when the international arbitration community is matured enough to attempt a general overhaul of the present judicial controls system and do away with the annulment mechanism altogether, other approaches may as well be considered. However, in any case, effective guarantee of arbitrating parties' most fundamental human rights, such as the right to a fair hearing and the right to an independent and impartial tribunal, must at all times be the cornerstone of international arbitration proceedings, irrespective of whether such proceedings are subjected to a more lenient or stringent system of judicial controls.

The second major point of focus of this book concerned the somewhat symbiotic issue of total lack of setting-aside proceedings in national arbitration law and the extent to which such a legislative vacuum may lead to a violation of the ECHR, in particular the right to a fair trial under Article 6(1) ECHR. The former Belgium's attempt to exclude the application of the annulment mechanism altogether attracted much criticism and scholarly discussions regarding the effectiveness and necessity of such a drastic approach to limiting judicial controls at the seat of arbitration. Presently, it is Latvia (and outside the reach of the ECHR—also Kyrgyzstan) that continues Belgium's notorious legacy in this regard and omits regulation of the annulment mechanism altogether. Considering this somewhat unique legislative approach to setting-aside proceedings, not many have addressed it in detail. Even less have looked at the said issue from the perspective of its compatibility with the ECHR.[4] The issue of total lack of setting-aside proceedings in national arbitration law indeed is somewhat unique and peculiar to few States only. In fact, at least among the ECHR Member States, Latvia is the only State adopting such an unprecedent approach to setting-aside proceedings. This, however, does not mean that the issue does not bear broader relevance. Considering recent scholarly debates on the necessity of the annulment mechanism in contemporary framework of international arbitration per se as well as recent developments in, e.g. the CJEU's jurisprudence, the analysis of the somewhat unique Latvian approach sits well also in a more international setting.

This book has demonstrated that a legislative regime not providing for a possibility to challenge arbitral awards before State courts arguably fails to satisfy not only the constituent elements of the *waiver theory*, but, more importantly, can be considered as violating parties' right of access to a court under Article 6(1) of the ECHR. The Latvian approach in this regard is unprecedented and limits the right of access to a court to the extent that the very essence of that right is impaired. As the author has argued, such a severe limitation of arbitrating parties' right of access to a court under Article 6(1) of the ECHR fails to pursue a legitimate aim and certainly falls short of the required degree of proportionality between the means employed and the alleged aim sought to be achieved. The extent of a violation of such a legislative approach with the ECHR is therefore self-explanatory—the *considerable discretion*[5] afforded to the ECHR Member States in regulating the question on which grounds an arbitral award should be quashed *shall not* extend to the *very existence* of such a remedy in national law. The indefinite distinction between *waivable* and *non-waivable* rights and its correlation with specific annulment grounds is in turn consequential to the very existence of setting-aside proceedings in national arbitration law in the first place.

So, do ECHR Member States have an absolute obligation to put in place an effective legislative framework providing for the annulment mechanism by means of which arbitrating parties may challenge the validity of arbitral awards before State courts at the seat of arbitration? The question must be looked at from two perspectives.

First, in the author's opinion, the absoluteness of the said obligation extends solely to the very existence of a remedy of setting-aside proceedings in national arbitration law. In other words, the ECHR Member States have a positive obligation to effectively legislate, i.e. to statutorily regulate setting-aside proceedings on a national level, in

[4]See, however, Jaksic (2002).

[5]*Suovaniemi and others v. Finland*, App. No. 31737/96, ECtHR, 23 February 1999.

order to guarantee individuals within their jurisdiction the respective right of access to a court.[6] The ECHR Member States' *margin of appreciation* in this regard shall be rather narrow, in particular considering the overall *European consensus* with regard to regulating the annulment mechanism in national law. Although certain ECHR Member States provide for a possibility to voluntarily exclude the application of the annulment mechanism, currently only Latvia goes as far to exclude the said remedy altogether.

Secondly, provided that the annulment mechanism per se is in place in national law, the author agrees with the ECtHR that the ECHR Member States shall be afforded *considerable discretion* in deciding the question on which particular grounds an arbitral award should be annulled. However, that discretion, despite being rather *considerable*, shall nevertheless be limited by means of the Court's own-made distinction between *waivable* and *non-waivable* rights of Article 6(1) of the ECHR and the fact that the right to a fair hearing and the right to an independent and impartial tribunal under Article 6(1) of the ECHR are generally not subject to a waiver. In other words, from the perspective of compatibility with the ECHR, in case of arbitration—an alternative dispute resolution mechanism not per se requested to satisfy all the guarantees of Article 6(1) of the ECHR—arbitrating parties must be afforded a possibility to challenge an arbitral award on the basis of annulment grounds that pertain to such parties' *non-waivable* rights under Article 6(1) of the ECHR, i.e. the right to a fair hearing and the right to an independent and impartial tribunal. The only exception, as confirmed also by the Court in the *Suovaniemi and others v. Finland* case, should be the renunciation of such rights *ex post*, i.e. after arbitrating parties became aware of the relevant circumstances potentially having effect on the validity of an arbitral award.

The above considerations and *de lege ferenda* recommendations may sound somewhat utopian, especially considering the current judicial controls system. Indeed, although such conclusions are fully compatible and compliant with the Court's established principles, especially with regard to the dichotomy between arbitration and the ECHR and the distinction between *waivable* and *non-waivable* rights under Article 6(1) of the ECHR, they may not reflect the reality of setting-aside proceedings in contemporary framework of international arbitration.

The majority ECHR Member States regulate setting-aside proceedings in their *leges arbitri* and provide arbitrating parties with a *non-waivable* right to challenge arbitral awards on the basis of violations of their most fundamental procedural human rights, such as the *non-waivable* rights under Article 6(1) of the ECHR. Their *leges arbitri* are either silent upon exclusion agreements or provide that the annulment mechanism cannot be voluntarily excluded by means of an agreement. At least in certain States the remedy of setting-aside proceedings is said to be either a mandatory provision of law or part of public policy, thus not subject to exclusion by parties.[7]

---

[6]See, e.g. *Golder v. United Kingdom*, App. No. 4451/70, ECtHR, 21 February 1975, para. 38; *Waite and Kennedy v. Germany*, 26083/94, ECtHR [GC], 18 February 1999, para. 59; *Sabeh El Leil v. France*, App. No. 34869/05, ECtHR [GC], 29 June 2011, para. 47.

[7]See Sect. 5.6.2.

From the Convention's perspective, therefore, the compatibility of the majority of ECHR Member States' regulatory framework providing for the remedy of setting-aside proceedings is not disputed.

Then there are those handful of ECHR Member States that permit exclusion of setting-aside proceedings in their *leges arbitri* and to whom the above *de lege ferenda* recommendations are particularly addressed. As explained, some of them, e.g. Germany (perhaps also Sweden with its distinction between grounds for annulment and invalidity, whereby the latter is not subject to exclusion) raise no compatibility issues with the ECHR—despite arbitrating parties being permitted under certain circumstances to exclude the annulment mechanism, different legislative techniques are used to nevertheless allow such parties to challenge arbitral awards on the basis of grounds pertaining to their *non-waivable* rights of Article 6(1) of the ECHR. In this regard, the German approach to setting-aside proceedings (and in particular to regulating exclusion thereof) seems to please both—arbitrating parties and their autonomy as well as the State at the seat of arbitration and its role as a supervisor of arbitration proceedings.

Others, on the other hand, regulate exclusion of setting-aside proceedings in a way that raises a question as to such approaches' compatibility with the ECHR. The above analysis and *de lege ferenda* recommendations are, in particular, addressed to these States. Understandably, without a general overhaul of the whole judicial controls system (and a subsequent uniform acceptance of such an overhaul by all ECHR Member States), the said German formula cannot be simply imposed on the rest of the ECHR Member States, in particular those adopting more lenient approaches to permitting exclusion agreements. To conclude otherwise would be to disregard the reality of the current judicial controls systems in international arbitration. At the same time, the author believes that the exclusion of setting-aside proceedings in contemporary framework of international arbitration can be and must be regulated in a way that better respects arbitrating parties' most fundamental procedural human rights, especially the *non-waivable* rights under Article 6(1) of the ECHR.

Lastly, there are those few States that omit regulation of setting-aside proceedings in national law altogether. Within the reach of the ECHR this is the case in Latvia. The Latvian approach and its extent, excluding the annulment mechanism in toto, as opposed to making the unavailability of such a mechanism conditional upon the connection of a dispute with the seat of arbitration (as formerly in Belgium) or the choice of applicable arbitration rules (as formerly in Malaysia), is notoriously unique and, as argued in this book, not only fails to satisfy the various requirements of the *waiver theory* under the Convention, but, more importantly, can be considered as violating arbitrating parties' right of access to a court under Article 6(1) of the ECHR. The *European consensus* with regard to regulation of setting-aside proceedings and the relatively scarce use of the possibility to exclude the annulment action, evidences that court scrutiny over arbitral awards generally promotes confidence and a more efficient arbitral process by enhancing fidelity of arbitrating parties' expectations.[8] Recent studies show that the quality of national arbitration law and the formal

[8] Park (2001), p. 595.

legal infrastructure at the seat of arbitration are among the most important reasons why certain arbitral seats are preferred over others.[9] In their choice for a particular seat of arbitration businesses seek sufficient assurances that their most fundamental human rights will be protected during arbitration proceedings and, if not, violation of their rights remedied through adequate court scrutiny over arbitral awards. Without a major overhaul in the system of judicial controls over arbitration, setting-aside proceedings will continue to serve as the primary mechanism to achieve that goal. A legal system that omits regulation of the annulment mechanism altogether not only loses its appeal in the eyes of the users of arbitration as a potential seat of arbitration, but can be considered as being at odds with the most fundamental human rights guarantees under the ECHR, in particular the right of access to a court under Article 6(1) of the ECHR.

Contemporary framework of international arbitration is characterized by a variety of different approaches to excluding the annulment mechanism. Although the above *de lege ferenda* recommendations on how to best approach exclusion of setting-aside proceedings in national law from the perspective of the ECHR may be fully compliant with the ECHR and its own established principles regarding the dichotomy between arbitration and the ECHR, without a general overhaul of the whole judicial controls systems in the contemporary framework of international arbitration, their relevance may seem merely theoretical. The question is therefore how to reconcile the above *de lege ferenda* considerations with the reality and variety of the different approaches to excluding setting aside proceedings that the ECHR Member States adopt in their national laws? Do parties choosing to arbitrate have sufficient assurances that their most fundamental human rights will be protected during arbitration proceedings and, if not, violation of their rights remedied through adequate court scrutiny over arbitral awards? Generally, the answer shall be yes.

[9]See Queen Mary University of London, White & Case (2018) 2018 International Arbitration Survey: The Evolution of International Arbitration, p. 10. http://www.arbitration.qmul.ac.uk/research/2018/. Accessed 21 May 2020.

Various institutional arbitration rules,[10] international arbitration instruments[11] and national arbitration laws[12] regulating arbitration proceedings all provide that arbitration proceedings shall conform to certain fundamental principles, such as the right to present one's case, the right to be treated equally or the right to be heard by independent and impartial arbitrators. In this sense, one has to agree with Jarrosson's critique to the application of the ECHR to arbitration—the Convention's rights and guarantees of due process are already being guaranteed by different international arbitration instruments, institutional arbitration rules and various national arbitration laws. In that respect, arbitrating parties' procedural human rights in most cases will be duly respected during arbitration proceedings, without the need to resort to State courts or the Convention's controlling bodies. This is even more so true when State courts are nevertheless required to assist parties in arbitration proceedings with various procedural tasks, or to exercise certain control over arbitration proceedings. Whenever a matter ancillary to arbitration proceedings, be it a request for the provision of interim measures, challenge to the validity of an arbitration agreement or an application for the setting-aside or recognition and enforcement of an arbitral award, reaches the domain of State courts, they have an obligation under the ECHR to apply the Convention's rights and freedoms and guarantee that arbitration proceedings are carried out in conformity with fundamental human rights.[13] In turn, whenever a State fails to remedy violations of the Convention's rights and freedoms, it essentially endorses such actions as its own and therefore may be held responsible both under the Convention and also internationally.[14] Therefore, in most of the cases, arbitrating parties can

---

[10]See, among others, art. 14(4) of the LCIA Arbitration Rules (2014); arts. 23(2) and 40 of the SCC Arbitration Rules (2017); art. 22(4) of the ICC Arbitration Rules (2017).

[11]For example, art. 18 of the UNCITRAL Model Law requires that 'the parties shall be treated with equality and each party shall be given a full opportunity of presenting his case.' Similarly, the fulfilment of parties' due process rights is implied in art. V of the New York Convention that provides that a foreign arbitral award may be refused recognition and enforcement if, inter alia, '[t]he party against whom the award is invoked was not given proper notice of the appointment of the arbitrator or of the arbitration proceedings or was otherwise unable to present his case' or '[t]he composition of the arbitral authority or the arbitral procedure was not in accordance with the agreement of the parties, or, failing such agreement, was not in accordance with the law of the country where the arbitration took place'. See also art. 17(1) of the 1976 UNCITRAL Arbitration Rules.

[12]National arbitration laws similarly require that parties' due process rights shall be respected during arbitration proceedings See, among others, art. 1699 of the BCCP, art. 1510 of the FCCP, sec. 18 of the Danish Arbitration Act, art. 1036(2) of the Dutch Code of Civil Procedure, sec. 732 of the Estonian Code of Civil Procedure, sec. 22 of the Finish Arbitration Act, sec. 1042(1) of the ZPO, art. 28(1) of the Lithuanian Law on Commercial Arbitration, arts. 19–23 of the Latvian 2015 Arbitration Law and many others.

[13]See, e.g. *Firma Heinz Schiebler KG v. the Federal Republic of Germany*, App. No. 18805/91, ECmHR, 2 December 1991; *Jakob Boss Söhn KG v. the Federal Republic of Germany*, App. No. 18479/91, ECmHR, 2 December 1991.

[14]Petrochilos (2004), pp. 112–113 in referring to Article 11 of the United Nations (UN) International Law Commission (ILC) Draft Articles on Responsibility of States for Internationally Wrongful Acts (2001) which states that a '[c]onduct which is not attributable to a State under the preceding articles shall nevertheless be considered an act of that State under international law if and to the extent

rest assured that their most fundamental rights, such as the *non-waivable* rights of a fair hearing and independent and impartial tribunal, will be duly respected and, if not, remedied by State courts at the seat of arbitration (or alternatively the place of recognition and enforcement). Inevitably, as it follows from the Court's *ratio decidendi* in cases, such as *Suovaniemi and others v. Finland,*[15] *Tabbane v. Switzerland,*[16] and *Transado-Transportes,*[17] if not remedied by State courts, the ECtHR, at least with regard to the *non-waivable* rights of Article 6(1) of the ECHR, will nevertheless *ex officio* verify alleged violations of such rights even if voluntarily waived by parties.

Does that mean that arbitrating parties should not think twice before agreeing on an exclusion agreement and excluding their rights to challenge the validity of an arbitral award before State courts? Certainly not. The continuous existence of the annulment mechanism per se in national *leges arbitri* and the fundamental rights it protects, as well as the scarce use of the possibility to exclude it in the various States where such an exclusion is statutorily permitted, serve as important reminders that parties should carefully consider before sacrificing their fundamental human rights and legal certainty over seeming rapidity and economy.

Does the above also mean that States should not reevaluate their adopted legislative approaches to excluding the setting-aside proceedings from their national *leges arbitri*? Certainly not. When providing a possibility to exclude the application of setting-aside proceedings, or, as the case may be in Latvia—when considering whether or not to do away with total exclusion of setting-aside proceedings and finally introduce the annulment mechanism in Latvian *lex arbitri*, States should not merely be guided by their outward appearance as seemingly attractive seats of arbitration, or, as the case may be, purely economic considerations, such as increase of court workload, especially if such *legitimate aims* are not achieved in practice. This book has shown that there is certainly more than that to the remedy of setting-aside proceedings—a mechanism that serves the broader purpose of protecting not only arbitrating parties' interests, but also those of third parties and the general public.

Does the above mean that the exclusion of setting-aside proceedings in national *leges arbitri* can be regulated in a way that more comprehensively respects arbitrating parties' most fundamental procedural human rights, especially those considered as *non-waivable* rights under Article 6(1) of the ECHR? Certainly yes. Although it cannot be expected that States currently permitting exclusion agreements change their legislative approaches overnight to permit the ECHR-compatible *ex post* exclusion agreements only, this book has highlighted that their current approaches at times fall short of complying with not only the different requirements of the *waiver theory*, but also with the *non-waivable* rights under Article 6(1) of the ECHR. In this sense, there is certainly room for legislative improvement.

---

that the State acknowledges and adopts the conduct in question as its own.' See also Jaksic (2007), p. 162, Benedettelli (2015), p. 642.

[15] *Suovaniemi and others v. Finland*, App. No. 31737/96, ECtHR, 23 February 1999.

[16] *Tabbane v. Switzerland*, App. No. 41069/12, ECtHR, 1 March 2016.

[17] *Transado-Transportes Fluviais Do Sado, S.A. v. Portugal*, App. No. 35943/02, ECtHR, 16 December 2003.

Although this book does not attempt to change the course of direction of the entire judicial controls system in the contemporary framework of international arbitration (as it is neither feasible, nor desirable), it nevertheless attempts to provide intellectual nourishment to a broad range of actors in international arbitration to look at the necessity of setting-aside proceedings in contemporary framework of international commercial arbitration from a somewhat different perspective—that of arbitrating parties' procedural human rights under the ECHR.

References

Benedettelli MV (2015) Human rights as a litigation tool in international arbitration: reflecting on the ECHR experience. Arbitr Int 31(4):631–659

Besson S (2006) Arbitration and human rights. ASA Bull 24:395–416

Briner R, Von Schlabrendorff F (2001) Article 6 of the European Convention on Human Rights and its bearing upon international arbitration. In: Briner R et al (eds) Law of International Business and Dispute Settlement in the 21st Century. Carl Heymanns Verlag KG, Liber Amicorum Karl-Heinz Bockstiegel

Gharavi HG (2002) The international effectiveness of the annulment of an arbitral award. Kluwer Law International

Jaksic A (2002) Arbitration and human rights. Peter Lang, Frankfurt am Main

Jaksic A (2007) Procedural guarantees of human rights in arbitration proceedings: a still unsettled problem? J Int Arbitr 24(2):159

Jarrosson C (1989) L'arbitrage et la Convention européenne des droits de l'homme. Rev Arbitr 4:573–607

Landrove JC (2006) European Convention on Human Rights' impact on consensual arbitration. An État des Lieux of Strasbourg Case-Law and of a Problematic Swiss Law Feature In: Besson et al (eds) Human rights at the center. Schulthess

Matscher F (1999) L'arbitrage et la Convention. In: Pettiti LE et al (eds) La Convention européenne des droits de l'Homme. Commentaire article par article, Économica

Mourre A (2000) Le droit français de l'arbitrage international face à la Convention européenne des droits de l'Homme. Gazette du Palais 337:16

Park WW (2001) Why courts review arbitral awards. In: Briner R et al (eds) Law of international business and dispute settlement in the 21st century, Liber Amicorum Karl-Heinz Bockstiegel. Carl Heymanns Verlag KG, Köln/Berlin/Bonn/München, pp 595–606

Paulsson MRP (2017) The 1958 New York convention on the recognition and enforcement of foreign arbitral awards from an unusual perspective: moving forward by parting with it. Indian J Arbitr L 5(2):23

Petrochilos G (2004) Procedural law in international arbitration. Oxford University Press

Radicati Di Brozolo LG (2012) The present—commercial arbitration as a transnational system of justice: the control system of arbitral awards: a pro-arbitration critique of Michael Reisman's "Architecture of international commercial arbitration". In: Van den Berg AJ (ed) Arbitration: the next fifty years. ICCA congress series volume. Kluwer Law International, pp 74–102

Reisman M, Richardson B (2012) The present—commercial arbitration as a transnational system of justice: an interpretation of the architecture of international commercial arbitration. In: Van den Berg AJ (ed) Arbitration: the next fifty years. ICCA congress series volume. Kluwer Law International, pp 17–65

Scherer M (2016) The fate of parties' agreements on judicial review of awards: a comparative and normative analysis of party-autonomy at the post-award stage. Arbitr Int 32:437–457

Van den Berg AJ (2014) Should the setting aside of the arbitral award be abolished? ICSID Rev 1–26. https://doi.org/10.1093/icsidreview/sit053

The manufacturer's authorised representative in the EU is Springer Nature Customer Service Centre GmbH, Europaplatz 3, 69115 Heidelberg, Germany. If you have any concerns regarding our products, please contact ProductSafety@springernature.com

Printed and bound by CPI Group (UK) Ltd, Croydon, CR0 4YY
22/09/2026
02221058-0018